THE VICTORIA HISTORY OF THE COUNTIES
OF ENGLAND

A HISTORY OF CHESHIRE
VOLUME V, PART 1

INSCRIBED TO THE MEMORY OF HER LATE MAJESTY

QUEEN VICTORIA

WHO GRACIOUSLY GAVE THE TITLE TO AND

ACCEPTED THE DEDICATION OF THIS HISTORY

THE VICTORIA HISTORY
OF THE COUNTIES OF
ENGLAND

THE UNIVERSITY OF LONDON

INSTITUTE OF HISTORICAL RESEARCH

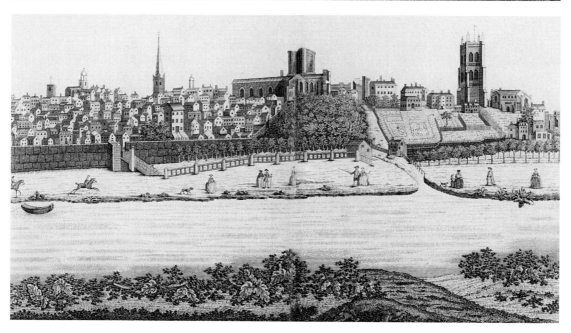

South-east prospect of Chester, 1760. Drawn by Lieut. Joseph Winder, engraved by J. Evans

A HISTORY OF
THE COUNTY OF
CHESTER

EDITED BY C. P. LEWIS AND A. T. THACKER

VOLUME V, PART 1

THE CITY OF CHESTER

GENERAL HISTORY AND TOPOGRAPHY

PUBLISHED FOR THE

INSTITUTE OF HISTORICAL RESEARCH

BY BOYDELL & BREWER · 2003

First published 2003

A Victoria County History publication
in association with The Boydell Press
an imprint of Boydell & Brewer Ltd
PO Box 9 Woodbridge Suffolk IP12 3DF UK
and of Boydell & Brewer Inc.
PO Box 41026 Rochester NY 14604–4126 USA
website: www.boydell.co.uk
and with the
University of London Institute of Historical Research

ISBN 1 904356 00 1

A catalogue record for this book is available from the British Library

Typeset by Joshua Associates Ltd, Oxford
Printed in Great Britain by
St Edmundsbury Press Ltd, Bury St Edmunds, Suffolk

CONTENTS OF VOLUME FIVE, PART ONE

PLATES

For permission to reproduce material in their possession thanks are offered to Cheshire County Council (Archives, Libraries, and Museums), the Chester Archaeological Society, Chester City Council (Chester Archaeology, Chester History and Heritage (formerly Chester Archives), and the Grosvenor Museum), and the Courtauld Institute of Art.

MAPS, PLANS, AND OTHER TEXT FIGURES

PREFACE

THIS VOLUME is the fourth to appear in the series for Cheshire. Planning for it was begun by Dr. B. E. Harris at a time when the staff of the Cheshire History, funded in full by Cheshire County Council and the Leverhulme Trust, consisted of himself as county editor and Dr. A. T. Thacker as assistant editor. The Leverhulme Trust, whose support had been instrumental in restarting the Cheshire History in 1971, continued its generous financial support until 1985, when the county council took on the whole burden of paying for research and writing. On Dr. Harris's death in 1988 he was succeeded as county editor by Dr. Thacker, who had been acting editor during Dr. Harris's long illness. Dr. J. S. Barrow was appointed as assistant editor in 1989 but resigned to take up a post at the University of Nottingham in 1990 and was not replaced. In 1990 an appeal for additional funds to enable the work of the Cheshire staff to continue was led by Mr. and Mrs. J. P. Hess of Chorlton Hall; its success ensured that the Cheshire History did not close down at that stage, and the warmest thanks are offered to Mr. and Mrs. Hess for their work. The names of those who gave money to the Cheshire Appeal are recorded with gratitude at the end of this volume. From 1992 to 1995 the University of London directly supported the Cheshire History by seconding Dr. C. P. Lewis part-time from the central staff of the Victoria History to assist Dr. Thacker. On Dr. Thacker's appointment as deputy editor of the Victoria County Histories in London in 1995, Dr. Lewis succeeded him as county editor and new arrangements were put in place for the management of the Cheshire History. Until 1995 the progress of the Cheshire volumes was supervised by an Editorial Board including representatives of Cheshire County Council, the Leverhulme Trust (until 1985), the Cheshire Appeal (from 1990), and the University of Liverpool. In 1995 the university agreed to become the employer of the Cheshire staff, and a new tripartite agreement was signed between itself, the county council, and the University of London as owner of the V.C.H. The work of the Cheshire History continued to be supported financially by the county council and the appeal, both of which were represented on an Advisory Committee set up by the University of Liverpool. The offices of the Cheshire History were moved from county council premises in Chester to the Department of History in Liverpool. The university's support was made possible through Professors C. T. Allmand, M. Elliott, and A. Harding of the Department of History and Professor J. N. Tarn, pro-vice-chancellor. Those arrangements, however, lasted only until 1998, when Cheshire County Council was unable to continue its financial support, and the University of Liverpool stepped in by re-appointing Dr. Lewis as a Lecturer in History and part-time county editor. The support of successive heads of the Department and later School of History at Liverpool, Professors Harding, Allmand, J. C. Belchem, and P. A. Stafford, is recorded here with sincere thanks.

A great many people have helped with the research and writing of this volume, and they are thanked in the footnotes to the appropriate chapters. The authors who were not members of staff of the Victoria History showed exemplary patience in the long delays – caused by the administrative changes and funding difficulties outlined above – in the publication of their chapters. The staff of record offices and libraries in Chester, London, and elsewhere readily made documents and books available and shared their knowledge of the collections in their care. A particular debt is owed to successive head archivists and staff of the Cheshire county and Chester city record offices.

ABBREVIATIONS

A.-S.	Anglo-Saxon
Acct(s).	Account(s)
Acts of P.C.	*Acts of the Privy Council of England* (H.M.S.O.)
Add. Ch.	Additional Charter(s)
Add. MS.	Additional Manuscript(s)
Alum. Cantab. to 1751	*Alumni Cantabrigienses, Part 1, to 1751*, comp. J. Venn and J. A. Venn
Alum. Cantab. 1752–1900	*Alumni Cantabrigienses, Part 2, 1752–1900*, comp. J. Venn and J. A. Venn
Alum. Oxon. 1500–1714	*Alumni Oxonienses, 1500–1714*, ed. J. Foster
Ann. Cest.	*Annales Cestrienses*, ed. R. C. Christie (R.S.L.C. xiv)
Ann. Rep.	*Annual Report*
App.	Appendix
Arch.	Archaeology, -ical
Archit.	Architecture, -al
Archives and Records, ed. Kennett	*Archives and Records of the City of Chester*, ed. A. M. Kennett
B.L.	British Library
Bk(s).	Book(s)
Bldg(s).	Building(s)
Blk. Prince's Reg.	*Register of Edward the Black Prince* (H.M.S.O.)
Bodl.	Bodleian Library, Oxford
Boro.	Borough
Brit.	Britain, British
Bull. John Rylands Libr.	*Bulletin of the John Rylands University Library of Manchester* (formerly *Bulletin of the John Rylands Library*)
Burne, *Chester Cath.*	R. V. H. Burne, *Chester Cathedral from its Founding by Henry VIII to the Accession of Queen Victoria*
Burne, *Monks*	R. V. H. Burne, *The Monks of Chester*
C.C.A.L.S.	Cheshire and Chester Archives and Local Studies (formerly Cheshire Record Office), Duke Street, Chester
C.H.H.	Chester History and Heritage (formerly part of Chester City Record Office), St. Michael's church, Bridge Street Row, Chester
C.J.	*Journals of the House of Commons*
Cal.	Calendar
Cal. Chanc. R. Var.	*Calendar of Chancery Rolls, Various, 1277–1326* (H.M.S.O.)
Cal. Chart. R.	*Calendar of the Charter Rolls preserved in the Public Record Office* (H.M.S.O.)
Cal. Ches. Ct. R.	*Calendar of County Court, City Court, and Eyre Rolls of Chester, 1259–97, with an Inquest of Military Service, 1288*, ed. R. Stewart-Brown (Chetham Soc. 2nd ser. lxxxiv)
Cal. Chester City Cl. Mins. 1603–42	*Calendar of Chester City Council Minutes, 1603–42*, ed. M. J. Groombridge (R.S.L.C. cvi)
Cal. Close	*Calendar of the Close Rolls preserved in the Public Record Office* (H.M.S.O.)
Cal. Doc. Irel.	*Calendar of Documents relating to Ireland preserved in the Public Record Office* (H.M.S.O.)
Cal. Fine R.	*Calendar of the Fine Rolls preserved in the Public Record Office* (H.M.S.O.)
Cal. Inq. Misc.	*Calendar of Inquisitions Miscellaneous (Chancery) preserved in the Public Record Office* (H.M.S.O.)
Cal. Inq. p.m.	*Calendar of Inquisitions post mortem preserved in the Public Record Office* (H.M.S.O.)
Cal. Justiciary R. of Irel.	*Calendar of the Justiciary Rolls of Ireland preserved in the Public Record Office of Ireland* (H.M.S.O.)
Cal. Lib.	*Calendar of the Liberate Rolls preserved in the Public Record Office* (H.M.S.O.)
Cal. Papal Reg.	*Calendar of Papal Registers: Papal Letters* (H.M.S.O. and Irish MSS. Com.)

Cal. Pat.	*Calendar of the Patent Rolls preserved in the Public Record Office* (H.M.S.O.)
Cal. S.P. Dom.	*Calendar of State Papers, Domestic Series* (H.M.S.O.)
Cal. S.P. Irel.	*Calendar of the State Papers relating to Ireland preserved in the Public Record Office* (H.M.S.O.)
Cal. S.P. Venice	*Calendar of State Papers and Manuscripts relating to English Affairs in the Archives of Venice and Northern Italy*
Camd.	Camden
Cart. Chester Abbey	*The Chartulary or Register of St. Werburgh's Abbey, Chester*, ed. J. Tait (2 vols., Chetham Soc. 2nd ser. lxxix, lxxxii)
Cat.	Catalogue
Cat. Anct. D.	*Descriptive Catalogue of Ancient Deeds in the Public Record Office* (H.M.S.O.)
Cath.	Cathedral
Census	printed reports of the decennial Census of Population
Cent.	Century, -ies
Ch.	Charter(s) *or* Church
Charters of A.-N. Earls	*The Charters of the Anglo-Norman Earls of Chester, c. 1071–1237*, ed. G. Barraclough (R.S.L.C. cxxvi)
Ches. Chamb. Accts.	*Accounts of the Chamberlains and other Officers of the County of Chester, 1301–60*, ed. R. Stewart-Brown (R.S.L.C. lix)
Ches. Hist.	*Cheshire History*
Ches. in Pipe R.	*Cheshire in the Pipe Rolls, 1158–1301*, ed. R. Stewart-Brown and M. H. Mills (R.S.L.C. xcii)
Chester Chron.	*Chester Chronicle* [newspaper]
Chester City Cl. Mins.	*Chester City Council Minutes* [printed and bound volumes from 1896]
Chester Customs Accts.	*Chester Customs Accounts, 1301–1566*, ed. K. P. Wilson (R.S.L.C. cxi)
Chrons.	*Chronicles*
Cl.	Council
Close R.	*Close Rolls of the Reign of Henry III preserved in the Public Record Office* (H.M.S.O.)
Colln.	Collection
Collns. Hist. Staffs.	Collections for a History of Staffordshire [published by the Staffordshire Record Society, formerly called the William Salt Archaeological Society]
Complete Peerage	G. E. C[okayne] and others, *The Complete Peerage* (2nd edn. 1910–98)
Ct. R.	Court Roll
Cttee.	Committee
D.K.R.	*Reports of the Deputy Keeper of the Public Records*
D.N.B.	*Dictionary of National Biography*
Diary of Henry Prescott	*The Diary of Henry Prescott, LL.B., Deputy Registrar of Chester Diocese*, ed. J. Addy and P. McNiven (3 vols., R.S.L.C., cxxvii, cxxxii, cxxxiii)
Dir.	*Directory*
Domesday Surv. Ches.	*Domesday Survey of Cheshire*, ed. J. Tait (Chetham Soc. N.s. lxxv)
E.E.T.S.	Early English Text Society
E.H.R.	*English Historical Review*
Eccl.	Ecclesiastical
Econ. H.R.	*Economic History Review*
Eg.	Egerton
Eng.	England, English
Eng. Hist. Doc.	*English Historical Documents*
Ex. e Rot. Fin.	*Excerpta e Rotulis Finium, Hen. III* (Record Commission)
f./ff.	folio, -s
Fam.	Family
G.E.C. Baronetage	G. E. C[okayne], *Complete Baronetage*
Gastrell, Not. Cest.	*Notitia Cestriensis, or Historical Notices of the Diocese of Chester*, by [Francis] Gastrell [Bishop of Chester], ed. F. R. Raines, i (Chetham Soc. [1st ser.] viii)
Gent. Mag.	*Gentleman's Magazine*
H.C.	House of Commons
H.L.	House of Lords
Harl.	Harleian

Harris, *Chester*	B. E. Harris, *Chester* (Bartholomew City Guides, 1979)
Hemingway, *Hist. Chester*	J. Hemingway, *History of the City of Chester* (2 vols., 1831)
Hewitt, *Med. Ches.*	H. J. Hewitt, *Medieval Cheshire: A Social and Economic History of Cheshire in the Reigns of the Three Edwards* (Chetham Soc. 2nd ser. lxxxviii)
Hist.	History, Historical
Hist. MSS. Com.	Historical Manuscripts Commission
Hist. Parl.	*History of Parliament*
Hist. Soc.	Historical Society
Hughes, *Stranger's Handbk.* (1856)	T. Hughes, *The Stranger's Handbook to Chester* ([1st edn.] 1856)
Ind.	Industry, -ies, -ial
Irel.	Ireland
J.C.A.S.	*Journal of the Chester Archaeological Society* (formerly called *Journal of the Chester and North Wales Architectural, Archaeological, and Historic Society,* and variants)
J.R.U.L.M.	John Rylands University Library of Manchester
Jnl.	*Journal*
Johnson, 'Aspects'	A. M. Johnson, 'Some Aspects of the Political, Constitutional, Social, and Economic History of the City of Chester, 1550–1662' (Oxf. Univ. D.Phil. thesis, 1971)
Jones, *Ch. in Chester*	D. Jones, *The Church in Chester, 1300–1540* (Chetham Soc. 3rd ser. vii)
King's Vale Royal	*The Vale-Royall of England, or, The County Palatine of Chester Illustrated* (publ. D. King, 1656; facsimile reprint 1972)
L. & P. Hen. VIII	*Letters & Papers, Foreign and Domestic, of the Reign of Henry VIII* (H.M.S.O.)
L.J.	*Journals of the House of Lords*
Lavaux, *Plan of Chester*	A. de Lavaux, *Plan of the City and Castle of Chester* [1745]
Leic.	Leicester
Leland, *Itin.* ed. Toulmin Smith	*Itinerary of John Leland,* ed. L. Toulmin Smith
Letter Books of Brereton	*The Letter Books of Sir William Brereton,* ed. R. N. Dore (R.S.L.C. cxxiii, cxxviii)
Lich.	Lichfield
List of Clergy, 1541–2	*A List of Clergy for Eleven Deaneries of the Diocese of Chester, 1541–2,* ed. W. F. Irvine (R.S.L.C. xxxiii)
Lond.	London
Lond. Gaz.	*London Gazette*
Lucian, *De Laude Cestrie*	*Liber Luciani de Laude Cestrie,* ed. M. V. Taylor (R.S.L.C. lxiv)
m./mm.	membrane, -s
Mins.	Minutes
Morris, *Chester*	R. H. Morris, *Chester in the Plantagenet and Tudor Reigns*
Morris, *Siege of Chester*	R. H. Morris, *The Siege of Chester, 1643–6,* ed. P. H. Lawson [also published in *J.C.A.S.* xxv]
MS.	Manuscript
N.S.	new series
O.E.D.	*Oxford English Dictionary*
O.S.	Ordnance Survey
o.s.	old series
orig. ser.	original series
Ormerod, *Hist. Ches.*	G. Ormerod, *The History of the County Palatine and City of Chester,* revised and enlarged edn. by T. Helsby (1882)
Oxf.	Oxford
P. & G. Dir. Chester	Phillipson and Golder, *Directory for Chester and its Immediate Neighbourhood* [various edns.]
P.N. Ches.	*The Place-Names of Cheshire,* ed. J. McN. Dodgson (English Place-Name Society)
Par.	Parish
Parl.	Parliament, -ary
Parl. Deb.	*Parliamentary Debates* [i.e. 'Hansard']
pers. comm.	personal comment
Pevsner, *Ches.*	N. Pevsner and E. Hubbard, *The Buildings of England: Cheshire*
P.R.O.	Public Record Office, Kew

Proc.	Proceedings
Q. Sess.	Quarter Sessions
R.O.	Record Office
R.S.L.C.	Record Society of Lancashire and Cheshire
Rec. Ser.	Record Series
Red Bk. Exch.	*Red Book of the Exchequer*, ed. H. Hall (Rolls Ser.)
REED: Chester	*Records of Early English Drama: Chester*, ed. L. M. Clopper
Reg.	Register(s)
Rep.	Report
31st Rep. Com. Char.	*Thirty-first Report of the Commissioners Appointed to Enquire Concerning Charities*, H.C. 103 (1837–8), xxiv
Rep. Com. Mun. Corp.	*Report of the Commission on Municipal Corporations*, H.C. 116 (1835), xxiii
Rev.	*Review*
Rolls Ser.	Rolls Series [officially called *Rerum Britannicarum Medii Aevi Scriptores*]
rot./rott.	rotulet, -s
s.n.	under the name (*sub nomine*)
s.v./s.vv.	under the word/words (*sub verbo/verbis*)
Sel. Cases concerning Law Merchant	*Select Cases concerning the Law Merchant*, ed. C. Gross and H. Hall (3 vols., Selden Soc.)
Sel. Cases in K.B.	*Select Cases in the Court of King's Bench*, ed. G. O. Sayles (7 vols., Selden Soc.)
Sel. R. Chester City Cts.	*Selected Rolls of the Chester City Courts, Late 13th and Early 14th Centuries*, ed. A. Hopkins (Chetham Soc. 3rd ser. ii)
ser.	series
Sheaf	*The Cheshire Sheaf* [preceded by series number, followed by volume number within the series]
Soc.	Society
sqq.	and following pages (*sequentia*)
T.H.S.L.C.	*Transactions of the Historic Society of Lancashire and Cheshire*
T.L.C.A.S.	*Transactions of the Lancashire and Cheshire Antiquarian Society*
Trans. R.H.S.	*Transactions of the Royal Historical Society*
Trans. Salop. Arch. Soc.	*Transactions of the Shropshire Archaeological and Historical Society*
TS.	Typescript
Univ.	University
V.C.H.	*Victoria County History*
Valor Eccl.	*Valor Ecclesiasticus, temp. Hen. VIII* (Record Commission)
Wilson, 'Port of Chester'	K. P. Wilson, 'The Port of Chester in the Later Middle Ages' (Liverpool Univ. Ph.D. thesis, 1965)

CLASSES OF ORIGINAL RECORDS

PUBLIC RECORD OFFICE

Palatinate of Chester
CHES 2   Exchequer of Chester: Enrolments
CHES 3   Exchequer of Chester: Various Inquisitions
CHES 19   Sheriffs' Tourn Rolls and Files
CHES 25   Chester County Court: Indictment Rolls and Files
CHES 29   Chester County Court: Plea Rolls
CHES 31   Final Concords and Recoveries Files
CHES 38   Miscellanea

Chancery
C 146   Ancient Deeds, Series C

Exchequer, King's Remembrancer
E 179   Records Relating to Lay and Clerical Taxation

Exchequer, Court of Augmentations
E 301   Certificates of Colleges, Chantries, and Similar Foundations
E 315   Miscellaneous Books

Exchequer, Trustees for Crown Lands and Fee-Farm Rents
E 317   Parliamentary Surveys

Home Office
HO 107   Census Returns, 1841 and 1851

Obsolete Lists
OBS 1   Obsolete Lists Associated with P.R.O. Holdings

Privy Council
PC 2   Registers

General Register Office
RG 11   Census Returns, 1881

Special Collections
SC 6   Ministers' and Receivers' Accounts
SC 11   Rentals and Surveys, Rolls

Secretaries of State
SP 12   State Papers Domestic, Elizabeth I
SP 16   State Papers Domestic, Charles I

Legal Records Relating to Wales
WALE 29   Palatinate of Chester: Ancient Deeds, Series F

War Office
WO 30   Miscellaneous Papers

Office of Works
WORK 14   Ancient Monuments and Historic Buildings: Registered Files

CHESHIRE AND CHESTER ARCHIVES AND LOCAL STUDIES

COUNTY AND DIOCESAN RECORDS

Estate and Family Papers
DAL   Aldersey of Aldersey
DBA   Barnston of Churton
DDX   Miscellaneous
DVE   Vernon of Kinderton

Diocesan Records
EDA   Administration
EDC   Consistory Court
EDD   Dean and Chapter
EDE   Episcopal Estates
EDT   Tithe

Church Commissioners
EEC   Chester Cathedral Chapter

Parish Records
P

Wills and Probate Records
WC   Diocesan Series (Disputed Wills)
WS   Supra Series

CHESTER CITY RECORDS

Assembly
ZAB   Assembly Books
ZAC   Assembly Committees
ZAF   Assembly Files
ZAP   Assembly Petitions

City Council
ZCA   Boundary Reports
ZCB   Council Minute Books
ZCCB   Committee Minute Books
ZCCF   Committee Files
ZCEA   Poll Books
ZCEB   Burgess Rolls
ZCEC   Ward Lists of Burgesses
ZCH   Charters
ZCHB   Cartularies
ZCHD   Corporation Deeds
ZCL   Corporation Lawsuits
ZCLB   Parliamentary Bills
ZCLC   Commissions of Inquiry and Public Inquiries
ZCX   Council Manuscripts

Private Records
ZCR 4   Williams and Co. (bankers)
ZCR 39   William Titherington (Dee Hills estate deeds)
ZCR 55   Chester Methodist Circuit

ZCR 56	Miscellaneous
ZCR 60	Thomas Hughes (antiquary)
ZCR 77	Lanceleys Ltd. (engineers)
ZCR 92	Butt and Co. Ltd. (jewellers)
ZCR 95	Thomas Welsby and Co. Ltd. (wine merchants)
ZCR 115	Roger Barnston's Volunteer Corps
ZCR 159	Chester Liberal Association
ZCR 164	Chester Council of Social Welfare and associated organizations
ZCR 204	Chester Council of Social Welfare
ZCR 210	Samuel Taylor Parry (mechanical engineer)
ZCR 256	Hydraulic Engineering Co. Ltd.
ZCR 294	Chester Co-operative Society Ltd.
ZCR 310	Richard Jones and Co. Ltd. (drapers and furnishers)
ZCR 352	Daniel Peck (merchant)
ZCR 366	J. H. Taylor and Sons (boat builders)
ZCR 388	Medical Officer of Health (printed report)
ZCR 420	Brookhirst Switchgear Ltd. (electrical engineers)
ZCR 469	Aldersey Family
ZCR 470	Chester Trades Council and Labour Party
ZCR 529	T. G. Burrell Ltd. (department store)
ZCR 558	Hendersons (Chester) Ltd. (furnishers)
ZCR 566	Chester Trustee Savings Bank
ZCR 572	Chester Evangelical Free Church Council
ZCR 586	Associated Lead Manufacturers (Chester Leadworks)
ZCR 600	Chester Municipal Charities (printed report)
ZCR 658	Browns of Chester (department store)

Accumulations of Deeds

ZD/HT	Henry Taylor (antiquary)
ZD/JWW	Jolliffe, Wickham, and Wood (solicitors)
ZD/PB	Potts and Ball (solicitors)

Council Departments

ZDH	Health
ZDHO	Housing
ZDLC	Town Clerk, Land Charges
ZDS	Surveyor
ZDTR	Treasurer

Guilds

ZG	Guild Records

Mayor

ZMB	Mayors' Books
ZMBB	Assize of Bread
ZMF	Mayors' Files
ZMIP	Inner Pentice Files
ZML	Mayors' Letters
ZMMP	Mayors' Military Papers
ZMR	Portmote Court Rolls

Murengers

ZMUB	Account Books
ZMUR	Account Roll
ZMUV	Vouchers

Coroners

ZQCI	Inquisitions

Crownmote

ZQCR	Court Rolls

Quarter Sessions

ZQRL	Licensed Victuallers
ZQSF	Quarter Sessions Files

Sheriffs

ZSB	Sheriffs' Books
ZSBC	Sheriffs' Court Books (Pentice Court)
ZSFB	Sheriffs' Files: Bonds
ZSR	Pentice Court Rolls

Treasurers

ZCAS	Assessments: Subsidies, Aids, and Taxes
ZTAA	Annuitants' Receipt Books
ZTAB	Account Books
ZTAR	Account Rolls and Rentals
ZTAV	Vouchers

Town Clerk

ZTCC	Papers Relating to Corporation Business
ZTCP	Papers Relating to Private Legal Practice

Statutory and Local Authorities

ZTRH	Hoole Urban District Council
ZTRI	Police (Improvement) Commissioners
ZTRP	Chester Civil Parish

Other Records

Cowper MSS.	Collectanea Devana of Dr. William Cowper

THE CITY OF CHESTER

THIS VOLUME, published in two parts, provides a full treatment of most aspects of Chester's history from Roman times to the year 2000.[1] The two parts are complementary. The chapters in Part 1 give a general account of the city, covering administrative, political, economic, social, and religious history, divided into six periods: Roman, Early Medieval (400–1230), Later Medieval (1230–1550), Early Modern (1550–1762), Late Georgian and Victorian (1762–1914), and Twentieth-Century (1914–2000). The topographies of Roman and 20th-century Chester form integral parts of the first and last chapters,[2] while a separate chapter deals with Topography 900–1914. Part 2 of the volume contains detailed accounts of particular topics, institutions, and buildings, grouped in five sections: Local Government and Public Services; Economic Infrastructure and Institutions; The Churches and Other Religious Bodies; Major Buildings; and Leisure and Culture. Part 2 has a full index to the whole volume, including subjects; Part 1 an index only of persons and places mentioned in that part.

DEFINING CHESTER

Until the 19th century what was meant by 'Chester' was unproblematic. The Roman fortress with its adjacent civilian settlement was succeeded in the early Middle Ages by a small fortified town on the same site. Probably in the 10th century two sides of the Roman walls were abandoned, and by the early 12th century the circuit of walls had reached its modern extent. Sizeable extramural suburbs grew up, including the separately named Handbridge south of the river, which has always been reckoned part of Chester. The suburbs were encircled by Chester's arable fields, meadows, and common pastures, with heaths to the north-east around Hoole, and a large area of marshland to the south-west at Saltney.

Beyond the immediate environs of walled town, suburbs, and farmland, an extensive territory depended upon Chester in the early Middle Ages, covering many townships with their own villages, hamlets, and farms. During the central Middle Ages many of the townships were incorporated into newly formed parishes, leaving a few outliers attached to the oldest Chester parishes of St. Oswald and St. John. They were never strictly speaking part of Chester, and their histories are not treated in this volume.

In the 10th and 11th centuries Chester hundred was one of twelve in Cheshire, but the creation of civic institutions in the 12th and 13th centuries led to the disappearance of the hundred and its replacement by the liberties of the city, the area within which the citizens enjoyed their various individual and corporate privileges. The liberties were first explicitly demarcated by a precise boundary in 1354 but must have existed long previously as a territory whose limits were generally known. They covered some 3,000 acres and included the abbot of Chester's manor north of the city, and an extensive area south of the Dee, focused on Handbridge. Both the manor of Handbridge and its open fields extended beyond the liberties into the township of Claverton to the south.[3]

On the north-east, north, and north-west the townships immediately beyond the liberties were Great Boughton, Hoole, Newton, Bache, and Blacon. The Hoole boundary was little more than ½ mile from the heart of Chester at the Cross (the central crossroads by St. Peter's church, also the site of the medieval High Cross). The approach to Great Boughton, 1½ miles distant from the Cross, lay through Chester's most important medieval and early modern suburb in Foregate Street and its continuation beyond the Bars, which was called Boughton. Right on the boundary from the early 12th century until the 1640s stood the leper hospital of St. Giles, occupying a tiny extra-parochial area called Spital Boughton. On the south-western side the boundary of the liberties coincided with the national boundary between England and Wales from 1536, when the Act of Union placed the lordship and parish of Hawarden in the newly created Welsh county of Denbighshire (it was transferred to Flintshire in 1541).[4]

From the 19th century Chester is less easy to define. The liberties circumscribed the formal extent of the city of Chester until minor adjustments were made in 1835, enlarging the municipal borough at the expense of Great Boughton, but already by then the town had spilled over the boundary through residential building in the adjoining parts of Great Boughton and Hoole. The arrival of the railway in the 1840s quickened the growth of Chester beyond the borough boundaries, creating new streets which were physically part of the city but administratively outside the remit of the borough council. North-east of the town, the main

1 Where not otherwise stated, what follows depends upon the findings presented more fully elsewhere in this volume.

2 A more detailed account of the topography of Roman Chester appeared in *V.C.H. Ches.* i. 117–85.

3 P. J. W. Higson, 'Pointers towards the Structure of Agriculture in Handbridge and Claverton prior to Parl. Enclosure', *T.H.S.L.C.* cxlii. 56–71.

4 R. R. Davies, *Lordship and Society in the March of Wales, 1282–1400*, 16, 48; *V.C.H. Ches.* ii. 7; G. Williams, *Recovery, Reorientation, and Reformation: Wales c. 1415–1642*, 268, 271.

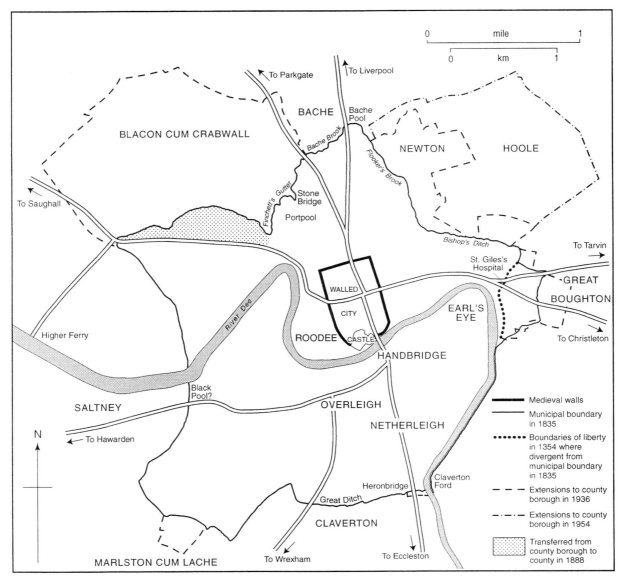

FIG. 1. *Chester: the city boundaries and neighbouring townships*

railway station was built on the boundary with Hoole, the nearer parts of which were rapidly built over. To the west, the railway brought industrial development and associated housing to a new suburb which straddled the boundary between Chester and the township of Saltney in Flintshire. For a variety of reasons there was no major extension of the city's boundaries until 1936, when the county borough incorporated parts of Great Boughton and Newton and most of Blacon, the last intended for a large new council-housing estate. Hoole remained a separate unit of local government (latterly an urban district) until it too was absorbed by Chester in 1954. Meanwhile the building of more new housing in the townships of Upton and Bache north of the city created a large built-up area which was not brought under Chester's control until 1974. Even after that date Saltney had to be excluded from Chester district because it was in

Wales and the national boundary was regarded by central government as inviolate.

The area described in both parts of this volume is essentially the medieval town and liberties, together with those parts brought within the borough boundary in 1835, 1936, and 1954, but only from the time of their incorporation into Chester. Saltney, Upton, Bache, and Great Boughton are discussed where appropriate, as in the accounts of 19th-century industry and 20th-century suburban housing. The earlier histories of all those townships are reserved for treatment elsewhere.

NAME AND SITUATION

The Roman name for the fortress built at the head of the Dee estuary was Deva, adopted directly from the British name of the river, and 'Deverdoeu' was still one of two alternative Welsh names for Chester in the late

12th century. Its other and more enduring Welsh name was Caerlleon, literally 'the fortress-city of the legions', a name identical with that of the great Roman fortress at the other end of the Marches at Caerleon (Mon.). The colloquial modern Welsh name is the shortened form, Caer. The early English-speaking settlers used a name which had the same meaning, 'Legacæstir', which was current until the 11th century, when – in a further parallel with Welsh usage – the first element fell out of use and the simplex name Chester emerged. From the 14th century to the 18th the city's prominent position in north-western England meant that it was commonly also known as Westchester.[1]

Chester's importance as a town has been shaped by its geographical position. The city centre and Handbridge occupy a ridge of sandstone interrupted by the river Dee. The western side of the ridge is a steep escarpment overlooking the Roodee, which until the 12th century was a tidal meadow at the head of a broad estuary extending some 20 miles to the open sea at Hilbre Island and Point of Ayr. The combination of factors made the site both the lowest point at which the river could be bridged (successively, and almost on the same spot, by the Romans and the Anglo-Saxons) and the limit of navigation in the estuary. Navigation and tides in the upper estuary were evidently restricted by a rocky natural feature underlying the man-made causeway or weir constructed just upstream from the Dee Bridge no later than the 1090s. Although little evidence of pre-Roman occupation of the site of Chester had come to light before 2000, local archaeologists then believed that there was likely to have been significant Iron Age activity in the vicinity.[2]

The geological strata underlying Chester comprise Pebble Beds to the east of Dee Bridge, the Roodee, and Bache, and Lower Mottled Sandstone to the west. Both are overlain by boulder clay except where the ridge protrudes in a line running from Heronbridge in the south through Handbridge and Queen's Park to the walled city. Further north there are pockets of glacial sands and gravels in Newton and Upton, while to the west the former bed of the upper estuary at Sealand, Lache, and the Roodee is composed of alluvium deposited as the river gradually assumed its modern course and width.[3] The Roman fortress did not occupy the highest point on the ridge, which lies at a little over 30 m. (100 ft.) just north of the city walls. To the north and east the land slopes gently down to about 23 m. (75 ft.) before rising again to a low ridge over 30 m. which runs south-east to north-west through Christleton, Hoole, Newton, and Upton. South and west of the Roman fortress there is a much steeper slope to below 5 m. (15 ft.) on the river bank and the Roodee. South of the river the land rises to about 24 m. (80 ft.) at the

southern boundary of the liberties. Within the city walls the natural ground levels have been much altered by almost two thousand years of building and demolition, with the effect of creating a much more level plateau.[4] The Dee describes a gently winding double bend through the city, flowing first north between Heronbridge and Handbridge on the left bank (within the liberties) and Great Boughton on the right (outside), turning sharply south-west around the meadows known historically as the Earl's Eye, passing in the relatively narrow gap between the walled city and Handbridge, and turning briefly north again around the Roodee. In ancient times the river flowed into the head of the open estuary at the Roodee but since the later Middle Ages it has been directed sharply south-west again for about a mile before finally turning north-west, after the 18th century into the straight canalized stretch which takes it through the reclaimed marshland of Sealand (Flints.) to the open part of the estuary below Flint.

CHESTER'S IMPORTANCE AND RANKING

Chester was for many centuries the most important place by far in north-western England. That was largely due to its location at the crossroads of the British Isles, where routes from southern Britain led into north Wales and the Irish Sea. On three occasions its role as the point of entry into the Irish Sea region for rulers based in the South made it prominent in national affairs. At the outset the Romans probably selected the site for their fortress because of its potential as a port for an assault on Ireland. In the 10th century the reoccupied fortress became the centre for attempts by English kings to dominate other rulers around the shores of the Irish Sea, notably in the carefully staged set-piece by which King Edgar demonstrated his overlordship by having them row him on the Dee in 973. Tribute in silver extracted from such rulers was turned into coin at Chester, whose mint was astonishingly prolific in the 10th century. Finally, the English conquest of north Wales in the 1270s and 1280s depended heavily on Chester as a base. The city's military and political importance to Edward I, which endured into the early 14th century, brought it great prosperity, notably through the victualling of armies and the supply of royal castles in north Wales.

Although never among the largest five or six English provincial towns, Chester was certainly in the second rank by the late Anglo-Saxon period and retained that status almost until 1700. Uncertainty about the numbers of inhabitants makes it impossible to assign a more precise ranking before 1801. In 1086 Chester was among a dozen towns with populations in the order of 2,000–2,500, behind seven with over 5,000 people

1 *P.N. Ches.* v (1:i), 2–7.
2 Inf. from Mr. Keith Matthews, Chester City Archaeology.
3 Geol. Surv. 1-inch map, sheets 108–9, solid and drift.

4 O.S. Map 1-inch, 7th ser., sheet 109 (1952 edn.); D. Mason, 'Chester: The Evolution and Adaptation of its Landscape', *J.C.A.S.* lix. 14–23.

each.[1] In the 1520s it was among sixteen towns with perhaps 3,500–5,000 inhabitants, when the six largest, other than London, had between 6,000 and 13,000 residents. By 1700 Chester's population was probably approaching 8,000, placing it in a second rank of some 25 towns with 5,000 or more people; the six largest towns after London then had between 10,000 and 30,000 people.[2] In the 18th century Chester continued to grow in absolute terms and it just about held its place, ranking 18th in England in 1801, the first year for which reliable population figures are available. It was then among the middling county towns, comparable with Shrewsbury, Worcester, Carlisle, Leicester, Derby, Oxford, Reading, Exeter, Cambridge, Colchester, and Ipswich but considerably smaller than such places as York, Norwich, Newcastle upon Tyne, and Bristol, let alone its near neighbours Liverpool and Manchester.[3] In the 19th century Chester slipped dramatically down the rankings as the new industrial towns of the North and Midlands swelled in size. By 1901 it was barely among the eighty most populous boroughs and cities, and even within Cheshire it had been overtaken by Stockport, Birkenhead, Crewe, and Wallasey.[4] In the 20th century Chester's prosperity and rising population allowed it to maintain that rank, overtaking many stagnant or declining northern towns (including Crewe and Wallasey) but eclipsed by a similar number of faster-growing towns, mostly in the South.[5]

At the time of the Norman Conquest Chester was in effect a provincial capital. With no larger place closer to it than York, Lincoln, and Oxford, it was the foremost town of western Mercia, covering the whole northwestern and central Midlands, the Welsh borders, and the upper North-West beyond the Mersey. Later in the Middle Ages Chester's region contracted: Bristol overtook it as the most important west-coast port at an early date; Coventry rose to become an economic capital for the heart of the Midlands; and, nearer at hand, Shrewsbury was almost certainly as big as Chester by 1300 and deprived it of any significant economic role in the central Marches and mid-Wales.

Chester survived as a regional capital through the Middle Ages and into the 18th century, with no rival nearer than Shrewsbury, but it dominated a much smaller region than cities such as Bristol, Exeter, Norwich, and Newcastle upon Tyne, as well as being a smaller place in absolute terms. Its hinterland was poorer than most of theirs, and its overseas trade was much more limited. The hinterland in economic terms covered the western half of Cheshire and much of north-east Wales; it was the main market for the

agricultural produce of that area, to which it also supplied manufactured goods, both locally produced and imported, and a variety of services. It continued to perform that role well into the 19th century, though the region which it dominated gradually diminished in size as rival towns such as Wrexham and Birkenhead grew in size. As a resort of the propertied and leisured classes, however, Chester had a much larger reach for much longer: even in the early 19th century, for example, the races were frequented and the infirmary was patronized by well-to-do families from south Lancashire, north Shropshire, north Staffordshire, and north Wales as far as Anglesey.

CHESTER AND THE GROSVENORS

Chester had no patron from the later Middle Ages onwards to match the Roman army, the 10th-century West Saxon kings, or Edward I, all of whom had put the city at the centre of national affairs. From the 17th century it did, however, have the Grosvenors. Seated at Eaton from the earlier 15th century,[6] holder of a baronetcy from 1622 and a peerage from 1761, the head of the family was Earl Grosvenor from 1784, marquess of Westminster from 1831, and duke of Westminster from 1874. In 1677 the family acquired the Middlesex manor of Ebury, in Westminster, and from the later 18th century it rose very quickly to become one of Britain's wealthiest. The basis of their wealth was initially lead mining in Flintshire, but that was very soon overtaken by the vast urban rents accrued from the successive development of Mayfair (1720s–1770s), Belgravia (1820s–1850s), and Pimlico (1830s and later) on their London estate. From the 18th century the Grosvenors played a large part in the life of Chester as landlords and patrons. Eaton Hall was only three miles from the Cross, though outside the liberties. A fitting approach from Handbridge along tree-lined avenues to Eaton was created through a very carefully managed parliamentary inclosure in 1805.[7]

From the late 17th century to the late 1820s Grosvenor patronage in Chester had an overtly political purpose: to dominate the Assembly (the governing body of the city) and monopolize Chester's parliamentary representation. The family's social leadership was significant even when it was divorced from direct political interests after the 1820s. During the rest of the 19th century and the early 20th the marquess and dukes of Westminster paid for schools, curates, a new parish church, two public parks, and a nurses' home; they owned the advowsons of two of the city's parish churches, were patrons of Chester races, major benefactors of the infirmary and the new Grosvenor

1 H. C. Darby, *Domesday Eng.* 302–9, 364–8.
2 C. G. A. Clay, *Econ. Expansion and Social Change: Eng. 1500–1700*, i. 166–70.
3 *Census*, 1801.
4 *Survey Gazetteer of Brit. Isles*, ed. J. G. Bartholomew (1904 edn.), 896.

5 *Census*, 1991, *Key Statistics for Urban and Rural Areas: Great Britain*, pp. 20–35.
6 Ormerod, *Hist. Ches.* ii. 833.
7 P. J. W. Higson, 'Landlord Control and Motivation in the Parl. Enclosure of St. Mary's-on-the-Hill Parish, Chester', *T.H.S.L.C.* cxxxvii. 93–116.

Museum, supporters of innumerable philanthropic activities, and had the new Grosvenor Bridge named after them. In the later 20th century their property interests in Chester included the largest of the city's shopping centres (the Grosvenor Centre) and a huge business park on the southern outskirts.

CHESTER'S WIDER CULTURAL CONNEXIONS

Although Chester has had close links with Wales and Ireland at nearly every period, its wider cultural links have always been rather meagre. There seems not to have been a Jewish community in the Middle Ages. Manxmen settled in Chester from the later Middle Ages, and a few Spanish merchants visited in the 16th century. Negligible numbers of displaced persons and Commonwealth immigrants arrived in the years after the Second World War, and in 1991 the non-white element amounted to little more than 1,000 people in a population of almost 90,000.[1] At only two periods have the streets been full of foreign voices: in Roman times, the legionary garrison was made up of soldiers drawn from across the provinces of the Empire, and late 20th-century tourism filled the city centre with thousands of visitors from western Europe, north America, and further afield.

The city's location, however, long gave it a pivotal role in the affairs of the Irish Sea region. In the 1120s the historian Henry of Huntingdon regarded Chester's distinct attribute as being 'near to the Irish' (not the Welsh).[2] As long as the Dee remained navigable, Ireland was Chester's chief overseas trading partner, and as such the main source of Chester merchants' prosperity in the later Middle Ages and the 16th century. The city's political importance to the English Crown from the 1590s into the early 18th century arose because it was the main staging post on the route between the two capital cities: about 185 miles from London by road and 150 from Dublin by sea. Connexions with Ireland were again evident in the brief flourishing of linen imports in the later 18th century, in famine-induced Irish migration to the city in the earlier 19th century, and in the comically abortive Fenian plot against Chester castle in 1867. The Roman Catholic presence in the city from the mid 19th century was very largely of Irish origin. Irish migration to Chester peaked in the mid 19th century and then declined somewhat: in 1851, in the immediate wake of the Potato Famine, some 7 per cent of Cestrians were Irish-born, account-

ing for about 2,000 people, but by 1901 the level had fallen to 3 per cent (though of a considerably larger total population), and in 1991 stood at about 2 per cent.[3]

Welsh links have been more obviously to the fore in Chester's history, but they were mostly restricted to the north-eastern corner of the principality and the districts along the north coast, areas closely bound into Chester's economic hinterland. At all periods since the 11th century or earlier Welshmen have frequented Chester's markets, fairs, and shops; Chester was the market for Welsh grain, livestock, coal, lead, and slates; Welsh soldiers were shipped from Chester to fight in Ireland in the 1590s, and a Welsh pirate allegedly sold his booty in the city in the 1560s.[4] Chester loomed large in the consciousness of the north Welsh: the city gates were regarded as the limits of Welsh territory in the 12th century,[5] and the 'men of Chester' were vilified in anti-English poetry of the 15th century,[6] but there was probably always much migration from Wales to the city, larger by far than any town in north Wales itself until the mid 19th century, and even then still larger than Wrexham. Before the later 18th century it seems that most migrants were rapidly Anglicized and assimilated, contributing to a rich stratum of Chester surnames of Welsh origin. Possibly as many as a third of the 1,200 freemen who voted in the shrieval election of 1818, for example, had Welsh surnames, many doubtless of families long established in the city.[7] Welsh-language books were printed in Chester from the early 18th century,[8] and Welsh newspapers from the 1790s,[9] the period when separate Welsh-speaking congregations were first formed in the city. The existence of Welsh churches suggests that the numbers of settlers were large enough to sustain the language beyond first-generation migrants. By the 1860s, when there were five Welsh-speaking congregations in Chester, St. David's Day was a focus of collective expression which transcended denominational boundaries. There had been a Chester Cymmrodorion Society, Anglican and Tory in orientation, from 1822 but it evidently died out after local politics became less polarized in the 1830s. The revival of a Chester Welsh Society (Cymdeithas Cymry Caer) in 1892 was evidently non-aligned in politics and religion.[10] The Welsh-born population formed 11 per cent of the total in 1851 and almost as much in 1901 and 1951.[11] In 1991 over 6 per cent of the residents of

1 Census, 1991, Key Statistics for Urban and Rural Areas: North, p. 50.

2 Henry of Huntingdon, Historia Anglorum, ed. D. Greenway, 20–1.

3 Census, 1851, Birthplaces, p. 664; 1901, Ches. p. 90; 1951, Ches. p. 82; 1991, Ches. p. 88: 1,801 people born in both parts of Ireland living in Chester district as a whole.

4 G. Williams, Recovery, Reorientation, and Reformation: Wales c. 1415–1642, 368, 372, 379.

5 R. R. Davies, Conquest, Coexistence, and Change: Wales 1063–1415, 16.

6 G. Williams, Recovery, Reorientation, and Reformation: Wales c. 1415–1642, 9.

7 Based on analysis of Poll-Bk. for Sheriff, with Concise Hist. and Papers (1818, publ. M. Monk).

8 M. Parry, 'Chester Welsh Printing', J.C.A.S. xxi. 57–67; D. Nuttall, 'Hist. Printing in Chester', ibid. liv. 51–9.

9 V.C.H. Ches. v (2), Newspapers.

10 T. Edwards, Chester Cambrian Societies, 1760–1906 (priv. print. 1906).

11 Census, 1851, Birthplaces, p. 664; 1901, Ches. p. 90; 1951, Ches. p. 82.

Chester district as a whole, wider than the city alone, had been born in Wales.[1]

THE CHARACTER OF CHESTER

Roman Chester is most plausibly represented and best understood as a military depot consisting of a walled fortress with a number of important extramural buildings, notably the amphitheatre, and an attendant civilian settlement. Archaeological investigations have revealed more about the fortress than about the town which served it.[2] There were long periods in which the Roman legion stationed at Chester was absent on duties elsewhere in Britain or further afield in the Empire, leaving only a skeleton garrison as depot caretakers. The ebb and flow of the military presence can hardly have failed to affect the civilian settlement, but it is difficult to say how far the latter may have had an independent existence. After the legion left for the last time, perhaps in 383, the character and extent of settlement at Chester is impossible to establish for a period of almost five centuries. It is clear that very substantial remains of the fortress walls and of stone buildings both inside and outside them survived for many centuries afterwards, and it seems probable that from the 7th century Chester was the centre of an extensive territory and had at least one major church.

Chester was re-established as a place of importance by the 10th century through the convergence of two circumstances. First, it was garrisoned again in the early 10th century during the course of Æthelflæd's military campaigns designed to secure the northern frontier of Mercia against the Vikings. In reoccupying Chester, Æthelflæd made it a centre of government, one of the fortified towns which later in the 10th century developed into the central places of the newly established Mercian shires. Cheshire was thus Chester's shire, and indeed was often known as Chestershire until the 15th century.[3] In addition, the city became a centre of trade for the Irish Sea region, with a small Hiberno-Norse quarter between the remains of the Roman fortress and the river Dee. Trade and government have been the mainstays of Chester's significance ever since.

Control of Chester in the early medieval period alternated between great regional magnates and the kings of England. Æthelflæd was ruler of a Mercia still partly independent of Wessex, but after her death Chester soon fell into the hands of the West Saxon kings, and on the eve of the Norman Conquest it was one of the series of sizeable Midland shire towns under royal lordship. After 1066 William I gave it to Earl Hugh, whose successors as earls of Chester ruled the city until 1237, when the earldom was annexed by the Crown. The fact that Chester belonged for over 150 years to Anglo-Norman earls rather than English kings, unlike most large towns, did not in practice make much difference to its development, though there may have been economic advantages from being the earls' headquarters. After 1237 the presence of senior palatine officials and a certain military presence at the castle affected the city's physical appearance and its prosperity. The palatine status of the county meant that Chester's administrative development was not straightforward. Cheshire had its law courts at Chester castle, in effect parallel to those at Westminster, and there were many conflicts of authority between the palatinate and the city's own courts. Chester did not return M.P.s to parliament until 1543. In many respects, however, the county palatine was assimilated to English administrative and judicial norms between the 1520s and the 1540s, though some of its distinctive institutions survived until the 1830s.[4]

In general the administrative development of Chester followed a course similar to that of other shire towns which were also regional capitals. Chester was already regarded as a city (*civitas*) in 1086. Institutions of self-government, notably the mayoralty, had developed by the 1230s, supplementing and eventually subordinating the sheriffs who had previously governed the city on behalf of the earls. Chester was created a county in its own right by the royal charter of 1506, and became successively a reformed municipal borough in 1835 and a county borough in 1889. Although the county borough was too small to resist absorption into a larger second-tier district council at local government reorganization in 1974, the style City of Chester was carried over as the name of the new district and the mayoralty was retained and indeed in 1992 elevated to a lord mayoralty.

Chester was also an ecclesiastical capital. For a few years after 1075 it served as the seat of the diocesan bishop earlier based at Lichfield and later at Coventry. The archdeaconry of Chester had a semi-independent status within the medieval diocese. The bishop's church in the city, St. John's, however, was always outranked by the great Benedictine abbey of St. Werburgh, founded by Earl Hugh in 1092. St. Werburgh's was rich and powerful, with a large monastic precinct within the city walls, a manor covering the northern part of the liberties, and control (initially) of the city's main annual fair. On the other hand, unlike abbeys in some smaller towns, St. Werburgh's was only one element in medieval Chester. The abbot and monks were frequently at loggerheads with the citizens, and as the civic authorities became more self-confident in the 14th and 15th centuries they gradually enlarged their rights at the expense of the abbey's, until the city's Great Charter of 1506 in effect confirmed Chester's independence from both St. Werburgh's and the county palatine.

Following the dissolution of the monastery in 1540

---

1 *Census*, 1991, *Ches.* p. 88.
2 D. J. P. Mason, *Roman Chester*, appeared after the chapter

on 'Roman Chester' in this volume was completed.
3 *P.N. Ches.* i. 1.   4 *V.C.H. Ches.* ii. 33–7.

the abbey church became the seat of a new diocesan bishop in 1541, the monastic precinct and many of its buildings being retained by the new establishment. The precinct was a place somewhat apart from the city until the 1920s. That separation, and the commercial bustle outside the precinct walls, prevented Chester from ever becoming a Trollopean backwater in the manner of the smaller cathedral cities: although the cathedral dominated the town centre as a building it was only one among several influences as an institution.

Chester was also for most of its history a garrison town, a consequence of its situation in relation to Wales and Ireland. The Roman fortress, Æthelflæd's *burh*, the small earthwork and timber castle of the Normans, and the larger stone castle created by Earl Ranulph III and Henry III were successively superimposed upon one another. From the 11th century to the late 13th the city was the gathering place for armies setting out into north Wales, and from the late 12th century to the late 17th for expeditions to quell rebellions in Ireland. Chester's military importance was reflected in the long siege which it endured at the hands of parliamentarian forces during the English Civil War. After the Glorious Revolution, however, that significance fell quickly away, notwithstanding the Jacobite scares of 1715 and 1745. The castle was garrisoned in the 18th century by companies of invalid soldiers, giving the second-in-command in 1760, Lieut. Joseph Winder, the leisure to amuse himself by drawing a detailed panoramic view of the city.[1] Even so, Chester's military role had not been entirely eroded: with the invention of county-based regiments and regional commands in the later 19th century, it became an important Army recruiting centre and the headquarters of Western Command.

The economy of the medieval town was based on Chester's position as a port, a market with an extensive hinterland, a place of craft manufacture, and a centre for servicing the needs of the abbey, several other religious houses, and the palatine administration and garrison at the castle. The port of Chester included outlying anchorages in the Dee estuary which became of greater significance as the head of the estuary silted up in the later Middle Ages and restricted access to the city's own quays. From 1559, when it was brought into the national customs system, Chester was administratively the head port for the whole stretch of coastline from Anglesey to Lancaster.[2] It remained the largest port on those coasts until eclipsed by Liverpool. Liverpool did not begin its meteoric rise as a transatlantic and international port until the later 17th century, but it was already encroaching on Chester's Irish trade by

1500. In the 16th century Liverpool's location closer to the burgeoning textile industries of south Lancashire, and on an open estuary but with a good natural harbour, gave it distinct advantages over Chester.

Coasting trade and especially the trade with Ireland were always Chester's mainstays; overseas contacts were extremely limited in comparison with those of Bristol or the main ports of the east and south coasts. Moreover the progressive silting of the Dee meant that coasting and long-distance vessels increasingly had to unload into carts or shallow-draught boats at the minor ports further down the estuary. Although ships were built at the Roodee shipyard as late as 1869 and small seagoing vessels still occasionally visited Crane Wharf in the 1940s, Chester's maritime importance had ended centuries earlier.

By the later Middle Ages, when abundant documentation allows a full picture of the city's economy to be drawn, Chester craftsmen were making an enormous variety of goods. Given the pastoral bias of the city's immediate hinterland, the most important area of specialization was leather manufacture in almost every branch. Textiles were never of any great moment. Much corn was also grown in the neighbourhood until the concentration on dairying in the later 19th century, and the Dee corn mills, powered by penning up the river at the causeway above the bridge, were large and profitable. They acquired national renown through the opening words of Isaac Bickerstaffe's comic song, *The Miller of the Dee*, written for a traditional tune in 1762: 'There was a jolly miller once, lived on the river Dee'.[3]

The sale of agricultural produce, locally manufactured goods, and imports of all kinds in Chester's markets and fairs contributed greatly to the city's prosperity from an early period into modern times. Despite the huge changes in the nature of the national economy and in the means by which goods were distributed, retailing remained of prime importance to the city at the end of the 20th century. A very large proportion of late 20th-century visitors to Chester came 'for the shops', and the city had a retail sector far larger than its own population would have warranted.

The 'long 18th century' has been seen as the period when Chester was transformed from a town of craft manufactures and artisans into a 'leisure town',[4] a 'historic regional centre . . . on the way to the pleasant obscurity of county rather than national fame'.[5] Although the characterizations contain some truth, they are cruder than Chester's complexity deserves. Its 18th-century 'leisure industries' – theatre, the races,

1 Above, frontispiece.
2 *Chester Customs Accts.* 3–7, 19, 73.
3 *Notes & Queries*, 3rd ser. iv. 49, 78, 277; R. Fiske, *Eng. Theatre Music in 18th Cent.* (2nd edn., 1986), 327–33, 343–4, 605; A. Nicholl, *Hist. of Eng. Drama, 1660–1900*, iii. 197–8, 237.
4 J. Stobart, 'Shopping Streets as Social Space: Leisure,

Consumerism and Improvement in an 18th-Cent. County Town', *Urban Hist.* xxv. 3–21; cf. P. Borsay, *The English Urban Renaissance: Culture and Society in the Provincial Town, 1660–1780*, 9, 20–1, 35–6.
5 E. A. Wrigley, 'Urban Growth and Agricultural Change', *The 18th-Cent. Town*, ed. P. Borsay, 48–9, 78–9.

and the comfortable lifestyles of coffee houses and conviviality described in the diaries of Henry Prescott, deputy registrar of the diocese between 1686 and 1719 – built on Chester's long-established position as a late-medieval and early-modern gentry capital. Craft manufacturing was certainly in slow decline throughout the later 18th century, but in a few trades did not die out until almost the end of the 19th. Moreover Chester did acquire some new heavy industries in association with the arrival of the canal (notably the canalside lead-works) and more particularly the railways, and has some claim to be regarded as a railway town, albeit one in which the railway diversified and strengthened a faltering local economy rather than creating a town from scratch, as at Crewe. A stress on Chester's standing as a Georgian resort also tends to underplay the significance of its leisure industries in the eras of the railway excursion and the mass ownership of motor cars. Already by 1896 the railways allowed noticeable numbers of American tourists and hordes of 'holiday-makers and pleasure-seekers' from Liverpool, Manchester, and the rest of Lancashire to make their way to Chester.[1] In the late 20th century the hordes became a torrent of millions of visitors each year and the fame of the most distinctive features of Chester's townscape – the city walls, the Rows, and the riverside – and of the most obvious aspects of its history and cultural heritage – notably the Romans and the mystery plays – spread world-wide, misunderstood and misrepresented though they frequently were.

1 G. L. Fenwick, *Hist. of Ancient City of Chester*, 253–4.

ROMAN CHESTER

FIRST ROMAN CONTACTS AND THE ESTABLISHMENT OF THE FORTRESS

The precise date of the first occupation of Chester by the Roman army remains uncertain,[1] but the potential uses to which the site could be put – a fine harbour at the highest navigable point on the Dee, a river crossing, and a defendable position – were doubtless well appreciated by Rome from an early date, perhaps even before Caesar's time.[2] The earliest Roman knowledge of the area was presumably through commerce: although proof is lacking, ships from the western Mediterranean and Gaul may occasionally have visited to engage in barter. Traces of cultivation on the site,[3] together with a few sherds of Iron Age pottery accidentally redeposited in the earliest Roman structures,[4] clearly attest to pre-Roman occupation, perhaps a small Cornovian fishing and farming settlement by the river bank, defended by a promontory enclosure on the site of the later castle. The place was potentially convenient for merchants trading with local people throughout the lower reaches of the Dee valley.[5] The river in time gave its name to the site in a Latinized form: Deva, 'the holy one'.[6]

Contacts with Rome presumably increased greatly after Claudius's successful invasion of south-eastern Britain in A.D. 43, and by the earlier 50s elements of the Roman army had probably arrived in the area during campaigns against the Ordovices and Deceangli in central and northern Wales and the Brigantes north and east of Cheshire.[7]

Further campaigns in Wales during the late 50s culminated in Suetonius Paulinus's attack on Anglesey in 60. Although there is no conclusive archaeological evidence, the Romans may well have used the harbour and crossing-point at Chester, defending them perhaps by a small fort. If so, their occupation then is likely to have been short-lived, since the Boudiccan uprising in

60 demanded the governor's immediate attention elsewhere and an abrupt cessation to his campaigns in north Wales.[8] It was only c. 70 that a new policy of total conquest of the British Isles led to the establishment of the first permanent military presence at Chester.[9]

As a prelude to implementing the new policy, the Ninth Legion was moved forward from Lincoln to York, and a new legion, the Second, called *Adiutrix* and recently raised by Vespasian from the marines of the Adriatic fleet, was sent to Britain with the new governor, Petillius Cerialis, and based initially at Lincoln.[10] It was soon moved west to construct a new legionary depot at Chester, probably under orders from Sextus Julius Frontinus as incoming provincial governor in or shortly after 74.[11]

During Frontinus's governorship (74–8) and in the first year of his successor, Gnaeus Julius Agricola, the Roman army completed the subjugation of the Silures and Ordovices in Wales by reconquering Anglesey in 78. Agricola was then free to complete the conquest of the Brigantes begun by Cerealis in the early 70s. The legionary depot and related installations at Chester were built during those years, with the finishing touches to the basic military requirements added by c. 80.[12]

Scarcely two years later Agricola had subdued Brigantia, occupied the Forth–Clyde isthmus, and was advancing towards the river Tay. Chester, with superb harbour facilities, played a key role in the seaborne support of the campaigns, and it was also adequately placed to keep watch on the Ordovices and southern Brigantes. At the same time the Roman army may have been preparing for the conquest of Ireland,[13] for which Chester was admirably situated to be the main embarkation point and supply base. Although never accomplished, the plan probably encouraged the development at Chester of a major military base.[14]

The idea that Chester's main role was naval is

---

1 *V.C.H. Ches.* i. 117–18. Thanks for help with this chapter are gratefully offered to the late Dr. G. A. Webster, the late Mr. F. H. Thompson, Dr. P. Carrington, Dr. D. J. P. Mason, Mr. S. Ward, and Dr. G. Lloyd-Morgan. *V.C.H. Ches.* i. 117–85 gives a fuller account of the layout and buildings of Roman Chester. D. J. P. Mason, *Roman Chester: City of the Eagles*, appeared after this chapter was completed.

2 Julius Caesar, *Gallic War*, ed. H. J. Edwards, 250–3; Diodorus Siculus, *Library of History*, ed. C. H. Oldfather and others, iii. 150–5; F. H. Thompson, *Roman Ches.* 6–7.

3 *V.C.H. Ches.* i. 115.

4 J. C. McPeake, M. Bulmer, and J. A. Rutter, 'Excavations in Garden of No. 1 Abbey Green, Chester, 1975–7: Interim Rep.' *J.C.A.S.* lxiii. 15.

5 J. and Ll. Laing, 'Mediterranean Trade with Wirral in Iron Age', *Ches. Arch. Bull.* ix. 6–8; *V.C.H. Ches.* i. 115.

6 A. L. F. Rivet and C. Smith, *Place-Names of Roman Britain*, 336–7.

7 G. Webster, *The Cornovii* (1991 edn.), 26–30; P. Carrington, 'Roman Advance into NW. Midlands before A.D. 71', *J.C.A.S.* lxviii. 5–22; G. Webster, *Rome against Caratacus*, 43–4.

8 G. Webster, *Boudica* (1978 edn.), 86–7; *J.C.A.S.* lxviii. 13.

9 K. Branigan, *Roman Britain*, 43; W. S. Hanson, *Agricola and Conquest of North* (1987 edn.), 115, 174; *V.C.H. Ches.* i. 115.

10 R. G. Collingwood and R. P. Wright, *Roman Inscriptions of Britain*, i, nos. 253, 258.

11 T. J. Strickland, '1st Cent. Deva', *J.C.A.S.* lxiii. 5–13; *V.C.H. Ches.* i. 118.

12 *V.C.H. Ches.* i. 118; *J.C.A.S.* lxiii. 8–9.

13 Tacitus, *Life of Agricola*, ed. M. Hutton, 70–1.

14 Hanson, *Agricola*, 151–2.

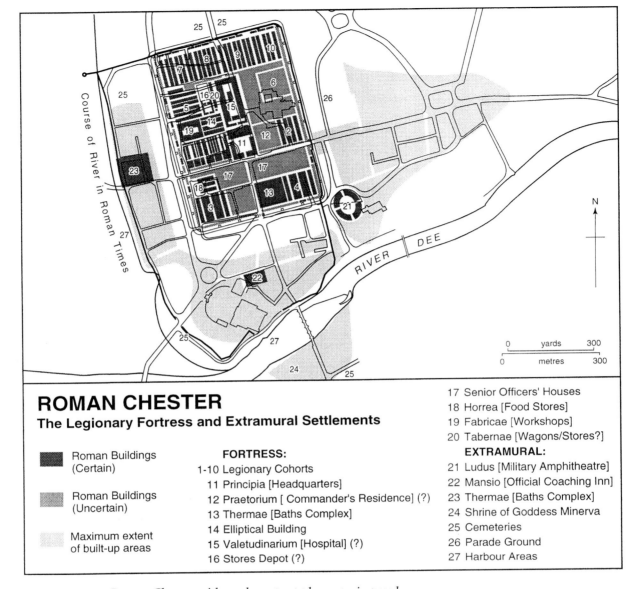

ROMAN CHESTER
The Legionary Fortress and Extramural Settlements

■ Roman Buildings (Certain)

▓ Roman Buildings (Uncertain)

░ Maximum extent of built-up areas

FORTRESS:
1-10 Legionary Cohorts
11 Principia [Headquarters]
12 Praetorium [Commander's Residence] (?)
13 Thermae [Baths Complex]
14 Elliptical Building
15 Valetudinarium [Hospital] (?)
16 Stores Depot (?)

17 Senior Officers' Houses
18 Horrea [Food Stores]
19 Fabricae [Workshops]
20 Tabernae [Wagons/Stores?]
EXTRAMURAL:
21 Ludus [Military Amphitheatre]
22 Mansio [Official Coaching Inn]
23 Thermae [Baths Complex]
24 Shrine of Goddess Minerva
25 Cemeteries
26 Parade Ground
27 Harbour Areas

FIG. 2. *Roman Chester, with modern street plan superimposed*

supported by the importance which the Roman army attached to seaborne operations, exemplified by the circumnavigation of northern Britain by its fleet in 84, and in particular by the positioning at Chester of the Second Legion, a unit with naval experience.[1] Other factors lend further support to the idea. First, the legionary depot at Wroxeter (Salop.) appears to have remained in commission, though perhaps merely under care-and-maintenance.[2] It was sufficiently well situated for campaigns in the Marches, central and north Wales, and probably southern Brigantia to make the relocation of a legionary depot to Chester merely to control the Ordovices and Brigantes unnecessary. Chester indeed may not have been well placed for

campaigns in north Wales, since a direct overland route was made difficult by marshlands to its southwest.[3] Moreover it was located somewhat away from the existing main roads leading north on the west side of the Pennines. Probably the main advantage of the site was that it was the highest navigation point on the Dee.[4]

THE SECOND LEGION AT CHESTER, 74–90

Acting as an essential reserve force (the meaning of *Adiutrix*),[5] supplying the northward-moving army by sea, and perhaps preparing for the conquest of Ireland, the men of the Second Legion are unlikely to have been heavily used by Agricola in his northern campaigns.

1 Hanson, *Agricola*, 115; V. E. Nash-Williams, *Roman Frontier in Wales* (1969 edn.), 11.
2 Webster, *Cornovii*, 43–5; *J.C.A.S.* lxiii. 10.

3 *J.C.A.S.* lxiii. 6–7; D. J. P. Mason, '*Prata Legionis* at Chester', *J.C.A.S.* lxix. 33.   4 *J.C.A.S.* lxviii. 17–18.
5 Nash-Williams, *Roman Frontier*, 11.

They were, moreover, deeply committed to the building of their depot and related installations at Chester, involved in supervising lead-mining operations in north-east Wales, and incidentally (with the support of various auxiliary regiments) kept some kind of watch over the Ordovices and southern Brigantes. During its service at Chester the legion, styled *Pia Fidelis* (Loyal and Faithful) for supporting Vespasian in the civil war of 69, comprised mostly men of Mediterranean origins, recruited in such regions as the eastern shore of the Adriatic, Thrace, northern Italy, and Greece.[1]

The new legionary depot at Chester was constructed in the manner typical of the period in Britain, mainly of timber-framed, wattle-and-daubed buildings. The *enceinte* consisted of a double turf-revetted rampart and palisade some 20 Roman feet (*c.* 6 metres) wide at base and 10 Roman feet (*c.* 3 metres) high, topped with a palisade 5 Roman feet high, to which were added wooden gates and towers probably 25 Roman feet (*c.* 7.4 metres) high, and with at least one substantial ditch outside.[2] Although of simple materials, many of the buildings, particularly the houses of the senior centurions, were finished to a high standard, with elaborate interior wall decoration, tiled roofs, and glazed windows.[3] A permanent piped water supply was laid from springs a short distance to the east, with subsidiary lead pipes connecting the main supply to the more important buildings.[4] There was also a main sewage and waste-water disposal system via rock-cut culverts set below the main streets and no doubt connected to both communal and private latrines, such as those for the centurions at Abbey Green.[5] Some buildings were of stone and concrete from the outset, among them the bath building and leisure complex alongside the *via praetoria* (Bridge Street), whose functions and status demanded a tall and structurally complex building. Its technical sophistication was comparable with that of similar buildings at the heart of the Roman Empire. While building continued, and at least until work on the depot itself was far advanced, the legionaries probably lived in temporary construction camps near by.[6]

Together with annexes for baggage trains and other surplus equipment, they appear to have been mainly east of the depot.[7]

Outside the ramparts the army probably gave priority to constructing harbour installations, a parade ground, a bridge (presumably at first entirely of timber), and various official establishments such as extramural baths,[8] posting houses,[9] and the amphitheatre. The amphitheatre was used for celebrating the many religious feasts in the legion's calendar, weapon training, drill, military parades and demonstrations, and, most important, public address. It was also designed for entertainment, initially largely for the soldiers, though the *cavea* (spectators' seating area) of the original wooden structure appears to have been too small for a full legion of *c.* 5,500 men.[10]

Attracted to Chester by the chance of a living from the large number of well-paid legionaries were local tribesmen, traders of all kinds from near and far, an army of servants and labourers (both slave and free), and officials employed to run the extramural posting houses, harbour facilities, and other official establishments. There were, too, retired soldiers, some probably from Wroxeter, who preferred to live close to their former comrades-in-arms in a lifestyle which retained a military flavour.[11] Many had wives and families. Thus, quite quickly, a sizeable settlement, known as the *canabae*,[12] grew up outside the walls of the fortress. It remained under direct military supervision, unlike the nearby independent and very large civil settlement at Heronbridge.[13]

In the early 80s part of the Second Legion was posted to the Rhine frontier. Although there was probably nothing new in the sending of detachments to other parts of the Empire while the main body of the legion remained in Britain, soon afterwards, in the late 80s, the remaining fighting strength of the legion was sent to the Danube.[14] Placed as it was in reserve at Chester, well south of the frontier zone, the Second was the legion which could most easily be spared. Its removal appears to have been related to the gradual abandonment of recent conquests in Scotland.[15]

Despite the withdrawal of the legion's fighting

---

1 *Rom. Inscr. Brit.* i, nos. 475–87.

2 T. J. Strickland, 'Defences of Roman Chester: Note on Discoveries made on North Wall, 1982', *J.C.A.S.* lxv. 25–36; idem, 'Defences of Roman Chester: Discoveries made on East Wall, 1983', *J.C.A.S.* lxvi. 5–11; *V.C.H. Ches.* i. 120–4; *Archit. in Roman Britain* (Council for British Archaeology, Research Rep. xciv), 104–19; *V.C.H. Ches.* v (2), City Walls and Gates: Roman.

3 *Ches. Arch. Bull.* iii. 38; *New Evidence for Roman Chester*, ed. T. J. Strickland and P. J. Davey, 11–12.

4 *J.C.A.S.* lxiii. 8–9.

5 e.g. ibid. 17–19; inf. on stone guttering discovered near Kaleyard Gate in 1994, from Mr. S. Ward, Chester City Council Arch. Service, Grosvenor Mus.

6 *Britannia*, xxi. 215–22. Cf. L. F. Pitts and J. K. St. Joseph, *Inchtuthil: Roman Legionary Fortress Excavations, 1952–65*, 203–46.

7 *New Evidence*, ed. Strickland and Davey, 32.

8 Ibid. 35–6.

9 D. J. P. Mason, *Excavations at Chester: 11–15 Castle St. and Neighbouring Sites, 1974–8*, 3–8.

10 F. H. Thompson, 'Excavation of Roman Amphitheatre at Chester', *Archaeologia*, cv. 134–44.

11 Webster, *Cornovii*, 47–8.

12 G. Webster, *Roman Imperial Army of 1st and 2nd Cent.* A.D. (1985 edn.), 209.

13 Ibid. 210; D. J. P. Mason, 'Prata Legionis' in Britain', *Britannia*, xix. 174–80; unpublished survey of Heronbridge by T. J. Strickland.

14 Hanson, *Agricola*, 135, 152, 160–1; *Inscriptiones Latinae Selectae*, ed. H. Dessau, i, no. 1025; iii (2), nos. 9193, 9200; Nash-Williams, *Roman Frontier*, 11.

15 Hanson, *Agricola*, 143–73.

strength it is unlikely that the army altogether abandoned the depot, which probably remained for a time nominally under the legion's command, many of its empty buildings being retained on a care-and-maintenance basis. The soldiers who stayed behind were presumably non-combatants involved in the administrative and other tasks of military depot life. The training of recruits probably continued unchanged.[1]

THE EARLY YEARS OF THE TWENTIETH LEGION, 90–122

By *c.* 90 the Second Legion had no further need of its base at Chester and the depot's future had to be decided. It was quickly realized that, since much of Brigantia was controlled by the army, and Wales had been subjugated, Chester was more usefully placed than Wroxeter, which was effectively landlocked. Accordingly, the legionary depot at Wroxeter was abandoned *c.* 90, and the Twentieth Legion, *Valeria Victrix*, established itself instead at Chester, possibly after a short stay at Gloucester.[2]

The Twentieth had been in Britain since the Claudian invasion in 43,[3] and had served in Brigantia and Scotland.[4] The legion, which during its early years at Chester was still recruiting heavily from Spain, northern Italy, the Adriatic, and southern France,[5] took over a depot at Chester in full working order, and the daily routine of training and repairs clearly continued. Many of the buildings were nearly twenty years old and required much replacement of rotting timbers. The defences may also have been refurbished,[6] and minor internal alterations were made to many buildings, particularly the officers' quarters *c.* 100.[7] Some buildings were completely reconstructed. At Abbey Green, for instance, a new timber-lined main sewage culvert was inserted alongside the *via sagularis* (the road running round the depot inside the defences) and new timber-framed cookhouses and mess huts were inserted alongside the ramparts.[8] In the *canabae* some official buildings were still being completely renewed in timber in the early 2nd century.[9]

Soon after the arrival of the Twentieth Legion, however, it was decided, apparently, to rebuild the entire depot in stone. An unlimited supply of building sandstone lay in the immediate neighbourhood, and quarries were opened on both sides of the Dee,[10] but the main reason for such a major undertaking may

have been a decision to make the Chester base permanent. Sound building in stone, or timber framing on stone sills, was potentially far more durable in a damp climate than timber framing alone. The scope of construction, the imposing major buildings, and the sophistication of even the barrack blocks, the verandas of which were supported on lathe-turned sandstone columns, suggest further that the legion was thinking on a grand scale in line with the general mood of confidence expressed in building and design throughout the Roman world at that time.[11]

Within the rebuilding programme some priority seems to have been given to the defences, which may still have been in their original form, though no doubt much repaired and patched during the previous 25 years or so.[12] In addition to the recutting of the ditch, the wooden interval towers and palisade appear to have been dismantled, though the turf-revetted rampart was retained. The gates were probably rebuilt then or soon after in stone on their original sites, and work began on an impressive stone revetment added to the front of the rampart.[13]

The extent and appearance of the defences *c.* 100 remain uncertain. If, as seems likely,[14] further work continued on them in the 3rd century, a hint of their intended strength is provided by the internal stone towers placed at regular intervals round the circuit. Although the towers were substantially rebuilt later, they probably originated in the late 1st or early 2nd century, and were fewer and more widely spaced than the original timber ones. It is perhaps more likely, however, that the walls under construction *c.* 100 were those which survived, albeit with later additions, on the north and east sides into modern times, constructed in *opus quadratum* (large dressed and squared blocks of stone), since there are striking similarities to the first wall at Gloucester and, to a lesser degree, the stone curtain wall at Inchtuthil (Perthshire), both built at about the same time at places associated with the Twentieth Legion.[15]

The rebuilding of the depot was conducted randomly rather than systematically, presumably because the cohorts made widely differing rates of progress. As previously, detachments would have been on duty elsewhere, and in their absence little building work may have been carried out in their parts of the depot. By the early 2nd century in the central area at least one large building and some barracks were rebuilt in

---

1 Webster, *Roman Imperial Army*, 113–14.

2 Webster, *Cornovii*, 45–6; H. R. Hurst, *Gloucester: Roman and Later Defences*, 118–19, 142.

3 R. S. O. Tomlin, '20th Legion at Wroxeter and Carlisle in 1st Cent.: Epigraphic Evidence', *Britannia*, xxiii. 145–6.

4 Pitts and St. Joseph, *Inchtuthil*, 279.

5 *Rom. Inscr. Brit.* i, nos. 492–3, 498, 500–4, 508.

6 *New Evidence*, ed. Strickland and Davey, 22; *V.C.H. Ches.* i. 124–5; *J.C.A.S.* lxvi. 8–10.

7 S. Ward and T. J. Strickland, *Excavations on Site of Northgate Brewery, Chester, 1974–5*, 3, 11–14.

8 *J.C.A.S.* lxiii. 17–19.

9 Mason, *Excavations at Chester: Castle St.* 4, 8–10.

10 *V.C.H. Ches.* i. 119, 226–7. Plate 1.

11 [R.] M. Wheeler, *Roman Art and Archit.* 8–9; *Archit. in Roman Britain*, 104–19.

12 *J.C.A.S.* lxvi. 5–11.

13 *V.C.H. Ches.* i. 124–7, 131; *V.C.H. Ches.* v (2), City Walls and Gates: Roman. Plate 2.

14 e.g. *J.C.A.S.* lxv. 34–5.

15 Hurst, *Gloucester Defences*, 119–21, 126–7; Pitts and St. Joseph, *Inchtuthil*, 279.

stone, or with stone sills,[1] whereas in the rearward areas progress appears to have been far slower, only a few cookhouses and mess huts near the north gate having been completed.[2] Curiously, replacement of some of the larger buildings seems to have been delayed. Indeed, the intended site of one major building, perhaps a stores compound, stood vacant from the first occupation by the Second Legion, being used instead for refuse pits.[3] The most essential requirements were satisfied first, other buildings receiving attention later as time and opportunity permitted, but curiously the headquarters building (*principia*) may not have been rebuilt in stone at all at that time.[4]

In the *canabae* the rebuilding programme seems scarcely to have begun by the 120s. One of the earliest extramural buildings reconstructed in stone was the amphitheatre, the various official functions of which presumably demanded priority. On a much grander scale than its predecessor, with seating for at least 7,000 spectators, more than the full strength of the legion, it reflected the expansion of the *canabae* and perhaps also the requirements of an increasing population, both military and civilian, for entertainments.[5] Such a major construction project also showed confidence in the future of Chester and its *canabae*.

The Dee bridge may also have received attention early in the 2nd century. In 2000 its remains, including pier bases, massive stones, and cornice fragments, lay scattered across the river bed a few metres downstream of its medieval successor, evidence of a very solid bridge of Roman military design, perhaps with a timber superstructure.[6]

In the extramural settlement between the waterfront and the western ramparts, a short distance outside the west gate, what appear to have been luxurious and extensive baths in stone and concrete were also already in use early in the 2nd century.[7]

THE 'MILITARY HIATUS', 122–97

In 122 Emperor Hadrian may have visited Chester on his way north to organize the construction of his great frontier works from the Solway Firth to the Tyne,[8] a project in which the Chester legion played a large part. Work continued on the frontier for the rest of Hadrian's reign (117–38) and into that of Antoninus Pius (138–61), still involving men from the Twentieth,[9] so that in Chester the reconstruction of the depot and its *canabae* in stone had to be severely curtailed.

In all parts of the depot and its extramural settlement there is abundant evidence of a halt in building between *c.* 120 and *c.* 130. In the left *retentura* (the rearward part of the depot) scarcely had work on the defences been completed and two cookhouses nearest the north gate rebuilt in stone, when the whole operation was abandoned; the remaining cookhouses, all the barracks, and even the main drains below the *via sagularis* were left in their original timber-framed form.[10] In the right *retentura* it seems that none of the cookhouses had yet been rebuilt, whereas work on the barracks had just started and at least one of the new centurions' houses was abandoned in a very incomplete state.[11] In the centre of the depot the barracks of one cohort, recently rebuilt in stone and reoccupied, seem to have been abandoned, and work on parts of a very large building immediately behind the headquarters may likewise have been cut short.[12] In the *canabae* just outside the south gate a second attempt at rebuilding a posting house in stone was abandoned incomplete by *c.* 130,[13] and other official establishments may have been similarly affected by the legion's preoccupations elsewhere. There is also circumstantial evidence that the amphitheatre may have fallen into neglect before *c.* 150.[14]

Events in northern Britain during the reign of Antoninus Pius continued to frustrate rebuilding at Chester. In particular, work was delayed by the lengthy involvement of the Twentieth Legion in a new campaign in Scotland and in building the Antonine Wall.[15] Legionaries from Chester manned some of the northern forts and at least one centurion from the Twentieth commanded an auxiliary regiment on the frontier.[16] Further trouble in the North in the 150s and 160s and the removal of troops from Britain to strengthen imperial armies elsewhere also probably

1 T. J. Strickland, 'Chester: Excavations in Princess St./Hunter St. Area, 1978–82: 1st Rep. on Discoveries of Roman Period', *J.C.A.S.* lxv. 9–11, 16–19.

2 Ward and Strickland, *Northgate Brewery*, 16–23; inf. from latest research on evidence from excavations at Abbey Green, 1975–8, forthcoming in D. J. P. Mason, T. J. Strickland, and others, *Excavations at Chester: Barracks of Roman Legionary Fortress* (Chester City Council).

3 *J.C.A.S.* lxv. 10–11.

4 *New Evidence*, ed. Strickland and Davey, 17–20; cf. Pitts and St. Joseph, *Inchtuthil*, 207–22.

5 *Archaeologia*, cv. 148–9, 163–4, 183–4.

6 T. J. Strickland, 'Roman Heritage of Chester: Survival of Buildings of *Deva* after Roman Period', *J.C.A.S.* lxvii. 25–7.

7 *V.C.H. Ches.* i. 176–7.

8 Cf. Webster, *Cornovii*, 50–1; *Rom. Inscr. Brit.* i, no. 288; M. Grant, *Roman Emperors* (1985 edn.), 78–9; Dio Cassius, *Roman History*, ed. E. Cary, viii. 440–3.

9 C. E. Stevens, *The Building of Hadrian's Wall* (Cumb. and Westmld. Antiq. and Arch. Soc. extra ser. xx); *Rom. Inscr. Brit.* i, nos. 1385, 1390–1, 1430, 1645, 1708, 1762, 1852, 2028, 2035, 2077–8.

10 Mason, Strickland, and others, *Excavations at Chester: Barracks* (forthcoming); C. LeQuesne and others, *Excavations at Chester: Roman and Later Defences, Pt. 1: Investigations 1978–90*.

11 Ward and Strickland, *Northgate Brewery*, 16–23.

12 *J.C.A.S.* lxv. 9–12, 19.

13 Mason, *Excavations at Chester: Castle St.* 4, 12–16.

14 *Archaeologia*, cv. 150–1, 169–70, 178, 182.

15 *Rom. Inscr. Brit.* i, nos. 2173, 2184, 2197–9, 2206, 2208, 2210; L. F. J. Keppie, 'Building of Antonine Wall: Arch. and Epigraphic Evidence', *Proc. Soc. Antiq. Scot.* cv. 151–65.

16 Nash-Williams, *Roman Frontier*, 14; *Rom. Inscr. Brit.* i, nos. 330, 1725.

affected Chester.[1] Certainly a detachment of the legion was employed in construction at Corbridge (Northumb.),[2] and deployment in the Danubian provinces is suggested by the fact that some of the 5,500 Iazygian cavalrymen drafted to Britain in the 170s found their way to Chester, where at least one was commemorated by a tombstone rediscovered in 1890.[3] A detachment from the legion was in Armorica in the reign of Commodus (180–92),[4] and the Twentieth may also have contributed to the token force sent to Rome to meet the emperor in 185. The legion was doubtless also involved, along with the rest of the provincial British army, in the succession struggles after Commodus's assassination in 192, in support of the British candidate for the purple, Clodius Albinus, defeated in 197 with heavy losses among the legions of Britain.[5]

Such commitments meant that the legion's base at Chester was run down for most of the 2nd century. The barracks in the left *retentura* appear to have fallen into a semi-derelict condition, and at least some were used for rubbish disposal.[6] In the right *retentura* the site of a centurion's house abandoned incomplete by *c.* 130 was also used as a rubbish tip for at least several decades.[7] A large building directly behind the headquarters had rubbish piled into one corner from *c.* 130 to as late as *c.* 240,[8] though other parts may have remained in use. Elsewhere in the *retentura* a very large open site was used for dumping refuse and metalworking waste.[9] A seemingly unique elliptical building appears also to have been abandoned incomplete and used as a rubbish tip until *c.* 230.[10]

The area housing the first cohort suffered similar neglect.[11] Three barracks in Crook Street and Goss Street had building activity in the early 2nd century, an accumulation of rubbish later in the century, and renewed building in the early 3rd. One was used for metalworking and another for a kiln or furnace. Stores or offices adjacent to the headquarters meanwhile became a makeshift latrine. In the extramural settlement the site of the posting house south of the depot was used as a rubbish dump, with urinal pits being

dug through the floors in the period *c.* 130 to *c.* 180.[12] In parts of the amphitheatre, too, rubbish accumulated.[13] Other sites in the *canabae*, however, seem to have experienced gradual expansion and improvement in the earlier 2nd century,[14] and perhaps only official buildings were run down.

Changes in the character of occupation after *c.* 130 may be explained by an intention, perhaps implied in an incomplete inscription found reused behind the headquarters, to demilitarize the site and establish an independent civilian settlement.[15] Nevertheless at least one senior officer of the legion was present at Chester in 154,[16] and Sarmatian cavalry were stationed there after *c.* 175,[17] indications that the site remained under military control. The garrison may have been small throughout the 2nd and early 3rd century, parts of the depot in effect being abandoned as accommodation for troops; on the other hand the extensive deposits of metalworking debris in the central parts of the depot, in at least one case associated with a building converted to workshops, imply intensive use.[18] The most likely explanation is that Chester was retained as a rearward works establishment, under the command of a senior officer, in which equipment was repaired and manufactured for the Roman army in the North.

THE SEVERAN DYNASTY AND AFTER, 197–250

In 197 Emperor Septimius Severus dispatched a new governor, Virius Lupus, to restore order in Britain, and a few years later campaigned there himself. No doubt the Twentieth Legion, brought back up to strength after 197, took part in his campaigns in Scotland. Severus died at York in 211 and soon afterwards his sons Caracalla and Geta withdrew from Britain.[19] Severus's intervention prompted great building activity at Chester, and within a generation or so every part of the depot appears to have been systematically refurbished.[20] The works included the completion of buildings planned a century before, most clearly the elliptical building, a building to its north with a walled com-

1 Pausanias, *Description of Greece*, ed. W. H. S. Jones, iv. 118–19; *Scriptores Historiae Augustae*, ed. D. Magie, i. 152–3, 186–7; Nash-Williams, *Roman Frontier*, 14.

2 *Rom. Inscr. Brit.* i, no. 1149.

3 Ibid. nos. 594–5; Dio Cassius, *Roman History*, ed. Cary, ix. 34–7; R. P. Wright, *Cat. of Roman Inscribed and Sculptured Stones in Grosvenor Mus.* 131, plate xxxiii.

4 Nash-Williams, *Roman Frontier*, 14.

5 Dio Cassius, *Roman History*, ed. Cary, ix. 88–91, 206–13.

6 Mason, Strickland, and others, *Excavations at Chester: Barracks* (forthcoming).

7 Ward and Strickland, *Northgate Brewery*, 3, 16–19.

8 *J.C.A.S.* lxv. 19–20; D. F. Petch, 'Praetorium at Deva', *J.C.A.S.* lv. 1–5; idem, 'Excavations on Site of Old Market Hall, Chester: 2nd Summary Rep. 1968–70', *J.C.A.S.* lvii. 3–20.

9 *J.C.A.S.* lxv. 10–12.

10 Inf. from Dr. D. J. P. Mason, formerly of Chester City Council Arch. Service; *Archit. in Roman Britain*, 77–92.

11 Para. based on Mason, Strickland, and others, *Excavations*

at Chester: Barracks (forthcoming), and on inf. from Dr. Mason.

12 Mason, *Excavations at Chester: Castle St.* 4, 15–16.

13 *Archaeologia*, cv. 150–1, 169–70, 178, 182.

14 Inf. from Mr. S. Ward, Chester City Council Arch. Service, and Dr. Mason; *New Evidence*, ed. Strickland and Davey, 35–7.

15 T. J. Strickland, '3rd Cent. Chester', *Roman West in 3rd Cent.* ed. A. King and M. Henig, ii (Brit. Arch. Rep. International Ser. cix (2)), 415–16; *J.C.A.S.* lvii. 21–6; inf. from the late Mr. F. H. Thompson, former curator of Grosvenor Mus.

16 *Rom. Inscr. Brit.* i, no. 452; M. J. Green, 'Tanarus, Taranis, and the Chester Altar', *J.C.A.S.* lxv. 37–8.

17 Wright, *Cat. of Roman Stones*, 137, plate xxxiv.

18 *New Evidence*, ed. Strickland and Davey, 20; *J.C.A.S.* lxv. 10–11.

19 Dio Cassius, *Roman History*, ed. Cary, ix. 260–73; Herodian, *History*, ed. C. R. Whittaker, i. 354–69.

20 *Roman West*, ed. King and Henig, 419–23; *J.C.A.S.* lxv. 34.

pound, and possibly even the headquarters. In the *canabae* major reconstruction and restoration also took place. As a result the early 3rd century could well be termed Deva's heyday.[1] The stimulus may have been the Severan dynasty's support for the army, together with reforms designed to make military life more agreeable for recruits.[2] Soldiers' dependants, for example, may have been given access to buildings such as the baths which had previously been purely for military use.[3] Work at some sites, including the elliptical building, however, continued until the later 3rd century.[4]

The programme included at least the repair of the defences and perhaps even completion of the curtain wall.[5] Many of the barrack blocks appear to have been completely rebuilt, frequently on new foundations sometimes themselves set amid earlier debris. Most notably the headquarters and other major buildings around it, perhaps including the commander's house (*praetorium*) to the east, were systematically rebuilt.[6]

Men of the Twentieth Legion were involved in the work,[7] and the legion presumably still provided much of the garrison. In the early 3rd century there is also evidence for the presence of men of the Second (*Augusta*) Legion,[8] and Chester may thus have housed a mixed garrison, like those stationed elsewhere in Britain, which included detachments of both those legions brigaded together with auxiliaries.[9] At the same time the changes introduced or encouraged by the Antonine constitution in the early 3rd century probably blurred the divisions between military and civilian.[10]

THE END OF ROMAN MILITARY OCCUPATION, 250–400

A unit called the Twentieth Legion was still at Chester in the middle of the 3rd century,[11] but it is not clear whether it comprised the fighting troops or merely the men maintaining the depot. Nevertheless the use of the legion's title implies some continuity in organization and structure, however superficial. As earlier, detachments were still active elsewhere both in northern Britain[12] and shortly after *c.* 250 on the Rhine and

Danube.[13] Men of the legion were present on Hadrian's Wall in the 260s,[14] and the Twentieth, with its traditional style *Valeria Victrix*, was in the army of the usurper Carausius in the late 3rd century.[15] Furthermore, if the presence of Carausius's coinage in Chester derives from regular payments to his troops, then presumably elements of the legion were still at their old depot too. Thereafter, however, it is not clear what troops were stationed at Chester: the depot was certainly occupied, but not necessarily only by soldiers.

Detachments of the military units based at Chester (by then not necessarily a legion in the traditional sense) would presumably have been used in Constantius Chlorus's campaigns in the North against the Picts in 306.[16] It used to be thought that many of the barracks had been systematically dismantled by that date,[17] but by the 1990s it was apparent that all parts of the depot, not least the barrack blocks, continued to be occupied. The internal alterations to buildings and reroofing carried out in the early 4th century may have been merely routine repairs, but they imply continued widespread use, and at least some are likely to have been undertaken to house soldiers living with their families.[18]

Intensive occupation continued both within and outside the walls until the later 4th century,[19] though the status of the occupants and the position of Chester within the reorganized military structure of Britain are obscure.[20] Soldiers based at Chester were still being paid in coins from the imperial mints until, but not during, the time of Magnus Maximus (383–8),[21] who perhaps removed the remaining regular troops from Chester when he invaded Gaul in 383.[22] The *Notitia Dignitatum*, a list of officials probably compiled *c.* 400, mentioned neither troops at Chester nor the Twentieth Legion elsewhere in Britain. The archaeological evidence available in 1996 was insufficiently clear to support definite conclusions, but probably a substantially civilian population continued to use the old legionary defences for security from raiders in the Irish Sea.[23]

1 *Archit. in Roman Britain*, 77–92. Cf. P. Salway, *Roman Britain*, 221–8.
2 *Rom. Inscr. Brit.* i, no. 505; G. R. Watson, *The Roman Soldier*, 137.
3 Cf. J. D. Zienkiewicz, *Legionary Fortress Baths at Caerleon*.
4 Inf. from Dr. Mason.
5 *J.C.A.S.* lxv. 25–36; lxvi. 5–11.
6 *Roman West*, ed. King and Henig, 415–44; *J.C.A.S.* lxv. 5–24; inf. from Dr. Mason.
7 *Rom. Inscr. Brit.* i, nos. 450, 465, 490, 491, 505, 507; cf. nos. 455, 462.
8 Ibid. no. 488.
9 Ibid. nos. 980, 1125, 1130, 1955, 1956.
10 Watson, *Roman Soldier*, 137, 140–2.
11 e.g. *Rom. Inscr. Brit.* i, no. 449.
12 Nash-Williams, *Roman Frontier*, 14.
13 *Corpus Inscriptionum Latinarum*, iii (1), no. 3228; xiii (2:i), no. 6780.

14 *Rom. Inscr. Brit.* i, no. 1956.
15 Carausius coin type nos. 82–3, 275: *Roman Imperial Coinage*, ed. H. Mattingly and E. A. Sydenham, v (2), pp. 470, 488.
16 M. Grant, *The Emperor Constantine*, 22–3.
17 e.g. *J.C.A.S.* lxiii. 19; *New Evidence*, ed. Strickland and Davey.
18 Mason, Strickland, and others, *Excavations at Chester: Barracks* (forthcoming); cf. P. T. Bidwell, 'Later Roman Barracks in Britain', *Roman Frontier Studies 1989: Proc. XVth International Congress*, ed. V. A. Maxfield and M. J. Dobson, 11–14.
19 S. Ward, *Excavations at Chester: 12 Watergate St.*, 1985, 16–21.
20 Cf. A. Dornier, 'Province of Valentia', *Britannia*, xiii. 253–60.
21 e.g. Salway, *Roman Britain*, 401–9; *New Evidence*, ed. Strickland and Davey, 41–4; inf. on coin finds from Dr. G. Lloyd-Morgan, formerly of Grosvenor Mus.
22 Salway, *Roman Britain*, 403–5; Webster, *Cornovii*, 124–8.
23 Salway, *Roman Britain*, 241, 369.

EARLY MEDIEVAL
CHESTER 400–1230

SUB-ROMAN AND EARLY ENGLISH
CHESTER

Although in the early 8th century Bede called Chester a city (*civitas*) and clearly knew of it as a Roman place, he said nothing about later activity there.[1] Nevertheless, despite the silence of the documentary sources, the site's enduring importance suggests that some form of occupation may have continued after the Roman army left. The legionary fortress had acquired an increasingly significant civilian role in the last century of its existence, and may have remained the focus of some kind of territorial unit. By the time of the Northumbrian king Æthelfrith's victory over the British in 616, Chester was in territory associated with the British kingdom of Powys and was perhaps the seat of a branch of the royal dynasty of the Cadelling, whose representatives were prominent in the battle. The fact that a little later, lands to the south, in Shropshire, were in the hands of a different dynasty suggests that the Cadelling who fought at Chester were confined to Cheshire and north Wales, and hence likely to have made use of the fortress.[2] Under their rule, too, the area was ecclesiastically important. The city was probably the scene of a synod of the British Church shortly after 600, and just to the south there seems to have been an early mother church at Eccleston. Further south was the great monastery of Bangor (Flints.), *c.* 1,200 of whose monks were allegedly slaughtered by the Northumbrians at the battle of Chester as they prayed for a British victory.[3]

The only material traces of the period from Chester are a few sherds of amphorae; dating perhaps from the 5th or 6th century and found within the legionary fortress, they are similar in form to vessels from other high-status sub-Roman sites in western Britain.[4] After 616 even such exiguous evidence is lacking. All that can safely be said is that, despite the Northumbrian

victory, Chester and its environs soon passed under Mercian domination, and that a 12th-century tradition that one of the city's two early minsters, St. John's, was founded by the Mercian king Æthelred in the late 7th century may therefore have something to commend it. The church's extramural site, its close association with the Anglo-Saxon bishops of Lichfield, and the burial rights which it shared with the other early minster, St. Werburgh's, all tend to confirm its antiquity.[5] The church was presumably a prominent building, and its clergy and their households an important constituent of the population; its location may show that settlement had moved away from the legionary fortress.

One other possible indication of early Anglo-Saxon occupation is the place-name Henwald's Lowe (later the Gorse Stacks), also extramural and just north-east of the Roman fortress. Henwald's Lowe became common land, and its name, a combination of an Old English personal name and Old English *hlaw*, 'mound' or 'hill', may indicate an early aristocratic burial.[6]

In 893 Vikings raided Chester, then 'a deserted city in Wirral'.[7] Although that description has led to the assumption that the site was waste from the 7th to the early 10th century,[8] it need not be so interpreted. The raid, which culminated in the Danes' occupying the city and being besieged there for two days while the English ravaged the surrounding districts, may well have been prompted by an awareness of the city's growing economic and strategic importance, lying as it did near a direct route between the already closely linked Scandinavian kingdoms of Dublin and York.[9] In any case, such desertion as there was can have been only temporary. The area south of the legionary fortress was occupied by the late 9th century; in particular, a site at Lower Bridge Street has yielded the remains of a small sunken-featured hut, a late

---

1 Thanks are due to Prof. J. Campbell, Dr. D. M. Metcalf, and Dr. N. J. Higham for reading and commenting on an earlier draft of this chapter. Bede, *Eccl. Hist.* ed. B. Colgrave and R. A. B. Mynors, 140.

2 *V.C.H. Ches.* i. 238–9.

3 A. T. Thacker, 'Chester and Gloucester: Early Eccl. Organization in Two Mercian Burhs', *Northern Hist.* xviii. 199–200; *P.N. Ches.* iv. 151; *V.C.H. Ches.* i. 239; Bede, *Eccl. Hist.* 140–2; cf. N. J. Higham, *Origins of Ches.* 85–7.

4 P. Carrington, *Eng. Heritage Bk. of Chester*, 53; cf. S. Ward

and others, *Excavations at Chester: Saxon Occupation within Roman Fortress*, 32–5; *V.C.H. Ches.* i. 238.

5 *Northern Hist.* xviii. 200–1.

6 *P.N. Ches.* v (1:i), 68–9; M. Gelling, *Signposts to the Past*, 134–7, 154–7.

7 *Two Saxon Chrons.* ed. C. Plummer and J. Earle, i. 87–8; *A.-S. Chron.* iii, ed. J. M. Bately, pp. xxv–xxxiv, 58.

8 e.g. G. Webster, 'Chester in the Dark Ages', *J.C.A.S.* xxxviii. 42–3; *A.-S. Chron.* ed. D. Whitelock (1961), 56.

9 *V.C.H. Ches.* i. 249.

9th-century brooch, and sherds of a Carolingian jar imported from northern France.[1] Moreover, from *c.* 890 Chester is the most likely site of a mint known to have operated in north-west Mercia.[2] By then, therefore, the city was presumably a place of some importance.

THE 10TH-CENTURY REFORTIFICATION AND REOCCUPATION

The history of medieval Chester can be said to begin only in 907 with the refortification of the site by the ruler of Mercia, King Alfred's daughter Æthelflæd.[3] The background to that event was the establishment of a Hiberno-Norse community in Wirral after its expulsion from Dublin in 902. It seems that the exiles, led by Hingamund, were granted land in Wirral by Æthelflæd and her husband Æthelred but soon afterwards cast covetous eyes on the wealth of Chester, only to be repulsed by the great army which she assembled in the city. The story, although preserved only in a late source, has been shown to be reliable in essentials, and confirms that any desertion of the city was temporary.[4]

The location of the walls erected *c.* 907 is unknown. That, as might be expected, Æthelflæd adapted or at least reused in part the Roman defences is suggested by the laying of a gravel road parallel to the inner side of the walls in the early 10th century.[5] Such an action implies that the Roman west wall, which later disappeared, was then largely intact; in the 12th century Holy Trinity church was apparently built upon the remains of its gate, and its line was still traceable in the 14th century, when refuse was dumped into the foundations.[6] The Roman walls were perhaps refurbished in their entirety as a defensible inner core, the total *enceinte* being enlarged by extending the north and east walls to the river to form an **L**-shaped fortification with the Dee as the main defence to the south and west. The length of walls kept in a defensible state seems to have been consonant with a formula recorded for Wessex in the Burghal Hidage, which stated that every hide of land assigned to the main-

tenance of a *burh* sufficed to provide one man, and that every pole (*c.* 5 metres) of fortress wall required four men to defend it. The formula probably applied to Chester, whose reeve in the mid 11th century used to call up one man from each hide of the county to repair the walls and bridge. Cheshire was probably notionally assessed at 1,200 hides, suggesting that the early medieval defences were *c.* 1,524 metres long. Though those measurements do not tally with the length of the Roman walls they would fit quite well with the postulated **L**-shaped arrangement.[7]

Defences in that form are also consistent with signs of late Anglo-Saxon, perhaps 10th-century, occupation in Lower Bridge Street, north of the river but outside the Roman defences.[8] Moreover there are indications that the wall which runs south from the south-east angle of the Roman fortress to the Dee dates from before 1066. Though it is no longer possible to accept without qualification the suggestion that Wolfeld's Gate, which was in that stretch of wall, bore a Scandinavian personal name most likely to have been used before 1066, the fact that the wall divided the *burh* proper from 'Redcliff' remains significant;[9] 'Redcliff' was the focus of the ecclesiastical enclave known as the bishop's borough, which was probably from early times surrounded by its own ditch.[10]

Evidence of late Anglo-Saxon occupation in the form of sherds of the locally produced pottery known to archaeologists as Chester ware has been found throughout the town, both within the legionary fortress, especially near the main central complexes and the Northgate, and further south between the fortress and the river.[11] Other indications of activity include the remains of a bone-working industry at Abbey Green near the Northgate,[12] and traces of domestic timber buildings, both simple sunken-featured huts and larger residential halls, in the centre of the fortress at Hamilton Place, Crook Street, Hunter Street, and Hunter's Walk.[13] It therefore appears that the refortification not only gave protection and fresh impetus to an existing extramural settlement near the river but also heralded a reoccupation of the legionary fortress itself.

1 Ibid. i. 250; D. J. P. Mason, *Excavations at Chester: 26–42 Lower Bridge St.* 2, 6–7, 34–5, 40, 61.

2 R. H. M. Dolley, 'Mint of Chester (Pt. 1)', *J.C.A.S.* xlii. 1–7; *A.-S. Coins*, ed. R. H. M. Dolley, 85; C. E. Blunt and others, *Coinage in 10th-Cent. Eng.* 21, 34–43.

3 *Two Saxon Chrons.* i. 94.

4 F. T. Wainwright, *Scandinavian Eng.* 79–87, 131–61; *V.C.H. Ches.* i. 249–50.

5 T. J. Strickland, 'Roman Heritage of Chester: Survival of Buildings of *Deva* after Roman Period', *J.C.A.S.* lxvii. 22; Ward and others, *Excavations at Chester: Saxon Occupation*, 72–4, 94–5, 122.

6 *J.C.A.S.* lxvii. 22; J. McN. Dodgson, 'Place-Names and Street-Names at Chester', *J.C.A.S.* lv. 48.

7 *V.C.H. Ches.* i. 250–1; Mason, *Excavations at Chester: Lower Bridge St.* 36–9; *Medieval Arch.* xiii. 92.

8 Mason, *Excavations at Chester: Lower Bridge St.* 2, 8–23; below, this chapter: Hiberno-Norse Community.

9 Mason, *Excavations at Chester: Lower Bridge St.* 38; *P.N. Ches.* v (1:i), 26; *J.C.A.S.* lv. 50–4.

10 Morris, *Chester*, 212, 214, 217; *P.N. Ches.* iv. 130; v (1:i), 77.

11 At Goss St., Hamilton Place, Hunter's Walk, Hunter St., Abbey Green, the legionary baths, and Lower Bridge St.: Ward and others, *Excavations at Chester: Saxon Occupation*, 32–6, 40–2, 51–2, 65, 85–91, 97; Mason, *Excavations at Chester: Lower Bridge St.* 40–57. Plate 3.

12 J. C. McPeake and others, 'Excavations in Garden of No. 1, Abbey Green, Chester, 1975–7: Interim Rep.' *J.C.A.S.* lxiii. 31; Ward and others, *Excavations at Chester: Saxon Occupation*, 92–3.

13 *J.C.A.S.* lxvii. 28–9; Ward and others, *Excavations at Chester: Saxon Occupation*, 21–7, 37–40, 48–9, 61–3; *A.-S. Studies in Arch. and Hist.* viii. 78.

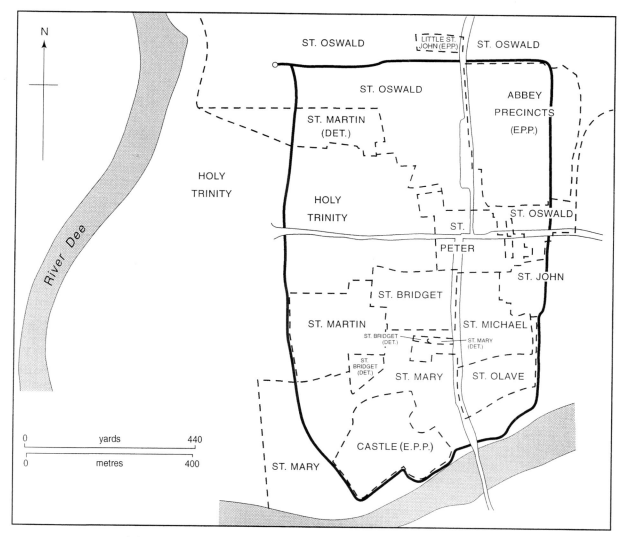

FIG. 3. *Parish boundaries within the walls*

CHESTER AND THE WEST SAXON RULERS, 907–40

Between 907 and 921 further forts were built over an area which stretched from north-east Wales to Manchester. Chester thus became the focus of complex garrisoning arrangements, initially to monitor Viking settlement.[1] Cestrians may at first have welcomed Æthelflæd: she was half Mercian and had married Æthelred (d. 911), the ruler (*patricius*) of Mercia, whose origins are unknown but who was almost certainly descended from the Mercian kings.[2] After Æthelflæd's death in 918, however, her brother King Edward the Elder seized and imprisoned the Mercian heir Ælfwynn, Æthelred and Æthelflæd's daughter.

That *coup d'état*, essentially a West Saxon takeover of the remains of Mercia, was clearly much resented. The king's visits to Cheshire and north Wales in 919 and 921, which resulted in the building of three new *burhs*, may well have been as much to suppress the consequent local unrest as to deal with the Vikings. Eventually, in 924, the men of Chester revolted in alliance with the Welsh. Edward went again to the North-West, took and garrisoned the city, but died shortly afterwards near by at Farndon. At the time Chester was thus clearly seen as a military centre of great importance, whose contacts with the Hiberno-Norse and north Wales rendered it particularly sensitive.[3]

The accession of Æthelstan in 924 restored the *burh*'s fortunes. The king, who had been brought up at the

1 *V.C.H. Ches.* i. 252–3; *A.-S. Studies in Arch. and Hist.* viii. 83–4; *T.L.C.A.S.* lxxxv. 193–222.

2 Asser, *Life of King Alfred*, ed. W. H. Stevenson, p. 24; *A.-S. Studies in Arch. and Hist.* ii. 213–21.

3 *Two Saxon Chrons.* i. 104–5; *V.C.H. Ches.* i. 254; Wainwright, *Scandinavian Eng.* 94, 127–9, 320–4; William of Malmesbury, *Gesta Regum*, ed. R. A. B. Mynors, R. M. Thomson, and M. Winterbottom (Oxford Medieval Texts), i. 210–11.

court of his aunt Æthelflæd, was popular with and well disposed towards his Mercian subjects.[1] During his reign Chester retained its strategic significance because of its command over the route to Dublin and its proximity to Wales, whose princes' relations with the West Saxons were always ambiguous. In 937 it may well have sheltered Æthelstan before his victory over the Scots and the Dublin Norsemen at 'Brunanburh' (probably nearby Bromborough),[2] and it was again crucially placed in 942 when there was collusion between the Welsh and the Scandinavian kingdom of York during King Edmund's campaign against the latter.[3]

Chester was the administrative as well as the military centre for the district involved in its maintenance as a royal fortress. Above all, it was the site of the court for a shire which may have originated in the early 10th century and certainly existed by 980.[4] The area involved was large: it presumably comprised the 12 hundreds of Cheshire listed in the Domesday Survey, and possibly for a while included south Lancashire as well.[5] The city had an important mint, whose activities, at least in the earlier 10th century, were almost certainly supervised by royal officials,[6] and whose exceptional productivity is a clear indication that Chester mattered to kings.[7] Its fortunes mirrored those of the city. Having flourished under Æthelflæd, when it produced coins of distinctive north-western design, it reverted to more standard types when Edward the Elder took over, probably because of the intrusion of new moneyers from the South.[8] Under Æthelstan, when coins first had a securely identifiable Chester mint-signature, a distinctive type was again issued, one which eschewed the portrait head of the alien West Saxon kings. Remarkably, the mint then became the most prolific centre of coin production in England, rivalling London in importance.[9]

The new *burh* was also the centre of important ecclesiastical developments. Late and unreliable traditions alleged that the body of St. Werburg was carried to Chester in 875 and installed in a minster refounded in her honour.[10] The minster undoubtedly existed by

958,[11] and on balance it seems likely that Æthelflæd was responsible for the translation and refoundation after 907, since she had engaged in similar activities elsewhere. By the 13th century St. Werburgh's was closely associated with the cult of St. Oswald, also favoured by Æthelflæd and perhaps also introduced by her to Chester.[12] The installation of such respected Mercian relics suggests that the *burh* was regarded not simply as a garrisoned fortress but as a major centre of authority, the focus of attempts to conciliate local resentment of the West Saxon incomers.

THE HIBERNO-NORSE COMMUNITY

Chester was well placed to take advantage of local traffic along the Dee and, more importantly, long-distance seaborne trade. From the 10th century onwards it developed connexions with Ireland and with Scandinavian settlements all round the Irish Sea. The importance which the Norse of Dublin, for example, attached to the link is apparent in their attempts to set up fortified quaysides, harbours, and navigation points along the north Welsh coast to ease the journey between the two ports.[13] Chester almost certainly contained a sizeable Hiberno-Norse community involved in the Irish trade, located south of the legionary fortress in the quarter next to the early harbour where the clearest evidence for pre-Conquest settlement has been found. Huts excavated in Lower Bridge Street have been interpreted as of the bow-sided type especially associated with Scandinavian sites in England, and what was perhaps the name of a gate in the city walls in that quarter, Clippe Gate, may have derived from the Old Norse personal name Klippr.[14] The dedications of the two churches in the area, St. Bridget and St. Olave, were also appropriate for a Hiberno-Norse community. St. Olave's cannot have come into being before the mid 11th century, since the dedicatee, the Norwegian king Olaf Haraldsson, was killed only in 1030; St. Bridget's, however, could well be earlier. The dedication was especially likely to have been favoured by immigrants from Ireland and was used also at West Kirby, in the Scandinavian settlement on Wirral. Moreover, since the medieval parish of

1 Malmesbury, *Gesta Regum*, i. 206–7, 210–11; *Two Saxon Chrons.* i. 105.

2 *V.C.H. Ches.* i. 260; *Saga-Bk. of Viking Soc.* xiv. 303–16; Higham, *Origins of Ches.* 125; but cf. *Saga-Bk. of Viking Soc.* xx. 200–17.

3 A. P. Smyth, *Scandinavian York and Dublin*, ii. 62–88; W. Davies, *Wales in Early Middle Ages*, 114, 116–17; *Welsh Hist. Rev.* x. 283–301.

4 *V.C.H. Ches.* i. 237; Higham, *Origins of Ches.* 115. For differing opinions about the date of shiring: P. H. Sawyer, *From Roman Britain to Norman Eng.* 197; *V.C.H. Salop.* iii. 3–4; *A.-S. Eng.* x. 162.   5 *V.C.H. Ches.* i. 252.

6 *Brit. Numismatic Jnl.* xlii. 116; xlviii. 35–8.

7 Ibid. xlii. 115; *V.C.H. Ches.* i. 260–1; *J.C.A.S.* xlii. 1–20; E. J. E. Pirie, *Sylloge of Coins of Brit. Isles* [v]: *Grosvenor Mus., Chester, I, Coins with Chester Mint-Signature*; below, this chapter: Mint and Trade.

8 *J.C.A.S.* xlii. 4–6; Blunt and others, *Coinage in 10th-Cent.*

Eng. 34–43, 51–2, 55, 72–81; below, this chapter: Mint and Trade.

9 *J.C.A.S.* xlii. 7–8, 13; Blunt and others, *Coinage in 10th-Cent. Eng.* 109–10; *Brit. Numismatic Jnl.* xlii. 97–9, 115; *A.-S. Monetary Hist.* ed. M. A. S. Blackburn, 142–4; below, this chapter: Mint and Trade.

10 R. Higden, *Polychronicon* (Rolls Ser.), vi. 126–8, 366; H. Bradshaw, *Life of St. Werburge of Chester* (E.E.T.S. orig. ser. lxxxviii), 149–52; *V.C.H. Ches.* iii. 132, where date wrongly given as 874.

11 *Cart. Chester Abbey*, i, pp. xviii, 8–13.

12 *Northern Hist.* xviii. 203–4, 209; *Midland Hist.* x. 18–19; *Oswald: Northumbrian King to European Saint*, ed. C. Stancliffe and E. Cambridge, 120; Bradshaw, *Life*, 152–3; *V.C.H. Ches.* v (2), Medieval Parish Churches: St. Oswald.

13 H. R. Loyn, *Vikings in Wales*, 18–21.

14 Mason, *Excavations at Chester: Lower Bridge St.* 18–22; *P.N. Ches.* v (1:i), 25–6; cf. *V.C.H. Ches.* v (2), City Walls and Gates: Gates, Posterns, and Towers (Shipgate).

St. Bridget's at Chester was in two portions, separated by parts of other parishes, it was perhaps once larger and had been eroded by later foundations. The church was probably the first to serve the Hiberno-Norse in Chester and dated from the period of their settlement in the city.[1]

The settlement may well have extended across the river into Handbridge, which in 1086 was assessed for tax in carucates rather than the hides normal in Cheshire. Carucates occurred elsewhere in the county in association with Scandinavian place-names, and appear to be evidence of Scandinavian settlement.[2]

Archaeological finds have confirmed a Hiberno-Norse presence in Chester. In particular, a brooch with Borre-Jellinge ornament found at Princess Street is identical with a brooch found in Dublin, and must have derived from the same mould.[3] There is evidence, too, for contact with the Isle of Man. Chester has yielded several ring-headed pins of a Hiberno-Norse type very like examples found in Man, and fragments of jewellery from a hoard deposited at Castle Esplanade c. 965 have also been interpreted as similar to material from a hoard found on the island.[4]

THE MINT AND TRADE IN THE 10TH CENTURY

The Hiberno-Norse community was much involved in coining. As early as the reign of Edward the Elder (899–924) one of the moneyers in north-western Mercia bore the name Irfara, a Norse nickname meaning 'the Ireland journeyer', and there continued to be a strong Scandinavian and Gaelic element among the names of Chester moneyers, much more pronounced than at other west Mercian mints, throughout the 10th century and beyond.[5] The discovery of an ingot mould in Lower Bridge Street suggests that metals may have been worked near the Hiberno-Norse settlement, perhaps in connexion with the mint.[6] The mint was involved in trade which passed along the Irish Sea routes, though the interpretation of its marked fluctuations in output is far from certain.[7]

The mint at Chester seems to have risen to prominence quite suddenly, c. 916–18, the time of Æthelflæd's

most notable victories over the Welsh and the Danes. At her death in 918 it was well established, with perhaps 16 moneyers.[8] Under Æthelstan (924–39) at least 25 moneyers worked there, with probably as many as 20 striking at any one time, compared with 10 in London and 7 in Winchester. That represented the zenith of Chester's activity.[9] Thereafter, though still relatively important, the mint lost something of its dominance. In the reigns of Edmund I (939–46) and Eadred (946–55) there were c. 17 moneyers, and in the troubled reign of Eadwig (955–7 in Mercia, 955–9 in Wessex) as few as 11.[10] Under Edgar (957–75) the mint became very active again, and there were c. 20 moneyers working there in 970.[11]

Despite the fluctuations the mint remained of at least regional importance until the early 970s: a Chester moneyer was chosen to strike a coin for the Welsh king Hywel Dda (d. 949 or 950),[12] and the city was a die-cutting centre for a region which included at least two other mints, Derby and Tamworth (Staffs.).[13] Chester moneyers were heavily involved in establishing the Derby mint in Æthelstan's reign,[14] and some sharing of moneyers, coin types, and dies among all three centres continued for most of the 10th century. In Edgar's reign before the reform of the coinage Chester sent dies and moneyers to other mints to help with production.[15]

Thereafter, however, the mint lost its importance. It took only a modest part in the reform of the coinage in 973, and in the late 10th century output declined steeply and die-cutting ceased entirely. Although there was a recovery in its activities in the early 11th century, it never again rivalled the great centres of London, York, and Winchester.[16]

The mint's extraordinary productivity in the earlier 10th century is rather puzzling. Proximity to the mines of north Wales, believed to have yielded silver along with the lead which was their chief product, has been adduced as a reason for its unusually high output, but there is no evidence that Wales ever produced silver in the quantity necessary for the vast numbers of coins minted in Chester. More plausibly, it has been suggested that the city was the centre for the collection of

1 N. J. Alldridge, 'Aspects of Topography of Early Medieval Chester', *J.C.A.S.* lxiv. 18–21.

2 *V.C.H. Ches.* i. 257–8, 297–8.

3 Ibid. i. 258, 285, 288, plate 24.

4 Ibid. i. 258.

5 *J.C.A.S.* xlii. 5, 8–11, 17 n.; *A.-S. Monetary Hist.* ed. Blackburn, 177–82; *Commentationes de Nummis Saeculorum IX–XI in Suecia Repertis*, ii. 191–276; *A.-S. Eng.* xvi. 233–308.

6 *V.C.H. Ches.* i. 285, 287; Mason, *Excavations at Chester: Lower Bridge St.* 64–5.

7 Dr. Metcalf is thanked for advice on what follows on the Chester mint.

8 *J.C.A.S.* xlii. 5–6; cf. Blunt and others, *Coinage in 10th-Cent. Eng.* 84.

9 *J.C.A.S.* xlii. 7–8, 13; *Brit. Numismatic Jnl.* xlii. 97–9, 115; Blunt and others, *Coinage in 10th-Cent. Eng.* 260; *Numismatic Chron.* clv. 43–5.

10 *J.C.A.S.* xlii. 8–9, 13–14; Blunt and others, *Coinage in 10th-Cent. Eng.* 120–1, 134–7, 150–1, 155–6, 260, 271, 273.

11 *J.C.A.S.* xlii. 9–11, 14–15; Blunt and others, *Coinage in 10th-Cent. Eng.* 163–4, 169–70, 260, 276; K. Jonsson, *New Era: Reformation of Late A.-S. Coinage*, 128–30.

12 Blunt and others, *Coinage in 10th-Cent. Eng.* 138, 271.

13 Jonsson, *New Era*, 65–8; *Brit. Numismatic Jnl.* xlii. 44–5, 97–103.

14 *Brit. Numismatic Jnl.* xlii. 93–4.

15 Ibid. 46–8; Jonsson, *New Era*, 49–51, 58–9, 65, 75–6, 128–32, 166–7; Blunt and others, *Coinage in 10th-Cent. Eng.* 163–4; *A.-S. Monetary Hist.* ed. Blackburn, 223; cf. *Numismatic Chron.* clv. 139–61.

16 Jonsson, *New Era*, 128–30; *Ethelred the Unready*, ed. D. Hill (Brit. Arch. Rep., Brit. Ser. lix), 184; *A.-S. Monetary Hist.* ed. Blackburn, 144; A. Freeman, *Moneyer and Mint in Reign of Edw. the Confessor* (Brit. Arch. Rep., Brit. Ser. cxlv), 55–8, 527–8.

bullion and tribute acquired by Æthelflæd and Æthelstan as a result of their military victories over the Danes and the Welsh princes.[1] Although there is nothing to suggest that Æthelstan ever exacted tribute on the scale or with the regularity necessary to sustain the output of the mint in his reign,[2] large amounts of bullion were probably obtained from the Vikings of the western Danelaw, either as plunder from those who had resisted and fled, or as offerings from those who wished to reach an accommodation with the new regime.[3]

The extensive coinage may also have been stimulated by a favourable balance of trade. Presumably Chester was a centre for the export of valuable commodities needed in Ireland, the bullion received in return being made into coin on the spot for circulation in England. That trade would naturally have been focused on Dublin, which by the mid 10th century had become the principal port of the Irish Sea and one of the richest of all Viking towns. The extent of the traffic between the two centres is apparent from the large amount of Chester ware exported to Dublin by the time of Æthelstan.[4] Other exports possibly included salt, much needed in Dublin to preserve fish and treat hides,[5] disc brooches and other items of Anglo-Saxon metalwork,[6] cloth, and slaves.[7] The importance and value of the last commodity has almost certainly been underestimated. The Dublin Norsemen's continuing need for slaves,[8] apparent from the long-lasting trade with Bristol,[9] was probably serviced, as later, by those penally enslaved and by captives taken on the turbulent frontier between England and Wales, for whom Chester would have been the obvious market.[10]

Trade between Chester and Dublin was not all one way. The large number of 10th-century coin hoards from Ireland and western Britain, in which Chester-minted coins were very prominent, points to a considerable outflow of silver from Chester.[11] Although the hoards may have been looted from England, the fact that their age-structure was consistently different from that of contemporary English ones suggests that the coins had a local circulation in a country otherwise lacking them, and hence that they were used in trade.[12] The avoidance of portraiture by the Chester mint before 970 may have been partly to accommodate the taste of the Norsemen of Dublin.[13]

Almost nothing is known of the goods imported into Chester from Dublin. Later evidence suggests that they were mainly furs, hides, fish, and agricultural produce. The only commodity known to have been imported before 1066 was marten furs, the subject of a royal right of pre-emption and therefore probably a high-value item. Almost certainly they came via Dublin, where they are known to have been a prized export.[14]

Chester, then, was probably a very busy emporium in the earlier 10th century. Yet excavated finds from the city have been few, especially from the area south of the legionary fortress where the early medieval harbour was located.[15] Possibly the main trading centre lay elsewhere; Meols, for example, at the north end of Wirral, appears to have been connected to Chester by a Roman road and has yielded a great variety of finds from the late Anglo-Saxon period, including metalwork, pottery, and a single Hiberno-Norse coin, though as yet no evidence of settlement.[16]

The discovery at Coppergate in York of a lead customs tag produced at the Chester mint in Eadwig's reign, and apparently attached to merchandise under the supervision of royal officials, suggests a cross-Pennine trade in Irish goods imported at Chester.[17] The prominence of Chester coins in southern England in the earlier 10th century during periods of fairly slack minting in London implies a further trade route running between the South-East and the North-West, along which Chester coin passed to purchase commodities in the South for export to Ireland and the Western Isles. The rise and fall of such different trade routes may help to explain fluctuations in the production of coin at Chester in the 10th century.[18]

The decline of the Chester mint has long been

1 e.g. *Brit. Numismatic Jnl.* xlii. 98; *J.C.A.S.* xlii. 3, 6, 10; *V.C.H. Ches.* i. 260.

2 *A.-S. Monetary Hist.* ed. Blackburn, 142–3.

3 Pers. comm. Mr. P. H. Sawyer; cf. Higham, *Origins of Ches.* 123–4.

4 *Untersuchungen zu Handel und Verkehr der vor- und frühgeschichtlichen Zeit in Mittel- und Nordeuropa,* iv: *Der Handel der Karolinger- und Wikingerzeit,* ed. K. Düwel and others, 200–45; *Comparative Hist. of Urban Origins in Non-Roman Europe,* ed. H. B. Clarke and A. Simms (Brit. Arch. Rep., International Ser. cclv), i. 130–9; *A.-S. Monetary Hist.* ed. Blackburn, 201–21, esp. 207–14.

5 *Untersuchungen,* iv, ed. Düwel and others, 215; *V.C.H. Ches.* i. 328–9.

6 *Untersuchungen,* iv, ed. Düwel and others, 220; *A.-S. Monetary Hist.* ed. Blackburn, 214–15.

7 C. N. L. Brooke, *Ch. and Welsh Border in Central Middle Ages,* 13.

8 *Untersuchungen,* iv, ed. Düwel and others, 222–3, 237; *A.-S.*

Monetary Hist. ed. Blackburn, 215; A. P. Smyth, *Scandinavian Kings in Brit. Isles,* 155–68.

9 Wm. of Malmesbury, *Vita Wulfstani* (Camd. 3rd ser. xl), 43, 91; *Atlas of Historic Towns,* ii, ed. M. D. Lobel, Bristol, p. 3.

10 Davies, *Wales in Early Middle Ages,* 114–15; *Hist. Gruffydd ap Cynan,* ed. A. Jones, 149; cf. ibid. 123, 125, 131, 137.

11 R. H. M. Dolley, *Sylloge* [viii]: *Hiberno-Norse Coins in Brit. Mus.* 9–54; *Irish Arch. Research Forum,* iii (2), 1–6; *A.-S. Monetary Hist.* ed. Blackburn, 134–5, 291–313.

12 Jonsson, *New Era,* 36; *A.-S. Monetary Hist.* ed. Blackburn, 149–50; *Proc. Royal Irish Academy,* lxxxvii, section C, 507–25.

13 *Jnl. Royal Soc. Antiq. Irel.* xci. 1–18; *V.C.H. Ches.* i. 261; *A.-S. Monetary Hist.* ed. Blackburn, 143–4.

14 *V.C.H. Ches.* i. 327, 342–3 (nos. 1c, 1d).

15 Ibid. i. 286–8.

16 Ibid. i. 257, 289; *T.H.S.L.C.* cxiii. 197–201.

17 *Aspects of Saxo-Norman Lond. II: Finds and Environmental Evidence,* ed. A. Vince, 335, 340.

18 *A.-S. Monetary Hist.* ed. Blackburn, 143–4, 153–6.

attributed to a Viking raid on Cheshire in 980.[1] Three of the four Anglo-Saxon coin hoards found in the city, those from Castle Esplanade, Pemberton's Parlour, and Eastgate Street,[2] have been assigned to roughly the same period and interpreted as linked to that raid.[3] A period of dereliction after the end of occupation in the harbour area in the south of the city has also been thought to reflect its effects, and it has been argued that the rise of Bristol and the beginning of Chester's eclipse as the principal port for the Dublin trade dated from that time.[4] Coherent though it is, that picture requires modification. In particular, it is clear that Chester did not play an important part in Edgar's reform of the coinage *c.* 973, well before the raid. The number of moneyers declined dramatically from *c.* 20 immediately before the reform to a mere five or so during the reform itself. Such small numbers continued throughout the reign of Edward the Martyr (975–8) and during the early issues of Æthelred II (978–1016), and were associated with a huge decline in output and the end of die-cutting at Chester. Die production for the Reform issue was centred upon London and Winchester, but most major mints quickly re-emerged as die-cutting centres, Chester alone among the great northern mints continuing to receive its dies from Winchester until the 990s.[5]

Assessment of the decline is also affected by re-datings of the Chester coin hoards. Those from Castle Esplanade and Eastgate Street were probably deposited *c.* 965 and *c.* 970 respectively, well before the renewal of Viking hostilities in the Irish Sea.[6] Only the Pemberton's Parlour hoard is likely to have been buried in 980 at the time of the Viking raid.[7] That raid has been overused as a reason for the decline of the Chester mint and cannot account for the catastrophic falling-off in 973, presumably part of some more general process since the other north-western mints, especially Derby, show a like pattern.[8] One possible explanation lies in long-term economic developments. The shift away from the north-western mints towards those of eastern England in the late 10th century may have owed as much to changes in trading patterns in response to the opening

up of the German silver mines in the 960s as to the disruption of traffic across the Irish Sea.[9]

CHESTER AND THE EALDORMEN AND EARLS OF MERCIA

Chester's economic fluctuations in the 10th century were accompanied by changes in the local administration, most notably by the rise of strong local ealdormen whose interest in the city eventually eclipsed that of the king. Such figures could be expected to take considerable profits not only from customs and tolls levied in the city but also from the mint.[10] Late Anglo-Saxon Chester was one of those towns where the moneyers made a payment in addition to the farm, which, like the dues rendered when the coinage was changed, was owed to king and earl in the proportion of two to one.[11]

It is not easy to ascribe territories to 10th-century ealdormen, but it seems that already in the 930s one of the districts ruled by such an official was north-west Mercia, the principal settlement in which was Chester.[12] The area had already emerged as a monetary region before Æthelstan's death in 939, and was characterized by a coinage distinct from the issues where there was direct royal control.[13] An ealdorman based in the North-West, Æthelmund, was among those appointed by King Edmund in 940,[14] and quite possibly his presence ensured the continuance of a north-western monetary region and an effective mint at Chester. After 965, however, his ealdormanry seems to have been absorbed into that of Ælfhere of Mercia, whose interests lay elsewhere.[15]

The rise of a local or at least Mercian ealdorman and the Mercian particularism fostered by Ælfhere meant that increasingly Chester lay on the fringes of royal authority. That was a further reason for the insignificant role assigned to its mint in the centralizing measures of 973.[16] Nevertheless, Chester was still a significant place, the scene of a notable expression of Edgar's imperial ambitions, the celebrated encounter with a group of Scots, Welsh, and Scandinavian rulers at which he was allegedly rowed on the Dee in token of submission.[17] The sources differ about the number and

1 R. H. M. Dolley and E. J. E. Pirie, 'Repercussions on Chester's Prosperity of Viking Descent on Ches. in 980', *Brit. Numismatic Jnl.* xxxiii. 39–44; *V.C.H. Ches.* i. 262.
2 J. D. A. Thompson, *Inventory of Brit. Coin Hoards, 600–1500*, nos. 84–6; *A.-S. Monetary Hist.* ed. Blackburn, 296–7 (nos. 144, 153, 174).
3 *Brit. Numismatic Jnl.* xxxiii. 44.
4 Mason, *Excavations at Chester: Lower Bridge St.* 23, 36; R. H. M. Dolley, 'Unpublished Chester Penny of Harthacnut', *Numismatic Chron.* 6th ser. xx. 191–3.
5 Jonsson, *New Era*, 86–94, 128–30; *Brit. Numismatic Jnl.* xlviii. 43–4.
6 Jonsson, *New Era*, 39–42, 68–70; Blunt and others, *Coinage in 10th-Cent. Eng.* 253–4.
7 Blunt and others, *Coinage in 10th-Cent. Eng.* 102–7; *Brit. Numismatic Jnl.* xxxviii. 43; G. F. Hill, 'Find of Coins of Eadgar, Eadweard II, and Æthelred II at Chester', *Numismatic Chron.* 4th ser. xx. 141–65.

8 Jonsson, *New Era*, 132.
9 *Brit. Numismatic Jnl.* l. 20–49; *A.-S. Monetary Hist.* ed. Blackburn, 133–57; cf. ibid. 191–9.
10 Jonsson, *New Era*, 185–8; *Brit. Numismatic Jnl.* xlviii. 37–8.
11 *V.C.H. Ches.* i. 343 (no. 1d); cf. *V.C.H. Hunts.* i. 338; *V.C.H. Leics.* i. 306.
12 C. R. Hart, *Early Chart. of Northern Eng. and N. Midlands*, pp. 287–8, 362.
13 *Brit. Numismatic Jnl.* xlii. 44–8; xlviii. 37–8.
14 H. M. Chadwick, *Studies on A.-S. Institutions*, 196–7; Hart, *Early Chart.* pp. 287–8.
15 *A.-S. Eng.* x. 143–72; Jonsson, *New Era*, 89–90.
16 e.g. Jonsson, *New Era*, 188–91.
17 *V.C.H. Ches.* i. 260; Ælfric, *Lives of Saints*, i (2) (E.E.T.S. orig. ser. lxxxii), 468–9; *Two Saxon Chrons.* i. 119; John of Worcester, *Chron.* ed. R. R. Darlington and P. McGurk, ii. 422–4; Malmesbury, *Gesta Regum*, ed. Mynors and others, i. 238–41; cf. Higham, *Origins of Ches.* 123–4.

identities of those involved, but it seems likely that Edgar did indeed take his fleet to Chester, where he met eight princes, including the kings of Scots and Strathclyde, the king of Gwynedd and other Welshmen, and the king of the Isles and another Norse ruler, perhaps from Wales or Cumbria. Although the account of the rowing from Edgar's palace on the Dee to the church of St. John and back appears only in post-Conquest sources, there was clearly a naval element in the ceremony. Taking place soon after Edgar's belated coronation at Bath in 973, it was undoubtedly a special occasion, although whether it was viewed by all the participants as a long-term submission to imperial authority is debatable.[1] Probably it set the seal on a more *ad hoc* relationship, a pact between parties interested in keeping Scandinavian raiders out of the Irish Sea.[2] As such, the episode illustrated the city's ambivalent position. Although an important harbour and naval base, it was relatively remote from the heartlands of English royal power, and hence a suitable setting for encounters with other ruling princes.

Edgar's death in 975 ended royal attempts at centralization, bringing a slackening of royal control over the coinage and a resumption of regional die-cutting. Chester nevertheless remained one of the few northern mints which continued to be supplied with dies from the South.[3] There seems to have been no senior ealdorman with a close interest in the North-West, and the area was perhaps under the control of a royal reeve. The city's relatively depressed state was indicated by the low output of its mint in the 980s and early 990s. From the 990s there were signs of a revival, and Chester may once again have become a die-cutting centre, albeit on a modest scale. Though it never regained its earlier pre-eminence, the mint was becoming more productive by 1000,[4] and by the reign of Cnut (1016–35) had reached a fresh peak of activity, with at least 16 moneyers active in his first substantive (Quatrefoil) issue. The mint cut its own dies, but they were not distributed elsewhere except for one pair cut perhaps *c.* 1020 for Sihtric III, king of Dublin. Chester coins were also imitated at a mint somewhere in the Irish Sea area during Cnut's reign, evidence that they commanded widespread acceptance.[5]

The changes may be connected with the appointment for western Mercia of a new ealdorman, Leof-

wine, whose sphere of influence probably included Chester.[6] Leofwine probably did not succeed immediately to the full authority of Ealdorman Ælfhere, for in 1007 he was subordinate to Eadric Streona when the latter was appointed earl of Mercia, and he remained so under Eadric's successor Eglaf (1017–23).[7] Even so, Leofwine's appointment had important political implications; it coincided with renewed royal efforts against the Northmen in the Irish Sea, in which Chester served in 1000 as the naval base for an attack on Cumberland and Man.[8] The city's military importance at that time was further demonstrated by the fact that it was the destination of Edmund Ironside and Earl Uhtred of Northumbria in their attempt to raise support against Cnut in 1016, and to harry Leofwine, whose loyalty was doubtful.[9]

After Eglaf's death in 1023 Leofwine's descendants succeeded to the whole Mercian earldom.[10] Western Mercia probably retained an especial importance: Leofwine's son, Earl Leofric (d. 1057), enriched several important churches and cult centres in the area, including the two minsters in Chester, St. Werburgh's and St. John's.[11] When Leofric's son Ælfgar revolted successfully in the 1050s, the western Marches were his centre of operations and he eventually sent his Irish Viking fleet to Chester to be paid off.[12] Clearly Chester was still an important naval base for his family.

Ælfgar's alliance with the Welsh king Gruffudd ap Llywelyn led to the latter's acquisition of lands west of the Dee, near Chester,[13] and when in 1063 Earl Harold attacked Gruffudd's palace at Rhuddlan in Flintshire he made the city his base.[14] Although with Gruffudd's defeat in the same year the lands beyond the Dee returned to English control, the main beneficiary was not the king but Ælfgar's youthful son and heir, Earl Edwin. By then the king had relinquished all his Cheshire lands to the earls of Mercia, leaving them in a position not so very unlike that of their post-Conquest successors at Chester.[15] Clearly by the mid 1060s the area held considerable potential for an energetic earl. One indication of the impact of such developments upon Chester itself was the fact that in Harold II's reign (January–October 1066) its mint was one of the few supplied with locally produced dies,[16] and the continuing close association of the city with the comital house was demonstrated when Harold's widow

1 D. E. Thornton, 'Edgar and the Eight Kings (A.D. 973): Textus et Dramatis Personae', *Early Medieval Europe*, x. 49–79; J. Barrow, 'Chester's Earliest Regatta? Edgar's Dee-Rowing Revisited', ibid. 81–93. Cf. J. L. Nelson, *Politics and Ritual in Early Medieval Europe*, 302–3; W. Davies, *Patterns of Power in Early Wales*, 59, 74–5; Davies, *Wales in Early Middle Ages*, 114. For a more sceptical view, rejected here: B. T. Hudson, *Kings of Celtic Scot.* 93–101.

2 Thanks are due to Ms. V. Wall for this suggestion.

3 Jonsson, *New Era*, 89–90, 92–3.

4 *Brit. Numismatic Jnl.* xlviii. 43–8.

5 G. C. Boon, *Welsh Hoards, 1979–81*, 1–35; *A.-S. Monetary Hist.* ed. Blackburn, 235–6, 246–8.

6 *A.-S. Monetary Hist.* ed. Blackburn, 223; *Brit. Numismatic Jnl.* xlviii. 45, 48, 50.

7 *A.-S. Eng.* x. 171 n.; Hart, *Early Chart.* pp. 344–5.

8 *Two Saxon Chrons.* i. 133; *Brit. Numismatic Jnl.* xlviii. 47, 50 n.

9 *Two Saxon Chrons.* i. 146–8; *V.C.H. Ches.* i. 262.

10 Hart, *Early Chart.* p. 342.

11 John of Worcester, *Chron.* ii. 582.

12 F. Barlow, *Edw. the Confessor*, 206–7; *Two Saxon Chrons.* i. 184–6.   13 *V.C.H. Ches.* i. 262–3, 344 (no. 7).

14 Barlow, *Edw. the Conf.* 207–12; *V.C.H. Ches.* i. 263.

15 *V.C.H. Ches.* i. 263, 316–17.

16 *A.-S. Monetary Hist.* ed. Blackburn, 225.

Ealdgyth was sent there by her brother Earl Edwin after the battle of Hastings.[1]

It thus appears that from the later 10th century the fortunes of the city and its mint depended greatly upon the presence of a sympathetic and effective local magnate. From the 990s the family of Leofwine probably performed that role. Their arrival in western Mercia coincided with a revival in minting activity, and their continued interest ensured the city's survival as a major provincial centre.

CHESTER IN 1066

By 1066 Chester was a prosperous town with a population of perhaps 2,500–3,000.[2] Rendering a farm of £45 and three timber of marten pelts (i.e. 120 skins), together with an additional payment from the moneyers,[3] it was assessed as a half hundred including the adjacent townships of Handbridge, Newton by Chester, 'Lee' (Overleigh and Netherleigh), and 'Redcliff', expressly said to be 'outside the city' but taxed with it. The city had its own laws and customs, administered by its hundredal court, over which presided 12 judges or doomsmen (*iudices civitatis*) drawn from the men of king, earl, and bishop, and liable to fines payable to the king and earl for failure to attend. The judges have been regarded as evidence of Scandinavian influence on the city's institutions and equated with the 'lawmen' (*lagemen* or *iudices*) of certain boroughs in the Danelaw. There is, however, no indication that they enjoyed the same status as the lawmen, who had extensive properties and judicial privileges. Indeed the laws of Chester, which were recorded in Domesday Book in exceptional detail, suggest that, as in other western towns dominated by a great local magnate, the status of its citizens was comparatively low. They were obliged to pay 10s. on taking up land in the city, and were also liable to heavy fines for failure to pay gavel or rent and for other misdemeanours.[4]

Late Anglo-Saxon Chester was in the hands of three lords, king, earl, and bishop, who all owned houses there. The earl was particularly influential, a reflection of his very powerful position in Cheshire as a whole. In contrast with those towns where he was simply allocated the normal third share of a fixed farm, in Chester he was entitled to a variety of renders and was represented by an agent, a reeve (*praepositus* or *minister*) who seems to have had similar status to the king's representative: his peace was protected from infringement by

the same fine of 40s. as that of the king's reeve.[5] The earl's reeve took a third of the forfeitures for criminal offences, a third of the payments for evasions of the tolls, and a third of the tolls themselves. The earl also received a third of the farm and his due share of the various payments made by the city's seven moneyers. The 12 doomsmen who presided over the city court were drawn from his men as well as the king's. Apart from the king's larger share of the forfeitures, tolls, and renders, the only expression of royal superiority appears to have been his right of pre-emption of marten furs.[6]

The earl's reeve was apparently, then, a very important official in pre-Conquest Chester, similar perhaps to the representatives of the Norman earl who succeeded him. His only local rival was the bishop of Lichfield, whose extensive property in and near the city included 56 houses, the manor of 'Redcliff', and the 'bishop's borough' with its complex of ecclesiastical buildings focused on St. John's church, apparently quit of tax. The bishop also had important customary rights in the city, mainly fines payable for various transgressions of the laws regulating trade on Sundays and other holy days.[7] His receipts from Chester were probably greater than in any other town in his diocese.[8]

Of Chester's two minsters, the larger and richer in 1066 was St. Werburgh's, with 12 canons and a warden (*custos*), all owning houses in the city, and an endowment assessed at *c.* 30 hides, in Cheshire and Flintshire, except for the manors of Hanbury and Fauld in Staffordshire.[9] Its precinct occupied part if not all of the north-eastern quarter of the Roman fortress, and it was the main ecclesiastical focus of the surrounding area, with a large extramural parish.[10] The cult which it housed apparently enjoyed something of a resurgence in the mid 11th century. A late 12th-century account told of the canons twice parading St. Werburg's shrine in defence of the city when it was besieged by a Welsh king called Griffin and by the rulers Harold of Denmark, Malcolm of Scotland, and the 'king of Goths and Galwedy'. Although ascribed to the reign of Edward the Elder (899–924), the first episode almost certainly alluded to Edward the Confessor and Harold Godwineson's conflict with Gruffudd ap Llywelyn, king of Gwynedd, in the 1050s and early 1060s.[11] The second story is more puzzling, but may represent some confused memory also of the 1050s, when Gruffudd intrigued with Earl Ælfgar of Mercia, Magnus, son of King Harald Hardrada of Norway, and the men of the

---

1 John of Worcester, *Chron.* ii. 604; *Jnl. Royal Soc. Antiq. Irel.* cix. 92–3.

2 *V.C.H. Ches.* i. 327, 342; *V.C.H. Ches.* v (2), Population.

3 *V.C.H. Ches.* i. 343 (no. 1d).

4 Ibid. i. 325–6, 342 (no. 1a), 344 (no. 10), 356 (nos. 181–3), 358 (nos. 210–12); cf. *V.C.H. Salop.* i. 309.

5 *V.C.H. Ches.* i. 342 (no. 1b).

6 Ibid. i. 326–7, 342–3.

7 Ibid. i. 269–70, 342–3.

8 *Domesday Surv. Ches.* 27.

9 *V.C.H. Ches.* i. 303, 344–5 (nos. 14–35), 348 (no. 70), 350 (no. 92); iii. 132–3; *Cart. Chester Abbey*, i, pp. x, xviii–xxi; *V.C.H. Staffs.* iv. 48 (no. 152).

10 Below, Topography, 900–1914: Early Medieval; *V.C.H. Ches.* v (2), Medieval Parish Churches: St. Oswald.

11 H. Bradshaw, *Life of St. Werburge of Chester* (E.E.T.S. orig. ser. lxxxviii), 154–5; *V.C.H. Ches.* i. 262–3; above, this chapter: Chester and the Ealdormen and Earls of Mercia.

Isles.[1] Other wonders attributed to the saint perhaps also date from the same period.[2]

St. John's had a dean (*matricularius*) and seven canons, all with houses in the city, and a parish much smaller than St. Werburgh's. In 1086 it was recorded as holding only the adjacent small manor of 'Redcliff', perhaps because its holdings were merged with those of the bishop.[3] A locally influential masons' workshop at the church used the soft red sandstone of 'Redcliff' to manufacture distinctive circle-headed grave crosses of a type found not only in Chester, but in Flintshire and Wirral.[4]

Industrial activities in the city included brewing, the working of bone, leather, and metal, and perhaps the manufacture of pottery: Chester ware has been found all over the city, which probably had its own kilns, like Stafford.[5] The importance of its external trade is indicated by the elaborate system of tolls, apparently of some antiquity, imposed on the cargoes of ships calling at the port.[6] Chester indeed was presumably highly dependent upon such trade.[7] Though only a middle-ranking borough in national terms, it was by far the largest settlement in an area of relatively low population. Even the Dee valley, the most densely settled of the surrounding districts, had a population of only *c.* 15 to the square mile, relatively insignificant in comparison with the 25–35 around other marcher towns such as Shrewsbury and Worcester.[8] Nor was Chester's hinterland in 1066 especially productive. It was notably worse off for ploughteams and corn mills than that of Shrewsbury, Hereford, and Worcester.[9] Chester, then, may have been dependent upon imported food. Indeed, in the 12th century, though it was well supplied with meat and fish, corn had to be imported from Ireland.[10]

The mint remained of provincial importance in 1066, with seven moneyers.[11] Despite its isolation, its standing was improving as rivals declined.[12] In sharp contrast with other western mints, Scandinavian and Irish names accounted for almost 40 per cent of the city's moneyers in the earlier 11th century, evidence that the Irish Sea trade remained significant.[13] On the

other hand English coins, especially Chester-minted ones, disappeared from Dublin during the period,[14] but not from north Wales, where several hoards deposited in Cnut's reign have been found. The suggestion of a collapse in the trade between Dublin and Chester is not, however, borne out by archaeological evidence which points to trade continuing without interruption throughout the 11th century; certainly it was in full vigour in the 12th.[15]

CHESTER AND THE ANGLO-NORMAN EARLS

Chester's close ties with the earls of Mercia led to its involvement in the rising of 1069–70. In 1069 the men of Chester in alliance with Eadric the wild and the Welsh besieged Shrewsbury. The Conqueror, then at York, responded by crossing the Pennines and bringing his army to Chester, where he built a castle. Resistance collapsed and Earl Edwin was soon replaced by a Fleming, Gherbod.[16] Identified as a centre of disaffection, the city was dealt with severely. The construction of William I's motte and bailey castle south-west of the legionary fortress almost certainly entailed considerable destruction; when Earl Hugh received the city, probably in 1071, the value of the farm had been reduced by a third to £30 and it was described as 'greatly wasted'. Of 487 houses standing in 1066, 205 had been lost and were perhaps not rebuilt before 1086. The increase in the farm of the city under Earl Hugh to £70 and a mark of gold (about its pre-Conquest level) perhaps indicates more burdensome exactions rather than returning prosperity.[17]

The new castle enhanced Chester's role as a military and administrative centre, and it quickly became the base for expeditions against both the Welsh and, in the 12th century, the Irish. Under Earl Hugh I the resources of the earldom were devoted to a prolonged campaign in north Wales, in which Chester was doubtless much concerned. It was there, for example, that the Welsh leader Gruffudd ap Cynan languished for 12 years, apparently fettered in the market place, after his capture in 1081.[18] In 1098 Earl Hugh marched from Chester as

1 Bradshaw, *Life*, 157–8; F. M. Stenton, *A.-S. Eng.* (3rd edn.), 574–5.

2 Bradshaw, *Life*, 162–9.

3 *V.C.H. Ches.* i. 302–3, 344 (nos. 10, 12); *V.C.H. Ches.* v (2), Collegiate Church of St. John.

4 *T.L.C.A.S.* lxviii. 1–11; *V.C.H. Ches.* i. 278–9.

5 *V.C.H. Ches.* i. 281–3, 343 (no. 1c); *Medieval Arch.* xx. 169–71; xxviii. 239–40.

6 *V.C.H. Ches.* i. 343 (no. 1c); *Domesday Surv. Ches.* 82; H. C. Darby, *Domesday Eng.* 290, 299.

7 *Domesday Geography of Northern Eng.* ed. H. C. Darby and I. S. Maxwell, 346–50; *Domesday Geography of Midland Eng.* ed. H. C. Darby and I. B. Terrett (1971 edn.), 134, 242.

8 What follows incorporates suggestions by Dr. C. P. Lewis.

9 *Domesday Geography Northern Eng.* 344, 376; *Domesday Geography Midland Eng.* 78, 98–101, 132, 147–51, 240, 259–61.

10 Lucian, *De Laude Cestrie*, 21–3, 44, 65.

11 E. J. E. Pirie, *Sylloge of Coins of Brit. Isles* [v]: *Grosvenor Mus., Chester, I: Coins with Chester Mint-Signature*, 335; *V.C.H. Ches.* i. 343 (no. 1d).

12 A. Freeman, *Moneyer and Mint in Reign of Edw. the Confessor* (Brit. Arch. Rep., Brit. Ser. cxlv), 55–8, 327–40, 528; *A.-S. Eng.* xvi. 248.

13 *A.-S. Eng.* xvi. 248.

14 R. H. M. Dolley, *Sylloge* [viii]: *Hiberno-Norse Coins in Brit. Mus.* 127; *Irish Arch. Research Forum*, iii (2), 1–6.

15 *Untersuchungen*, iv, ed. Düwel and others, 209–10; *A.-S. Monetary Hist.* ed. Blackburn, 208–13; Boon, *Welsh Hoards*, 4–6, 14–15.

16 Orderic Vitalis, *Eccl. Hist.* ed. M. Chibnall, ii. 228, 234, 236.

17 *V.C.H. Ches.* i. 343 (no. 1e); cf. *V.C.H. Ches.* v (2), Population.

18 *Hist. Gruffydd ap Cynan*, 63, 131–3; Orderic, *Eccl. Hist.* iv, pp. xxxv–xxxvii, 144.

joint leader of an ill-fated expedition to Anglesey.[1] Later comital expeditions became the stuff of legend. One led by Earl Richard (1101–20), for example, was believed to be the occasion of a relief march by the constable of Chester and of a miracle of St. Werburg.[2] The story is probably mythical, for it is closely related to another, regarded as explaining the origin of the Chester court of minstrels, which told of the rescue of Ranulph III at Rhuddlan by the constable Roger de Lacy (d. 1211) at the head of an unruly band of fiddlers, players, cobblers, and reprobates of both sexes from Chester.[3]

Other, more authentic expeditions were royally led. In 1157, during the minority of Earl Hugh II, Henry II received the homage of Malcolm IV, king of Scots, in Chester before invading north Wales.[4] In 1165 Henry used Shrewsbury as his base but after the campaign visited Chester to meet the ships which he had ordered to harry Gwynedd.[5] Shortly afterwards Chester appears to have been involved in a further attack, for in 1170 Hugh II was said to have built a mound at Boughton out of the heads of Welshmen killed at the 'bridge of Baldert', possibly Balderton (in Dodleston), south of Chester.[6] In 1211 King John also attacked the Welsh from Chester.[7]

Chester remained a major point of embarkation for Ireland, and in the 12th century a steady stream of visitors passed through *en route* for Dublin and elsewhere. Important travellers, such as the bishop of Louth, the abbot of Buildwas (Salop.), and Richard de Limesey, marshal in Ireland, usually stayed in the abbey rather than the castle, the residential buildings of which had yet to receive the lavish improvements provided by Henry III and his successors.[8] Nevertheless, the castle was undoubtedly used as a base for armed expeditions bound for Ireland, apparently first contemplated by Henry II in 1164 and increasingly important thereafter.[9] In 1185, when the city was in royal hands during Ranulph III's minority, some two hundred notabilities, including royal officials and military commanders, sailed thence to Ireland with their men, equipment, and provisions to join the king's son, Prince John.[10] In 1186 John himself visited Chester, only to be recalled by Henry II while awaiting a favourable wind for Ireland. Even though he did not

go himself, many others did, including John de Courcy and the prior of Dublin.[11]

It is not clear how often the earls resided in their city. Their presence was only recorded at special occasions, such as Hugh I's attendance at the ceremonies marking the establishment of St. Werburgh's abbey in 1092,[12] and Ranulph III's visits to meet Llywelyn ap Iorwerth in 1220 and 1231.[13] Nevertheless, there were certainly other less public visits. One such was a gathering of leading Angevin supporters convened in Chester by Ranulph II in 1147–8, which included his nephew Earl Gilbert of Clare, Earl Roger of Hereford, Cadwaladr ap Gruffudd, younger brother of the ruler of Gwynedd, and William Fitz-Alan of Oswestry (Salop.).[14] Another was in 1224, when the disgraced Fawkes de Breauté fled to Chester and Ranulph III wrote to Henry III in his defence.[15] Both Hugh II, after his release from prison in 1177, and Ranulph III, who had probably been brought up there, issued charters at Chester and may have harboured ambitions to make it the centre of an independent principality.[16] One sign of Hugh's attitude was perhaps the sheltering at Chester of hermits who claimed, bizarrely, to be Harold II of England and the German Emperor Henry V. Although clearly fantastic, in both cases their claims cast doubt on Angevin legitimacy: Harold for obvious reasons, the emperor because his survival would have bastardized Henry II of England. Unlike Hugh, Ranulph III remained loyal to the house of Anjou; nevertheless, the fact that the hermit stories continued to circulate during his rule perhaps tells something of the political culture and pretensions of his capital.[17]

The personal presence and ambitions of the earls made little difference to the city's role as the administrative centre of their earldom.[18] Important comital officials such as the justice and the two chamberlains must often have been present, and even those lower down the scale, such as the constable of the castle, bulked large in city life. In the 1180s, for example, during Ranulph III's minority, the constable administered the earl's Cheshire lands for the Crown and received payments from the burgesses.[19] Another

1 R. R. Davies, *Conquest, Coexistence, and Change: Wales 1063–1415*, 28–36; Orderic, *Eccl. Hist.* v. 222–4.

2 Bradshaw, *Life*, 179–81; Morris, *Chester*, 3–4.

3 Ormerod, *Hist. Ches.* i. 36.

4 *Brut y Tywysogyon: Peniarth MS. 20 Version*, ed. T. Jones, 59–60; *Brut y Tywysogyon: Red Bk. of Hergest Version*, ed. T. Jones, 135–7; Davies, *Wales 1063–1415*, 51–2; *D.N.B.* s.n. Malcolm IV.

5 *Brut: Peniarth 20*, 63–4; *Brut: Red Bk.* 145–7; Davies, *Wales 1063–1415*, 53; J. E. Lloyd, *Hist. of Wales*, ii. 577.

6 *Ann. Cest.* 25.

7 Lloyd, *Hist. Wales*, ii. 634–5.

8 *Ches. in Pipe R.* 12, 18, 21–2; Lucian, *De Laude Cestrie*, 30, 58; *V.C.H. Ches.* v (2), Castle: Buildings.

9 *Brut: Peniarth 20*, 64; *Brut: Red Bk.* 147; Hewitt, *Medieval Ches.* 2 n.

10 *Ches. in Pipe R.* 17, 22.

11 Ibid. 18, 22; *Ann. Cest.* 25; Lucian, *De Laude Cestrie*, 32, 61–2.

12 *Cart. Chester Abbey*, i, pp. xxiii–xxiv; Eadmer, *Life of St. Anselm*, ed. R. W. Southern (1972 edn.), 63; Eadmer, *Historia Novorum in Anglia* (Rolls Ser.), 27–9.

13 *Ann. Cest.* 50, 58.

14 *Charters of A.-N. Earls*, nos. 64, 84–5.

15 Ibid. no. 415.

16 A. T. Thacker, 'The Earls and Their Earldom', *J.C.A.S.* lxxi. 13–15.

17 A. Thacker, 'Cult of King Harold at Chester', *Middle Ages in NW.* ed. T. Scott and P. Starkey, 164–5, 175; below, this chapter: Church in Anglo-Norman Chester.

18 Cf. D. Crouch, 'Administration of Norman Earldom', *J.C.A.S.* lxxi. 69–95.

19 *Ches. in Pipe R.* 8–9, 12–14, 16–17.

important figure was the head of the earl's secretariat.[1] Comital clerks resided in Chester as early as the time of Ranulph II (1129–53), when a certain John the clerk stated that he had written a charter there at the earl's command.[2] Later, under Ranulph III (1181–1232), the clerk Thomas, sometimes designated the earl's chancellor, was often in Chester.[3] The impact such a figure could make upon the local scene is apparent from the career of Peter, his successor as the earl's principal clerk and sometimes termed the clerk of Chester: the earl was godfather to one of his sons, and he had a grand stone house in Bridge Street and important privileges within the city.[4]

THE CITY SHERIFF AND THE PORTMOTE

The Norman earls dominated the government of the city still more than had their English predecessors. By 1071 the borough had been mediatized and royal officials had been excluded. The earl's reeve, however, remained. As late as c. 1210 Ranulph III could refer to one of his grantees, William of Barrow, as 'my reeve of Chester', an indication that the city 'was still in effect a seigneurial borough'.[5] The duties of the earl's reeve are obscure. In particular, it is uncertain how they related to those of another representative of the earl, mentioned much more often: the sheriff of the city. The earliest reference to the sheriff of Chester, the first for any English borough, was in the 1120s in Ranulph I's charter granting jurisdiction over the summer fair to St. Werburgh's abbey, in which provision was made for the amount received in fines by the monks to be deducted from the farm which the city sheriff rendered to the earl's chamberlains.[6] The sheriff evidently accounted for the city's revenues, an arrangement whose origins perhaps date from before the 1070s, when the farm of the city was already distinguished from that of the earl's pleas in the shire and hundred courts, though both were held by the same person, the earl's man Mundræd.[7]

The city shrievalty existed from c. 1070, early holders of the post including Winebald, Pain, William Gamberell, and Richard Pierrepont.[8] Their status is not easy to assess. In the 1070s Mundræd, a landowner and tenant of the honor of Chester in Cheshire and Suffolk and of Roger de Montgomery in Shropshire, had clearly been a person of consequence.[9] In the 12th

century Ranulph I's sheriff, Winebald, had a house in the market place, while Pain (d. by 1178) was evidently a member of a local family with holdings in Chester. Richard Pierrepont, sheriff c. 1210–15, though not a Cheshire man, had property in both city and county. Pierrepont's standing in Chester is indicated by his obligation to find a doomsman for the city court and by the use of his counterseal to warrant a private deed conveying land in the city.[10] That by then the sheriff was regarded as the earl's principal representative in Chester is apparent from the prominence of Pierrepont and his successor as witnesses of local charters, and from Ranulph III's express mention of the sheriff's office when prohibiting any infringement of a grant of fishing rights to Peter the clerk.[11]

From an early period the sheriff's duties included policing. In the time of Earl Ranulph II, for example, he and the abbot's officials were charged with the arrest and detention of merchants who offended against the regulations governing trading at St. Werburgh's fair.[12] The sheriff probably also, as later, presided over the portmote court, in existence by 1200, when Peter the clerk was exempted from attending it.[13] Almost certainly the portmote represented a continuation of the hundred court of Chester, mentioned in 1086. Apart from the exemption of the castle precincts and St. Werburgh's abbey, probably under Earl Hugh I, the area of its jurisdiction was much the same, though its business may have been modified by the exclusion of the most serious criminal cases, the earl's pleas, known in Ranulph III's time as the pleas of the sword.[14] In the 13th century the portmote heard all kinds of cases except Crown pleas, though it was especially associated with disputes relating to real estate. Its procedures involved doomsmen (judices or judicatores), who interpreted civic custom and may have been the direct successors of the Anglo-Saxon judges. Responsibility for finding doomsmen rested with particular urban holdings; in the early 13th century, for example, worthies such as Peter the clerk and the sheriff Richard Pierrepont held property which obliged them to provide a doomsman, a duty from which they were exempted by the earl.[15] By the early 13th century the doomsmen appear to have been well-to-do individuals who attested charters alongside the sheriff.[16] Probably, however, the court

1 Cf. T. Webber, 'Scribes and Handwriting of Original Charters', J.C.A.S. lxxi. 137–51.

2 Cart. Chester Abbey, i, p. xlvii, quoting B.L. Harl. MS. 2079, f. 7v.

3 e.g. Charters of A.-N. Earls, nos. 228, 245–7, 250, 256–7, 268.

4 Ibid. nos. 280–6; Cart. Chester Abbey, i, pp. xlviii–xlix.

5 Charters of A.-N. Earls, no. 373; cf. no. 403.

6 Ibid. nos. 13, 26; Cart. Chester Abbey, i, pp. xlix–l, 47–8.

7 V.C.H. Ches. i. 343 (no. 1e).

8 Charters of A.-N. Earls, nos. 192, 372; 3 Sheaf, xxx, pp. 60–1.   9 V.C.H. Ches. i. 315.

10 Charters of A.-N. Earls, nos. 13, 28, 192, 372; W. F. Irvine,

'Chester in 12th and 13th Cent.' J.C.A.S. n.s. x. 19; 3 Sheaf, xxx, pp. 60–1.

11 Charters of A.-N. Earls, no. 280; J.C.A.S. n.s. x. 17–18, 20, 23.

12 Cart. Chester Abbey, i, pp. xlix–l, 52–3; Charters of A.-N. Earls, no. 23.

13 Charters of A.-N. Earls, nos. 281, 372.

14 Ibid. nos. 3, 27; Morris, Chester, 107–11; Cart. Chester Abbey, i, pp. 21, 23, 38–9, 67; J. Tait, Medieval Eng. Boro. 44; V.C.H. Ches. ii. 3–4.

15 Charters of A.-N. Earls, nos. 282, 372; Sel. R. Chester City Cts. pp. xiv–xxiii, l–liv.

16 J.C.A.S. n.s. x. 20; Tait, Medieval Eng. Boro. 300.

remained very much under the influence of the earl. Some indication of how that influence was exercised, and the kind of business with which the court might deal, is given by Ranulph III's charter of liberties granted in the 1190s, which among other things regulated the rights of citizens who bought stolen goods. If a citizen bought goods in open market which a Frenchman or an Englishman afterwards claimed were stolen, he would be quit of action by the earl and his bailiffs upon restoring the goods in question. If, however, a Welshman made a similar claim he had to repay the citizen his purchase price. The involvement of the earl's representatives in the city's judicial procedures is further implied in the exemption of the citizens from the obligation to obtain leave of the sheriff or the earl's bailiffs before taking surety for the recovery of chattels which they had lent.[1] Though it is not clear whether the sheriff in question was from the city or the county, it seems likely that it was the former in view of his other responsibilities in Chester.

THE BURGESSES AND THE EMERGENCE OF THE GUILD MERCHANT

By 1066 land in the city was held by varied forms of tenure. Burgesses clearly existed in the later 11th century,[2] but their number and tenurial conditions are uncertain. As elsewhere, burgage holdings were heritable and obliged to pay gavel (*gablum*) to the 'chief lords': before 1066 the king, the earl of Mercia, and the bishop of Lichfield; afterwards the Norman earls and bishops of Chester.[3] Such tenements were distinguished from land belonging to a rural manor, which was exempt from customary dues and tenanted by villeins (*hospites*) rather than burgesses.[4] Burgages in Chester were evidently well worth having; in the early 12th century, for example, one was valued highly enough to be exchanged for half the manor of Warburton.[5] Several of the earl's principal tenants also apparently thought it worth while to maintain a residence or tenanted houses in the shire town. Thus in 1086 Osbern fitz Tezzon had 15 burgesses there attached to his chief manor of Dodleston, and Hamon de Massey a house attached to Dunham Massey.[6]

Gradually the emphasis in the citizens' relations with their lord changed from duties to privileges, and by the late 12th century the occasional personal services for which they had been liable had largely disappeared. About 1178, for example, Earl Hugh II granted Pain, nephew of Iseult, land in the city as a free customary tenant, with quittance from toll, taking and guarding prisoners, taking distresses, carrying writs, doing night watch, and all other similar 'customs and vexations'.[7] That such privileges were not new is indicated by Ranulph III's charter confirming the liberties and free customs which the citizens enjoyed under his predecessors. By then they included freedom from inquest (*recognitio*) and assize (*proportamentum*), to which Ranulph added the right to make valid wills whether death occurred within the city or elsewhere, and a restriction on the liability of citizens who purchased stolen goods.[8] Such a body of personal rights and privileged tenure perhaps originated in the liberties of the two minsters, both of which held houses in the city free of all custom by 1066.[9]

Other privileges were linked with trade. In the earliest surviving city charter Henry II confirmed the burgesses' right to buy and sell in Dublin under the same terms as their ancestors in the time of Henry I.[10] Later charters of John, both as lord of Ireland and as king, and of Walter de Lacy, lord of Meath (Irel.), enlarged those rights, which related mainly to the trade in corn.[11] Further grants covered the citizens' commercial activities nearer home. A lost charter of Earl Hugh II, probably dating from his last years (1177–81), confirmed a grant of Ranulph II (1129–53) that the burgesses of Chester were to enjoy their customary liberties in fairs and markets throughout Cheshire.[12] In the early 13th century Ranulph III conceded a monopoly of trade within the city except during the two fairs.[13] Such privileges were linked with the beginnings of corporate action by the burgesses, first evidenced by their responsibility for paying at least part of the city farm during Ranulph III's minority (1181 to perhaps 1188).[14] Ranulph III soon afterwards, in the early 1190s, conceded a guild merchant.[15] The terms of that grant did not indicate whether the guild was created then or existed already, nor did they explain the nature of the organization involved. Even so it undoubtedly prepared the way for the emergence in the 1230s of a mayor and sheriffs responsible to the citizens rather than to the earl.[16]

1 *Charters of A.-N. Earls*, no. 256.
2 *V.C.H. Ches.* i. 343 (no. 1e); *Cart. Chester Abbey*, i, p. 17; cf. *Facsimiles of Early Ches. Charters*, ed. G. Barraclough, pp. 34–5.
3 *V.C.H. Ches.* i. 342 (no. 1b); *J.C.A.S.* N.S. x. 29–30, 37, 40; Tait, *Medieval Eng. Boro.* 100–1.
4 *V.C.H. Ches.* i. 343 (no. 1e); *Domesday Surv. Ches.* 29; Tait, *Medieval Eng. Boro.* 88–9.
5 *Cart. Chester Abbey*, i, p. 52.
6 *V.C.H. Ches.* i. 359 (no. 227), 367 (no. 334); cf. ibid. 346 (no. 36), 366 (no. 320), 367 (no. 334); cf. S. Reynolds, *Introduction to Hist. of Eng. Medieval Towns*, 94.
7 *Charters of A.-N. Earls*, no. 192; Tait, *Medieval Eng. Boro.* 134; cf. *Charters of A.-N. Earls*, no. 267; *Facsimiles*, ed. Barra-

clough, pp. 34–5.
8 *Charters of A.-N. Earls*, no. 256.
9 *V.C.H. Ches.* i. 344 (nos. 12–14).
10 J. H. Round, *Feudal Eng.* (1964 edn.), 353–4; Morris, *Chester*, 480; C.C.A.L.S., ZCH 1.
11 Morris, *Chester*, 11, 484–5; C.C.A.L.S., ZCH 2–3, 6; ZCHB 2, f. 31.
12 B.L. Eg. MS. 3872, f. 11.
13 *Charters of A.-N. Earls*, no. 258.
14 *Ches. in Pipe R.* 13, 17.
15 *Charters of A.-N. Earls*, no. 257; C.C.A.L.S., ZCH 5.
16 Below, Later Medieval Chester: City Government, 1230–1350.

TRADE AND ECONOMIC LIFE, 1070–1230

In the 12th century, though Chester was clearly regarded as a prosperous town, there are hints that it was very dependent on external trade. William of Malmesbury, for example, noted that while its hinterland abounded in beasts and fish, especially salmon, it was unproductive of cereals, which had to be imported from Ireland.[1] Somewhat later the monk Lucian also praised the woods, pastures, beasts, and fisheries of the Cestrians, but also remarked that they were well placed to obtain supplies not only locally but from Wales and Ireland.[2] In the early 13th century the citizens obtained corn from the Irish lands of Walter de Lacy under arrangements of some antiquity; he remitted the customary charges and granted the Cestrians freedom to buy all kinds of corn, malt, and flour.[3]

Despite the troubled relations between the Norman earls and the princes of Gwynedd, the Cestrians' need was such that the Welsh were encouraged to trade in the city's market, supplying especially cattle and meat. They were not, however, accorded equal status with the English and French. The less generous treatment which they received when their goods were stolen shows their inferior status at the end of the 12th century.[4] So too does the disdainful attitude of the Cestrian monk Lucian: 'The native [Cestrian] knows how savagely our neighbour often approaches, and stimulated by hunger and cold haunts the place, and then cannot help but compare the difference in supplies. Yet he returns, but with hostile glance and evil thoughts envies the citizen within the walls.'[5]

The trade with Ireland was perhaps crucial to Chester's economy. Besides food, the city imported animal pelts, especially marten.[6] Its exports are much less certain. As earlier, they presumably included salt, needed for Dublin's trade in hides and fish, and some at least of the English pottery which in the absence of home-based manufactures Dublin continued to use in considerable quantities before 1200.[7] That such trading remained significant after the English conquest of Dublin and the grant of the city to the men of Bristol is clear from the city charters, all of which post-date those events.[8] Evidently Henry II's predilection for loyalist Bristol did not have as much effect on Chester

as has sometimes been suggested, and there was no sudden rupture of Chester's relations with Dublin in the late 12th century.

Ireland was not Chester's only international link. In the late 12th century, for example, ships from Aquitaine, Spain, and Germany brought cargoes of wine into the harbour on the south side of the city.[9] Wine was clearly a valuable import, for in 1238 it formed the basis of the rent which the burgesses paid the new royal earl for one of the Dee Mills.[10] All that activity was reflected in the city's markets and fairs. There was undoubtedly a market in Chester well before it was first documented c. 1080,[11] in the city centre immediately south of St. Peter's church. A focal point, it was fronted in the 1120s by important buildings, including the sheriff's house and a 'great shop' (magna sopa).[12] In the 1090s Gruffudd ap Cynan was supposedly exhibited there in chains and released by a young Welshman visiting 'to buy necessities'.[13] A second market place was established in front of St. Werburgh's abbey gate by Earl Ranulph II.[14] Commodities on sale there were mainly provisions, both local and imported, including cereals, cattle and meat, and fish from the Dee and Ireland.[15]

The city also had two annual fairs, at Midsummer and Michaelmas. Their origins are uncertain. From an early period the monks of St. Werburgh's claimed that Earl Hugh I (d. 1101) had granted them the right to hold a fair on the three days around the feast of St. Werburg's translation on 21 June.[16] Although the grant was not mentioned in Earl Richard's confirmation of Hugh's charter to the abbey, on balance the claim is likely to have been correct.[17] Almost certainly, however, the fair was reorganized in the 1120s by Ranulph I, who provided new regulations governing its hours of opening.[18] Further regulation took place under Ranulph II (1129–53), who permitted stalls and a market to be set up before the abbey gate, and prohibited trading elsewhere in the city while the fair lasted.[19] Ranulph later pledged his peace to all attending the fair and extended responsibility for its policing to the barons of Cheshire.[20] By the early 13th century the fair was associated with the feast of St. John the Baptist, Midsummer Day (24 June), and had evidently been extended to probably at least a week.[21] The origins

1 Wm. of Malmesbury, *Gesta Pontificum* (Rolls Ser.), 308; cf. R. Higden, *Polychronicon* (Rolls Ser.), ii. 78.
2 Lucian, *De Laude Cestrie*, 65; cf. ibid. 44.
3 Morris, *Chester*, 11, 484–5.
4 *Charters of A.-N. Earls*, no. 256.
5 Lucian, *De Laude Cestrie*, 31, 52.
6 Round, *Feudal Eng.* 353–4.
7 *Untersuchungen*, iv, ed. Düwel and others, 213–14; *A.-S. Monetary Hist.* ed. Blackburn, 217–18; *Ceramics and Trade*, ed. P. Davey and R. Hodges, 275–80; *Comparative Hist. of Urban Origins*, ed. Clarke and Simms, i. 136.
8 Morris, *Chester*, 11; C.C.A.L.S., ZCHB 2, f. 31.
9 Lucian, *De Laude Cestrie*, 46.
10 *Ches. in Pipe R.* 34, 59.
11 Orderic, *Eccl. Hist.* iv. 136; *Charters of A.-N. Earls*, no. 1.
12 *Cart. Chester Abbey*, i, pp. 41, 45; ii, pp. 288–9; *Charters of A.-N. Earls*, nos. 11, 13, 28.
13 *Hist. Gruffydd ap Cynan*, 133.
14 *Cart. Chester Abbey*, i, pp. 52–3; *Charters of A.-N. Earls*, no. 23.
15 Lucian, *De Laude Cestrie*, 24–5, 44, 47.
16 *Charters of A.-N. Earls*, no. 4; *Cart. Chester Abbey*, i, pp. xiii, 21.
17 *Charters of A.-N. Earls*, nos. 8, 12; cf. ibid. no. 22.
18 Ibid. no. 13.
19 Ibid. nos. 22–3; *Cart. Chester Abbey*, i, pp. 52–3.
20 *Charters of A.-N. Earls*, no. 24.
21 Ibid. nos. 258, 448.

of the Michaelmas fair are even more obscure. It was certainly held in the early 13th century, and may have been much older. It was never, however, as important or long-lasting as the Midsummer fair.[1]

The city did not depend simply upon trade. In the 12th century industrial workers included leather-dressers and artisans,[2] and probably potters making wares for local use and export to Dublin.[3] Provisioning the city and its environs was especially important. Brewing, recorded in 1086, was regulated by a charter of Earl John (1232–7) which limited the levy (*capcio*) on beer to himself and his justiciar while they were present in the city, and restricted the amount taken from each brewing to 4 sesters (24 gallons).[4] Milling was of prime importance. The Dee Mills, located at the bridge, seem to have existed by the late 11th century.[5] By 1238 there were six mills there, farmed separately from the city for the very large sum of £100.[6] From an early date all citizens, except the monks of St. Werburgh's and their tenants, were required to grind their corn there and pay the earl a toll for the service.[7] Though the customs governing the monopoly, apparently systematized by Ranulph III, were later regarded as benefiting the city, among contemporaries they seem to have occasioned resentment, and after the death of Earl John in 1237 the mills were destroyed by the inhabitants.[8]

Another important activity was fishing, especially the taking of salmon from the Dee, where they abounded.[9] The earls had a fishery by the Dee Bridge,[10] and by the 1140s they had assigned the monks of St. Werburgh's a tithe of the fish taken there and in other fisheries.[11] Throughout the later 12th century they continued to grant boats on the Dee to various ecclesiastical establishments, including in the 1150s the newly established nuns of Chester and the monks of Much Wenlock (Salop.).[12] In the 1160s Hugh II's similar grant to Trentham priory (Staffs.) expressly allowed for fishing 'above and below the bridge', evidently that at Chester.[13] Hugh clearly valued his fisheries highly, and he and his predecessors perhaps had a monopoly.[14] His successor Ranulph III, however, was apparently much more prodigal of his rights on the Dee, and from *c.* 1200 increasing numbers of citizens held stalls, nets, or boats on the river.[15]

The mint at Chester survived the Conquest with six or seven moneyers. By the 1070s, however, the number was reduced to four, and thereafter the earls of Chester probably received the profits, although they never issued coins in their own name.[16] The number of moneyers, which perhaps dwindled further under King Stephen, fell to two after Henry II's reforms in 1158, and in 1180 the mint closed.[17]

THE CHURCH IN ANGLO-NORMAN CHESTER

The Normans brought many changes to the religious life of the city, of which the most dramatic was the transfer of the north-west Mercian see in 1075 from Lichfield to St. John's, already an episcopal possession.[18] The reasons for the move were mixed. Chester was much larger and more important than Lichfield, and the bishop already had considerable property there.[19] The new Norman bishop, Peter, may also have seen a chance for diocesan expansion in tandem with the earl's plans for the conquest of north Wales. There was then no neighbouring bishop at St. Asaph (Flints.),[20] and Peter may have felt that if large territories in north-east Wales were to come under his jurisdiction, Chester would be a more central base than Lichfield. His ambitions were probably stimulated by claims, inherited from his Anglo-Saxon predecessor, in the area of English occupation immediately west of the Dee.[21] In the event, by 1087 those claims had been rejected or ignored, and in 1098 the Norman attempt to conquer north Wales suffered a severe setback. Moreover the prospect of gaining control of the rich abbey of Coventry tempted Peter's successor Robert de Limesey away from Chester.[22] Although any chance of a return ended with the collapse of the earl's hopes of conquering north Wales in the 1140s, and although St. John's had lost its cathedral status by 1100 and the chapter its rights in episcopal elections by 1237, the bishops continued to use Chester in their official style and to maintain a presence in the city. In the 12th century St. John's remained the centre of an ecclesiastical enclave, including the minster of St. Mary, the chapel of St. James, a hermitage, and residences for the bishop and archdeacon of Chester.[23] The archdeaconry,

1 *Charters of A.-N. Earls*, no. 258; *V.C.H. Ches.* v (2), Fairs.

2 *Charters of A.-N. Earls*, no. 23.

3 *Comparative Hist. of Urban Origins*, ed. Clarke and Simms, i. 136.

4 *Charters of A.-N. Earls*, no. 448.

5 Ibid. no. 8; *V.C.H. Ches.* v (2), Mills and Fisheries: Dee Corn Mills.

6 *Ches. in Pipe R.* 34.

7 R. Bennett and J. Elton, *Hist. of Corn Milling*, iv. 55–67.

8 *Ches. in Pipe R.* 27.

9 e.g. *V.C.H. Ches.* i. 346 (no. 48).

10 *Charters of A.-N. Earls*, no. 8.

11 Ibid. no. 26; cf. no. 28.   12 Ibid. nos. 99, 109.

13 Ibid. no. 151.   14 Cf. ibid. no. 152.

15 e.g. ibid. no. 268; *J.C.A.S.* N.S. x. 21; B.L. Add. Ch. 72201–2, 72204, 75142.

16 *Sylloge* [v], 35; G. C. Brooke, *Cat. of Eng. Coins in Brit. Mus.: Norman Kings*, i, p. clxvii; R. H. M. Dolley, *Norman Conquest and Eng. Coinage*, 13–14; *New Hist. of Royal Mint*, ed. C. E. Challis, 57.

17 *Sylloge* [v], 35–6; *The Anarchy of King Stephen's Reign*, ed. E. King, 145–205, esp. 190; D. F. Allen, *Cat. of Eng. Coins in Brit. Mus.: Cross-and-Crosslets Type of Hen. II*, p. cxxviii.

18 *V.C.H. Ches.* i. 325, 342 (no. 1a).

19 Ibid. i. 270–1; *Domesday Surv. Ches.* 27–8.

20 C. N. L. Brooke, *Ch. and Welsh Border in Central Middle Ages*, 9–10, 12–13; R. R. Davies, *Wales 1063–1415*, 183.

21 *V.C.H. Ches.* i. 271–3, 302. Plate 5.

22 F. Barlow, *Eng. Ch. 1000–1066*, 64.

23 *V.C.H. Ches.* i. 344 (no. 11); *Vita Haroldi*, ed. W. de Gray Birch, 96–9; below, this section; below, Topography, 900–1914: Early Medieval; *V.C.H. Ches.* v (2), Collegiate Church of St. John.

probably in existence by the late 11th century and certainly by 1151, was closely associated with St. John's, where the archdeacon's court was held throughout the Middle Ages.[1]

The Normans also established regular monasticism within the city. In 1092 Anselm, then abbot of Bec (Eure), visited Chester at Earl Hugh I's invitation to refound the minster of St. Werburgh's as a community of Benedictine monks. The new monastery received large endowments from the earl and his principal tenants, and from the beginning was clearly intended as their pantheon.[2] Earl Hugh's cousin and leading baron, Robert of Rhuddlan, was initially buried in the abbey in 1093 or 1094, before his removal to Saint-Evroul (Orne), and all the Norman earls except Richard, drowned in the *White Ship*, were also interred there.[3]

St. Werburgh's also played an important part in the life of the community. The greatest landowner in Chester, it held a large manor, centred on the chapel of St. Thomas Becket outside the Northgate, where the abbot held court for his tenants.[4] The abbey's holding included numerous properties in Northgate Street, Parsons Lane, and Bridge Street, and much extramural territory outside the Northgate, extending from the walls to the city limits and taking in most of the fields east of Bache Way.[5] Exempted by the earls from the jurisdiction of their officials and those of the citizens, it had its own corn mill, controlled the Midsummer fair, and administered the city's principal parish, which under an arrangement probably already ancient by the 13th century was focused on the altar of St. Oswald within the abbey church.[6] Through its parochial responsibilities it was guardian of two of the city's principal burial grounds: that immediately south of the abbey church, in being by the 12th century, and another outside the Northgate.[7] St. Werburgh's and St. John's, which held the city's other main graveyard, took good care to defend their burial rights. In the 12th and early 13th century they negotiated agreements with new religious foundations within the city, including hospitals and friaries, to prevent them establishing burial grounds for any but their own inmates or those especially closely connected with them.[8]

The refoundation of the abbey seems to have revitalized the cult of its patron saint. A translation feast, probably commemorating Werburg's removal to Chester and apparently known in Abingdon (Berks.) before the Conquest, was revived by being made the focus of the city's summer fair.[9] By 1150 Werburg's association with Chester was sufficiently well known for William of Malmesbury and Henry of Huntingdon erroneously (but apparently independently) to make the city the scene of the saint's resurrection of a goose that had been cooked and eaten. The story was an embellished version of a miracle in the earliest surviving Life of the saint, probably compiled at Ely (Cambs.), and may reflect a separate tradition preserved in Chester by the monks of the new abbey.[10]

Legends about the saint, together with a Life, probably that attributed to Goscelin of Saint-Bertin, were said in the 16th century to be preserved in a book called the 'third passionary'.[11] The corpus of miracle stories was probably put together in the late 12th century: it comprised wonders associated with both the canons of the old minster and the monks of the new abbey, extending, it was claimed, from the reign of Edward the Elder (899–924) to 1180.[12]

The 12th-century material included the story of Earl Richard's rescue by his constable, William fitz Niel, aided by St. Werburg's miraculous intervention, which in turn elicited from William the gift of Newton by Chester.[13] A later episode told of fire breaking out in the city but being contained when the community took out the saint's shrine and bore it in procession, chanting litanies and prayers.[14] That story was undoubtedly current almost immediately after the events it purported to describe, since it was also recorded by Lucian in his *De Laude Cestrie*, written at the abbey in the 1190s.[15] The evidence suggests that in the 12th century the monks of St. Werburgh's were actively presenting their patroness as the special protector of the earls and their city. Lucian indeed included a long and prolix eulogy of the saint which presented her in precisely that role.[16]

Other religious foundations followed the introduction of the Benedictines into St. Werburgh's. The most important was the Benedictine nunnery established first in Handbridge by Earl Ranulph II and later moved by him to a site near the castle.[17] Always much poorer than St. Werburgh's, it nevertheless received a number of important privileges in the city

1 *V.C.H. Staffs.* iii. 30; *V.C.H. Ches.* v (2), Collegiate Church of St. John.

2 *Cart. Chester Abbey*, i, pp. xxii–xxv, 13–37; *Charters of A.-N. Earls*, no. 3; *V.C.H. Ches.* iii. 132–3.

3 Orderic, *Eccl. Hist.* iv, pp. xxxiv–xxxviii, 140–2; *Complete Peerage*, iii. 164–9; Ormerod, *Hist. Ches.* i. 258.

4 *Cart. Chester Abbey*, i, p. 132; *Cal. Ches. Ct. R.* pp. 158–9, 161, 164, 166; Burne, *Monks*, 42–3; Ormerod, *Hist. Ches.* i. 352.

5 C.C.A.L.S., EDD 12/1; 12/4.

6 *Cart. Chester Abbey*, i, pp. 21, 42, 47–8, 67–9, 113–14, 117–19; *V.C.H. Ches.* v (2), Mills and Fisheries: Dee Corn Mills; Medieval Parish Churches: St. Oswald.

7 *Cart. Chester Abbey*, i, pp. 132, 251; ii, p. 274.

8 Ibid. ii, pp. 299–302.

9 Ibid. i, p. xlii; M. R. James, *Descriptive Cat. of MSS. of Corpus Christi Coll. Camb.* i. 117; *Bishop Æthelwold*, ed. B. Yorke, 62–3.

10 Malmesbury, *Gesta Pontificum*, 308–9; Henry of Huntingdon, *Historia Anglorum*, ed. D. Greenway, 692–3; *Acta Sanctorum, Feb.* (ed. J. Carnandet, Paris, 1863), i. 388.

11 H. Bradshaw, *Life of St. Werburge of Chester* (E.E.T.S. orig. ser. lxxxviii), 188.

12 Ibid. 153–88.

13 Ibid. 179–81.

14 Ibid. 185–8.

15 Lucian, *De Laude Cestrie*, 55.

16 Ibid. 54–60.

17 *Charters of A.-N. Earls*, no. 97; *V.C.H. Ches.* iii. 146.

and probably always attracted more affection from the citizens.[1] Other foundations included the hospitals of St. John without the Northgate and St. Giles, Boughton. The former, established by Ranulph III in the 1190s to care for the poor, seems to have had a limited parochial function from an early date. It was allowed to offer the sacrament to visiting strangers, and, by permission of St. Werburgh's and St. John's, to bury the poor who died there, the brethren themselves, and those in confraternity with them. St. Giles's, probably founded in the time of Ranulph II, was for lepers. It too had a burial ground, in which the heads of Welshmen killed in battle with the earl were reputed to have been buried in 1170. Both hospitals had considerable privileges within the city, including rights to fish in the Dee and to take certain tolls. Their landed endowments came not only from the earl but from his officials and associates such as Robert the chamberlain.[2]

In addition to the religious communities, sometimes perhaps attached to them, there were hermits. In the 12th century Chester seems to have had a reputation for them. Gerald of Wales, who accompanied Archbishop Baldwin when he went to Chester in 1188 to preach the Crusade, told of two famous personages locally reputed to have become hermits in Chester and to be buried there: King Harold and the German emperor Henry IV (or V).[3] The notion that Harold lived on after Hastings appeared in several stories,[4] and a link with Chester was current by the later 12th century. It occurred in its fullest form in the *Vita Haroldi*, an anonymous work written c. 1200. There, Harold was said to have been taken to Winchester after the battle and nursed back to health, to undergo adventures abroad before returning as an old man to England. He eventually went to Chester, where he became a hermit in the cell of St. James, attached to St. John's church. There he died and was buried, confirming his true identity in his last hours.[5] Despite its absurdity, the story was undoubtedly being told in late 12th-century Chester. The author of the *Vita Haroldi* ascribed the tale to a priest of St. John's named Andrew, perhaps the Canon Andrew of St. John's who attested grants to St. Werburgh's in the period c. 1150–80.[6] Probably a respected anchorite did indeed die at Chester in the later 12th century claiming

to be Harold. At all events the tradition had a long life. In 1332 an incorrupt body, allegedly Harold's, was discovered in St. John's, and in the mid 14th century the story of the hermit was recounted by the local historian Ranulph Higden, together with the tale of the German emperor, by then believed to have taken the name Godescall and to have been associated with St. Werburgh's, where his tomb was certainly later displayed.[7] Though clearly absurd, and doubted even by Higden, the stories suggest the presence of hermits in 12th-century Chester. In particular, the claim of the *Vita Haroldi* that Harold had both a predecessor and a successor in his cell at St. John's provides evidence that the hermitage undoubtedly associated with that church in the 14th century existed much earlier.[8]

Besides the minsters and the later religious foundations, lesser urban churches were also emerging. By 1086 they certainly included the church (*templum*) of St. Peter in the market place, and the minster (*monasterium*) of St. Mary, which stood near St. John's, to which it was linked liturgically.[9] It seems likely that St. Bridget's and perhaps St. Olave's and St. Michael's also existed by then.[10] In any case, all Chester's nine medieval parish churches had been founded by c. 1150; doubt attaches only to the chapel of St. Chad, for which there is no evidence before the earlier 13th century.[11]

The main responsibility of the lesser churches was presumably as centres for the administration of the sacraments; probably none, except St. Mary's on the Hill, with its large extramural parish, had a burial ground.[12] How many parish boundaries within the city were already fixed is not clear; it may be in some instances that, as elsewhere, the main factor was the pattern of occupation rather than the ownership of property. Nevertheless, the city's parochial structure was probably established before 1200.[13] The largest parish was that of St. Werburgh. Though the abbey precinct was itself extra-parochial, the parish church attached to it had responsibility not only for areas of the city within and without the walls, but for numerous rural townships as well; in part at least the remnants of the early minster territory, they also seem to have included some of the abbey's later endowments.[14] St. John's parish was much smaller, largely confined to the bishop's estates east of the walled town, and extending

1 *Charters of A.-N. Earls*, no. 99; below, Later Medieval Chester: Religion (Religious Communities).

2 *V.C.H. Ches.* iii. 178–81; *Charters of A.-N. Earls*, nos. 198, 221.

3 Gerald of Wales, *Opera* (Rolls Ser.), i. 186; vi. 139–40; *Middle Ages in NW.* ed. T. Scott and P. Starkey, 155–76.

4 *The Anglo-Saxons: Studies presented to Bruce Dickins*, ed. P. Clemoes, 122–36; *Trans. Battle and District Hist. Soc.* xxiii. 14–16.

5 *Vita Haroldi*, 30, 77, 81–99.

6 Ibid. 97–8; *Cart. Chester Abbey*, i, p. 94; ii, p. 336; *Middle Ages in NW.* 160–2; cf. *Foundation of Waltham Abbey*, ed. W. Stubbs, 30–1; *Waltham Chron.* ed. L. Watkiss and

M. Chibnall, 54–6.

7 Higden, *Polychronicon*, vii. 244, 446–8; *Middle Ages in NW.* 162–4.

8 *Vita Haroldi*, 78, 96.

9 *V.C.H. Ches.* i. 343 (no. 1e), 344 (nos. 10–12); Lucian, *De Laude Cestrie*, 63.

10 *V.C.H. Ches.* v (2), Medieval Parish Churches.

11 Ibid.; *J.C.A.S.* lxiv. 5–31.

12 Below, Later Medieval Chester: Religion (Parish Churches).

13 Cf. D. Keene, *Survey of Medieval Winchester*, ii. 107, 116, 125.

14 *Northern Hist.* xviii. 199–206; *V.C.H. Ches.* v (2), Medieval Parish Churches: St. Oswald.

to Boughton,[1] but another large extramural area was attached to St. Mary's on the Hill, a church founded in the mid 12th century to serve the castle and the administration based there; possibly that parish was shaped by the territories attached to the castle.[2] Of the remaining churches, St. Peter's was wholly intramural, occupying an irregular area in the centre of the city perhaps determined by the urban estate on which it seems to have been founded.[3] To the south lay the two churches with Hiberno-Norse dedications, of which St. Bridget's with its larger and dispersed parish was probably earlier.[4] Between the main intramural portion and the extramural Earl's Eye lay not only St. Olave's but also St. Michael's, while to the west lay St. Martin's. The origins of the last two cannot be determined, though St. Martin's at least was probably relatively late.[5]

1 *V.C.H. Ches.* v (2), Collegiate Church of St. John.
2 Ibid. Medieval Parish Churches: St. Mary.
3 Ibid.: St. Peter; *J.C.A.S.* lxiv. 16–17.

4 *V.C.H. Ches.* v (2), Medieval Parish Churches: St. Bridget, St. Olave.
5 Ibid.: St. Martin, St. Michael.

LATER MEDIEVAL CHESTER 1230–1550

CITY AND CROWN, 1237–1350

Although the Crown's annexation of the Norman earldom of Chester in 1237 made no immediate impact upon the city's institutions, it brought it into direct contact with the king and royal officials for the first time since 1066. Henry III was anxious to be seen as the legitimate successor of the Norman earls, and especially of Ranulph III. As early as 1232 he granted £3 a year from the manor of Newcastle-under-Lyme (Staffs.) to support a chaplain at Chester abbey to pray for Earl Ranulph's soul, and in 1238 he ordered the arrears to be paid.[1] Royal confirmations of Ranulph's three charters to the citizens, guaranteeing their liberties, free customs, and guild merchant, were issued in 1237 and 1239.[2] Henry also took over the earls' charitable responsibilities within the city. In 1239, for example, he provided for three beds for the poor and infirm in St. John's hospital without the Northgate, as Ranulph III had done,[3] and in 1241 he ordered that William of the chamber was to have his wages for keeping the king's buildings and garden at Chester castle, in the same manner as his ancestors under the Norman earls.[4]

The farm of the city was fixed in 1237 at the very high sum of £200 a year, besides £100 for the Dee Mills; it was, however, reduced in the two succeeding years, so that in 1239–40 it stood at £130.[5] An allowance was also made to the city bailiffs or sheriffs for keeping town and bridge in 1240.[6] Such generosity was counterbalanced by a tallage of 50 marks assessed on the city in the same year, and by loans totalling 300 marks which the king extracted from the citizens in 1244 and 1246.[7]

In 1241 Henry first visited Chester, on his way to and from Rhuddlan (Flints.) to receive the submission of the Welsh prince Dafydd ap Llywelyn.[8] Those visits saw the inauguration of work on the castle and the dispatch of building implements and military equipment from Chester to Rhuddlan.[9] The king was also in Chester in 1245, at the head of a large army which relieved Dyserth castle (Flints.) and established a new fortress at Deganwy (Caern.). He again returned to England by way of the city.[10] During such expeditions men were mustered at Chester, and the city became a major source of provisions, equipment, and weapons.[11] The royal financial administration, the wardrobe, was temporarily established there, and received from Ireland and elsewhere large sums of money which were stored in the castle and the abbey.[12]

In 1257 in a rising against the officials of Henry III and his son the Lord Edward, the Welsh apparently penetrated as far as Chester.[13] In response Henry and Edward organized a further expedition into Wales, mustering men and equipment in the city.[14] Envoys from Prince Llywelyn ap Gruffudd visited the king there,[15] and the royal wardrobe and its staff were again brought thither.[16] After a fortnight's stay Henry and Edward set out on what was to be the king's last invasion of Wales. They returned to Chester less than a month later after a brief campaign.[17] Although plans for further expeditions were frustrated by Henry's difficulties in England,[18] in 1260 Edward raised substantial loans from the city.[19]

During the Barons' Wars Chester was held for the Lord Edward by the justice, William la Zouche, who in

---

1 *Cal. Chart. R.* 1226–57, 169; *Cal. Lib.* 1226–40, 350, 495–6; *Close R.* 1237–42, 226.

2 C.C.A.L.S., ZCH 9–11; Morris, *Chester*, 488–90.

3 *Cal. Lib.* 1226–40, 405; cf. ibid. 451.

4 Ibid. 1240–5, 53.

5 Ibid. 1226–40, 423; 1240–5, 21; *Ches. in Pipe R.* 34.

6 *Cal. Lib.* 1240–5, 59.

7 *Ches. in Pipe R.* 58; *Cal. Pat.* 1232–47, 431–2, 435, 492; *Cal. Lib.* 1245–51, 47; *Close R.* 1242–7, 383; cf. *Cal. Pat.* 1232–47, 467; *Cal. Lib.* 1245–51, 258.

8 *Ann. Cest.* 62; *Close R.* 1237–42, 325–8, 341, 362; *Cal. Pat.* 1232–47, 257–8; *Cal. Lib.* 1240–5, 68–71, 75; J. E. Lloyd, *Hist. of Wales*, ii. 698; R. R. Davies, *Conquest, Coexistence, and Change: Wales 1063–1415*, 301.

9 *Cal. Lib.* 1240–5, 69–70; *Ches. in Pipe R.* 38, 45, 52, 54, 59, 71.

10 *Ann. Cest.* 64; *Close R.* 1242–7, 334–6, 363, 367–8, 471;

Cal. Lib. 1240–5, 319–21; 1245–51, 1–2; *Cal. Chart. R.* 1226–57, 287–8; *Cal. Pat.* 1232–47, 459, 465; Lloyd, *Hist. Wales*, ii. 703–5; Davies, *Wales 1063–1415*, 302.

11 *Cal. Pat.* 1232–47, 456.

12 Ibid. 256–7, 466; *Cal. Lib.* 1240–5, 69, 320–1; 1245–51, 1, 3; *Close R.* 1242–7, 332, 336.

13 Matthew Paris, *Chronica Majora* (Rolls Ser.), v. 594.

14 *Cal. Pat.* 1247–58, 564, 573; *Close R.* 1256–9, 79, 139, 220–1.   15 *Cal. Lib.* 1251–60, 388, 390, 407, 523.

16 Ibid. 426; *Cal. Pat.* 1247–58, 576, 620.

17 *Ann. Cest.* 74; *Close R.* 1256–9, 85–9, 91–3, 145–50; *Cal. Pat.* 1247–58, 573–5, 577–9, 596–8, 600–1, 606; *Cal. Chart. R.* 1226–57, 472–5; 1257–1300, 5; *Cal. Lib.* 1251–60, 392, 403; Lloyd, *Hist. Wales*, ii. 721–2; Davies, *Wales 1063–1415*, 310.

18 *Close R.* 1256–9, 294–7, 299, 480–1; 1259–61, 191–4, 200–1; *Cal. Pat.* 1247–58, 627–8.

19 *Cal. Doc. Irel.* 1252–84, no. 682.

1263 took violent possession of St. Werburgh's and in 1264, apparently at the suggestion of one of the city sheriffs, began a defensive ditch immediately north of the city walls, destroying property belonging to the abbey in the process.[1] Despite William's efforts, the city and county were given to Simon de Montfort in 1264, and in 1265 Simon's son Henry went there to receive homage from the citizens and the men of the shire.[2] After Edward's escape from baronial custody, however, the royalists besieged Luke de Taney, Montfort's justice of Chester, in Chester castle. Taney surrendered upon news of Montfort's defeat at Evesham,[3] and Edward himself occupied Chester, from where he sent out instructions described as his 'first recorded act of state' as a 'responsible adviser of the Crown'.[4] In 1270 he ordered that nothing except due prises (customs duties) were to be taken from the city's merchants.[5] In return he seems to have expected more loans; in the early 1270s, for example, he was repaying a debt of £400 owed to the mayor and citizens.[6]

After 1267 Llywelyn ap Gruffudd's annual payments in return for recognition as prince of Wales and other concessions made in the treaty of Montgomery were handed over to the king's envoys at St. Werburgh's abbey.[7] By 1274, however, the prince was falling into arrears,[8] and his failure to appear at Chester in 1275, after Edward I had journeyed there to receive his submission,[9] proved a turning point in his relations with the king.[10] By then preparations were in train to establish Chester as the base for a major expedition against him. Already in 1274 the king had ordered that the royal demesne in Chester be tilled and sown, and dilapidated houses within the castle replaced,[11] and in 1275 his grant of the Dee Mills to the royal master mason Richard the engineer was accompanied by provision for grinding corn free of toll in time of war.[12]

With the outbreak of Edward's first Welsh war in 1277, Chester was made one of the three military commands from which Llywelyn's principality was attacked; royal forces operating from the city under the command of William de Beauchamp, earl of Warwick, quickly brought northern Powys to submission.[13] As in previous campaigns, workmen, soldiers,

timber, ammunition, victuals, and boats were assembled in the city.[14] The royal wardrobe was also brought there in five carts.[15] With the city thus established as the chief base for operations in north-eastern Wales, in July Edward himself arrived to lead a large force of infantry on the culminating campaign.[16] He returned to the city in September when it was clear that Llywelyn would be forced to surrender.[17]

Chester retained its pivotal role in the aftermath of that campaign. It was there that Llywelyn was required to pay annual instalments of the huge debt to the king which he had incurred as the price of his disobedience. It was there too, in St. John's church, that 10 hostages from the leading men of Gwynedd were released after swearing loyalty on the Holy Cross of Chester.[18] Chester's functions as an administrative and financial centre were enhanced by the activity generated by Edward's new castles in north-east Wales, placed under the supervision of an officer of the palatinate, the justice of Chester.[19] In 1276 the citizens were formally granted the farm of the city, together with the fishery at the Dee Bridge, for an annual payment of £150.[20] In 1280 the justice was ordered to establish an exchange in the city for trafficking in precious metals, and £1,000 was sent from London for the purpose.[21] Two local merchants were placed in charge, and in 1281 were ordered to deliver £1,250 to the keeper of the wardrobe for the expenses of the royal household.[22] In 1281 further payments were made into the wardrobe at Chester, and the city provided one of the locations for an inquiry into the laws and customs of the Welsh.[23]

The Welsh rebellion in 1282 greatly enhanced Chester's military and administrative importance. As in 1277, the city formed the base of one of three military commands, and was put in the charge of the trusted Reynold de Grey, aided by the sheriffs of Lancashire and Shropshire.[24] Reynold was quickly placed in control of a cavalry force, and provisions from all over the king's dominions, but especially Ireland, Ponthieu, and the bishopric of Winchester, flowed into Chester.[25] Weapons, in particular quarrels for crossbowmen, were sent to the city,[26] and workmen

1 *Ann. Cest.* 86, 88.

2 Ibid. 90; *Cal. Pat.* 1258–66, 487.

3 *Ann. Cest.* 94, 96; *Cal. Pat.* 1258–66, 487.

4 F. M. Powicke, *King Hen. III and Lord Edw.* ii. 504.

5 C.C.A.L.S., ZCH 12; Morris, *Chester*, 499–500.

6 *Cal. Doc. Irel.* 1252–84, no. 891.

7 *Cal. Pat.* 1266–72, 123, 175, 299–300, 306, 370, 391.

8 Davies, *Wales 1063–1415*, 322–3, 326–7.

9 Ibid. 327–8; *Cal. Close*, 1272–9, 241; *Ann. Cest.* 102; *Chrons. of Reigns of Edw. I and Edw. II* (Rolls Ser.), i. 85.

10 Davies, *Wales 1063–1415*, 328; *Cal. Close*, 1272–9, 325, 359–60.   11 *Cal. Close*, 1272–9, 141.

12 *Cal. Fine R.* 1272–1307, 52.

13 Davies, *Wales 1063–1415*, 333–4; Lloyd, *Hist. Wales*, ii. 758–9; J. E. Morris, *Welsh Wars of Edw. I*, 115, 140.

14 *Cal. Close*, 1272–9, 372; *Cal. Pat.* 1272–81, 227–8; Davies,

Wales 1063–1415, 334; Morris, *Welsh Wars*, 118–20, 127–8, 130.

15 *Cal. Pat.* 1272–81, 209; T. F. Tout, *Chapters in Administrative Hist. of Medieval Eng.* ii. 44–5.

16 *Cal. Fine R.* 1272–1307, 81, 86; *Cal. Chart. R.* 1257–1300, 204.

17 *Cal. Fine R.* 1272–1307, 82; *Cal. Chart. R.* 1257–1300, 278.   18 *Cal. Chanc. R. Var.* 169.

19 Morris, *Welsh Wars*, 143–5.

20 *Cal. Fine R.* 1272–1307, 92; *Ches. in Pipe R.* 112, 117, 132.

21 *Cal. Pat.* 1272–81, 415.   22 Ibid. 450.

23 *Cal. Close*, 1279–88, 104; *Cal. Chanc. R. Var.* 191–4.

24 Davies, *Wales 1063–1415*, 349; Morris, *Welsh Wars*, 152–5.

25 *Cal. Close*, 1279–88, 150; *Cal. Chanc. R. Var.* 214, 226, 246, 250, 257–8.

26 Morris, *Welsh Wars*, 91.

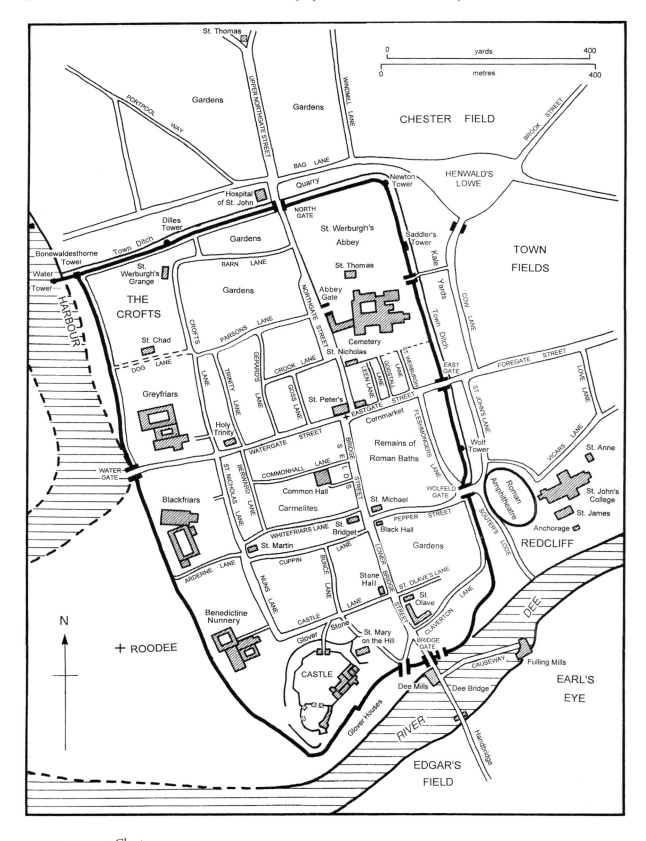

FIG. 4. *Chester, c. 1500*

gathered there, including a muster of 1,010 diggers and 345 carpenters from all parts of England.[1] A special wardrobe account was kept for the campaign, and the royal wardrobe was once more moved to Chester.[2]

Edward himself arrived in the midst of that activity, and took command of the cavalry already mustered there.[3] With him came the royal court and chancery, and during 1282 and 1283 chancery enrolments were made at Chester.[4] Edward moved on into north Wales after staying in the city for over three weeks and leaving orders for 1,000 woodcutters to be assembled there and sent on to Rhuddlan to help clear pathways for his men.[5] The city remained a major centre for provisioning the army; late in 1282, for example, the justice of Chester and the sheriffs of some 15 counties were ordered to ensure that it was continuously supplied with victuals and other merchandise.[6]

Edward returned to Chester after his victory in summer 1283.[7] He was there again in 1284, *en route* to north Wales,[8] but made no further visits until after the launch of his third campaign against the Welsh in 1294.[9] In response to the rebellion of that year Edward established three commands, the northernmost at Chester under Reynold de Grey and John de Warenne, earl of Surrey.[10] By the end of the year, when the king himself arrived in Chester, 16,000 infantrymen had been mustered.[11] Edward proceeded swiftly to Conwy (Caern.),[12] arranging for supplies to be transmitted from Chester, in particular large quantities of wood to make crossbows and hurdles.[13] As before, the city formed an administrative base, and in 1295, while the king was at Conwy, the chancellor, John Langton, stayed there.[14] With the restoration of peace the city was the scene of the recruitment of 100 masons to work on Caernarfon castle.[15]

Edward's decisive victory over the rebels in 1294–5 ended resistance to his rule in Wales, and he seems to have paid only one further visit to Chester, in 1301.[16] The Welsh campaigns, however, left their impact on the city. By 1295, for example, the portmote had evolved the custom that in time of war it did not

meet except to hear pleas of novel disseisin, darrein presentment, and dower.[17] The city, moreover, retained its role as a supply centre, albeit on a much reduced scale, when Edward turned his attentions to Scotland. In 1300, for example, Henry de Lacy, earl of Lincoln, sent envoys to Chester to obtain provisions for his mission to Scotland on the king's behalf, and in 1306 ten ships were gathered in the port to carry corn to the North.[18]

In 1300, perhaps in recognition of the city's special role in his Welsh campaigns, Edward granted Chester a new charter, for the most part a confirmation of developments which had occurred informally over the previous century.[19] By that means the king recognized the existence of the mayoralty (never the subject of a formal grant), officially recorded for the first time that the farm was in the hands of the citizens, and fixed that farm at £100, the figure customarily paid throughout his reign.[20] There was, however, one important innovation: the exceptional, indeed at that time unique grant to the mayor and sheriffs of the right to hold the pleas of the Crown. The implications of the concession were considerable, and the charter may justly be regarded as a landmark in the city's history.[21] Its issue was preceded by Chester's addition a few weeks earlier to the select group of towns with exchanges, that established in 1280 presumably having lapsed after the conquest of Wales.[22]

In 1301 Edward I's son, Edward of Caernarfon, was made prince of Wales and earl of Chester. He was not seen at Chester until 1309, when as Edward II he made his first and apparently only visit, in order to meet his favourite, Piers Gaveston, returning from Ireland.[23] During his reign Chester remained a base from which supplies could be obtained for royal enterprises in Scotland and elsewhere. In 1309, for example, William (III) of Doncaster, the most prominent of the Chester merchants, supplied the king with 5,000 horseshoes, 8,000 large nails, and 60,000 small nails.[24] In 1310 the justice of Chester was requested to find victuals for the king's intended war against Robert Bruce, and in 1311

1 Davies, *Wales 1063–1415*, 350; *Cal. Chanc. R. Var.* 247–8, 251.

2 *Cal. Chanc. R. Var.* 219, 238; *Cal. Pat.* 1281–92, 33, 60–1, 67, 71, 110.

3 *Cal. Chanc. R. Var.* 223–31, 253; *Cal. Chart. R.* 1257–1300, 262–3; *Cal. Close,* 1279–88, 191; *Cal. Fine R.* 1272–1307, 163–5; Morris, *Welsh Wars,* 158–9.

4 *Cal. Close,* 1279–88, 190–3, 195, 230–1, 235, 237; *Cal. Chanc. R. Var.* 242; *Cal. Pat.* 1281–92, 27, 60.

5 *Cal. Chanc. R. Var.* 232.

6 Ibid. 257–8; cf. ibid. 246, 270.

7 *Cal. Fine R.* 1272–1307, 189; *Cal. Chart. R.* 1257–1300, 268.

8 *Cal. Fine R.* 1272–1307, 206; *Cal. Chart. R.* 1257–1300, 278; Davies, *Wales 1063–1415,* 357–8.

9 *Cal. Fine R.* 1272–1307, 349; *Cal. Pat.* 1292–1301, 125, 127, 158; *Cal. Close,* 1288–96, 406–7.

10 Morris, *Welsh Wars,* 244–7, 253–4; *Cal. Chanc. R. Var.* 359–60.

11 *Cal. Chanc. R. Var.* 355, 359; Davies, *Wales 1063–1415,* 383.

12 Davies, *Wales 1063–1415,* 383–4.

13 *Cal. Inq. Misc.* i, p. 475.

14 *Cal. Close,* 1288–96, 443, 445.

15 Ibid. 413.

16 *Cal. Chart. R.* 1300–26, 9.

17 C.C.A.L.S., ZMR 1, rot. 1d.; *Sel. R. Chester City Cts.* 10.

18 *Cal. Pat.* 1292–1301, 505; *Cal. Close,* 1302–7, 385.

19 C.C.A.L.S., ZCH 13; Morris, *Chester,* 490–3; *Cal. Chart. R.* 1257–1300, 480–6.

20 Cf. *Ches. in Pipe R.* 112, 117, 122; *Cal. Fine R.* 1272–1307, 92.

21 Below, this chapter: City Government, 1230–1350 (Charter of 1300).

22 *Red Bk. Exch.* (Rolls Ser.), iii. 990.

23 *V.C.H. Ches.* ii. 9; *Cal. Fine R.* 1307–19, 27, 43–4; *Cal. Pat.* 1307–13, 163; *Cal. Close,* 1307–13, 161; *Chrons. of Edw. I and II,* ii. 161.

24 *36 D.K.R.* App. II, p. 150.

the mayor and citizens were asked to supply two ships.[1] Further requests were made after the king's defeat at Bannockburn had opened the way for Scottish raiding throughout the North. Thus in 1316 payments were made for 1,000 footmen sent from Glamorgan to Chester and thence to Scotland, and safe-conducts were issued to merchants of Chester to buy corn in Ireland for the king's needs.[2]

Edward's political difficulties had their repercussions in the North-West, and in 1318 disorder broke out in Chester. A great multitude of armed men came there on a day when the county court was due to be held, besieged the city, wounded and killed some of its defenders, and burned suburban houses. Thereafter they maintained a guard on the river Dee to prevent merchants from entering or leaving, and attacked those who tried to do so. Sir Roger Mortimer, justice of Wales, John de Warenne, earl of Surrey, Sir John Grey, and the sheriffs of Lancashire, Shropshire, and Staffordshire were commissioned to repress the disorder.[3] Though its cause is not known, it was clearly related to Edward's quarrel with his cousin Thomas, earl of Lancaster. The attackers apparently included Thomas's men, and the earl intervened to ensure that those imprisoned in Chester castle were delivered to his own officials.[4]

Chester was evidently a centre of disaffection after Edward II's deposition in 1327. Among the very many included in the general pardon of that year were William of Basingwerk and Richard of the Peak, both local men.[5] Later, just as an invasion was planned by the Scots, the justice of Chester received an order to arrest a group of malefactors in the city and adjacent ports.[6] Within a month, the former mayor Richard le Bruyn had also been arrested and accused of adherence to Donald, earl of Mar (d. 1332), one of the Scottish leaders.[7] Thereafter, fines ranging from £30 to £200 were extracted from several leading citizens, including William of Doncaster the elder, presumably William (III),[8] and 18 of their sons were briefly imprisoned in Chester castle as sureties.[9]

By the end of 1327 relations between city and Crown had improved, and four Chester merchants were given letters of protection and safe conduct for a year.[10] In 1329 the mayor and citizens were granted a murage (a tax for repairing the walls) for four years.[11] Despite the appointment of a commission in 1330 to inquire into their alleged misappropriation of large sums collected under an earlier grant of murage,[12] relations thereafter with the new regime seem to have been unexceptionable. In 1333 Edward III's young son, Edward of Woodstock, later known as the Black Prince, was created earl of Chester; he did not, however, visit the city until 1353.[13]

CITY GOVERNMENT, 1230–1350

By the 1230s it is possible to trace in Chester emergent civic institutions, responsible to the citizens rather than the earl. In the 1230s the dominant figures were still the city sheriffs but by 1300 the mayor was established as the senior civic official. Throughout the period the main institutions of city government remained the city courts and the guild merchant.

THE SHERIFFS AND THEIR COURTS, 1230–1300

The shrievalty appears first to have been divided in the 1220s or 1230s, during the tenure of Stephen Fresnell, and there were certainly two sheriffs by 1244.[14] Possibly the division of the office marked its transfer to civic control; elsewhere the right to appoint borough officials was linked with responsibility for the farm, a privilege which the Cestrians had acquired by 1238.[15]

One indication that the office had been vested in the citizens, and had perhaps become elective, is the greater frequency with which it changed hands from the mid 13th century; the fact that at least 11 different combinations of holders served during the mayoralty of Richard the clerk (c. 1251–68), for example, strongly suggests that by then appointments were for one year only.[16] Indeed, in the mid 14th century the sheriffs alleged that the citizens had been granted the power to elect two sheriffs by the Lord Edward as earl of Chester after 1254.[17]

Throughout the period the principal city court remained the portmote.[18] Clearly a court of record, where the principal citizens of Chester witnessed one another's land grants, by the mid 13th century it probably dealt with other forms of civil business relating to property, and with minor criminal offences.

1 *Cal. Close*, 1307–13, 213, 353.
2 Ibid. 1313–18, 299, 364–5; *Cal. Pat.* 1313–17, 470, 568.
3 *Cal. Pat.* 1317–21, 200; *Cal. Close*, 1318–23, 12.
4 *Cal. Close*, 1318–23, 23–4.
5 *Cal. Pat.* 1327–30, 48.
6 Ibid. 153.
7 Ibid. 183; *Cal. Close*, 1327–30, 142; N. Fryde, *Tyranny and Fall of Edw. II*, 201, 209, 212.
8 *Cal. Close*, 1327–30, 169, 273, 278, 448.
9 Ibid. 169, 187–8.
10 *Cal. Pat.* 1327–30, 183, 196–7.

11 Ibid. 455.
12 Ibid. 559; 1330–4, 62.
13 *Cal. Chart. R.* 1327–41, 300.
14 *V.C.H. Ches.* i. 326, 343; *J.C.A.S.* n.s. x. 20; *Cal. Pat.* 1232–47, 431–2; *Ancestor*, vi. 33.
15 *Ches. in Pipe R.* 40, 42, 46; J. Tait, *Medieval Eng. Boro.* 185–93.
16 *V.C.H. Ches.* v (2), Lists of Mayors and Sheriffs.
17 C.C.A.L.S., ZCHB 2, ff. 66v.–67.
18 Para. based on *Sel. R. Chester City Cts.* pp. x, xxi, xxiii–xlix; *Cal. Ches. Ct. R.* pp. 4, 26.

By the 1290s, when it met every two to three weeks (occasionally consecutively) on Mondays, with long recesses at Christmas, Easter, Midsummer, and harvest, it dealt with every kind of action apart from the Crown pleas, but was especially concerned with pleas of real estate, initiated by both plaint and writ.

Business in the portmote remained in the hands of doomsmen, holders of certain properties within the city: such an obligation, for instance, went with the land and buildings in Bridge Street granted by Simon Whitchurch, abbot of St. Werburgh's (1265–91), to David the miller, who thereafter witnessed charters in the portmote, acted as doomsman, and eventually became sheriff in the 1290s. The property so conveyed was clearly large by Chester standards, since David paid £2 a year rent for it.[1] Presumably all such properties were of some size and standing. Certainly, the only one from the period that can be identified, also in Bridge Street and adjoining St. Olave's church, was a major stone house owned by another prominent citizen, Edward I's master mason Richard the engineer.[2]

Almost certainly the sheriffs continued to preside over the portmote throughout the 13th century. The position, however, is complicated by the fact that although in the 1240s and 1250s they often headed witness lists recorded in the portmote,[3] sometimes apparently even when the mayor was present,[4] from the later 1250s the mayor took precedence.[5] Moreover, in 13th-century royal records the principal local officials were generally referred to ambiguously as 'bailiffs'.[6] The term was useful to the Crown: embracing the holder of any bailiwick, it was applied to urban officials known locally by a variety of titles.[7] When, for example, in 1241 the king ordered that the bailiffs of Chester be paid their expenses for keeping the town and bridge, the officials so designated probably comprised the serjeants of the four main gates as well as the sheriffs.[8] In the county court, too, the presidents of the portmote were invariably termed bailiffs,[9] although the same court also referred to the city's sheriffs in a manner which suggests that it regarded them as the officials principally responsible for bringing to justice those offending within the city limits. In cases which involved the citizens' privileges and immunities, however, the mayor seems also to have been involved.[10]

The shrieval office was still very influential, and in 1264 the St. Werburgh's annalist vehemently denounced one of its holders for urging the demolition of houses belonging to the abbey in order to make the north wall of the city more defensible.[11] The sheriffs' standing was further enhanced when in the mid 13th century they began to hold a separate summary court, distinct from the portmote and meeting in the Pentice, a structure built against the south wall of St. Peter's church, which seems to have served as the shrieval office. Though the Pentice court apparently dealt with much the same kind of business as the portmote, cases were determined personally by the sheriffs, and there were no doomsmen.[12] The court, which was well established by 1288, was particularly concerned with the regulation of the markets, dealing with offences such as forestalling and regrating, and also heard all pleas during the fairs, when the portmote was suspended.[13]

Serious crimes, earlier dealt with by the county court, had by the 1280s become the preserve of separate sessions, presided over by the justice of Chester or his deputy, and known as the king's court in the city.[14] By then it had been recognized that cases of simple trespass and the fines arising from them were to be left to the sheriffs in the Pentice.[15] The sheriffs also executed the orders of the king's court and the city courts; within the liberties they were responsible for arrest, attachment, and distraint, for summoning defendants and bringing juries, for keeping prisoners secure and producing them in court, for taking bail, and for taking charge of and accounting for disputed property.[16]

The king's court in the city nevertheless continued to refer to the presiding officials of the portmote as bailiffs. In 1292, for example, a citizen alleged at the king's court that he had been falsely amerced on the orders of the bailiffs and judgers of the portmote for not answering a plea at the proper hour. It was then established, on the evidence of the mayor and community, that it was customary at the portmote for parties in suits to appear at the third call 'after the horn had been sounded and the bailiffs had taken their seats'.[17] A further indication of the bailiffs' role is provided by an order of 1293 that they were to bring

1 *Cart. Chester Abbey*, ii, p. 341; *J.C.A.S.* N.S. ii. 154–5; v. 429–30; x. 38, 43–4, 46; *Cal. Ches. Ct. R.* p. 172.

2 *Cat. Anct. D.* ii, C 3291; below, this chapter: Economy and Society, 1230–1350 (Leading Merchants and Citizens).

3 *Ancestor*, vi. 33; *J.C.A.S.* N.S. x. 24; A. Kennett, 'Origin and Early Hist. of Mayors of Chester' (TS. at C.H.H.), 6; B.L. Add. Ch. 49982–3, 49986.

4 e.g. J.R.U.L.M., Arley Deeds, box 25, no. 24; B.L. Add. Ch. 49981, 49987; cf. C.C.A.L.S., DVE 1/EI/5.

5 e.g. B.L. Add. Ch. 49994, 49997, 50000, 72209, 72215–16, 72219–20, 72224–6; *J.C.A.S.* N.S. x. 25–7.

6 e.g. *Close R.* 1237–42, 146.

7 Cf. Tait, *Medieval Eng. Boro.* 186, quoting *Brit. Boro. Charters, 1042–1216*, ed. A. Ballard, 231.

8 *Cal. Lib.* 1240–5, 59; cf. *Cal. Pat.* 1247–58, 628; 1258–66, 262.

9 *Cal. Ches. Ct. R.* p. 26.

10 Ibid. p. 18.

11 *Ann. Cest.* 86–8.

12 *Cal. Ches. Ct. R.* p. 154; *Sel. R. Chester City Cts.* pp. xv, xviii–xix; *V.C.H. Ches.* v (2), Law Courts: Middle Ages (Pentice).

13 e.g. C.C.A.L.S., ZSR 11, rot. 1; ZSR 12, rot. 7; ZSR 13, rot. 1; ZSR 25, rot. 1.

14 *Cal. Ches. Ct. R.* pp. 18, 156, 159.

15 Ibid. pp. 169, 177, 197.

16 e.g. ibid. pp. 152, 187, 189–94, 196, 203; *Sel. R. Chester City Cts.* p. xx; C.C.A.L.S., ZMR 3–4.

17 *Cal. Ches. Ct. R.* pp. 176–7.

the record of the portmote into the king's court after a complaint of false judgement.[1]

Occasionally the county court used the term bailiff to refer to officials performing actions otherwise ascribed to the sheriffs, such as making arrests and taking charge of pledges.[2] In one instance there was an unambiguous reference to an official as both bailiff and sheriff: in 1288 Hugh Payn as bailiff obtained the release of a load of malt detained at the Dee Mills, and as one of the sheriffs was assaulted in his own court, the Pentice.[3] Clearly the term bailiff had no very specific meaning in the records of the king's court at Chester. If any distinction was intended between bailiff and sheriff, then the most that can be said is that the former was more comprehensive and could include officers other than the sheriff, in particular their executive officers, the serjeants.[4]

The records of the portmote itself, which survive only from 1295, generally used the term sheriff, although on at least one occasion bailiff was substituted.[5] They suggest that until 1300 the sheriffs were expected to preside; in particular, dating seems to have been by shrieval terms as well as regnal years.[6] The sheriffs' role is further confirmed by the fact that until the early 14th century royal writs enrolled at the court, including original writs, were invariably addressed to them alone.[7]

THE SERJEANTS OF THE CITY

Serjeanties occurred in a variety of contexts in 13th-century Chester. The crucial group was the serjeanties of the four main gates, Eastgate, Northgate, Bridgegate, and Watergate, offices which were initially held of the earl. Although they remained in the earl's gift until the end of the Middle Ages,[8] they nevertheless acquired civic functions, often exercised by keepers and deputies. There thus developed a body known as the serjeants of the city, charged with policing, supervising the city watch, and servicing the city courts.[9] Almost certainly, as later, the four gates and the four main streets entered through them were the basis of the city's administrative subdivisions: a serjeanty of Bridge Street, for example, existed by 1340.[10] The serjeants of the gates thus became responsible for supervising the watch and collecting tolls at the gates (a function which by the 1290s they were already abusing). The serjeant

of the Northgate also had charge of the city prison, gallows, and pillory.[11] They assisted the sheriffs in making arrests, summoning defendants and juries, taking charge of the goods of those found guilty of serious crimes,[12] and ensuring the security of prisoners.[13] That association led to their inclusion among the 'bailiffs of the city', and perhaps enabled the more senior among them occasionally to preside over the portmote in the absence of the sheriffs.[14]

THE EMERGENCE OF THE MAYORALTY

Unlike the sheriffs and serjeants, the mayors originated as representatives of the citizens themselves. As elsewhere the mayoralty was never the subject of a formal grant. The earliest known holder of the office, William the clerk, was first named as mayor c. 1240, though he had been a senior civic figure, attesting documents, since the 1220s.[15] The sudden occurrence of a clutch of royal letters and orders addressed to the mayor between 1244 and 1251 suggests that his office was a recent creation. The business with which he was required to deal, occasionally alone but more often in conjunction with the sheriffs and other prominent citizens, included a request for a loan, an adjudication on the closure of a lane near the Franciscan friary, overseeing paving and royal works within the city, and disposing of the remains of the king's wine after a royal visit.[16]

The rise of the mayor to prominence in civic administration coincided with the growth of royal interest in the city, stimulated by Henry III's expeditions into Wales.[17] Thereafter, in charters of the 1250s, the mayor was accorded a primacy of honour in the attestation of grants recorded at the portmote, yielding precedence only to the justice of Chester.[18] Gradually, too, he seems to have taken on the role of chief representative and negotiator on behalf of the citizens in a variety of matters relating to the city's rights and privileges. In the 1260s he was associated with the sheriffs in defending Chester's legal privileges in the county court, and by the 1290s he was expected to adjudicate on civic custom and to prosecute the city's claims to immunity at the King's Bench.[19]

A further responsibility came with the grant of the right to hold the seal of Statute Merchant. The larger portion of the seal was kept by the mayor, the smaller

1 *Cal. Ches. Ct. R.* p. 181.
2 Ibid. pp. 152, 179, 198.
3 Ibid. pp. 152, 154.
4 e.g. ibid. pp. 169, 189, 194.
5 C.C.A.L.S., ZMR 3, rot. 2d.
6 e.g. ibid. ZMR 2, rot. 1; ZMR 3, rott. 13, 16d.; ZMR 5, rot. 1.
7 e.g. *Sel. R. Chester City Cts.* 5, 14, 18–19.
8 *V.C.H. Ches.* v (2), City Walls and Gates: Medieval and Later.
9 *Cal. Ches. Ct. R.* pp. 181–2, 184, 189, 192, 194.
10 B.L. Add. Ch. 75151–2; *Talbot Deeds, 1200–1682* (R.S.L.C. ciii), p. 24; Morris, *Chester*, 553–4.
11 Morris, *Chester*, 554–8; *Cal. Ches. Ct. R.* pp. 181–2.

12 *Cal. Ches. Ct. R.* p. 198; C.C.A.L.S., ZMR 1, rot. 1d.; ZMR 3, rot. 8; ZMR 5, rot. 2.   13 Cf. *Cal. Ches. Ct. R.* p. 196.
14 Ibid. pp. 189, 192, 194.
15 *J.C.A.S.* n.s. x. 22–3, 25–6; *Coucher Bk. or Chartulary of Whalley Abbey*, i (Chetham Soc. [o.s.], x), pp. 27–8; J.R.U.L.M., Arley Deeds, box 25, no. 24; B.L. Add. Ch. 49981, 49984–5, 49988–9.
16 *Cal. Pat. 1232–47*, 431–2; *1247–58*, 93; *Close R. 1242–7*, 339, 423, 430.
17 Above, this chapter: City and Crown, 1237–1350.
18 *J.C.A.S.* n.s. x. 23, 29.
19 *Cal. Ches. Ct. R.* pp. 18, 26, 203; *Sel. Cases in K.B.* iii (Selden Soc. lviii), p. 39.

by a new associate, the clerk for the recognizance of debt. Early holders of the latter post, first recorded in 1291,[1] included the son of a former mayor and a royal clerk.[2] The grant of the seal made Chester a regional centre for the registration of debt and conditional bonds, some of which involved very large notional sums; by the 1340s proceedings were held before the mayor and clerk and enrolled among the records of the portmote.[3]

Despite such wide responsibilities, the mayor did not apparently act as a judge within the city or preside over the city's courts before 1300; his involvement in judicial processes was apparently limited to punishing those convicted in the king's court of minor marketing offences.[4] Occasionally, indeed, the sheriffs were expected to act against mayors who exceeded their role. In 1293, for example, the king's court empowered the sheriffs to attach the mayor, Robert the mercer, on a charge of inflicting the punishment of being drawn on hurdles.[5]

Such evidence suggests that the mayoralty originated informally as the headship of some association of the civic élite, probably the guild merchant; a local tradition that before the citizens had a mayor, the warden or alderman of the guild was their civic head, although erroneous, perhaps adds substance to that view.[6] It is also uncertain how the early mayors were chosen. If it was by election, then no term seems to have been put upon the successful candidate's tenure: mayors such as William the clerk, Walter de Livet, Richard the clerk, and John Arneway apparently held the office for uninterrupted periods of 10 years or more. From 1278, however, the mayors changed more frequently, although the same men often reappeared.[7] That may well suggest a more open method of selection, perhaps accompanying the extension of the mayor's role in the late 13th century.

CIVIC GOVERNMENT, 1230–1300

The emergence of a mayor implies a growing sense of common identity among the citizens, and it is perhaps significant that in contemporary court records the mayor was often mentioned in association with the commonalty.[8] Royal reference to 'good men' (*probi* or *boni homines*) suggests that the men of Chester were regarded by the Crown as analogous to other urban

élites in the mid 13th century.[9] Some sense of common identity was perhaps already apparent in the divisions between the king's men and bishop's men in Chester which flared into violence in 1238; the king's men included John son of Ulketel, probably John Ulkel, later a doomsman and sheriff.[10] By then, too, the citizens' control of the farm was reflected in its reduction by £30 or £40 from the high sum of £200 originally demanded.[11]

The men of Chester assumed other responsibilities at an early date, especially the maintenance of streets and defences. Under the terms of the earliest surviving grants of pavage and murage, in 1246 and 1249, they could apparently be called to account for the moneys collected for those purposes.[12] Similarly, in 1246 their consent was required to allow the Franciscans to breach the city walls to bring in materials for their new buildings.[13] In 1288 maintenance of the Dee Bridge became a further duty.[14]

Taxation was the principal means by which the men of Chester were liable to be treated as a community by the Crown. In 1240, for example, the king received £50 as aid from Chester.[15] Tallages were also levied on the city community as a whole and could relate to local projects. Building works begun at the castle in 1249 were paid for by a tallage levied on the city and on the king's men in the county.[16] In addition to such taxes the citizens were required to make loans in both cash and kind.[17]

The 13th-century burgesses also acted as a group in managing the town fields in Newton and Claverton[18] and their long-standing rights of common pasture on Saltney marsh, where in 1249 a dispute between the 'king's burgesses' of Chester and Roger of Mold over a ditch which Roger had caused to be dug was resolved in their favour.[19]

The townspeople's main instrument of common action was the portmote, whose doomsmen retained their dominance in civic life throughout the 13th century[20] and as late as 1305 adjudicated on such major issues as the presidency of the court.[21] With their power to determine custom, their role in the attestation of local land grants, and their high social standing, they seem to have formed the principal element in the administration of the 13th-century city,[22] and the main civic officials were chosen from

1 *Sel. Cases concerning Law Merchant*, iii (Selden Soc. xlix), p. lvii.
2 *Cal. Pat. 1307–13*, 224; *1313–17*, 390.
3 C.C.A.L.S., ZMR 40; B.L. Add. Ch. 50148.
4 *Cal. Ches. Ct. R.* p. 205.
5 Ibid. p. 183.
6 Tait, *Medieval Eng. Boro.* 232; C. Gross, *Gild Merchant*, ii. 41–2.
7 *V.C.H. Ches.* v (2), Lists of Mayors and Sheriffs.
8 e.g. *Cal. Ches. Ct. R.* p. 18.
9 e.g. *Close R. 1237–42*, 146.
10 Ibid. 23.
11 *Cal. Lib. 1240–5*, 21; cf. *Cal. Fine R. 1272–1307*, 92.

12 *Close R. 1242–7*, 423; *Cal. Pat. 1247–58*, 49.
13 *Close R. 1242–7*, 408.
14 *28 D.K.R.* 7; *3 Sheaf*, xxi, pp. 32–3.
15 *Cal. Lib. 1240–5*, 10.
16 Ibid. *1245–51*, 47, 258.
17 Ibid. *1240–5*, 70; *Cal. Pat. 1232–47*, 431–2, 435, 492; *Cal. Doc. Irel. 1252–84*, no. 682.
18 *J.C.A.S.* N.S. x. 33, 35–6, 45, 47.
19 *Close R. 1247–51*, 236, 262, 347, 360, 419–20.
20 Para. based on *Sel. R. Chester City Cts.* pp. l–liv; C.C.A.L.S., ZMR 1, rott. 1d.–2d.; ZMR 3, rott. 7, 11.
21 C.C.A.L.S., ZMR 9, rot. 15d.
22 Tait, *Medieval Eng. Boro.* 300.

their ranks. The connexion between the portmote and the guild merchant, even in the late 14th century, is obscure. Almost certainly presided over by the mayor, the guild merchant was probably, as elsewhere, much more than a society of private traders independent of the city.[1] In the 13th century its membership was drawn from the ruling élite, especially the doomsmen and civic officers, as was that of the otherwise unknown and possibly related guild of St. Mary which met in the house of the former mayor John of Brickhill in 1330. Many of the 48 members of St. Mary's guild either belonged to families which had produced senior civic officers or were pledged by such prominent citizens. The record of those admitted on that occasion seems to have been kept with the archives of the city treasurer.[2]

The membership and privileges of the burgesses were ill-defined, and there is no evidence to identify them as a group with the guild merchant.[3] Burgage tenure was linked primarily with payment of gavel, the money rent owed to the king or chief lord,[4] which by the 13th century was perhaps reduced to a quitrent,[5] and specific civic obligations were attached to certain burgage holdings.[6] Nothing, however, is known of any council of twelve or twenty-four such as came into being elsewhere. Nor was there any communal seal, although in the early 13th century one sheriff, Richard Pierrepont, had his own privy seal, as did the mayor a little later.[7] How the men of Chester acted in concert to discharge the responsibilities laid upon them by royal orders is not clear, and there is no indication of how they chose their senior officials. The sheriffs and perhaps the mayors were elected in the later 13th century, the sheriffs presumably in the portmote, the mayors in the guild merchant. Other officials, such as the overseers of pavage and the king's works, were nominated by the Crown, presumably on the recommendation of the portmote or guild.[8] Some, such as the collectors of murage, were simply required to be two men of the town, and must have been appointed locally.[9] The *cursus honorum* for Chester's élite is well illustrated by the career of Richard the clerk. The son of a former mayor, William the clerk, he was probably already active in the portmote of Chester by c. 1250, and soon became sheriff and eventually mayor.[10] In

1253, however, he paid to avoid service as a viewer, presumably a less desirable office.[11]

Chester's urban élite formed a tightly knit group. Difficult though it is to be sure whether family names were being passed on from father to son, there are clear indications that the principal civic offices were very largely the preserve of a few prominent families: the same surnames or patronymics occurred again and again among the mayors, sheriffs, and doomsmen. One such family was that of William and Richard the clerk, which may also have included Philip the clerk, sheriff 1277–8.[12] Another was the Saracens, well established by 1200, when one of its members was a doomsman, and still represented in the portmote in the 1270s, by which time it had produced at least one long-serving sheriff.[13] Similarly the Hurrell family supplied mayors, sheriffs, doomsmen, a clerk for the recognizance of debt, and a collector of customs between the mid 13th century and the 1330s.[14] Especially important in the later 13th and much of the 14th century was the Doncaster family, whose fortunes were founded by William, prior of St. Werburgh's (d. 1259).[15] In the late 13th and early 14th century his relative, William (III), brought the family's prosperity to its apogee with his activities as mayor and doomsman, purveyor to the royal armies, collector of royal customs, and warden and searcher of money in Chester and north Wales.[16] His son and grandson, both also called William, continued to play a prominent role in civic affairs, William (IV) being sheriff in 1313–14 and William (V) sheriff 1343–4.[17] Such examples could easily be multiplied, especially for the better documented 1290s and early 14th century, when notable families included the Payns, the Brickhills, and the Dunfouls. The Payns seem to have been especially important in the 1280s and 1290s, when Hugh Payn owned extensive property within the liberties, held the office of sheriff, accounted for the city's amercements at the Chester exchequer, and made a grant of seven messuages which enabled the Carmelites to establish themselves on a permanent site.[18] A relative, Nicholas Payn, was twice sheriff in the same period.[19] The Brickhill family also accumulated offices. One Hugh was sheriff in the 1280s, and another many times

1 Morris, *Chester*, 379–81.

2 B.L. Harl. MS. 2158, f. 41v.

3 But cf. *Chester: 1900 Years of Hist.* ed. A. M. Kennett, 26; Morris, *Chester*, 380.

4 Cf. distinction in 1086 between burgesses' land rendering custom, and land free from custom: *V.C.H. Ches.* i. 342–4; Tait, *Medieval Eng. Boro.* 88–9.

5 Tait, *Medieval Eng. Boro.* 102–3; *J.C.A.S.* N.S. x. 37–8, 40.

6 Above, this section (Sheriffs and their Courts).

7 For Pierrepont: *Facsimiles of Early Ches. Charters*, ed. G. Barraclough, pp. 27–8; W. de G. Birch, *Cat. of Seals in Department of MSS. in Brit. Mus.* ii. 53.

8 *Close R.* 1242–7, 423; 1247–51, 433–4; *Cal. Pat.* 1247–58, 93.

9 *Cal. Pat.* 1247–58, 49.

10 B.L. Add. Ch. 49982, 49987, 72206, 72209, 72219–20, 72222; *J.C.A.S.* N.S. x. 32.

11 *Ex. e Rot. Fin.* (Rec. Com.), ii. 159.

12 Ibid.; *Cal. Fine R.* 1272–1307, 268; *Cal. Ches. Ct. R.* p. 163.

13 *J.C.A.S.* N.S. x. 16–17, 19, 22, 24–9, 31–2.

14 Ibid. 33–5, 37–9; *Cal. Ches. Ct. R.* p. 163; *Cal. Pat.* 1307–13, 224; *Cal. Fine R.* 1319–27, 146–7.

15 *Ann. Cest.* 76–7.

16 *Sel. R. Chester City Cts.* p. lxvii; *Cal. Fine R.* 1272–1307, 467, 476; 1307–19, 33, 68, 80; C.C.A.L.S., ZMR 3, rot. 12; ZMR 8, rot. 6d.

17 *V.C.H. Ches.* v (2), Lists of Mayors and Sheriffs.

18 *Cal. Ches. Ct. R.* pp. 152, 154, 192–3; *J.C.A.S.* N.S. x. 50.

19 *Cat. Anct. D.* iii, C 4044, 6335, 6341; *V.C.H. Ches.* iii. 176; *J.C.A.S.* xxxi. 7–8.

mayor in the period 1293–1314, while William was three times sheriff and six times mayor between 1306 and 1332, and a third member of the family, John, was mayor in 1320–1 and perhaps in 1321–2.[1]

THE CITY AND THE COUNTY COURT BEFORE 1300

The city's growing independence was evident in its relations with the county court. In the 13th century the portmote's competence was restricted to civil cases and minor criminal offences. Crown pleas were dealt with by a court under the justice of Chester, which by the 1280s was known as the king's court in the city.[2] Like the portmote, it met on Mondays, though not usually more than once a month and with recesses at Christmas, Easter, Midsummer, and harvest.[3] It met within the city, possibly at the castle,[4] and included judgers drawn, like those of the portmote, from the senior citizenry of Chester.[5] Increasingly its sessions were distinguished from those of the normal county court. In the mid 13th century its proceedings were included with the rest of the county business, but by the 1280s they were recorded on a separate roll, and indeed included some property transactions of the kind frequently enrolled at the portmote.[6] At the same time business relating to Chester at such sessions of the county court passed more and more into the hands of civic officials, so that by the 1280s presentments were made by the city coroners or the 12 'jurors for the city', and orders were executed by the city sheriffs.[7]

The king's court in the city heard appeals from the portmote and Pentice, though by the 1290s in so doing it consulted with the mayor and commonalty about the city's customs.[8] Equally, however, cases initiated in the king's court could be referred to the city courts,[9] notably certain minor offences which were referred back to the sheriffs to be heard summarily in the Pentice.[10] On occasion the overlap between the two jurisdictions gave rise to dispute. The competence of the city courts was restricted to the city liberties, yet many citizens had important interests outside, especially in the immediately adjacent town fields in Newton and Claverton.[11] There was uncertainty over which was the appropriate court to deal with disputes between citizens about property in such areas. Thus in 1294 a case involving the distraint of eight oxen, presumably working in one of the town fields outside the liberties, was initially determined in favour of the plaintiff by the 12 city jurors, but was deferred when

the defendant claimed that he ought not to answer in the king's court in the city for an offence in the county. By then the king's court in the city was recognized as separate from the county court proper, and its competence was restricted to the area covered by the portmote and Pentice.[12]

Increasingly, the city sought to limit or at least define the court's role. In 1295 the mayor, Hugh of Brickhill, and Roger of Mold's steward appeared before the court of King's Bench to argue that no royal official except the justice of Chester had ever held any plea in the city, but were forced to admit that they had no charter to justify their claim save the king's confirmations of the customs of the county.[13]

THE CHARTER OF 1300 AND CITY GOVERNMENT 1300–50

The case of 1295 perhaps prompted the citizens to seek a formal definition of their rights. In 1300 they achieved their aim with Edward I's charter, the product of royal interest in the city which culminated during the Welsh wars.[14] The charter, which confirmed all the citizens' gains during the previous century, recognized the offices of mayor and city coroner and the grant to the citizens of the fee farm, set at £100 a year, only half of what had been demanded in the 1230s.[15] In one area it innovated. The grant of the Crown pleas to the citizens, at the time a unique privilege,[16] replaced the king's court in the city with a new court presided over by the mayor and 'bailiffs' (that is, the city sheriffs). The association of the latter with the mayor in a new judicial role affected the standing of both offices. The charter did not specify the nature of the court which was to hear the Crown pleas, beyond implying that it was in some sense the successor to the king's court in the city. Initially, it seems, no separate court was held. The earliest Crown pleas were enrolled with the records of the portmote, and were presumably heard at its sessions, thus giving rise to certain procedural problems.[17] Because the mayor had suddenly acquired a new role in the ancient city court, litigants began to argue about whether in his absence the sheriffs alone could still determine cases as they had before 1300. When in 1305 the plaintiff in a plea of novel disseisin argued that according to the usages of the city the sheriffs could hear and determine all pleas without the mayor, the sheriffs, by then unsure of their rights, adjourned the case. Clearly the new judicial role accorded the mayor

1 C.C.A.L.S., ZMR 3, rot. 18; *V.C.H. Ches.* v (2), Lists of Mayors and Sheriffs.
2 *Cal. Ches. Ct. R.* pp. 156, 159.
3 Ibid. pp. xxi, 152–206 *passim*.
4 Ibid. pp. 158–9.
5 Ibid. pp. xxvii–xxviii, 158, 163, 172, 177, 180.
6 e.g. ibid. p. 170.
7 Ibid. pp. xxix, 152, 187, 189–94, 196.
8 Ibid. pp. 176–7, 180–1.   9 Ibid. pp. xxvii–xxix.

10 Ibid. pp. 203–6.
11 Below, this chapter: Economy and Society, 1230–1350 (Trades and Industries).
12 *Cal. Ches. Ct. R.* p. 189.
13 *Sel. Cases in K.B.* iii, p. 39.
14 Morris, *Chester*, 490–3; C.C.A.L.S., ZCH 13.
15 *Cal. Lib.* 1226–40, 423.
16 Tait, *Medieval Eng. Boro.* 345.
17 C.C.A.L.S., ZMR 9, rott. 13, 22; ZMR 10, rot. 1.

in the charter of 1300 had rendered the presidency of the portmote uncertain.[1]

By 1305 the mayor had taken over the presidency of the portmote for civil as well as criminal cases. By then, too, the portmote roll was dated by reference to both mayor and sheriffs, instead of the sheriffs alone, as had been customary earlier.[2] In 1306 a deed was enrolled before the mayor in the portmote, and by 1313 original writs enrolled in the record were addressed to both mayor and sheriffs.[3] Though by 1316 the city had started to keep a separate record of Crown pleas, as late as 1358 they were still deemed to be held in the portmote.[4] As a result, by the time that a separate court of Crown pleas, the crownmote, eventually emerged, the mayor's position as president of the portmote had been firmly established.[5] The long process by which the mayoralty had gradually displaced the shrievalty as the principal civic office was more or less complete.

The growth of mayoral power in the portmote also affected the sole remaining shrieval court, the Pentice. For a brief period, *c.* 1320–40, it was presided over by the mayor together with the sheriffs.[6] When once again it became exclusively shrieval, much of its business had been eroded. Fair-time pleas and market offences were dealt with by the mayor in the portmote, and as a result proceedings in the Pentice became more and more routine.[7]

Inevitably the new arrangements led occasionally to dispute. In 1320, for example, the mayor and sheriffs, grounding themselves on Edward I's charter, refused to produce a man indicted at the eyre of the justice of Chester and committed to prison in Chester pending trial at the next session of the county court.[8] On the whole, however, in the early period there seems to have been relatively little friction between the two jurisdictions, and it was not until the mid 14th century that fresh controversy arose with the removal of cases from the city to the county court through writs of false judgement and of error.[9] By then a few criminal cases from Chester seem as a matter of routine to have strayed into the county court, by which means the latter had regained some residual jurisdiction over the city.[10]

ECONOMY AND SOCIETY, 1230–1350

By the 1230s Chester was a prosperous trading centre with a market of regional importance, two fairs, and a port. Its economy continued to expand, stimulated by royal interest and its role as a supply centre for royal enterprises in Wales, which more than compensated for the resultant temporary interruptions to the Welsh trade.[11] The late 13th and early 14th century probably saw the peak of the city's prosperity in the Middle Ages.

THE CITY AND ITS HINTERLAND

One pillar of Chester's economy remained its dominance over an extensive, if relatively impoverished hinterland. Its twice-weekly market was without serious rival between north-east Wales and the Marches to the west, Derby to the east, Shrewsbury to the south, and Lancaster and perhaps beyond to the north.[12] Marketing was concentrated in the two open spaces by St. Peter's church and the abbey gate, but also spread into the main streets.[13] The main commodities were agricultural. Cattle were kept by the citizens on the town fields and on Saltney marsh (Flints.) and were brought into Chester from the Dee valley, Wirral, and north Wales; pigs were driven to market from forests as far distant as Ewloe (Flints.) and Delamere.[14] Livestock entered the city at the Eastgate and the Bridgegate, the beast market probably being located (as later) near the latter, while dairy produce and meat were sold at or near the Cross.[15] War undoubtedly stimulated the local market; besides the large quantities of victuals brought into the city by royal order to supply the army, the merchants of Chester were expected to find further provisions themselves.[16]

The fish market served a wide area including the Welsh Marches.[17] Salmon, lampreys, and eels were taken from the earl's fishery by the Dee Bridge,[18] while sea fish such as herring, cod, flatfish, and sparling, and shellfish such as oysters, mussels, and whelks were caught locally or imported from Ireland and the Isle of Man.[19] Herring from the Irish Sea was especially important.[20] By the earlier 14th century tolls were taken on fish at all the main gates, especially the

1 C.C.A.L.S., ZMR 9, rott. 8, 15d.   2 Ibid. rot. 20.

3 Ibid. ZMR 11, rot. 4d.; ZMR 19, rot. 1; cf. *J.C.A.S.* xxxi. 9–10.

4 C.C.A.L.S., ZQCR 1–5; cf. *Blk. Prince's Reg.* iii. 291–2.

5 e.g. C.C.A.L.S., ZMR 20, rot. 3d.; ZMR 24; *Sel. R. Chester City Cts.* 29.

6 C.C.A.L.S., ZSR 33, rot. 1d.; ZSR 39, rot. 1; ZSR 42, rot. 1; ZSR 48, rot. 1; ZSR 50.

7 *V.C.H. Ches.* v (2), Law Courts: Middle Ages (Pentice).

8 P.R.O., CHES 29/32, m. 17d. Thanks are due to Mr. P. H. W. Booth, Liverpool Univ., for this ref.

9 P.R.O., CHES 29/78, m. 25; *Blk. Prince's Reg.* iii. 291–2.

10 P.R.O., CHES 25/4, m. 27d.

11 e.g. *Cal. Chanc. R. Var.* 247.

12 e.g. Morris, *Chester,* 562.

13 *V.C.H. Ches.* v (2), Markets: General Produce Markets.

14 e.g. *Ches. Chamb. Accts.* 9; Hewitt, *Med. Ches.* 125.

15 Morris, *Chester,* 556–7; Hewitt, *Med. Ches.* 84.

16 e.g. *Close R.* 1242–7, 383.   17 Morris, *Chester,* 562.

18 e.g. P.R.O., SC 6/788/2, m. 3.

19 Hewitt, *Med. Ches.* 125; cf. K. P. Wilson, 'Port of Chester in Later Middle Ages' (Liverpool Univ. Ph.D. thesis, 1966), i. 83.

20 C.C.A.L.S., ZCR 469/542, f. 18[A] verso; Morris, *Chester,* 556, 562; *Ches. Chamb. Accts.* 10–11; *New Hist. of Irel.* ii, ed. A. Cosgrove, 505.

Watergate and the Northgate, the point of entry for sea fish and shellfish landed at the outports in the Dee estuary.[1]

Corn was much less abundant. Though there was a corn market in Eastgate Street by the 1270s, and though some corn was undoubtedly grown in the county and by the citizens themselves in the town fields, considerable quantities of wheat and barley had to be brought in from further afield, principally Ireland.[2] The grain was not simply for home consumption: the city also acted as a centre for distribution throughout its region. Although trade with the native Welsh was suspended during Edward I's campaigns, such disruption was more than counterbalanced by the citizens' provisioning of the English armies,[3] and with the establishment of peace Chester resumed its wider distributive role.[4] The extremely high farm of the Dee Mills throughout the 13th and earlier 14th century perhaps reflected toll income resulting from Chester's role as an entrepôt for wheat, oats, barley, and malt.[5]

Pre-eminent among raw materials marketed in the city was salt, brought there from the Cheshire wiches and sold as far afield as Dublin and Ruthin (Denb.).[6] Additional commodities included coal, mined at Ewloe and Buckley (Flints.) by the early 14th century and carried to Chester by both land and water.[7] Lead mined at Holywell, and iron mined at Ewloe and smelted in Hopedale (all Flints.) were also conveyed to the city, especially for use in the royal castles of Chester and Beeston.[8] In 1311 the lead mines of Englefield were leased to the important merchant William (III) of Doncaster, whose home was in Chester.[9]

Chester and its environs were plentifully supplied with timber and brushwood, used for making weapons for the royal army in Wales and for fuel. The main sources of supply were the woods of the abbey and the earl. Citizens were licensed to take timber from and make charcoal in certain of the earl's woods and also obtained fuel from his park at Shotwick, which in the mid 14th century supplied a Chester baker with 10,000 faggots.[10] Bark was also brought from local woods and further afield for use in the tanning industry.[11]

The city's importance as a regional market was reinforced by its role as the capital of the earldom. The fact that the castle was the seat of the justice of Chester or his representative, of the chamberlain and clerks of the exchequer, and of a county court which did not itinerate and which acknowledged no superior jurisdiction, entailed the permanent presence of important officials and encouraged the attendance of the local gentry as doomsmen and suitors.[12] The grand stone house which the Thorntons inherited from Peter the clerk,[13] and the stone chamber built by Ranulph of Oxford, chamberlain of Chester,[14] were a measure of their impact on the city. Local gentlemen were also involved in city life as serjeants of the principal gates; the Raby family, for example, as heirs of Philip the clerk held the Bridgegate, together with land in the city and Claverton, and the manor of Raby in Wirral.[15] In addition rich merchants from a wide area were attracted to Chester to register bonds enforcing agreements under Statute Merchant.[16] The presence of such people encouraged a market in expensive domestic articles, including fine pottery, bronze bowls and cauldrons, ecclesiastical and secular plate, and jewellery.[17]

Chester's continuing importance as an ecclesiastical centre provided further economic stimulus. St. Werburgh's remained the richest abbey in the North-West, with far-flung possessions and a wide range of influential contacts. The maintenance of its forty monks and its considerable hospitality to visitors, especially grandees travelling to Ireland and north Wales, required a wide range of commodities.[18] St. John's also retained importance as the seat of the archdeacon of Chester and his court.[19] Though its canons were often non-resident, well-to-do 'masters' (*magistri*, perhaps ecclesiastical lawyers) maintained property in its environs and elsewhere within the city.[20]

By the 13th century Chester's Midsummer fair lasted a month and the Michaelmas fair a fortnight.[21] The significance of the Midsummer fair is attested by the citizens' largely successful struggle in the late 13th century to wrest control from the abbot of St. Werburgh's.[22] Commodities included salt, coal, horses, cattle, sheep, pigs, sacks of wool, pelts, and

1 Morris, *Chester*, 554–8.

2 Ibid. 555; below, this section (Trades and Industries).

3 *Cal. Close*, 1272–9, 314; above, this chapter: City and Crown, 1237–1350.

4 *Ct. R. of Lordship of Ruthin or Dyffryn-Clwydd*, ed. R. A. Roberts, 41.

5 *Blk. Prince's Reg.* iii. 317; C.C.A.L.S., ZMR 5, rot. 5d.

6 *Ct. R. Ruthin*, 45.

7 *Flints. Ministers' Accts. 1328–53* (Flints. Hist. Soc. Rec. Ser. ii), pp. xli–xlii, 17–18, 34–5, 76, 92; *36 D.K.R.* App. II, pp. 129, 176, 259–60, 388, 441, 535; *Cal. Pat.* 1272–81, 311; 1330–4, 181; *Ches. Chamb. Accts.* 102, 109, 112, 121, 161, 208, 224, 249, 263.

8 *Flints. Ministers' Accts. 1328–53*, pp. lxiii–lxxi, 6–7, 9, 19, 22, 45, 52–9, 68, 71, 88, 113; *Ches. Chamb. Accts.* 6; Hewitt, *Med. Ches.* 85.

9 *Cal. Close*, 1307–13, 380; *Cal. Fine R.* 1307–19, 109.

10 *Cal. Inq. Misc.* i, p. 475; *Cal. Pat.* 1272–81, 255–6; Hewitt, *Med. Ches.* 126.

11 *Ches. Chamb. Accts.* 97, 104, 121, 128, 208, 263.

12 Ibid. pp. xi–xxiii; *V.C.H. Ches.* ii. 3–5, 18–25; *Cal. Ches. Ct. R.* pp. xvi–xxxviii.

13 B.L. Add. Ch. 50177; P.R.O., SC 6/784/7, m. 4; Ormerod, *Hist. Ches.* ii. 14–16.

14 B.L. Add. Ch. 72224.

15 Ibid. Add. Ch. 75151–2, 75162; *Cal. Ches. Ct. R.* p. 166; Ormerod, *Hist. Ches.* i. 356.

16 C.C.A.L.S., ZMR 40; B.L. Add. Ch. 50148.

17 *Sel. R. Chester City Cts.* pp. lxii, lxiv.

18 *V.C.H. Ches.* iii. 132–46.

19 *V.C.H. Ches.* v (2), Collegiate Church of St. John.

20 e.g. Geoffrey of Meols: P.R.O., WALE 29/31, 132, 320, 330.

21 *V.C.H. Ches.* v (2), Fairs.

22 *Cal. Ches. Ct. R.* pp. 122–3; P.R.O., CHES 29/5, m. 2.

copper or bronze pots and bowls.[1] Cloth was also important.[2]

The growing commercial importance of the fairs is suggested by arrangements made *c.* 1260, whereby Wymark, widow of John the tailor, divided her property with Hugh the tailor, presumably her son, and agreed to take down the wall which separated her holding from his during fair time, thus giving Hugh extra space which he presumably required at a busy time.[3] The impact of the fairs upon the region as a whole is indicated by the fact that policing fell in part upon landholders living as far away as Crewe (in Coppenhall),[4] and by the existence within the county of rural serjeants of passage who protected routeways to Chester during fair time.[5]

There was perhaps a sequence of local small-scale summer fairs in the environs of Chester, linked with the main one in the city. Thus the dates of Bromborough fair, established in 1278, were timed to dovetail exactly with the opening of Chester's Midsummer fair.[6]

THE PORT AND LONG-DISTANCE TRADE

The port and its anchorages, which extended from Portpool at the edge of the liberty along the western shore of Wirral to Redbank in Thurstaston,[7] were the focus of longshore trade with north Wales, involving not only fish, timber, bark, and coal, but also slate and millstones from as far afield as Ogwen (Caern.) and Anglesey. In the other direction, there was traffic with Cheshire ports such as Frodsham and Runcorn.[8] There was also long-distance trade, above all with Ireland, which by 1237 was a major source of foodstuffs.[9] The province sent large quantities of victuals to Chester whenever the king visited the city or made an expedition into north Wales. Irish corn was Chester's speciality;[10] for wine Bristol and Boston (Lincs.) were much more important.[11]

The Irish trade continued under Edward I,[12] and was promoted by the abbot of Vale Royal and his Chester agent, Robert le Barn.[13] It rose to a peak during the campaign of 1282–3, when foodstuffs, including peas, beans, wine, salmon, cheese, and salted meat as well as corn, flowed through Chester in quantities which far exceeded those from any other province apart from Ponthieu.[14] The extraordinary demands imposed by Edward left the city itself starved of supplies.[15] The 1290s, and especially Edward's third campaign, saw renewed activity, with Dublin still the main point of contact,[16] although there were also more casual links with other ports in south-east Ireland, including Wexford and Waterford.[17] William (III) of Doncaster and other leading Chester merchants continued to supply Irish victuals to the king's castles in Wales,[18] and occasionally to the royal armies until the 1320s,[19] but thereafter the trade seems to have declined in importance, reviving only at the end of the century.[20]

Besides corn and other foodstuffs Ireland was also a source of cloth,[21] and more importantly of furs and hides. Furs were evidently a significant and characteristic element in Chester's trade in the mid 13th century,[22] and pelts were still being sold at the fairs in the earlier 14th.[23] Hides and lambskins were sold in the city itself and occasionally exported in small quantities.[24] The presence of tawyers in Chester by the 1290s[25] indicates a trade in light fine skins, which probably came largely from Ireland.[26]

Chester's exports to Ireland are less certain. They included pottery, mainly tableware, floor tiles, and roof tiles,[27] small quantities of wool and hides,[28] and occasionally live animals from the royal parks and forests.[29] As later, the Irish also undoubtedly imported

1 P.R.O., CHES 29/59, m. 23; Morris, *Chester*, 554–8; Ormerod, *Hist. Ches.* i. 287–8.

2 C.C.A.L.S., ZMR 3, rott. 2d., 5.

3 B.L. Add. Ch. 49997, 50004; cf. E. W. Moore, *Fairs of Medieval Eng.* 143–5, 232–9, 306–9.

4 *Cal. Inq. p.m.* iv, p. 179; Ormerod, *Hist. Ches.* iii. 303.

5 *Cal. Inq. Misc.* ii, p. 62; Ormerod, *Hist. Ches.* ii. 337; cf. *36 D.K.R.* App. II, p. 27 (Bechton, 1311). Thanks are due to Mr. P. H. W. Booth for these references.

6 Ormerod, *Hist. Ches.* i. 288.

7 *V.C.H. Ches.* v (2), Water Transport: River.

8 e.g. *Ches. Chamb. Accts.* 10, 121, 126, 208, 241, 249; *Sel. R. Chester City Cts.* p. lix; Wilson, 'Port of Chester', i. 149; cf. *Cal. Inq. Misc.* ii, p. 11.

9 *Close R.* 1237–42, 115.

10 Ibid. 325; cf. ibid. 359–60, 420, 432; *Cal. Lib.* 1240–5, 314, 317; 1245–51, 1–2, 41.

11 e.g. *Cal. Lib.* 1226–40, 337–8; 1240–5, 298, 309, 312; 1251–60, 516; *Close R.* 1237–42, 61; *Cal. Pat.* 1247–58, 628.

12 *Cal. Close,* 1272–9, 314, 372; *Cal. Pat.* 1272–81, 208, 227–8.

13 *Cal. Pat.* 1272–81, 265.

14 *Cal. Chanc. R. Var.* 214; cf. ibid. 226; *Cal. Close,* 1279–88, 150.

15 Hewitt, *Med. Ches.* 82–3; *Cal. Pat.* 1281–92, 59, 116; *Cal.*

Chanc. R. Var. 266.

16 Cf. *Chartularies of St. Mary's Abbey, Dublin* (Rolls Ser.), i. 132, 216–17, 219, 222–3, 246, 441, 461; *Reg. of Abbey of St. Thomas, Dublin* (Rolls Ser.), 222, 271, 274, 385–6, 391, 406.

17 *Cal. Justiciary R. of Irel.* 1295–1303, 157; 1305–7, 118; *Cal. Ches. Ct. R.* p. 191.

18 *Cal. Doc. Irel.* 1293–1301, 59, 159.

19 *Cal. Pat.* 1307–13, 503; 1313–17, 470, 568; 1321–4, 27, 114–18; *Cal. Close,* 1313–18, 299; *Cal. Doc. Irel.* 1302–7, 94.

20 Hewitt, *Med. Ches.* 135; below, this chapter: Economy and Society, 1350–1550 (Port and Overseas Trade: Irish and Coastal); cf. *New Hist. Irel.* ii. 515.

21 For cloth, below, this section (Trades and Industries).

22 *Eng. Hist. Doc.* iii, ed. H. Rothwell, p. 883.

23 Ormerod, *Hist. Ches.* i. 287–8.

24 Wilson, 'Port of Chester', ii. 2; *Chester Customs Accts.* 20.

25 e.g. C.C.A.L.S., ZMR 3, rott. 14d., 16d.; ZMR 5, rott. 2d., 4d.; P.R.O., SC 6/787/2, m. 1; SC 6/787/7, m. 1.

26 *Sel. R. Chester City Cts.* p. lix.

27 E. S. Eames and T. Fanning, *Irish Medieval Tiles,* 34–5, 41–3; *Ceramics and Trade: Production and Distribution of Later Medieval Pottery in NW. Europe,* ed. P. Davey and R. Hodges, 226, 230.

28 *Ches. in Pipe R.* 165.

29 *Cal. Doc. Irel.* 1171–1251, 398.

salt,[1] and by the earlier 14th century Chester may also have been one of the ports through which they obtained fine cloth from London and the Midlands.[2]

Other important overseas contacts were with Gascony, particularly noted as the source of wine, shipped from Bordeaux. The prestige attached to the trade is evident from the high status of Chester's vintners, at least two of whom were sheriffs of the city in the 13th century,[3] and from the fact that in 1237 the burgesses offered two tuns of wine for the rent of one of the Dee Mills.[4] There is, however, no evidence of a prise (customs duty) being exacted on wine in the earlier 13th century, and it is uncertain whether what was on sale had been imported directly from abroad or represented the castle's surplus from purchases elsewhere in England.[5]

By the mid 13th century royal activity was stimulating demand in the Chester market. As early as 1241 the justice, John le Strange, purchased wine there to be sent to Shrewsbury and Rhuddlan.[6] The quantities obtainable in Chester were, however, insufficient for the king's needs. Wine was bought at Boston fair in 1238, 1245, and 1258, at Bristol in 1245 and 1260, and from Ireland in 1241.[7] By *c.* 1260 it was also imported directly from Bordeaux.[8] Besides the king, who stored wine in the castle,[9] importers and purchasers included in the 1270s the abbot of Vale Royal,[10] and in 1304 William (III) of Doncaster, acting partly on behalf of Henry de Lacy, earl of Lincoln.[11] In 1322 William was also involved, with seven other leading Chester merchants, in shipping merchandise including 105 tuns of wine from Bordeaux to Chester, but the vessel which they chartered was attacked by armed men off Anglesey and its cargo was lost or damaged.[12] The trade remained an exotic feature of Chester's economy throughout the earlier 14th century. Yet despite the involvement of many important local men, among whom at least five citizens owned ships which made the journey to Bordeaux, the amounts of wine imported appear to have been very small in comparison with the trade of London and Bristol, a reflection of Chester's underpopulated and underdeveloped hinterland.[13]

Pottery, especially the mottled green and polychrome jugs of Saintonge, came with the wine. Similar wares found at castles and monasteries in north Wales perhaps also arrived with wine imported at Chester. Their disappearance from the city and elsewhere after the mid 14th century was the result of economic decline, or at least of the disruption of trade with the onset of the Hundred Years' War.[14] Small quantities of English pottery contemporaneous with that from Saintonge included Ham Green wares, the Bristol provenance of which may also indicate an association with the wine trade.[15] There were also small amounts of pottery from northern France, and Stamford or 'Midlands' ware.[16]

Hampered by the slender resources of its hinterland, Chester participated in only a modest way in the wool trade. Its merchants obtained small quantities of wool for export or to supply the local gentry mainly from monasteries in north Wales.[17] Sacks of wool were also sold at the Chester fairs.[18] International trade was hindered by Chester's lack of integration into the national customs system; although collectors of customs were appointed from time to time, the city was never included among the staple towns and never received the cocket seal, the royal authorization for the export of wool, wool fells, and hides.[19] Hence a rich local merchant such as Doncaster exported wool from east-coast ports.[20]

The city thus played only a limited role in the king's efforts to raise revenue through the vast wool purchases of the late 1330s. By 1338 the four leading merchants of Chester who had been appointed takers and buyers of wool in Cheshire and Flintshire had purchased only 200 sacks, a fraction of what was obtained in adjacent counties.[21] Similarly, only three of Chester's merchants were among those lending to the king in 1338–9. The modest sums involved were to be repaid by a reduction of the wool custom for which the lenders were liable, and for all three Cestrians the port at which the allowance was made was London; like William of Doncaster before them, Chester merchants who participated in the wool trade in the 1330s did so through the capital.[22] Such activity as there was in their home

---

1 R. Higden, *Polychronicon* (Rolls Ser.), ii. 18; *Chester Customs Accts.* 103; cf. *New Hist. Irel.* ii. 236–7.

2 *New Hist. Irel.* ii. 505–6; cf. Wilson, 'Port of Chester', i. 81, 87–91.

3 i.e. Adam and Laurence: *V.C.H. Ches.* v (2), Lists of Mayors and Sheriffs.

4 *Ches. in Pipe R.* 39–40.

5 Ibid. 48–9, 59, 67–8; *Cal. Lib. 1240–5*, 21; Wilson, 'Port of Chester', i. 4.

6 *Cal. Lib. 1240–5*, 69–70.

7 Ibid. 298, 309, 312; 1251–60, 516; *Close R. 1237–42*, 61, 325; *Cal. Pat. 1247–58*, 628.

8 *Cal. Pat. 1272–81*, 79.

9 Ibid. 212; *Cal. Close, 1272–9*, 274.

10 *Cal. Pat. 1272–81*, 315.

11 Wilson, 'Port of Chester', ii. 2; *Chester Customs Accts.* 20; *Cal. Fine R. 1272–1307*, 492.

12 *Cal. Close, 1318–23*, 453–4; *Cal. Pat. 1321–4*, 114.

13 Wilson, 'Port of Chester', i. 108–12, 141; *Chester Customs Accts.* 20–1.

14 *Medieval Ceramics*, i. 17–30; Wilson, 'Port of Chester', i. 112. Plate 4.

15 S. W. Ward, *Excavations at Chester: Lesser Medieval Religious Houses*, 150, 192.

16 Pers. comm. Mrs. J. Axworthy Rutter, formerly of Chester City Archaeology.

17 Hewitt, *Med. Ches.* 46–8; *Cal. Pat. 1272–81*, 68, 235; 36 *D.K.R.* App. II, pp. 150, 207, 281, 355; cf. *Ches. in Pipe R.* 165.

18 Ormerod, *Hist. Ches.* i. 287–8.

19 Wilson, 'Port of Chester', i. 8–12; *Chester Customs Accts.* 3–4.

20 *Cal. Close, 1307–13*, 141.

21 Ibid. 1337–9, 148–50, 188, 270, 274; Hewitt, *Med. Ches.* 47–8.

22 *Cal. Close, 1337–9*, 430; 1339–41, 54; cf. ibid. 1339–41, 214, 440, 471, 476; 1343–6, 152, 402.

town was largely illicit; in 1343 Chester was named as a place to which wool bought below the fixed price was taken to evade customs.[1]

Chester's participation in the cloth trade was also modest. Some cloth was made locally, for there were fulling mills on the south bank of the Dee by the mid 14th century,[2] but the material was probably limited in both quality and quantity. In 1245, indeed, Henry III had to buy cloth at Boston to meet his needs at Chester,[3] and although by the 1270s merchants of the city were supplying the royal garrisons at Chester and Beeston, they were probably importing material for that purpose.[4] In the late 13th and early 14th century one source of supply was Ireland.[5] Others included London and Coventry, which sent good quality cloth to Chester for export and presumably also for local use.[6] By 1300 a wide variety of cloth was marketed in Chester, including green worsted, bluet, and linen from Normandy,[7] an important means of distribution being the fairs.[8]

TOLLS, CUSTOMS, AND PRISES

Tolls were taken at the city's gates by the late 13th century and probably long before.[9] In the reign of Edward II (1307–27), when they were recorded in detail, they were levied on the goods of 'foreign' merchants as they entered and left the city, the citizens themselves being exempt. At the Eastgate, the principal entry for landborne traffic and the only gate at which tolls could be paid in cash, there was a tariff for wool, salt, coal, timber, 'long boards', bark for tanning, turf, knives, cups, dishes, and tankards. Merchandise produced within Cheshire, including corn, malt, lead, iron, steel, and livestock, was exempt.[10] At the Northgate the serjeant took toll on a wide variety of sea fish and shellfish, ale, fruit, sheep, timber, shingles, coal, firewood, and turf. At the Bridgegate tolls were taken on cattle brought in from Wales, fish and shellfish of various kinds, hops, nuts, firewood, turf, coal, timber, shingles, laths, bark for tanning, knives, cups, and dishes. Levies were presumably also made at the two adjacent gates, the Shipgate and the Horsegate, for which the serjeant of the Bridgegate was also responsible. The commodities which passed through the

Watergate were similar, and included barley, various kinds of fish, coal, cups, dishes, and knives.[11]

In the late 13th century the tolls levied at the gates were disputed. In 1290, for example, the citizens challenged the serjeant Hugh of Raby's rights at the Bridgegate, and in 1293 the serjeant of the Eastgate, Robert of Bradford, was charged with taking unauthorized customs.[12] Others charged with taking illegal tolls included the abbot of Chester, who was extracting levies (*vadia*) from traffic on the road from Portpool to the Northgate,[13] and one of the serjeants of the city, who had taken prises from dealers and fishermen bringing fish into Chester by water.[14] The problem remained unresolved in the early 14th century,[15] and in 1314 the keepers of all four gates were found guilty of abusing their position, in particular of taking unauthorized custom on commodities produced in the shire and from fishing boats coming to the anchorage at Portpool and to the harbour proper.[16] Even so, in 1349 the serjeant of the Eastgate was still maintaining his right to tolls on many items declared exempt in 1314.[17]

All that is known of the port customs between the mid 11th and late 13th century is that 'due prises' existed. By the 1270s, however, it is clear that wine was among the items on which prisage was taken.[18] In the 1280s or early 1290s a collector was appointed, an eminent Chester merchant,[19] and in the early 14th century the money so raised was treated as revenue of the earldom. Prisage, which was also levied on timber, bark, and coal as well as wine,[20] was distinguished from custom, in theory levied upon alien merchants, but apparently not collected until the 1380s, presumably because alien merchants did not import wine through Chester in the earlier 14th century.[21]

In other respects Chester's relationship to the national customs system is obscure. Although not included in the custom on wool, wool fells, and hides, inaugurated in 1275,[22] it was mentioned in the new custom of 1303, when two former mayors were appointed collectors in the city and the Welsh ports as far south as Haverfordwest (Pemb.).[23] Despite a trickle of royal instructions thereafter,[24] custom on wool, wool

1 *Cal. Close*, 1343–6, 78; *Cal. Pat.* 1343–5, 164; Hewitt, *Med. Ches.* 134.

2 *V.C.H. Ches.* v (2), Mills and Fisheries: Dee Fulling Mills.

3 *Cal. Pat.* 1232–47, 460.

4 *Ches. in Pipe R.* 109.

5 C.C.A.L.S., ZSR 2, rot. 16; *Sel. R. Chester City Cts.* p. lxi.

6 *New Hist. Irel.* ii. 505–6.

7 C.C.A.L.S., ZMR 7, rot. 4; *Sel. R. Chester City Cts.* p. lxi.

8 C.C.A.L.S., ZMR 3, rott. 2d., 5; B.L. Add. Ch. 49997, 50004.

9 e.g. *Cal. Ches. Ct. R.* pp. 166, 181–3; Morris, *Chester*, 559–60; B.L. Harl. MS. 2074, f. 98v.; P.R.O., CHES 29/59, m. 23.

10 C.C.A.L.S., ZMR 5, rot. 4; Morris, *Chester*, 555–6.

11 Morris, *Chester*, 556–7.

12 *Cal. Ches. Ct. R.* pp. 166, 181–4.

13 Ibid. pp. 188, 190, 199, 204.   14 Ibid. p. 189.

15 *Cal. Inq. Misc.* ii, p. 11.   16 Morris, *Chester*, 556–8.

17 Ibid. 561–2; P.R.O., CHES 29/59, m. 23.

18 C.C.A.L.S., ZCH 12; Morris, *Chester*, 499–500; *Cal. Chart. R.* 1257–1300, 198; *Cal. Close*, 1272–9, 297; 1279–88, 308, 499; 1288–96, 2; 1296–1302, 180, 270; *Ches. in Pipe R.* 118.

19 *Cal. Fine R.* 1272–1307, 350.

20 *Ches. Chamb. Accts.* 42, 44, 85, 87, 91, 93, 102, 109, 112, 121, 161, 208, 224, 249, 263.

21 Wilson, 'Port of Chester', i. 12–13; *Chester Customs Accts.* 4–5; *Cal. Pat.* 1307–13, 149; *Cal. Fine R.* 1307–19, 10, 33–4, 68.

22 Para. based on Wilson, 'Port of Chester', i. 2–19; *Chester Customs Accts.* 2–4.

23 *Cal. Fine R.* 1272–1307, 466–7, 475–6.

24 Ibid. 1307–19, 336–8; 1319–27, 145–7, 204–5; 1327–37, 54–5; *Cal. Pat.* 1313–17, 15, 56; *Cal. Close*, 1318–23, 16; 1327–30, 390; 1339–41, 450–1.

fells, and hides was levied only in that year, when local merchants paid duty amounting to just over £19 to the chamberlain of Chester.[1] Thereafter no further payment was recorded and from 1320 the chamberlain noted that custom was not taken at Chester because the cocket seal had not been issued to the port.[2] In 1343 the city was expressly excluded from the national customs system and closed to the export of wool.[3] It was again excluded from collection when the custom on cloth was extended to native merchants in 1347.[4]

Tolls were also levied by the citizens themselves. Indeed, in the later 1270s a 'custom of boats' and minor tolls were included with the revenues of the city.[5] Such customs had probably been regulated from the mid 13th century by the guild merchant, which certainly by 1319 exacted payment from alien merchants for the sale of merchandise including herring, salmon, and eels.[6]

Further taxes levied on merchandise by the citizens included murage and pavage for repairing the walls and paving the streets. Murage was the subject of a royal grant to the citizens from the mid 13th century, but usually there is no indication of how the money was raised. In 1279, however, the mayor and citizens were granted a three-year pavage of ½*d.* on every cartload of firewood or coals brought into the city.[7] Later, the leavelookers, as the wardens of the guild merchant became known, made a fixed levy on all merchandise sold by aliens within the city whenever a murage was granted.[8]

TRADES AND INDUSTRIES

Agriculture was of prime importance. Besides the rich and successful who bought rural manors,[9] many Cestrians had holdings in the town fields, which lay all round the city, both within the liberties[10] and just outside, in the townships of Bache,[11] Claverton,[12] and Newton by Chester.[13] They were divided into strips and in some areas, such as Newbold and the Gorse Stacks, included both arable and non-arable land.[14] In addi-

tion, the citizens had common rights of pasture on Hoole heath and on the meadows situated beside the Dee in Saltney, both lying outside the liberties.[15] They also kept cattle on private pastures north of the city.[16]

The most productive fishery remained that by the Dee Bridge, which belonged to the earl and from the 1270s was leased to the farmers of the Dee Mills for the large annual rent of £50.[17] In addition, St. Werburgh's and other local religious houses had their own 'free' boats on the Dee, and by *c.* 1300 the privilege had been extended to several prominent citizens, including Sir Peter Thornton, Geoffrey of Meols, Richard the clerk, Robert the chamberlain, and Hugh the mercer.[18] Others owned or leased stalls and nets in the river,[19] or had rights in more distant fisheries off Wirral.[20]

The mills, which retained their monopoly over grinding and their remarkable profitability, were probably also used, as later, by inhabitants of nearby areas outside the liberties. Throughout the period they produced huge amounts of malt and flour;[21] the scale of operations at their peak is indicated by the fact that in 1283 the king reduced the farm by only a fourth to compensate for the grinding of 1,752 quarters of wheat for his men during seven months in the previous year.[22]

The earl's millers enforced their rights vigorously,[23] and their impact on city life was considerable. In the 1260s and 1270s they witnessed numerous grants of property within the liberties,[24] and held land and rents in Castle Lane and Lower Bridge Street.[25] By the 1290s there were at least five millers, serving as judgers, jurymen, and pledgers in the city sessions of the county court.[26] Some operated at the Dee Mills,[27] others probably at the abbot's mill at Bache.[28] Among the latter, David the miller was especially notable: sheriff at least twice in the 1280s and 1290s,[29] and a frequent witness to enrolments in the portmote,[30] he owned property in Northgate Street and Bache and a malt kiln in or near the corn market, and was tenant of all the abbot's holdings in Bridge Street, for which he

1 Wilson, 'Port of Chester', ii. 2; *Chester Customs Accts.* 20.

2 *Chester Customs Accts.* 3–4, quoting *Ches. Chamb. Accts.* 91, 102, 121, 159–60, 224, 263.

3 *Cal. Close, 1341–3,* 647–8; *1343–6,* 78; *Cal. Fine R. 1337–47,* 222–3, 264–5, 336.

4 *Cal. Close, 1346–9,* 290–1.

5 Wilson, 'Port of Chester', i. 3; *Ches. in Pipe R.* 112, 117, 122, 133–4, 138.

6 C.C.A.L.S., ZCR 469/542, f. 18[A] verso.

7 *Cal. Pat. 1272–81,* 311.

8 *Chester Customs Accts.* 15; C.C.A.L.S., ZCR 469/542.

9 Below, this section (Leading Merchants and Citizens).

10 B.L. Add. Ch. 50138, 72201–2, 72217, 72226, 72229.

11 P.R.O., WALE 29/246, 250–2, 255–6, 258.

12 B.L. Add. Ch. 50114, 72205, 72268, 75142; C.C.A.L.S., ZMR 31, rot. 3.

13 B.L. Add. Ch. 50035; *J.C.A.S.* n.s. x. 35–6, 45–7, 59.

14 B.L. Add. Ch. 50138, 72201–2.

15 *Close R. 1247–51,* 236, 262, 347, 360, 419–20; *28 D.K.R.* 36.

16 *Cal. Ches. Ct. R.* pp. 181, 199, 204.

17 *V.C.H. Ches.* v (2), Mills and Fisheries: Dee Fisheries.

18 *Ches. Chamb. Accts.* 73–5.

19 C.C.A.L.S., DAL 489; B.L. Add. Ch. 72271; *Ches. Chamb. Accts.* 73.

20 *Cat. Anct. D.* iii, C 3649; cf. ibid. vi, C 4323.

21 *V.C.H. Ches.* v (2), Mills and Fisheries: Dee Corn Mills.

22 *Cal. Close, 1279–88,* 202–3.

23 P.R.O., CHES 25/1, m. 4.

24 e.g. B.L. Add. Ch. 72224, 72229, 75138–41, 75145, 75239; Eaton Hall, CH 84.

25 Eaton Hall, CH 48, 53–4.

26 *Cal. Ches. Ct. R.* pp. 160, 162–3, 169, 177, 182–3, 185, 205.

27 e.g. ibid. pp. 179, 182.

28 e.g. ibid. pp. 163, 180.

29 During the mayoralties of Robert the mercer (B.L. Add. Ch. 72249) and Hugh of Brickhill (B.L. Add. Ch. 72256; C.C.A.L.S., ZMR 2, rot. 1d.; ZD/HT 40).

30 *Cal. Ches. Ct. R.* p. 177; B.L. Add. Ch. 50052, 50054, 50058, 72242; P.R.O., WALE 29/272; C.C.A.L.S., ZD/HT 1.

returned a doomsman to the portmote.[1] After 1300, although still apparently numerous, millers became less prominent in city life.[2]

The city's role as a regional capital, a stopping place on the routes to Ireland and Wales, and a centre for the production and sale of malt, ensured that brewing remained important. By 1306 there were at least 19 brewers, but many had additional occupations; among those involved were such notable personages as William (III) of Doncaster, and Hugh, agent of the abbot of Vale Royal, whose Chester tenants included several brewers. Others were of much humbler status, including a cook and two women amerced 'for defect of hops'.[3]

Retailing was a major activity within the city from the earlier 13th century, taking place not only at the stalls set up at markets and fairs, but in permanent premises already called 'shops' (*shopae*). The shops were generally small, sometimes little more than a lock-up 3 metres by 2 metres,[4] and at most the size of the ground floor of a modest plot, say 8.5 metres by 2.5 metres.[5] By the earlier 14th century such structures were found not just in the four main streets, but in many of the lesser ones, including Castle Street, Pepper Street, Parsons Lane (later Princess Street), Fleshmongers Lane (later Newgate Street), and St. John's Lane.[6] They were especially numerous outside the Eastgate in Foregate Street, where by the mid 14th century the bishop of Lichfield held 15 shops with gardens.[7] Initially, however, the main concentration was in the centre of the city around St. Peter's. At least four abutted the church itself by 1220, and from the mid 13th century shops also stood next to it in Northgate and Watergate Streets, and opposite it in Eastgate and Bridge Streets.[8] By the late 13th century in the main streets they were on two levels, in the arrangement already known as the Rows.[9]

From the first, shops were often grouped by trade. In the city centre Rows were devoted to butchers, bakers, cooks, ironmongers, and cobblers by the early 14th century, and in Foregate Street there were jewellers.[10] Similar groupings of traders also occurred in the selds,

which in Chester, as elsewhere, are most plausibly viewed as 'private bazaars' into which were gathered a number of stalls selling a particular form of merchandise, such as skins or woollen cloth, perhaps under specially privileged regulations.[11] The Chester selds, which were almost invariably in the ownership of prominent civic families, were concentrated on the west side of Bridge Street in front of the common hall and northwards to the Cross. Their heyday was the later 13th century, when commercial pressures were such that they were being subdivided[12] and occasionally enlarged at the expense of private accommodation. The Tailors' seld, for example, appears to have originated as a large house near the common hall which was progressively given over to trade in the 1260s and 1270s, and at least in part retained the same functions in 1315, when it belonged to the Erneys family.[13] By the mid 14th century the selds were in decline; their multiplicity of owners was reflected in physical subdivision into sections, some at least of which were vacant and unlettable.[14]

Especially prominent among the retailers were the purveyors of victuals. The butchers, who profited from the demand created by the garrisons of the royal castles,[15] were numerous and well organized and seem to have enjoyed comparatively high status, making frequent appearances in city suits and pleas.[16] By the mid 14th century they had evolved common codes of practice which from time to time brought them into conflict with the city authorities; they were by then being required to reduce the nuisance which they caused in the city centre by obstructing the highway and hanging carcasses above their *tabulae*, possibly stallboards in front of Fleshers' Row.[17] By 1349 they were subject to competition from country butchers, who were allowed to trade in the city on Mondays.[18]

Other victuallers located near the Cross included the fishmongers, whose fishboards were at the east end of Watergate Street.[19] On the other side of the Cross, in Eastgate Street, were the bakers, whose premises were in Bakers' Row, conveniently close to the corn market

1 P.R.O., WALE 29/249, 272; *36 D.K.R.* App. II, p. 35; *Cart. Chester Abbey*, ii, p. 341.

2 Cf. *Cal. of Deeds and Papers of Moore Fam.* (R.S.L.C. lxvii), no. 999; B.L. Add. Ch. 50099.

3 C.C.A.L.S., ZSR 5, rott. 2, 4; Morris, *Chester*, 455; *Cal. Ches. Ct. R.* p. 190.

4 e.g. C.C.A.L.S., ZD/HT 2; *J.C.A.S.* n.s. vi. 49–51.

5 B.L. Add. Ch. 50053, 50078; cf. ibid. 50099, 50136; C.C.A.L.S., ZMR 3, rot. 12d.

6 e.g. B.L. Add. Ch. 49982, 50053, 50068, 50134, 50136, 50143, 50152, 50196, 50203, 72317, 72319, 75154; P.R.O., CHES 25/1, m. 4; CHES 29/60, m. 12; E 315/47; C.C.A.L.S., ZD/HT 42–3; ZMR 3, rot. 21d.; ZMR 29, rot. 3; ZMR 35.

7 C.C.A.L.S., ZD/HT 31–4; *J.C.A.S.* n.s. iv. 183–4; 3 *Sheaf*, xxiii, no. 5372.

8 e.g. B.L. Add. Ch. 49975; *J.C.A.S.* n.s. x. 17; P.R.O., CHES 25/1; C.C.A.L.S., ZCHD 2/1; *28 D.K.R.* 58; *Cal. Deeds Moore Fam.* no. 993.

9 *V.C.H. Ches.* v (2), The Rows: Origin

10 Ibid.; *J.C.A.S.* n.s. iv. 178–85.

11 D. Keene, *Survey of Medieval Winchester*, i. 137–8; ii. 1091–2, 1098; D. Keene, *Cheapside before Gt. Fire*, 12–13; *V.C.H. Ches.* v (2), The Rows: Physical Form (Selds).

12 e.g. C.C.A.L.S., ZMR 5, rot. 5; cf. P.R.O., CHES 31/1A.

13 B.L. Add. Ch. 49997, 50004, 50117–18; 3 *Sheaf*, xxviii, p. 79.

14 e.g. C.C.A.L.S., ZMR 42; Eaton Hall, MS. 321; P.R.O., SC 6/784/5, m. 5; SC 6/784/7, m. 4; SC 6/784/11, m. 4; *Blk. Prince's Reg.* iii. 486–7.

15 *Flints. Ministers' Accts. 1301–28* (Flints. Hist. Soc. Rec. Ser. iii), 18; *Ches. Chamb. Accts.* 10.

16 e.g. *Cal. Ches. Ct. R.* pp. 162, 166, 169, 173–4, 202; C.C.A.L.S., ZMR 3, rott. 1–2, 4, 7d., 8 and d.; ZMR 5, rot. 4.

17 C.C.A.L.S., ZQCR 5; cf. ibid. ZQCR 11.

18 P.R.O., CHES 29/59; cf. Morris, *Chester*, 562.

19 *V.C.H. Ches.* v (2), Markets: General Produce Markets.

and to St. Giles's bakehouse, which by the 14th century they rented from the Doncasters, who leased it from St. Giles's hospital.[1] Other bakehouses in which prominent merchants held shares were presumably near by.[2] Numbering about 16 in 1300, the bakers formed a prominent group in the city, acting as pledgers and assessors in the county court;[3] they served a wide area, and were prosperous enough to be fined heavily for offences against the assize of bread.[4]

Of even higher status were the spicers and vintners. In the later 13th century members of both groups served as sheriffs, doomsmen, jurors, and witnesses to land grants enrolled in the portmote.[5] Some were clearly men of property.[6] As a luxury trade, wine in particular attracted rich merchants who dealt with a wide variety of expensive merchandise, men such as Hugh of Brickhill, William (III) of Doncaster, and Richard Russell.[7]

Lower down the social scale, the cooks,[8] saucemakers,[9] water carriers,[10] and taverners[11] rarely if ever achieved civic office. The cooks, who appear to have been especially numerous, were sufficiently well organized by the earlier 14th century to be concentrated in a Row,[12] but the taverners were more scattered, operating throughout the main streets from undercrofts beneath the Rows.[13]

Among the city's most numerous and important traders were those involved in the preparation and sale of furs and leather: skinners, tanners, cordwainers or corvisers, cobblers, tawyers, saddlers, and glovers. The skinners were especially prominent in the earlier 13th century, when one of their number was a doomsman of the portmote who witnessed numerous local charters

and held land in Bridge Street, probably within the prime commercial area of the selds.[14] In the later 13th century other members of the craft were active in the abbot's manor court and sold land to William (III) of Doncaster in the 1290s.[15] After 1300, however, they seem to have been less prominent in civic life.

The tanners were much less grand,[16] and because of the noisome nature of their trade were located outside the walls, especially in St. John's Lane.[17] They probably always held themselves apart from the tawyers, cordwainers, and cobblers who were particularly numerous in Chester,[18] with premises in Foregate Street, Pepper Street, and especially Corvisers' Row in front of the selds in Bridge Street.[19] By the mid 14th century the terms cordwainer, corviser, and cobbler seem to have become interchangeable, and those so designated formed a single powerful group, the shoemakers (*sutores*), one of the first to distinguish itself as a separate craft. By 1351 they were embarked upon an ultimately successful challenge to the tanners' long-established monopoly over the preparation of leather.[20]

The saddlers and glovers apparently formed separate groups.[21] The saddlers were established in a Row in Bridge Street by the 1340s and perhaps by the 1290s, when the Erneys family owned three shops 'among the saddlers', perhaps associated with their seld.[22] Glovers were established in Eastgate Street and Foregate Street in the earlier 13th century,[23] and perhaps dressed their leather at features known as glover stones, located near the castle, the Eastgate, and the churches of St. Peter and St. Michael.[24]

Cloth had probably been sold in the selds from the mid 13th century,[25] presumably by the mercers who by

---

1 P.R.O., CHES 25/1; C.C.A.L.S., ZD/HT 18, 24; ZMR 30; B.L. Add. Ch. 50151; *J.C.A.S.* n.s. ii. 166–8; x. 103–4.

2 *J.C.A.S.* xxii. 119; C.C.A.L.S., ZMR 35.

3 e.g. *Cal. Ches. Ct. R.* pp. 152, 172, 174, 178, 183, 188, 195; cf. *Sel. R. Chester City Cts.* 38, 59–60; C.C.A.L.S., ZMR 3, rott. 5d., 8–9; ZMR 7, rot. 14.

4 B.L. Harl. MS. 2162, f. 6; *Sel. R. Chester City Cts.* pp. xviii, lxii; C.C.A.L.S., ZSR 1, rot. 4; ZSR 2, rott. 2, 4; Morris, *Chester*, 454–5, 512.

5 *Cal. Ches. Ct. R.* p. 179; *Sel. R. Chester City Cts.* 77; B.L. Add. Ch. 49981, 50010, 50081–2, 72203, 72206–7, 75239; C.C.A.L.S., ZD/HT 1, 19, 39; P.R.O., CHES 25/1, m. 1; *J.C.A.S.* n.s. ii. 155.

6 P.R.O., WALE 29/272; *Ches. Chamb. Accts.* 45, 74, 93; 3 *Sheaf*, xx, p. 47.

7 *Chester Customs Accts.* 20; Wilson, 'Port of Chester', ii. 2–3; *Ches. Chamb. Accts.* 79, 93; below, this section (Leading Merchants and Citizens).

8 *Cal. Ches. Ct. R.* pp. 173, 177; *Sel. R. Chester City Cts.* pp. xxxv, xlii, xliv, lxv, 9, 31, 45, 56, 86, 92–4; C.C.A.L.S., ZMR 2; ZMR 3, rott. 4d., 16d.; ZMR 4, rot. 1; ZMR 7, rot. 4d.

9 *Sel. R. Chester City Cts.* 61–2, 69, 84; B.L. Add. Ch. 50134, 75154; C.C.A.L.S., DBA 35; 3 *Sheaf*, xvii, pp. 95–6; xlii, no. 8938.

10 *Sel. R. Chester City Cts.* 49; *Cal. Ches. Ct. R.* pp. 155, 159, 183; C.C.A.L.S., ZMR 5, rot. 4d.; B.L. Add. Ch. 50079–80.

11 *Sel. R. Chester City Cts.* 30, 46, 69, 90; C.C.A.L.S., ZMR 3, rot. 11.

12 C.C.A.L.S., ZMR 30, rot. 3; ibid. DVE 1/CI/22.

13 e.g. ibid. ZMR 3, rot. 11.

14 B.L. Add. Ch. 49973, 72224, 72226, 72228–9, 75139–42, 75145; Eaton Hall, CH 45, 53; J.R.U.L.M., Arley Deeds, box 25, no. 23; C.C.A.L.S., DVE 1/CI/41; *J.C.A.S.* n.s. x. 18.

15 Eaton Hall, CH 32; C.C.A.L.S., DVE 1/CI/4; 3 *Sheaf*, lvi, pp. 63–4.

16 e.g. *Cal. Ches. Ct. R.* pp. 157, 161, 169, 186, 190; C.C.A.L.S., ZMR 5, rott. 1d., 4d., 5d., 9, 12.

17 J.R.U.L.M., Arley Deeds, box 22, no. 8; B.L. Add. Ch. 50017, 72248–9, 72257–8, 72265–6; P.R.O., CHES 25/1, m. 3.

18 e.g. *Cal. Ches. Ct. R.* pp. 153–4, 157, 162, 165–71, 173, 175–8, 185–8, 192, 201, 205; C.C.A.L.S., ZMR 3, rott. 2, 3 and d., 14d., 16d.; ZMR 5, rott. 1d., 2d., 4d.; ZMR 7, rott. 4d., 5d.

19 B.L. Add. Ch. 50053; C.C.A.L.S., DVE 1/CI/13.

20 *Blk. Prince's Reg.* iii. 50, 428, 472, 486; 36 D.K.R. App. II, p. 93; P.R.O., SC 6/785/10, m. 1; SC 6/786/1, m. 1; SC 6/786/2, m. 1; SC 6/786/6, m. 1; SC 6/786/10, m. 1; SC 6/787/7, m. 1; SC 6/787/8, m. 1.

21 B.L. Add. Ch. 50102, 72209; C.C.A.L.S., ZMR 3, rott. 3, 20d.; P.R.O., CHES 25/1.

22 B.L. Add. Ch. 50152; P.R.O., CHES 25/1, m. 3; *Ches. Chamb. Accts.* 74.

23 B.L. Add. Ch. 72209; 3 *Sheaf*, xxxiii, pp. 86–8.

24 e.g. C.C.A.L.S., ZD/HT 43; *J.C.A.S.* n.s. ii. 175; *Coucher Bk. or Chartulary of Whalley Abbey*, ii (Chetham Soc. [o.s.], xi), pp. 343–5; *P.N. Ches.* v (1:i), 45–6.

25 Above, this subsection.

then constituted an important element in the civic élite, serving as mayors and sheriffs, county escheators, and collectors of local prises and customs.[1] As elsewhere, they probably dealt primarily in fine textiles,[2] though in Chester their concerns extended beyond a single commodity. In the late 13th and early 14th century, for example, Robert le Prudemercer (d. 1295) and his son and grandson not only traded in cloth but had a boat on the Dee and shops and other property in the Rows, Watergate Street, Fleshmongers Lane, the Crofts, and elsewhere.[3]

The tailors were of more varied status. Apparently numerous, they often witnessed property transactions and were occasionally doomsmen, pledgers, and the owners of selds.[4] They seem to have developed a sense of corporate identity relatively early for Chester: by the early 14th century they apparently met annually at an exclusive feast,[5] and if accused of bad workmanship put themselves upon the protection of their fellows.[6] Such solidarity seems to have given them an advantage over the drapers, who were said to be losing ground to them in the mid 14th century.[7]

Clothworkers were a late and relatively junior group within the city. Nevertheless, by the 1290s Chester contained a number of fullers or walkers, presumably employed at the mills at the Handbridge end of the weir.[8] The presence of dyers,[9] chaloners,[10] and shearmen[11] suggests that the main activity was finishing rather than making cloth.[12]

Pottery, made from local boulder clays, was a significant industry throughout the period, much of it produced by the city's religious communities.[13] There were kilns within the precincts of St. Werburgh's, the nunnery, and at least one of the friaries,

and also on an extramural site north of Foregate Street and east of Frodsham Street.[14] Products included tableware and tiles, especially line-impressed floor tiles bearing distinctive and consistent patterns. From the late 13th century such tiles were installed in high-quality and elaborate assemblages in the religious houses which produced them,[15] and were also sold to local merchants for use in their own dwellings and for export, especially to Ireland.[16] Their number and quality were such that their designs were widely copied in and around Dublin.[17] Similar wares were also produced in north Wales, perhaps because in the late 13th century potters were sent from the city to work alongside Edward I's English builders.[18]

Goldsmiths played an important part in city life from an early date, serving as doomsmen in the portmote and jurors at local inquisitions.[19] Concentrated in Eastgate Street and Foregate Street,[20] they were clearly relatively numerous; at least seven may be identified, for example, in the decade 1292–1302.[21] Other metalworkers included bellfounders, cutlers, and smiths, working in forges in Lower Bridge Street and Foregate Street.[22] More distinctive were the quite numerous craftsmen involved in making and maintaining armour and weaponry in the late 13th and early 14th century, including bowyers, fletchers, and furbishers.[23] The castle was a centre of expertise in those trades and contained officials such as an artillery maker, who serviced weaponry in Flint and Rhuddlan.[24]

The castle presumably formed an important base for the building trades in the late 13th and early 14th century. Although masons occurred only rarely in the records,[25] the city was the home of Richard the engineer and his son Amaury, and Robert the mason

---

1 e.g. C.C.A.L.S., ZD/HT 4–5; *Cal. Fine R. 1272–1307*, 350; *1307–19*, 54, 68; *Cal. Ches. Ct. R.* p. 168.

2 Cf. Keene, *Winchester Studies*, i. 320–1.

3 P.R.O., SC 6/771/5, m. 14; SC 6/784/5, m. 5; C.C.A.L.S., ZD/HT 39; ZMR 3, rott. 2d., 11; Eaton Hall, MS. 321; *Cal. Fine R. 1272–1307*, 350.

4 C.C.A.L.S., ZMR 3, rott. 3d., 5; ZMR 5, rot. 4d.; ZMR 7, rot. 4 and d.; P.R.O., CHES 25/1, m. 1; B.L. Add. Ch. 49982–3, 72214, 72241–2; *Sel. R. Chester City Cts.* pp. xlv, lxv, 61, 67, 73, 122; *Cal. Ches. Ct. R.* pp. 151, 166–7, 179, 196.

5 *Ches. Chamb. Accts.* 37, 74; P.R.O., SC 6/771/3, m. 8; SC 6/771/5, m. 14.   6 C.C.A.L.S., ZMR 7.

7 Ibid. DBA 35; *Blk. Prince's Reg.* iii. 50.

8 *Ches. Chamb. Accts.* 230; *Blk. Prince's Reg.* iii. 209–10; *Cal. Close, 1288–96*, 77, 182; *Sel. R. Chester City Cts.* 86, 90; C.C.A.L.S., ZMR 3, rot. 5.

9 *Cal. Ches. Ct. R.* p. 170; *Sel. R. Chester City Cts.* 59, 68; C.C.A.L.S., ZMR 3, rott. 5–6, 16d., 20d.

10 *Cal. Ches. Ct. R.* pp. 154, 185–6, 206; *Sel. R. Chester City Cts.* 67; C.C.A.L.S., ZMR 5, rot. 4d.

11 *Cal. Ches. Ct. R.* pp. 158, 162, 165–6, 168, 170, 175, 182, 185.

12 Cf. below, this chapter: Economy and Society, 1350–1550 (Trades and Industries: Textiles and Clothing).

13 Thanks are due to Mrs. J. Axworthy Rutter for much help with this para.; Ward, *Excavations at Chester: Lesser Religious Houses*, 254–5.

14 *Medieval Pottery from Excavations in NW.* ed. P. J. Davey, 86–91; Ward, *Excavations at Chester: Lesser Religious Houses*, 95–114, 138–63, 192–3, 210–20; *Liverpool Annals of Arch. and Anthropology*, xxiii. 47–50.

15 Ward, *Excavations at Chester: Lesser Religious Houses*, 14–15, 95–114, 139–63, 192–3, 202–6, 210–20, 229–79.

16 *J.C.A.S.* lxvii. 57–8, 66.

17 *Medieval Arch.* xix. 205–9; *Proc. Royal Irish Academy*, lxviii, section C, pp. 131, 152; lxxviii, section C, pp. 127–98; E. S. Eames and T. Fanning, *Irish Medieval Tiles*, 34–43, 136–9.

18 Ward, *Excavations at Chester: Lesser Religious Houses*, 220.

19 B.L. Add. Ch. 50064, 50089, 50109, 72249; P.R.O., WALE 29/272; C.C.A.L.S., ZMR 5, rot. 1d.; *J.C.A.S.* n.s. x. 18; *Cal. Ches. Ct. R.* p. 179.

20 C.C.A.L.S., ZD/HT 18–19, 31–4; P.R.O., CHES 25/1, m. 3; *J.C.A.S.* n.s. iv. 178–85.

21 C.C.A.L.S., ZD/HT 18–19, 31–2; ZMR 5, rott. 1d., 2d.; P.R.O., CHES 25/1, m. 3; *Cal. Deeds Moore Fam.* no. 997; *Cal. Ches. Ct. R.* pp. 179, 185, 201.

22 *J.C.A.S.* n.s. x. 34; *Cal. Ches. Ct. R.* pp. 157, 176, 181, 189, 197; J.R.U.L.M., Arley Deeds, box 3, no. 4; C.C.A.L.S., ZMR 3, rot. 20d.; ZMR 5, rot. 1d.; ZMR 7; B.L. Add. Ch. 75151; P.R.O., WALE 29/333; *Ches. Chamb. Accts.* 74.

23 *Cal. Ches. Ct. R.* pp. 178, 184–6, 192–3, 195–6; *Sel. R. Chester City Cts.* p. lxiv; C.C.A.L.S., ZMR 3, rott. 1, 3–7.

24 *Flints. Ministers' Accts. 1301–28*, 35, 37, 47.

25 e.g. *Sel. R. Chester City Cts.* 66.

rented the Northgate in 1303–4.[1] Carpenters were more prominent, and seem to have been located especially in Castle Lane and Bridge Street.[2] Other workers in wood included numerous turners[3] and coopers.[4]

LEADING MERCHANTS AND CITIZENS

At the peak of Chester's commercial community stood a small group of merchants, often interrelated and dealing with a wide range of commodities, mostly of high value and distributed through long-distance or overseas trade. They had few if any foreign rivals.[5] Such men belonged to families which had led the guild merchant since the early 13th century and had obtained an increasing grip on the principal civic offices, including the shrievalty, as the century progressed.[6] Their activities are well illustrated by the operation of the wine trade. By the late 13th century the shipping of wine was in the hands of men like Hugh of Brickhill, whose ship the *Nicolase* was sent to Gascony in 1283 stocked with hides and armour for the king's knights, and was commissioned to return with wine and other victuals for the royal army in Wales.[7] By the early 14th century William (III) of Doncaster had become a leading shipper.[8] Such men were also involved in retail and distribution; William of Doncaster and Roger Blund, for example, stored wine in their cellars before selling it to customers who included the royal earl.[9] They were not, however, specialist wine merchants. Even a merchant like Richard Spillering, who bought wine for the abbot of Vale Royal in 1279 and supplied the royal earl in the early 14th century, purchased goods other than wine on his trips overseas.[10]

For a brief period in the late 13th and early 14th century, when Chester was probably at the height of its medieval prosperity, the city was the home of figures of national significance, such as Richard the engineer and William of Doncaster, both of whom served as mayor. Richard followed his profession locally, supervising projects at Chester abbey[11] and royal works throughout

Cheshire,[12] and was also heavily involved in quite different trades as farmer of the Dee Mills and fishery from the 1270s until his death in 1315.[13] He was active in farming, especially cattle,[14] and also held much property in the city, including a mansion next to St. Olave's church in Lower Bridge Street and other houses in Bridge Street and Watergate Street.[15] Mayor in 1305–6,[16] his influence on Chester was clearly considerable.[17]

Richard's career illustrates the scale on which rich Cestrians might invest in land in the environs of the city. By the 1290s he already owned three messuages and 50 acres of land in Hoole.[18] His most important acquisitions, however, lay south of the city. From 1284 he was buying land in Eccleston and Pulford, and in 1294 he settled the manor of Eaton on his daughter when she married.[19] He continued to deal in land in the area and eventually assembled a large estate focused on Belgrave (in Eaton), a manor house whose elaborate moat he may well have constructed himself.[20] The family ceased to reside in Chester in 1321, when the house in Lower Bridge Street was sold, presumably because Richard's sons preferred to establish themselves as country gentlemen at Belgrave and elsewhere.[21]

The Doncasters, who provide an even more striking instance of wide-ranging commercial activity and the accumulation of multifarious assets, continued to live in Chester for at least a century (*c.* 1250–1350). The earliest known member of the family, William, prior of St. Werburgh's, died in 1259.[22] A second William was buying land near St. Peter's in the 1270s,[23] and by 1300 he and his relatives had acquired land all over Chester.[24] Their principal residence was in Watergate Street, a large mansion associated with shops and undercrofts, for which a doomsman was returned to the portmote and which was decorated with paintings in 1297.[25] Their holdings were especially concentrated upon the commercially valuable land at the city centre, where they included Row properties with shops and undercrofts in Watergate and Northgate Streets, a

1 *Ches. Chamb. Accts.* 73.

2 *Cat. Anct. D.* vi, C 5270; *Cal. Ches. Ct. R.* pp. 178, 184, 201; 27 *D.K.R.* 98; P.R.O., CHES 29/22, m. 40d.; J.R.U.L.M., Arley Deeds, box 25, no. 5; B.L. Add. Ch. 50129.

3 B.L. Add. Ch. 50066; C.C.A.L.S., DDX 405/1; *Cal. Ches. Ct. R.* p. 190.

4 *Cal. Ches. Ct. R.* p. 187; C.C.A.L.S., ZMR 3, rott. 5–6.

5 *Sel. R. Chester City Cts.* pp. lxiv–lxx.

6 Above, this chapter: City Government, 1230–1350 (esp. Sheriffs and their Courts, Emergence of the Mayoralty).

7 *Cal. Chanc. R. Var.* 267.

8 *Chester Customs Accts.* 20; Wilson, 'Port of Chester', ii. 2–3.

9 *Ches. Chamb. Accts.* 79.

10 Ibid. 45; *Chester Customs Accts.* 20; *Cal. Pat. 1272–81*, 315.

11 *J.C.A.S.* lxvi. 41–3.

12 *Hist. of King's Works*, ed. H. M. Colvin, i. 468.

13 *V.C.H. Ches.* v (2), Mills and Fisheries: Dee Corn Mills, Dee Fisheries.

14 *Cal. Ches. Ct. R.* p. 181.

15 3 *Sheaf*, xix, pp. 72–3; *King's Works*, i. 468 n.; *J.C.A.S.* N.S. v. 429–30; B.L. Add. Ch. 72253; Eaton Hall, CH 159.

16 *Cal. Close, 1302–7*, 417.

17 J. Harvey, *Eng. Medieval Architects* (1984 edn.), 178–80; *King's Works*, i. 468.

18 P.R.O., CHES 29/8, m. 6; 26 *D.K.R.* 44.

19 Rest of para. based on *J.C.A.S.* lxix. 59–77.

20 C.C.A.L.S., DVE 1/EI/1–3, 14; Eaton Hall, CH 96, 153; W. Beamont, *Cal. of Ancient Charters preserved at Eaton Hall, Ches.* 19.

21 Beamont, *Cal. Chart. Eaton*, 20; 3 *Sheaf*, xix, pp. 72–3; Ormerod, *Hist. Ches.* ii. 826.

22 *J.C.A.S.* N.S. ii. 155.

23 Ibid. N.S. vi. 52–3.

24 Ibid. N.S. ii. 159–61, 164–6; v. 429–30; vi. 53, 55; C.C.A.L.S., ZD/HT 4, 40, 42–3; ibid. DBA 35; DVE 1/CI/3.

25 C.C.A.L.S., ZMR 3, rot. 12; ZMR 8, rot. 6d.; *J.C.A.S.* N.S. v. 429–30; cf. P.R.O., CHES 25/1, m. 4.

bakehouse in Eastgate Street, and a seld in Bridge Street,[1] but they also had extensive holdings in the town fields, a mill, at least two messuages, 50 acres of arable, and 6 acres of meadow in Upton and Newton, and *c.* 36 selions and 4 acres of meadow in Bache.[2]

Further afield, the Doncasters held land in Wirral,[3] and by 1300 were acquiring land and offices in Flint, Maelor Saesneg, Rhuddlan, and Anglesey.[4] Two especially important grants were the keepership of the royal manor of Mostyn (Flints.) in 1309, initially for a term of years and later for life,[5] and the lease of the lead mines of Englefield in 1311.[6] Much of their enrichment was the work of William (III). Active in the portmote and in royal service by 1295,[7] mayor for a part term in 1301 and for two full terms and another part thereafter,[8] his success was founded on the provision of victuals and raw materials for the royal army and garrisons in north Wales.[9] He had especially strong contacts with Ireland,[10] from which his ship, the *Mariota* of Chester, transported goods to north Wales in the 1290s.[11] His influence at court was apparent in a variety of royal appointments in the early 14th century, including collector of customs and searcher of money in the ports of Chester and north Wales, and in the retaliatory orders made in response to his complaints about the seizure of his goods and money at Antwerp in 1301.[12]

William survived until 1330 or later, and although much of his commercial activity was not conducted from Chester, the city remained his principal base and, at least in his later years, his home.[13] After the deposition of Edward II in 1327, however, he seems to have fallen from favour, together with other prominent Cestrians. In 1328 he was found to have debts to the late king totalling £166 13*s.* 4*d.*, among which was included a fine of £30 for an unspecified misdemeanour.[14] Thereafter he and his family retired from the national stage.

In Chester and north Wales, however, the Doncaster family remained important. William (III)'s son William (IV), sheriff in 1313–14,[15] purchased the serjeanty of the Watergate and other lands and rents from the Stanlow family in 1325,[16] and in 1330 received from his father at least six tenements in Eastgate Street, together with the family holdings in Mold (Flints.).[17] By the 1340s the family's main Chester properties were held by William (V), sheriff in 1343–4.[18] At his death the direct line came to an end, his holdings passing by marriage to the Hope family.[19] Although others bearing the name of Doncaster still had property in the city, after 1344 none held civic office.[20]

Another family which remained firmly identified with the city while investing in land in the surrounding countryside was the Brickhills. They presumably came from the earl of Chester's estate at Brickhill (Bucks.),[21] and first emerged as leading citizens in the 1280s, when Hugh (d. 1292) became sheriff and perhaps mayor.[22] A second Hugh was mayor 15 times between 1293 and 1314. The family had a house in Bridge Street, property in Bakers' Row, Watergate Street, and Fleshmongers Lane, and owned a ship, the *Nicolase*.[23] By the 1280s they were sufficiently rich for one of the Hughs to become, albeit briefly, a partner with Richard the engineer in farming the Dee Mills,[24] and in the 1290s they were also buying land in the town fields.[25] They also acquired offices: Hugh (II), the mayor, was appointed collector of customs in the ports of Chester and north Wales in 1303, and probably became chamberlain of Chester *c.* 1312.[26]

Other prominent members of the family included William Brickhill (or Birchills), dean of St. John's and rector of Mold in the 1290s,[27] John Brickhill, mayor 1320–2,[28] and William, son of Peter Brickhill, a royal clerk, who was sheriff three times and mayor five times

1 *J.C.A.S.* N.S. ii. 161, 166–7; C.C.A.L.S., ZMR 3, rot. 2d.

2 P.R.O., CHES 29/20, m. 5; CHES 29/32, m. 13d.; CHES 29/35, m. 14A; OBS 1/819, p. 23; WALE 29/256; 27 *D.K.R.* 94, 117, 120; *J.C.A.S.* N.S. x. 106.

3 P.R.O., CHES 29/39, m. 14; OBS 1/819, p. 31.

4 *J.C.A.S.* N.S. ii. 156, 160–3, 168–70, 177–9; vi. 56–7; *Cal. Pat.* 1307–13, 163; 1313–17, 287.

5 *Cal. Fine R.* 1307–19, 52, 70; *Cal. Close,* 1307–13, 380.

6 *Cal. Close,* 1307–13, 380; *Cal. Fine R.* 1307–19, 109.

7 C.C.A.L.S., ZMR 1, rot. 3; *Sel. R. Chester City Cts.* 5, 7; *Cal. Close,* 1288–96, 445; 1296–1302, 84.

8 Wm. (III) the merchant is probably to be identified with Wm. senior, the mayor, husband of Felice, and active in Chester *c.* 1295–*c.* 1330. He is to be distinguished from his son, Wm. junior, husband of Alice, who was probably sheriff 1313–14: B.L. Add. Ch. 50064, 50117–18, 72263, 75148; *Cal. Close,* 1313–18, 294; C.C.A.L.S., ZCR 469/542, f. 18[B] verso; *V.C.H. Ches.* v (2), Lists of Mayors and Sheriffs.

9 *Cal. Pat.* 1292–1301, 135; cf. ibid. 134; *Cal. Fine R.* 1272–1307, 492; *Cal. Close,* 1302–7, 160–1; 36 *D.K.R.* App. II, p. 150.

10 *Cal. Doc. Irel.* 1293–1301, 59, 346; 1302–7, 94; *Cal. Pat.* 1292–1301, 126, 134; 1301–7, 143; 1307–13, 6, 20, 503.

11 *Cal. Doc. Irel.* 1293–1301, 159, 272–3.

12 e.g. *Cal. Fine R.* 1272–1307, 467, 476; 1307–19, 10, 33–4,

68, 80; *Cal. Pat.* 1301–7, 57; 1307–13, 149, 190; *Cal. Close,* 1296–1302, 439, 540; 1307–13, 112, 181–2.

13 Cf. *J.C.A.S.* N.S. ii. 170–3.

14 *Cal. Close,* 1327–30, 273, 278, 490.

15 *V.C.H. Ches.* v (2), Lists of Mayors and Sheriffs.

16 *J.C.A.S.* N.S. v. 428.

17 Ibid. N.S. ii. 174.

18 Ibid. 166–7, 177–8; v. 430–1; *V.C.H. Ches.* v (2), Lists of Mayors and Sheriffs.

19 *J.C.A.S.* N.S. ii. 158–9.

20 e.g. ibid. 157, 174.

21 Ibid. lxxi. 47, 63.

22 *V.C.H. Ches.* v (2), Lists of Mayors and Sheriffs.

23 P.R.O., CHES 25/1; WALE 29/400; C.C.A.L.S., ZMR 7, rot. 4d.; *J.C.A.S.* N.S. v. 429–30; *Cal. Chanc. R. Var.* 267.

24 *Cal. Ches. Ct. R.* pp. 82, 123–5.

25 J.R.U.L.M., Arley Deeds, box 1, no. 53; P.R.O., CHES 29/31, m. 10; 27 *D.K.R.* 115.

26 *Cal. Fine R.* 1272–1307, 467, 476; M. Sharp, 'Contributions to Hist. of Earldom and Co. of Chester, 1237–1399' (Manchester Univ. Ph.D. thesis, 1925), 13.

27 Jones, *Ch. in Chester,* 123; *Cal. Pat.* 1292–1301, 286.

28 B.L. Add. Ch. 72268–9; *V.C.H. Ches.* v (2), Lists of Mayors and Sheriffs.

between 1306 and 1332,[1] and who married Cecily, heiress of the manor of Thurstaston in Wirral.[2]

Other leading merchant families, such as the Russells, Hurrells, Payns, and Dunfouls, also combined the ownership of commercial property in the city with civic and royal office-holding and investment in agricultural land.[3] Most remained resident in the city, but occasionally they made the transition to country gentlemen while retaining their urban links. An outstanding example was the Blund family, which rose to prominence under John, mayor 1316–17, who bought the manor of Little Neston and Hargrave shortly before his death in 1317.[4] His descendant, another John, who was mayor 14 times between 1334 and 1360, evidently adopted the life of a country gentleman, hunting with greyhounds at Little Neston.[5] In other instances members of local gentry families rose to prominence in city life. In particular, the Bruyn family of Bruen Stapleford produced a mayor, Richard le Bruyn, in the early 14th century.[6]

In the late 13th and early 14th century, the activities of the interrelated group of merchant families who dominated Chester produced a very active market in land, and property seems to have changed hands rapidly.[7] Holdings were assembled by purchase, or through leases and rents, and the sources of wealth were similarly diverse, including both trade in luxury goods and royal patronage. The leading men of Chester appear to have been assimilated into the local gentry, with whom they intermarried and who in turn rose to high office in the city. Such developments, which imply considerable prosperity, reached their high point in the early 14th century. After the 1330s, however, Chester's citizens seem to have bought and sold land less frequently.

The leading men of Chester lived in style. The townhouses of those who remained resident were quite ostentatious, combining first-floor living quarters, which included large halls and solars, with commercial premises comprising undercrofts and groups of as many as five Row-level shops. They were often located at corner sites, probably because they afforded better access and extra window space, and usually fronted the main streets. The best surviving examples are nos. 48–52 Bridge Street and 38–42 Watergate Street, perhaps the home of the Doncasters.[8] Others are known only from contemporary descriptions. They include the mansion of Richard the engineer in Lower Bridge Street, which not only had a stone tower but was intimately linked with St. Olave's church, perhaps once its chapel,[9] and the Black Hall, the house of the mayoral family of the Daresburys, which stood in Pepper Street and contained stone and painted chambers as well as stables.[10]

CITY AND CROWN, 1350–1550

In 1351, as part of a more general investigation of his earldom's franchises, the Black Prince instituted quo warranto proceedings in Chester. For a ratification of their charters and a declaration of the bounds of their liberties, the citizens agreed to a fine of £300, which because they were impoverished was to be paid by instalments over five years.[11] Royal officials delayed the matter until the prince himself went to Chester in 1353.[12] His visit, which lasted some two months, involved a meeting in the city at which the men of the shire paid a fine of 5,000 marks to maintain their franchises.[13] Chester itself, in accordance with its exempt status, did not contribute,[14] and in 1354 obtained a charter defining the boundaries of the liberty, confirming its admiralty powers over the Dee, and further excluding royal officials by annexing its escheatorship to the mayoralty.[15] The payments promised in return for those privileges were extracted by the prince only with considerable difficulty.[16]

The Black Prince again visited Chester briefly in 1358, but is not known otherwise to have gone there.[17] The links of his son, Richard II (1377–99), with the city and shire developed only in the later years of his reign. The king visited Chester for the first time in 1387 and granted the citizens a murage for the repair of their ruined bridge.[18] His favourite, Robert de Vere,

1　*Cal. Pat.* 1292–1301, 139, 519; *V.C.H. Ches.* v (2), Lists of Mayors and Sheriffs.

2　P.R.O., CHES 29/38, m. 5; *27 D.K.R.* 122; cf. Ormerod, *Hist. Ches.* ii. 503; *28 D.K.R.* 22; P.R.O., CHES 29/40, m. 19; OBS 1/819, pp. 28, 32–3.

3　*Sel. R. Chester City Cts.* pp. lxviii–lxix; 3 *Sheaf*, lvi, p. 69; C.C.A.L.S., DVE 1/CI/22; ibid. ZMR 30, rot. 3; P.R.O., SC 6/784/5, m. 5; SC 6/784/7, m. 4; Eaton Hall, MS. 321.

4　P.R.O., CHES 29/30, m. 21d.; *27 D.K.R.* 113.

5　*Blk. Prince's Reg.* iii. 351.

6　Ormerod, *Hist. Ches.* ii. 317–18, 322; *27 D.K.R.* 112–14; *36 D.K.R.* App. II, pp. 63–4; *V.C.H. Ches.* v (2), Lists of Mayors and Sheriffs.

7　Para. based on sources cited throughout this subsection.

8　C.C.A.L.S., ZMR 3, rot. 12; ZMR 8, rot. 6d.; *V.C.H. Ches.* v (2), The Rows: Physical Form (Domestic Accommodation).

9　*Cal. Ches. Ct. R.* p. 204; 3 *Sheaf*, xix, pp. 72–3.

10　J.R.U.L.M., Arley Deeds, box 25, no. 13.

11　*Blk. Prince's Reg.* iii. 3–4, 13–14, 20–1, 29–31; *V.C.H. Ches.* ii. 30–1.

12　*Blk. Prince's Reg.* iii. 242–3.

13　Ibid. 112–25, esp. 115; *36 D.K.R.* App. II, p. 92; *Northern Hist.* xii. 16–31.

14　*V.C.H. Ches.* ii. 24; D. J. Clayton, *Administration of Co. Palatine of Chester, 1442–85* (Chetham Soc. 3rd ser. xxxv), 59.

15　*Blk. Prince's Reg.* iii. 152, 181; Morris, *Chester*, 495–9; C.C.A.L.S., ZCH 18.

16　*Blk. Prince's Reg.* iii. 100, 105–6, 182, 242–3.

17　Ibid. 271, 307–8, 316, 333, 344.

18　P. Morgan, *War and Society in Medieval Ches. 1277–1403* (Chetham Soc. 3rd ser. xxxiv), 187; Morris, *Chester*, 503; C.C.A.L.S., ZCH 20.

earl of Oxford, whom he made justice of Chester, established his household in the city and while based there raised the army which was defeated at Radcot Bridge (Oxon.) later in 1387.[1] The failure of Vere's campaign was celebrated locally by his enemy Richard FitzAlan, earl of Arundel, who from his base in Holt (Denb.) caused a copy of the appeal against the royal favourite to be nailed to the door of St. Peter's church.[2] In 1389, after the king had reasserted his personal authority, the men of the shire met at Chester and granted a subsidy of 3,000 marks.[3]

In 1393 there was a mysterious rising in Cheshire, apparently aimed primarily against Richard II's hated enemy Thomas of Woodstock, duke of Gloucester, then justice of Chester. The king proclaimed his innocence of any involvement, but the fact that he found it necessary to do so casts doubt upon his protestation. At all events it provided him with a pretext to remove Gloucester from the post of justice and enabled him to consolidate his authority over city and county.[4] The result of those manoeuvrings became apparent in 1394, when Baldwin Radington, controller of the royal household, at Chester to recruit for the king's expedition to Ireland, broke into the abbot of St. Werburgh's lodgings, detained two of his servants, and raided the neighbouring houses. The mayor, John Armourer, having intervened in the dispute, Radington attacked the sheriffs; during the affray one of his own men was killed and in retaliation he and his supporters rode out 'in manner of war', terrorizing the city and its environs, an outrage to which the king's only response was to indict one of the sheriffs for the death of Radington's follower.[5]

Royal involvement in the city's affairs brought benefits as well as problems. In the 1390s royal favour secured for the monks of St. Werburgh's the long-sought licences to appropriate their livings.[6] The resumption of building work at the crossing of the abbey church may also be attributed to royal interest, contact with a refined and sophisticated court being a factor in the community's acquisition of such accomplished works as the late 14th-century choir stalls.[7] At St. John's, too, royal patronage may have played a part in the refoundation in 1393 of the fraternity of St. Anne, the chaplains of which were to pray daily for the king and his family.[8] In his last years Richard visited the capital of his new principality with increasing frequency, staying there at least six times in 1398–9.[9] His growing fondness for the city was demonstrated in 1398 when he granted an exemplification of its charters and extended its privileges by authorizing the outlawing of any foreign or unpropertied defendants who failed to respond to summonses to appear in its courts.[10]

Despite such favoured status, in 1399 the city surrendered to Henry Bolingbroke, duke of Lancaster, without a fight.[11] Before the king's arrest the duke stayed at Chester castle for 12 days, drinking the king's wine, wasting fields, and pillaging houses. While there, he also secured the arrest and execution of Sir Peter Legh of Lyme, one of Richard's leading retainers in Cheshire.[12] Richard himself, captured at Flint some two weeks later, was taken to Chester and detained for a few days in the castle, while Bolingbroke received a deputation from the city of London renouncing fealty to the prisoner.[13]

Early in 1400 there was a revolt in Cheshire, linked with the Earls' Rising. Those involved included prominent members of Richard's Cheshire retinue and a large group of townsmen from Chester, who, dressed in the livery of the deposed monarch, removed Legh's head from the Eastgate and unsuccessfully besieged the castle, then held by the chamberlain of Chester, the sheriff of Cheshire, and the constable, William Venables of Kinderton.[14] Clearly there remained some sympathy for Richard II among the civic élite.[15] The Chester Carmelites, themselves well favoured by the citizens, also apparently harboured Ricardian sympathies, and gave burial to Legh's mutilated body, together with the head after its retrieval from the Eastgate.[16]

The new dynasty exacted a price for such attitudes. Some notable local offices changed hands in 1399–1400, including the constableship of the castle and the tenancy of the Dee Mills.[17] The Carmelites' complaint of poverty in 1400 perhaps stemmed partly from Bolingbroke's ravaging in 1399.[18] There was a reckoning, too, for St. Werburgh's: in 1400 Thomas Arundel, archbishop of Canterbury, ordered a visitation to investigate the monastery's financial administration.

1 Morgan, *War and Society*, 187–8.

2 R. R. Davies, 'Ric. II and Principality of Chester, 1397–9', *Reign of Ric. II*, ed. F. R. H. Du Boulay and C. M. Barron, 259, citing P.R.O., SC 6/1234–5.

3 *36 D.K.R.* App. II, pp. 95–6; *Cal. Chart. R. 1341–1417*, 313–15.

4 Morgan, *War and Society*, 193–6.

5 Ibid. 196–7; *Eng. Hist. Doc.* iv, ed. A. R. Myers, pp. 1222–3; Morris, *Chester*, 29–30; C.C.A.L.S., ZCHB 2, ff. 37, 66.

6 *V.C.H. Ches.* iii. 141.

7 *V.C.H. Ches.* v (2), Cathedral and Close: Monastic Buildings to 1541.

8 *Cal. Pat. 1391–6*, 248–9.

9 *Reign of Ric. II*, 272; *Cal. Close, 1396–9*, 382.

10 *Reign of Ric. II*, 261; *36 D.K.R.* App. II, p. 99; cf. Morgan, *War and Society*, 189, 201.   11 *Reign of Ric. II*, 276.

12 *The Chronicle of Adam of Usk, 1377–1421*, ed. C. Given Wilson, 56–9; Morgan, *War and Society*, 203–4; *J.C.A.S.* xxxi. 36; Ormerod, *Hist. Ches.* iii. 672.

13 *Chronicle of Adam of Usk*, 58–61; Morris, *Chester*, 35–7.

14 P. McNiven, 'Ches. Rising of 1400', *Bull. John Rylands Libr.* lii. 387–9; Morgan, *War and Society*, 205–7.

15 *Cal. Pat. 1399–1401*, 285–6, 385–6.

16 *J.C.A.S.* xxxi. 16.

17 *36 D.K.R.* App. II, pp. 454, 491; Morgan, *War and Society*, 207; *V.C.H. Ches.* v (2), Castle: Administrative and Military Functions.

18 *36 D.K.R.* App. II, p. 101.

Although Abbot Sutton survived, he was subjected to humiliating restrictions, and soon afterwards the appropriations of livings which Richard II had approved were revoked.[1]

The civic authorities appear nevertheless to have reached a somewhat uneasy *modus vivendi* with the new dynasty. The leading citizens were pardoned for their role in the rising,[2] and in 1401 Henry, prince of Wales, confirmed the charters.[3] Late in 1400 the mayor and sheriffs were required to supply provisions protected by an armed guard for an expedition planned by the king and prince,[4] and the portmote was suspended while they fulfilled their commitments.[5] In 1402 the city evidently agreed to provide and man a barge and three small ships in the king's service, and later it was required to furnish all the richer citizens with equipment necessary for its defence.[6] Despite Chester's co-operation, the new dynasty continued to be distrustful, taking sureties to ensure that supplies sold in the city were used to provision royal troops rather than the rebels.[7]

In 1403 Sir Henry Percy ('Hotspur'), lately justice of Chester, stayed in the city and raised the standard of revolt there before the battle of Shrewsbury.[8] The citizens were far less involved with the rebels than in 1400, and indeed the mayor and the constable of the castle were present at Shrewsbury in the king's retinue.[9] After Percy's defeat one of the quarters of his body was sent to Chester, together with the heads of Sir Richard Venables and Sir Richard Vernon.[10] The continuing insecurity of both the new dynasty and the city authorities was demonstrated in the instructions issued by Prince Henry in response to defections in north Wales in the weeks after the battle. The corporation was required to impose a curfew upon all Welshmen visiting Chester, and to ensure that they left their arms at the city gates and did not gather in groups of more than three; all Welsh residents were expelled and any who stayed overnight were threatened with execution. Such measures against the Welsh were the most extreme to be proclaimed in any English city during Owain Glyn Dŵr's revolt.[11] Shortly after their issue the mayor and citizens were pardoned for their role in Hotspur's rebellion, in return for a payment of 300

marks or for supplying shipping for men going to the relief of Beaumaris castle (Ang.).[12]

In 1404 the government still found it necessary to order the citizens not to sell arms or merchandise to the rebels and to commission keepers of roads out of Chester.[13] In 1405 Prince Henry visited the city,[14] and by 1407, when grants of murages were resumed, relations had probably been restored to some semblance of normality.[15] As the Welsh revolt crumbled, Chester witnessed a steady stream of prominent local Welshmen making their way to the castle to submit to the English authorities.[16] Even so, in 1409 the Crown nominated a governor temporarily to replace the Welsh mayor, and in 1412 intervened again when some citizens banded together to prevent a free election.[17] After the Welsh threat receded, no royal visits of note were recorded, a sign perhaps that relations with the Crown remained distant.

In 1442 Chester castle was chosen for the imprisonment of Eleanor Cobham, whose husband, Henry VI's uncle Humphrey, duke of Gloucester, had been justice of Chester 1427–40.[18] The king himself visited Chester in 1445 and reduced the annual farm from £100 to £50, on the grounds that trade had suffered from the silting of the port and that 'restrictions and charges' had been imposed by the Welsh rebellion.[19] His visit marked a period of warmer relations between the city and the Crown. The king's son Edward was created prince of Wales and earl of Chester in 1454, and in 1455 Queen Margaret apparently visited the city to seek support. The queen and the prince and very probably Henry himself were all again in Chester in 1456. After the battle of Blore Heath (Staffs.) in 1459, two of the Yorkist leaders, the earl of Salisbury's sons Thomas and John Neville, were imprisoned in Chester castle.[20]

Despite such links between Chester and the house of Lancaster, in 1460 Richard, duke of York, granted the city's mayor, John Southworth, an annual pension of £10 for past services.[21] In 1461 Edward IV renewed the reduction of the farm, but his anxieties about the city were reflected in a proclamation requiring the mayor and sheriffs of Chester to arrest all within the shire who supported the king's Lancastrian enemies.[22] In 1472

1 *V.C.H. Ches.* iii. 141.

2 e.g. *Cal. Pat.* 1399–1401, 285–6, 385–6.

3 C.C.A.L.S., ZCH 23; Morris, *Chester*, 506.

4 *36 D.K.R.* App. II, p. 101.

5 Morgan, *War and Society*, 211.

6 *36 D.K.R.* App. II, pp. 102, 348.

7 Morris, *Chester*, 43; R. R. Davies, *Revolt of Owain Glyn Dŵr*, 256.

8 *Cal. Close,* 1399–1402, 24, 26; Ormerod, *Hist. Ches.* i. 63; Morris, *Chester*, 43.

9 P. McNiven, 'Men of Ches. and Rebellion of 1403', *T.H.S.L.C.* cxxix. 12, 21.

10 *Cal. Pat.* 1401–5, 293; Morris, *Chester*, 45.

11 Morgan, *War and Society*, 211; Davies, *Owain Glyn Dŵr*, 290–1; *36 D.K.R.* App. II, p. 102.

12 *Cal. Pat.* 1401–5, 330; *36 D.K.R.* App. II, p. 103; Morris, *Chester*, 507–8; C.C.A.L.S., ZCH 24.

13 *36 D.K.R.* App. II, pp. 4, 103, 334, 539.

14 C.C.A.L.S., ZCHB 1, f. 4.

15 Ibid. ZCH 25; *36 D.K.R.* App. II, pp. 103–4.

16 Davies, *Owain Glyn Dŵr*, 123, 296–7.

17 *36 D.K.R.* App. II, pp. 104, 504; C.C.A.L.S., ZCR 469/542; ZMB 2, ff. 62v.–63, 81, 83v., 84v., 85v., 91; Morris, *Chester*, 47.

18 Morris, *Chester*, 54; *V.C.H. Ches.* ii. 13–14.

19 *37 D.K.R.* App. II, p. 137; Morris, *Chester*, 54, 511–14; C.C.A.L.S., ZCH 28.

20 Clayton, *Administration*, 74–90; Morris, *Chester*, 56.

21 *Cal. Pat.* 1461–7, 129.

22 Clayton, *Administration*, 99, quoting P.R.O., CHES 2/134, rot. 8d.

Edward again renewed the reduction of the farm, and in 1484 Richard III cut it further to £30.[1] Even so, by 1485 the citizens' sympathies seem to have been with the Tudors. Their mayor from 1484 to 1486, Sir John Savage (d. 1495), had close links with the Stanleys, and his son, also Sir John (d. 1492), led the left wing of Henry Tudor's forces at Bosworth and was afterwards well rewarded.[2] The serjeant of the Bridgegate, Sir William Troutbeck, also fought for Henry at that battle.[3]

The citizens received their reward in 1486 when Henry VII reduced the annual farm to £20 in perpetuity.[4] The king visited Chester with his queen and his mother in 1493 or 1495, and in 1498 or 1499 his son Prince Arthur attended a performance of an Assumption Day play and presented a silver badge to the Smiths, Cutlers, and Plumbers' company.[5] The main mark of the king's favour was his grant in 1506 of the Great Charter, which constituted the city a county in its own right.[6]

Henry VIII had few dealings with Chester. In 1522 the city was called upon to supply forces to defend the Scottish borders, and the mayor mustered a force of sixty soldiers to serve with Thomas Howard, earl of Surrey.[7] The Dissolution passed largely without incident, although in 1536 one of the city's merchants was imprisoned together with the abbot of Norton and Randle Brereton in Chester castle.[8] In 1543 the city acquired parliamentary representation at Westminster; henceforth it was to return two M.P.s, selected by the aldermen and presented to the freemen for election.[9]

CITY GOVERNMENT AND POLITICS, 1350–1550

THE DECAY OF THE GUILD MERCHANT

By the mid 14th century the roles of the main civic officers had been largely defined. The dominance of the mayor, already well established, was enhanced by the grant of the escheatorship in 1354, and by his increasing control over market offences, presented at inquests held in the courts over which he presided.[10] The activities of the sheriffs, by then elected annually, were gradually restricted to the collection of local dues, policing, and the administration of summary justice for minor offences.[11] The principal institutions remained those of a century before, the portmote and the unitary guild merchant. There was as yet no trace of a body of aldermen and common councilmen, although by 1356 the city authorities (called the mayor and commonalty) collectively owned property in Bridge Street near the Cross.[12]

Although in 1358, in accordance with the charter of 1300, the county sheriff confirmed at the Pentice that Chester was a 'free city',[13] definition of the citizens' liberties continued to trouble relations with the palatinate, especially during the 1350s,[14] and was never fully resolved in Chester's favour. Throughout the later 14th and the 15th century the county court heard cases of theft and assault committed within Chester's liberties, usually it seems because the offenders or their victims were of relatively high status.[15] Occasionally, too, city officers were brought before the shire court for offences committed within the liberties, including illegal trading and extortion, and when there were serious disturbances in the city.[16]

The palatine administration apparently had difficulty in dealing with such matters, especially over its handling in 1349–50 of the murder of the mayor, Bartholomew of Northenden. The culprits were never fully brought to justice: pardons were issued in the early 1350s and 1360 to two of them, and others seem to have gone to Gascony with the Black Prince.[17] Chester, indeed, was apparently notorious for its lawbreakers: in 1354 the prince asserted that there were more evil-doers within the city than in the entire shire outside it, and there were further complaints in 1357.[18]

One source of strife lay in the gradual disintegration of the unitary guild merchant. Signs of conflict were apparent by 1351, when the Black Prince responded to claims by the citizens that 'substantial men of the commonalty' were combining related crafts such as tailoring and drapery, or shoemaking and tanning.[19] In 1361 the city's tanners paid the Black Prince to

1 *37 D.K.R.* App. II, pp. 139–40, 142; Morris, *Chester*, 516–21; C.C.A.L.S., ZCH 30.

2 Ormerod, *Hist. Ches.* i. 713–14; Clayton, *Administration*, 109, 115, 179–80; C. Ross, *Ric. III*, 220.

3 Clayton, *Administration*, 115.

4 Morris, *Chester*, 521–4; C.C.A.L.S., ZCH 31.

5 Morris, *Chester*, 63–4; Ormerod, *Hist. Ches.* i. 234; *REED: Chester*, pp. xliii, 514.

6 C.C.A.L.S., ZCH 32.

7 Morris, *Chester*, 67.

8 Ibid.; Ormerod, *Hist. Ches.* i. 502.

9 *V.C.H. Ches.* ii. 98, 110–11.

10 C.C.A.L.S., ZCH 18; ZQCR 2, 4–5, 10–11; *Sel. R. Chester City Cts.* p. xviii.

11 C.C.A.L.S., ZCHB 2, ff. 66v.–67.

12 Ibid. ZCHD 2/1.

13 Ibid. ZCHB 2, ff. 66v.–67.

14 e.g. *Blk. Prince's Reg.* iii. 291.

15 P.R.O., CHES 25/10, m. 12; CHES 25/14, m. 24d.; CHES 25/16, m. 15. Thanks are due to Dr. Jane Laughton for these and the following references.

16 P.R.O., CHES 25/8, mm. 1–4, 14, 16; CHES 25/10, mm. 33d., 36d.; CHES 25/12, mm. 6–7; CHES 29/129, m. 1; CHES 29/110, mm. 4d., 7d.

17 *Blk. Prince's Reg.* iii. 10, 15, 29; *36 D.K.R.* App. II, pp. 146, 166, 192; Morris, *Chester*, 24.

18 *Blk. Prince's Reg.* iii. 161, 271; cf. *Cal. Pat. 1348–50*, 411.

19 *Blk. Prince's Reg.* iii. 50.

establish a monopoly in the production of leather, but despite attempts to prevent the shoemakers from encroaching on their craft, by 1370 the ruling had been reversed.[1] Evidently such disputes could no longer be regulated within the unitary guild, and several occupational groupings were near to constituting themselves into separate corporations. Relations within and between the crafts could still affect the general peace, as in the great affray which took place in front of St. Peter's church in 1399, when a group of master craftsmen involved in clothmaking attacked their own journeymen. Such tensions perhaps diminished as the craft guilds consolidated their position in the early 15th century.[2]

THE EMERGENCE OF THE ASSEMBLY

The gradual dissolution of the earlier medieval framework of government was accompanied by the emergence of new civic structures, a process which seems to have crystallized in the 1390s, when the city was the object of Richard II's especial favour. Of the new institutions, the most significant was the aldermanate or Twenty-Four, in place by the early 1390s.[3] Its early members, who despite their precise collective designation varied in number from 26 to over 30,[4] were mostly former mayors and sheriffs and were associated with the current office-holders in making ordinances for the city; they met with the mayor to deliberate on the common good, and accompanied him on civic business, duties enforceable by fines exacted by the sheriffs.[5]

By the 1390s Chester had also acquired a treasurer to account for the city rents[6] and a 'common clerk of the city', evidently the successor of the custodian of the seal of Statute Merchant, charged with legal business and soon known as the clerk to the Pentice.[7] Except for the clerk, civic officers were evidently elected, although the nature of the franchise is not clear.[8] By the 1390s, then, the city had a nascent corporation; indeed, in 1391 its governing body expressly referred to itself in such terms when it sought to lease the Dee Mills from the Crown.[9]

The period also saw the creation of the Mayor's Book, containing a mixture of administrative and judicial business.[10] In 1407 the earliest surviving orders attributed to the Assembly were recorded, prohibiting the use of royal writs to the prejudice of the city courts.[11] Other early orders, not so attributed and issued from the 1390s, *inter alia* regulated the duties of freemen and the trading activities of the city's butchers, fishmongers, bakers, brewers, and cooks, prohibited the throwing of rubbish into the streets, and set a fine for bringing a cart with iron-bound wheels across the renovated bridge.[12]

By the 1430s accounts were presented to the Assembly annually by two treasurers.[13] The corporation then owned shops throughout the city, including seven beneath the Pentice and others at the Cross, in Ironmongers' Row, next to the Eastgate, and in Watergate Street. It also owned property in Commonhall and Cow Lanes, by the quarry outside the Northgate, near Capelgate and the mills, and in the Crofts. By 1442 the rents amounted to over £12 a year. Other more variable sources of income derived from fees payable for entry into the freedom and for writs of error,[14] and from local customs collected by the sheriffs on merchandise entering and leaving the city.[15] By 1440 the civic officials also included two murengers, responsible for maintaining the defences and using income derived from customs levied at the gates and other duties.[16]

The emergent corporation was closely connected with the old guild merchant, admissions to which were recorded from the 1390s in the Mayor's Book and equated with the freedom of the city.[17] Obtainable by inheritance or payment of a large entry fine, and perhaps dependent upon a residential qualification, the freedom brought with it the duty to contribute to the city's administrative burdens and expenses.[18] It probably also helped to secure membership of the guild of St. Anne, revived in 1393 as a chantry foundation for the civic élite.[19]

Beneath the Assembly, a further tier of administration developed from the ancient serjeanties. Granted before the charter of 1300, those offices were essentially benefices held of the earl and sat uncomfortably with newer civic institutions, which derived their authority from the citizens themselves.[20] Gradually they lost their early policing functions, although the administrative subdivisions of the city remained based on the four principal gates and streets. By the late 14th century, a group of 16 leading property holders or 'custumaries' (*custumarii*) supervised policing activities within those

1 Ibid. 472.
2 C.C.A.L.S., ZMB 1, ff. 55v.–56; *REED: Chester*, 5–6; *36 D.K.R.* App. II, p. 99.
3 C.C.A.L.S., ZQCR 10–11; ZMB 1, ff. 16v., 62v.
4 e.g. ibid. ZMB 1, f. 62v.; ZMB 4, f. 50.
5 e.g. ibid. ZAF 1, f. 1; ZMB 1, ff. 16v., 61v.; ZQCR 10–11.
6 e.g. ibid. ZMB 1, f. 41v.
7 Ibid. ZMB 2, f. 54; *36 D.K.R.* App. II, p. 97; Morris, *Chester*, 204; *Archives and Recs. of Chester*, ed. A. M. Kennett, 35.
8 C.C.A.L.S., ZAF 1, f. 1.
9 *36 D.K.R.* App. II, p. 96.
10 C.C.A.L.S., ZMB 1, *passim*.
11 Ibid. ZAF 1, f. 2.

12 Ibid. ff. 3–4v.; ZMB 1, ff. 16 and v., 19–20; Morris, *Chester*, 383.
13 B.L. Harl. MS. 2158, ff. 31–66.
14 Ibid. ff. 31v.–34v.
15 *Chester Customs Accts.* 8–11.
16 Ibid. 15–16; C.C.A.L.S., ZMUB 1; ZMUR 1.
17 C.C.A.L.S., ZMB 1, ff. 9, 42; ZMB 2, ff. 14v.–15; ZMB 3, ff. 15v.–16, 25, 56–7, 105, 106v.; ZMB 4, ff. 45–6; Morris, *Chester*, 383.   18 Morris, *Chester*, 383.
19 Below, this chapter: Religion (Guilds, Confraternities, and Chantries).
20 Thanks are due to Mr. P. H. W. Booth for discussion of the serjeanties.

subdivisions, including guarding condemned felons and keeping the Christmas watch; other duties were performed by bailiffs, answerable to the sheriffs, whose main responsibility was the collection of sums of money, known as estreats (*extracta*), four times a year. The nature of the estreats is not clear but the sums involved were quite large, ranging from *c.* £3 to over £16 for a single street in a single term.[1]

THE CIVIC ÉLITE

Throughout the later 14th and earlier 15th century the main civic offices were dominated by a relatively small group of families, mostly merchants, such as the Blunds, Bellyetters, Hopes, Hattons, Ewloes, and Whitmores. Mayors generally held office repeatedly. John Blund, for example, was mayor for eight terms in the 1350s and John Armourer for seven between 1385 and 1395.[2] Such men were often rich: Armourer, for instance, left 60 pounds of silver in 1396 to establish a chantry in Holy Trinity church,[3] and John Ewloe (mayor 1405–10, d. 1418) owned property in Bridge Street, Watergate Street, Cuppin Lane, and Cow Lane, land in the fields of Handbridge and Claverton, and fishing stalls in the Dee, as well as extensive holdings in right of his first wife in and near the city.[4] A similar linkage of city tenements and local rural manors is evident in the estate of John Whitmore (mayor 1412–15), who at his death in 1438 held 15 messuages, 15 gardens, and an undercroft in Chester together with considerable property in the environs, including the manor of Thurstaston, and land and fisheries in Caldy and Guilden Sutton.[5]

Such men played a dominant role in city life, not always on the side of law and order. John Walsh, member of a mayoral family if not himself mayor, and in the early 1390s farmer of the Dee Mills, was in 1393 indicted for a killing and briefly imprisoned.[6] John Armourer was a leading figure in the dispute with Richard II's courtiers in 1394.[7] Though they were not in office at the time, both John Ewloe and John Whitmore were involved in disorder in 1416, while the then mayor William Hawarden was actually imprisoned.[8]

A notable element within the city élite was a powerful group of Welsh descent. Their presence caused especial difficulty during Owain Glyn Dŵr's revolt in the early 15th century, when under pressure from Prince Henry and the palatine administration, the

city promulgated harsh decrees against Welsh residents and visitors.[9] Such tensions culminated in 1408 in a serious dispute between the civic authorities, then led by the Welshman John Ewloe, and William Venables, constable of the castle. Venables and over fifty members of his retinue were bound to keep peace with the mayor and sheriffs, and in 1409 both Venables and Ewloe were suspended from office. To replace the mayor, the Crown appointed Sir William Brereton, sheriff of Cheshire, as 'keeper and governor' of the city, and his deputy presided over the portmote and crownmote until Ewloe was re-elected later in 1409. The case provoked such discord within the city that the following election, in 1410, was disrupted by the armed intervention of Robert Chamberlain, a former sheriff and apparently a member of Venables's affinity. He was evidently unsuccessful, since the new mayor, Roger Potter, was one of the leading litigants against the former constable. In 1411 a 'day of reconciliation' (*dies amoris*) was celebrated between Venables and the leading townsmen, and in 1412, under the terms awarded by the arbitrators, Venables and his affinity agreed to pay reparations to various citizens.[10] Nevertheless, the city apparently remained riven by feud. A further attempt at armed interference in the elections of 1412 caused the Crown to commission the current mayor and other nominees to choose the next mayor,[11] while in 1416 Ewloe, his son Edmund, and their Welsh retainers attacked another citizen in Eastgate Street. Shortly afterwards Edmund and his fellow Welshmen broke into the house of John Hope, lately sheriff and soon to be mayor.[12] Further disturbances in the same year included an attack on two citizens with the connivance of the mayor, William Hawarden, who was briefly imprisoned in Chester castle but after the lapse of a year regained the mayoralty.[13] The fact that other leading citizens, including William Venables and two former mayors, were required to give guarantees to keep the peace suggests considerable discord among the civic élite at that time.[14]

CITY GOVERNMENT, 1430–1506

From the 1430s the long mayoral tenures characteristic of the 13th and 14th centuries ceased, and except for a few two- or three-year terms in the 1440s, 1450s, and 1470s the office changed hands every year.[15] Although the openings for a powerful individual to exercise a prolonged ascendancy were thereby diminished, the

1 Morris, *Chester*, 553–4; C.C.A.L.S., ZMB 1, ff. 3, 44v.–46, 65, 67; ZMB 2, ff. 12–13, 32v., 47v.–49, 61–3, 98, 109; ZMB 3, ff. 19–20; ZMB 4, f. 36.
2 *V.C.H. Ches.* v (2), Lists of Mayors and Sheriffs.
3 P.R.O., WALE 29/291.
4 Ibid. CHES 3/30, no. 10; *25 D.K.R.* 42.
5 *37 D.K.R.* App. II, p. 790.
6 *36 D.K.R.* App. II, pp. 96, 504; P.R.O., SC 6/790/3, m. 3.
7 Above, this chapter: City and Crown, 1350–1550.
8 Ibid.; *37 D.K.R.* App. II, p. 789.

9 Above, this chapter: City and Crown, 1350–1550.
10 *36 D.K.R.* App. II, pp. 90, 104, 387, 493; C.C.A.L.S., ZAF 1, f. 1; ZCHB 2, ff. 67v.–68.
11 *36 D.K.R.* App. II, pp. 104, 504.
12 Morris, *Chester*, 48–9; *37 D.K.R.* App. II, pp. 96, 267; *V.C.H. Ches.* v (2), Lists of Mayors and Sheriffs.
13 Morris, *Chester*, 49; *37 D.K.R.* App. II, pp. 354, 459, 759–60; *V.C.H. Ches.* v (2), Lists of Mayors and Sheriffs.
14 *37 D.K.R.* App. II, pp. 96, 167, 354, 459, 737.
15 *V.C.H. Ches.* v (2), Lists of Mayors and Sheriffs.

power of the mayor continued to increase. By the early 15th century he had control of the markets, dealing with the more serious trading offences, suppressing illegal markets, and issuing regulations relating to prices, hours of sale, disposal of waste, and the killing of beasts.[1] By the late 1440s although his court met less often, its sessions lasted longer, and its competence had been extended with the holding of indictments relating to every type of offence.[2]

In 1450 it was alleged that the citizens had 'from ancient time' assembled in the common hall to choose the mayor, sheriffs, and other officials of the corporation, evidence that by then freemen were participating in civic elections.[3] Shortly afterwards, a formal body of common councilmen, the Forty-Eight, was added to the Assembly. As with the aldermen, numbers fluctuated, on occasion rising to over sixty; in 1453 the names were arranged by the four quarters of the city, which perhaps played a part in the selection procedures. Two complete sections of the list each comprised 22 names, of which 10–12 were marked as 'sworn'.[4] The councilmen's duties are uncertain, but as representatives of the citizens their main role was probably, as later, to watch over civic finances; in the 1450s, for example, a committee of four aldermen and eight councilmen audited the treasurers' accounts.[5] The councilmen presumably also played a part in the election of the city sheriff, who seems to have been chosen by the Assembly as a whole.[6]

Almost certainly the emergence of the common councilmen was linked with changes in the admission to the freedom, from 1452 made in full portmote and limited to resident citizens.[7] That restriction, evidently an innovation, marked the emergence of a division between the franchise and the guild merchant, which thereafter seems to have been primarily concerned with non-residents involved in the city's trade under the supervision of officials known as leavelookers, apparently first recorded in 1454–5. By the 1470s the leavelookers, already perhaps regarded as the leaders of the common councilmen, were responsible for receiving entry subscriptions from non-freemen and for levying a modest tax on their merchandise to pay for the entertainment of distinguished visitors to Chester. By then, too, such foreign members of the guild paid the local customs on goods entering and leaving the city.[8] Henceforth, it seems, the crucial

qualification for participation in civic government was the freedom, which was linked with membership of an appropriate craft guild.[9]

By the later 15th century the city's government was thus in the hands of an Assembly which comprised the mayor and sheriffs, the aldermen or Twenty-Four, and the councilmen or Forty-Eight. It was served by three groups of annually elected officials: two treasurers, chosen from the aldermen; two leavelookers, chosen from the common councilmen; and two murengers, also chosen from the councilmen but by the aldermen alone. Former sheriffs automatically became aldermen.[10] Other salaried officials included the recorder, swordbearer, and serjeants-at-mace who attended the mayor and sheriffs.[11] Throughout the late 15th century the Assembly's finances continued to depend upon rents from its property, fairly stable at £12–£16 a year, and more variable income from fees and tolls.[12] It sufficed for the fixed annual expenditure on the officers' fees, but exceptional costs, such as the rebuilding of the Pentice in the 1460s, had to be financed by a special levy on the citizens.[13]

A further institution linked with the Assembly was the fraternity of St. George, like that of St. Anne primarily a religious guild, which was housed in St. Peter's church, probably in the south aisle. First mentioned in 1462, when it was governed by four masters or wardens,[14] it received bequests from leading mayoral and aldermanic families in the late 15th and early 16th century and by then was so much part of civic government that its stewards or seneschals were listed in the Mayor's Books with the civic dignitaries.[15]

Somewhat less closely associated with the Assembly were the craft guilds, which by 1450 numbered over twenty. Governed by stewards and aldermen, they derived their generally modest income from fees payable on admission and annually thereafter.[16] Although they had considerable independence in the conduct of their affairs, they were ultimately subordinate to the Assembly, which settled disputes within the membership of a particular guild or between guilds, and on occasion decided the level of entry fees; they played a large part in civic life, most notably in the mystery plays and in regulating economic activity, especially through the definition of trading standards, the purchase of raw materials, and the determination of the terms of apprenticeship and journeymen's

1 C.C.A.L.S., ZAF 1, ff. 3–4; ZMB 1, ff. 2, 5, 6v.–7, 16v., 36, 37v., 52v., 69; ZMB 4, ff. 34, 53; ZSB 5, f. 35 and v.; Morris, *Chester*, 400–1.
2 C.C.A.L.S., ZMB 4.
3 Johnson, 'Aspects', 42, citing C.C.A.L.S., ZSB 15.
4 C.C.A.L.S., ZMB 4, f. 55v.
5 B.L. Harl. MS. 2158, f. 44; cf. C.C.A.L.S., ZMB 5, f. 46v.
6 Johnson, 'Aspects', 46, 50.
7 C.C.A.L.S., ZAF 1, f. 15v.
8 Ibid. ZMB 5, f. 180; ZMB 6, f. 1; B.L. Harl. MS. 2158, f. 44; *Chester Customs Accts.* 16; *Archives of Chester*, 14, 25–6; cf. Morris, *Chester*, 381.

9 Johnson, 'Aspects', 251–2.
10 Ibid. 56–7; C.C.A.L.S., ZMB 5, ff. 46v., 69v.–70, 180–181v.; J. Laughton, 'Prolegomena to Societal Hist. of Late Medieval Chester' (Leicester Univ. M.A. thesis, 1987), 8, 13.
11 B.L. Harl. MS. 2158, f. 44; cf. ibid. ff. 48, 63; Morris, *Chester*, 527–8, 534, 536.
12 B.L. Harl. MS. 2158, ff. 44–66; C.C.A.L.S., ZTAR 1/2–4.
13 B.L. Harl. MS. 2158, ff. 45–7, 49–50.
14 Ibid. Harl. MS. 2063, f. 113.
15 e.g. C.C.A.L.S., ZMB 12, f. 4; ZMB 13, f. 2.
16 Rest of para. based on Johnson, 'Aspects', 247–9; *V.C.H. Ches.* v (2), Craft Guilds: Origins, Organization before 1750.

employment. Nevertheless, there was not, as elsewhere, a close linkage of guild and civic office, although company stewards on occasion became constables or common councilmen.[1]

The administrative subdivisions of the city remained focused upon the four main streets, from the 1460s together with occasional additional units based on Foregate Street, Handbridge, and Upper Northgate Street. By then, although they had ceased to be the vehicle for the collection of estreats, they provided the framework for imposing assessments and amercements and accounting for civic property.[2] From c. 1450 they were associated with constables, who could number as many as five or even nine in a large division such as Eastgate Street or Bridge Street. Like the common councilmen, constables were often listed in the Mayor's Book grouped by administrative division, with a note about whether they had been sworn in.[3] Their main duties appear to have been carrying out the Assembly's orders. In 1487, for example, when the administrative areas for which they were responsible were known as wards, they were ordered to summon the city's brewers to have their measures stamped.[4]

Power lay above all with the mayor and aldermen, the latter generally former mayors and sheriffs holding office for life. Such men continued to be drawn mainly from the leading merchant families, often interrelated and including mercers, drapers, goldsmiths, glovers, ironmongers, and dyers.[5] Mayors might also include members of the local gentry, such as the Masseys, Savages, and Southworths.[6] Sheriffs were largely drawn from the major civic families.[7] By the late 15th century, although they included junior members of aldermanic families, the common councilmen were more likely to be drawn from the city's prosperous artisans.[8]

THE CHARTER OF 1506

In 1506 the city was given county status and its constitution was formalized by royal charter.[9] The arrangements appear generally to have been those in operation in the later 15th century, with a few minor amendments. The number of aldermen was fixed at 24 but the councilmen were reduced to 40. The freemen were deemed part of the corporation and given the right to elect the aldermen and councilmen. The charter also prescribed the procedures for electing the principal civic officers: the mayor was to be chosen by the aldermen and sheriffs from two aldermen named

by the freemen; one of the two sheriffs, the king's, was to be nominated by the aldermen, while the other, the city's, was elected by the whole Assembly. In confirmation of his long-exercised responsibilities, the mayor was made clerk of the market.

The charter also amended the structure of the city's courts. While confirming that the portmote, Pentice, and crownmote were to be held as formerly, it added two others, the county court of the city and quarter sessions. The county court of the city, a necessary aspect of its new status, had very little business. Quarter sessions, on the other hand, was responsible for trying all misdemeanours and most felonies on the city's behalf; in practice it took some business from the portmote but most from the crownmote, for which only the most serious felonies were reserved. Its justices were the mayor, recorder, and former mayors, who constituted the senior aldermen.[10]

Another administrative change probably introduced in the early 16th century was a rearrangement of the wards and their association with aldermen. Although in 1507–8 the councilmen and constables continued to appear in the civic record in unequal groups drawn from the four main streets, by then the constables were further subdivided according to the wards of named aldermen, numbering nine altogether.[11] By the 1530s there were 15 wards, to each of which was attached an alderman and one or two constables, and each equipped with a pair of stocks. The 12 wards within the walls were named after the eight intramural parish churches, together with Eastgate, Northgate, Cornmarket (southern Northgate Street), and Beastmarket (Lower Bridge Street) wards; the three outside were St. Giles's and St. John's to the east and St. Thomas's to the north.[12] Arrangements appear still to have been relatively fluid. In 1538–9 twenty-three constables were listed in ten groups, each a ward associated with an alderman, while in 1548–9 the constables were arranged by the four main streets.[13]

CITY AND SHIRE IN THE EARLY 16TH CENTURY

Although the terms of the charter were adhered to for about a decade after 1506, thereafter its provision for annual elections of aldermen and councilmen was progressively undermined. In 1518 a bylaw provided that aldermen who died during their term could be replaced without election, and shortly afterwards it became customary for the Assembly to make such

1 e.g. C.C.A.L.S., ZMB 6, ff. 3v., 30, 166v.–170.

2 B.L. Harl. MS. 2158, ff. 45–7, 51v.–52v.; C.C.A.L.S., ZMB 6, f. 83v.; ZMB 7, ff. 2v., 120; ZMB 9; ZSB 1, f. 136.

3 C.C.A.L.S., ZMB 4, f. 21; ZMB 5, ff. 41, 69v., 180–1; ZMB 6, ff. 3v., 33v.

4 Ibid. ZMB 6, ff. 166v.–170.

5 e.g. Laughton, 'Prolegomena', 20–1, 24.

6 Ibid. 14; Clayton, *Administration*, 179–81; Jones, *Ch. in Chester*, 97, 155; *V.C.H. Ches.* v (2), Lists of Mayors and Sheriffs.

7 Laughton, 'Prolegomena', 14–15.

8 Ibid. 13–16.

9 Acct. of charter based, except where stated otherwise, on Morris, *Chester*, 524–40; Johnson, 'Aspects', 37, 42–3, 46, 52; C.C.A.L.S., ZCH 32.

10 Johnson, 'Aspects', 180–1.

11 C.C.A.L.S., ZMB 9, unfol. (1507–8).

12 Ibid. ZAB 1, ff. 36–37v.

13 Ibid. ZMB 13, f. 2; ZMB 15.

appointments for life. By 1533 the annual election of councilmen had also been subverted, some even being appointed purely on the nomination of the mayor. Such infringements of the charter were further compounded from the 1520s by the emergence in the Assembly of a group known as the sheriff-peers, consisting of former sheriffs and holding office for life.[1]

The main civic offices were dominated by drapers, merchants, and mercers, with terms served by a variety of other craftsmen.[2] Whatever their occupational identity, many office-holders were engaged in Continental trade, including in the period 1500–60 over half the mayors and just under half the sheriffs. A wider range of twenty or so occupations was represented among the common councillors.[3] Repeated service as mayor was quite common: 10 men served twice, 4 three times, and Thomas Smith eight or nine times.[4] Such a limited circulation of office does not suggest an oligarchy of new men pushing hard for access to political power commensurate with their wealth, but rather a group with established associations linked to the county and continually strengthening its connexions and drawing in new blood by marriage and business contacts.

Civic office was held by members of established county families such as the Alderseys, Balls, Davenports, Duttons, Smiths, and Staffordshire Sneyds. The close weave of county and city relationships is illustrated by the Aldersey family, seated at Aldersey and Spurstow in east Cheshire, which provided five office-holders. Men such as Ralph Aldersey, sheriff in 1541, maintained contact with their gentry relatives, with grandees such as William Brereton, and with leading merchants from the city itself.[5] Similarly, Fulk Dutton (d. 1558), a draper and three times mayor, had links with such county families as the Leghs, Savages, and Egertons, and with leading urban officials including the recorders of Chester and Liverpool.[6]

County influence was especially visible in Chester during the mayoralties of Sir Piers Dutton, elected three times in succession from 1512; resentment in some quarters is evident from the fact that on the third occasion the election was declared unlawful and Dutton was replaced as mayor.[7] Accusations of county interference in civic elections also surfaced under the reforming mayor Henry Gee.[8]

Other reasons for suspicion of the county emanated

from the civic courts. In 1506 Chester's independence from the shire was reaffirmed when it was declared a county of itself. Nevertheless, by then the city courts had already been affected by the development of business at the palatinate exchequer court, which offered a pragmatic approach and balanced and workable solutions. Even in the late 15th century men arrested by the city sheriffs for debt had successfully appealed to the exchequer on the grounds that they were avowry men under the special protection of the palatinate. The sheriffs were summoned by writ to appear in the exchequer to explain their actions, and the justice and chamberlain eventually decreed that they should desist from imprisoning privileged tenants of the earl, conceding, however, the right to exact reasonable fines if the avowry men in question had merchandise or exercised a craft within the city.[9] The growth of such jurisdiction during the early 16th century, and the regular evocation of cases to the exchequer by writs of *certiorari*, caused tension between the city courts and those at the castle.[10] Although such actions were often taken simply to ensure relatively speedy and balanced results, they might also be used more controversially, against the city's courts and officials; there were cases, for example, in which the city sheriffs were accused of wrongful imprisonment or neglecting their duties towards the plaintiffs.[11] By 1540, when the Assembly ruled that no suits could be taken out of the city except by licence from the mayor, signs of friction between the two jurisdictions were becoming evident.[12]

HENRY GEE AND THE REFORM OF CIVIC GOVERNMENT[13]

By the 1530s the city was developing a strong sense of its identity, fostered by emphasis upon its ceremonial and by the first stirrings of an interest in and embellishment of a partly mythic civic past.[14] Such developments were especially evident during the two mayoralties of Henry Gee (1533–4, 1539–40). In his first term Gee, who was determined to invest the city's government with a proper sense of dignity and order, began the Assembly Book, a record of the Assembly's orders, the first entries of which included a list of previous office-holders, a description of the city's boundaries, and a list of local customs duties and

1 Ibid. ZAB 1, ff. 74, 85; Johnson, 'Aspects', 37–9.

2 Following three paras. are by Dr. J. I. Kermode.

3 K. P. Wilson, 'Port of Chester in Later Middle Ages' (Liverpool Univ. Ph.D. thesis, 1966), i. 162; C.C.A.L.S., ZMB 8, ff. 10–11; ZMB 12, ff. 73v., 76; ZMB 12, ff. 221–4; ZMB 14, f. 3.

4 *V.C.H. Ches.* v (2), Lists of Mayors and Sheriffs.

5 Ormerod, *Hist. Ches.* iii. 739–40; Wilson, 'Port of Chester', i. 163–4; *39 D.K.R.* 3.

6 C.C.A.L.S., WS 8/1; Ormerod, *Hist. Ches.* iii. 374; *Lancs. and Ches. Wills and Inventories*, ii (Chetham Soc. [o.s.], li), 93, 214.

7 C.C.A.L.S., ZCX 3, f. 51.

8 Ibid. ZAB 1, ff. 58–9.

9 T. J. Thornton, 'Political Society in Early Tudor Ches. 1480–1560' (Oxf. Univ. D.Phil. thesis, 1993), 114–15, 117–18, 121; R. Stewart-Brown, 'Avowries of Ches.' *E.H.R.* xxix. 41–55; *V.C.H. Ches.* ii. 4.

10 Thornton, 'Political Society', 113–28, 137.

11 Ibid. 124–5.

12 C.C.A.L.S., ZAB 1, f. 72; cf. ibid. f. 118.

13 This acct. was written by Dr. J. I. Kermode; cf. J. Kermode, 'New Brooms in Early Tudor Chester', *Government, Religion, and Society in Northern Eng. 1000–1700*, ed. J. C. Appleby and P. Dalton, 144–58.

14 *V.C.H. Ches.* v (2), Plays, Sports, and Customs before 1700.

officials' fees. Especially concerned about the quality of government, Gee sought to prevent mayoral nomination of aldermen, and decreed that henceforth all elections to the Forty should be by the Assembly meeting in the Pentice.[1] During his second mayoralty he addressed another abuse, that of non-freemen holding civic office, blaming favouritism on the part of mayors, and the general decay of the body of freemen. To prevent 'gentlemen's servants of the county being preferred to the offices and rooms [of the city]', it was agreed that only properly admitted freemen were to hold office, and that the mayor and sheriffs could remove anyone who was not so qualified, or otherwise incompetent, and replace him on the advice of the aldermen.[2]

Although there is no evidence that the city's finances were particularly weak, Gee complained in 1539–40 about mayoral irresponsibility and ordered that the whole council be consulted about expenditure, and that only honest men be allowed in the city's exchequer and then only when accompanied by a sheriff. Other orders made during his second mayoralty included a ban on the sale of common lands to protect the city's rent income, and the regulation of the appointment of the city recorder and lesser officials.[3]

Both puritan and reforming, Gee had a wide range of concerns. He acted against unlawful gaming, drink, and excessive celebrations on Christmas Day. He introduced regulations concerning women's proper dress and parties accompanying childbirth and churching. He proposed to list legitimate beggars by ward, and required the able-bodied to present themselves for work each day and all children aged six to attend school. He even forbade women aged between 14 and 40 to serve ale, invoking the need to preserve the city's good reputation in order to attract visitors.[4]

Although Gee's attempts to end the nomination of councilmen by mayors met with little success,[5] periodic efforts were made to maintain a high standard of civic service for the common good. In 1549–50, for example, candidates for the shrievalty were required first to have served as leavelookers, those evading office were fined, and members of the common council were

required to wear their tippets. In 1554 the election of new councillors was placed under the control of the existing council as well as the mayor, and attempts were made to ensure better attendance at the city quarter sessions. The worship of the aldermen, in their capacity as justices of the peace, was emphasized by ordering them to wear their scarlet robes on eight popular holy days.[6] Aldermen in particular had a penchant for enhancing the aura of civic office, and several left silver or gilt goblets or other treasures for the use of the mayor, at home or in the Pentice.[7]

The cost of running the city government continued to be met, in part, by rent from the corporate estate, which from the 1530s had a book value of *c.* £25 and a collected rent income of just under £20; as earlier, the remainder of the city's income of *c.* £50 was derived from tolls and fees. Expenditure hovered around £45 in 1547–8 and 1558–9, some £22 accounted for in salaries. Civic officers and servants were also paid a fixed percentage of local tolls and customs, and some, such as the serjeants-at-mace and the yeoman of the Pentice, received some victuals in addition to their livery. The city accounts apparently maintained a healthy surplus each year, but following complaints that city money was spent unwisely, from 1540 expenditure had to be sanctioned by the whole council.[8]

Clearing ditches and watercourses, supplying water, paving the main streets, and repairing the walls were constant concerns of the Assembly.[9] Public works, both inside and beyond the city walls, benefited from charitable bequests. Prominent citizens left cash towards the repair of the bridges at Bridge Trafford and Tilston, the roads between Chester and Hawarden (Flints.), the new quay in Wirral, and the lanes in the city.[10] As part of its interest in maintaining law and order, the Assembly ordered in 1503 that a curfew be observed after eight o'clock, and that former mayors, sheriffs, and innkeepers should hang a lighted lantern outside their houses during winter months.[11] A similar concern that the city should not become a haven for felons led the mayor to act promptly to prevent parliament from transferring the right of sanctuary to Chester from Manchester in 1542.[12]

ECONOMY AND SOCIETY, 1350–1550

Medieval Chester housed no industry of national importance and, as a west-facing port, was unable to participate in Continental trade to any significant extent. The city's economy was broadly based but its

activities were small in scale and none dominated. Although Chester did not share the spectacular success enjoyed by towns more closely associated with the wool and cloth trades, it was spared the consequences of the

1 C.C.A.L.S., ZAB 1, f. 74.
2 Ibid. ff. 58–9.   3 Ibid. ff. 69–70v., 74v.
4 Ibid. ff. 60, 62, 70, 72.   5 Cf. ibid. f. 85.
6 Ibid. ff. 74v., 79v.–80, 83, 85–6, 92.
7 Ibid. f. 81; ibid. WS 5/1, 6/7, 8/1, 3; EDA 2/1, ff. 163–4; 3 *Sheaf,* xviii, pp. 88–9, 99.
8 C.C.A.L.S., ZTAR 1/7, 10; ZAB 1, ff. 41–9, 53–8, 74v.

9 Ibid. ZAB 1, f. 78v.; ZMUB 1–4, *passim;* Morris, *Chester,* 265–6, 275, 281–3.
10 3 *Sheaf,* xvii, p. 69; xviii, pp. 88, 92, 99; xxiii, p. 37; *Lancs. and Ches. Wills and Inventories,* ii (Chetham Soc. [o.s.], li), 8; C.C.A.L.S., EDA 2/1, ff. 163–4; WS 6/7, 8/3.
11 Morris, *Chester,* 274–5; C.C.A.L.S., ZAB 1, f. 66v.
12 C.C.A.L.S., ZAB 1, f. 75.

dramatic slumps in those industries. Even so, for much of the period the city was far from prosperous, and occasionally, as in the 1450s, in considerable decay. The citizens claimed in 1484 that it was 'wholly destroyed' because of the silting of the harbour, and in 1486 that it was 'thoroughly ruined . . . nearly one quarter destroyed' because access for shipping had been impossible for 200 years and Welsh traders avoided it because of high tolls.[1] Although such claims were undoubtedly exaggerated, they may well have reflected a depressed economy. By the 1490s, however, there were signs of revival and in the early 16th century Chester prospered.[2]

Throughout the period, commercial property remained dense around the High Cross, under the Pentice, up Northgate Street, down Bridge Street, and to a lesser extent westwards down Watergate Street.[3] In the early 16th century, while some plots were 'void' or in decay,[4] there was new building in Love Lane, Lower Bridge Street, and in the 'Boll Yard' near the corn market.[5] Commercial potential determined property values, with the highest rents of 27s.–30s. on the shops under and next to the Pentice, and on a house and cellar by the Eastgate.[6]

CHESTER AND ITS REGION

Chester continued to play a role as the provincial capital of the north-western plain. The city served as an important market, an administrative and ecclesiastical centre, and the premier port of the region. The origin of outsiders using its courts, although they accounted for no more than 7 per cent of cases in the early 16th century, was indicative of the extent of that region.[7] Those from elsewhere in Cheshire and the Welsh were the biggest groups. The former were drawn mainly from north and west Cheshire, with a few from market towns in mid Cheshire such as Frodsham, Northwich, Middlewich, and Nantwich.[8] Most Welsh

litigants came from Denbigh, Wrexham, Mold, and Flintshire, a few from Beaumaris, Caernarfon, Conwy, and Colwyn (Denb.).[9] After them, the largest group was from Lancashire, especially Manchester and its region.[10]

The Rural Hinterland. Even in 1550 Chester had strong agricultural interests. Pigs roamed the streets in 1549 and freemen grazed sheep and other livestock on the city commons. Arable land was rented from the corporation, people had barns for storage, and farming was a common byemployment.[11] Several overseas merchants had large country estates and farms, or were members of established gentry families such as the Alderseys and Bostocks. Most of their property was probably inherited rather than newly acquired.[12]

Livestock was the mainstay of the local agrarian economy. Chester's market, protected by the prohibition in 1357 of new markets within 4 leagues of the city,[13] continued to be closely linked with the marshland pastures around the Dee and Mersey estuaries, and more importantly with the mixed farming of the rich townships to its south and east.[14] The city had especially close connexions with Christleton parish, barely 2 miles east of the Cross,[15] where farmers concentrated on fattening livestock and there was an occasional cattle market.[16] The city also obtained grain and above all meat from neighbouring parts of Wales.[17] Townsmen continued to buy land near Chester, seeing it as a source of wealth and status. In the early 15th century, for example, John Ewloe owned land in Handbridge, Claverton, and Mollington,[18] and John Whitmore in Caldy and Guilden Sutton;[19] both men served several terms as mayor.[20] Cestrians also owned fishgarths and fishtraps along the western shore of Wirral.[21]

The inhabitants of the hinterland used Chester's credit facilities and enforced debts at the Pentice

1 Morris, *Chester*, 516–21.
2 This acct. is based on the research which underlies J. W. Laughton, 'Aspects of Social and Econ. Hist. of Late Medieval Chester, 1350–*c.* 1500' (Camb. Univ. Ph.D. thesis, 1994), and J. Kermode, 'Trade of Late Medieval Chester, 1500–50', *Progress and Problems in Medieval Eng.* ed. R. Britnell and J. Hatcher, 286–307.
3 e.g. C.C.A.L.S., ZAB 1, ff. 53–8; ibid. EDA 2/1, ff. 123–4.
4 Ibid. ZAB 1, f. 38v.; 3 *Sheaf*, xxii, pp. 43–4.
5 C.C.A.L.S., ZAB 1, ff. 39v., 55, 70v.–71; cf. *P.N. Ches.* v (1:i), 10.
6 C.C.A.L.S., ZAB 1, ff. 53–54v.
7 *Progress and Problems*, 299–301.
8 e.g. C.C.A.L.S., ZSR 443, rot. 4; ZSR 445, rot. 1d.; ZSR 506, rot. 64d.; ZSB 7, f. 70v.
9 e.g. ibid. ZSR 504, rott. 10–11, 29, 35–6; ZSR 506, rot. 73d.; ZMR 111, rot. 1; ZSBC 1, f. 6; ZSBC 7, ff. 66, 107.
10 e.g. ibid. ZSR 522, rot. 13; ZSR 535, rott. 12, 25d., 40; ZSR 543, rot. 12; ZSR 554, rott. 1, 6 and d.; ZSBC 1, ff. 50, 64, 69v.; ZSBC 7, f. 34.
11 Ibid. ZAB 1, f. 82; ibid. WS 6/7; WS 17/1; EDA 2/1, ff. 188–9; Morris, *Chester*, 263.
12 C.C.A.L.S., EDA 2/1, ff. 188–9; WS 5/1; WS 6/3–4; WS 6/7;

WS 8/1; WS 8/3; 3 *Sheaf*, xi, pp. 1–2; xvii, p. 30; *Colln. of Lancs. and Ches. Wills* (R.S.L.C. xxx), 189–90; *Lancs. and Ches. Wills and Inventories*, iii (Chetham Soc. [o.s.], liv), 25–30.
13 *Blk. Prince's Reg.* iii. 261.
14 e.g. P.R.O., CHES 25/11, m. 6; CHES 25/12, m. 31d.; CHES 25/15, mm. 5, 52; CHES 29/165, m. 15d.
15 e.g. ibid. CHES 25/11, m. 21; CHES 25/12, mm. 6, 10, 23, 31d., 32d.; CHES 25/14, m. 23d.; CHES 25/15, mm. 38d., 51d.; CHES 25/16, m. 2d.
16 Ibid. CHES 25/9, m. 37; CHES 29/177, m. 42; cf. CHES 25/12, m. 3d.; CHES 29/167, m. 23d.; CHES 29/186, m. 17d.; CHES 29/187, m. 37.
17 e.g. P.R.O., CHES 25/14, m. 13; CHES 29/107, m. 17; C.C.A.L.S., ZMB 4, f. 62v.; ZSR 122, rot. 1; ZSR 135, rot. 1d.; ZSR 136, rot. 1; ZSR 155, rot. 1d.; ZSR 168, rot. 1; ZSR 169, rot. 1; ZSR 196, rot. 1d.; ZSR 251, rot. 1d.; ZSR 255, rot. 1; ZSR 281, rot. 1; ZSR 318, rot. 1d.; ZSR 349, rot. 3d.; ZSR 367, rot. 1d.; ZSR 380, rot. 1.
18 C.C.A.L.S., ZMR 69, rot. 1 and d.
19 P.R.O., SC 6/796/3, m. 13.
20 *V.C.H. Ches.* v (2), Lists of Mayors and Sheriffs.
21 P.R.O., CHES 25/16, m. 11d.; SC 6/796/3, m. 13; SC 6/801/8, m. 2d.

court.[1] Although the city provided casual employment, especially for men carting goods to and from the anchorages further down the Dee estuary,[2] and for women in domestic service[3] and brewing,[4] there was apparently no annual hiring fair or fixed day in the year on which terms of service began.[5] Nor did the presence of fulling mills encourage the development of much textile production in the neighbourhood.[6] The area as a whole remained relatively underdeveloped in the period. Although the city's outports were busy, the volume of goods carried into the city and their final destination are unknown. A county regularly skimmed by its royal earls for cash to maintain English garrisons in Wales,[7] and routinely exploited by the earls' numerous lessees for short-term profit,[8] may have represented a limited market for imported goods. Some local gentry families certainly preferred to shop in London for major items and luxuries, such as cloth for liveries, jewellery, silver, and saddles.[9]

The Wider Region. The city's capacity to attract migrants from a distance may have been relatively limited. Few new freemen apparently came from beyond Cheshire,[10] but the fairs continued to attract traders from far afield. Although both sold goods of every kind, the Midsummer fair probably specialized in cloth and mercery wares,[11] and the Michaelmas fair in livestock.[12] By the 15th century the Midsummer fair had a core period of a week around 24 June, when receipts from gate tolls reached their peak. Receipts during Michaelmas week also rose slightly, but never matched those for Midsummer, and the Michaelmas fair was perhaps less well attended. The sums involved were very small, and the fairs may not have drawn large crowds in the 15th century.[13] The inauguration of the Midsummer show, perhaps in the 1490s, may have been an attempt by the civic authorities to enhance the fair's attractions.[14] By the early 16th century the city's horse fairs drew large numbers, especially from Shropshire and north Wales,[15] and drovers from Cheshire, north Wales, and Lancashire were bringing herds of up to 200 animals to Chester, supplying the city's important leather industry as well as butchers from as far afield as Warrington.[16]

Traders from beyond the region visiting Chester at other times of year included men from Staffordshire, Warwickshire, and the Marches as far south as Worcester, who came primarily for fish. By the 1390s they paid an annual fine to the city authorities, who recorded their names: in the 15th century numbers ranged from 9 to 24 in any one year.[17] They brought specialities of their own region for sale, including fruit and wood-ash from Worcestershire,[18] knives, hilts, and pommels from Shrewsbury,[19] metal horse-trappings from Newcastle-under-Lyme and Walsall (both Staffs.),[20] and scythes from Birmingham.[21] In the earlier 16th century country fishmongers regularly paid fines to retail in Chester,[22] from whose markets fish was sent to Nantwich and Shrewsbury among other places.[23]

Merchants from east of the Pennines were fewer in number and most used Chester merely as the port of embarkation for Ireland. In the early 15th century, when the English colony in Ireland was under sustained attack, they were almost invariably bowyers from Yorkshire, at least one of whom became a freeman of Chester;[24] later they were superseded by merchants from Halifax, Pontefract, and Bradford,

1 e.g. C.C.A.L.S., ZSR 161, rot. 1d.; ZSR 169, rot. 1; ZSR 206, rot. 1d.; ZSR 359, rot. 1d.; ZSR 371, rot. 1d.

2 e.g. ibid. ZSR 67, rot. 1d.; ZSR 75, rot. 1; ZSR 104, rot. 1; ZSR 118, rot. 1; ZSR 148, rot. 1; ZSR 184, rot. 1; ZSR 239, rot. 1; ZSR 349, rot. 3; ZSR 372, rot. 1d.; ZSR 380, rot. 1; ZSR 402, rot. 1.

3 Ibid. ZSR 197, rot. 1d.; ZSR 223, rot. 1d.; ZSR 239, rot. 2d.; ZSR 334, rot. 1; ZSR 387, rot. 1d.; P.R.O., CHES 25/16, m. 5.

4 C.C.A.L.S., ZSR 112, rot. 1; ZSR 219, rot. 1d.; ZSR 258, rot. 1.

5 Ibid. ZSR 118, rot. 1d.; ZSR 123, rot. 4; ZSR 128, rot. 4; ZSR 197, rot. 1d.; ZSR 261, rot. 3; ZSR 300, rot. 1d.; P.R.O., CHES 25/16, m. 5.

6 P.R.O., CHES 25/12, m. 22d.; CHES 25/14, m. 14; C.C.A.L.S., ZMB 3, f. 75v.; ZSR 118, rot. 1d.; ZSR 235, rot. 1; ZSR 237, rot. 1d.; ZSR 415, rot. 1.

7 A. E. Curry, 'Demesne of Co. Palatine of Chester in Early 15th Cent.' (Manchester Univ. M.A. thesis, 1977), 284 sqq.

8 e.g. *Letters and Accts. of Wm. Brereton of Malpas* (R.S.L.C. cxvi), 15, 48.

9 Ibid. 238, 241; *Lancs. and Ches. Wills and Inventories*, i (Chetham Soc. [o.s.], xxxiii), 139–42; ii (Chetham Soc. [o.s.], li), 65, 126; iii (Chetham Soc. [o.s.], liv), 43.

10 e.g. C.C.A.L.S., ZMB 1, f. 9; ZMB 2, ff. 48v., 73; ZMB 3, ff. 15v., 56, 57 and v., 105 and v.

11 Ibid. ZMR 3, rott. 2d., 5; ZSR 51, rot. 2; ZSR 81, rot. 2d.; ZSR 135, rot. 1; ZSR 295, rot. 1d.; ZSR 308, rot. 1; ZSR 349, rot.

3; ZSR 375, rot. 1d.; ZSR 391, rot. 1d.; ZSR 449, rot. 1; P.R.O., CHES 25/16, m. 15d.

12 *Blk. Prince's Reg.* i. 19; P.R.O., CHES 25/11, m. 12; CHES 25/15, m. 16d.; CHES 29/137, m. 35d.; CHES 29/165, m. 15d.; C.C.A.L.S., ZSR 288, rot. 1d.; ZSR 351, rot. 7d.; ZSR 420, rot. 1; ZSR 423, rot. 1d.; ZSR 424, rot. 1d.; ZSR 425, rot. 1; ZSR 427, rot. 1.

13 C.C.A.L.S., ZMB 3, f. 67 and v.; ZMUB 1, ff. 1–6v.; ZMUR 1, mm. 1–2; ZSB 3, ff. 86v.–88.

14 *V.C.H. Ches.* v (2), Plays, Sports, and Customs before 1700: City Watches and Midsummer Show (Midsummer Watch).

15 *Letters of Wm. Brereton*, 43, 45–6; Johnson, 'Aspects', 234.

16 C.C.A.L.S., ZSB 5, f. 61; ZSB 6, f. 19v.; ZSR 504, rott. 23, 37.

17 Ibid. ZMB 1, f. 36; ZMB 3, f. 62v.; ZMB 4, f. 27; ZSB 2, f. 24; ZSB 3, f. 70v.; ZSB 4, f. 12; ZSR 109, rot. 1; ZSR 123, rot. 1; ZSR 130, rot. 1d.; ZSR 195, rot. 1d.; ZSR 245, rot. 1d.; ZSR 277, rot. 1d.; ZSR 311, rot. 1; ZSR 315, rot. 1d.; ZSR 334, rot. 1; ZSR 337, rot. 1; ZSR 359, rot. 1d.

18 Ibid. ZSR 231, rot. 1d.; ZSR 237, rot. 1d.; ZSR 243, rot. 1.

19 Ibid. ZSR 190, rot. 1; ZMB 4, f. 40v.; ZSB 1, f. 38v.

20 Ibid. ZSR 249, rot. 1; ZSR 376, rot. 1.

21 Ibid. ZSR 389, rot. 1d.

22 e.g. ibid. ZSB 4, ff. 5–7, 11–12; ZSB 5, f. 47v.

23 Ibid. ZMB 6, f. 36 and v.; ZSR 445, rot. 1d.

24 Ibid. ZMB 3, ff. 100 and v., 105v.; *New Hist. of Irel.* ii, ed. A. Cosgrove, 529–30, 533–56.

exporting cloth from the West Riding and returning with Irish furs.[1] The few Yorkshiremen who did business in Chester itself supplied dyestuffs in the early 15th century, and cloth later.[2]

Chester had strong trading and social links with Liverpool,[3] whose Irish trade had perhaps already eclipsed its own by the late 15th century.[4] The city had close links with other Lancashire towns and villages which gave surnames to several prominent families, such as the Eccleses, Farringtons, Hales, Heywoods, Rainfords, and Rochdales. In the late 14th and early 15th century Chester continued to attract immigrants from the North-West, while other Lancastrians came to trade in cloth or travel to Ireland.[5]

By the early 16th century Lancastrians, in particular men from Manchester and its region, were increasingly active in the textile trade.[6] Business relations merged into closer ties, with members of the Gee and Aldersey families of Chester marrying into families from Manchester.[7] Men from Kendal (Westmld.) also appeared from time to time in the city courts, and Kendal cloth was sold and exported through Chester in the 16th century.[8] In 1547 specific imposts were demanded from Kendal and Manchester men selling in the city.[9]

Until the later 15th century the city with which Chester was most strongly linked was Coventry. Its merchants regularly passed through Chester *en route* for Ireland, taking with them cloth, dyestuffs, and occasionally the sweet wines of the Mediterranean, and perhaps returning with hides.[10] Such men, some of whom visited Chester as many as five times a year,[11] also traded in the city, selling cloth, wine, and dyestuffs, and buying horses, furs, and fish.[12] In Chester they registered debts owed to them by merchants from

other towns, and turned to the Pentice court to enforce payment.[13] A few loaned money to Cestrians.[14] Some at least became freemen of Chester, and wealthy Cestrians in their turn joined Coventry's Trinity guild.[15] The number of Coventry merchants active in Chester fell after the mid 15th century, reflecting the decline of their own city.[16] None seems to have joined Chester's guild merchant after *c.* 1453, when it became an organization of privileged foreign traders.[17]

By the 15th century Cestrians had regular contact with Londoners, including skinners and fishmongers on their way to Ireland.[18] Londoners also sold fine woollen cloth and mercery wares, sweet wines, dyestuffs, paper, figs, and raisins in Chester itself.[19] Chester never attracted the leading London merchants, and those who did trade there often had local connexions, like Hugh Wych, who had kinsmen in Nantwich.[20] A few Londoners rented shops in the city,[21] and others may have invested liquid capital by providing loans for local merchants in order to facilitate trade.[22] Some visited or invested sufficiently to make membership of the guild merchant worth while.[23]

In the earlier 16th century several Londoners appeared in the city courts as plaintiffs pursuing local debtors. They included a brewer, a grocer, haberdashers, a mercer, merchants, salters, and aldermen.[24] Some Londoners shipped goods from Spain to Chester,[25] but their claim to trade there toll-free was disputed, and there was concerted opposition in 1533 to prevent a London grocer from retailing wine.[26]

As the taxation and customs centre for the region, Chester had a key role in the circulation of coins and the extension of credit. There was an unusually large number of goldsmiths working in the city, a group

1 C.C.A.L.S., ZSB 1, f. 133v.; ZSB 3, f. 63; ZSR 255, rot. 1d.

2 Ibid. ZSR 128, rot. 4d.; ZSR 290, rot. 1d.; ZSR 295, rot. 1d.; P.R.O., CHES 25/15, m. 53.

3 e.g. M. J. Bennett, *Community, Class, and Careerism: Ches. and Lancs. Society in the Age of Sir Gawain and the Green Knight*, 13.

4 C.C.A.L.S., ZSB 4, ff. 15v.–16, 63, 81v.; C. N. Parkinson, *Rise of Port of Liverpool*, 18–20.

5 C.C.A.L.S., ZMB 1, f. 9; ZMB 2, f. 73; ZSB 1, ff. 29v., 30v., 38v., 71, 78–9; ZSB 2, ff. 66v.–67, 70; ZSB 3, ff. 5, 48, 56v.; ZSB 4, f. 102v.; ZSR 123, rot. 2; ZSR 219, rot. 1d.; ZSR 273, rot. 1d.

6 K. P. Wilson, 'Port of Chester in Later Middle Ages' (Liverpool Univ. Ph.D. thesis, 1966), i. 100; *Pleadings and Depositions in Duchy Court of Lancaster*, iii (R.S.L.C. xl), 6–10.

7 C.C.A.L.S., EDA 2/1, ff. 188–9; ibid. ZSR 554, rot. 6; *Lancs. and Ches. Wills and Inventories*, i (Chetham Soc. [o.s.], xxxiii), 159.

8 e.g. C.C.A.L.S., ZMR 111, rot. 6; ZSFB 2/11–12; ZSBC 1, ff. 20, 30; Wilson, 'Port of Chester', i. 103.

9 C.C.A.L.S., ZAB 1, f. 77 and v.

10 Ibid. ZMB 3, ff. 35, 58, 95v.   11 Ibid. ZMB 1, f. 60v.

12 Ibid. f. 53; ZMB 2, f. 100v.; ZSB 1, ff. 30v.–31; ZSR 135, rot. 1; ZSR 160, rot. 1d.; ZSR 190, rot. 1; ZSR 206, rot. 1d.; ZSR 220, rot. 1; ZSR 277, rot. 1; ZSR 316, rot. 1; ZSR 327, rot. 1; ZSR 359, rot. 1d.; ZSR 394, rot. 1d.

13 Ibid. ZSR 124, rot. 1 and d.; ZSR 160, rot. 1d.; ZSR 220, rot. 1.

14 Ibid. ZSR 220, rot. 1d.; ZSR 316, rot. 1; ZSR 331, rot. 1.

15 Ibid. ZMB 3, f. 56; *Reg. of Guild of Holy Trinity, St. Mary, St. John the Baptist, and St. Katherine of Coventry*, i (Dugdale Soc. xiii), 2, 13, 28, 37, 64, 91, 93.

16 Wilson, 'Port of Chester', i. 91.

17 C.C.A.L.S., ZMB 5, f. 180; ZMB 6, ff. 3, 33, 88.

18 Ibid. ZSB 2, ff. 9, 53; ZSB 3, f. 111v.; ZSR 107, rot. 1d.; ZSR 156, rot. 1d.; ZSR 204, rot. 1d.; ZSR 210, rot. 1; ZSR 238, rot. 1d.; ZSR 261, rot. 3.

19 Ibid. ZSB 1, f. 155; ZSR 111, rot. 1d.; ZSR 115, rot. 1d.; ZSR 261, rot. 1; ZSR 351, rot. 3d.; ZSR 360, rot. 1d.; ZSR 371, rot. 1; ZSR 413, rot. 1d.

20 e.g. Wm. Wettenhall, Hugh Wych, Ral. Verney, and Thos. Cottingham: S. L. Thrupp, *Merchant Class of Medieval Lond. 1300–1500*, 371, 373–6; C.C.A.L.S., ZMB 4, f. 22v.; ZMR 96, rot. 1; ZSB 1, ff. 31v., 57v., 127, 128v., 172v.; ZSR 294, rot. 1.

21 C.C.A.L.S., ZTAR 1/4, m. 1.

22 Ibid. ZSR 233, rot. 1d.; ZSR 319, rot. 1d.

23 e.g. Jas. Wells: ibid. ZMB 5, f. 180; ZSB 2, ff. 9, 33v., 34v., 47, 68v.–74v.; ZSB 3, ff. 11, 28v.–29, 31v., 35, 49v., 52, 102v., 111v.

24 Ibid. ZSR 504, rott. 36, 36Ad.; ZSR 522, rott. 5, 30d.; ZSR 535, rot. 27d.; ZSR 554, rott. 1, 3, 7; ZSBC 1, ff. 3, 25v., 35, 45, 53v.; ZSBC 7, ff. 5, 49, 52, 78, 98, 103, 122–3; ZMR 111, rot. 2.

25 Ibid. ZAB 1, f. 78v.; *Chester Customs Accts.* 76–9, 83, 85–6, 88, 90, 94, 96, 99.

26 *L. & P. Hen. VIII*, vi, p. 92.

commonly associated with money lending, and they made regular appearances before the city courts as both plaintiffs and defendants.[1] Credit and perhaps cash loans flowed into Chester from further afield. A Dubliner impleaded a Chester goldsmith in 1540 for a 30s. debt, and in 1551 a London goldsmith was pursuing a Chester merchant for a debt of £10.[2] There is evidence of a bullion shortage in Cheshire in the early 16th century. Orders were sent to the mayor of Chester in 1499 that all coins were to be accepted in the city, however small, with the exception of Irish 'spurred' pennies,[3] and in 1535 counterfeit coins were said to be circulating from Valle Crucis abbey (Denb.) and Norton priory.[4] A shortage of good coins may have exacerbated a local problem. Pawning was quite common in the city, notably in the 1530s,[5] and there may have been some hoarding of coins.[6]

THE PORT AND OVERSEAS TRADE

In 1361 the citizens of Chester claimed that they lived by trade,[7] and even in the early 16th century the corporation continued to believe that the city's economic future depended upon its overseas contacts.[8] In the later Middle Ages, however, the port suffered from facing west, away from the Continent, and also perhaps from the silting of the Dee estuary, as was frequently alleged.[9] Ships with very heavy cargoes, such as wine and millstones, unloaded at anchorages in Wirral, the goods then being transferred to smaller craft or carts,[10] but the city's own harbour at Portpool handled fish, Welsh slates, woollen cloth, hardware, and malt,[11] and at high tide the smallest vessels could reach the New Tower at the north-western corner of the city walls.[12]

The records do not permit statistical analysis or quantification of Chester's trade in the late 14th and 15th century.[13] All that can safely be said is that an average of 49 ships arriving each year in the 1420s dropped to 40 in the 1450s, 35 in the 1460s, and 30 in the 1470s, but then apparently rose to 44 in the 1490s. The busiest single year was 1500–1, with 57 ships. Such totals were small in comparison with major ports on the east and south coasts,[14] and included tiny boats with only one or two crewmen.[15] Chester's overseas

trade probably declined after the 1420s, reached its nadir in the 1470s, and began to improve in the 1490s, a recovery which ran counter to the citizens' claims about silting.[16]

In the early 16th century overseas trade with Ireland, Spain, Portugal, and Brittany expanded, but only merchants with a sizeable turnover could carry the heavy costs which arose from carriage from anchorages down the estuary and from high customs duties. The share of the port's trade controlled by Cestrians fluctuated. Dubliners dominated the Irish Sea trade, and there was strong competition for the rest of the overseas trade from English, Welsh, and Continental merchants. In 1538–42, during Chester's trading zenith, 40–45 per cent of traders were Chester freemen.[17] Most were probably only occasionally involved, and between 1500 and 1550 there were forty or so significant Chester merchants who shipped through the port.[18] Their trade was predominantly in importing iron and wine and exporting hides and cloth, but few were specialists. Even though Richard Grimsditch's main trading effort was with the Continent, for example, he also bought Irish cloth,[19] while Henry Gee in 1532 shared a cargo which included canvas, buckram, glass, honey, black soap, velvet, trenchers, a round table, and a bedcase.[20]

Irish and Coastal Trade. Throughout the 15th century the Irish trade dominated the port, and until the 1480s, when numbers of local vessels increased, most of the ships involved were themselves Irish.[21] The main ports from which they came were within the Pale: Dublin, Howth, Malahide, Rush, and Drogheda. Commodities exported from Ireland included sea fish and salmon from the Bann fisheries, hides, cloth, and yarn.[22] In the other direction Chester handled salt until *c.* 1450, and wine, high-quality woollens and other textiles, and a range of manufactured goods such as metal pots and pans throughout the period.[23]

By the later 15th century Irishmen were prominent in Chester's guild merchant; at least 6 of the 17 men entering the guild in 1474 came from Dublin and a seventh from Drogheda.[24] Others opted for citizen-

1 e.g. C.C.A.L.S., ZSBC 1, ff. 38v., 69v.; ZSFB 2/17.
2 Ibid. ZSR 543, rot. 6; ZSR 554, rot. 1.
3 *37 D.K.R.* App. II, p. 144; cf. C. E. Challis, *Tudor Coinage*, 53.
4 *Letters of Wm. Brereton*, 40–1.
5 C.C.A.L.S., ZSB 5, ff. 130–1, 157; ZSB 7, ff. 9, 31, 67, 85.
6 Ibid. ZSR 554, rot. 1.   7 *Blk. Prince's Reg.* iii. 415–16.
8 C.C.A.L.S., ZAB 1, *passim*.   9 Ibid. ZCH 28–31.
10 Ibid. ZMB 6, f. 83; K. P. Wilson, 'Port of Chester in 15th Cent.' *T.H.S.L.C.* cxvii. 3, 6; *Chester Customs Accts.* 20–62; P.R.O., SC 6/785/5, m. 1d.
11 C.C.A.L.S., ZSB 3, f. 94v.; ZSR 457, rot. 1d.; ZSR 454, rot. 1d.; ZSR 376, rot. 1d.; ZSR 467, rot. 1d.
12 Ibid. ZSR 104, rot. 1d.; ZSR 121, rot. 1.
13 Para. based on ibid. ZMB 2, ff. 37v.–42v.; ZMB 3, ff. 85v.–86v.; Wilson, 'Port of Chester', ii, App. H.
14 Cf. *Brokage Book of Southampton, 1443–4* (Southampton Rec. Ser. iv, vi); *Local Port Book of Southampton for 1439–40*

(ibid. v); *Customs Accts. of Hull, 1453–90* (Yorks. Arch. Soc. Rec. Ser. cxliv); *Overseas Trade of Lond.: Exchequer Customs Accts. 1480–1* (Lond. Rec. Soc. xxvii), p. xxxviii.
15 C.C.A.L.S., ZSB 1, f. 127; ZSB 4, f. 138.
16 Ibid. ZCH 28–31.
17 Wilson, 'Port of Chester', i. 163.
18 C.C.A.L.S., ZSB *passim*; *Chester Customs Accts. passim*.
19 C.C.A.L.S., ZSB 9, f. 68v.
20 *Chester Customs Accts.* 64; Wilson, 'Port of Chester', i. 164–8.
21 Cf. *New Hist. Irel.* ii. 512–14.
22 C.C.A.L.S., ZMB 2, ff. 37v., 39v.–40v., 41v., 72; ZMB 5, f. 214v.; ZMUB 1, ff. 7–8v.; ZSB 4, ff. 138, 139v., 140v.–141; ZSR 245, rot. 1; ZSR 314, rot. 1d.; ZSR 364, rot. 1; ZSR 366, rot. 1.
23 Ibid. ZMB 2, ff. 37v.–38v., 80v., 82; ZMB 3, ff. 58, 100v.; ZSB 1, f. 70v.
24 Ibid. ZMB 5, f. 180.

ship.[1] Robert Nottervill, mayor of Chester in 1478–9, had apparently twice served as mayor of Drogheda.[2] Not all Irish immigrants were of high status, and in the early 15th century they included male and female labourers, and women who turned to keeping brothels in Chester.[3]

There was also a coastal trade with Anglesey. Ships from the island, mostly based in Beaumaris, regularly carried fish, wool, and cloth to Chester, and returned with metal, wine, almonds, and felt caps.[4] Occasionally men from the island married into city families.[5] By the 14th century Manxmen also settled in the city,[6] including the mayor John Armourer.[7] Although relatively few Manx ships visited Chester in the early 15th century, perhaps because the island's trade was only just developing under the lordship of the Stanley family,[8] by the 1450s there was regular trade with Castletown and other ports, especially in fish and cloth.[9] Manxmen also came to Chester to work as labourers, many as tenants of the nunnery, living in an area of poor housing in Nuns Lane.[10]

During the earlier 16th century changes in the pattern of trade around the Irish Sea initially boosted Chester's port activity but eventually led to its decline. From the 1490s the south-east Lancashire textile industry began to develop, trade with the Iberian peninsula and Brittany expanded, ships from Chester's outports in Lancashire began to appear south of the Ribble, and Welsh merchants increasingly took over the sea trade of west Wales.[11]

By 1500 Irish and coastal trade accounted for over 75 per cent of all inward sailings to Chester, rising to 95 per cent in 1548–9.[12] There was an active re-export trade between Chester and Ireland in both directions, suggesting that Irish merchants picked up what they could as return cargoes, and were perhaps more concerned with selling in Chester than with buying. Some traditional commodities had disappeared from Anglo-Irish trade. Cheshire salt was not exported via Chester after 1450 and had been replaced by salt from

the bay of Bourgneuf carried in Breton and Gascon ships.[13] Irish corn imports faded after a ban in 1472.[14] Most cargoes were a mixture of cloth, fish, hides and skins, linen (both cloth and yarn), wool (fells, flocks, and yarn), honey, tallow, wax, and occasional re-exports such as silk.[15] The trade was concentrated in the Pale, and not with wealthier Waterford, Cork, and Kinsale.[16]

Fish exceeded any other single commodity in quantity.[17] Eels, cod, herring, and salmon were regularly imported in ships from Ireland, Chester, Cumberland, the Isle of Man, and Wales. Salmon was the most valuable species, paying custom at more than double the rate for herring,[18] but accounting for far smaller quantities. In 1525–6 over 103 tons of herring was shipped but only ½ ton of salmon. A Chester merchant leased the Bann salmon fishery in 1519 and shipped its products to his native city in the 1520s.[19] Irish salmon continued to find a market in Chester and over 5 tons and 260 butts was imported in 1543–4.[20]

Both tanned and raw hides were sent from Ireland to Chester, together with tallow used in waterproofing, but skins were considerably more numerous. In 1525–6, for example, Chester received some 2,200 hides, over 13,000 lambskins, 10,200 sheepskins, 2,300 badger pelts, 1,100 calfskins, 640 marten and otter skins, 300 fox skins, 90 goatskins, and 50 hart skins.[21] Alum and oil, used by glovers and tawyers to prepare light leathers, also came from Ireland.[22] Prices for skins in the luxury market rose fast between 1500 and 1550, marten tripling in price and otter quadrupling, and Irish skins were sold in London after preparation in Chester.[23]

The pattern of Chester's textile trade with Ireland was transformed in the early 16th century. The falling demand for clipped wool in the textile industry of Coventry[24] meant that only small quantities were imported through Chester after 1500.[25] Coarse friezes, checkers, mantles, blankets, and rugs accounted for most imports to Chester.[26] Checkers predominated and

1 Ibid. ZMB 3, ff. 56, 105v.; *New Hist. Irel.* ii. 520; P.R.O., CHES 29/166, m. 8; CHES 29/167, m. 3.

2 3 *Sheaf,* xxix, p. 40.

3 *Cal. Pat.* 1436–41, 281; C.C.A.L.S., ZSB 2, f. 8; ZSR 160, rot. 1d.; ZSR 190, rot. 1.

4 C.C.A.L.S., ZSR 126, rot. 2; ZSR 159, rot. 1d.; ZSR 320, rot. 1d.; ZSR 363, rot. 1d.; ZSR 364, rot. 1; ZSR 394, rot. 1; ZSR 399, rot. 1; ZSR 466, rot. 1.

5 *Cal. of Deeds and Papers of Moore Fam.* (R.S.L.C. lxvii), no. 1028.

6 C.C.A.L.S., ZSR 60, rot. 1d.; ZSR 81, rot. 1d.

7 P.R.O., WALE 29/291.

8 Bennett, *Community, Class, and Careerism,* 130–1, 217, 220; C.C.A.L.S., ZMB 3, f. 33v.

9 C.C.A.L.S., ZSB 1, f. 108v.; ZSB 2, ff. 49, 52; ZSB 3, ff. 11, 12v., 75, 77v.; ZSB 4, ff. 14, 15, 18v., 37, 56v., 103, 140v.–141v.; ZSR 318, rot. 1d.; ZSR 327, rot. 1d.; ZSR 401, rot. 1d.

10 *J.C.A.S.* xiii. 105–9.

11 *Progress and Problems,* 286–307.

12 Wilson, 'Port of Chester', i. 105–7.

13 *New Hist. Irel.* ii. 507; C.C.A.L.S., ZSB 5, f. 176.

14 T. O'Neill, *Merchants and Mariners in Medieval Irel.* 27.

15 e.g. C.C.A.L.S., ZSB 5, ff. 174–5.

16 Wilson, 'Port of Chester', i. 96; *New Hist. Irel.* ii. 495.

17 O'Neill, *Merchants and Mariners,* 31–40.

18 C.C.A.L.S., ZAB 1, f. 41.

19 Ibid. ZSB 5, f. 177v.; O'Neill, *Merchants and Mariners,* 31–40.

20 C.C.A.L.S., ZSB 8, ff. 39–99.

21 Ibid. ZSB 5, ff. 174–197v.; ZSB 8, ff. 59–93; *Chester Customs Accts.* 132–42; cf. O'Neill, *Merchants and Mariners,* 78–9.

22 C.C.A.L.S., ZSB 5, f. 176.

23 A. K. Longfield, *Anglo-Irish Trade in 16th Cent.* 62–3; E. M. Veale, *Eng. Fur Trade in Later Middle Ages,* 169; D. M. Woodward, 'Chester Leather Ind. 1558–1625', *T.H.S.L.C.* cxix. 71.

24 Wilson, 'Port of Chester', i. 91; C. Phythian-Adams, *Desolation of a City: Coventry and Urban Crisis of Late Middle Ages,* 33–67.

25 C.C.A.L.S., ZSB 5, ff. 174–187v.

26 Ibid. f. 178; ZSB 8, ff. 39–99; Longfield, *Anglo-Irish Trade,* 80–1.

at least 2,000 yards and 1,500 pieces were imported in 1525–6, together with at least 300 yards and 550 pieces of linen cloth. Yarn was also important, some 8,000 lb. being sent to Chester in 1525–6.[1] By 1550 the composition of the trade had shifted from finished cloth to sheepskins and yarn for the expanding Lancashire textile industry.[2] Small quantities of Irish barley, rye, wheat, butchered beef, and honey were also shipped into Chester and re-exported to the Continent,[3] and some battery, brass, pewter, glass, and turpentine were also imported.[4] Chester's exports to Ireland in the early 16th century probably, as at Bristol in 1504, included coal and cloth.[5] Salt, wine, and Breton canvas were re-exported from Chester to Ireland and vice versa.[6]

In the early 16th century the composition of the merchants involved in trade between Chester and Ireland was transformed. Coventry men virtually disappeared: only eight were active in 1500–1, two in 1508–9, and one or two thereafter. Occasionally a Coventry draper appeared in the Pentice court to recover debts from Cestrians.[7] From 1500 Drogheda merchants also abandoned the city in favour of Liverpool. Dubliners remained to dominate the Irish trade through Chester, a group which between 1520 and 1540 included several who rose to be mayors and bailiffs of their home city.[8] Perhaps only one in ten of the merchants involved in the Irish trade were based in Chester.[9]

A separate development after 1500 was the presence at Chester of more ships from Cumberland and Lancashire carrying herring, salmon, cod, and hides.[10]

Continental Trade. A few Cestrians were shippers of wine from Gascony and iron from Spain in the early 15th century,[11] but many more of the ships involved were based in the West Country, at Totnes, Dartmouth, and Plymouth in Devon, Fowey, Falmouth, and St. Ives in Cornwall,[12] and Bristol.[13] After the truce with France in 1463 a few alien vessels joined the trade, especially from St. Malo in Brittany.[14] Although the treaty of Picquigny in 1475 allowed greater freedom of trade, numbers remained low[15] until the late 1480s, when Spanish ships began to arrive, bringing wine,

iron, and oil, and returning to their home ports in the bay of Biscay with calfskins, tallow, and coloured woollen cloth.[16]

The involvement of the city's leading merchants appears to have ceased between the 1460s and the 1490s. Thereafter, however, their share increased until in the 1510s they were dominant. Such merchants, generally aldermen or councillors, were engaged mainly in the Spanish trade but also maintained an interest in the Irish and coastal trade.[17] The number of ships owned by Cestrians in the late 14th and 15th century was small, until the 1490s never accounting for more than 13 per cent of vessels entering the port, and falling as low as perhaps 8 per cent in the 1450s and 3 per cent in the 1480s.[18] Indeed, in 1484 the citizens claimed that Chester had no merchant ships of its own, and in 1496, when they were licensed to trade with Gascony, they were allowed to use foreign vessels since they themselves had none suitable. In 1497–8, however, three Chester-owned ships accounted for 8 of the 49 recorded entries into the port.[19] Even when Chester's merchants began to trade further afield in the early 16th century and shipowning was increasing, most preferred to venture their cargoes in ships from other ports.[20]

After the treaty of Medina del Campo opened up trade with the Iberian peninsula in 1489, Spanish iron, and wine from Portugal, Spain, and Gascony became the basis for a dramatic expansion in Chester's overseas trade, which allowed other Mediterranean commodities to reach the city, and provided new markets for hides and cloth. Chester's trade with Spain focused on the Basque region. Iron imports from there rose from 939 tons in 1490–1500 to 4,273 tons in 1530–40, and although dropping below 1,000 tons thereafter, survived international tension as a regular item in Chester's trade. It was carried in both local and Iberian ships, but before 1540 alien merchants shipped the largest quantities: 77 per cent in 1490–1500, 36 per cent in 1510–20, 61 per cent in 1523–30, 52 per cent in 1530–40, and 28 per cent in 1540–50.[21] Besides iron, small quantities of angora, silk and velvet, liquorice, train oil, woad, and Cordovan skins were sometimes

1 e.g. C.C.A.L.S., ZSB 5, ff. 175, 177.

2 Longfield, *Anglo-Irish Trade*, 77.

3 e.g. C.C.A.L.S., ZSB 5, f. 179v.; ZSB 7, f. 97v.; ZSB 8, ff. 23, 81v., 82v., 84, 89.

4 e.g. ibid. ZSB 5, f. 178v.; ZSB 10, f. 175; Longfield, *Anglo-Irish Trade*, 126–7.

5 Longfield, *Anglo-Irish Trade*, 170; Wilson, 'Port of Chester', i. 87.

6 e.g. C.C.A.L.S., ZSB 5, ff. 174, 179.

7 e.g. ibid. ZSFB 2/13; ZSBC 1, f. 13v.

8 Wilson, 'Port of Chester', i. 94.

9 Ibid. i. 166.

10 Ibid. i. 97–8; C.C.A.L.S., ZSB 5, ff. 11v., 79v., 103, 125, 146–7, 174; ZSB 6, ff. 3v., 15; ZSB 7, ff. 5, 23, 62, 74v., 98v., 126v.; ZSB 8, ff. 66v., 71v.

11 *Chester Customs Accts. passim.*

12 C.C.A.L.S., ZSB 1, f. 56v.; ZSB 2, f. 96v.; ZSB 3, ff. 33, 54, 76, 80v.; ZSB 4, ff. 15v.–16, 139, 147v., 150v.

13 Ibid. ZSR 156, rot. 1; ZSB 1, ff. 108, 125, 127; ZSB 2, f. 78v.; ZSB 3, ff. 12v., 14v.

14 e.g. ibid. ZSB 2, ff. 53, 71, 74; ZSB 3, f. 55.

15 Ibid. ZSB 3, ff. 71v., 78v., 81v.

16 e.g. ibid. ff. 102v., 105 and v., 111v.; ZSB 4, ff. 16–17, 34v., 39, 62, 129, 147v.

17 *Chester Customs Accts. passim*; Wilson, 'Port of Chester', i. 162–4; ii, App. H.

18 Wilson, 'Port of Chester', ii, App. H; cf. C.C.A.L.S., ZSB 1, ff. 28v.–35v.; ZSB 2, ff. 68–75.

19 C.C.A.L.S., ZSB 4, ff. 102–108v.

20 Wilson, 'Port of Chester', i. 96, 148–9.

21 Ibid. i. 124, 137; *Chester Customs Accts.* 69–71; D. M. Woodward, *Trade of Elizabethan Chester*, 130.

carried.[1] Trade with Portugal and Andalusia through the northern Spanish ports brought cork, dyestuffs, figs and raisins, litmus, pepper and herbs, oil, sugar, wax, and sweet wines to Chester from *c.* 1509.[2] Never extensive, it dwindled to only two shipments between 1542 and 1560.[3] From 1494–5 or earlier small loads of Spanish wine reached Chester, and occasionally southern ships also carried cargoes of Gascon wine.[4]

Cloth, hides, and skins comprised the main return cargoes. In 1539 Manchester cottons, friezes, kerseys, broad dozens, and goatskins were carted from Chester to four Spanish ships at anchor in the Dee estuary.[5] In 1536 Chester was brought into the national customs system for leather and in 1537–8 customs duties were paid on 10,681 tanned hides in five Spanish and five Chester ships. Figures for later years ranged from 700 to 1,600 hides, with Spanish merchants exporting the larger share.[6]

Chester was the most north-westerly port in England regularly handling wine, perhaps often as the terminus of voyages which had already called at Bristol or Dublin and intermediate ports.[7] Chester's wine imports doubled from 1,131 tuns in 1490–1500 to a peak of 2,451 in 1510–20. Imports remained high in the 1520s and 1530s before falling to 698 tuns in the 1540s. Chester regularly accounted for 3–4 per cent of national imports, except in 1509–10 when, remarkably, it took 9 per cent. Gascony was the main source, Portugal and Spain supplying only tiny quantities.

Ships from Gascony also carried alum, dyestuffs, honey, linen cloth, pitch, tar, train oil, salt, vinegar, and woad, some of which may have been taken aboard *en route* at Breton ports. Breton ships also carried Gascon products to Chester, as well as Breton canvas. Return cargoes were probably mainly hides and cloth.[8]

Trade with distant markets brought foreign merchants, who sued and were sued in the city courts.[9] In 1532 a Spaniard was killed in the city during a fracas with his fellows.[10] Trade was conducted directly by Cestrians at the port of dispatch or through agents.[11] Relations between the citizens and their Spanish and Portuguese counterparts were apparently good,[12] and

Henry Gee, twice mayor between 1533 and 1540, left £5 to a Spanish business acquaintance.[13]

Overall, the period 1500–40 was a time of increasing imports, ended by hostilities with Spain and growing competition with other north-western ports.[14] Chester's administrative dominance over its outports guaranteed the palatinate's income from customs but not the presence of merchants or the carriage of goods into Chester. The north Wales ports were becoming busier, with coastal trade increasingly in the hands of Welsh merchants,[15] though a number of Chester merchants imported Breton canvas, iron, and wine through Beaumaris between 1517 and 1520.[16] Beaumaris also encroached upon Chester's role as a port of military embarkation for Ireland in the 1530s.[17]

Chester's greatest and ultimately triumphant rival was Liverpool. Competition was fiercest over the Anglo-Irish trade in yarn and cloth, and Chester's Assembly legislated against its own and Dublin citizens shipping through Liverpool. It forbade Cestrians to bargain with Irish merchants at Liverpool or elsewhere in 1532,[18] and to buy Irish goods which had not been through the city's customs registration system or to ship goods through Liverpool even in chartered vessels in 1549 or 1550.[19] The prohibition may have had little effect, for in 1535 Liverpool was described as the natural entrepôt for Irish yarn.[20] In the mid 16th century, while Chester exported more cloth to the Continent than Liverpool did,[21] Liverpool had overtaken Chester in the Anglo-Irish trade.[22] Liverpool's success was due in part to its location closer to the textile centres in Lancashire and in part to Chester's reluctance to adapt to market forces. No exemptions from Chester's local customs were allowed, except in a reciprocal agreement with Wexford.[23] While Chester freemen made a single payment of 4*d.* a vessel, outsiders had to pay on every major item imported and exported.[24] Dubliners claimed the lower dues payable at Liverpool as a major attraction in 1533,[25] and in 1550 the mayor of Dublin complained to his counterpart in Chester that increases in customs dues encouraged merchants to sail elsewhere.[26] Chester merchants,

1 Wilson, 'Port of Chester', i. 130; e.g. C.C.A.L.S., ZSB 5, f. 167; ZSB 7, ff. 21v., 23v., 59, 61, 141.
2 e.g. C.C.A.L.S., ZSB 5, ff. 164v., 176v., 179; ZSB 7, ff. 4, 58, 73v.; ZSB 8, f. 44v.; *Chester Customs Accts.* 138–9, 142.
3 Wilson, 'Port of Chester', i. 13.
4 C.C.A.L.S., ZSB 4, ff. 52–62v.; *Chester Customs Accts.* 35.
5 C.C.A.L.S., ZSB 7, ff. 122v., 125–126v.; cf. ibid. f. 74.
6 *Chester Customs Accts.* 57–62.
7 Para. based on ibid. esp. 70–2; Wilson, 'Port of Chester', i. 119, 121, 124.
8 Wilson, 'Port of Chester', i. 135–6; C.C.A.L.S., ZSB 5, ff. 103, 164–165v., 176v.; ZSB 7, ff. 5, 7, 22, 38–54, 58, 73v.; ZSB 8, f. 16.
9 e.g. C.C.A.L.S., ZMR 111, rott. 6, 11; ZSR 535, rott. 28, 37; ZSR 543, rot. 1; ZSFB 2/30.
10 Liverpool Univ. Libr. MS. 23.5, f. 52.
11 e.g. C.C.A.L.S., ZMR 111, rott. 8–11; ZMR 112, rot. 8d.
12 e.g. ibid. ZSB 5, f. 121.
13 Ibid. EDA 2/1, ff. 188–9; *V.C.H. Ches.* v (2), Lists of Mayors

and Sheriffs.
14 Wilson, 'Port of Chester', i. 128.
15 E. A. Lewis, 'Contribution to Commercial Hist. of Medieval Wales', *Y Cymmrodor*, xxiv. 99, 129–33, 170–88.
16 Ibid. 172–4.
17 R. Bagwell, *Irel. under the Tudors*, i. 169; C.C.A.L.S., ZSB 7, f. 121.
18 C.C.A.L.S., ZAF 1, f. 18.
19 Ibid. ZAB 1, ff. 81v.–82v.; Wilson, 'Port of Chester', i. 169.
20 Wilson, 'Port of Chester', i. 102; Leland, *Itin.* ed. Toulmin Smith, v. 40–1.
21 Wilson, 'Port of Chester', i. 102; N. Lowe, *Lancs. Textile Ind. in 16th Cent.* (Chetham Soc. 3rd ser. xx), 79.
22 Woodward, *Trade of Eliz. Chester*, 7–8, 13, 15.
23 B.L. Harl. MS. 2057, f. 129.
24 C.C.A.L.S., ZAB 1, ff. 41–2.
25 *L. & P. Hen. VIII*, vi, p. 148.
26 C.C.A.L.S., ZML 5/1.

too, were driven away: Edmund, son of the incorruptible mayor Henry Gee, was importing wine with a Spanish partner into Liverpool in 1546.[1]

TRADES AND INDUSTRIES

By 1350 a great variety of specialist craftsmen worked in Chester. About 170 occupations were recorded during the later 14th and 15th century, a number which compares favourably with Winchester (163) and even London (almost 200).[2] Even allowing for those that were rare or indicative merely of a change in terminology there were still in 1476–7, for example, some 60 trades followed by the 288 townsmen whose occupations are known. Most crafts fell into three main groupings: victualling, the production of clothing, and leather working. By the early 16th century textile workers were the largest group, comprising 28 per cent of new freemen; leather workers came next with 20 per cent, followed by the victuallers (14 per cent), merchants and traders (10 per cent), metal workers (8 per cent), and building workers (2 per cent). After the 1530s the basis of the city's economy shifted towards leather and away from the textile trades.[3]

Victualling Trades. With perhaps 3,500 or more inhabitants in 1463,[4] Chester required considerable quantities of grain. In the later 14th century some of its needs were still met from Ireland,[5] and merchants from Drogheda and Malahide occasionally took wheat and malt there in the early 15th century.[6] By 1419, however, the use of Irish wheat by the city's bakers was unusual, and no shipments were recorded after 1420.[7] Other supplies came from Wirral, the Welsh Marches,[8] and the town fields.[9] Many leading citizens owned arable land and produced grain for sale in the market.[10]

Although all purchases were supposed to be made in the corn market, occasionally bakers were discovered intercepting supplies *en route* to the city.[11] They also regularly flouted their obligation to have corn ground at the royal mills on the Dee and went instead to the abbot's mill at Bache or to mills at Trafford and Eccleston.[12] Armed affrays between the bakers and the Dee millers were common.[13] By the mid 15th century the mills' profits had declined sharply; the quantities of grain which they handled decreased and prices fell, perhaps because of dwindling population.[14]

By the 1390s at least twelve bakers worked in the city.[15] Thereafter numbers seem to have fluctuated, often falling to as few as six and occasionally in the early 16th century rising to twenty or more.[16] They commonly included one or two women, an indication that it was perhaps normal for a widow to continue her late husband's business.[17]

The bakers' everyday customers included people from the Marches, whose withdrawal because of Owain Glyn Dŵr's rebellion allegedly contributed to the city's decay.[18] By the late 15th century, except for large orders met directly by bakers, distribution was largely in the hands of women, often the *femmes soles* whose legal status allowed them to trade independently of their husbands.[19] Horse-bread made from peas and beans was also produced,[20] and in times of dearth served for human consumption.[21] Prices were regulated by statute and fixed with reference to the price of grain. As elsewhere, they were monitored by the assize of bread, held several times a year, often on market days. The mayor presided and two prominent citizens and two city bakers acted as assessors.[22]

Between the 1390s and the 1500s the number of butchers varied between nine and twenty.[23] The leading butchers were wealthy men and in the 15th century provided nine sheriffs. As earlier they occupied premises in both the Row and the undercrofts of

---

1 *Pleadings and Depositions in Duchy Court of Lancaster*, iii (R.S.L.C. xl), 135–7.

2 D. Keene, *Survey of Medieval Winchester*, i. 250; *The English Medieval Town: Reader in Urban Hist.* ed. R. Holt and G. Rosser, 7, 127.

3 Analysis based on *Rolls of Freemen of Chester*, i (R.S.L.C. li); D. M. Palliser, 'Revised List of Chester Freemen' (TS. at C.H.H.); C.C.A.L.S., ZMB *passim*.

4 *V.C.H. Ches.* v (2), Population.

5 *Cal. Pat. 1391–6*, 17.

6 C.C.A.L.S., ZMB 2, ff. 40v.–41, 42, 51.

7 Ibid. ZMB 3, f. 112v.; ZSR 143, rot. 1d.; cf. *Studies in Eng. Trade in 15th Cent.* ed. E. Power and M. M. Postan, 199; *New Hist. Irel.* ii. 485.

8 C.C.A.L.S., ZSR 135, rot. 1d.; ZSR 155, rot. 1d.; ZSR 165, rot. 1d.; ZSR 196, rot. 1d.; ZSR 284, rot. 1; ZSR 352, rot. 1d.; ZSR 402, rot. 1d.; cf. H. Taylor, *Historic Notices of Boro. and Co. Town of Flint*, 103.

9 C.C.A.L.S., ZSR 164, rot. 1d.; ZSR 359, rot. 1d.; ZSR 401, rot. 1; ZSR 404, rot. 1; ZSR 417, rot. 1.

10 e.g. ibid. ZMR 69, rot. 1 and d.; ZSR 238, rot. 1; ZSR 280, rot. 1d.; ZSR 353, rot. 1d.; ZSR 386, rot. 1d.; ZSR 412, rot. 1; P.R.O., SC 6/796/3, m. 13.

11 P.R.O., CHES 25/10, m. 10.

12 Ibid. CHES 25/10, m. 33; CHES 25/12, mm. 4, 38d.; CHES 25/14, m. 3d.

13 Ibid. CHES 25/11, mm. 1, 5, 8, 22; CHES 25/12, mm. 18d., 38d.; CHES 25/13, m. 1; CHES 25/14, m. 3d.

14 *V.C.H. Ches.* v (2), Mills and Fisheries: Dee Corn Mills.

15 C.C.A.L.S., ZMB 1, ff. 5–7v., 40.

16 Ibid. ZMB 2, ff. 9, 36, 52, 75v.; ZMB 3, f. 15; ZMB 4, f. 44v.; ZMB 6, f. 121v.; ZSB 3, f. 116; ZSR 174–93 *passim*.

17 Ibid. ZMB 7, ff. 104v., 156; ZMB 8, ff. 60v., 128; ZMB 9A, f. 4v.; ZMB 9B, f. 15v.; ZMB 9C, f. 5; ZMB 9E, f. 12; ZMB 9G, f. 5.

18 Ibid. ZCH 30; *36 D.K.R.* App. II, pp. 60, 78, 225–6, 230, 247, 475, 544; cf. P.R.O., CHES 29/59, m. 23.

19 C.C.A.L.S., ZSR 360, rot. 1d.; ZSR 365, rot. 1; ZSR 386, rot. 1; ZSR 400, rot. 1; ZSR 406, rot. 1; ZSR 414, rot. 1d.; ZSR 420, rot. 1d.

20 *Letters of Wm. Brereton*, 245.

21 Ormerod, *Hist. Ches.* i. 233.

22 C.C.A.L.S., ZMB 1, ff. 5–7v., 37v.; ZMB 2, ff. 9 and v., 35v.–36v., 52v.–53, 102 and v.; ZMB 3, ff. 15, 47, 50v., 112 and v.

23 Ibid. ZMB 1, f. 2; ZMB 2, ff. 29, 78; ZMB 3, ff. 62, 102v.; ZMB 6, f. 122; ZMB 7, ff. 120, 159; ZMB 8, ff. 60v., 128; ZMB 9A, f. 4v.; ZMB 9E, f. 12; ZMB 10, f. 2v.; ZQCR 10, m. 1; ZQCR 11, m. 1; ZSB 3, f. 65; P.R.O., CHES 29/109, m. 11d.

Fleshmongers' Row near the Cross;[1] councillors and constables of that quarter of the city invariably included one or two of their number.[2] Butchers also had shops in Foregate Street, and kept livestock in the Crofts and in the town fields east of Cow Lane.[3] They were frequently in trouble for slaughtering beasts in their shops, hanging carcasses outside the doors, and discarding the heads and entrails into the streets.[4] They were also regularly accused of regrating and forestalling, perhaps in reality a device for licensing their trade.[5]

Apart from sheep from the Frodsham area, most livestock sold in Chester came from Wales. The town was the destination of two main droving routes, one from the west through Northop and Hawarden, the other from the south through Eccleston and Christleton.[6] Chester butchers had especially close relations with Welsh dealers, whom they often represented in court.[7]

Chester's butchers sold beef, veal, mutton, lamb, and pork. A few also dealt in fish. Sales, which by the late 15th century were supervised by elected representatives of the wards,[8] were to customers ranging from the abbot of St. Werburgh's to cooks and artisans.[9] The byproducts of butchering, notably hides, both untreated and tanned, were sold to Chester's numerous leather workers.[10] Butchers also produced tallow.[11] By the early 16th century they acted as middle men, trading in both light skins from Ireland and heavier hides from neighbouring counties.[12]

Inshore fishing was in the hands of leading citizens who owned stalls in the Dee, and fishermen who rented fishgarths and traps along the estuary shore.[13] The King's Pool by the bridge remained the most important fishery. The prime catch was salmon, often salted and available throughout the year, but lamprey, bass, eels,

and sprats were also taken.[14] From deeper waters herring was routinely landed in the city, and Irish and Manx fish importers were prominent among those paying custom duties. The herring was generally preserved, either in brine or by smoking. Haddock and cod were also landed, together with the occasional seal, porpoise, sturgeon, and stockfish.[15]

In the later 14th century perhaps between 10 and 13 fishmongers regularly traded in Chester.[16] In the early 15th century numbers seem to have declined,[17] rising again only in the 1440s and 1450s.[18] In the late 15th century the trade was apparently concentrated in fewer hands. Its main focus was the Watergate, near which the Fishmongers' guild rented land,[19] and Watergate Street, in and around which lived fishermen and netmakers, and at the east end of which was the fish market.

Throughout the period Chester's wealthiest fishmongers owned seagoing vessels and traded on a relatively large scale. In the early 15th century, for example, Richard Smith traded with men from Carrickfergus, Drogheda, and Beaumaris, perhaps salting some of the fish he imported. Smith owned a cookshop on a prime site in Eastgate Street and also dealt in wine and cloth.[20] In 1436 a steward of the Fishmongers' guild sold salt and wine as well as salmon, herring, haddock, and whitefish,[21] and by 1500 fish was among the wide range of commodities handled by the most prominent city merchants.[22]

The city's cooks bought fish, meat, poultry, pigeons, and occasionally luxuries such as currants.[23] They perhaps only ever numbered six at any one time, but were nevertheless organized into a guild and put on their own pageant.[24] The cooks had close links with the

1 C.C.A.L.S., ZMB 2, f. 95v.; ZMB 5, ff. 1, 41v.; ZMR 64, rot. 1d.; ZMR 72, rot. 1; ZMR 78, rot. 1; ZSR 126, rot. 2d.; *36 D.K.R.* App. II, p. 98; 3 *Sheaf*, xliii, pp. 6–7.

2 e.g. C.C.A.L.S., ZMB 5, ff. 85v., 109v., 129v.; ZMB 6, ff. 33v., 83v.; ZMB 7, f. 156; ZMB 8, f. 127v.

3 Ibid. ZMR 78, rot. 1; ZSB 2, f. 40; ZSB 3, f. 64v.; B.L. Harl. MS. 2158, ff. 193–5, 197, 198v., 200, 204, 212v., 213v., 218.

4 e.g. C.C.A.L.S., ZMB 1, f. 16; ZMB 2, f. 19; ZSB 3, ff. 60v., 65, 94v.; ZSB 4, f. 32v.; ZSB 5, ff. 35, 137.

5 Ibid. ZMB 2, ff. 29, 78; ZMB 3, f. 62, 102v.

6 Ibid. ZSR 122, rot. 1; ZSR 155, rot. 1d.; ZSR 160, rot. 1d.; ZSR 168, rot. 1; ZSR 197, rot. 1; ZSR 239, rot. 4; ZSR 253, rot. 1d.; ZSR 255, rot. 1; ZSR 281, rot. 1; ZSR 268, rot. 1 and d.; ZSR 362, rot. 1; ZSR 369, rot. 1d.; ZSR 374, rot. 1; ZSR 383, rot. 1; ZSR 402, rot. 1d.

7 e.g. ibid. ZSR 169, rot. 1; ZSR 261, rot. 3; ZSR 316, rot. 1d.; ZSR 349, rot. 3d.; P.R.O., CHES 25/15, m. 38d.

8 C.C.A.L.S., ZCHB 2, f. 82v.

9 Ibid. ZSR 170, rot. 1; ZSR 244, rot. 1d.; ZSR 262, rot. 1; ZSR 294, rot. 1; ZSR 349, rot. 3; ZSR 376, rot. 1; ZSR 399, rot. 1.

10 Ibid. ZSR 150, rot. 1; ZSR 177, rot. 1; ZSR 239, rot. 4d.; ZSR 304, rot. 1; ZSR 315, rot. 1d.; ZSR 329, rot. 1.

11 Ibid. ZSR 173, rot. 1d.; ZSR 227, rot. 1; ZSR 385, rot. 1d.; ZSR 427, rot. 1d.

12 *T.H.S.L.C.* cxix. 68–73.

13 C.C.A.L.S., ZMR 69, rot. 1 and d.; ZSB 2, f. 6; ZSR 296, rot. 1d.; P.R.O., SC 6/784/2, m. 12; SC 6/787/8, m. 2; SC 6/791/5, m.

3; SC 6/797/1, m. 1d.

14 P.R.O., SC 6/787/9 to SC 6/796/10.

15 C.C.A.L.S., ZSR 130, rot. 1d.; ZSR 267, rot. 1d.; ZSR 275, rot. 1d.; ZSR 359, rot. 1; ZSR 372, rot. 1; ZSR 381, rot. 1.

16 Ibid. ZQCR 4, m. 1; ZQCR 10, m. 1.

17 Ibid. ZMB 3, f. 102v.; P.R.O., CHES 25/9, m. 37; CHES 29/108, m. 15d.; CHES 29/109, m. 11d.

18 Rest of para. based on C.C.A.L.S., ZMB 1, f. 36; ZMB 3, f. 62v.; ZMB 4, f. 27; ZSR 104, rot. 1; ZSR 135, rot. 1; ZSR 237, rot. 1d.; ZSR 245, rot. 1d.; ZSR 254, rot. 1d.; ZSR 315, rot. 1d.; ZSR 323, rot. 1d.; ZSR 359, rot. 1d.; ZSR 394, rot. 1d.; ZSR 442, rot. 1d.; ZSR 458, rot. 1d.

19 B.L. Harl. MS. 2158, f. 193.

20 C.C.A.L.S., ZSR 129, rot. 2d.; ZSR 135, rot. 1; ZSR 143, rot. 1d.; ZSR 165, rot. 1d.; ZSR 168, rot. 1d.; ZSR 190, rot. 1; ZMB 3, f. 86v.; *Cal. of Deeds and Papers of Moore Fam.* (R.S.L.C. lxvii), no. 1028.

21 C.C.A.L.S., ZSR 229, rot. 1d.; ZSR 263, rot. 1; ZSR 274, rot. 1; ZSR 275, rot. 1; ZSR 277, rot. 1; ZSR 312, rot. 1 and d.

22 e.g. ibid. ZSR 403, rot. 1 (Tudor ap Thomas); ZSR 429, rot. 1d. (Jn. Walley); ZSR 432, rot. 1 (Jas. Manley); ZSR 449, rot. 1d. (Hugh Hurlton).

23 e.g. ibid. ZSR 170, rot. 1; ZSR 266, rot. 1d.; ZSR 282, rot. 1d.; ZSR 346, rot. 2; ZSR 371, rot. 1d.; ZSR 408, rot. 1d.

24 Ibid. ZMB 1, f. 2; ZQCR 10, m. 1; ZQCR 11, m. 1; ZSB 1, f. 156v.; ZSB 2, ff. 26, 40, 85v.; ZSB 3, ff. 2v., 37, 94v.; ZSR 356, rot. 1.

bakers, and the Rows of the two trades adjoined, both probably forming part or an extension of the Dark Row at the corner of Northgate Street and Eastgate Street.[1] The wealth and status of cooks varied enormously, from men who served as sheriff down to traders with only a scarcely licit hearth obstructing a pavement.[2]

Few of the city's merchants traded as specialist spicers or grocers, and their commodities may have been sold by mercers.[3] Brewing, which catered for visitors and the immediate rural hinterland as well as residents,[4] was profitable, and leading citizens participated; they owned malt kilns,[5] employed bailiffs to oversee production,[6] and exported malt to Wales, a prohibited practice apparently licensed by fining it.[7] Large quantities of malt, especially unmilled oat malt, were handled and paid tolls at the Dee Mills.[8]

Brewing was a domestic activity and much of it was in female hands.[9] Some of Chester's wealthiest households brewed on a considerable scale under the wife's supervision, and female servants were employed both to produce and sell ale, often from the cellar beneath the family home.[10] Cellars were regularly named after their aldermanic owners, an association which perhaps explains the unusual absence of named alehouses and hostelries in late medieval Chester.[11]

The wives and widows of middling townsmen brewed on a smaller scale, often doing no more than sell their small household surplus from time to time. The more ambitious traded as *femmes soles* from rented cellars, some remaining in business for a decade or more.[12] All were regularly in trouble with the authorities for using false measures, adulterating their ale, or selling too dear; in 1497, for example, 94 people allegedly used false measures.[13] Most of the city's tapsters were based in the Eastgate Street district, many of them outside the walls in Foregate Street. Throughout the period numbers of men also sold ale, but their interest in the drink trade may have grown once the introduction of beer, perhaps as late as the 1470s,[14] allowed production on a commercial scale. By the 16th century women were effectively excluded.

Only the wealthiest Cestrians traded in wine. Most were prominent merchants involved with many commodities, and were rarely described as vintners.[15] The trade was probably modest, but the few ships paying prise may have been a poor indicator, since the tax was perhaps exacted at other ports while the wine was *en route* to the city. The trade may have grown in the 1490s and earlier 16th century, when it was dominated by Chester freemen.[16]

Although at least five taverners were recorded in the 1390s, they later dwindled in number, and disappeared entirely after 1451. Wine was probably retailed by the vintners, who may, as later, have used their undercrofts for both storage and sales.[17] In the 1530s several leading merchants certainly owned taverns.[18]

Textiles and Clothing. Throughout the period many workers in Chester produced textiles, both woollen and linen, and the city served as a cloth finishing centre for a wider hinterland. The industry, which produced cheap and coarse goods for local consumption, failed to attract large entrepreneurs and was small in scale. Wool came from Wirral, Anglesey,[19] and further afield, including Coventry and Derbyshire.[20] The workforce included female kempsters in the later 14th century, and cardmakers, who initially migrated from centres such as Oswestry (Salop.) and perhaps Tamworth (Staffs.) and Coventry, in the 15th.[21] Spinning was a female monopoly, partly organized under the putting-out system, with entrepreneurs providing both the spinning wheels and the raw material; sometimes, however, women sold their own yarn.[22]

The weavers, although poor, were one of the largest occupational groups. They were found in every quarter of the city and worked at home, often assisted by their wives. Linen weaving and woollen weaving may have been separate crafts, with the linen weavers occupying a

---

1 B.L. Harl. MS. 2158, f. 216.

2 *Cal. Deeds Moore Fam.* no. 1028; C.C.A.L.S., ZQCR 10, m. 1; ZQCR 11, m. 1; ZMB 2, ff. 59, 92; ZMB 3, ff. 101–2.

3 e.g. *Lancs. and Ches. Wills and Inventories* (Chetham Soc. N.S. iii), 1–4.

4 *36 D.K.R.* App. II, pp. 78, 211, 230, 247, 373, 523, 544.

5 P.R.O., SC 6/784/5, m. 5; B.L. Harl. MS. 2063, f. 122; C.C.A.L.S., ZMR 77, rot. 1.

6 C.C.A.L.S., ZSR 285, rot. 1d.

7 e.g. ibid. ZSB 2, ff. 24v.–25, 27v.; ZSB 3, ff. 25v., 69v., 94, 96v.

8 P.R.O., SC 6/784/5, m. 3; SC 6/787/9 to SC 6/801/2.

9 This para. and next based on J. Laughton, 'The Alewives of Later Medieval Chester', *Crown, Government, and People in the 15th Cent.* ed. R. E. Archer, 191–208.

10 e.g. P.R.O., CHES 25/12, m. 18d. (Alice wife of Jn. Armourer); C.C.A.L.S., ZMB 1, f. 15v. (Margaret wife of Wm. Hawarden); ZMB 2, f. 4 (Margery wife of Jn. Walsh).

11 e.g. C.C.A.L.S., ZMB 3, ff. 12v., 71v.; ZSB 1, ff. 42, 47.

12 e.g. Alice Duy: ibid. ZSR 167, rot. 1d.; ZSR 266, rot. 1; ZSR 272, rot. 1; ZSR 295, rot. 1d.; ZSR 309, rot. 1d.; Alice Buccy: ZMB

6, f. 166v.; ZSR 351, rot. 1; ZSR 367, rot. 1; ZSB 4, ff. 50, 94.

13 Ibid. ZSB 4, f. 94 and v.

14 Ibid. ZSB 3, f. 69 (first ref. to beer in Chester).

15 e.g. ibid. ZMB 3, f. 64.

16 K. P. Wilson, 'Port of Chester in Later Middle Ages' (Liverpool Univ. Ph.D. thesis, 1966), i. 124; ii, App. A; *Chester Customs Accts.* 71.

17 C.C.A.L.S., WS 1618, Button; WS 1621, Throppe; WS 1625, Aldersey; cf. H. Swanson, *Medieval Artisans: An Urban Class in Late Medieval Eng.* 22.

18 *L. & P. Hen. VIII*, vi, p. 92.

19 e.g. C.C.A.L.S., ZSR 118, rot. 1; ZSR 123, rot. 2d.; ZSR 466, rot. 1.   20 Ibid. ZMB 2, f. 100v.; ZMB 3, f. 98v.

21 Ibid. ZSR 66, rot. 1d.; ZSR 69, rot. 1d.; ZSR 71, rot. 1; ZSR 106, rot. 1d.; ZSR 108, rot. 1d.; ZSR 110, rot. 1d.; ZSR 113, rot. 1; ZMB 2, f. 39; ZMB 3, f. 97v.; cf. Keene, *Survey of Medieval Winchester*, i. 299–300; R. H. Britnell, *Growth and Decline in Colchester, 1300–1525*, 75; *Eng. Medieval Industries: Craftsmen, Techniques, Products*, ed. J. Blair and N. Ramsay, 324.

22 C.C.A.L.S., ZSR 142, rot. 1; ZSR 240, rot. 1; ZSR 245, rot. 1; ZSR 263, rot. 1d.; ZSR 280, rot. 1d.; ZSR 295, rot. 1.

subordinate position; often non-citizens paying an annual fine to work in Chester, they apparently congregated in Northgate Street[1] and probably produced coarse materials such as canvas.[2] The men who commissioned the weaving and supplied the yarn (often the city's walkers, dyers, or drapers) perhaps provided poorer craftsmen with equipment; more affluent weavers owned their own looms and undertook commissions in their own right.[3] The most prosperous acted as entrepreneurs themselves, buying raw wool, having it prepared for weaving, and distributing the yarn to weavers in the city and perhaps neighbouring villages.[4]

In the early 15th century Chester's chaloners, specialist weavers of bedding, were relatively prosperous craftsmen who perhaps congregated in the vicinity of St. John's Lane.[5] By 1550 their status had declined and the craft became the preserve of Welsh immigrants based in Handbridge.[6]

By the early 16th century some 70 per cent of Chester's textile workers were engaged in finishing, making up, and selling.[7] The dyers or hewsters, many of whom lived in or near St. John's Lane,[8] and whose dyestuffs and equipment were expensive, were the richest,[9] and were usually prominent citizens: 10 became sheriff between 1380 and 1509. After the early 15th century their numbers never fell below 10, even in the difficult 1440s and 1450s, perhaps in part because Chester finished cloth woven in Wales.[10] The city also supplied Welsh dyers with dyestuffs.[11] Woad and madder were probably the most commonly used, suggesting that grey and brown russets were the standard local product, but small amounts of the scarlet dye called grain were occasionally purchased.[12] In the early 15th century Yorkshire merchants visited

Chester with dyestuffs but in later years Londoners apparently monopolized the trade.[13]

Fulling (or walking) and shearing were carried out by distinct groups, with the former dominant, occasionally employing shearmen or providing their tools.[14] Chester's leading walkers, who congregated around the Dee fulling mills, were considerable entrepreneurs who purchased wool, commissioned its weaving and dyeing, and sold the finished product. They included men who held high civic office.[15] By the late 14th century the fulling mills were leased by the Crown to the citizens.[16] Rebuilt in the early 1390s, when production appears to have reached a peak, their profitability thereafter is uncertain and the lessees were often in arrears.[17] There were especial difficulties between the 1450s and the early 1480s when the mills were in disrepair and the number of walkers declined.[18]

The cloth made at Chester, like the Welsh cloth brought to the city for finishing, was generally coarse, including fustian, falding, blanket, russets, and frieze.[19] Finer woollen textiles, manufactured especially in Coventry and the West Riding of Yorkshire, were marketed by the city's drapers, whose numbers apparently increased in the 1490s.[20] The drapers were wealthy men and over the period 1380–1509 provided 17 sheriffs and 9 mayors, their power being especially marked after 1460. Although they may have clustered in Northgate Street, where they apparently sold cloth from their own shops, no cloth hall was ever built in Chester and there was not even a distinct drapers' Row.[21]

By contrast the mercers were concentrated in an extensive Row on the eastern side of Bridge Street,[22] a prime site in keeping with the distinction enjoyed by their guild, which commonly occupied the first place in

1 Ibid. ZSB 1, ff. 118, 139; ZMB 3, ff. 45 and v., 60v.; ZMB 4, f. 41.

2 e.g. ibid. ZSR 115, rot. 1d.; ZSR 124, rot. 1d.; ZSR 261, rot. 1; ZSR 319, rot. 1d.

3 Ibid. ZSR 119, rot. 1d.; ZSR 153, rot. 1; ZSR 289, rot. 1d.; ZSR 302, rot. 1; ZSR 319, rot. 1.

4 e.g. Jn. Herford: ibid. ZSR 197, rot. 1d.; ZSR 235, rot. 1; ZSR 237, rot. 1d.; ZSR 281, rot. 1d.; ZSR 285, rot. 1; ZSR 287, rot. 1d.

5 Ibid. ZSR 111, rot. 1d.; ZSR 122, rot. 1; ZSR 123, rot. 2; ZMB 1, ff. 11, 13.

6 Ibid. ZSR 338, rot. 1; ZSR 352, rot. 1; ZSR 371, rot. 1d.; ZSR 372, rot. 1d.; ZSR 455, rot. 1.

7 Analysis based on ibid. ZMB *passim*; *Rolls of Freemen of Chester*, i; Palliser, 'Revised List' (TS. at C.H.H.).

8 e.g. C.C.A.L.S., ZSR 140, rot. 1d.; ZSR 210, rot. 1d.; ZSR 226, rot. 1d.; ZSR 237, rot. 1d.

9 Ibid. ZSB 3, f. 59; ZSR 128, rot. 4d.; ZSR 236, rot. 1d.; ZSR 247, rot. 1d.; ZSR 259, rot. 1d.; ZSR 268, rot. 1; ZSR 368, rot. 1; ZSR 442, rot. 1d.; ZSR 449, rot. 1.

10 Ibid. ZSR 142, rot. 1d.; ZSR 191, rot. 1; ZSR 230, rot. 1; ZSR 237, rot. 1d.

11 Ibid. ZSR 159, rot. 1; ZSR 236, rot. 1d.; ZSR 360, rot. 1d.; ZSR 372, rot. 1d.

12 Ibid. ZSR 128, rot. 4d.; *Lancs. and Ches. Wills and Inventories* (Chetham Soc. N.S. iii), 1–4.

13 C.C.A.L.S., ZMB 2, f. 82; ZSR 128, rot. 4d.; ZSR 320, rot.

1d.; ZSR 360, rot. 1d.; ZSR 370, rot. 1; cf. *Business Hist. Rev.* lxv. 475–501.

14 C.C.A.L.S., ZSR 259, rot. 1; ZSR 288, rot. 1; ZSR 346, rot. 2d.; ZSR 373, rot. 1d.; ZSR 448, rot. 1d.

15 e.g. Adam Rainford: ibid. ZSR 198, rot. 1; ZSR 239, rot. 1d.; ZSR 251, rot. 1; ZSR 267, rot. 1d.; ZSR 273, rot. 1d.; ZSR 279, rot. 1; ZSR 282, rot. 1d.; Hamon Goodman: ibid. ZSR 354, rot. 1; ZSR 420, rot. 1; ZSR 462, rot. 1; ZSR 471, rot. 1d.

16 P.R.O., SC 6/787/9, m. 3; SC 6/788/2, m. 3; SC 6/788/6, m. 3; SC 6/789/5, m. 3; SC 6/789/7, m. 3.

17 Ibid. SC 6/790/5, m. 4; SC 6/790/7, m. 4; SC 6/795/1, m. 7; SC 6/801/1, m. 4d.

18 e.g. ibid. SC 6/798/4, m. 7; SC 6/799/1, m. 7d.; SC /799/9, m. 4d.; SC 6/800/1, m. 4d.; SC 6/800/4, m. 4d.; SC 6/800/5, m. 4d.; SC 6/800/8, m. 4d.; SC 6/801/1, m. 4d.

19 C.C.A.L.S., ZSR 78, rot. 1; ZSR 148, rot. 1; ZSR 166, rot. 1; ZSR 180, rot. 1; ZSR 209, rot. 1; ZSR 212, rot. 1; ZSR 224, rot. 1d.; ZSR 293, rot. 1d.; ZSR 303, rot. 1; ZSR 327, rot. 1; ZSR 344, rot. 1; ZSR 385, rot. 1d.; ZSR 396, rot. 1; ZSR 399, rot. 1; ZSR 458, rot. 1.

20 Ibid. ZSR 148, rot. 1d.; ZSR 169, rot. 1; ZSR 180, rot. 1; ZSR 195, rot. 1d.; ZSR 206, rot. 1d.; ZSR 290, rot. 1d.; ZSR 295, rot. 1d.; ZSR 338, rot. 1d.; ZSR 419, rot. 1d.; P.R.O., CHES 25/15, m. 53.

21 C.C.A.L.S., ZMB 7, f. 81v.; ZTAR 1/4; B.L. Harl. MS. 2158, ff. 197–9, 201v., 212v., 213v., 216 and v., 221v., 223v.

22 *P.N. Ches.* v (1:i), 21.

any list of companies.[1] The leading mercers included some of the city's most influential men. Between 1380 and 1509 twenty-five mercers became sheriff and fifteen mayor. Although they sold costly silks, velvets, damasks, and the fine linens of Flanders and Brabant,[2] until the late 1480s there was evidently little local demand for such fabrics and they also stocked other items, including ribbons, points (laces for fastening clothing), spices, and paper,[3] commodities probably largely obtained from London merchants.[4]

The tailors, one of the largest groups of craftsmen, included wealthy men who also sold cloth[5] and occasionally acted as pledges for members of the local gentry.[6] Most tailors, however, were poor, many of them Welsh immigrants, and few achieved civic office. They were concentrated in Bridge Street and Castle Lane.[7]

Although the boundaries between the clothing trades were fluid and some tailors also made hose,[8] there was a distinct craft of cappers in the late 14th and earlier 15th century, later replaced by the feltcappers, who were well established by the 1480s and shared a guild with the skinners.[9]

Leather Trades.   Tanning and leather working were important enough to be among the earliest crafts to develop guilds.[10] Although the shoemakers emerged victorious from the dispute of the 1360s,[11] and thereafter some of their number were engaged in tanning,[12] the tanners remained active and apparently congregated in and around Barkers Lane (later Union Street), close to the company altar in St. John's church.[13] Hides were imported from Ireland,[14] or supplied by the city's butchers and other local traders.[15] The cobblers, always

among the largest and humblest occupational groups,[16] had a Row in Bridge Street,[17] but were also scattered throughout the city.[18] The saddlers, who in the 14th century also had a Row in Bridge Street, may well have had a further base in Eastgate Street and beyond the walls, near the tanners. Never as numerous as the cobblers, they were apparently richer and occasionally held civic office.[19] Other leather workers included a few parchment makers, also perhaps based outside the Eastgate,[20] and glovers, mainly in Lower Bridge Street. The status of the latter and the importance of their trade apparently increased in the late 15th century, when three became sheriff and one mayor. By then, although Bridge Street apparently remained the focus of manufacture, retailing may have been in Eastgate Street, where Glovers' Row was recorded in 1426.[21] Skinners, who were particularly prominent in civic life in the mid 15th century, declined in numbers thereafter. They traded especially in squirrel,[22] although rabbit, fox, and beaver were also known.[23]

Metal Trades.   Iron, bronze, pewter, gold, and silver items were made in Chester throughout the period. Among the most indispensable were horseshoes and iron tools, by the later 14th century in part produced from metal shipped from Spain,[24] and forged in smithies outside the walls, near the city gates and at the Bars, where the smiths also provided bread and ale for travellers and fodder and grazing for their horses.[25] Ironmongers were among the city's leading merchants, active in overseas trade and by the early 16th century combined in one powerful company with the mercers.[26] The smiths shared a guild with the declining number of marshals or specialist farriers.[27]

1 e.g. C.C.A.L.S., ZMB 6, f. 30.

2 Ibid. ZSR 115, rot. 1d.; ZSR 124, rot. 1d.; ZSR 132, rot. 1d.; ZSR 162, rot. 1; ZSR 267, rot. 1d.; ZSR 333, rot. 1d.; ZSR 334, rot. 1; ZSR 351, rot. 3; ZSR 362, rot. 1d.; ZSR 365, rot. 1; ZSR 367, rot. 1; ZSR 368, rot. 1; ZSR 384, rot. 1.

3 e.g. *Lancs. and Ches. Wills and Inventories* (Chetham Soc. N.S. iii), 1–4.

4 e.g. C.C.A.L.S., ZSR 115, rot. 1d.; ZSR 261, rott. 1, 2.

5 e.g. ibid. ZSR 135, rot. 1; ZSR 144, rot. 1; ZSR 160, rot. 1; ZSR 231, rot. 1d.; ZSR 408, rot. 1d.

6 e.g. ibid. ZSR 239, rot. 1.

7 Ibid. ZSR 93, rot. 1; ZSR 94, rot. 1; ZSR 118, rot. 1d.; ZSR 129, rot. 2d.; ZSR 142, rot. 1; ZSR 149, rot. 1d.; ZSR 170, rot. 1d.; ZSR 216, rot. 1; ZSR 228, rot. 1; ZSR 247, rot. 1; B.L. Harl. MS. 2158, f. 195v.

8 e.g. Jn. Pennington: C.C.A.L.S., ZSR 307, rot. 1; ZSR 326, rot. 1d.

9 Ibid. ZSR 84, rot. 1; ZSR 133, rot. 1; ZSR 235, rot. 1; ZSR 310, rot. 1; ZSR 333, rot. 1.

10 *V.C.H. Ches.* v (2), Craft Guilds: Origins.

11 Above, this chapter: City Government and Politics, 1350–1550 (Decay of the Guild Merchant).

12 C.C.A.L.S., ZSR 243, rot. 1 and d.

13 Ibid. ZSR 136, rot. 1d.; ZSR 148, rot. 1d.; ZSR 158, rot. 1; ZSR 330, rot. 1.

14 e.g. ibid. ZMB 2, f. 41v.; ZMB 3, ff. 92, 93; ZCAM 1, ff. 16–17v.

15 Ibid. ZSR 139, rot. 1; ZSR 150, rot. 1; ZSR 173, rot. 1d.;

ZSR 174, rot. 1; ZSR 209, rot. 1d.; ZSR 244, rot. 1; ZSR 246, rot. 1d.; ZSR 272, rot. 1; ZSR 306, rot. 1; ZSR 329, rot. 1; ZSR 370, rot. 1; ZSR 457, rot. 1.

16 Ibid. ZSR 122, rot. 1d.; ZSR 147, rot. 1; ZSR 217, rot. 1; ZSR 277, rot. 1; ZSR 360, rot. 1.

17 *P.N. Ches.* v (1:i), 21.

18 e.g. C.C.A.L.S., ZSR 346, rot. 1; ZSR 448, rot. 1.

19 Ibid. ZSR 59, rot. 1; ZSR 90, rot. 1; ZSR 121, rot. 1d.

20 e.g. ibid. ZSR 235, rot. 1.

21 P.R.O., CHES 25/16, m. 15 (Ric. Wirral); C.C.A.L.S., ZMB 5, ff. 69v. (Jas. Norris), 129v. (Jn. Evans); ZMB 7, f. 158v. (Nic. Newhouse); ZMR 81, rot. 1d.; ZSB 3, f. 27v.

22 e.g. C.C.A.L.S., ZSR 113, rot. 1; ZSR 130, rot. 1d.; ZSR 208, rot. 1; ZSR 317, rot. 1d.; P.R.O., CHES 25/10, m. 26d.

23 C.C.A.L.S., ZSR 119, rot. 1; ZSR 191, rot. 1d.; ZSR 262, rot. 1; ZSR 369, rot. 1.

24 Ibid. ZQCR 7, m. 1; Wilson, 'Port of Chester', ii, p. ii.

25 C.C.A.L.S., ZMUR 1, f. 3; ZSR 174, rot. 1d.; ZSR 196, rot. 1; ZSR 277, rot. 1; ZSR 289, rot. 1d.; ZSR 290, rot. 1d.; ZSR 315, rot. 1 and d.; ZSR 338, rot. 1; ZSR 357, rot. 1d.; ZSR 363, rot. 1d.; ZSR 368, rot. 1; ZSR 401, rot. 1; ZSR 429, rot. 1d.; ZSR 458, rot. 1d.

26 Ibid. ZSR 103, rot. 1; ZSR 126, rot. 2; ZSR 154, rot. 1d.; ZSR 174, rot. 1d.; ZSR 238, rot. 1d.; ZSR 317, rot. 1d.; ZSR 400, rot. 1d.; ZSR 429, rot. 1; Johnson, 'Aspects', 277.

27 C.C.A.L.S., ZSR 165, rot. 1d.; ZSR 166, rot. 1d.; ZSR 230, rot. 1d.; ZSR 233, rot. 1d.; ZSR 237, rot. 1d.; ZSR 264, rot. 1d.; ZSR 292, rot. 1d.

Lorimers, located in a Row near the abbey, were few and apparently disappeared by *c.* 1460.[1] The spurriers maintained their craft and were occasionally rich, although never numerous.[2] The cutlers declined in number throughout the 15th century. Occasionally men of considerable status,[3] but more usually not,[4] their decline suggests that knives were brought into town rather than manufactured there.[5]

A few pinners, cardmakers, and wiredrawers worked in late medieval Chester, occasionally combining the various crafts.[6] Locksmiths found steady employment,[7] and furbers, although never numerous, were in regular demand: weapons were routinely carried by many townsmen,[8] and the civic élite regularly bequeathed body armour, steel caps, swords, and daggers.[9]

Bells were cast in the city,[10] and pewter vessels were used there by 1391.[11] Pewterers, first recorded in 1429, increased in number in the late 15th and early 16th century,[12] when there was briefly a separate guild of founders and pewterers.[13]

Goldsmiths remained concentrated in Eastgate Street and Foregate Street in the late 14th and 15th century.[14] Their numbers were fairly constant even in the 1440s and 1450s, when other crafts perhaps declined. In the early 16th century they were a significant presence among the freemen, perhaps 1 per cent of the total. In general they were not rich, and few held high civic office. Some were involved in an additional craft, and one bore the surname Tinker.[15] Gold objects were rare in medieval Chester, although some residents owned silver-gilt cups and gilded buckles,[16] and the city's goldsmiths worked mainly in silver.[17] Leading craftsmen also perhaps offered their stone-built cellars

for the storage of valuable goods,[18] and lent money, sometimes considerable sums.[19] As elsewhere, their role corresponded to that of a banker, although they themselves commonly fell into debt.[20]

Building Trades. Although most buildings in late medieval Chester were timber-framed, and stone buildings were thus prominent landmarks,[21] masons and stonecarvers were needed for the city's walls, castle, religious buildings, bridge, and the paving in thoroughfares such Eastgate and Bridge Streets.[22] Stone was available from quarries outside the Northgate and near the river. There seems to have been little new building between 1350 and the late 15th century, and in 1486 the citizens claimed that a quarter of the city lay in ruins. Thereafter new work at the abbey and some of the churches apparently led to an increase in the number of masons.[23] Brickmen were recorded from 1459, perhaps working with clay tiles rather than bricks as such.[24]

Carpenters and wrights were the most numerous of the building craftsmen. Although one became sheriff,[25] most were low-paid non-citizens who supplemented their income with small-scale retailing and casual labouring.[26] At the pinnacle of the craft were the master carpenters of the palatinate, some of whom participated in the life of the town and the guilds.[27]

Other building workers included thatchers and slaters. Because of fire risk, thatchers, who apparently lived mostly in Foregate Street, were employed chiefly on buildings outside the walls.[28] Slaters were more numerous and in 1407 were among those whose wages the city governors sought to control.[29] Although

1 Ibid. ZSR 251, rot. 1; ZSR 324, rot. 1; *P.N. Ches.* v (1:i), 22–3.

2 e.g. Freget fam.: ibid. ZSR 134, rot. 1; ZSR 266, rot. 1; ZSR 270, rot. 1; ZSR 272, rot. 1d.; ZSR 273, rot. 1d.; ZSR 307, rot. 1; ZMB 3, f. 16; ZMB 4, f. 68v.; ZTAR 1/3, m. 1.

3 e.g. Jn. Hey: P.R.O., CHES 25/10, m. 1.

4 C.C.A.L.S., ZSR 298, rot. 1; ZSR 367, rot. 1d.; ZSR 385, rot. 1; ZSR 466, rot. 1d.

5 Ibid. ZMB 4, f. 40v.; ZSB 1, ff. 38v., 70v.; ZSR 190, rot. 1; cf. Keene, *Survey of Medieval Winchester,* i. 280.

6 e.g. Rob. Leche: C.C.A.L.S., ZSR 419, rot. 1; ZSR 449, rot. 1.

7 e.g. ibid. ZSR 193, rot. 1; ZSR 254, rot. 1; ZSR 304, rot. 1; ZSR 386, rot. 1; ZSR 459, rot. 1.

8 e.g. ibid. ZSR 126, rot. 2; ZSR 230, rot. 1d.; ZSR 289, rot. 1; ZSR 301, rot. 1d.; ZSR 361, rot. 1; ZSR 455, rot. 1.

9 Ibid. ZSR 461, rot. 1; P.R.O., WALE 29/291; 3 *Sheaf,* xvii, p. 105; xxxvi, p. 9.

10 C.C.A.L.S., ZSR 153, rot. 1d.; ZSR 157, rot. 1; ZSR 228, rot. 1; ZSR 404, rot. 1; ZSR 427, rot. 1d.; ZMB 8, f. 101v.

11 Ibid. ZSR 104, rot. 1; ZSR 158, rot. 1; ZSR 250, rot. 1; ZSR 383, rot. 1d.; ZSR 457, rot. 1.

12 Ibid. ZMB *passim; Rolls of Freemen of Chester,* i; Palliser, 'Revised List' (TS. at C.H.H.).

13 *V.C.H. Ches.* v (2), Craft Guilds: List.

14 B.L. Harl. MS. 2158, ff. 197, 200, 218, 221v.

15 Analysis based on *Rolls of Freemen of Chester,* i; Palliser, 'Revised List'; C.C.A.L.S., ZMB *passim;* Ral. Mutlow: ibid. ZSR 250, rot. 1d.; ZSR 253, rot. 1d.; Wm. Tinker: ibid. ZSB 2, f. 6v.

16 C.C.A.L.S., ZSR 133, rot. 1; ZSR 143, rot. 1d.; ZSR 169, rot. 1d.; ZSR 241, rot. 1d.; ZSR 309, rot. 1; ZSR 341, rot. 1d.; ZSR

351, rot. 3; ZSR 376, rot. 1d.; ZSR 386, rot. 1; ZSR 419, rot. 1; ZSR 446, rot. 1; ZSR 453, rot. 1d.; ZSR 458, rot. 1.

17 Ibid. ZSR 381, rot. 1d.; ZSR 410, rot. 1; ZSR 427, rot. 1d.; ZSR 440, rot. 1.

18 Ibid. ZSR 136, rot. 1; ZSR 156, rot. 1; ZSR 177, rot. 1; ZSR 216, rot. 1d.; ZSR 243, rot. 1d.; ZSR 260, rot. 1; ZSR 380, rot. 1; ZSR 438, rot. 1; ZSR 467, rot. 1.

19 e.g. ibid. ZSR 535, rot. 26; ZSR 543, rot. 12; ZSR 554, rot. 1; ZSBC 1, ff. 38v.–39, 69v.

20 Ibid. ZSR 123, rot. 1d.; ZSR 159, rot. 1d.; ZSR 174, rot. 1d.; ZSR 187, rot. 1; ZSR 207, rot. 1; ZSR 249, rot. 1d.; ZSR 361, rot. 1; ZSR 389, rot. 1d.; ZSR 422, rot. 1; ZSR 444, rot. 1.

21 e.g. P.R.O., CHES 25/12, m. 6d.; B.L. Harl. MS. 2037, f. 173v.; 3 *Sheaf,* lvi, p. 59.   22 C.C.A.L.S., ZMUR 1, m. 3.

23 Below, this chapter: Religion (Religious Communities, Parish Churches).

24 C.C.A.L.S., ZSR 312, rot. 1d.; ZSR 332, rot. 1d.; ZSR 419, rot. 1.

25 *Some Obits of Abbots and Founders of St. Werburgh's Abbey* (R.S.L.C. lxiv), 91.

26 P.R.O., SC 6/784/5, m. 5d.; SC 11/890, m. 1; C.C.A.L.S., ZMB 6, ff. 167, 170; ZSB 1, ff. 41v., 102; ZSB 3, f. 41; ZSR 175, rot. 1d.; ZSR 180, rot. 1; ZSR 239, rot. 3; ZSR 287, rot. 1d.; ZSR 290, rot. 1; ZSR 316, rot. 1d.

27 36 *D.K.R.* App. II, pp. 158, 425; 3 *Sheaf,* xxxvi, p. 54; C.C.A.L.S., ZMB 3, f. 25.

28 C.C.A.L.S., ZSR 237, rot. 1; ZSR 337, rot. 1d.; ZSR 351, rot. 1d.; ZSR 399, rot. 1d.; ZSR 418, rot. 1d.; cf. B.L. Harl. MS. 2037, f. 309v.   29 C.C.A.L.S., ZQCR 11, m. 1.

their pay was not high, in the early 15th century the trade attracted immigrant labour from Kendal and Ruthin, both towns in areas which perhaps also supplied slates.[1] None of Chester's resident slaters grew wealthy and they were scattered throughout the city with perhaps a concentration in Northgate Street.[2] They worked closely with other roofing craftsmen including tilers[3] and shinglers.[4]

Plumbers were never numerous and often worked in association with glaziers, a group with skills developed in the 14th century, when Chester was an important centre for window glass.[5] There is no evidence of glazing in domestic buildings, and the glaziers shared a guild with stainers and painters, all of whom presumably worked most commonly for ecclesiastical patrons.[6] Painters, however, occasionally decorated the principal chambers of the houses of important townsmen,[7] obtaining their colours from leading city merchants, notably the mercers.[8]

Other Trades. Weapon makers such as bowyers, fletchers, and stringers remained sufficiently numerous to form a craft guild,[9] the members of which occasionally attained civic office in the later 15th century. Ropers, porters, and coopers worked particularly in the distributive services associated with the harbour area. Cestrians also became carters and mariners.[10]

THE CORPORATION AND THE REGULATION OF TRADE

By the mid 14th century market offences were presented at inquests held before the mayor and sheriffs, and dealt with in the portmote or crownmote.[11] At a comprehensive inquest of 1407 the city's butchers, fishmongers, and poulterers were indicted for trading offences 'both in the market and without', and the smiths, cutlers, goldsmiths, skinners, barbers, coopers, and slaters for trading without paying toll and custom to the earl and for paying excessive wages contrary to the Statute of Labourers.[12] By then the mayor was also responsible for regulating prices, hours of sale, the disposal of waste, and slaughtering.[13] He also dealt

with all the more serious market offences, including raising prices, evading tolls, and holding illegal markets in private houses or outside the city liberties.[14] In 1506 the Great Charter established him as clerk of the market.[15]

Tolls were payable at the city gates, but the amounts collected were small; much Cheshire produce was exempt and a proportion was perhaps appropriated by the holders of the serjeanties of the gates.[16] From the late 15th century the markets were increasingly tightly regulated.[17] Already in the 1470s there were complaints that fishmongers who were not citizens sold fish outside the market,[18] and in 1506 the Great Charter required that all fish and flesh had to be retailed in the customary place.[19] During the 16th century the Assembly tightened its control over the economy as a whole by supporting guild monopolies and freemen's privileges.[20] Aliens born outside England and Wales were subjected to an entry fine of at least £10, and able non-free merchants were encouraged to take up the freedom of the city. Guild regulations were subjected to the mayor's approval from 1529.[21] The Tailors were extremely energetic in protecting their monopoly, and other guilds pursuing 'foreign' craftsmen in the city courts included the Carpenters, Dyers, Skinners, Tanners, and Smiths.[22]

The conduct of the city's food markets came under closer supervision from the 1530s, particularly over the conditions and times of sale; freemen had priority in buying, followed by resident non-freemen and then outsiders. The sale of corn and fish were of especial concern.[23] The Assembly pursued a strongly protectionist policy to discourage sales by or to non-freemen except during the two fairs.[24] It was, however, difficult to prevent private sales between citizens and foreigners in the scattered city markets, and in 1546–7 a common hall was built in Northgate Street where all goods brought to the city in bulk had to be deposited before being offered for sale. A clerk or keeper of the common hall was appointed and a scale of tolls was levied; Kendal and Manchester merchants were singled out to pay extra tolls.[25] Orders control-

---

1 C.C.A.L.S., ZMB 3, ff. 8, 70v.; ZSR 401, rot. 1d.; ZSR 457, rot. 1d.

2 e.g. ibid. ZSB 1, f. 65; ZSB 3, ff. 46, 70; ZSB 5, f. 5v.; ZSR 162, rot. 1; ZSR 238, rot. 1; ZSR 243, rot. 1d.; ZSR 329, rot. 1d.; ZSR 404, rot. 1.

3 Ibid. ZMB 1, f. 32v.; ZMB 4, f. 53v.; ZSB 3, f. 20; ZSB 4, ff. 53, 74; ZSR 362, rot. 1d.

4 Ibid. ZMB 8, f. 46; ZSR 366, rot. 1.

5 *Eng. Medieval Ind.* ed. Blair and Ramsay, 277.

6 C.C.A.L.S., ZMB 4, f. 63; ZSR 59, rot. 1; ZSR 342, rot. 1; ZSR 358, rot. 1d.; ZSR 383, rot. 1d.; ZSR 419, rot. 1d.

7 e.g. J.R.U.L.M., Arley Deeds, box 25, nos. 13–14.

8 C.C.A.L.S., ZSR 142, rot. 1d.; ZSR 288, rot. 1; ZSR 300, rot. 1.

9 *V.C.H. Ches.* v (2), Craft Guilds: List; cf. C.C.A.L.S., ZSR 165, rot. 1d.; ZSR 238, rot. 1d.; ZSR 242, rot. 1; ZSR 273, rot. 1d.; ZSR 297, rot. 1; ZSR 326, rot. 1; ZSR 465, rot. 1; ZSR 471, rot. 1.

10 C.C.A.L.S., ZSR 287, rot. 1; ZSR 290, rot. 1d.; ZSR 303, rot.

1d.; ZSR 311, rot. 1; ZSR 315, rot. 1d.; ZSR 378, rot. 1d.; ZSR 449, rot. 1; ZSR 465, rot. 1d.

11 Ibid. ZQCR 2, 4–5, 10; *Sel. R. Chester City Cts.* p. xviii.

12 C.C.A.L.S., ZQCR 11.   13 Ibid. ZAF 1, ff. 3–4.

14 e.g. ibid. ZMB 1, ff. 2, 5, 6v.–7, 16v., 36, 37v., 52v., 69; ZMB 4, ff. 34, 53; Morris, *Chester*, 401–2.

15 C.C.A.L.S., ZCH 32.

16 Ibid. ZMB 3, f. 67 and v.; ZMUR 1, mm. 1–2; ZSB 3, ff. 27, 34 and v., 86v.–88; P.R.O., CHES 29/59, m. 23 and d.

17 Johnson, 'Aspects', 229, 244–5; Morris, *Chester*, 522.

18 Morris, *Chester*, 402.

19 C.C.A.L.S., ZCH 32.   20 e.g. ibid. ZAB 1, f. 79v.

21 Johnson, 'Aspects', 245; C.C.A.L.S., ZAB 1, ff. 65v.–66, 69.

22 C.C.A.L.S., ZSR 445, rot. 1; ZSR 504, rot. 9; ZSR 506, rott. 51d., 56d., 60d.; ZSR 522, rot. 33; ZSR 535, rott. 23, 32.

23 Ibid. ZAB 1, ff. 61, 64v.; Morris, *Chester*, 397.

24 Johnson, 'Aspects', 231.

25 C.C.A.L.S., ZAB 1, ff. 76v.–77; Morris, *Chester*, 399–400.

ling wholesale trade were issued in 1549, banning all foreigners from the common hall and prohibiting freemen from acting as their agents under pain of a £2 fine for the first offence, and loss of citizenship for the second.[1]

An attempt to improve port facilities was under way by 1541, with the construction of a quay at Neston some 10 miles down river from Chester.[2] A committee of four, including three aldermen, was set up to supervise the work, voluntary contributions were gathered in each parish, and a customs levy was dedicated to the project.[3] The New Haven was used even though it remained uncompleted.[4]

The council continued to regulate food supply through the assize of bread and ale and the close supervision of bakers and butchers, whose names were recorded in the Mayor's Book.[5] The bakers took an oath before the mayor to abide by the assize and to bake wholesome bread, and in 1505 their monopoly was confirmed on condition that they baked enough to feed the city. They had to join the Bakers' company and leave copies of their marks in the Pentice.[6]

Dearth prompted action to ensure a free market. Regulations controlling the movement of grain were issued across the county in 1485, 1496, and 1507–8.[7] In 1536, when the price of barley rose, the council inveighed against regraters and forestallers and regulated the trade in barley and malt.[8]

The council supervised external trade through its management of a system of local customs which favoured the freemen.[9] Customs duties were dedicated to individual city officials.[10] All duties payable to the sheriffs were doubled for a fortnight before and after Midsummer and for one week before and after Michaelmas. Common bargains, the sale of forfeit goods, were also managed to the citizens' advantage. Because merchants incurred extra costs by using the Dee estuary ports, the council stipulated precise rates for off-loading into lighters and for carrying goods overland to the city. Portering rates were regulated, with set charges for transport from anchorages and within the city, and for installing goods in cellars.

CHESTER AS A COUNTY CAPITAL

The presence of the palatinate and county courts brought a constant flow of visitors to the castle, including officials, lawyers, attorneys of absent recognitors, sureties, jurors, and suitors.[11] At the Chester exchequer, recognitors and their sureties alone numbered 363 between October 1512 and May 1513.[12] For a Cheshire gentleman, personal attendance at Chester was as vital as going to Westminster, giving access to patronage and important gossip.[13] The palatinate government had innumerable small posts to be filled, some carrying pensions, which were as eagerly sought as its major offices. Patronage was a powerful magnet, drawing men from beyond as well as within Cheshire.[14]

The local gentry were needed particularly to serve on the numerous juries empanelled at the palatinate courts. The county court, for example, which met eight or more times a year, usually for at least two or three days,[15] might require as many as 116 individual jurors for a single session.[16] There were also grand jury panels, drawn from the gentry in the area closest to Chester. Between 1523 and 1536 an average of 14 jurors were chosen from panels averaging 27, and during the early 16th century panels came to represent a higher social rank and it was routine to include the names of Cheshire's leading knights, albeit as absentees.[17]

Other courts generating visitors included those of the archdeaconry and after 1541 the diocese of Chester.[18] From 1543 the palatinate court of Great Sessions notionally met twice a year in Chester for sessions lasting six days.[19] The city's own courts also brought in well-to-do outsiders: in the late 1540s, in particular, the mayor's court was used to enrol statutory bonds for extraordinary sums ranging from £200 to £5,000[20] and to pursue actions with Cestrians for debt.[21]

The convenience of the city and palatinate courts may have attracted some merchants and others to negotiate agreements and enrol debts even though their goods never entered the city.[22] Although many actions were between Welshmen,[23] no group was dominant and business spanned Chester's region in

1 C.C.A.L.S., ZAB 1, f. 79.

2 B.L. Harl. MS. 2082, f. 14; Morris, *Chester*, 459–60.

3 C.C.A.L.S., ZAB 1, f. 91.

4 E. Rideout, 'Chester Companies and the Old Quay', *T.H.S.L.C.* lxxix. 141–74.

5 C.C.A.L.S., ZMB *passim*.

6 Ibid. ZAB 1, f. 69; B.L. Harl. MS. 2025, f. 8; Morris, *Chester*, 416.

7 37 *D.K.R.* App. II, pp. 47, 96, 142, 362, 365, 436, 463, 597, 623–4, 772, 806.   8 C.C.A.L.S., ZAB 1, f. 65.

9 *Chester Customs Accts.* 8–17.

10 Rest of para. based on C.C.A.L.S., ZAB 1, ff. 41–46v.

11 T. J. Thornton, 'Political Society in Early Tudor Ches. 1480–1560' (Oxf. Univ. D.Phil. thesis, 1993); *V.C.H. Ches.* ii. 18–25; D. J. Clayton, *Administration of Co. Palatine of Chester, 1442–85* (Chetham Soc. 3rd ser. xxxv), 19, 241–3.

12 P.R.O., CHES 5/1 (4 Hen. VIII).

13 e.g. Bodl. MS. Lat. misc. c.66, f. 63.

14 37 *D.K.R.* App. II, *passim*.

15 *Letters and Accts. of Wm. Brereton of Malpas* (R.S.L.C. cxvi), 238, 240.

16 Clayton, *Administration*, 134, 230–1; pers. comm. Dr. T. J. Thornton, Huddersfield Univ.

17 P.R.O., CHES 24/86–7; pers. comm. Dr. Thornton.

18 *V.C.H. Ches.* v (2), Law Courts: Middle Ages (Ecclesiastical Courts).

19 *V.C.H. Ches.* ii. 35, 38.

20 C.C.A.L.S., ZMR 112, rott. 1–2, 5–7.

21 e.g. ibid. rot. 4d.; ZSR 554, rot. 3.

22 e.g. ibid. ZSR 554, rott. 2, 7.

23 Ibid. ZSFB 2/1–6; cf. ZSR 504, rot. 37; ZSR 506, rott. 68, 69d., 73d.

its widest sense, involving men from as far away as Kendal and Halifax.[1]

By the 16th century there was considerable intermingling of civic, county, and regional affairs. Citizens were drawn into county matters through acting as sureties for gentlemen and knights, presumably for some consideration.[2] They owned property throughout the region, including Lancashire and north Wales, and left money to men in Denbigh and to churches in Denbigh, Lymm, Tarvin, and Warrington.[3] The city's churches were similarly remembered by Cestrians in exile in Bristol and London.[4]

County figures in return participated in civic matters: the commission supervising the dissolution of Chester's religious houses, for example, comprised civic dignitaries together with Sir Piers Dutton and William Brereton,[5] while another commission appointed to inquire into disorder in 1547 included the mayor with four knights and four gentlemen.[6] County knights were invited in to arbitrate in quite minor disputes,[7] and together with other local gentlemen owned and leased property in the city for personal use or as an investment.[8]

By the early 16th century Chester was quite cosmopolitan, and in general relations with outsiders were cordial, those with north Wales being usually close. Welshmen rented and owned property in the city, became freemen, and were buried in the city churches,[9] while Chester merchants had similar ties with Denbighshire and mid Wales.[10] There was a strong Welsh presence in the city, both residents and traders using the markets and courts, and Welsh was spoken in the streets.[11] Spaniards traded and took disputes to the courts in person, and at least one married and settled in Chester, conducting an illegal trade in local cloth.[12] The Irish, on the other hand, although Chester's chief trading partners, were apparently rarely more than visitors. Occasionally tensions within and between the different groups erupted violently. There was an affray involving Welshmen in 1514, and in 1532 the mayor intervened in a murderous squabble between Spaniards. His successor bravely calmed a significantly larger disturbance in 1549, reputed to have involved 500 Irishmen in a bloody fight with the citizens.[13]

RELIGION, 1230–1550

RELIGIOUS COMMUNITIES

Although Chester had few parish churches for a town of its size, it was home to several religious communities which played a correspondingly large role in town life. Their precincts were extensive, and their inmates formed sizeable and occasionally troublesome groups within the population.[14] The grandest religious house in the city by far remained the abbey of St. Werburgh, which continued until the Dissolution to enjoy an income ranking among the top twenty or so English Benedictine monasteries.[15] The annexation of the earldom brought it for the first time into close contact with the Crown, and thereafter the abbot entertained important guests and often took custody of money and treasure *en route* to Westminster from Ireland.[16] By the 1290s it also provided corrodies for royal servants. In

the 13th century, despite difficulties during the Barons' Wars, when its property and privileges were attacked, it enjoyed a period of stability, and an ambitious building programme was initiated.[17] After the long and successful abbacy of Simon Whitchurch (1265–91), in the early 14th century the abbey suffered internal dissension and financial mismanagement; the troubles grew worse after the 1340s when Abbot William Bebington obtained exemption from episcopal control for his servants and for the abbey's parish of St. Oswald, and culminated in the deposition of the next abbot, Richard Sainsbury, in 1362.[18] The mid 14th century was nevertheless marked by great progress with the conventual buildings, and by the writing of Ranulph Higden's world history, the *Polychronicon*, the only scholarly work of the first rank produced by the community.[19] By 1364, however, Higden was dead

---

1 C.C.A.L.S., ZSR 506, rot. 41; ZSFB 2/8; ZSFB 2/15.

2 37 *D.K.R.* App. II, pp. 48, 246, 502.

3 C.C.A.L.S., WS 8/1; WS 8/3; 3 *Sheaf*, xi, pp. 1–2; xvii, p. 69; xviii, pp. 37, 90, 92.

4 3 *Sheaf*, xvi, pp. 56–7; xvii, p. 21; xviii, pp. 97, 101; *Colln. of Lancs. and Ches. Wills* (R.S.L.C. xxx), 168–9.

5 J. Beck, *Tudor Ches.* 98; Morris, *Chester*, 149.

6 C.C.A.L.S., ZAB 1, f. 78v.

7 e.g. ibid. ZSR 504, rot. 18d.

8 Ibid. ZAB 1, ff. 37v.–40, 53–8; ZMR 112, rot. 8; *Colln. of Lancs. and Ches. Wills* (R.S.L.C. xxx), 85; *Lancs. and Ches. Wills and Inventories*, i (Chetham Soc. [o.s.], xxxviii), 169, 179.

9 e.g. 3 *Sheaf*, xviii, p. 101.

10 Ibid. p. 92; C.C.A.L.S., WS 8/1; WS 8/3.

11 e.g. C.C.A.L.S., ZSB 5, f. 37v.; ZSBC 1, f. 64 and *passim*;

ZSR 504, rot. 36; ZSR 535, rot. 23.

12 Ibid. ZSB 5, f. 166v.; ZSB 7, ff. 12–13; ZSR 535, rot. 37; ZSR 543, rot. 1; *L. & P. Hen. VIII*, ix, no. 794; Wilson, 'Port of Chester', i. 133.

13 Morris, *Chester*, 66, 69; B.L. Harl. MS. 2125, f. 206; C.C.A.L.S., ZAB 1, f. 76v.; Liverpool Univ. Libr., MS. 23.5, ff. 257, 274, 291.

14 Jones, *Ch. in Chester*, 10–38.

15 Ibid. 59–60.

16 e.g. *Cal. Pat.* 1232–47, 466; 1247–58, 68, 70, 105, 118, 136, 151, 203, 361; *Cal. Lib.* 1245–51, 370; 1251–60, 6, 44, 152.

17 *V.C.H. Ches.* iii. 133–7; *V.C.H. Ches.* v (2), Cathedral and Close: Abbey Church to 1541.

18 Burne, *Monks*, 79; *V.C.H. Ches.* iii. 139.

19 A. Gransden, *Historical Writing in Eng.* ii. 43–57.

and the greatest period of building was over. Apart from the installation of the magnificent choir stalls in the 1380s, perhaps through the patronage of Richard II, little was done to the fabric until the late 15th century, and the community appears to have been impoverished and often riven by internal strife.[1]

The abbey's impact upon the life of the citizens was considerable and diverse. It held the advowsons of three city churches, St. Mary, St. Peter, and St. Olave, and in the early 13th century appropriated a fourth, that of its own parish, St. Oswald.[2] Its privileges bore most heavily upon Cestrians in the early 1390s when it finally succeeded in its long-standing ambition to appropriate the rich living of St. Mary's and united it with the impoverished rectory of St. Olave's. In 1397 Abbot Henry Sutton obtained papal licences to suppress the vicarages of St. Mary's and St. Oswald's, leaving both large parishes in the cure of ill-paid stipendiary chaplains. The changes were opposed by the bishop of Lichfield and in 1402 were reversed by the archbishop of Canterbury.[3]

As the greatest landowner in the city, with extensive jurisdictional privileges and exemptions from toll, the abbey's relations with the citizens were never easy. During the 13th century, however, it received numerous small grants of property in and around Chester. In 1278, for example, the late mayor, John Arneway, left property in Blacon, Crabwall, and the city in return for his burial in St. Werburgh's and for the maintenance in perpetuity of two chaplains to celebrate daily masses for his own and his wife's souls at the altar of St. Leonard in the abbey church and at St. Bridget's.[4] Eventually, however, the abbey's rights, especially its trading monopoly during St. Werburgh's fair, became a source of friction, and by a settlement made in 1284 they were eroded.[5] There were also difficulties about the abbey manor. In the 1280s and 1290s the citizens unsuccessfully contested the abbot's right to hold a manor court at St. Thomas's chapel outside the Northgate, and tried to prevent him from treating a road from St. John's hospital to the anchorage at Portpool as his private property. There were also complaints that he had blocked the road to the stone cross outside the Northgate and encroached on the highway by building a bakehouse.[6] In the early 14th century there was further friction over the exemption of the abbey and its tenants from tolls,[7] and in 1323 the abbot was

forced to back down over access through the city wall to the monastic Kaleyards.[8]

With the onset of conflict in the late 13th century the citizens' generosity seems to have dried up;[9] for the following two centuries few if any chose to be buried or commemorated in the abbey, and the only chantries established there were for the community's own abbots and monks.[10] Unloved by the citizens, the abbey became a focus for disorder. In 1394, for example, there was an affray involving Baldwin Radington, controller of the royal household,[11] and in the 15th century monks and servants of the abbey were involved in brawls on several occasions. Abbot Richard Oldham (1455–85) had a particularly turbulent career: imprisoned in the castle in 1461, he was bound over in 1478 to keep the peace towards the mayor, John Southworth, and again, with a large group of the city's tradesmen, in 1480.[12]

In the late 15th century there was a revival in the fortunes and discipline of the monastery under Abbots Simon Ripley (1485–93) and John Birkenshaw (1493–1524). The abbey church was completed and St. Oswald's was rebuilt.[13] Leading citizens, including the former mayors John Southworth and Ralph Davenport (d. 1506), once again chose to be buried there, and by c. 1530 there was a school for local boys.[14] Even so, the abbey continued to be worsted in its conflicts with the citizens. The most telling evidence of its weakness was the curtailment of the abbot's jurisdiction over the Michaelmas fair in 1485.[15]

No other religious community in Chester could rival the wealth and influence of St. Werburgh's. Indeed, all had financial problems. The nunnery, for example, never well endowed, in 1331 had barely sufficient income to support its inmates, and in the earlier 15th century was regularly exempted from taxation because of poverty. In lieu of proper endowment it had been granted various annuities and privileges, some of which represented potential sources of conflict with the citizens. Particularly controversial was the exemption of its tenants from tolls and other local levies. That privilege, first granted by the founder in the mid 12th century, was rendered even more distasteful by grants of 1303 and 1358 which freed the nuns' tenants from all obligations to the city, including jury service;[16] in the 1350s matters reached a climax when the prioress, Helewise, was indicted in the portmote for setting up

1 *V.C.H. Ches.* iii. 139–42.

2 *V.C.H. Ches.* v (2), Medieval Parish Churches.

3 Jones, *Ch. in Chester*, 13–14, 177–8.

4 *Cart. Chester Abbey*, ii, pp. 463–4, 468–70.

5 *V.C.H. Ches.* v (2), Fairs.

6 *Cal. Ches. Ct. R.* pp. 155–6, 159, 163–5, 188, 190, 199, 204; cf. C.C.A.L.S., ZCHB 1, f. 17 and v.; ZCHB 2, f. 84 and v.

7 C.C.A.L.S., ZMR 19; Morris, *Chester*, 378–9.

8 Burne, *Monks*, 62; 1 *Sheaf*, ii, p. 33.

9 e.g. *Cart. Chester Abbey*, i, pp. 237–44; ii, pp. 339–52.

10 e.g. 29 *D.K.R.* 51–2; Burne, *Monks*, 97–101; 3 *Sheaf*, xviii,

p. 94 (citing P.R.O., CHES 29/82, m. 27).

11 Above, this chapter: City and Crown, 1350–1550.

12 Morris, *Chester*, 129; Burne, *Monks*, 125–7, 129–33; C.C.A.L.S., ZSB 2, f. 45v.

13 *V.C.H. Ches.* v (2), Cathedral and Close: Abbey Church to 1541.

14 3 *Sheaf*, xxiii, pp. 37–8; Burne, *Chester Cath.* 9.

15 C.C.A.L.S., ZMB 6, f. 101.

16 *V.C.H. Ches.* iii. 146–8; *Cal. Chart. R.* 1226–57, 310; 1341–1417, 287–8; Ormerod, *Hist. Ches.* i. 346; C.C.A.L.S., ZCHB 2, f. 69.

an unlicensed court for her tenants.[1] Even so the nunnery appears to have been held in some affection by the citizens. The prioress, generally a member of the local gentry, entertained their women and children at her table, and the nuns ran a school.[2] Unlike the monks they continued to receive grants throughout the period.[3] Chantries were established at the nunnery by Cecily Compton in 1353 and the widow of Robert Paris, chamberlain of Chester, in 1379.[4] By the late 15th century the nuns had houses and tenements bringing annual rents of some £25, scattered throughout the city.[5] Their local standing was reflected in the prioress's participation in the foundation of St. Ursula's hospital for needy members of the corporation in 1509, when she was given the right to nominate to vacancies unfilled by the city authorities.[6] By then, with the revival of the city's economy, the number of bequests to the nuns was growing, and *c.* 1520 they embarked upon a new cloister.[7] Nevertheless, no citizens' burials were recorded in the church or its precincts until 1535.[8]

In the 13th century three friaries were permanently established in the town. The Dominicans, first to arrive, probably in the 1230s, were quickly followed in 1238 by the Franciscans, and some time before 1277 by the Carmelites. For a brief period in the late 13th century there was also a community of Friars of the Sack. All the friaries received some royal support during the 13th century, and the Franciscans regarded themselves as a royal foundation.[9] None was ever rich. The three main communities were all apparently popular with the citizens, many of whom entered into confraternity with them,[10] and from the mid 14th century they attracted numerous small bequests.[11] By the 15th century they also enjoyed close relations with certain of the craft guilds and other groupings, notably the Carmelites with the Carpenters, and the Franciscans with the merchants and sailors.[12]

The friars' churches were favoured places of burial. The Carmelites appear to have attracted most support and by the Dissolution had become the largest and least

impoverished of the three. They received the body of the executed rebel Sir Peter Legh in 1399, and their church housed the tombs of members of prominent families, including John Hope (d. 1439), Roger Smith (d. 1508), and John Hawarden (d. 1496). Fewer burials were recorded at the churches of the Franciscans and Dominicans, whose popularity was probably greater among the less well off.[13]

By the later 15th century the friars were frequently involved in disorder in the town. The Carmelites were especially unruly. In 1454, for example, three of their brethren were charged with wandering armed through the city to the terror of the populace,[14] and in 1462 another was bound over for feuding with a monk of St. Werburgh's.[15] Most scandalously of all, throughout the 1490s the entire community, including the prior, appears to have taken part in a succession of brawls and internal disputes.[16] The other friaries were not immune from such problems. In 1454 the prior of the Dominicans and several of his brethren attacked a servant of Abbot Richard Oldham, who as bishop of Man had held ordinations in their church in 1452.[17] The feud with Oldham evidently continued, and members of the community, including another prior, were bound over to keep the peace in 1459, 1462, and 1463.[18] In 1464 one of the friars was accused of murdering a baker outside the friary gate, and the prior of abetting him.[19] In the 1490s the prior was involved in an affray against the prior of the Carmelites, and in 1510 or 1511 one of his successors was accused of assault.[20] Even the Greyfriars had their share of trouble: their prior was attacked in 1427,[21] and one friar was accused of assaulting another and a second man in 1502 or 1503.[22]

Building activity by the lesser religious houses largely followed the same rhythms as St. Werburgh's. Much work was done during the 13th and earlier 14th century, and all the friaries were enlarged within a century or so of their foundation, the Carmelites in particular greatly extending both precinct and buildings in the 1350s. Thereafter, except perhaps at the

1 C.C.A.L.S., ZQCR 5.

2 *Blk. Prince's Reg.* iii. 310; Jones, *Ch. in Chester,* 91.

3 e.g. *Cal. Pat.* 1399–1401, 296–304; *J.C.A.S.* xiii. 96–9, 101–3; 1 *Sheaf,* ii, p. 84; 3 *Sheaf,* xvii, p. 38; xviii, pp. 92–4; xxi, p. 2; xxiii, pp. 37–8; xxxvi, pp. 59–60; Jones, *Ch. in Chester,* 104; D. L. Broughton, *Rec. of an Old Ches. Fam.* 86–7; *Reg. Chichele* (Cant. & York Soc.), ii. 42; P.R.O., CHES 38/25/7; WALE 29/291.

4 Jones, *Ch. in Chester,* 104, 107, 109; 3 *Sheaf,* xxi, pp. 2, 5–9; P.R.O., CHES 3/2, no. 3; CHES 38/25/7.

5 Jones, *Ch. in Chester,* 61–2.

6 *V.C.H. Ches.* iii. 183.

7 e.g. *Lancs. and Ches. Wills and Inventories,* ii (Chetham Soc. [o.s.], li), 6–12; 3 *Sheaf,* xv, p. 42; xviii, pp. 87, 92; xxi, p. 9; xxiii, pp. 37–8; *V.C.H. Ches.* v (2), Sites and Remains of Medieval Religious Houses: Benedictine Nunnery.

8 *V.C.H. Ches.* iii. 147; *Cart. Chester Abbey,* ii, pp. 300–1; 3 *Sheaf,* xxi, p. 9.

9 *V.C.H. Ches.* iii. 171–2, 174, 176, 178.

10 Jones, *Ch. in Chester,* 98.

11 e.g. C.C.A.L.S., ZMR 42; P.R.O., WALE 29/291; B.L. Harl. MS. 2061, f. 24v.; Harl. MS. 2176, f. 276; J. P. Earwaker, *Hist. of Church and Par. of St. Mary-on-the-Hill,* 30; 3 *Sheaf,* xiii, pp. 90–1; xiv, pp. 8–9; xvii, pp. 23, 69–70, 105; xviii, pp. 24–5, 87, 92–4; xx, pp. 67, 71; xxi, p. 9; xxii, p. 62; xxiii, pp. 37–8; *J.C.A.S.* xxiv. 27; Ormerod, *Hist. Ches.* i. 648.

12 *V.C.H. Ches.* iii. 172, 176.

13 Ibid. 172–7.

14 C.C.A.L.S., ZSB 1, f. 132; Morris, *Chester,* 351.

15 C.C.A.L.S., ZMB 5, f. 74.

16 e.g. ibid. ZMB 7, f. 171; ZMB 8, f. 40v.; ZSB 4, ff. 48, 51v., 110, 119–22; *V.C.H. Ches.* iii. 177; *J.C.A.S.* xxxi. 19; Morris, *Chester,* 148.

17 C.C.A.L.S., ZSB 1, f. 131; Morris, *Chester,* 146.

18 C.C.A.L.S., ZMB 5, ff. 48, 76; Morris, *Chester,* 130.

19 P.R.O., CHES 29/169, m. 25.

20 C.C.A.L.S., ZSB 4, ff. 119–20; ZSB 5, f. 114 and v.

21 P.R.O., CHES 25/12, m. 15d.

22 C.C.A.L.S., ZSB 5, f. 6.

Blackfriars, there appears to have been little further activity until the late 15th century, when the Dominicans started to reconstruct their church and the Carmelites built a steeple. Work continued until the 1520s or later; the Dominicans, for example, planned a new nave and rebuilt their frater.[1]

The hospitals of St. John and St. Giles continued to receive favours from the earl and the citizens in the 13th century, though neither was exceptionally successful or well endowed. St. John's, the richer, owned much property both locally and further afield,[2] but its good beginnings were largely vitiated by the improvidence of its wardens; in 1316 the prior of Birkenhead, into whose hands care of the hospital had passed, complained of numerous improper alienations of lands and rents. Similar abuses appear to have taken place in the mid 14th century and again in the late 15th and early 16th.[3] Compounded by resentment that the hospital sheltered paupers not native to the city, they evidently ensured that it received few new benefactions.[4] Confidence was so low in 1509 that the city corporation used a bequest of Roger Smith, a former sheriff, to establish a new hospital, St. Ursula's, to care for those among its own members who fell on hard times. St. Ursula's did not prosper, and from 1547 was reduced to the status of almshouses.[5]

The other older hospital, the leper house of St. Giles, was never well endowed. Apart from its site in Boughton its most important possession appears to have been a bakehouse in Bakers' Row in Eastgate Street.[6] Its privileges, which included the right to levy a toll on all provisions brought for sale in Chester market, involved it in extensive litigation during the 14th century, especially with the tenants of St. Werburgh's. In 1537 the city authorities were sufficiently hostile to point out that whereas the grant of the market toll had been to support the sick, the inmates were in general 'mighty whole and sound persons, able to labour'. The hospital was threatened with the loss of its privileges unless admissions were confined to the sick.[7]

The religious community which enjoyed closest relations with the citizens was the collegiate church of St. John. Staffed by a dean and seven canons whose liturgical duties were generally performed by ill-paid

vicars choral, from the 13th century it was the citizens' favoured church for burial and chantries.[8] Burials were encouraged by the establishment of the fraternity of St. Anne;[9] in 1396, for example, one of the latter's benefactors, the former sheriff John Hatton, made provision to be laid beside his first wife Agnes in the Lady chapel and for four years of requiems.[10] The church seems to have enjoyed particular popularity as a place of burial in the early 16th century, when interments included those of the wealthy rector of Holy Trinity, Henry Rainford (d. 1505),[11] Nicholas Deykin (d. 1518) and his wife,[12] Richard Broster, a former sheriff (d. 1523), and his wife,[13] and Ranulph Pole, rector of Hawarden (d. 1538).[14] For a while the college also maintained contacts with the citizens through its schools. In 1353 there was a grammar school and a music school, the latter held in the White chapel in the graveyard.[15] A grammar school, presumably the same, was in the care of a clerk named John Whitby in 1368,[16] but both institutions evidently disappeared long before the dissolution of the college.[17]

St. John's, which was never rich and owned comparatively little property in the city, nevertheless built ambitiously in the later Middle Ages. The major work, the extension of the eastern chapels, was perhaps connected with the establishment of the Thornton chantry in 1348. An elaborate north-western tower was added in the early 16th century.[18] The church remained in the patronage of the bishop throughout the Middle Ages. Although it claimed exemption from the archdeacon of Chester, until 1541 it continued as the main centre of diocesan administration within the city.[19] It was there that the bishop on occasion conducted ordinations[20] and that the archdeacon, or more usually his official, held court.[21] Members of the chapter from time to time held the offices of archdeacon and official,[22] and under Bishop Robert Stretton (1358–85) penitentiaries for the archdeaconry or county were frequently chosen from the clergy or the hermits attached to the college.[23]

PARISH CHURCHES

By the early 13th century the city had received its full, if comparatively modest, complement of nine parish

1 *V.C.H. Ches.* v (2), Sites and Remains of Medieval Religious Houses.

2 *V.C.H. Ches.* iii. 178–82; Jones, *Ch. in Chester*, 65–6.

3 Jones, *Ch. in Chester*, 87.

4 Ibid. 44; *T.H.S.L.C.* lxxviii. 67.

5 *V.C.H. Ches.* iii. 183–4.

6 Above, this chapter: Economy and Society, 1230–1350 (Trades and Industries).

7 *V.C.H. Ches.* iii. 178–9; Jones, *Ch. in Chester*, 43–4; B.L. Harl. MS. 2063, f. 58v.; 3 *Sheaf*, xxx, p. 66; xxxv, pp. 50–1.

8 *V.C.H. Ches.* v (2), Collegiate Church of St. John.

9 Below, this section (Guilds, Confraternities, and Chantries).

10 3 *Sheaf*, xxxvi, p. 9.   11 Ibid. xviii, pp. 93–4.

12 Ibid. xiv, pp. 8–9.   13 Ibid. pp. 37–8.

14 *T.H.S.L.C.* lxv. 174.   15 Jones, *Ch. in Chester*, 111.

16 *Lich. Episcopal Reg. V: 2nd Reg. of Bp. Rob. de Stretton, 1360–85* (Collns. Hist. Staffs. N.S. viii), p. 120.

17 Jones, *Ch. in Chester*, 111; *V.C.H. Ches.* iii. 230.

18 J. M. Maddison, 'Decorated Archit. in NW. Midlands' (Manchester Univ. Ph.D. thesis, 1978), 265–6.

19 *V.C.H. Ches.* iii. 6, 10.

20 e.g. *Reg. Stretton, 1360–85*, p. 217; cf. Morris, *Chester*, 146.

21 Jones, *Ch. in Chester*, 113; *V.C.H. Ches.* iii. 8–10; C.C.A.L.S., EDC 1/1–10.

22 Jones, *Ch. in Chester*, 18, 20, 128, 131, 133, 139, 143, 149, 152, 154, 158.

23 Ibid. 160, 163; *Reg. Stretton, 1360–85*, pp. 11, 21, 32, 42, 47.

churches.[1] Besides St. John's and the monks' parish of St. Oswald, they comprised the churches of St. Mary on the Hill, Holy Trinity, St. Peter, St. Michael, St. Martin, St. Bridget, and St. Olave. By the 1250s there was also a chapel dedicated to St. Chad in the Crofts, though it is uncertain whether it was ever parochial. The mother churches' monopoly over burial rights appears to have persisted until relatively late, and there were evidently no graveyards at the other churches until the 14th century. The first seems to have been at St. Mary's, the only church apart from St. Oswald's to have a large parish outside the city liberties. Few of the livings were adequately endowed. The richest was St. Mary's, a church closely associated with the castle and which retained its independence throughout the Middle Ages, despite repeated attempts to appropriate it by the monks of St. Werburgh's. Though the rector was often an absentee, he had a chaplain and the church possessed abundant ornaments and vestments. It also attracted bequests from eminent citizens, several of whom were buried there.

Another rich living, St. Oswald's, was appropriated by the monks in the 13th century and was served by a perpetual vicar. Originally meeting within the abbey church at the altar of St. Oswald, its parishioners acquired a separate building only *c.* 1348. Like the abbey it seems to have been held in little affection by local people, though by the later 15th century it had become the special responsibility of the corporation: in 1488 Abbot Simon Ripley negotiated with the mayor, sheriffs, and leading members of the Assembly for help in reconstructing it. Two other churches, St. Peter's and Holy Trinity, survived as rectories. Never well endowed, they were usually staffed by chaplains. Both were the scene of a few grand burials or chantries; burials in Holy Trinity, for example, included the mayors John Whitmore (d. 1374) and John Armourer (d. 1396),[2] and in St. Peter's Alderman Thomas Middleton (d. 1535).[3]

The other four churches were poor. All were served by chaplains, St. Martin's and St. Bridget's having been appropriated to St. John's in the 14th century, and St. Michael's and St. Olave's apparently lacking sufficient income to support a rector. None appears to have attracted much interest from the more well-to-do of the city, apart from the occasional burial or minor bequest towards buildings and furnishings. St. Michael's, with two known burials and a chantry served by two chaplains, was perhaps the most favoured.[4]

The pattern of building at the parochial level was closely related to that in the religious communities. At St. Peter's, for example, there was work connected with that at St. Werburgh's in the early 14th century. Activity peaked in the late 15th and early 16th century: St. Mary's was largely rebuilt, St. Nicholas's chapel, serving as the parish church of St. Oswald's, was greatly enlarged in 1488, and St. Michael's acquired a new chancel. In the 1530s St. Peter's was doubled in size, a work assisted by Fulk Dutton, a draper who owned the buildings demolished for the extension.

THE CLERGY

In late medieval Chester the clergy formed a significant proportion of the population. In the earlier part of the period they were dominated by the monastic communities,[5] but by the later 14th century there were fewer religious and more minor posts for seculars, as chaplains serving fraternities, chantries, and private individuals. The impact of the secular clergy was reinforced by the presence of the archidiaconal court and the representatives or officials of the largely absentee archdeacons.[6] The city was, moreover, the centre of a rural deanery, under an official styled the 'dean of Christianity'.[7]

The richer benefices tended to be held by absentees. The canons of St. John's in particular had little incentive to reside, since the commons which they received were comparatively low. They were often civil servants or ecclesiastical administrators, especially before the steep decline in the value of their prebends in the early 15th century. Since they were collated by the bishop, many were also canons at Lichfield.[8] The dean, whose benefice, the richest in the city, was also in the bishop's gift, more often resided, partly no doubt because his archidiaconal jurisdiction over the college and its appropriated churches was regarded as incompatible with pluralism. Nevertheless, some deans were absentee, and in the early 15th century, after the losses sustained by the church in the wars with the Welsh, their pluralism was regularized by papal dispensations.[9]

After the deanery the richest benefice in the city was the rectory of St. Mary's, the incumbents of which were also often absentee. They included royal clerks and ecclesiastical administrators, partly because the living belonged to the abbot of St. Werburgh's.[10] The only other relatively wealthy living, that of the petty canon or senior cantarist at St. John's, remained in the gift of a local family, the descendants of its founder, and was generally held by resident members of the local gentry.[11]

The occupants of the lesser benefices, more often

---

1 Account based, except where stated otherwise, on details in *V.C.H. Ches.* v (2), Medieval Parish Churches.

2 *J.C.A.S.* n.s. vi. 42–8; P.R.O., WALE 29/291.

3 3 *Sheaf*, xviii, p. 87.

4 Ibid. xvii, p. 105; xxxvi, pp. 59–60; B.L. Harl. MS. 2061, f. 25; *Cat. Anct. D.* vi, C 5282.

5 Jones, *Ch. in Chester*, 11–12.

6 *V.C.H. Ches.* v (2), Law Courts: Middle Ages (Ecclesiastical Courts).

7 e.g. C.C.A.L.S., ZMR 3, rott. 5, 7; cf. P.R.O., CHES 25/1.

8 Jones, *Ch. in Chester*, 12, 17–19.

9 Ibid. 32, 126; *Cal. Papal Reg.* vi. 270; vii. 282.

10 Jones, *Ch. in Chester*, 13, 25, 33–4, 173–6.

11 Ibid. 14, 21–2, 25.

resident, probably made greatest impact upon the life of the city. Occasionally, they included men of wealth, such as Alexander le Bel, a kinsman of former mayor John Arneway, who held Holy Trinity in the early 14th century, or Robert of Bredon, farmer of the Dee Mills and rector of St. Peter's from 1350 to 1377.[1] In general, however, they seem to have had modest backgrounds. Much of the daily pastoral work was performed not by the beneficed clergy but by a miscellaneous group of chaplains, whose numbers proliferated in the later Middle Ages. They included the vicars choral at St. John's, and chaplains to the hospitals, chantries, confraternities, and castle.[2] Many of the richer citizens had oratories in their houses, licensed by the diocesan, and some apparently also maintained chaplains.[3] The duties of such clerics were various: the vicars choral at St. John's, for example, were employed primarily to fulfil the choir duties of the absent canons, but they also served the appropriated parishes of St. Bridget and St. Martin and undertook chantry commissions from laymen.[4] In addition there were hermitages attached to St. John's and other churches, including St. Martin's and St. Chad's. At St. John's the eremitic tradition extended from the 12th century to the mid 14th or later,[5] and included figures of some local importance such as John of Chorlton, established in a cell beside the collegiate church in 1363, and appointed penitentiary for the archdeaconry of Chester for two years in 1366 and for Cheshire during the bishop's pleasure in 1369.[6] A further hermitage, established by John Spicer before 1358, was situated by the bridge at Chester, and was probably identical with that of St. James in Handbridge, whose occupant, John Benet, was in 1450 accused of sheltering malefactors and keeping a brothel.[7]

RELIGIOUS CULTS

Chester contained a number of images regarded with especial veneration, including those of Our Lady variously at the abbey, the nunnery, Blackfriars, and St. Mary on the Hill; of St. Catherine and St. Stephen at St. Mary's; and of St. Michael at St. Michael's.[8] More significant cult objects included the girdle of St. Thomas Becket at the nunnery, the remains of St. Werburg at the abbey, and the Holy Rood at St. John's. Nothing is known of the nuns' relic beyond

the fact of its existence in 1536;[9] the two major cults were those of St. Werburg and the Holy Rood. That of St. Werburg, earlier and initially more important, appears to have fluctuated with the fortunes of its host community. By the 13th century it was in decline. Despite the lavish rebuilding of the saint's shrine c. 1340, there is little to suggest that she was then the object of interest within the city, apart from a procession held in her honour by an Abbot Thomas, probably Birchills (1291–1323).[10] Possibly she exerted more attraction in the wider world: late medieval pilgrim badges adorned with geese and found in London may have alluded to a celebrated miracle performed by St. Werburg, and were perhaps tokens acquired at her shrine in Chester.[11] The cult locally revived a little in the late 15th and early 16th century, when bequests were left for tapers before the shrine,[12] and the Chester monk Henry Bradshaw compiled a vernacular verse Life, culled from ancient sources in the monastic library.[13] A further relic, the saint's supposed girdle, was said in 1536 to be in great request for comforting women at childbirth.[14]

From the late 13th century the most significant relic in Chester was the Holy Rood at St. John's, a silver-gilt crucifix containing wood from the True Cross. Its origins are uncertain. Perhaps it was brought from the East by Earl Ranulph III, who was on Crusade in 1219–20.[15] On the other hand it may have been associated with the cult of King Harold, boosted in 1332 by the discovery within the church of his alleged remains, still fragrant and clad in leather hose, golden spurs, and crown. Harold's links with the cult of the Holy Rood and in particular with the miracle-working crucifix of Waltham (Essex), perhaps suggested the introduction of an analogous devotion into Chester.[16]

The relic was first mentioned in 1256 or 1257, when Fulk of Orby left a mark of silver a year for lights in its honour. Its reputation increased steadily in the later 13th and early 14th century, and for a while St. John's was known as the church of the Holy Cross.[17] By the early 14th century at least one of the ships which plied from the city, the property of William (III) of Doncaster, was known as the *Holy Cross of Chester*,[18] and women kept vigil before the Rood.[19] The relic's fame extended well beyond the city. In the 14th century the oath 'by the rood of Chester' was evidently

1 Ibid. 25, 167.
2 Ibid. 10–11, 22–7.
3 *Reg. Stretton, 1360–85*, pp. 12, 14, 31, 34, 59, 64, 74, 81, 83; *Cat. Anct. D.* vi, C 4044.
4 *V.C.H. Ches.* v (2), Collegiate Church of St. John.
5 Ibid.; *V.C.H. Ches.* iii. 127.
6 *Reg. Stretton, 1360–85*, pp. 32, 47; 3 *Sheaf*, lv, pp. 48–9, 68.
7 *36 D.K.R.* App. II, p. 436; *Blk. Prince's Reg.* iii. 457; *Reg. Stretton, 1360–85*, p. 38; Morris, *Chester*, 169; *V.C.H. Ches.* iii. 127.
8 *J.C.A.S.* xxxi. 9; *Cal. of Deeds and Papers of Moore Fam.* (R.S.L.C. lxvii), no. 992; 3 *Sheaf*, xxi, p. 9.
9 *L. & P. Hen. VIII*, x, p. 141.

10 *J.C.A.S.* xxxi. 9. Plate 6.
11 M. Mitchiner, *Medieval Pilgrim and Secular Badges*, p. 191; London Museum, *Medieval Catalogue*, plate 72, no. 45.
12 3 *Sheaf*, xix, p. 4; xxiii, pp. 37–8.
13 H. Bradshaw, *Life of St. Werburge of Chester* (E.E.T.S. orig. ser. lxxxviii).
14 *L. & P. Hen. VIII*, x, p. 141.
15 3 *Sheaf*, xxii, pp. 37–40.
16 A. Thacker, 'Cult of King Harold at Chester', *Middle Ages in NW.* ed. T. Scott and P. Starkey, 158–64.
17 *V.C.H. Ches.* v (2), Collegiate Church of St. John.
18 *Chester Customs Accts.* 21.
19 Morris, *Chester*, 172.

commonplace, being mentioned in both William Langland's great poem the *Vision of Piers the Ploughman* and the less famous *Richard the Redeless*.[1] The Rood was especially venerated in Wales; in 1278, for example, certain Welshmen swore on it not to bear arms against the king, and in the later 14th century it was the subject of several odes by the poet Gruffudd ap Maredudd (fl. 1352–82), who seems himself to have made a pilgrimage to the relic.[2] Its reputation was even carried abroad to Gascony by Cheshire men; in 1411, for example, Henry Champayne, a burgess of Libourne (Gironde), presumably inspired by the cult at St. John's, bequeathed to the city of Chester a gilt shrine containing a piece of the Holy Cross, though it is uncertain whether it ever reached Chester.[3]

At their height, offerings to the Rood amounted to perhaps £70 a year and constituted by far the biggest item in the revenues of the collegiate church;[4] they presumably helped to fund the four canonries which by the early 15th century were termed the prebends of the Holy Cross.[5] The high tide of the relic's popularity had perhaps been reached before the mid 14th century, when offerings were in decline.[6] Nevertheless, money, treasure, and candles continued to be left to the Rood, pilgrimages were made, and requiems were offered at its altar until its removal in the 1530s.[7]

GUILDS, CONFRATERNITIES, AND CHANTRIES

Chester had relatively few religious guilds and their impact upon city life was correspondingly limited. In the early 14th century the guild of St. Mary comprised some 48 members of the civic élite, but its purpose is unknown and it was probably short-lived. Thereafter the city never had more than three confraternities. The earliest and most important was that of St. Anne, probably founded in 1361, when its members successfully petitioned the Black Prince for a licence to hold lands and rents in Chester to maintain a chantry and two chaplains in St. John's church.[8] It received few gifts in the later 14th century,[9] but in 1393 its refoundation by John Woodhouse, dean of St. John's, led to numerous grants of land in the city and its environs. The new

arrangements provided for two wardens and two chantry priests, and originally for endowments worth up to £20 a year. By the later 15th century, although new endowments had long since ceased, income had risen to almost £40, and the fraternity had property all over the city.[10]

The fraternity was open to both men and women, and its members seem usually to have comprised twenty-five or thirty of the city's governing élite. The wardens or masters were often apparently drawn from the clergy of St. John's; between 1396 and 1420, for example, they included Ranulph Scolehall, chaplain of the Orby chantry, who was presumably a relative of John Scolehall, escheator of Cheshire 1365–70.[11] The fraternity's chantry seems originally to have been within the collegiate church, but later, presumably after the refoundation, a separate building was established in the precinct east of St. John's.[12]

A second religious guild, that of St. George, was housed in St. Peter's church, probably in the south aisle.[13] First mentioned in 1462, when it was governed by four masters or wardens, it too was open to both men and women, with two chaplains apparently required to pray for the souls of benefactors at St. George's altar.[14] Its property within the city, which included shops in Watergate Street near the church, was sufficient to require two rent collectors.[15] In 1489 Nicholas Southworth, son of a former mayor and clerk to the kitchen of Edward IV, gave it the large sum of £40 for ornaments.[16] In the 1530s the guild's chaplain occupied a chamber 'over the door' of St. Peter's, and in 1548 it had property bringing in annually some £12.[17] The guild, like the church which housed it, had close links with the city government, and in the early 16th century its stewards were listed in the Mayor's Books after the civic dignitaries.[18] It was still receiving bequests from aldermen in 1535.[19]

A third fraternity, that of St. Ursula, was established in 1509 to support Roger Smith's hospital, chapel, and chantry. Also open to both sexes, it was governed by two wardens or masters and maintained a chaplain to provide services for the inmates of the hospital and to pray for the souls of the founder, his kin, and all departed members of the fraternity. It was never

1 Wm. Langland, *Vision of William Concerning Piers the Plowman*, ed. W. W. Skeat, i (E.E.T.S. orig. ser. xxviii), p. 65; ii (ibid. xxxviii), p. 82; iii (ibid. liv), p. 471; cf. wrong interpretation of rood as cross on Roodee: ibid. iv (E.E.T.S. orig. ser. lxvii), p. 125.
    2 *Cal. Chanc. R. Var.* 169; 3 *Sheaf*, xxii, pp. 37–40.
    3 Hemingway, *Hist. Chester*, i. 138.
    4 Jones, *Ch. in Chester*, 78–9.
    5 Ormerod, *Hist. Ches.* i. 313; *Valor Eccl.* (Rec. Com.), v. 203.
    6 Jones, *Ch. in Chester*, 78.
    7 *V.C.H. Ches.* v (2), Collegiate Church of St. John.
    8 *Blk. Prince's Reg.* iii. 408–9, 450.
    9 e.g. 3 *Sheaf*, xxxvi, pp. 24, 59–60, 66.
    10 Ibid. xxxvi, *passim*; *Cal. Pat.* 1391–6, 248–9; 1396–9, 156–7; 1408–13, 242–3; P.R.O., SC 11/890–1; SC 12/6/24, ff. 19v.–26;

Jones, *Ch. in Chester*, 64–5, 98.
    11 3 *Sheaf*, xxxvi, *passim*; lv, p. 86; *V.C.H. Ches.* ii. 25–6.
    12 *Blk. Prince's Reg.* iii. 409; Jones, *Ch. in Chester*, 64–5; P.R.O., WALE 29/291.
    13 Jones, *Ch. in Chester*, 65; 3 *Sheaf*, xxi, pp. 62–3; xxiii, pp. 2–3; Ormerod, *Hist. Ches.* i. 354; C.C.A.L.S., ZMB 5, ff. 176–7; B.L. Harl. MS. 2158, ff. 39, 40v.
    14 B.L. Harl. MS. 2063, f. 113; 3 *Sheaf*, xvii, p. 69; xxiii, pp. 2–3; Jones, *Ch. in Chester*, 11, 98, 117; *List of Clergy, 1541–2*, 1; P.R.O., E 301/8/1.
    15 C.C.A.L.S., ZMB 5, ff. 176–7.   16 3 *Sheaf*, xix, p. 4.
    17 *Cal. Pat.* 1549–51, 411; P.R.O., E 301/8/1; B.L. Harl. MS. 2150, f. 165.
    18 e.g. C.C.A.L.S., ZMB 12, f. 4; ZMB 13, f. 2.
    19 3 *Sheaf*, xviii, p. 87.

popular with the citizens and may have lapsed before the Dissolution.[1]

The city had numerous chantries, established by citizens and members of the local gentry. The fully developed perpetual foundation was never very popular, and many were temporary.[2] The principal focus of chantry endowments was St. John's. The tradition there began with the foundation of a perpetual chantry by Philip of Orby (d. 1229), served by two cantarists of whom the senior, the petty canon, enjoyed a benefice ultimately worth more than the full canonries. He was bound to be resident and was probably often the senior clergyman at St. John's. A further chantry was established there in 1349 by Sir Peter Rutter of Thornton le Moors. It was served by two chaplains chosen by the dean. Later foundations, often temporary, were encouraged by the existence of a body of chaplains and vicars choral available to perform the necessary duties. Their consolidated endowments were known later as the obit lands.

Elsewhere in the city, a few perpetual chantries were established in the conventual churches. At St. Werburgh's the most notable foundations were all 13th-century: the king's for Earl Ranulph III, established in 1238, and those honouring the mayor John Arneway (*c.* 1270) and Sir Philip Burnel of Malpas (1281).[3] The nunnery and the friaries enjoyed longer-lasting patronage; perpetual chantries were established, for example, at the nunnery in the later 14th century,[4] at the Greyfriars by the priest John of Barrow in 1294,[5] and at the Carmelites by Sir Gilbert Haydock in 1348.[6] Analogous, if less formal, arrangements for daily commemoration at the conventual mass were made in 1367 by Thomas Stathom and his wife at the Carmelites and in 1467 by Sir William Tarbock and his wife at the Dominicans.[7] At the Dissolution three chantries survived at St. Werburgh's and there were two chantry priests at the nunnery; provision at the friaries was not recorded.[8]

Among the parish churches the most lavish chantry foundation was that made in 1433 at St. Mary's by William Troutbeck, serjeant of the Bridgegate, complete with its own sumptuous chapel.[9] Apart from Arneway's foundation at St. Bridget's in the 1270s, and that founded by the chamberlain in the castle chapel of St. Mary de Castro in the 1530s, there was little else of note.[10] The most ambitious scheme appears

never to have been realized. In 1369 Sir John Delves bequeathed the profits of seven manors to establish a chantry for himself and his family in Handbridge; nothing more, however, is heard of it.[11] In 1548 the chantry commissioners recorded chantries at St. Mary's and the castle chapel, and stipendiaries at St. Mary's, St. Michael's, Holy Trinity, and St. Bridget's.[12]

The craft guilds, established by the early 15th century, provided a further means of lay involvement in the life of the church, in particular through their role in religious processions and drama. Above all they had a crucial role in staging the mystery plays. First recorded in 1422, the plays were initially associated with a procession from St. Mary's to St. John's on the feast of Corpus Christi. By the early 16th century they had been transferred to Whitsun, a move which seems to have been associated with growing civic control. The Whitsun plays, which by the 1520s were spread over three days, were performed less regularly than the annual Corpus Christi production, and it is possible that a play was still performed on the feast day of Corpus Christi under the patronage of the Chester clergy, although if so it did not survive the Edwardian reforms.[13]

THE DISSOLUTION

There was no lack of vitality in the church in Chester in the earlier 16th century: building, supported by local people, was in progress at several religious houses up to the 1520s and in at least one parish church as late as the 1530s; and the city's principal relics, above all the Holy Rood, continued to attract veneration and oblations until their removal. The first signs of a failure of confidence came in the 1530s with changes in royal attitudes and the advent of a reforming mayor, Henry Gee.[14] Investment in the city's religious communities came to a standstill. The reconstruction of St. Werburgh's petered out *c.* 1530, and by the mid 1530s the warden and priors of the friaries were granting away their property on very long leases, presumably expecting dissolution.[15] The initial moves took place in 1536 when the royal commissioners Richard Layton and Rowland Lee, bishop of Lichfield, recorded incontinency among the inmates of St. Werburgh's, the nunnery, and St. John's, and noted the relics of St. Werburg and St. Thomas Becket.[16] They made no reference to the Holy Rood at St. John's, which may

1 *J.C.A.S.* xxxii. 104–6; *V.C.H. Ches.* iii. 183–4.

2 Para. based on details given in *V.C.H. Ches.* v (2), Collegiate Church of St. John; P.R.O., SC 12/6/24, ff. 10, 19, 27v.

3 Jones, *Ch. in Chester*, 103; *Cart. Chester Abbey*, ii, p. 469; *Cal. Lib.* 1226–40, 350, 496; *Close R.* 1237–42, 226.

4 Jones, *Ch. in Chester*, 104; 2 *Sheaf*, i, p. 84; P.R.O., CHES 3/2, no. 3; CHES 38/25/7.

5 *Cal. Close*, 1288–96, 372; *Cal. Inq. Misc.* i, p. 471.

6 W. Beamont, *Hist. of House of Lyme*, 26.

7 *V.C.H. Ches.* iii. 176; *J.C.A.S.* xxxix. 48.

8 *Valor Eccl.* (Rec. Com.), v. 206.

9 Earwaker, *Hist. St. Mary*, 31–3.

10 *Cart. Chester Abbey*, ii, p. 469; *Valor Eccl.* v. 208.

11 Broughton, *Rec. of Old Ches. Fam.* 16–19; 3 *Sheaf*, xxxvi, pp. 67–8.

12 P.R.O., E 301/8/1; SC 12/6/24, ff. 5–31; cf. *List of Clergy, 1541–2*, 1–3.

13 *V.C.H. Ches.* v (2), Plays, Sports, and Customs before 1700: Chester Plays.

14 J. Kermode, 'New Brooms in Early Tudor Chester', *Government, Religion, and Society in Northern Eng. 1000–1700*, ed. J. C. Appleby and P. Dalton, 144–58.

15 *V.C.H. Ches.* iii. 173, 175, 177; *J.C.A.S.* xxiv. 33, 37–8; xxxi. 27; xxxix. 50–1.   16 *L. & P. Hen. VIII*, x, pp. 141–2.

already have been removed by Bishop Lee himself.[1] Their visit was followed by the surrender of the three friaries to Richard Ingworth, bishop of Dover, in 1538.[2] As a house with an annual income under £200 the nunnery should also have been dissolved, but in 1537 the prioress had paid £160 for exemption. It survived until 1540, when both it and St. Werburgh's were suppressed.[3] There was evidently no resistance at any of the monastic houses.

Of the city's remaining religious corporations, the college of St. John was clearly under threat from the late 1530s and by the early 1540s was disposing of its property in a succession of long leases. The removal of the Holy Rood c. 1536 occasioned such a loss in offerings that the number of clergy had to be reduced, a change especially affecting the petty canons' chantry, which was apparently discontinued in 1543.[4] The college itself and the city's remaining chantries and confraternities were all suppressed in 1547.[5] Only the hospitals escaped.[6]

At St. Werburgh's change proceeded relatively slowly. In 1541 the abbey was refounded as the cathedral church of the new see of Chester, and the entire precinct was handed over to the newly constituted dean and chapter.[7] In the short term there was much continuity. Though the dedication was changed, to Christ and the Blessed Virgin, and some eighteen months elapsed between dissolution and resurrection, the break was more apparent than real. At the dissolution the monastery contained c. 28 monks, of whom 10 were made members of the new cathedral establishment; of the senior clergy of the latter only three were not ex-monks of St. Werburgh's. The dean and former abbot, Thomas Clarke, continued to occupy his old lodgings, and the organist and choirmaster was the former master of the monastic school.

The principal building in the precinct, the former abbey church, was still unfinished at the dissolution. In 1539, when the monastery clearly had little time left, the parishioners of St. Oswald's had been moved into the large and recently completed south transept, perhaps an attempt by the monks to preserve their threatened church, but more likely due to the desire of the parishioners, in particular the civic authorities, to obtain grander premises.[8] Presumably services continued in the south transept throughout 1540 and 1541. The interior fittings were probably not much disturbed, since the high altar in the choir was still in place in 1541, when the dying Dean Clarke ordered that his body was to be interred in front of it. The only

major structure inside the building likely to have been dismantled is the shrine of St. Werburg.[9]

The new cathedral had an establishment headed by a dean and six prebendaries, with a large inferior staff.[10] Draft statutes issued in 1544 were never formally confirmed, but achieved authority on the basis of custom and tradition. The dean and prebendaries, provided their income did not fall below a certain level, were expected to keep separate houses within the precinct, but the minor canons, choirmaster, conducts, and schoolmasters were supposed to eat together in a common hall, under the presidency of the precentor, a requirement evidently observed until 1600 or later.

The community at the new cathedral preserved many of the functions of the abbey, reciting the ancient offices and fulfilling its predecessor's eleemosynary and educative role. The old ceremonies were retained until 1547: money was spent on observing Corpus Christi Day and on censers, the sacrament house, and the canopy under which on certain feast days the Host was carried in procession. The preservation of a relatively undisturbed semi-monastic regime probably owed much to the first two deans, Clarke and his successor, Henry Man (1541–7), both former monks. By 1544, however, the character of the chapter was changing; only two of the original appointments remained and the newcomers were probably not from a monastic background. William Cliffe, appointed dean in 1547, came from York Minster, a cathedral of the old foundation, and was a conformer who contrived to achieve promotion under Henry VIII and Edward VI and to retain his preferments under Mary. Changes were introduced in 1548, when the dean and chapter sold a cross and two silver censers. In 1550 stones were carried away from the altars, and shortly afterwards the great high altar was 'laid' (perhaps meaning buried) and replaced by a wooden holy table. In 1553, when the royal commissioners visited Chester, the cathedral's ornaments seem already to have been depleted, and after their departure the church must have seemed bare indeed.

At other religious houses in the city there was more disruption. The sites of the nunnery and friaries were all sold in the 1540s. The nunnery and part of the Whitefriars were converted to residential use; the Blackfriars and Greyfriars were left to decay. The physical appearance of the extensive monastic precincts in the west of the city was thereby much altered.[11] At St. John's, too, there was much disruption. When the college was dissolved in 1547 the whole eastern limb

1 L. & P. Hen. VIII, xiv (1), p. 96; 3 Sheaf, xviii, pp. 27–8.
2 V.C.H. Ches. iii. 173, 175, 177.
3 Ibid. iii. 143–4, 149.
4 V.C.H. Ches. v (2), Collegiate Church of St. John.
5 P.R.O., E 301/8/1.
6 V.C.H. Ches. iii. 179, 181.
7 Ibid. iii. 144, 188; rest of para. based on A. T. Thacker, 'Reuse of Monastic Bldgs. at Chester, 1540–1640', T.H.S.L.C.

cxlv. 24–5.
8 Burne, Monks, 136, 139; 3 Sheaf, xxx, p. 2.
9 V.C.H. Ches. v (2), Cathedral and Close: Cathedral Church from 1541.
10 This and next para. based on V.C.H. Ches. iii. 188; T.H.S.L.C. cxlv. 24–5.
11 V.C.H. Ches. v (2), Sites and Remains of Medieval Religious Houses.

was appropriated by the king. Although revenues were set aside to support a vicar and curate, and the nave survived as a parish church, the east end and the subordinate chapels, oratories, and hermitages were abandoned and the ornaments and vestments were largely dispersed.[1]

In the parishes there was apparently little protestant activity before 1547, and Catholic worship seems to have continued until comparatively late in all the richest churches. St. Oswald's, for example, received a bequest of a mass vestment for the parochial altar as late as 1543.[2] At St. Peter's, a bequest was made for a window in the new aisle in 1539, and in 1541 Robert Goulburne directed that he was to be buried near the choir door, 'before the Blessed Sacrament'.[3] At Holy Trinity in 1539 Ralph Rogers remitted to the parishioners his outlay on the 'making of the cross', and at St. Mary's money was left to maintain services at the altars

of St. Mary and St. Catherine in 1547.[4] The last two churches retained their comparatively abundant ornaments intact until 1547, but thereafter they were swiftly removed. The process began at St. Mary's, where in 1547 the rood was taken down and the church was whitewashed, presumably to obliterate sacred pictures. The appurtenances of the new rite, a Prayer Book, two psalters, and the Paraphrases, were introduced in 1549, and in 1550 the altars and holy water stoup were removed and the parson married. At Holy Trinity the altars and tabernacle were removed in 1549, and in 1551 there were sales of vestments and ornaments. In 1553 the royal commissioners found little of value in the city's churches, except for St. Mary's, where, despite half-hearted attempts by parishioners to keep back some of the more precious possessions, almost everything was dispersed.[5]

1 *V.C.H. Ches.* v (2), Collegiate Church of St. John.
2 B.L. Harl. MS. 2079, f. 50.
3 Ibid. f. 49v.; Harl. MS. 2176, f. 146; 3 *Sheaf,* xviii, pp. 99–100.

4 B.L. Harl. MS. 2076, f. 146; *Colln. of Lancs. and Ches. Wills* (R.S.L.C. xxx), 174–5.
5 *V.C.H. Ches.* v (2), Medieval Parish Churches.

EARLY MODERN
CHESTER 1550–1762

IN 1550 Chester was a regional capital whose trade and political importance to the government were largely based on the city's links with Ireland.[1] Although not one of the very largest provincial towns, it was the only sizeable place in the North-West, and its standing had recently been enhanced by the acquisition of county status, a cathedral, and parliamentary representation.[2] The city declined over the following two centuries, not in absolute terms, but in relation to similar regional capitals and to other places in its own region, especially Liverpool. A long blockade during the Civil War, and the severe epidemic which immediately followed, were destructive only in the short term, and Chester's long-term decline was caused more by the loss to Liverpool of its position as the main port for Ireland. The city, however, retained and in many ways enhanced its standing as a cultural capital for an extensive region.

DEMOGRAPHY

POPULATION STATISTICS

Five types of data allow Chester's demographic history during the early modern period to be traced: full surveys of inhabitants at seven dates between 1563 and 1728, parish Easter books, evidence about household size, parish registers, and bills of mortality.

Full Surveys of Inhabitants. The full surveys were of heterogeneous origin and usually need to be corrected by supplying omissions. The figures for mean household size used to calculate numbers of inhabitants from the numbers of households are discussed below. All the corrected figures are necessarily approximations.

The diocesan returns of 1563 recorded 966 'families' by parish.[3] That figure included perhaps 70 households in the townships of St. Oswald's and St. John's parishes which lay outside the liberties, and excluded perhaps 40 households of clergy and others in the cathedral precincts. Negligence led to undercounting by c. 15 per cent.[4] The corrected figure was thus 1,041 households, representing 4,685 inhabitants.

The murage assessment of 1629 named 1,117 'citizens and inhabitants' (that is, householders) by ward.[5] St. John's Lane was omitted, but 78 householders were assessed there in 1630.[6] The poor were exempt from paying the murage, but a survey of 1631 numbered c. 250 pauper households.[7] The total number of households in 1629 was thus 1,445, representing 6,503 inhabitants.

The people of Chester were counted individually towards the end of the siege in January 1646, householders being listed by name along with the size of their 'families', including children, lodgers, and billeted soldiers. Civilians totalled 4,268 in 772 households, a mean household size of 5.53, higher than normal because of the siege.[8] Perhaps another 1,600 people lived in areas missing from the enumeration: c. 300 households in St. Olave's ward and c. 25 on the east side of Northgate Street. Civilians thus numbered an estimated 6,056. There were 387 soldiers in billets among c. 3,000 stationed within the walls.[9]

In the assessment list for the 1660 poll tax 1,307 householders were named by ward,[10] but those in receipt of alms and exempt from the tax amounted to at least another 20 per cent,[11] suggesting a real household total of 1,568 and a population of 6,742.

The hearth tax assessment of September 1664 named 1,648 householders, probably omitting only 18 almsmen.[12] The exempt were among those listed, and

1 Thanks are offered to Dr. A. M. Johnson for generously making available his unpublished thesis, 'Some Aspects of the Political, Constitutional, Social, and Economic History of the City of Chester, 1550–1662' (Oxf. Univ. D.Phil. thesis, 1971). What follows makes extensive use of his work.

2 A. R. Myres, 'Tudor Chester', *J.C.A.S.* lxiii. 53, 57.

3 B.L. Harl. MS. 594, f. 97.

4 Cf. C.C.A.L.S., P 65/8/1, ff. 18–20v.; A. Dyer, 'Bishops' Census of 1563: Significance and Accuracy', *Local Population Studies,* xlix. 35.

5 C.C.A.L.S., ZMB 32, ff. 136–41.

6 B.L. Harl. MS. 2082, ff. 157–69.

7 C.C.A.L.S., ZQSF 75, ff. 6–18; cf. *Cal. Chester City Cl. Mins. 1603–42,* 154–5, 159, 162.

8 B.L. Harl. MS. 2135, ff. 98–132.

9 Morris, *Siege of Chester,* 149; cf. ibid. 146, 242.

10 P.R.O., E 179/244/29.

11 Cf. *Northwich Hundred: Poll Tax 1660 and Hearth Tax 1664* (R.S.L.C. cxix), 22; *Trans. Salop. Arch. Soc.* lix. 109.

12 P.R.O., E 179/86/146, printed in *Miscellanies relating to Lancs. and Ches.* v (R.S.L.C. lii); B.L. Harl. MS. 1989, f. 74v.; Harl. MS. 2150, ff. 57, 259.

amounted to 26 per cent of the total. The population of the city may thus be reckoned as 7,164.

Bishop Gastrell's census of *c.* 1725 numbered 2,311 'families' by parish, a figure which included the residents of rural townships outside the liberties.[1] The corrected figures are 1,888 households and 8,118 inhabitants. In 1728 it was reported that a recent count had revealed *c.* 1,300 dwelling houses and 7,800 inhabitants.[2] The estimate was imprecise but independent of Gastrell's census, the general accuracy of which it confirms.

Parish Easter Books. For the periods between the full surveys rougher estimates can be made from partial surveys. Annual lists of householders paying parish rates or tithes, recorded in parish Easter books, can be used as the basis for such estimates where the proportion of the city's population living in a parish with an Easter book can be determined. When two or more Easter books survive for the same date, projections from each of them are a means of verifying the estimates, as is comparison with the full surveys (Table 1, p. 94).[3] The diocesan survey of 1563 and the protestation returns of 1642 allow the proportion of the city's population living in five of the parishes to be estimated for the later 16th and the earlier 17th century (Table 2, p. 94). The change in proportions coincided with a major epidemic.

Household Size. Mean household size varied over time,[4] and the multipliers adopted in this section in order to derive population figures from counts of households are 4.5 for the period 1547–1644,[5] and 4.3 for the period 1660–1725.[6]

Parish Registers. The value of parish registers for estimating Chester's population is limited by their coverage, since they are only 33 per cent complete for the period 1560–81, between 63 and 98 per cent for 1582–1644, 92 per cent for 1660–91, and 100 per cent thereafter, but probably with increasingly defective registration. Even when coverage was partial, however, the annual numbers of baptisms and burials indicate trends in the natural growth of the population (Table 3, p. 94).

Bills of Mortality. Bills of mortality can be used to assess the numbers of dead in two major epidemics when parochial registration of burials broke down. They survive for 1647.[7] For 1603–5 death tolls were reported in the town annals (Table 4, p. 95).

DEMOGRAPHIC HISTORY

Chester's population in 1563 of *c.* 4,700 (or *c.* 5,200 if mean household size was 5) put it in the second rank of provincial towns, half the size of York and a third that of Norwich.[8] Within the North-West, however, it was the largest town for sixty miles around.[9] The city probably reached that population after half a century of growth following the recession of the later Middle Ages. It evidently grew quickly between 1563 and 1586, reaching perhaps 6,130, an estimate projected from the single parish of St. Michael's, which had 72 householders in 1563 and 94 in 1586. Such growth is consonant with Chester's known economic expansion over the same period.[10] A population rise of 30.4 per cent in 23 years, or 1.32 per cent a year, far exceeded the likely natural growth, and must have been fuelled by immigration. The number of freemen increased from *c.* 400 in 1555 to *c.* 600 in 1573.[11] New freemen were able to practise their trade legally and thus establish a family and employ workmen,[12] so that economic growth could lead directly to a larger population.

A population of *c.* 6,130 in 1586, however, was the highest level reached in the 16th century. If St. John's and St. Michael's parishes were typical, numbers fell to *c.* 5,610 in 1597 and *c.* 5,220 in 1602 (Table 1). The decline was reflected in the number of tenants on the former nunnery estate, a mixture of suburban and intramural property, which fell from 114 in 1588 to 102 in 1597.[13] New building, including 86 properties first rented from the corporation between 1590 and 1603,[14] was industrial, commercial, and agricultural

1 Gastrell, *Not. Cest.* 98–124.

2 3 *Sheaf,* xlviii, p. 47.

3 N. Alldridge, 'Population Profile of an Early Modern Town: Chester 1547–1728', *Annales de démographie historique* (1986), 119–20; cf. S. J. Wright, 'Easter Books and Parish Rate Books', *Urban Hist. Yearbook* (1985), 30–45.

4 G. Cabourdin and G. Viard, *Lexique historique de la France d'Ancien Régime* (Paris, 1978), 136, s.v. feu; P. Laslett, 'Mean Household Size in Eng. since 16th Cent.' *Household and Fam. in Past Time*, ed. P. Laslett and R. Wall, 125–58.

5 N. Goose, 'Household Size and Structure in Early Stuart Cambridge', *Tudor and Stuart Town: Reader in Eng. Urban Hist. 1530–1688*, ed. J. Barry, 74–120, esp. 119; C. Phythian-Adams, *Desolation of a City: Coventry and Urban Crisis of Late Middle Ages*, 238–48; N. Goose, 'Eccl. Returns of 1563: Cautionary Note', *Local Population Studies*, xxxiv. 46–7; ibid. xlix. 20–6.

6 Cf. T. Arkell, 'Multiplying Factors for Estimating Population Totals from the Hearth Tax', *Local Population Studies*, xxviii. 55.

7 B.L. Harl. MS. 1929, f. 36; 1 *Sheaf,* i, pp. 183–4.

8 P. Clark and P. Slack, *Eng. Towns in Transition, 1500–1700*, 33–61, esp. 46–7; D. M. Palliser, *Age of Elizabeth: Eng. under Later Tudors, 1547–1603*, 203; P. J. Corfield, 'Urban Developments in Eng. and Wales in 16th and 17th Cent.' *Tudor and Stuart Town*, ed. Barry, 39–51.

9 N. Alldridge, 'Mechanics of Decline: Population, Migration, and Economy in Early Modern Chester', *Eng. Towns in Decline, 1350–1800*, ed. M. Reed, 2–3 and table 1; Palliser, *Age of Eliz.* 217; Phythian-Adams, *Desolation of a City*, 15.

10 Below, this chapter: Economy and Society, 1550–1642.

11 E. Rideout, 'Chester Companies and the Old Quay', *T.H.S.L.C.* lxxix. 163–74; C.C.A.L.S., ZMMP 2–3; *Rolls of Freemen of City of Chester*, i (R.S.L.C. li).

12 e.g. P.R.O., SP 12/110, f. 111; C.C.A.L.S., ZCAS 1, ff. 234–9; cf. *Trans. Salop. Arch. Soc.* lxiv. 37–8.

13 P.R.O., SC 11/143; SC 11/145; B.L. Harl. MS. 2039, ff. 13–14.

14 C.C.A.L.S., ZTAR 2/23, mm. 3–4; cf. Johnson, 'Aspects', 93.

FIG. 5. *Chester from the west, 1585*

rather than residential. Chester was simultaneously prospering and losing population probably because of the Irish wars. Chester supplied and shipped the huge armies involved,[1] but local military recruitment drained off potential migrants to the city and even enticed away some inhabitants.[2]

The importance of migration to Chester is underlined by the trends in natural growth (Table 3). There were perhaps 1,000 more baptisms than burials throughout the city between 1560 and 1579, but a baby-boom then would not have led to larger numbers of householders until at least twenty years later. The increasing numbers of householders as early as the 1560s must instead have been due to an influx of young adults from the countryside.[3] Between 1580 and 1599 the number of baptisms grew in accordance with the larger population of young adults, but the burial rate was simultaneously rising even faster, and the net natural growth in population fell to nil by 1600.

Higher mortality cannot be ruled out as an explanation, since the trend elsewhere in Cheshire and nationally was also towards lower natural growth.[4] Chester, however, seems to have escaped disease and famine in the 1580s and 1590s, even in 1596, a year of dearth elsewhere.[5] Possibly newcomers to the city in earlier decades were beginning to die off by the 1580s, whereas some young men who had been baptized in Chester were perhaps leaving in the 1580s and 1590s as colonists and soldiers in Ireland, and so neither raising families in the city nor adding to the local death rate.

The widespread and severe epidemic of bubonic plague in 1603–5 was unusual in Chester in falling into two contrasting phases (Table 4).[6] The first was long drawn out but relatively mild: 933 dead out of *c*. 5,220 inhabitants over 83 weeks represented a death rate of 11 per cent a year, four times the annual rate of the previous decade but not as severe as that experienced elsewhere.[7] The second phase killed 1,041 people

1 Below, this chapter: Military and Political Affairs, 1550–1642 (Military Affairs).

2 B.L. Harl. MS. 2125, ff. 44–6; C.C.A.L.S., ZQSF 53, ff. 35–6; cf. ibid. DDX 358/1, f. 26; J. J. N. McGurk, 'Recruitment and Transportation of Elizabethan Troops and Service in Irel. 1594–1603' (Liverpool Univ. Ph.D. thesis, 1983), 97–103, 227, 262.

3 For apprentices: 3 *Sheaf*, vii–viii *passim*; cf. D. M. Woodward, 'Chester Leather Ind. 1558–1625', *T.H.S.L.C.* cxix. 94–5.

4 E. A. Wrigley and R. S. Schofield, *Population Hist. of Eng. 1541–1871*, 528–9, 531; their Ches. sample was 13 parishes (16.1 per cent of 1563 pop.): Christleton, Eastham, Eccleston, Heswall, Wallasey, Woodchurch (par. registers at C.C.A.L.S.), Bunbury, Frodsham, Gawsworth, Nantwich, Neston, Sandbach, Wilmslow

(data kindly provided by Cambridge Group for Hist. of Population and Social Structure). Cf. C. B. Phillips and J. H. Smith, *Lancs. and Ches. from 1540*, 10–11; D. Palliser, 'Dearth and Disease in Staffs. 1540–1670', *Rural Change and Urban Growth, 1500–1800*, ed. C. W. Chalklin and M. A. Havinden, 60.

5 3 *Sheaf*, ix, p. 22; cf. Ormerod, *Hist. Ches.* i. 236–7.

6 J. F. D. Shrewsbury, *Hist. of Bubonic Plague in Brit. Isles*, 264–93, 312.

7 Cf. T. S. Willan, 'Plague in Perspective: Manchester in 1605', *T.H.S.L.C.* cxxxii. 29–40; W. A. Champion, 'Population Change in Shrewsbury, 1400–1700' (TS. 1983, in Salop. R.O.), 98; Palliser, *Age of Eliz.* 51–2; *Rural Change and Urban Growth*, ed. Chalklin and Havinden, 63.

overcrowded housing; and a ban on the Michaelmas fair and Christmas watch in 1604 to prevent crowds from gathering.[5] The spontaneous flight of gentlemen's households may have had the helpful effect of thinning the population.[6] Coincidentally trade through Chester declined: fewer merchants brought goods in,[7] maritime trade was in the doldrums, and cloth exports in 1604 were only a tenth of their level in 1602.[8] Such factors placed obstacles in the way of a build-up of infection which might have led to an explosive outbreak.

On the other hand the first phase was evidently prolonged, at a low level, by the repeated arrival of outsiders lacking immunity.[9] The dead of Chester certainly seem to have been replaced between 1602 and 1604: new tenants were found for the former nunnery estate;[10] in St. Michael's parish the number of householders actually increased;[11] and membership of the guilds was kept up by new admissions.[12] Immigration was at odds with the council's policy of quarantine, though the mayor himself tried to recall an alderman from Wrexham to pay his taxes.[13] During the epidemic the Assembly's expenditure was higher and its revenue lower, so that the burden of paying for relief grew and urban landlords, churchwardens, and guild stewards needed to find replacements for dead tenants, ratepayers, and company freemen.[14]

Such considerations may also have made the citizens overhasty in relaxing their guard against disease. In May 1605, after a six-week lull, the plague returned,[15] either from incubating bacilli or a fresh infection. Its increased severity was apparent from a broader impact across the social range. It struck first not in the suburbs but in the city centre, and so made the civic élite unusually vulnerable. One of the first victims was the previous year's mayor, John Aldersey.[16] Two gentlemen's families and four aldermen's were hit in Aldersey's parish, and the mayor, Edward Dutton, paid for remaining in the city by having his house twice infected and losing some of his children and servants. In all a third of the dead were from the middling ranks of the freemen and just over half from the lowest orders.[17]

There are several explanations for the increased severity of the second phase. Earlier replacement meant that there were as many people susceptible to

in 34 weeks, or 20 per cent a year among a population probably as large as in 1603. Shorter periods of plague normally inflicted greater proportionate losses,[1] but the differences between the two phases in Chester and especially a fresh outbreak in May 1605 require separate explanation.

The first outbreak was not, apparently, of a more benign strain: in one house it killed seven people in a short time,[2] it was accompanied by 'other diseases' (probably smallpox),[3] and when it was carried from Chester to Nantwich in June 1604 it killed 430 people in 10 months, a mortality of between 23 and 28 per cent.[4] Preventive measures taken in Chester by the Assembly in 1603–5 may have retarded the spread of infection, even though they were conventional and crude: erecting pesthouses on the outskirts to isolate the sick; destruction of infected bedding; orders against

---

1 T. H. Hollingsworth, *Historical Demography*, 365.

2 B.L. Add. MS. 39925, f. 25v.

3 Ibid. Harl. MS. 2125, f. 46v.; cf. *Par. Registers of Holy Trinity, Chester*, ed. L. M. Farrall, 75–6, 78, 80, 99; J. Ley, *A Monitor of Mortality* (1643), 42.

4 J. Lake, *Great Fire of Nantwich*, 20.

5 B.L. Harl. MS. 2125, f. 123; C.C.A.L.S., ZMB 28, f. 152; ZTAR 2/23, mm. 7–9; ZQSF 51, ff. 39–45; *Cal. Chester City Cl. Mins. 1603–42*, 7–10, 20–1.

6 B.L. Harl. MS. 2125, f. 46v.; *Cal. Chester City Cl. Mins. 1603–42*, 2.

7 *Cal. Chester City Cl. Mins. 1603–42*, 17.

8 W. B. Stephens, 'Cloth Exports of Provincial Ports, 1600–40', *Econ. H.R.* 2nd ser. xxii. 236, 246; idem, 'Overseas Trade of Chester in Early 17th Cent.' *T.H.S.L.C.* cxx. 23–4; D. M. Wood-

ward, 'Overseas Trade of Chester, 1600–50', *T.H.S.L.C.* cxxii. 27–8; idem, 'Anglo-Irish Livestock Trade of 17th Cent.' *Irish Hist. Studies*, xviii. 515.

9 *Biology of Populations*, ed. B. K. Sladen and F. B. Bang (New York, 1969), 357.

10 B.L. Harl. MS. 2039, ff. 13–14.

11 C.C.A.L.S., P 65/8/1, ff. 166v.–170v.

12 e.g. ibid. ZG 6; *T.H.S.L.C.* cxix. 96.

13 *Cal. Chester City Cl. Mins. 1603–42*, 2.

14 Johnson, 'Aspects', 253–4, 258.

15 B.L. Harl. MS. 2125, f. 123.

16 C.C.A.L.S., WS 1606, Jn. Aldersey (will, deposition); *Par. Reg. Holy Trin.* ed. Farrall, 72.

17 B.L. Harl. MS. 2125, f. 47; ibid. Add. MS. 39925, f. 25; *Par. Reg. Holy Trin.* ed. Farrall, 72–3.

TABLE 1: *Population estimates from Easter books, 1547–1644*

Date	Estimated from full surveys	Estimated from Easter books					Maximum divergence between estimates
		Holy Trinity	St. John's	St. Michael's	St. Oswald's	St. Peter's	
1547		5,240					
1557		4,640					
1559		4,640					
1563	4,685			4,700			
1586				6,130			
1597			5,610	5,610			0.0%
1602				5,220			
1612				6,700	6,680		0.3%
1619		6,960					
1620			6,700	6,770	6,550		6.3%
1629	6,503			6,615		6,140	7.7%
1641			7,600	7,875		7,460	5.6%
1642			7,360	7,640			3.8%
1643	7,550						
1644			7,600	7,640		7,810	2.8%

Sources: B.L. Harl. MS. 2177, ff. 21–52 (Holy Trinity); C.C.A.L.S., P 29/7/2 (St. Oswald's); P 63/7/1 (St. Peter's); P 65/8/1 (St. Michael's); ibid. ZCR 65/39–42 (St. John's); ZCAS 1, ff. 6–12, 115–40 (poll tax for St. John's parish, 1641).

TABLE 2: *Proportion of total city population in each of five parishes, 1547–1644*

Period	Holy Trinity	St. John's	St. Michael's	St. Oswald's	St. Peter's
1547–1605	12.0%	23.7%	14.5%	14.4%	10.0%
1606–44	13.0%	24.0%	17.5%	14.0%	11.2%

Sources: B.L. Harl. MS. 594, f. 97 (for 1547–1605); House of Lords R.O., Protestation Returns (Chester City) and B.L. Harl. MS. 2107, ff. 118–21 (for 1606–44). The relative size of St. John's and St. Oswald's was established by comparing Easter book lists.

TABLE 3: *Baptisms and burials, 1560–1729*

Period	Coverage	Total baptisms	Total burials	Surplus baptisms
1560–9	33%	471	248	+ 223
1570–9	33%	485	348	+ 137
1580–9	63%	1,090	949	+ 141
1590–9	73%	1,248	1,246	+ 2
1606–9	70–78%	577	390	+ 187
1610–19	70–91%	1,542	1,181	+ 361
1620–9	73–98%	2,168	1,951	+ 217
1630–9	73–98%	2,242	2,251	− 9
1640–4	68–73%	1,326	1,340	− 14
1660–9	92%	2,419	2,345	+ 74
1670–9	92%	2,583	2,544	+ 39
1680–9	92%	2,863	3,178	− 315
1690–9	100%	3,108	2,967	+ 141
1700–9	100%	2,840	2,723	+ 117
1710–19	100%	2,877	2,540	+ 337
1720–9	100%	3,152	3,269	− 117

Sources: *Par. Reg. Holy Trin.* ed. Farrall; B.L. Harl. MS. 2177 (St. Bridget's, printed in 3 *Sheaf*, xv–xviii); C.C.A.L.S., P 16/1/1 (St. Martin's); P 20/1/1 (St. Mary's); P 29/1/1 (St. Oswald's); P 51/1/1 (St. John's); P 63/1/1 (St. Peter's); P 64/1/1 (St. Olave's); P 65/1/1 (St. Michael's).

infection as ever. Although the Midsummer show and fair were cancelled, citizens seem to have flouted safety measures: John Aldersey, for example, was moved from Eastgate Street to Watergate Street while sick. Richer citizens, perhaps more worried about the state of their businesses after the first phase than about the disease itself, may have delayed flight too long. William Aldersey, another former mayor, left only when the weekly death-toll reached 58 and his next-door neighbour's family had been decimated.[1] The community as a whole was poorer, and among the poorest ill-nourishment and bad housing may have made many people less resistant.[2] On the other hand Chester's desperate state seems to have discouraged immigration, and for the first time there were gaps in rate- and rent-rolls.[3] The epidemic's greater intensity thus ensured its briefer duration.

In the long term, the double epidemic of 1603–5 was

1 B.L. Add. MS. 39925, f. 25; cf. C.C.A.L.S., WS 1605, Wm. Allen (will, admin., deposition); Ellen Allen (will).

2 Cf. P. Slack, 'Mortality Crises and Epidemic Disease in Eng. 1485–1610', *Health, Medicine, and Mortality in 16th Cent.* ed. C. Webster, 48–9; cf. *Q. Sess. Recs. of Ches. 1559–1760* (R.S.L.C. xciv), 53–6.

3 C.C.A.L.S., P 65/8/1, f. 172; B.L. Harl. MS. 2029, ff. 13–14.

TABLE 4: *Deaths during the plague of 1603–5*

Phase	Period	Number of weeks	Deaths from plague	Deaths from other diseases	Total deaths	Deaths per week
First	24 Aug. 1603 to 19 May 1604	38.5	349	39	388	10.0
	20 May to 13 Oct. 1604	22.0	311	22	333	15.2
	14 Oct. 1604 to 20 Mar. 1605	22.5	152	60	212	9.2
	Sub-total	83.0	812	121	933	
Lull	21 Mar. to 30 Apr. 1605	6.0				
Second	1 May to 10 Aug. 1605	14.5	457	35	492	33.9
	11 Aug. to 31 Dec. 1605	19.5	503	46	549	28.2
	Sub-total	34.0	960	81	1,041	
Tail	1 Jan. to 14 Mar. 1606	12.0	26	0	26	
Total		135.0	1,798	202	2,000	

Sources: B.L. Add. MS. 39925, f. 25; Harl. MS. 2125, ff. 46v.–47v., 123; Stowe MS. 811, f. 60.

not a serious demographic setback for Chester. Only in the final year was there a net loss in numbers of householders. For a time afterwards families may have been on average smaller, though there seems to have been an immediate baby-boom (Table 3). The excess of baptisms over burials in the years 1606–9 was *pro rata* comparable with that in the 1560s, and in St. Michael's parish the number of householders was back to its pre-plague level by 1610. By 1612 pre-plague levels had been surpassed by a large margin and Chester was embarked upon its period of fastest growth in early modern times. Projections of the total population from the balanced cross-section of the city represented by St. Michael's and St. Oswald's parishes point to as many as *c.* 6,700 inhabitants. St. John's, a suburban parish containing a quarter of the total population, lagged behind in pace of growth, but it was more populous than before the epidemic and its rate of growth had caught up by 1620.

The growth in population in the early 17th century seems to have occurred in two well spaced bursts: a sudden acceleration between 1606 and 1612 (averaging 4.04 per cent a year), a pause or even a slight decline until *c.* 1629, when there were *c.* 6,500 inhabitants, and a fresh leap to *c.* 7,650 in 1644 (averaging a growth of 1.18 per cent a year).[1] On the eve of the siege Chester's population reached a level not exceeded until the early 18th century. Recovery from the epidemic of 1603–5 thus inaugurated a new period of prosperity.[2] The growth in population was, as earlier, powered by economic developments. The similarity of the relative numbers of baptisms and burials with those of the late 16th century suggests that the same forces were at work

(Table 3). The birth rate rose each decade between the later 1600s and the earlier 1640s, but the surpluses of baptisms over burials were inexorably eroded by rising numbers of burials. By 1630 there was no natural growth, despite a rise in the actual population. Presumably there was considerable immigration to Chester, the effect of which towards the end of the forty-year period was to increase the numbers dying there. Elsewhere in the county there were certainly large rural surpluses in population throughout the period, especially between 1600 and 1629,[3] and much of the increase was probably drawn to Chester. The proportion of Chester apprentices from outside the city, for example, grew to two thirds after 1600.[4]

The siege of Chester between late 1644 and February 1646, and the ensuing epidemic, put an end to population growth. The initial influx of royalists and exodus of parliamentarians probably cancelled each other out,[5] but soon the city also housed *c.* 3,000 soldiers and the many women and children who accompanied them.[6] The resulting overcrowding worsened as the suburbs were evacuated and burnt in 1645. Randle Holme II, a former mayor, estimated the refugees at *c.* 1,600.[7] At the end of the siege civilians still numbered *c.* 6,000, cooped up inside the walls with the soldiers. The exceptionally high mean household size of 5.53 and a density of 9 people per house in Northgate Street indicate the degree of overcrowding. Much new accommodation was jerrybuilt and insanitary.[8] Although disease did not strike during the siege, crowding and poor hygiene persisted throughout 1646 and early 1647, partly because rebuilding was delayed.[9] The plague arrived in June 1647, perhaps with

1 Cf. W. A. Champion, 'Frankpledge Population of Shrewsbury, 1500–1720', *Local Population Studies*, xli. 54, 56.
2 Below, this chapter: Economy and Society, 1550–1642.
3 Cf. Phillips and Smith, *Lancs. and Ches. from 1540*, 11–12.
4 3 *Sheaf*, vii–viii, xxvi, *passim*.
5 Morris, *Siege of Chester*, 44–5.
6 Ibid. 149; B.L. Harl. MS. 2135, ff. 40–1.

7 B.L. Harl. MS. 2135, f. 40; cf. ibid. f. 108.
8 Ibid. Harl. MS. 7568, f. 137; C.C.A.L.S., ZAF 39A, f. 25; Hist. MSS. Com. 7, *8th Rep. I, Chester*, p. 365; S. Ward, *Excavations at Chester: 12 Watergate St.* 54.
9 P.R.O., E 317/Ches. 6A, 7, 10A, 13A; *Lancs. and Ches. Ch. Surveys, 1649–55* (R.S.L.C. i), 223–4, 232–8; cf. Morris, *Siege of Chester*, 211.

troops bound for Ireland.[1] The onslaught was unprecedented. In 16 weeks, 1,863 people died. The first week alone claimed 64 victims, more than the week of highest mortality in 1605. The peak was the seventh week, with 209 dead, and the worst of the epidemic was over in the sixteenth week with 52 dead, after which there was a long tail of intermittent deaths, lasting until April 1648 and numbering 236.[2] The plague was reported as taking its victims 'very strangely, strikes them black of one side, and then they run mad; . . . they die within a few hours'.[3] It was evidently bubonic plague, and Chester was one of two places in the British Isles hit hardest in the outbreak.[4] Total deaths between June 1647 and April 1648 amounted to 2,099, perhaps 35 per cent of the population if it had remained stable after the end of the siege. The incidence of deaths varied greatly among the parishes: in St. Peter's, one of the most uniformly prosperous parts of the city, there were only 75 dead in a population of 700–800, whereas in Holy Trinity, where rich and poor lived side by side, 232 died out of *c.* 600, four times the rate.

The outbreak started in the city centre, probably in St. Michael's parish. In the first week 70 per cent of fatalities occurred in the five intramural parishes where habitational densities were highest in the multi-storeyed mansions lining the main streets. In that sense the epidemic can be attributed to overcrowding caused by the siege. Nevertheless it quickly spread outwards, and by the fourth week 65 per cent of deaths were occurring in the suburban and partly suburban parishes. By the end three quarters of all deaths had been in those parishes, despite the sparsity of housing left in the suburbs after the siege. Evidently the normal social selectivity of plague was reasserted.[5] The course of the epidemic implies great impoverishment among the mass of citizens, and indeed it was asserted at the time that almost all the wealthy had left the city.[6] The intensity of the onslaught, however, combined with the quarantining effect of widespread flight, slack trade, and little immigration, hastened the decline of infection, especially as winter approached.

By contrast with the epidemic of 1603–5, recovery was slow. In the 1650s even prosperous parishes like St. Peter's and St. Michael's had only two thirds of their pre-plague population (Table 5). St. Mary's in 1657 had only three quarters the number of households of a

TABLE 5: *Number of households in four parishes, 1643–57*

Date	Holy Trinity	St. Mary's	St. Michael's	St. Peter's
1643	129			
1644			97	155
1647	111			150
1648			65	
1649	64		65	
1650			64	96
1652	117			
1653			69	
1654	111			
1655	132		62	
1657		168		

Sources: B.L. Harl. MS. 2177, ff. 21–52 (Holy Trinity); C.C.A.L.S., P 20/13/1 (St. Mary's); P 63/7/1 (St. Peter's); P 65/8/1 (St. Michael's).

century before. Holy Trinity parish was the exception, perhaps because squatters settled on the Crofts. Not until the Restoration did the population recover beyond the level at the end of the siege: *c.* 6,750 inhabitants in 1660, rising to *c.* 7,160 in 1664, still well below the pre-Civil War peak of *c.* 7,650. Chester did not recover from the combined effects of the siege and the epidemic until perhaps 1700.

One immediate cause of the delay in recovery was the prevalence of plague or other diseases in the region around Chester until 1665.[7] Another was the slow rebuilding of the devastated suburbs, not under way until the mid 1660s.[8] The underlying cause, however, was Chester's impoverishment and the political blight which it suffered in the 1650s for its royalist sympathies. The siege caused an estimated £200,000 worth of damage, liquidated the city's assets, and completely dislocated its trade.[9] As elsewhere, the arrival of plague was particularly serious for a town already at a low ebb.[10]

Natural growth, absent in the 1630s and earlier 1640s, did not resume after the epidemic: between 1655 and 1669 there was a net natural loss of 17. The loss of capital and trade had also greatly reduced net migration to the city, and much if not all of the increase in the number of householders between 1646 and 1664 was due to the return of at least 258

1 *Cal. S.P. Venice*, 1643–7, pp. 318, 320; *Cal. S.P. Irel.* 1633–47, 535; cf. *Letters and Papers relating to Irish Rebellion, 1642–6*, ed. J. Hogan, 197.

2 B.L. Harl. MS. 1929, f. 36; 1 *Sheaf*, i, pp. 183–4; cf. Hollingsworth, *Hist. Demog.* 366–7, 371.

3 1 *Sheaf*, i, p. 330.

4 Shrewsbury, *Hist. Bubonic Plague*, 422.

5 *Health, Medicine, and Mortality in 16th Cent.* ed. Webster, 48–9.

6 Morris, *Siege of Chester*, 210.

7 *Hist. MSS. Com. 7, 8th Rep. I, Chester*, p. 386; B.L. Harl.

MS. 1929, ff. 8v., 19v.; C.C.A.L.S., ZAB 2, f. 94v.; *Cal. S.P. Dom.* 1664–5, 461; Chetham Soc. [o.s.], lxxxiii. 27; *Rural Change and Urban Growth*, ed. Chalklin and Havinden, 66–7; W. E. A. Axon, 'Chronological Notes on Visitations of Plague in Lancs. and Ches.' *T.L.C.A.S.* xii. 90–7.   8 C.C.A.L.S., ZAF 34–38c.

9 Below, this chapter: Civil War and Interregnum (City Government, 1646–60; Economy and Society, 1646–60); B.L. Harl. MS. 2135, ff. 40–3; Johnson, 'Aspects', 212, 214, 223.

10 Cf. P. Slack, *Impact of Plague in Tudor and Stuart Eng.* 188; J. Dupaquier, 'Sur la population française au xviie et au xviiie siècle', *Revue historique*, ccxxxix. 58.

freemen who had fled earlier. With their families, they perhaps represented 1,100 inhabitants, the whole of Chester's 'growth' between 1646 and 1664.[1] Outsiders and non-free traders, in contrast, were systematically discouraged as likely to be a burden to the city.[2] An apparently smaller surplus population in Chester's hinterland in the 1650s and 1660s, in part due to disease,[3] also reduced the number of potential migrants to Chester.

After the Restoration Chester was still regarded as 'the head of the region',[4] but in fact its provincial standing was permanently reduced. By the yardstick of the hearth tax both Shrewsbury and Manchester were as big, and soon after 1700 Chester was outstripped by Liverpool, Manchester, Birmingham, and Dublin.[5] Georgian Chester was perhaps only the 30th largest city in England.[6] Chester's 18th-century decline has been traced to the combined blows of siege and plague,[7] but that explanation ignores both the wider changes in the region and Chester's later capacity for growth: to over 8,000 inhabitants in 1725 and 13,000 by 1775.[8] In fact Chester's decline was not absolute but relative to its urban neighbours. It is significant, however, that the mid 17th-century disasters coincided with a crucial turning point in Chester's history when, like many other old-established towns, it was disadvantaged by fundamental economic transformations in its region.[9]

Between 1664 and 1725 the population rose modestly from *c.* 7,160 to *c.* 8,120 inhabitants. No doubt the progression was not smooth but its exact course cannot be traced because the later 17th-century Easter books are unreliable. The natural increase of 381 between 1665 and 1724 did not account for the total

TABLE 6: *Comparative vital indices, 1660–1729*

Period	Chester	North of England	England and Wales
1660–9	1.03	no data	1.00
1670–9	1.02	no data	1.03
1680–9	0.90	no data	0.98
1690–9	1.05	1.15	1.10
1700–9	1.04	1.32	1.19
1710–19	1.13	1.25	1.13
1720–9	0.96	0.98	0.99

Note: A figure higher than 1.0 denotes natural population growth; a figure lower than 1.0 denotes natural population decline.
Sources: Chester: as Table 3; N. Eng.: *Hist. Geography of Eng. and Wales*, ed. R. A. Dodgshon and R. A. Butlin (1978), 230; Eng.: Wrigley and Schofield, *Population Hist. of Eng.* 532–3.

rise, so there must have been net immigration, but it can only have been at moderate levels since, unlike earlier periods of growth, burials rarely exceeded baptisms. The relatively slow increase in Chester was similar to that experienced nationally in the same years.[10] Although the ratio of births to deaths dipped further locally than nationally in the 1680s, and rose less high in the 1700s, the pattern of fluctuations was remarkably similar and actual rates in each decade were often the same or close (Table 6). There were greater differences between Chester and the North of England, suggesting that the natural growth of the rural population throughout the North-West and west Midlands was being channelled to towns other than Chester.[11]

CITY GOVERNMENT, 1550–1642

THE ASSEMBLY

Chester was governed under its charter of 1506 by an Assembly comprising the mayor, two sheriffs, 24 aldermen (the Twenty-Four), and 40 common councilmen (the Forty), unofficially augmented in the earlier 16th century by the sheriff-peers (former sheriffs not yet promoted to the rank of alderman).[12] The annual election of aldermen and councillors had been under-

mined before 1550, elections being held only when vacancies occurred. The right of freemen to vote even on those occasions was gradually eroded, despite a lawsuit in 1573, though the Assembly managed to prevent mayors from simply nominating new councilmen. The irregular position of the sheriff-peers was questioned in 1599–1600, but in 1606 it was agreed to follow custom, irrespective of the literal sense of the charter. As there were usually between 15 and 20

1 Based on comparison of names in B.L. Harl. MS. 2135, ff. 98–132; *Miscellanies*, v (R.S.L.C. lii); and *Rolls of Freemen of Chester*, i.

2 C.C.A.L.S., ZAF 29, f. 19; ZAF 31, f. 12; ZQSF 78, ff. 3–6v., esp. 3v.; Morris, *Siege of Chester*, 209.

3 Data from 13 Ches. pars. as above, p. 92 n. 4.

4 Rutgerus Hermannides, *Britannia Magna* (Amsterdam, 1661), 177.

5 *Eng. Towns in Decline*, ed. Reed, 3–5, table 1; J. de Vries, *European Urbanization, 1500–1800*, 139–44.

6 C. W. Chalklin, *Provincial Towns of Georgian Eng.: A Study*

of the Building Process, 1740–1820, 5, 9, 18.

7 Shrewsbury, *Hist. Bubonic Plague*, 423.

8 J. Haygarth, 'Observations on Population and Diseases of Chester in 1774–5', *Philosophical Trans. of Royal Soc.* lxviii (1), 139.

9 A. D. Dyer, 'Influence of Bubonic Plague in Eng. 1500–1667', *Medical Hist.* xxii. 313.

10 R. A. Houston, *Population Hist. of Brit. and Irel. 1500–1750*, 28.

11 Cf. D. C. Coleman, *Economy of Eng. 1450–1750*, 97–9.

12 Morris, *Chester*, 524–5; *Tudor Chester*, ed. A. M. Kennett, 10.

sheriff-peers, the Assembly sometimes comprised more than 80 members who served for life.[1]

Limited popular participation survived in mayoral elections, which took place annually in October. Under the charter the freemen were to select two aldermen, from whom the aldermen and sheriffs elected one as mayor, but by 1567 the initiative lay with the aldermen, who presented two or more candidates to the freemen for approval and chose one as mayor themselves. By 1600 the first choice of candidates was made by the senior aldermen (former mayors, known as aldermen J.P.s); four separate votes were made by the other aldermen and the sheriffs, the sheriff-peers, the councilmen, and the freemen; and finally the aldermen alone elected as mayor one of the two candidates who had gained most votes in the earlier stages. Usually the man favoured at the first meeting of the aldermen J.P.s was successful, but the freemen took a great interest in the proceedings: 905 voted in 1629, 928 in 1634, and more than 1,000 in 1638.[2] By contrast, the freemen played little or no part in electing sheriffs: one was usually nominated by the aldermen, the other by the whole Assembly.[3]

The mayor and aldermen J.P.s dominated the Assembly, initiating measures and determining policy. From the early 17th century they met privately in the inner Pentice to discuss matters such as the mayoralty and financial affairs,[4] though councilmen were consulted on important questions, including finance, and some business still went to a vote of the whole Assembly. Membership of the latter was confined to freemen, and from 1583 vacancies were to be filled within a week in order to circumvent external pressure.[5] Fines were levied, though rarely, on absentees, and the Assembly kept a strict order of precedence and insisted on the wearing of tippets and gowns.[6] Meetings were summoned by the mayor and normally held on Fridays, but their frequency varied greatly, averaging seven a year during the 17th century.[7]

By 1600 a regular order of business had developed: the filling of vacancies in the Assembly and civic offices; financial matters; business introduced by members; the award of charitable funds; admissions to the freedom; and the consideration of petitions, presented in increasing numbers by guild officers and individual citizens.[8] The Assembly often defended its corporate rights and privileges,[9] co-operated with central government in implementing statutes and orders, supervised city officials, devised and enforced local regulations, and upheld civic dignity. The last was bolstered by ceremonies which involved displaying the civic mace and sword, as well as the coat of arms granted in 1580 and confirmed, probably with the motto, in 1613.[10] The book of civic memoranda begun in the mayoralty of Henry Gee (1539–40) was continued in an increasingly systematic way until it became during the 1570s the Assembly minute book; by then arrangements had been made to preserve the city's other records.[11]

ELECTED OFFICERS

Aspirants to civic office normally moved through a *cursus honorum* which could lead from common councilman through leavelooker, sheriff, and alderman to the mayoralty. A councillor had perhaps only a one in three chance of becoming an alderman, after 10 or 15 years in most cases, and as aldermen were elected for life but sheriffs served for only a year many failed to reach the highest offices. At least 18 men bypassed the shrievalty and were appointed aldermen because of their social standing. Little more than attendance at the Assembly was required of councilmen, who at first represented the wards. Two each year were elected as leavelookers, responsible for collecting tolls, and were thereafter senior members of the Forty. Two more served as murengers (another subsidiary financial office) and two as coroners.[12]

The two sheriffs, also appointed annually, had usually already served as leavelookers. Their most onerous duties were legal: they held the Pentice, passage, and county courts, collected fines and forfeitures, served writs, and had custody of prisoners in the Northgate gaol. They also had a general responsibility for public order, especially during fairs, and after 1543 conducted parliamentary elections. Two treasurers were elected from among the aldermen.[13]

The mayor's wide-ranging duties involved much detailed administration and paperwork. He led the Assembly and had considerable judicial powers in the portmote and crownmote courts and the city quarter sessions. He was *ex officio* clerk of the market, and was usually appointed by the government as a commissioner for taxation.[14] A small allowance, £13 6s. 8d. in the 1620s besides some casual fees, did not meet the

1 C.C.A.L.S., ZAB 1, ff. 85, 128, 129v.–130, 208, 236v.–264, 266; *Cal. Chester City Cl. Mins. 1603–42*, 15, 25; Johnson, 'Aspects', 36–42.

2 Johnson, 'Aspects', 42–5.

3 Ibid. 46.

4 C.C.A.L.S., ZAF 11/26; ZAF 14/3–5; ZAF 17/3–4; ZAF 21/9; ZAF 24/1, 3; ZMB 28, ff. 348v.–349v.

5 Ibid. ZAB 1, ff. 58–9, 196.

6 Ibid. ff. 83, 92, 94, 233; Morris, *Chester*, 182–3, 186.

7 C.C.A.L.S., ZAB 1, ff. 131–57; *Cal. Chester City Cl. Mins. 1603–42*, App. 1.

8 *Cal. Chester City Cl. Mins. 1603–42*, *passim*; C.C.A.L.S.,

ZAF 7–8, *passim*.

9 Below, this chapter: Economy and Society, 1550–1642 (Occupations and Economic Regulation, Merchants).

10 M. J. Groombridge, *Guide to Charters, Plate, and Insignia of City of Chester*, 44–5.

11 *J.C.A.S.* lxiii. 53; *Tudor Chester*, ed. Kennett, 34; *Archives and Records*, ed. Kennett, 13.

12 Johnson, 'Aspects', 47–57; *Archives and Records*, 95, 97; below, this section (Financial Administration).

13 Johnson, 'Aspects', 55–7; *Archives and Records*, 26; below, this section (Legal Administration, Financial Administration).

14 C.C.A.L.S., ZMB 28, *passim*.

heavy expenses incurred.[1] In the 1550s fines were imposed for refusal to serve as mayor, sheriff, or leavelooker, but by 1566 it was possible to decline the mayoralty or resign an aldermanship.[2]

Most influential men willingly undertook civic office,[3] and 62 of the mayors between 1550 and 1642 came from only 26 families. In general the aldermen were drawn from the wealthier occupations, notably drapers, merchants, mercers, ironmongers, and vintners. Merchants were mayors more often than any others, but tanners, glovers, shoemakers, innholders, and brewers also held the office frequently. Many, for example Henry Hardware, William Goodman, and the Gamulls, owned property in the city; the Gamulls, William Glazier, John Cowper, John Brereton, and others had rural property, mostly near by.[4]

Some leading civic families made marriage alliances with the county gentry, among them the Alderseys, Duttons, and perhaps most mayors. Partly as a result the gentry were increasingly willing to accept civic office, including (as mayor) Sir Laurence Smith, Sir John Savage the elder, Sir Randle Mainwaring, Sir John Savage the younger, and Sir Thomas Smith. Many aldermanic families were linked by marriage, like the Smiths and Mainwarings, Brerewoods and Ratcliffes, Gamulls and Bavands, and Thropps and Cowpers,[5] and some served for long periods over several generations. The average length of aldermanic tenure was more than 15 years, and 10 mayors served in the Assembly for more than 30 years. One of the most prolific office-holding families was that of Brerewood: Robert I was sheriff, Robert II mayor three times, his son John sheriff, and the latter's son, Robert III, recorder and alderman. At least six other families, Aldersey, Smith, Dutton, Hardware, Goodman, and Ratcliffe, had similar records.

PROFESSIONAL OFFICERS

The mayor's principal officers were the swordbearer, the serjeant of the peace (who was macebearer), four serjeants-at-mace, the yeoman of the Pentice (a janitor), and the city crier. All received small wages, partly from the mayor, partly from city funds, and the swordbearer also received meat, drink, a gown, and

extra payments at Assembly elections.[6] The serjeant of the peace was responsible for attachments (seizure of goods) and at first shared with the swordbearer tolls of the malt market and fees at admissions to the freedom. The serjeants-at-mace had the exclusive right of acting as attorneys in the city courts, and initially were also paid out of the market tolls and received food and drink. Income from tolls was replaced in 1589 by annual wages.[7]

The sheriffs' main officers were the four serjeants of the Pentice, who could only attach 'strangers' (non-citizens) and were not permitted to act as attorneys. They took fees for attachments and tolls at the fairs, over which they squabbled until the 1630s, when fixed wages were substituted.[8] All the offices were normally filled on petition to the Assembly, sometimes accompanied by attempts to use outside influence, since they provided both status and a livelihood.[9]

The professional offices of recorder and clerk of the Pentice (or town clerk) were far more important. The recorder, always a lawyer and an alderman, was elected by the Assembly, his primary duties being to provide legal advice in the city courts and informally, and to act as a J.P.[10] The recorder was also an almost automatic choice as one of the city's M.P.s.[11] In 1606 James I tried to have his own nominee appointed, but the Assembly stood on the charter of 1506 and the king withdrew.[12]

The clerk of the Pentice was central to the city's administration. Always a lawyer, he was clerk of the courts and the Assembly, and served as the sheriffs' attorney at the Chester palatinate exchequer. By the 1620s he employed three under-clerks.[13]

OFFICE AND FACTION

Clerks of the Pentice seem to have been appointed by the recorder and sheriffs, not the Assembly. In 1587, however, Secretary of State Sir Francis Walsingham and the earl of Derby, Henry Stanley, blatantly sought the reversion for Peter Proby, a Cestrian lawyer. The interference caused much ill-feeling and the matter was not settled until 1590, when Proby was offered an annuity as a solicitor for the city.[14] When the incumbent died in 1598 the Assembly appointed his successor,[15] but on the latter's death in 1602 the mayor, John

1 Ibid. ZAB 1, f. 110; Johnson, 'Aspects', 53; *Cal. S.P. Dom.* 1627–8, 63; Morris, *Chester*, 179–81.

2 *Tudor Chester*, ed. Kennett, 10; Morris, *Chester*, 179–81; Johnson, 'Aspects', 52–3.

3 Except where otherwise stated, biographical details based on *V.C.H. Ches.* v (2), Lists of Mayors and Sheriffs; T. S. Alexander-Macquiban, 'Mayors of Chester, 1525–1640' (TS. at C.H.H.).

4 Transcripts of probate material at C.C.A.L.S. kindly supplied by Mr. A. H. King through the good offices of Mr. P. H. W. Booth; *Lancs. and Ches. Wills and Inventories*, iii (Chetham Soc. [o.s.], liv); [vi] (ibid. N.S. xxxvii), *passim*.

5 Alexander-Macquiban, 'Mayors'; *Ches. and Lancs. Funeral Certificates, 1600–78* (R.S.L.C. vi), *passim*.

6 C.C.A.L.S., ZAB 1, ff. 43 sqq., 211v.

7 Ibid. f. 226v.

8 *Cal. Chester City Cl. Mins. 1603–42*, 116, 152, 177, 185.

9 Ibid. 102; Johnson, 'Aspects', 60–1.

10 *Cal. Chester City Cl. Mins. 1603–42*, 54; Morris, *Chester*, 525.

11 Below, this chapter: Military and Political Affairs, 1550–1642 (Parliamentary Representation).

12 *Cal. Chester City Cl. Mins. 1603–42*, 22–3; H. T. Dutton, 'Stuart Kings and Chester Corporation', *J.C.A.S.* xxviii. 185–6; Johnson, 'Aspects', 61–3.

13 Johnson, 'Aspects', 63–5; *Archives and Records*, 35–6.

14 C.C.A.L.S., ZML 5/91–5, 176–217; *Acts of P.C. 1587–8*, 42; 1588–9, 285; Johnson, 'Aspects', 67.

15 C.C.A.L.S., ZAB 1, ff. 255, 259v.–260, 270; Johnson, 'Aspects', 67–8.

Ratcliffe, intruded a nominee of Lord Keeper Sir Thomas Egerton, Robert Whitby, by simply giving him the keys to the Pentice. In retaliation 40 members of the Assembly, including six former mayors, pressed for a free election, though they were not personally hostile to Whitby, whom they elected to the clerkship in the same year.[1]

Prolonged factional division in Chester's civic life followed.[2] Within five years Whitby had become a common councilman and clerk of the peace for Cheshire, and had his son Thomas elected as joint clerk of the Pentice, a position previously unknown. In 1612 Robert was elected mayor, Thomas became sheriff, and another son, Edward, was appointed recorder. The bishop and dean of Chester, George Lloyd and Thomas Mallory, openly alleged corruption, and during the next five years growing opposition to the Whitbys was orchestrated by Robert Brerewood. The Assembly was divided, and detailed evidence of the Whitbys' misconduct and maladministration was forthcoming in abundance. After the privy council insisted on a local resolution of the matter Robert and Thomas Whitby were examined formally in the inner Pentice in 1618, and the Assembly then dismissed them as joint clerks and appointed Robert Brerewood in their place.

The dispute spilled over into the parliamentary election of 1621, for which Edward Whitby, still recorder, was a candidate; after much intrigue he was returned with Alderman John Ratcliffe, evidently an ally.[3] The recorder remained actively hostile to Brerewood, and in 1627, with the help of Sir Thomas Savage, Mayor Nicholas Ince manipulated the Assembly into suspending Brerewood and appointing an acting clerk. They then sidestepped any counter-move by Brerewood's supporters, usually a majority in the Assembly, by secretly persuading the privy council to assume jurisdiction. The privy council at first committed the case to four commissioners, but after a disorderly mayoral election instead appointed Savage, one of Brerewood's adversaries, to examine the allegations against him. They included extortion and neglect of duty over three years. Brerewood resigned and was replaced in January 1628 by Savage's nominee.

The rivalry continued through the parliamentary election of 1628, when Recorder Whitby and John

Ratcliffe were again returned, but differences were resolved by 1633, when (at the third attempt) Brerewood was made one of the city's counsel. Six years later, on Whitby's death, he was elected recorder.

LEGAL ADMINISTRATION[4]

Administration was often hampered by strained relations between the mayor and sheriffs, as amateur judges of the portmote and Pentice respectively, and the recorder, who was a professional lawyer. From the late 16th century a dispute developed about the recorder's fee, payable by the sheriffs,[5] and there was repeated argument about the fees charged to litigants by the clerk of the Pentice, at its height during the joint clerkship of the Whitbys. After their dismissal the Assembly confirmed a fixed scale of fees in 1621.[6]

A more serious jurisdictional conflict with the palatinate arose in part because the exchequer court of the chamberlain of Chester (the palatinate court) had long served as a court of equity for the city, valued by the citizens even though the Assembly tried to discourage resort to it.[7] In the early 1560s the vice-chamberlain of Chester, William Glazier, an alderman, tried to collect customs duties in the city and took cognizance of an action for debt brought against Alderman Thomas Green, who had the mayor's support.[8] Both sides pressed their claims at Westminster, and in 1563, almost simultaneously, the chamberlain of Chester (Edward Stanley, earl of Derby) obtained the right to remove cases from the city to the Chester exchequer, while the corporation secured a change of wording in its charter which exempted the city from the exchequer's jurisdiction. The exchequer continued to assert its rights, and in 1568 disposed of another rival by obtaining a ruling which freed both the county palatine and the city from the authority of the Council in the Marches of Wales. It persisted in accepting actions entered by citizens and in issuing writs to remove cases from the city courts. City officers retaliated by ignoring the writs and disfranchising the vice-chamberlain and two others.[9]

In 1574 the privy council upheld the exchequer's claims, ordered the reinstatement of those disfranchised, and confirmed the city's charter without the wording which excluded the exchequer.[10] Some time before, the new chamberlain, Robert Dudley, earl of

1 B.L. Harl. MS. 2105, ff. 231–2.

2 Except where otherwise stated what follows is based on B.L. Harl. MSS. 2091, 2105; P.R.O., SP 16/98, f. 111; C.C.A.L.S., ZAB 1, ff. 272, 276; *Cal. S.P. Dom.* 1627–8, 94, 260; *Acts of P.C.* 1627, 157–8, 372–3, 484–5; 1627–8, 12–14, 177; *Cal. Chester City Cl. Mins.* 1603–42, 36–7, 59, 69, 89, 91, 96, 133, 143, 146, 156, 173, 199. For Whitby family: J. W. Laughton, 'House that John Built', *J.C.A.S.* lxx. 99–103; J. K. Gruenfelder, 'Parl. Election at Chester, 1621', *T.H.S.L.C.* cxx. 35–44. For Brerewood: *D.N.B.*

3 *T.H.S.L.C.* cxx. 35–44; below, this chapter: Military and Political Affairs, 1550–1642 (Parliamentary Representation).

4 The portmote, Pentice, quarter sessions, crownmote, and

county court of the city are treated in *V.C.H. Ches.* v (2), Law Courts: Early Modern.

5 Johnson, 'Aspects', 161; C.C.A.L.S., ZAB 1, f. 247v.; *Cal. Chester City Cl. Mins.* 1603–42, 96.

6 C.C.A.L.S., ZAB 1, ff. 48, 255, 273v.; *Cal. Chester City Cl. Mins.* 1603–42, 89–90, 104–8; Johnson, 'Aspects', 162–3.

7 C.C.A.L.S., ZAB 1, ff. 72, 118, 131–2; Johnson, 'Aspects', 167–9.

8 C.C.A.L.S., ZAB 1, ff. 96, 105; Johnson, 'Aspects', 170–1.

9 Johnson, 'Aspects', 172–3; *Cal. Pat.* 1560–3, 471–3; P. Williams, *Council in Marches of Wales under Eliz. I*, 198–9.

10 *Acts of P.C.* 1571–5, 203, 225–7; Morris, *Chester*, 545–9; Johnson, 'Aspects', 173–5; *V.C.H. Ches.* ii. 39.

Leicester, had urged compromise,[1] and thereafter open strife gave way to mutual respect. Occasional clashes still took place, but the city benefited from the exchequer's involvement in several important cases, including the protracted arguments about the clerkship of the Pentice and about liberties in the city.[2]

FINANCIAL ADMINISTRATION

The corporation's finances were mainly administered by the treasurers, two in number and elected annually, other revenues being managed by the sheriffs, murengers, and leavelookers.[3] Before 1584 the mayor could authorize payments independently of the treasurers, and from 1573 the accounts of all four sets of officers were drawn up annually and submitted to auditors elected by the Assembly from its senior members.[4] The most important sources of income were rents from property, fees for grazing and haymaking rights on the Roodee, and payments for admission to the freedom, which between them normally accounted for over half the total. In addition there were receipts from tolls at the gates, miscellaneous fees, the prisage of wine, and surpluses from charitable endowments and occasional trading deals.[5]

Income from property grew absolutely and as a proportion of the total, from £25–£30 a year in the later 16th century to c. £65 by 1640, through higher rents, stricter leasing arrangements, and new building on city-owned land. The number of tenancies rose from 68 in 1573 to almost 370 in 1642, though arrears remained a problem. Payments for grazing animals on the Roodee at 10s. a head normally produced c. £30 a year. Fees paid by entrants to the freedom were more variable. New freemen admitted by patrimony paid only 3s. 4d., and those qualifying by apprenticeship £1 3s. 4d., but the corporation could exact what it chose from others. The total yield was rarely less than £20 a year and occasionally could be over £60.[6]

In the early 17th century the prisage on wine, farmed by royal patentees, brought in only c. £30 a year, but in 1639 the city secured the exclusive right to collect it, and during the first 15 months raised over £352.[7] The endowments of charitable funds under corporation control were administered by the treasurers, who used surpluses for civic purposes and could on occa-

sion (in 1634, for example) borrow capital from the loan charities to meet deficits in their accounts.[8]

The city's expenses included salaries, wages, fees, administrative costs, and the maintenance of its properties. Annual payments to office-holders amounted to c. £30 during the later 16th century but had almost doubled by 1640. The recorder's fee, for instance, was raised in 1611 from £1 6s. 8d. to £13 6s. 8d., largely to compensate for increased legal business in London, and after 1618 a muster master was paid £10 a year to train the militia.[9] The other large increase was on the city's own lawsuits.[10]

The finances of the other accounting officers are more obscure. The sheriffs collected court fines, customs duties, tolls at fairs, and other lesser dues, amounting to little more than £25 a year in the early 17th century; from that they were required to pay the fee-farm rent of £20 and some minor fees.[11] The sheriffs were frequently at fault from the 1570s in both collecting and accounting, and clearly avoided their financial duties whenever possible. Eventually, in 1621 the Assembly ordered them to pay the fee-farm rent from their official income or their own pockets, allowing them to keep a quarter of any surplus.[12]

The murengers continued to collect murage, imposed on merchandise entering the city by sea and used for repairs to the walls, gates, and streets. The leavelookers took tolls on goods brought in for sale by non-freemen, and had to pay, among other things, for the crier and the chimes at St. Peter's church.[13] Even before 1600 the funds of both were insufficient, and the problem was not resolved until 1627–8, when the Assembly ordered them to collaborate, the leavelookers collecting all the duties, and the murengers dealing with payments.[14]

Before the 1580s the treasurers usually handled £50–£60 a year; thereafter the figure regularly reached £160, and from the mid 1620s was almost four times greater than in the 1550s. Nevertheless the accounts were in surplus perhaps only one year in two.[15] There seems to have been no stock of capital, and whenever the regular income proved insufficient the authorities had to make a special assessment. During the later 16th century such levies were required for the house of correction, the waterworks, and especially the New Haven at

1 C.C.A.L.S., ZAB 1, ff. 133–5.
2 Johnson, 'Aspects', 176–8; W. J. Jones, 'Palatine Performance in 17th Cent.' *Eng. Commonwealth, 1547–1640*, ed. P. Clark and others, 198–9.
3 *Cal. Chester City Cl. Mins. 1603–42*, pp. xiv–xvii; Johnson, 'Aspects', 90–112.
4 C.C.A.L.S., ZAB 1, ff. 131v., 197.
5 *Cal. Chester City Cl. Mins. 1603–42*, pp. xvi, xxxii–xxxiii, 214–19.
6 B.L. Harl. MS. 2173, f. 90 sqq.; C.C.A.L.S., ZTAR 1/1 to ZTAR 3/49 *passim*; Johnson, 'Aspects', 91–5.
7 C.C.A.L.S., ZTAR 3/47.
8 *Cal. Chester City Cl. Mins. 1603–42*, 172, 180, 214–19.
9 Ibid. 54, 92; C.C.A.L.S., ZTAR 1/21; ZTAR 2/36; ZTAR

3/42, 44, 49.
10 Johnson, 'Aspects', 100–1.
11 Ibid. 103; *Cal. Chester City Cl. Mins. 1603–42*, pp. xiv–xv, 222–3.
12 C.C.A.L.S., ZAB 1, ff. 113, 124, 137, 166–8, 178, 254v., 259v.; *Cal. Chester City Cl. Mins. 1603–42*, 93, 110.
13 B.L. Harl. MS. 2158, ff. 2, 40; C.C.A.L.S., ZAB 1, f. 265; *Chester Customs Accts.* 14–16, 144–5; *Cal. Chester City Cl. Mins. 1603–42*, pp. xv, xvii, 61, 192, 209; Johnson, 'Aspects', 106–7.
14 *Cal. Chester City Cl. Mins. 1603–42*, 16–17, 78, 81–2; Johnson, 'Aspects', 106–8.
15 C.C.A.L.S., ZTAR 1/1 to ZTAR 3/49 *passim*; Johnson, 'Aspects', 90–2.

Neston;[1] in 1605 the renewal of the charter needed a general assessment of £100;[2] and from that date to 1642 there were no fewer than seven assessments for the murengers' works.[3] The levies were burdensome for the constables and aldermen of the wards who collected them, and sometimes aroused argument about liability. The corporation was thus usually reluctant to undertake costly new projects.

ECONOMY AND SOCIETY, 1550–1642

Chester's economy grew steadily from 1550 to *c.* 1600, not least because in the early 1580s and later 1590s the passage of troops bound for Ireland created more demand for goods and services. Recovery from the plagues of 1603–5 was hampered by national economic difficulties and by recurrent, though limited, local epidemics, but from the mid 1620s prosperity returned.[4]

OCCUPATIONS AND ECONOMIC REGULATION

From the mid 16th century the Assembly was more closely involved in economic regulation, both through the guilds and directly. It confirmed that only freemen could trade in the city, and in 1557 fully recognized admission to the freedom by purchase or apprenticeship, allowing outsiders to purchase their freedom especially when they followed a useful occupation.[5] Among those admitted in that way were victuallers, a currier, and weavers, but a scheme in the early 1580s to promote woollen textiles by instituting a staple for Lancashire or Welsh cottons was strongly opposed by the authorities of Shrewsbury and failed.[6]

From 1540 to 1644 at least 3,440 freemen were admitted. There were probably *c.* 500 in 1567 and more than 900 in 1641,[7] and the average annual rate of admissions increased from 25 in 1540–59 to 42 in 1620–44. High admissions of newcomers in 1573 to satisfy a demand for labour, and in 1601–2, when there were large troop movements to Ireland, suggest that the Assembly tried to match the level of enfranchisements with the opportunities for skilled employment.[8] There were more than sixty crafts and trades in the city by 1600.[9] Between 1550 and 1649 in all 53 per cent of admissions were in the manual crafts, 27 per cent in services, and 20 per cent in the wholesale and distributive trades. Services took an increasing share and the distributive trades less. The three basic occupations – catering, clothing and textiles, and building – accounted for some 40 per cent of admissions. Purveyors of food and especially drink became more numerous, mainly after 1600. In the clothing trades, weavers and cloth finishers declined steadily, but feltmakers multiplied before 1600 and again after 1620.[10]

Leather was the most important manufacturing industry, employing perhaps more than 250 workers in the late 16th century. Shoemakers, glovers, tanners, saddlers, skinners, and curriers together formed more than a fifth of the freemen admitted between 1558 and 1625, with shoemakers first, glovers second, and tanners fourth among all occupations. The tanners, curriers, and wealthier glovers sold wholesale, whereas poorer glovers and the shoemakers and saddlers bought tanned leather and sold their products retail. Sources of skins and hides included Ireland as well as butchers and graziers in the neighbourhood, and some tanners had their own farms. One of the most successful leather manufacturers was Robert Brerewood, who died in 1601 with goods valued at almost £1,600: he worked as both a glover and a tanner, was (untypically) also a retailer, and also dealt in wool from sheepskins and timber purchased for the bark.[11]

Other rich Cestrians included William Dodd (d. 1598), a mercer worth £1,840; Robert Bennet (d. 1616), another mercer worth £1,288; Alderman Edward Button (d. 1618), an innkeeper worth £713; George Warrington (d. 1640), a brewer worth £940; and Alderman Thomas Thropp the elder (d. 1620), a vintner worth £2,475. Butchers who also grazed their own livestock were a particularly affluent group.[12] So, too, were the lessees of the Dee Mills, which remained vital to the city economy and highly profitable. The

1 Below, this chapter: Economy and Society, 1550–1642 (Social Conditions); *V.C.H. Ches.* v (2), Public Utilities: Water; Water Transport: River.

2 *Cal. Chester City Cl. Mins. 1603–42*, 17.

3 Ibid. 17, 41, 108, 134, 154, 174, 211.

4 Above, this chapter: Demography.

5 C.C.A.L.S., ZAB 1, f. 91; Morris, *Chester*, 386–8, 403–4, 437, 443–4; D. Woodward, *Men at Work: Labourers and Building Craftsmen in Towns of N. Eng. 1450–1750*, 54–7.

6 C.C.A.L.S., ZAB 1, f. 91; *Cal. Chester City Cl. Mins. 1603–42*, 189; Morris, *Chester*, 446–7; *Tudor Chester*, ed. Kennett, 17; D. M. Woodward, *Trade of Elizabethan Chester*, 88–94; T. C. Mendenhall, *Shrewsbury Drapers and Welsh Wool Trade*, 133–5; Salop. R.O., 1831, box 21.

7 N. J. Alldridge, 'Loyalty and Identity in Chester Parishes, 1540–1640', *Parish, Church, and People: Local Studies in Lay Religion, 1350–1750*, ed. S. J. Wright, 106; Morris, *Chester*, 448–50.

8 *Rolls of Freemen of Chester*, i (R.S.L.C. li), pp. xiii–xvi and passim; Johnson, 'Aspects', 9–10; *Eng. Towns in Decline, 1350–1800*, ed. M. Reed, table 7.

9 *T.H.S.L.C.* cxix. 96–7; P. M. Giles, 'Felt-hatting Ind. c. 1500–1850', *T.L.C.A.S.* lxix. 106–7; F. Simpson, 'City Gilds of Chester: Barber-Surgeons', *J.C.A.S.* xviii. 171, 174; A. M. Kennett, *Loyal Chester*, 10; Johnson, 'Aspects', 27, 277.

10 Analysis based on figures compiled from *Rolls of Freemen of Chester*, i, by Miss S. Richardson; *T.H.S.L.C.* cxix. 67.

11 *T.H.S.L.C.* cxix. 65–111; Woodward, *Men at Work*, 47; Johnson, 'Aspects', 26–7.

12 Probate inventory transcripts from C.C.A.L.S. kindly supplied by Mr. A. H. King.

lessees' attempt to enforce a monopoly of grinding corn led to a lengthy dispute with the citizens.[1]

The city had an important role as a distributive centre,[2] and its shops, markets, and fairs all throve in the century after 1550. The staples traded in the city were wool, linen yarn, iron, lead, leather goods, corn (chiefly barley, rye, and oats), livestock (especially cattle), fish, and cheese. Fine fabrics and other light luxury goods, dyes, hops, and supplies for troops bound for Ireland were brought from London in return for cloth, skins, and salmon. Customers from gentlemen's households in Lancashire and Cheshire bought silk, soap, hair powder, spices, sack, wine, and other luxuries.[3] Clay tobacco pipes began to be made in Chester (at a kiln in the Crofts), rather than imported from London, in the 1630s.[4] Chester's fairs already had a reputation for the sale of horses, drawing local dealers and customers from as far as Yorkshire. Sellers from Shropshire and north Wales dominated the fairs, which specialized in the small Border horses used in transport.[5]

The markets and fairs were closely supervised respectively by the mayor and sheriffs.[6] Concessions to merchants who were not freemen were rare, but in 1607 non-free importers of Irish yarn were permitted to sell it without restriction in an attempt to divert them from Liverpool.[7] At fair times London dealers were accused of abusing the privilege of unrestricted trading, but local traders apparently benefited from the willingness of some Londoners to extend credit from fair to fair.[8] In the retail markets new regulations reflected continuing concerns to keep basic foodstuffs freely available, reasonably priced, and wholesome, especially when bad harvests or the presence of expeditions bound for Ireland in the 1580s and 1590s threatened to raise prices.[9]

Close supervision of the sale of ale, bread, and meat brought the mayor and Assembly into conflict with brewers, bakers, and butchers. In 1557, after a year of tight price regulation, the Bakers' company defied the assize of bread and refused to bake, whereupon the mayor threw the trade open, confiscated the guild's

charter, and briefly disfranchised its members. Disputes continued until 1586, when finally the Assembly allowed anyone to sell bread on the two market days. The bakers continued to be aggrieved about innkeepers who baked their own bread and about unfree bakers at Gloverstone, an enclave in front of the castle which lay outside the city's jursidiction.[10] Butchers were frequently in trouble for bad meat and high prices. In 1578 the Assembly therefore opened a new flesh shambles for country butchers, and kept it open in the face of persistent hostility from the city butchers.[11] There was also conflict about brewers breaching the assize of ale.[12]

One means of alleviating shortages was the 'common bargain', whereby imported bulk supplies had first to be offered to the city for up to 40 days, during which time the mayor could purchase them for resale to the citizens at reasonable prices. It was apparently first used in the iron trade, but by 1550 had been extended to wine, oil, corn, fish, and other commodities. The procedure was followed for corn supplies in 1585 and 1597 to counter a dearth. In 1587 the time allowed for the bargain was reduced to 10 days.[13] The levying of tolls at the gates caused difficulties with outsiders, among the officers responsible, and between the city and Sir Randle Crewe, owner of those at the Eastgate. Some tolls were very small, there were exemptions, and collection often proved difficult.[14]

MARITIME TRADE

Throughout the 16th century Chester was the largest port in north-west England, although it carried only a small proportion of the country's trade, ranking 12th in a list of 18 provincial ports in 1594–5. It had few, if any, ships of over 100 tons, and was unfavourably located for trading with England's main markets overseas. Although well situated for trade with Ireland, its hinterland was not heavily populated or industrially developed, and competition from Liverpool gradually became more serious.[15]

Chester was the head port of the North-West, with Liverpool, the north Wales ports, and Lancaster as its

1 *V.C.H. Ches.* v (2), Mills and Fisheries: Dee Corn Mills.
2 Ibid. Roads and Road Transport: Long-Distance Road Transport.
3 T. S. Willan, *Inland Trade*, 5–6, 29, 39; Woodward, *Trade of Eliz. Chester*, 69–72; *T.H.S.L.C.* cxix. 75–8; *Agrarian Hist. of Eng. and Wales*, iv. 80–4, 470.
4 *Past Uncovered: Quarterly Newsletter of Chester Arch.* Autumn 1998.
5 P. Edwards, 'Horse Trade of Chester in 16th and 17th Cent.' *J.C.A.S.* lxii. 91–8.
6 C.C.A.L.S., ZAB 1, ff. 76v.–77, 79, 106–7, 112; *Cal. Chester City Cl. Mins. 1603–42*, 63–4, 79; Morris, *Chester*, 394–5.
7 *Cal. Chester City Cl. Mins. 1603–42*, 30–1; C. Armour, 'Trade of Chester and State of Dee Navigation, 1600–1800' (Lond. Univ. Ph.D. thesis, 1956), 47–8.
8 P.R.O., PC 2/47, ff. 366–7, 451; Johnson, 'Aspects', 233.
9 C.C.A.L.S., ZMMP 2, 8–9, *passim*; ZMB 28, *passim*; Morris, *Chester*, 395–400, 437–8, 442; *Cal. Chester City Cl. Mins. 1603–*

42, 173; *Tudor Chester*, ed. Kennett, 18; Johnson, 'Aspects', 235–6.
10 C.C.A.L.S., ZAB 1, ff. 88v.–90, 207; Morris, *Chester*, 415–22; Johnson, 'Aspects', 235, 237–8.
11 C.C.A.L.S., ZAB 1, ff. 174, 207, 230, 277v.; ZAB 2, f. 124; Morris, *Chester*, 438–42.
12 C.C.A.L.S., ZAB 1, ff. 97v.–98; ZAF 15/33; *Acts of P.C.* 1600–1, 24–5; *Cal. S.P. Dom.* 1636–7, 374, 406; 1637, 110–11; Johnson, 'Aspects', 238–9.
13 C.C.A.L.S., ZAB 1, ff. 68, 121v.–122, 203–4, 208v., 251; Morris, *Chester*, 390–3, 399–400; Woodward, *Trade of Eliz. Chester*, 49–51; *Cal. Chester City Cl. Mins. 1603–42*, 40, 57, 59, 76, 173; Armour, 'Trade of Chester', 46–7; Kennett, *Loyal Chester*, 14–15.
14 C.C.A.L.S., ZML 6/81; *Cal. Chester City Cl. Mins. 1603–42*, pp. xxv, 160–5; Johnson, 'Aspects', 240–3.
15 Woodward, *Trade of Eliz. Chester*, 1–4; Johnson, 'Aspects', 2.

members, but the silting of the Dee put it at a disadvantage even after the New Haven at Neston came permanently into use *c.* 1570, since the river channel was not improved.[1] Most ships, and all the larger ones engaged in Continental trade, either discharged their cargoes downstream or transhipped them into lighters which could sail up to Chester, either way incurring extra charges.[2]

The Irish trade was already the backbone of the city's commerce in 1550, and grew from a third of Chester's imports and three quarters of its exports by value in 1582–3 to two thirds of imports and nine tenths of exports a decade later. The balance of trade, initially in Ireland's favour, quickly reversed, and Chester's exports far outstripped its imports by value. Chester and Liverpool at first had complementary roles, Chester handling most exports and Liverpool most imports. Chester's exports were increasingly diverse: cloth above all, but also Welsh coal, re-exported iron and soap, salt, miscellaneous manufactured goods, foodstuffs, and wine. The most important imports from Ireland were raw materials: skins and hides for the local leather industry, wool, linen yarn, small amounts of tallow and timber, and large quantities of fish, especially herring. Between 80 and 90 per cent of the Irish trade was with Dublin, and Dublin merchants dominated it, numbering more than 100 by 1592–3. Chester's own merchants were more involved with other Irish ports, especially those in Ulster in the late 16th century. Some Cestrians, including the very successful Thomas Tomlinson, acted as factors for merchants from elsewhere.[3]

Trade with the Isle of Man and south-west Scotland, the latter beginning in the 1580s, was on a very small scale and essentially similar to that with Ireland: imports of skins, hides, wool, and fish in exchange for cheap basic manufactures. Most of it was conducted by Manx and Scots merchants, but in the 1580s several Chester craftsmen began importing raw materials from Man for their own use.[4]

Chester was central to the coastal trade of the North-West and north Wales, sending out large amounts of grain (except in years of local scarcity), but also wine, foreign fruits and other re-exports, and manufactured and household goods. Coastal imports to Chester included Irish merchandise transhipped from Liverpool, grain from Lancashire, and fish from south-western England. Chester merchants regularly brought from London large miscellaneous cargoes of wine, chalk, iron, fuller's earth, and other commodities.[5]

During the later 16th century there was a small trade with the Baltic, chiefly imports of naval stores, and rye in times of scarcity, but Chester's Continental trade remained mainly with Spain and France. From Spain came some large cargoes of train oil, but the main import was iron, as much as 363 tons in 1562–3. Regular imports from France included fruits, spices, and above all wine. Exports to France and Spain included cloth, coal, and lead, but at first consisted mainly of the woollen cloth known as Lancashire cottons to Spain. From the mid 1580s cottons were overtaken by tanned calfskins, exported under a royal licence of 1584 which permitted Chester merchants to ship 10,000 dickers (i.e. 100,000 skins) over 12 years. On the outbreak of war with Spain in 1585 the trade switched to Saint-Jean-de-Luz (Pyrénées-Atlantiques), from where calfskins could be taken into Spain to exchange for iron; even so, fewer than 3,000 dickers had been exported by 1598 when the licence was renewed for nine years. Much of the trade was carried in Chester-owned ships, which normally made two round voyages a year. From the 1570s many were lost through shipwreck, piracy, and enemy attack. As their capacity averaged only *c.* 40 tons, larger vessels from other ports were also used. Trading prosperity was high during the early 1560s with flourishing wine and iron imports, and lower during the later 1560s and the 1570s because of the loss of ships and an embargo on trade with Spain. During the early 1580s a boom was fed by imports of French wine, and difficulties accompanying the war with Spain were overcome to prolong prosperity into the 1590s.[6]

Between 1600 and the Civil War there was little change in the city's maritime commerce. Wine imports from France and to a lesser extent Spain expanded rapidly in the 1630s to 1,053 tuns in 1638, but then fell sharply.[7] Iron imports from Spain did not recover in the same way.[8] Exports were still dominated by calfskins, but also included cloth and in good years corn, as well as the beginnings of a large trade in lead. However, no new markets were opened until the 1630s. Chester's coastal trade continued, but Ireland remained the city's main commercial outlet.[9] Exports included growing quantities of coal and cloth. Imports of sheep and cattle surged from the 1620s, reaching 18,000 animals, chiefly cattle, in 1639.[10] Coal exports and livestock imports had little direct effect on the city: both were shipped at anchorages in the estuary, mainly by Irish merchants in vessels not owned locally. Nevertheless,

1 *V.C.H. Ches.* v (2), Water Transport: River.

2 Woodward, *Trade of Eliz. Chester*, 3.

3 Ibid. 5–34, 131–3.

4 Ibid. 35–6.

5 Ibid. 66–9, 133–4.

6 Ibid. 37–58, 130–3; N. Lowe, *Lancs. Textile Ind. in 16th Cent.* (Chetham Soc. 3rd ser. xx), *passim*; *T.H.S.L.C.* cxix. 85–9; cf. below, this section (Merchants).

7 *T.H.S.L.C.* cxx. 23–34; W. B. Stephens, 'Eng. Wine Imports, *c.* 1603–40', *Tudor and Stuart Devon*, ed. T. Gray and others, 144–7.

8 Rest of para. based mainly on *T.H.S.L.C.* cxx. 23–34; cxxii. 25–42.

9 T. S. Willan, *Eng. Coasting Trade, 1600–1750*, 91, 97, 103–5, 107–9, 180–1; Armour, 'Trade of Chester', 303–4.

10 Woodward, *Trade of Eliz. Chester*, 127 n.

Chester in 1640 was still more important in overseas trade than Liverpool, especially in exports.

MERCHANTS AND MERCHANTS' COMPANIES

Chester's own merchants regularly handled 90 per cent of the cloth and calfskins exported to the Continent and up to 70 per cent of the iron and wine imported. During the later 16th century a small number of merchants came to predominate: 31 traded with France and Spain in 1565–6, for example, but only 15 in 1602–3, and the share taken by the biggest operators grew. Some of the smaller merchants spent time on the Continent as factors for richer ones.[1]

Two local families were pre-eminent. Six Alderseys traded with the Continent between 1558 and 1603, and family members owned property in and near the city and held civic office. Their wealth became largely concentrated in the hands of the third William Aldersey (d. 1625), who left a personal estate worth over £2,300 and credits of £1,700. The Gamulls, not quite as wealthy, also held civic office and had interests in the Dee Mills and a salt-works. Another rich overseas merchant was Richard Bavand, mayor and M.P., who died in 1603 owning goods worth *c.* £400, more than 20 properties in the city, and land outside.[2] Merchants supplemented their profits with advantageous marriages, investment in shipping, farming, property rents, retailing, loans to the Crown, and in some cases smuggling and evasion of tolls.[3] Nevertheless, even the most prominent were less affluent than their counterparts in the main provincial ports, and Chester was not dominated by a merchant oligarchy.[4]

In 1554 a group of overseas traders secured the incorporation by royal grant of a company of merchants, to be governed by a master and two wardens and enjoy the privileges normally granted to such companies. Membership was to comprise merchants trading with the Continent ('mere merchants') and exclude craftsmen and retailers. There was immediate opposition in Chester on the grounds that it would exclude some freemen from foreign trade contrary to long-established practice, but the company renewed its charter in 1559 and even came to include a few retailers.[5] Indeed, after Chester was brought within

the national customs system in 1559 the corporation and the company collaborated in opposing higher customs rates on certain goods than were charged elsewhere.[6]

Such co-operation dissolved after 1577, when some local merchants joined the newly formed Spanish Company in order to share in its monopoly of trade with Spain and Portugal.[7] By 1581 they were attempting to exclude the city's retailers from the Iberian trade. The corporation, which included many retailers, took a stand against the merchants, and the dispute became bogged down in a welter of petitions, legal opinions, and abortive adjudications.[8] In 1584 the grant of a royal licence to export calfskins complicated the dispute, for it was granted to the merchants alone, and there were allegations that it had been obtained by deceit. Finally, in 1589 the privy council settled matters: the charter of the Merchants' company was confirmed, retailers were allowed to join it and trade overseas, and in return merchants were permitted to retail (in one trade only) and join the appropriate guild.[9] At first the compromise had limited effects, since the war had restricted direct trade with Spain. Most Chester merchants lost interest in the Spanish Company, and only four were members in 1605.[10]

Disputes continued, however, over other privileges sought by leading merchants. In 1605 Chester's exemption from prisage on imported wines was deemed to have ended, and competition ensued for the right to collect the tax. At first the corporation was allowed to farm it from the royal grantee, with William Gamull and other prominent merchants as its subfarmers from 1611. In 1624 a new farmer of prisage instead sublet his rights for £650 a year exclusively to five major wine merchants, William and Andrew Gamull, William Aldersey, Thomas Thropp, and William Glegg.[11] The arrangement had been secured in secret and was challenged by William Edwards, a new councilman already embattled against Gamull's clique for preventing his admission to the Merchants' company.[12] In 1629 the dispute took another twist when William Gamull and his friends, supposedly negotiating a renewal of the licence to export calfskins on behalf of the city generally, instead secured a monopoly for themselves. The privy council finally ruled that all

1 Ibid. 41, 57–65.

2 Ibid. 59–60, 106–12, 135; cf. ibid. 96, 103; Armour, 'Trade of Chester', 28, 202; Lowe, *Lancs. Textile Ind.* 74–5.

3 Woodward, *Trade of Eliz. Chester*, 62–3, 114–17; Morris, *Chester*, 394–5.

4 Woodward, *Trade of Eliz. Chester*, 122–3; R. Grassby, *Business Community of 17th-Cent. Eng.* 58, 250.

5 Woodward, *Trade of Eliz. Chester*, 73–5; Morris, *Chester*, 463–4; C.C.A.L.S., ZML 5/226, 265–8.

6 C.C.A.L.S., ZAB 1, ff. 95–6, 98–101, 128, 132v.; Woodward, *Trade of Eliz. Chester*, 75–8.

7 Woodward, *Trade of Eliz. Chester*, 79–82.

8 Ibid. 82–7; C.C.A.L.S., ZAB 1, ff. 183, 184v.–186; ZML

5/269; Morris, *Chester*, 463–8.

9 C.C.A.L.S., ZAB 1, ff. 180, 219v., 220v.–223; ZML 5/251–64; Morris, *Chester*, 467–8; Woodward, *Trade of Eliz. Chester*, 94–103.

10 Woodward, *Trade of Eliz. Chester*, 83–4, 102–4.

11 C.C.A.L.S., ZCHB 3, f. 104; ZML 6/51; *Cal. Chester City Cl. Mins. 1603–42*, pp. xxvii, 72, 76–7, 87, 127–8; A. M. Johnson, 'Politics in Chester during Civil Wars and Interregnum, 1640–62', *Crisis and Order in Eng. Towns, 1500–1700*, ed. P. Clark and P. Slack, 205.

12 *Cal. Chester City Cl. Mins. 1603–42*, 125, 127–9; *Acts of P.C. 1626*, 356; *Crisis and Order*, ed. Clark and Slack, 205–6; Johnson, 'Aspects', 302–3.

merchants should benefit, though perhaps only on Gamull's terms.[1]

In 1630 Gamull and others were still allegedly refusing to allow Edwards to share in the freighting of ships, and two years later Edwards and his associates were accused of diverting cargoes of wine to Beaumaris (Ang.) in order to avoid paying prisage at Chester. Edwards's campaign seems to have won him support, however, for he became an alderman in 1631 and was mayor in 1636–7. By 1640 conflict among the merchants had died down: the corporation had resumed the right to levy the prisage on wines, and negotiations for a new licence to export calfskins were conducted in the name of the mayor and citizens.[2] The Merchants' company remained in being, with 46 members in 1639.[3]

GUILDS

Much of Chester's economic life between 1550 and the Civil War was controlled by the craft guilds, which in theory, and often in practice, prevented any master craftsman or trader from working in the city without first qualifying as a freeman and being admitted to the appropriate guild.[4] There were nevertheless many disputes about working practices within guilds. Some members of the company of Joiners, Turners, and Carvers, for example, bought partly finished pieces of furniture from country producers and completed the work themselves; having failed to stamp out the abuse, the guild officers licensed it, but then discovered in 1622 that the main culprit was the senior guild alderman. In companies like the Smiths', where men specialized in related crafts, there were repeated demarcation disputes. Rules against guild members' having more than one shop were flouted, notably among the Saddlers and the Shoemakers, one of whom was ordered in 1626 to close his second outlet in Wrexham.[5] The Tanners maintained stringent rules about the purchase of raw materials in order to prevent stocks from being cornered: each member could make an annual agreement with one country butcher for a supply of skins but was otherwise allowed to buy only one a day. The Brewers' company was divided between large-scale wholesale brewers and small-scale retailers. The former were required to sell beer only in

36-gallon barrels, but after the company was chartered in 1607 some of them began retailing in small quantities, and in 1618 they were ordered to desist.[6]

There were also rivalries between guilds. The Tailors complained against the Drapers, the Mercers against the Linendrapers, and the Weavers against the Embroiderers.[7] The monopoly granted to the Brewers' company by its royal charter of 1634 (unlike its charter of 1607 from the Assembly) provoked fierce opposition, and eventually the company had to accept a privy council ruling that innkeepers could brew beer for their guests.[8]

Two controversies raised points of principle about guild privileges. In 1615 Thomas Aldersey, a 'mere merchant' who wished to carry on the ironmongery business of the widow whom he had married, attempted to take advantage of the privy council's order of 1589 allowing merchants to engage in one retail trade and join the appropriate guild. The Ironmongers tried to insist that he serve a seven-year apprenticeship, but were not supported by the mayor, Aldersey's father. Aldersey's apprentices allegedly assaulted two senior members of the guild, and his shop was picketed, then attacked. Eventually the privy council reaffirmed the order which allowed Aldersey to trade, but he nevertheless moved the business to the exempt jurisdiction of Gloverstone, where he traded for 10 years before being admitted to the company at a much enhanced fee.[9] A later dispute questioned whether enfranchisement and guild membership were both required for the exercise of a particular trade. An embroiderer who began trading as a mercer was challenged by the Mercers' guild and disfranchised in 1619. The assize judges ruled in 1622 that he should be readmitted only to the freedom, allowing him to work legally only as an embroiderer, and when he persisted in trading as a mercer he was fined and his shop was closed.[10]

The guilds found it less easy to enforce their rights against competitors based in Gloverstone and the cathedral precincts, not least because the dean and chapter were rarely supportive,[11] and against country craftsmen who sold cheap wares illegally in Chester, despite privy council support against country feltmakers in the late 1620s.[12]

1 *Crisis and Order*, ed. Clark and Slack, 206–7; Johnson, 'Aspects', 303–5.

2 *Cal. Chester City Cl. Mins. 1603–42*, 166, 169–70, 202, 207; *Crisis and Order*, ed. Clark and Slack, 207; Johnson, 'Aspects', 305–6.

3 B.L. Harl. MS. 2054, ff. 50–1.

4 *V.C.H. Ches.* v (2), Craft Guilds: Economic Regulation; M. J. Groombridge, 'City Gilds of Chester', *J.C.A.S.* xxxix. 98–9; *T.H.S.L.C.* cxix. 93, 98–100; Woodward, *Men at Work*, 30–5; Johnson, 'Aspects', 230, 251–60; C.C.A.L.S., ZAB 1, ff. 116v., 259v.

5 C.C.A.L.S., ZAB 1, f. 277; *Cal. Chester City Cl. Mins. 1603–42*, 1–2, 140; F. Simpson, 'City Gilds of Chester: Smiths, Cutlers, and Plumbers', *J.C.A.S.* xx. 15–17; ibid. xxxix. 99; Woodward, *Men at Work*, 78–9; Johnson, 'Aspects', 263–70.

6 C.C.A.L.S., ZAB 1, ff. 238v., 252v., 270; *Cal. Chester City Cl.*

Mins. 1603–42, 7; Johnson, 'Aspects', 270–6.

7 Morris, *Chester*, 404–5, 409, 435–6; *J.C.A.S.* xxxix. 99–100; Woodward, *Men at Work*, 18.

8 *Cal. Chester City Cl. Mins. 1603–42*, 29, 185–6; *Cal. S.P. Dom. 1635–6*, 371–2; 1637, 49–50; Johnson, 'Aspects', 289–92.

9 *Cal. Chester City Cl. Mins. 1603–42*, 78; *Acts of P.C. 1615–16*, 66, 651–2; Johnson, 'Aspects', 279–86.

10 C.C.A.L.S., ZML 6/139–41; *Acts of P.C. 1618–19*, 159–60, 327–8; 1621–3, 296–7; *Cal. S.P. Dom. 1611–18*, 565; *Cal. Chester City Cl. Mins. 1603–42*, 97–8, 121, 124–5; Johnson, 'Aspects', 286–9.

11 *Cal. Chester City Cl. Mins. 1603–42*, 132; C.C.A.L.S., ZAB 2, f. 21v.; Johnson, 'Aspects', 295–6.

12 P.R.O., PC 2/38, ff. 230, 501; PC 2/39, f. 385; PC 2/41, f. 373; PC 2/42, f. 478; PC 2/44, f. 292; *Cal. S.P. Dom. 1628–9*, 340, 545; Johnson, 'Aspects', 292–5.

SOCIAL CONDITIONS

Disease was an ever-present threat, and the corporation took action against its spread from the 1570s (when it appointed a city surgeon), aiming to exclude people arriving from plague-infected areas and to isolate citizens who contracted plague.[1] In 1625, when plague was raging elsewhere, it enforced a 24-hour watch at the gates against persons and goods from infected places, and ordered innkeepers to check their guests. The Michaelmas fair was cancelled during further epidemics in 1631 and 1636.[2]

Poverty and vagrancy were intractable problems throughout the period. Beggars came from Wales, the Isle of Man, Ireland, and poorer parts of the North-West, drawn no doubt by the prospect of alms, pickings, or casual work.[3] In 1539–40 Chester was one of the first places to regulate them in response to national legislation distinguishing between the deserving and undeserving poor. A census of the indigent was taken, beggars were listed and licensed to beg in only one designated ward, and other workless men were required to present themselves for hire.[4] In the mid 16th century *c.* 60 beggars were licensed, and there were further surveys of the poor in 1555 and 1572.[5] In 1586 and 1591, as their number grew, the Assembly ordered the magistrates to conduct monthly searches for rogues and vagabonds.[6] Other measures included a ban in 1604 on converting buildings into small separate dwellings.[7]

The 'deserving' poor were relieved under an Act of 1563 by compulsory charitable donations, which raised £98 in 1567 from 342 donors. Recipients numbering 121 were mostly paid between 1*d.* and 4*d.* weekly.[8] The needy probably exceeded that number, and the introduction of compulsory poor rates under legislation of 1572 plainly did not solve the problem. The Assembly soon began to supervise the administration of parish poor rates,[9] and the new poor law of 1598 was implemented after a joint meeting of the mayor, aldermen J.P.s, constables, and parish overseers.[10]

In 1572 the corporation raised an assessment to pay for a house of correction, with equipment and raw materials for clothmaking, on which the able-bodied poor could be set to work. The house opened outside the Northgate in 1576, under the supervision of three aldermen and the management of two masters.[11] The Weavers' guild opposed the scheme in vain. In 1577 the master was required to employ 20 poor people and take up to five others named by the magistrates as in need of correction, the numbers later being doubled.[12] After 1600 difficulties repeatedly arose about the master's terms and the sale of the cloth produced, despite competition for the mastership and a review of arrangements in 1625. In 1638 two new masters, both clothworkers, were appointed to replenish the stock and employ at least 100 people.[13]

Despite all discouragements vagrants and beggars continued to enter the city. In the early 17th century the Assembly called for monthly, and even fortnightly, searches for lodgers and vagrants, and required aldermen to check their wards for beggars, bone-lace weavers, and other undesirables. In 1638, after a further census of beggars and vagrants, some were given relief, some set to work, and some expelled.[14] The numbers relieved in the earlier 17th century are not known.[15] The corporation provided some work by making loans to craftsmen for training the poor, for example in weaving braid and fustians or knitting stockings.[16] During emergencies in the 1580s the proceeds of common bargains were set aside for the poor,[17] and in 1603–5 the corporation spent heavily on poor plague victims, in part using a grant from the county magistrates.[18] Efforts to control grain supplies and prices in times of dearth also benefited the poorest.[19]

Some parishes were well provided with charitable benefactions, especially from civic families.[20] More important were those administered by the corporation,

---

1 Above, this chapter: Demography; Morris, *Chester*, 78–9; Shrewsbury, *Hist. Bubonic Plague*, 272–3; C.C.A.L.S., ZCHB 3, f. 13v.

2 *Cal. Chester City Cl. Mins. 1603–42*, 135–7, 167–8, 188–90; Johnson, 'Aspects', 216.

3 A. L. Beier, *Masterless Men: The Vagrancy Problem in Eng. 1560–1640*, 36–7, 39, 72.

4 C.C.A.L.S., ZAB 1, f. 60; Morris, *Chester*, 355–7; P. Slack, *Poverty and Policy in Tudor and Stuart Eng.* 119, 123; Johnson, 'Aspects', 191–2.

5 C.C.A.L.S., ZAB 1, f. 126v.; Morris, *Chester*, 355–7; Johnson, 'Aspects', 191–2, 197, 203.

6 C.C.A.L.S., ZAB 1, ff. 211v., 231v., 232v.; Morris, *Chester*, 359.

7 Morris, *Chester*, 192, 452; Beier, *Masterless Men*, 83, 148; Slack, *Poverty and Policy*, 68; *Cal. Chester City Cl. Mins. 1603–42*, 9–10; C.C.A.L.S., ZMB 28, *passim*; cf. 31 Eliz. I, c. 7.

8 Johnson, 'Aspects', 192–5.

9 Ibid. 196; *Tudor Chester*, ed. Kennett, 24–5; Morris, *Chester*, 366; Slack, *Poverty and Policy*, 126.

10 C.C.A.L.S., ZAB 1, f. 254.

11 Ibid. ff. 126v., 164, 169v., 170v.; Morris, *Chester*, 362–4; Slack, *Poverty and Policy*, 125; Johnson, 'Aspects', 197–9.

12 Morris, *Chester*, 408–9; Johnson, 'Aspects', 199–200.

13 *Cal. Chester City Cl. Mins. 1603–42*, 37–8, 41, 46–7, 51 n., 53, 91, 97, 117, 132–3, 159, 179, 194–6, 220; Johnson, 'Aspects', 200–1.

14 *Cal. Chester City Cl. Mins. 1603–42*, 55, 88, 125, 134, 152–3, 160, 196.

15 C.C.A.L.S., ZML 6/32, 34; ZQSF *passim*.

16 *Cal. Chester City Cl. Mins. 1603–42*, 46–7, 90, 123, 197.

17 C.C.A.L.S., ZAB 1, ff. 204, 214v., 218; Woodward, *Trade of Eliz. Chester*, 53.

18 C.C.A.L.S., ZAB 1, f. 278v.; ZML 2/173; ZML 3/177; ZTAR 2/23; *Cal. Chester City Cl. Mins. 1603–42*, 8–9; *Q. Sess. Recs. of Ches. 1559–1760* (R.S.L.C. xciv), 53–5.

19 Morris, *Chester*, 428–31; Woodward, *Trade of Eliz. Chester*, 49–53.

20 *V.C.H. Ches.* v (2), Charities for the Poor: Parochial Charities.

mostly established between 1575 and 1620 by wealthy citizens or successful Londoners with local connexions, such as John Vernon and three members of the Offley family, Hugh, Robert, and William. As well as direct poor relief they provided loans to give work to the poor and working capital for newly qualified traders and artificers. The sums for poor relief amounted to almost £84 a year.[1] The mayor and Assembly considered requests for grants or loans, and competition was often keen: in 1612, for example, 127 applicants petitioned for the 24 portions of Robert Offley's charity.[2] Sometimes there were difficulties in obtaining the interest payable on loans or recovering the principal, and some funds were lost through default or mismanagement.[3]

A few small charitable grants provided for civic junketing and anniversary sermons, but there was no large bequest for religious purposes and only one for education, Robert Offley's exhibition at Brasenose College, Oxford. There is no other evidence of civic concern with education during the period, when the King's school was administered by the dean and chapter.[4]

CULTURAL PURSUITS

The presence in Chester of many clergy, teachers, lawyers, palatinate officials, gentlemen, and other educated people stimulated literary interests. By the early 17th century there were stationers and a printer, but as yet apparently no bookseller.[5] Local authors included clergy who published religious tracts, and Robert Rogers (d. 1595), archdeacon of Chester, who collected materials for a history of the city, the 'Breviary', which was completed by his son David in several versions. Civic pride was also reflected in Alderman William Aldersey's list of mayors and sheriffs, augmented by annalistic entries; by an account of the city's institutions by William Webb (fl. *c.* 1580–1620), a clerk in the mayor's court; and by the copies of the plays, mayoral lists, annals, and other documents made by George Bellin, a parish and guild clerk. Particularly important were the antiquarian labours of members of the Chaloner and Holme families, heraldic painters. Thomas Chaloner was a deputy herald, whose widow married Randle Holme I (*c.* 1571–1655). Holme and

his son, Randle II (1601–59), both served as churchwardens at St. Mary's, aldermen of the company of Painters, Glaziers, Embroiderers, and Stationers, deputy heralds, and mayors; industrious and accurate, they amassed large collections from the city records, monumental inscriptions, genealogies, and gentlemen's papers. Their work preserved records of Chester's institutions, officials, ceremonies, and customs, promoted a sense, partly artificial, of the antiquity of its liberties, and established a tradition of local scholarship.[6]

Creativity in the arts was otherwise almost confined to a few goldsmiths who produced domestic and church plate, the busy heraldic painters, and above all musicians and actors. Among musicians Francis Pilkington had a family connexion with the service of the earl of Derby, chamberlain of Chester; he became a singing-man at the cathedral *c.* 1602, and wrote madrigals and other compositions. His contemporary Thomas Bateson was cathedral organist from *c.* 1599 to 1608; among his works were an anthem, an important group of madrigals, and a setting of a cathedral service used until the early 18th century.[7] The city waits performed the music at official and private events and gave public recitals; some also taught music and dancing. Their rivals locally were the minstrels licensed by the Dutton family, and there was a fracas between the two in 1610.[8] The city's dramatic traditions were upheld most spectacularly in a staging of 'Aeneas and Dido' in 1564 and a pageant in 1610 in honour of Henry, prince of Wales and earl of Chester.[9]

Official disapproval in a changed religious climate ended the Whitsun play after 1575 and modified other traditional public spectacles and observances. The Midsummer show was shorn of its more unseemly features after 1600 but continued as a popular carnival.[10] In the 1550s Christmas mumming and the Christmas breakfast for the poor were prohibited as the cause of unbefitting levity; the Christmas watch, with its torchlight procession and fireworks, survived only with less eating and drinking.[11] Participation in the Sheriffs' breakfast on Easter Monday was severely restricted in 1640.[12] Even in their modified form, however, the popular shows and celebrations promoted a sense of civic community

1 *V.C.H. Ches.* v (2), Charities for the Poor: Municipal Charities; *Cal. Chester City Cl. Mins. 1603–42*, 214–19; Johnson, 'Aspects', 204–7.

2 C.C.A.L.S., ZAF 9/37; ZAF 10/100; ZAF 11 *passim*; Johnson, 'Aspects', 209.

3 *Cal. Chester City Cl. Mins. 1603–42*, 20, 37, 148, 154, 158, 219; Johnson, 'Aspects', 210.

4 *V.C.H. Ches.* v (2), Education: Before 1700; *V.C.H. Ches.* iii. 230.

5 J. P. Earwaker, 'Four Randle Holmes of Chester, Antiquaries, Heralds, and Genealogists, *c.* 1571–1707', *J.C.A.S.* N.S. iv. 113–14, 160.

6 *REED: Chester*, pp. xxiii–xxxvi, 320–6, 351–5; P. Clark, 'Visions of Urban Community', *The Pursuit of Urban Hist.* ed. D. Fraser and A. Sutcliffe, 110–12; A. T. Thacker, 'Ches.' *Eng.*

County Histories, ed. C. R. J. Currie and C. P. Lewis, 72–4; *J.C.A.S.* N.S. iv. 115–35.

7 J. C. Bridge, 'Two Chester Madrigal Writers', *J.C.A.S.* N.S. vi. 60–4; idem, 'Organists of Chester Cath.' *J.C.A.S.* xix. 73, 75–6.

8 *REED: Chester*, pp. li, lix; Morris, *Chester*, 348; *V.C.H. Ches.* v (2), Plays, Sports, and Customs before 1700: Music and Minstrelsy.

9 *V.C.H. Ches.* v (2), Plays, Sports, and Customs before 1700: Private Patronage.

10 Ibid.: Chester Plays (Whitsun Play: History); City Watches and Midsummer Show.

11 *REED: Chester*, pp. xlvi, 56, 323–4, 352–3; *Tudor Chester*, ed. Kennett, 22.

12 *V.C.H. Ches.* v (2), Plays, Sports, and Customs before 1700: Sporting Customs (Sheriffs' Breakfast).

and counteracted the social frailty caused by tensions and hardship.

Other public entertainments included occasional days of national rejoicing, an annual round of civic and guild ceremonies, and from 1609 the St. George's Day horse race on the Roodee.[1] Visiting dignitaries were welcomed with pomp and merry-making; Robert Dudley, earl of Leicester, for example, in 1584; Charlotte de la Trémouille, dowager duchess of Thouars and mother-in-law of James Stanley, Lord Strange (the heir of William Stanley, earl of Derby), in 1630; and James I himself in 1617.[2] Everyday pastimes included football, bowls, cock fighting, and bull and bear baiting, the last of which the authorities tried in vain to suppress.[3] The quality of Chester's beer was commended by the poet John Taylor (d. 1653).[4] Chester's public spectacles, entertainments, and races enhanced the position it already enjoyed as a social centre for the region.

RELIGION, 1550–1642

FROM THE EDWARDIAN REFORMATION TO THE ELIZABETHAN SETTLEMENT

The Henrician reformation had been received in Chester with acquiescence tempered by conservatism and expediency. Prominent townsmen who bought or rented ecclesiastical property included William Sneyd, Hugh Aldersey, and William Goodman, all former mayors, and the Dutton family.[5] The more extreme official line taken under Edward VI was also accepted. At the cathedral Dean William Cliffe (1547–58) quickly ordered the destruction of traditional fittings, while some of the vestments may have been handed over for use in the Whitsun plays.[6] The poorer parish churches, including St. Peter's, had little to lose, but the effects on the richest parishes were severe. St. John's, formerly a well endowed college, became a rather poor parish church, while Holy Trinity, where many leading citizens worshipped, and St. Mary's lost many ornaments, sacred vessels, and vestments. The abolition of chantries resulted in fewer clergy, and many city benefices were too poor to allow stipendiary curates to be recruited.[7]

There is little indication of enthusiasm for new doctrines in Chester, which contained no notable protestant laymen, and whose overseas trade was not with ports where protestantism was entrenched. John Bradford, a renowned protestant proselytizer, preached in the city during the 1550s, and John Bird, bishop of Chester 1541–54, took a strongly protestant line, but in general the clergy probably remained conservative and compliant.[8] The Marian reaction in the city was thus limited. The married incumbent of St. Mary's and Bishop Bird were deprived. The latter's two successors, George Coates (1554–5) and Cuthbert Scott (1556–9), reorganized the church courts to revitalize Catholic worship throughout the diocese. Parishioners rebuilt altars, set up roods and images of the Virgin anew, and replaced vestments and vessels.[9] Changes at the cathedral were modest. Two canons resigned.[10] The only indication of lay resistance came in 1555, when one of the sheriffs, John Cowper, led an unsuccessful attempt to rescue a heretic, George Marsh, from being burnt at Spital Boughton on the outskirts of the liberties.[11]

There was apparently little overt opposition to the Elizabethan settlement, but the interregnum between the deprivation of Bishop Scott in June 1559 and the appointment of Bishop William Downham in May 1561 left the diocesan machinery in the hands of Marian officials.[12] The cathedral chapter was scarcely affected: Dean Cliffe died in 1558 and was replaced by Richard Walker, the last dean of St. John's, a conformer since 1540; two of the Henrician canons remained, along with four from Mary's reign. The Palm Sunday liturgical observances continued at first, but the cathedral soon acquired the Prayer Book of 1559 and the Psalter, and set up a table of the Commandments.[13] In the parishes the Marian alterations were undone, sometimes reluctantly.[14] The heavy

1 *V.C.H. Ches.* v (2), Chester Races.

2 *Tudor Chester*, ed. Kennett, 20; *Cal. Chester City Cl. Mins. 1603–42*, 84, 94, 103, 121; *J.C.A.S.* xxviii. 186; xxxviii. 154; Kennett, *Loyal Chester*, 8.

3 Morris, *Chester*, 331–6; *Cal. Chester City Cl. Mins. 1603–42*, 164, 200; *J.C.A.S.* xxxix. 100–1; *REED: Chester*, pp. lviii–lix; *Urban Hist. Yearbook*, xviii. 12.

4 C.C.A.L.S., ZQSF 52–6; P. Clark, *The Eng. Alehouse: A Social Hist. 1200–1830*, 73, 79, 98; *Tudor Chester*, ed. Kennett, 26.

5 Above, Later Medieval Chester: Religion (The Dissolution); Burne, *Monks*, 173; *V.C.H. Ches.* iii. 175, 177; *Cal. of Lancs. and Ches. Exchequer Depositions* (R.S.L.C. xi), 108–10.

6 Burne, *Chester Cath.* 19, 22–6; *Tudor Chester*, ed. Kennett, 28; J. Beck, *Tudor Ches.* 87; S. E. Lehmberg, *Reformation of Cathedrals*, 116, 178–80; *V.C.H. Ches.* v (2), Cathedral and Close: Cathedral Church from 1541.

7 *V.C.H. Ches.* v (2), Medieval Parish Churches.

8 C. Haigh, *Reformation and Resistance in Tudor Lancs.* 169; F. Sanders, 'John Bird, D.D., Bishop of Chester 1541–54', *J.C.A.S.* xiii. 110–26; *V.C.H. Ches.* iii. 16–18.

9 *V.C.H. Ches.* iii. 18–19; Haigh, *Reformation and Resistance*, 196–7; J. R. Beresford, 'Churchwardens' Accts. of Holy Trinity, 1532–1633', *J.C.A.S.* xxxviii. 98, 115–20; *Tudor Chester*, ed. Kennett, 28; *V.C.H. Ches.* v (2), Medieval Parish Churches.

10 Burne, *Chester Cath.* 19, 29, 33; Beck, *Tudor Ches.* 87–8; Lehmberg, *Reformation of Cathedrals*, 129–30.

11 Haigh, *Reformation and Resistance*, 183–5; *V.C.H. Ches.* iii. 17; Beck, *Tudor Ches.* 88.

12 *V.C.H. Ches.* iii. 20; *Ch. and Society in Eng.: Henry VIII to James I*, ed. F. Heal and R. O'Day, 46, 111.

13 Burne, *Chester Cath.* 35–40; Lehmberg, *Reformation of Cathedrals*, 150–2; *REED: Chester*, p. viii.

14 *V.C.H. Ches.* v (2), Medieval Parish Churches.

cost of making church buildings suitable for protestant worship hampered the maintenance of cathedral and parish churches alike, notably at St. John's, which became partly ruinous. The churchyard of St. Oswald's was desecrated by its use as a rubbish dump.[1] Many problems remained in the 1580s. St. Oswald's and St. Michael's, and St. Martin's and St. Bridget's were obliged to share ministers because of their poverty, while several parishes sometimes needed to levy Easter rates to pay their ministers and parish clerks.[2] In 1592 six out of nine lacked the Book of Homilies and Bishop Jewell's *Reply*; there was no catechizing at St. John's and St. Michael's, and no sermons at St. Mary's; and at St. Peter's and Holy Trinity there were complaints about clerical absenteeism and negligence.[3] Nevertheless, some important senior clergymen held office in Elizabethan Chester, among them Bishops William Chadderton and Richard Vaughan (later promoted to Lincoln and London respectively), Dean John Piers (eventually archbishop of York), and Dean William Cliffe, a member of the commission which drew up the Henrician *King's Book*.[4]

CONFORMITY AND PURITANISM, 1558–1619

Initial efforts to enforce conformity were less than urgent under the lax regime of Bishop Downham, but in 1564 he presented a report, not wholly accurate, which cast doubt on the religious loyalties of several aldermen, including the mayor (Richard Poole) and three of his predecessors (John Smith, William Aldersey, and Randle Bamvill). There were also a few suspect absentees from church services, notably Fulk Aldersey and his wife, but open recusancy was clearly negligible.[5] During the later 1560s heavier pressure was brought to bear on conservatives, and by 1580 a score of recusants had been dealt with. About the same time convicted Cheshire recusants and priests were moved from Chester castle to Manchester, partly because Chester was thought more sympathetic. The decision was later reversed, mistakenly, because supervision at the castle proved to be slack.[6] There were few recusants in the city, and the authorities' main concern was that

Catholics were entering Chester in order to escape by ship to Ireland.[7]

Enthusiastic protestantism developed only slowly. During the 1560s and 1570s there were attempts to promote good behaviour in church and some agitation against the Whitsun plays,[8] but the turning point came only in the 1580s, when Bishop Chadderton (1579–95) established monthly exercises, dominated by puritans, and encouraged clergy to attend. Among the participants was the Revd. Christopher Goodman, who returned to Chester in 1584 and soon gathered influential support among the laity. Active at the cathedral at the same time were Prebendary John Nutter as a preacher and Thomas Hitchens as a lecturer.[9] In 1583 the corporation established a weekly Friday lecture at St. Peter's, which became a centre of puritan preaching. After Goodman associated himself with St. Bridget's it too displayed puritan leanings, and in other parishes, Holy Trinity for example, there were complaints about incumbents who failed to preach regularly.[10] The growing attachment to puritan teachings was both reflected in, and encouraged by, the corporation's eventual concern with personal behaviour. It repeatedly attempted to curb excessive drinking and vice, attacking church ales, Welsh weddings, unlawful games, bowling, football, and bull and bear baiting. In 1583 the authorities banned Sunday trading and exhorted Cestrians to attend church whenever sermons were preached and twice on Sundays and holy days; the corporation set an example by attending services with due formality. Opposition to Mayor Henry Hardware's interference with the Midsummer show in 1600, however, suggests that the citizens' enthusiasm for high-minded reforms was limited.[11]

The 'godly' and more conservative elements continued to differ during the early 17th century about the Midsummer show and visiting players.[12] From 1610 to 1612 successive mayors ordered strict observance of the Sabbath, encouraged the corporation to attend sermons at St. Peter's, and took control of the races on St. George's Day in order to prevent misbehaviour.[13] A distinctive lay puritan temper thus steadily

1 *V.C.H. Ches.* v (2), Cathedral and Close: Cathedral Church from 1541; ibid. Medieval Parish Churches.

2 *V.C.H. Ches.* v (2), Medieval Parish Churches; *Parish, Church, and People*, ed. Wright, 92.

3 W. F. Irvine, 'Bishop of Chester's Visitation Book, 1592', *J.C.A.S.* n.s. v. 408–12.

4 *V.C.H. Ches.* iii. 188; Burne, *Chester Cath.* 3, 19, 29–30, 37, 60, 67; *J.C.A.S.* lxiii. 56.

5 K. R. Wark, *Elizabethan Recusancy in Ches.* chapter 1 *passim*; *V.C.H. Ches.* iii. 20–1.

6 Wark, *Eliz. Recusancy*, chapters 2–4 *passim* and pp. 67–8, 106, 123; Haigh, *Reformation and Resistance*, 250–1; B. Coward, 'Lieutenancy of Lancs. and Ches. in 16th and Early 17th Cent.' *T.H.S.L.C.* cxix. 59, 63–4.

7 Wark, *Eliz. Recusancy*, 56, 70, 72–3, 82, 85, 88–101, 108, 114–18, 132.

8 R. H. Morris, *Chester* (Diocesan Histories ser.), 133.

C.C.A.L.S., ZAB 1, ff. 162v.–163, 165v.–166; *V.C.H. Ches.* v (2), Plays, Sports, and Customs before 1700: Chester Plays.

9 *V.C.H. Ches.* iii. 23–4; P. Collinson, *Elizabethan Puritan Movement*, 65–6, 170, 210–11; R. C. Richardson, 'Puritanism and Ecclesiastical Authorities', *Politics, Religion, and Eng. Civil War*, ed. B. Manning, 5; Lehmberg, *Reformation of Cathedrals*, 162, 277.

10 Johnson, 'Aspects', 16; *Tudor Chester*, ed. Kennett, 28, 30; *V.C.H. Ches.* v (2), Medieval Parish Churches.

11 Morris, *Chester*, 331–6, 359, 425–31; R. C. Richardson, *Puritanism in NW. Eng.* 147–8; *Urban Hist. Yearbook*, xviii. 11–13; *V.C.H. Ches.* v (2), Plays, Sports, and Customs before 1700.

12 P. Collinson, *Birthpangs of Protestant Eng.* 58; *V.C.H. Ches.* v (2), Plays, Sports, and Customs before 1700; *Cal. Chester City Cl. Mins. 1603–42*, 79–80.

13 C.C.A.L.S., ZML 2/242; *Cal. Chester City Cl. Mins. 1603–42*, 50, 52, 55.

developed before 1620, and it was not effectively countered by openly conservative opinion or by outright recusancy.

Clerical support for puritanism is not easy to measure. William Barlow, dean 1603–5, was a prominent and strongly anti-puritan member of the Hampton Court conference in 1604,[1] but Bishop Richard Vaughan (1597–1604) sympathized with many puritan opinions.[2] The next bishop, George Lloyd (1604–15), a former divinity lecturer at the cathedral, was an active preacher and apparently a moderate who tolerated puritan clergy in Chester.[3] His successor, Thomas Morton (1616–19), however, was of firmly Anglican views and pressed the puritans to conform.[4] His task was made more difficult by the ministrations of Nicholas Byfield, a Calvinist polemicist and a powerful preacher, who was rector of St. Peter's 1608–15, where his congregation included the well known puritan gentleman John Bruen of Bruen Stapleford, a supporter of private prayer meetings in the parish.[5] Members of the corporation attended Byfield's services, and the mayor of 1611–12, John Ratcliffe, had his official pew in the church until it was removed on the orders of Bishop Lloyd.[6] Besides Byfield there were two or three special sermons every week by lecturers funded at different times by the corporation, guilds, and private gifts.[7] Their work and the sermons of visiting ministers made St. Peter's the main preaching centre in Jacobean Chester.[8] Otherwise the parish churches suffered from neglect and petty dissension. The poorer ones were served only by reading ministers, often pluralists, some of whom were also petty canons in the cathedral and had a well founded reputation for laxity in their duties.[9]

THE RULE OF BISHOP BRIDGEMAN, 1619–42

John Bridgeman's early years as bishop were marked by attempts to improve the conduct of the cathedral clergy,[10] but he was not fully supported by the dean, Thomas Mallory (1607–44), and perhaps achieved little. Moreover Bridgeman soon became embroiled in a triangular dispute involving the dean and chapter

and the corporation. There had already been a symbolic clash between corporation and cathedral in 1607, when the mayor had tried to enter the cathedral with the city's sword erect, according to custom, and a scuffle ensued when a prebendary endeavoured to lower the sword. Soon afterwards the swordbearer died and his funeral cortège, headed by civic dignitaries, was refused entry at the west door. A court judgement in the corporation's favour strengthened its position in the cathedral.[11] A new dispute about pews, pulpits, and sermons in St. Oswald's, the parish church occupying the south transept, lasted from 1624 to 1638.[12]

Contention also arose about Abbey Court, long a source of friction because unfree craftsmen could set up shop there exempt from the city's trading regulations. In 1630 Prebendary William Case, pursuing a private dispute, sought permission for a stranger to keep a stationer's shop in Abbey Court and later threatened to arrange for more shops to be opened there. Case was a quarrelsome man who neglected his cure, and whose incumbency of St. Oswald's (1626–34) can have done little to assuage the conflict there.[13] Bridgeman himself wished to reserve buildings in the Court for the cathedral's officers, but the dean and chapter complied only in 1638 after intervention by Archbishop Laud.[14]

Eventually Bridgeman's campaign for 'beautification' brought about changes in the fabric of the cathedral and most of the city's churches, where repairs were accompanied by new paving, uniform seating, altars, and rails.[15] At first he showed little inclination to interfere with services in the city churches[16] even though several were not conducted to his satisfaction. As a result puritan teaching became more thoroughly entrenched.[17] Outstanding among the puritan clergy was John Ley, an active pamphleteer, a prebendary by 1627, and later subdean at the cathedral, who was appointed city preacher at St. Peter's in 1630. Ley was on good terms with Bridgeman and James Ussher, archbishop of Armagh, and was himself a moderate reformer, though a strong Sabbatarian whose sermons in defence of Byfield's teachings led to his temporary

1 *D.N.B.*

2 K. Fincham, *Prelate as Pastor: The Episcopate of James I*, 272.

3 Ibid. 193, 272; *V.C.H. Ches.* iii. 26–7.

4 *V.C.H. Ches.* iii. 28–9; Fincham, *Prelate as Pastor*, 227, 253, 257, 260.

5 P. Collinson, *Religion of Protestants: The Church in Eng. Society, 1559–1625*, 243; Richardson, *Puritanism in NW.* 147.

6 Richardson, *Puritanism in NW.* 147; *Cal. Chester City Cl. Mins. 1603–42*, 52; *V.C.H. Ches.* v (2), Medieval Parish Churches.

7 C.C.A.L.S., ZAB 1, ff. 246, 279; ZAF 10/61; ZML 6/88; *Cal. Chester City Cl. Mins. 1603–42*, 21, 31 n., 78, 82; Wark, *Eliz. Recusancy*, 127.

8 Collinson, *Religion of Protestants*, 146 n.; M. J. Crossley Evans, 'Clergy of City of Chester, 1630–72', *J.C.A.S.* lxviii. 97, 105–6.

9 *J.C.A.S.* lxviii. 98–100.

10 *V.C.H. Ches.* iii. 29–30; Fincham, *Prelate as Pastor*, 76–7,

171–2; Burne, *Chester Cath.* 99–100; *J.C.A.S.* lxviii. 99, 103.

11 *Cal. Chester City Cl. Mins. 1603–42*, 27; Burne, *Chester Cath.* 87–8; *J.C.A.S.* lxviii. 101.

12 *V.C.H. Ches.* v (2), Medieval Parish Churches: St. Oswald.

13 C.C.A.L.S., ZAF 15/34; *Cal. Chester City Cl. Mins. 1603–42*, 160–1; Burne, *Chester Cath.* 97, 100, 108–11; *J.C.A.S.* lxviii. 102–3.

14 *V.C.H. Ches.* v (2), Cathedral and Close: Precinct from 1541.

15 Burne, *Chester Cath.* 107, 116–17; E. Barber, 'Chester Cath.: Jacobean Work', *J.C.A.S.* n.s. xii. 5–21; M. H. Ridgway, 'Coloured Window-Glass in Ches. 1550–1850', ibid. xlix. 15; *J.C.A.S.* lxviii. 108; *V.C.H. Ches.* v (2), Medieval Parish Churches.

16 *J.C.A.S.* lxviii. 104–5.

17 *V.C.H. Ches.* iii. 29, 31–3; B. W. Quintrell, 'Lancs. Ills, the King's Will, and the Troubling of Bishop Bridgeman', *T.H.S.L.C.* cxxxii. 67–102.

removal from the lectureship.[1] Ley had three close allies: John Glendal, chosen and paid by the parishioners of St. Peter's as a stipendiary preacher; John Bruen's nephew Nathaniel Lancaster, a follower of Byfield and a lecturer at St. Peter's who also preached at St. Michael's and St. Olave's; and Nicholas Conney, divinity lecturer at the cathedral, vicar of both St. John's and (after 1634) St. Oswald's. The work at St. Peter's enhanced its status as the main puritan church in the city, enjoying civic support during the conflict at St. Oswald's and attracting larger congregations.[2]

For some time puritan clergy and laity were not harried, not only because of the bishop's lenience but also because some churchwardens were in collusion with their ministers. Pressure mounted when the diocesan authorities were spurred on by Richard Neile, archbishop of York from 1632, who was convinced that Chester was a hotbed of puritanism. The bishop and his officers therefore took a closer interest in both services and clergy, singling out lecturers for ignoring the prescribed liturgy, attempting to enforce ritual observances, presenting clergy for nonconformity or neglect of duty, and pressing for improvements to church fabrics.[3] Episcopal pressure seems to have had little effect, and the growing acceptance of puritan convictions was demonstrated in the welcome given to the radical puritan William Prynne in 1637, when, on his way to prison at Caernarfon, he was entertained by local sympathizers, including Calvin Bruen and Robert Ince (both former sheriffs), Alderman Thomas Aldersey, and Peter Ince, a stationer. The ecclesiastical authorities reacted sharply: sermons against Prynne were ordered in all the city churches, his alleged supporters were examined, the home of Peter Ince (who was suspected of distributing puritan literature) was searched, and heavy fines and public penances were handed down.[4]

The severe punishments imposed on Prynne's supporters helped to polarize religious attitudes in the city. Soon afterwards, when the bishop visited St. John's he was met with a show of disapproval by the churchwardens, who were then belatedly obliged to 'beautify' the church. There was controversy about the incumbents of St. Martin's and St. Mary's and further ill

feeling about Dean Mallory's behaviour over the mayor's stall in the cathedral choir. Despite the bishop's opposition to the Ratcliffes' brewery in Abbey Court, Ley praised the work of John Ratcliffe, the Sabbatarian mayor and patron of Byfield, at his wife's funeral. When a visiting puritan preacher, Thomas Holford, found himself before the consistory court in 1638 for expressing extreme views in a Friday lecture at St. Peter's, clerical opinion was divided. Holford escaped punishment and later preached unhindered. The levy of a clerical assessment to help fund the war against the Scottish Covenanters revealed further divisions: some clergy paid (including the dean and chapter), but others refused.[5]

During 1640–1, as the bishop's authority weakened, the city's puritans developed a more radical edge, popular, anti-episcopal, and nonconforming. Puritan publications were distributed. John Ley issued Sabbatarian addresses, but also, paradoxically, a defence of Bridgeman's use of a supposedly popish altar in the cathedral.[6] Other puritan clergy were less balanced, encouraging citizens to attack Laudian furnishings: altar rails, screens, and other costly fittings were swept away in parish churches; there and at the cathedral walls were whitened, images were obliterated, and painted glass was removed. Calvin Bruen toured the churches in order to report on the destruction to the mayor.[7] Simultaneously Prayer Book services were abandoned and in 1641 Samuel Eaton, recently returned from New England, preached an inflammatory sermon at St. John's in favour of congregationalism,[8] to which a preacher at the cathedral replied attacking puritans and popish innovators alike. Conney and the subdean, William Bispham, signed a petition against innovations in religion, but Conney also joined in a moderate puritan petition regretting the king's estrangement from parliament. Sir Thomas Aston's counter-petition in favour of episcopacy and the liturgy was supported in the city, but Calvin Bruen alleged that he had secured signatures by deceitfully pretending to favour reform.[9] Whatever their impact on the townspeople at large, however, by 1642 such exchanges were subsumed in wider political argument.

1 C.C.A.L.S., ZCHB 3, ff. 133v.–134; ZML 2/273–4; *Cal. S.P. Dom. 1631–3*, 279; *Cal. Chester City Cl. Mins. 1603–42*, 160; J. S. Morrill, *Ches. 1630–60: County Government and Society*, 20; *J.C.A.S.* lxviii. 106–8.
2 *J.C.A.S.* lxviii. 102–3, 105; *V.C.H. Ches.* v (2), Medieval Parish Churches.
3 *Cal. S.P. Dom. 1633–4*, 443; *Politics, Religion, and Eng. Civil War*, ed. Manning, 26; Richardson, *Puritanism in NW.* 39, 82–3; *V.C.H. Ches.* iii. 31–5; *J.C.A.S.* lxviii. 108.
4 *Ches. Hist.* xxxvii. 26–35; *Politics, Religion, and Eng. Civil*

War, ed. Manning, 25; *Cal. Chester City Cl. Mins. 1603–42*, 195; *V.C.H. Ches.* iii. 35; *J.C.A.S.* lxviii. 108–9.
5 *J.C.A.S.* lxviii. 104, 108–10; Burne, *Chester Cath.* 112; *Parish, Church, and People*, ed. Wright, 115–16.
6 Burne, *Chester Cath.* 117–19; *J.C.A.S.* lxviii. 111–12.
7 *J.C.A.S.* lxviii. 111; Burne, *Chester Cath.* 123–4; Morrill, *Ches. 1630–60*, 36; *V.C.H. Ches.* v (2), Medieval Parish Churches.
8 *J.C.A.S.* lxviii. 111; Morrill, *Ches. 1630–60*, 37.
9 *J.C.A.S.* lxviii. 112; A. Fletcher, *Outbreak of Eng. Civil War*, 289–90.

MILITARY AND POLITICAL AFFAIRS, 1550–1642

MILITARY AFFAIRS

Although not involved in the rebellions following the Reformation, the city took precautions as fear of a Spanish invasion mounted during the mid 1580s: military supplies were purchased, foot soldiers trained, and a watch was kept for hostile shipping in the Dee. The defeat of the Armada was duly celebrated, but the authorities remained cautious and in the early 1590s required new freemen to arm themselves, reviewed the trained bands, and inspected munitions stored locally.[1]

After the outbreak of rebellion in Ireland in 1579 Chester was the main port used for sending English troops levied in other parts of the country, who passed through the city frequently and in growing numbers. The mayor and other officials were often fully occupied with receiving them and arranging quarters, food, and money. Ships were requisitioned and provisioned, and supplies of food, drink, stores, and ammunition were sent to Ireland. The repeated demands strained local markets, especially during the shortages of the later 1590s: prices rose, ships' masters demanded large payments, there were difficulties with the authorities of Liverpool, disaffected men deserted in droves and were rarely captured, weapons were often found to be defective, moneys were embezzled, profiteering was rife, and Chester earned a reputation as a 'robber's cave'. The city's expenses were supposedly reimbursed by the treasurers-at-war, but funds were short or delayed and loans had to be obtained locally. Disorderly conduct was frequent, especially when troops were delayed by bad weather or lack of ships. To contain it, in 1594 the mayor erected a gibbet at the High Cross.[2]

Chester's military obligations grew when the Irish campaign intensified in the 1590s. During the two years from early 1600 many reinforcements passed through the port, the mayor received a stream of orders from the privy council, and there were further problems of supply and unruly behaviour.[3] Even after the effective end of the rebellion in 1603 the shipment of men and munitions continued periodically, and the

mayor was called upon to collect funds for measures against pirates.[4]

The corporation remained responsible for the city's militia and vigorously upheld the right to organize it independently of the county,[5] appointing a professional soldier as muster master to train the men.[6] In 1626 the lord lieutenant of Cheshire was ordered to establish a magazine in Chester castle at the county's expense, and an artillery yard was eventually laid out near Cow Lane (later Frodsham Street), powder and match for the trained bands being bought from city funds despite the Assembly's reluctance to establish a precedent.[7]

PARLIAMENTARY REPRESENTATION

In 1543 Chester was made a double-member constituency. It may have sent representatives to parliament in 1545, but its first recorded M.P.s were returned in 1547. It seems likely that until the later 17th century the electorate comprised all adult males. In practice, as there were perhaps no formally contested elections except those of 1621 and 1628, the franchise was initially exercised by the corporation, which selected or at least approved the candidates. In 1621 the victors were accused of canvassing people not qualified to vote, but there was no objection to non-freemen voters as such, and the number participating in 1628, over 900, suggests a male inhabitant franchise.[8]

The city resisted attempts by outsiders to nominate candidates or stand themselves.[9] Instead, leading townsmen were usually elected: between 1547 and 1659 only two of 32 M.P.s were neither aldermen nor fee'd lawyers. The recorder was almost invariably chosen, with the result that some, notably Richard Sneyd, William Gerard, and Edward Whitby, acquired extensive parliamentary experience. Otherwise, repeated election was infrequent.[10] During the later 16th century the city's M.P.s helped secure provisions favourable to Chester in legislation concerning recognizances, the removal of weirs in the Dee, poor relief, and the regulation of taverns. In 1554 they were asked to complain about the incorporation of the Merchants'

1 C.C.A.L.S., ZMMP 2 *passim*; Beck, *Tudor Ches.* 19–20; *Tudor Chester*, ed. Kennett, 31–2.

2 C.C.A.L.S., ZMMP 2–7 *passim*; Morris, *Chester*, 84–92; C. G. Cruickshank, *Elizabeth's Army* (2nd edn., 1966), 62–9, 83, 140–1; *European Crisis of 1590s*, ed. P. Clark, 46, 52, 55; *Tudor Chester*, ed. Kennett, 32–3.

3 *Acts of P.C.* 1599–1600, 101–4, 412–16, 558–9, and *passim*; 1600–1, 12–13, 86–7, and *passim*; 1601–4, 46–7, 71, and *passim*; Woodward, *Trade of Eliz. Chester*, 24.

4 C.C.A.L.S., ZML 6/21, 35, 118–37; ZMMP 15 *passim*; *Acts of P.C.* 1615–16, 690–1, 700; 1616–17, 20; 1618–19, 358–9, 363–4, 410; 1623–5, 371–2, 472–3, 485; 1625–6, 80–1; *Cal. S.P. Dom.* 1619–23, 24, 28, 43, 104, 412; 1625–6, 5, 8, 12, 54; Armour,

'Trade of Chester', 232–7.

5 *Acts of P.C.* 1595–6, 284–5; G. P. Higgins, 'Militia in Early Stuart Ches.' *J.C.A.S.* lxi. 39.

6 *Cal. Chester City Cl. Mins.* 1603–42, 66–8, 92, 141 n.

7 Ibid. 141, 163; *J.C.A.S.* lxi. 42; *T.H.S.L.C.* cxix. 52.

8 *Hist. Parl.*, *Commons*, 1509–58, i. 44–5; D. Hirst, *Representative of the People? Voters and Voting in Eng. under Early Stuarts*, 94–6; *V.C.H. Ches.* ii. 99–100.

9 *Hist. Parl.*, *Commons*, 1558–1603, i. 121–2; *V.C.H. Ches.* ii. 111–12; Morris, *Chester*, 191 n.

10 *Hist. Parl.*, *Commons*, 1509–58, i. 44–5, 302–3; ii. 205–6, 560, 585–6; iii. 334–5, 345; 1558–1603, i. 121–2, 405–6, 439, 486; ii. 164, 182–3, 186–8, 194–5; iii. 398, 577–8, 682; *V.C.H. Ches.* ii. 110.

company, during the later 1580s to secure a grant for the New Haven, and in 1610 to seek a reduction in the duty on Irish yarn imports.[1]

Sometimes local quarrels influenced the choice of M.P.s. During Mary's reign one of the seats alternated between Thomas Massey and William Aldersey, possibly because of the controversy over the Merchants' company. Similarly, the choice of William Glazier in 1571 and 1572 may have been an attempt to compromise in the dispute with the palatinate exchequer.[2] Factionalism focused upon the Whitby family played a large part in the contested elections of 1621 and 1628.[3]

ROYAL TAXATION

Attempts to secure reductions in the city's tax assessment failed in 1611 and 1625–6.[4] There were also problems over a voluntary gift for a projected expedition against Barbary pirates in 1618–19, and over the corporation's attempt to make the inhabitants of Gloverstone liable to tax. Conversely, the forced loan of 1626–7 was paid quickly, perhaps because the various factions in the Assembly hoped to win privy council favour in their disputes.[5] More serious arguments arose about the assessments for Ship Money.[6] At the outset Chester was aggrieved at having to pay a quarter of the county's total under the first writ of 1634, a proportion later reduced. The city authorities then exempted citizens who had contributed to its own assessment from payment for property held in Cheshire, provoking the county to complain successfully to the privy council. Chester retaliated in 1635 by assessing the sheriff of Cheshire, Sir Thomas Aston, Bt., on profits received in the city from his farm of duties on French wine imports. The county backed Aston, and by 1636 also supported the dean and chapter, the inhabitants of Gloverstone, and Sir William Brereton, Bt., in their disputes with the city over liability.[7] In 1638 the privy council ordered Aston to pay with the city and declared Gloverstone exempt, and in 1639 the dean and chapter paid with the county. The arguments allowed both county and corporation to protect their interests without openly challenging the king. The dispute was mostly about

jurisdiction and did not seriously disrupt collection. Chester's contributions were fully paid at first, though delays began in 1636, and by 1640 the privy council was upbraiding the corporation for widespread resistance.

THE DRIFT TO CIVIL WAR, 1640–2

During autumn 1640, with the Scottish army in north-eastern England, the Assembly set up a nightly watch, strengthened the defences at the Eastgate, Newgate, and Bridgegate, and ordered members of the corporation and others to supply corselets, muskets, halberds, and calivers within a month. Arrears of an earlier assessment to replenish the magazine were called in, and ordnance and carriages were brought from Wirral. The trained bands were to be brought up to their full strength of 100 men and placed under the captaincy of Alderman Francis Gamull.[8] There were no military threats during the following months, but the Assembly did not meet between December 1640 and June 1641. During that time, however, the city's M.P.s seem to have followed a moderate and sometimes non-committal line in the Commons.[9]

Defensive preparations remained half-hearted, with the arrears for the magazine never fully collected,[10] and funds for repairing the city walls having to be borrowed from the proceeds of the prisage on wines until an assessment could be levied.[11] Later in 1641, when the Assembly was transacting very little business, it faced growing threats to public order. First, the arrival of protestant refugees from the Irish rebellion set off anti-popish hysteria,[12] culminating in January 1642 in a skirmish just outside the city between Catholics and protestants, with loss of life on both sides.[13] By then troops bound for Ireland had begun to arrive in the city,[14] and the authorities were embroiled in the usual problems: shortage of shipping and delays in embarking troops, unruly and violent behaviour by waiting soldiers, rising prices of food and fodder, and delays in repayment for quarters.[15] The main puritan preachers had curtailed their ministrations and some of the lectureships had fallen vacant, although John Ley, Nathaniel Lancaster, and Thomas Holford were still in the district and in

1 C.C.A.L.S., ZAB 1, f. 219; ZML 2/233; *Hist. Parl., Commons, 1509–58*, i. 45; *Tudor Chester*, ed. Kennett, 11.

2 *V.C.H. Ches.* ii. 110–11; above, this chapter: City Government, 1550–1642 (Legal Administration).

3 Above, this chapter: City Government, 1550–1642 (Office and Faction).

4 B.L. Harl. MS. 2173, ff. 10, 17, 74; C.C.A.L.S., ZML 6/83–4, 87.

5 C.C.A.L.S., ZML 6/118–37; Johnson, 'Aspects', 116–18; R. Cust, *Forced Loan and Eng. Politics, 1626–8*, 121–2.

6 What follows is based on B.L. Harl. MS. 2093, ff. 90–173; Harl. MS. 2173, ff. 19–40; P. Lake, 'Collection of Ship Money in Ches. during 1630s', *Northern Hist.* xvii. 44–71; E. Marcotte, 'Shrieval Administration of Ship Money in Ches. 1637', *Bull. John Rylands Libr.* lviii. 148–9, 160–1; Johnson, 'Aspects', 120–37.

7 *Cal. S.P. Dom.* 1637, 1, 4–5, 42, 116; *Northern Hist.* xvii. 47–8; *J.C.A.S.* xxviii. 187–8.

8 *Cal. Chester City Cl. Mins. 1603–42*, 205–6.

9 Morrill, *Ches. 1630–60*, 40–1, 43–4; M. F. Keeler, *Long Parl. 1640–1: Biographical Study*, 182–3, 341–2.

10 *Cal. Chester City Cl. Mins. 1603–42*, 208, 211.

11 Ibid. 207.

12 Armour, 'Trade of Chester', 237 sqq.; Fletcher, *Outbreak of Eng. Civil War*, 202; *J.C.A.S.* lxviii. 111.

13 *V.C.H. Ches.* iii. 89; R. Clifton, 'Popular Fear of Catholics during Puritan Revolution', *Rebellion, Popular Protest, and Social Order in Early Modern Eng.* ed. P. Slack, 137, 155–6.

14 *Cal. S.P. Dom.* 1641–3, 205.

15 *Letter Books of Sir William Brereton* (R.S.L.C. cxxiii, cxxviii), ii, pp. 538–9, 541–2.

early summer were threatened with legal action for failing to publish royal declarations in their churches.[1]

The prevailing mood in Chester in summer 1642 was a wish for accommodation between Charles I and parliament, reflected in the city's neutralist petition in August and in its reaction to the parliamentary commission of lieutenancy and the royal commission of array. The Assembly stood fast against both an attempt by James Stanley, Lord Strange, to secure the county magazine in the castle for the royalists, and Alderman William Edwards's and Sir William Brereton's effort to take control of the city's trained bands for parliament.[2]

Nevertheless, Bishop Bridgeman, his son Orlando (vice-chamberlain of Chester), other lawyers, and prominent figures were apparently trying to encourage royalist sympathies among leading citizens.[3] On 6 September Mayor Thomas Cowper secured a majority vote in the Assembly for an immediate assessment of 100 marks to fortify the city.[4] The decisive event, however, was the arrival of the king himself in Chester on 23 September. In an upsurge of loyalty he was greeted with popular enthusiasm, pageantry, bellringing, and a loyal address. The king's supporters seized their opportunity. The houses of known opponents, such as Brereton and Aldermen Edwards and Aldersey, were searched for arms; county gentlemen favourable to parliament were rounded up; and parliamentary supporters in the corporation left. When the king departed five days later, with a gift of money from the corporation, the parliamentarian presence in the city had all but gone, and the royalist hold on Chester had finally been consolidated.[5]

THE CIVIL WAR AND INTERREGNUM, 1642–60

THE CIVIL WAR, 1642–6

Chester had great strategic importance during the Civil War. It could readily be garrisoned and defended, was the principal port for Ireland and the gateway to royalist north Wales, had road connexions with north-western and midland counties, and was close to the western route to Scotland. During the early months of the Civil War, when people flocked into the city as a refuge from lawlessness in rural Cheshire, the king's adherents strengthened its defences. Commissioners of array brought in men for the garrison, and the corporation raised 300 'volunteers'. Armed watchmen guarded the gates continuously (paid for by a monthly assessment on all inhabitants), muskets were stored in the Pentice, and the trained bands and 'volunteers' were mustered. In December 1642 the Assembly ordered a further assessment for arms, ammunition, ordnance, and additional fortifications.[6]

The city's involvement in the Civil War fell into four phases: January 1643 to March 1644, March to November 1644, November 1644 to September 1645, and September 1645 to February 1646.[7]

The first phase began with the arrival of the corpor-

ation's old opponent Sir William Brereton as parliamentary commander in Cheshire, headquartered at Nantwich.[8] To meet the threat the king appointed Sir Nicholas Byron as military governor of Chester, and the corporation agreed to continue the assessment for soldiers' pay and to levy £500 for more elaborate defences.[9] The work, supervised by Colonel Robert Ellis, a soldier with experience of Continental warfare, was completed by the summer. Earthen mounds were raised behind the walls to strengthen them, and new drawbridges were installed at the Northgate, Eastgate, and Bridgegate. Extensive outworks were made in the form of an earthen rampart with a ditch, dug in straight lengths with salients and flanks, mounts for cannon, pitfalls, and heavy gates. The line of the outworks, 3 km. long, ran from midway between the Water Tower and the Northgate in a north-westerly direction, then eastwards across Upper Northgate Street and Flooker's brook to Flookersbrook Hall, then south to Cockpit hill, east to Boughton, and thence to the Dee.[10]

During early 1643, although trade was dislocated, there was little military activity, and the Assembly met regularly for routine business.[11] In June all able-bodied

1 Ibid. ii, p. 545; Morrill, *Ches. 1630–60*, 62; *J.C.A.S.* lxviii. 112–13.

2 *Letter Books of Brereton*, ii, App. X (iii); *Tracts relating to Civil War in Ches. 1641–59* (Chetham Soc. N.S. lxv), 47–8; Morris, *Siege of Chester*, 23–4, 215; J. L. Malcolm, *Caesar's Due: Loyalty and King Charles, 1642–6*, 84; Morrill, *Ches. 1630–60*, 59 n.; Fletcher, *Outbreak of Eng. Civil War*, 394; *J.C.A.S.* xxviii. 188.

3 Edward [Hyde], Earl of Clarendon, *Hist. of Rebellion and Civil Wars in Eng.* ed. W. D. Macray, ii. 469–70; Morrill, *Ches. 1630–60*, 129.

4 *Cal. Chester City Cl. Mins. 1603–42*, 211.

5 Ibid. 212; *Tracts relating to Civil War*, 59–75; Morris, *Siege of Chester*, 25–31, 217; Fletcher, *Outbreak of Eng. Civil War*, 331,

333; *J.C.A.S.* xxviii. 188–9; *Letter Books of Brereton*, ii, pp. 592–3; *Crisis and Order*, ed. Clark and Slack, 208–10.

6 Fletcher, *Outbreak of Eng. Civil War*, 402; C.C.A.L.S., ZAB 2, ff. 59–60; Morris, *Siege of Chester*, 33–4; Morrill, *Ches. 1630–60*, 60–4, 75, 128–9, 134. This section also draws on B.L. Harl. MS. 2155, ff. 108–26, printed in Morris, *Siege of Chester*, 215–36.

7 S. Ward, *Excavations at Chester: Civil War Siegeworks, 1642–6*, 2.

8 R. N. Dore, 'Early Life of Sir William Brereton', *T.L.C.A.S.* lxiii. 4–5, 18–20, 23–4; idem, *Civil Wars in Ches.* 25–8.

9 C.C.A.L.S., ZAB 2, f. 61; Morrill, *Ches. 1630–60*, 135.

10 Ward, *Civil War Siegeworks*, 5–6, 11; Morris, *Siege of Chester*, 35.

11 C.C.A.L.S., ZAB 2, ff. 58v.–63v.; Johnson, 'Aspects', 99.

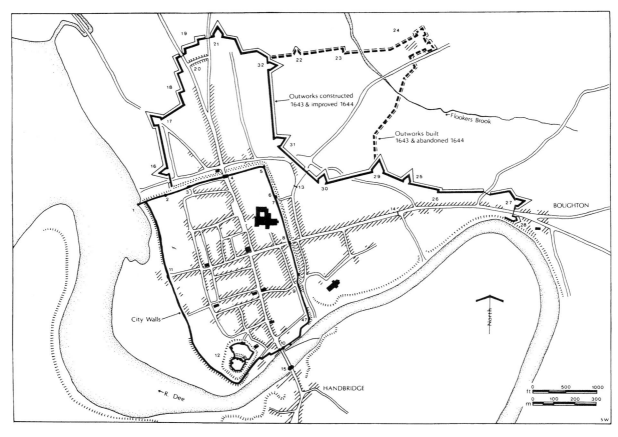

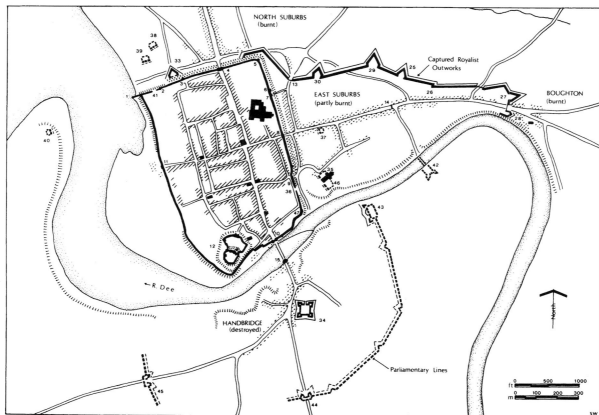

men between 16 and 60 not already in the trained bands were enlisted for Francis Gamull's town guard. Soon afterwards Brereton's troops launched a probing attack against the new defences but were driven off and for three months thereafter were occupied elsewhere. During the lull the city's defenders demolished buildings at Boughton which could provide shelter for attackers. The corporation meanwhile took charge of *c.* £928 of the city's charitable endowments,[1] raised three troops of horse, stockpiled foodstuffs, and issued orders in the event of an alarm.[2] In November Brereton's forces moved into north Wales to cut the city's supply lines, while Chester was reinforced from Oxford and Ireland. The city rejected a summons to surrender, and the royalist army drove Brereton's troops from north Wales and weakened his position in Cheshire, although it was defeated in January 1644 while trying to capture Nantwich.[3]

The Irish soldiers stationed in Chester, ill-supplied with clothing and food, were a burden on the city, and there was pilfering and disorder.[4] Other sources of dissent included rivalries between the royalist officers in the city and the county commissioners of array, and between the military commanders and the mayor. The deputy governor's decision in November to demolish the whole of Handbridge, later extended to all buildings outside the Northgate, was much resented.[5]

The second phase of the war began when the governor, Sir Nicholas Byron, was captured in March 1644. The king recommended in his place the colonel of the town guard, Francis Gamull, but he was highly unpopular with the citizens and opposed by other royalist leaders, and Byron was replaced by his nephew John, Lord Byron.[6] Prince Rupert's visit of two days from 11 March heralded a strengthening of the outworks. The salient reaching to Flookersbrook Hall was cut off, the hall itself and other buildings being demolished; new works with mounts for cannon were built outside the north-eastern corner of the city and nearer the walls; ramparts were raised and ditches deepened; and there was more demolition in the suburbs.[7]

The governor's headquarters in the castle lay outside the city's jurisdiction, and from there he kept civic office-holders under surveillance. During the mayoralty of Randle Holme II, a strong royalist, the Assembly apparently did not meet between December 1643 and April 1644, and when it did, attendance had to be enforced. Some normal business was transacted, but the non-payment of rent and avoidance of market regulations suggest that the city's administration was disrupted.[8] A greater problem was the overcrowding caused by soldiers and their followers, royalist sympathizers, and refugees, who swelled the population to perhaps 7,600 by Easter 1644, increasing the pressures on supplies and the dangers of disorder and fire.[9]

The burdens on the city were increased in July, when, after the heavy royalist defeat at Marston Moor, Rupert returned to Chester, lodging in the bishop's palace and endeavouring to impress foot soldiers and collect funds. There was disaffection

1 C.C.A.L.S., ZAB 2, ff. 63–4; ZML 2/288; Morris, *Siege of Chester*, 41; Johnson, 'Aspects', 92, 99.

2 C.C.A.L.S., ZAB 2, f. 64; ZML 2/292, 294, 295A, 295B, 296; Morris, *Siege of Chester*, 42–5.

3 Morris, *Siege of Chester*, 45–9, 55–7; Kennett, *Loyal Chester*, 23.

4 C.C.A.L.S., ZAB 2, f. 64v.; ZML 2/290; J. Lowe, 'Campaigns of Irish Royalist Army in Ches. Nov. 1643 to Jan. 1644', *T.H.S.L.C.* cxi. 59; M. H. Ridgway, 'Chester Goldsmiths from Early Times to 1726', *J.C.A.S.* liii. 83.

5 C.C.A.L.S., ZML 2/289, 293; Morris, *Siege of Chester*, 47–8; Morrill, *Ches. 1630–60*, 130 sqq.; Malcolm, *Caesar's Due*, 118; Johnson, 'Aspects', 312.

6 *Crisis and Order*, ed. Clark and Slack, 211–12; Kennett, *Loyal Chester*, 20.

7 Ward, *Civil War Siegeworks*, 11; C.C.A.L.S., ZAB 2, f. 67v.; ZAF 26/6; Morris, *Siege of Chester*, 58–9.

8 C.C.A.L.S., ZAB 2, ff. 63v.–69.

9 S. Porter, *Destruction in Eng. Civil Wars*, 52; above, this chapter: Demography.

FIG. 6 (OPPOSITE) *Civil War defences and siege works*

Above: medieval defences and conjectural line of royalist defences, 1643–4.

Below: conjectural lines of royalist defences and parliamentarian siege works, 1645–6. Modern names, where different from the 17th-century ones, are given in parentheses.

Medieval defences: 1 New Tower (Water Tower); 2 Goblin Tower (Pemberton's Parlour); 3 raised platform (Morgan's Mount); 4 Northgate; 5 Phoenix Tower (King Charles's Tower); 6 Saddlers' Tower; 7 Kaleyards Gate; 8 Eastgate; 9 Newgate; 10 Bridgegate; 11 Watergate; 12 castle; 13 Cowlane Gate; 14 the Bars; 15 Further Bridgegate.

Earlier royalist outworks: 16 Morgan's Mount, first phase; 17 mount; 18 flank; 19 flank; 20 Rock Lane; 21 Dr. Walley's Mount; 22 mount; 23 flank; 24 Flookersbrook Hall; 25 Horn Lane Mount; 26 flank; 27 mount; 28 mount.

Later royalist outworks: 29 Cockpit Mount; 30 Justing Croft Mount; 31 Phoenix Tower Mount; 32 Reeds Mount; 33 Morgan's Mount, second phase; 34 Handbridge fort.

Parliamentarian siege works and breaches: 35 battery in St. John's churchyard; 36 breach near the Newgate; 37 battery in Foregate Street; 38 first northern battery; 39 second northern battery; 40 battery on Brewer's Hall hill; 41 breach near Goblin Tower; 42 bridge of boats and lower mount; 43 higher mount; 44 Eccleston Lane; 45 Hough Green; 46 battery in the bowling green; 47 Barnaby's Tower.

among the citizens, not least about the Irish soldiers,[1] and resistance to the garrison's financial demands, especially in September when the corporation decided to raise £600 over six weeks.[2] The limits to support for the royal cause were marked in the mayoral election of 1644. The first nominees of the aldermen J.P.s were Sir Francis Gamull (newly made a baronet) and Sir Thomas Smith, the city's M.P.s who by then were disabled from sitting. Eventually, however, Charles Walley was chosen with strong support from the freemen; a former mayor, he was a reluctant candidate who held no military or political post and was likely to put local interests first.[3]

Chester was too well defended for Brereton to take it by either assault or blockade. Nevertheless, during the third phase of the war the parliamentarians slowly established a siege in the face of occasional royalist attempts at relief. In late October 1644 an attack on the city was driven off, but by January 1645, with Brereton's garrisons as near as Christleton and after an unsuccessful sortie by the governor,[4] the position was serious. The Assembly agreed to a further assessment of £20 a week for eight weeks and the surrender of another £100 worth of plate for conversion into coin.[5]

Meanwhile the appearance of Prince Maurice's troops obliged Brereton to raise the close siege on 19 February. The prince concluded that the outer defences were still too long to hold and decided to abandon them round the northern suburbs and demolish buildings there; the new outworks began near the north-eastern corner of the city and extended to Boughton and the river, and a new bastion for a heavy cannon was erected on the north wall. Maurice, who was joined for a time by Prince Rupert, departed in mid March, taking some of Chester's most seasoned defenders with him.[6] The parliamentarians, briefly reinforced by Scottish troops, quickly resumed the siege. In April they were less than a mile from the outworks on the Cheshire side and had drawn forces into north Wales after a diversionary attack on Handbridge. They had fortified camps but were insufficiently strong to hold off a relieving army or enforce a total blockade: the besieged grazed their cattle in Hoole, and a ship landed stores of powder and match. For Brereton the capture of Chester was the key to the parliamentarian hold on north Wales and much of north-western England, and he repeatedly pressed for reinforcements and a tighter blockade on the river.[7] For the royalists Chester was by now the only major garrison in the region.

As the siege was tightened conditions became more difficult. The weekly assessment of £20 was renewed in April 1645 for a further two months, there were signs of popular antagonism towards Sir Francis Gamull and Welsh soldiers, and fresh provisions were increasingly scarce and expensive.[8] Before the internal situation could deteriorate Brereton was ordered to abandon his advanced positions and withdraw his main forces beyond the Mersey because of the reported approach of a royalist army.[9] In mid June the parliamentary county committee took control of the war in Cheshire and scaled back military operations. With the siege less close, the city's defenders were able to send out foraging parties, clean the streets, and build a new fort at Handbridge to protect the approaches to the Dee Bridge.[10]

The final phase of the siege began on 20 September 1645 when parliamentarian troops under Colonel Michael Jones and Major James Lothian overran the eastern outworks and captured the eastern suburbs up to the Eastgate, a loss which the governor later blamed on the slackness of Mayor Walley and Gamull. The mayor's house in Foregate Street was captured (and with it the civic sword and mace) and became Brereton's headquarters. The defenders were now confined within the walls.[11] Immediately the besiegers began to use St. John's church tower as an observation post and stationed a battery in its churchyard, from which a breach in the walls was made near the Newgate on 22 September. The attackers, however, were repulsed,[12] and royal forces arrived the next day under Charles I himself, who stayed at Gamull's house. On 24 September the king's army engaged the parliamentarians on Rowton moor, where, after initial success, it was defeated with heavy losses; the king left the city the next day, giving permission for surrender if there was no relief within 10 days.[13] The first summons to surrender on 26 September, however, was rejected,

1 *Cal. S.P. Dom.* 1644, 392, 394; Morris, *Siege of Chester*, 63–4; Morrill, *Ches. 1630–60*, 134; Malcolm, *Caesar's Due*, 198–9.

2 C.C.A.L.S., ZAB 2, f. 68; *Cal. S.P. Dom.* 1644–5, 67–8, 95; Morris, *Siege of Chester*, 65–6; Dore, *Civil Wars in Ches.* 43; Morrill, *Ches. 1630–60*, 135–6.

3 *Crisis and Order*, ed. Clark and Slack, 212–13; *Letter Books of Brereton*, ii, pp. 82, 590; Keeler, *Long Parl.* 183, 342.

4 *Letter Books of Brereton*, i, pp. 9–10; Morris, *Siege of Chester*, 68–73; Dore, *Civil Wars in Ches.* 43 sqq.; Kennett, *Loyal Chester*, 23–4.

5 C.C.A.L.S., ZAB 2, ff. 69v.–70; *J.C.A.S.* liii. 83.

6 Ward, *Civil War Siegeworks*, 4, 11; *Letter Books of Brereton*, i, nos. 7, 39, 141; ii, p. 86; Morris, *Siege of Chester*, 74–5, 78–9; Dore, *Civil Wars in Ches.* 47.

7 *Letter Books of Brereton*, i, nos. 89, 130, 158, 177, 181, 238, 273, 289, 345, 375, 379, 408, 499.

8 Ibid. nos. 119, 125, 193–5, 315; C.C.A.L.S., ZAB 2, ff. 70v.–72; Morris, *Siege of Chester*, 76–85.

9 *Letter Books of Brereton*, i, nos. 238, 315, 545–6, 570–1, 601; Dore, *Civil Wars in Ches.* 49.

10 Ward, *Civil War Siegeworks*, 4; C.C.A.L.S., ZAB 2, f. 72; Morris, *Siege of Chester*, 96–8, 102–5; Dore, *Civil Wars in Ches.* 48–9.

11 Ward, *Civil War Siegeworks*, 4, 11; *Letter Books of Brereton*, ii, pp. 83 n., 86 n., 190, and no. 809; Morris, *Siege of Chester*, 107–9.

12 Ward, *Civil War Siegeworks*, 5, 12; *Memorials of Civil War in Ches.* (R.S.L.C. xix), 181–2; Morris, *Siege of Chester*, 109–10.

13 *Tracts relating to Civil War*, 134–45; Morris, *Siege of Chester*, 110–12, 121; Dore, *Civil Wars in Ches.* 50–2; *J.C.A.S.* xxviii. 189–90.

the garrison was reinforced, and the damaged walls were repaired.[1]

The parliamentarians responded by occupying the northern suburbs, and by supplementing their battery at St. John's with newly acquired siege guns placed in Foregate Street and opposite the battery on the north wall, where the defenders' large cannon was soon destroyed and a breach made; breastworks were built near the gates for musketeers, and the besiegers used the captured outworks for their own protection. The guns at St. John's were turned on the Dee Mills, the Bridgegate waterworks, and the south-east corner of the walls. On the Welsh side the royalists still held the fort at Handbridge, from where they assailed parliamentarian troops in the villages beyond. In response the parliamentarians built a battery for a large artillery piece on Brewer's Hall hill, and linked their positions on either side of the river with a bridge of boats from Dee Lane to the Earl's Eye, protected by gun emplacements at the south end.[2] After a fruitless second summons to surrender on 8 October the besiegers mounted another heavy bombardment and attempted to storm the city; the defences were breached in several places but the onslaught was beaten off after heavy fighting.[3]

By then the corporation's business was almost entirely confined to raising money for the garrison, amid growing reluctance to pay.[4] Opposition to the royalist cause, a source of anxiety to the governor and already evident in the suspension of seven sheriff-peers and five councilmen in the spring, found further expression in the mayoral election. The royalist Sir Francis Gamull, although first choice of the aldermen J.P.s, received no votes from the freemen, and eventually a reluctant Alderman Walley was persuaded to serve again.[5]

There were no further attempts to storm the city after October 1645. Instead, the besiegers relied on a mixture of persuasion and intimidation: the forced removal of the remaining inhabitants of the suburbs into the city to put further pressure on accommodation and provisions; the use of St. John's tower by snipers, one of whom killed Sheriff Randle Richardson; and intermittent bombardments, which damaged the mills and the waterworks, threatening supplies of bread and drinking water. Papers offering inducements to sur-

render were shot into the city. The parliamentarians, again under Brereton's command from late October, were hampered by shortages of food and pay and fears of a relieving army. For their part Chester's defenders maintained an obstinate resistance: they made several sorties, shot burning arrows to set fire to any suburban buildings which remained to shelter the enemy, and frequently circumvented the blockade to bring in small stocks of food.[6] Hopes of improvement in royalist fortunes were dashed by the parliamentarian victory at Denbigh and the capture of Beeston castle, and on 18 November the city received a further summons to surrender. It was intended to sow dissension between the military and the citizens with an assurance that honourable terms would be granted, but the mayor and governor jointly rejected it.[7]

Brereton returned to intimidation during the following weeks, bombarding the city as heavily and frequently as his limited supply of ammunition allowed. His aim, however, was to force Chester's capitulation, not to destroy it, and to that end he endeavoured to tighten the already close siege. The royalists countered with a sortie across the Dee Bridge and by trying to float fire boats loaded with powder against the bridge of boats, but neither venture succeeded. Even when in December ice floes temporarily broke the bridge of boats and a large detachment of the besiegers was drawn off to counter a royalist force at Whitchurch (Salop.), the defenders were unable to take advantage, apart from bringing in a small quantity of wheat and oatmeal.[8] During the later part of December and early January 1646 the blockade in the Dee was tightened further.[9]

Morale in Chester was undermined by the bombardment, the continuing absence of a relief force, and the shortage of food and fuel, made worse by severely cold weather.[10] Civic government was disrupted and disaffection spread among civilians and soldiers alike, Governor Byron and his entourage finding themselves increasingly unable to rely on the support of the mayor and influential citizens.[11] Brereton, aware of the divisions, appealed to the townspeople on 3 January to force a surrender, but a formal summons four days later was without result. The governor tried to temporize, and even took a census of householders and food stocks to gauge the prospects of continuing resistance.

1 Morris, *Siege of Chester*, 127–9; Dore, *Civil Wars in Ches.* 52–3.

2 Ward, *Civil War Siegeworks*, 12–13, 32 sqq.; *Letter Books of Brereton*, ii, no. 840 and p. 86 n.

3 Ward, *Civil War Siegeworks*, 5; *Letter Books of Brereton*, ii, nos. 671–2, 682; Morris, *Siege of Chester*, 127–31.

4 C.C.A.L.S., ZAB 2, ff. 72–3; ZAF 27/15–16; ZML 2/295A, 295B; *Letter Books of Brereton*, ii, no. 884; Morris, *Siege of Chester*, 139.

5 Johnson, 'Aspects', 316–18; idem, 'Politics in Chester', 213–14.

6 *Letter Books of Brereton*, ii, nos. 684, 739, 742, 752, 766, 780–1, 790, 830–1; *Memorials of Civil War in Ches.* 185–6;

Morris, *Siege of Chester*, 144–6.

7 *Letter Books of Brereton*, ii, nos. 873, 878–9, 882; Morris, *Siege of Chester*, 141–3.

8 *Letter Books of Brereton*, ii, nos. 895, 928, 936–7, 975, 1009–10, 1066–7, 1107, 1112, 1116–17, 1133, 1146, 1153–4, and p. 591; *Memorials of Civil War in Ches.* 190–1; Morris, *Siege of Chester*, 143, 150, 152–7; Porter, *Destruction*, 50–1, 61.

9 *Letter Books of Brereton*, ii, nos. 1139, 1143–4, 1236–9, 1247–9.

10 Ibid. nos. 928, 978, 1018, 1071, 1155, and pp. 5–6; C.C.A.L.S., ZAB 2, ff. 73–4; Morris, *Siege of Chester*, 157–63, 168 sqq.

11 *Letter Books of Brereton*, ii, pp. 584–92.

On 12 January the mayor joined him in rejecting another call to surrender, but within three days had persuaded him to negotiate.[1] The fighting ceased, and on 20 January tortuous negotiations began, each side initially offering terms which the other was likely to reject. The articles of surrender, agreed on 31 January and 1 February, included the following terms: the officers and a few soldiers were allowed to march out with arms and limited amounts of money; other soldiers were to leave their arms and horses behind; the governor and others were allowed to march to Conwy without hindrance; Welsh soldiers were permitted to go home, but those of Irish parentage were to be prisoners; the persons and goods of citizens were to be protected; no churches were to be damaged; imprisoned parliamentarians were to be released; and the city and castle were to be delivered to Brereton.[2] Chester surrendered for several reasons: the general collapse of the royal cause; the fact that its 1,600 defending soldiers were heavily outnumbered by Brereton's force; the effects of the blockade and the threat of starvation; the risk of a storming assault; and the absence of any prospect of relief. On 3 February Byron and those in the garrison who had chosen to stay with him marched out, and Brereton's forces marched in.[3]

Within a few days of the surrender Brereton reported that a garrison of 1,500 foot and 200 horse would be required to hold the city.[4] Colonel Michael Jones was appointed governor, and Alderman William Edwards took command of the town guard; arms, armour, and ordnance were collected in the castle.[5] The Assembly was suspended, the main royalist aldermen were removed or ceased to act, and the city was controlled jointly by the military and the remaining parliamentarian aldermen until the corporation could be formally reconstituted.[6] Between the citizens and the garrison there was ill feeling about parliamentary taxes, especially the excise, and complaints of thefts and indiscipline by soldiers.[7] Growing poverty resulted from the interruption of markets and overseas trade, the effects of the siege, the costs of defence, and military operations in the hinterland;[8] the city's funds were exhausted, its plate converted to coin, its charitable funds used largely for public purposes. The siege

had caused widespread destruction, and it was said that a quarter of the city had been burnt.[9]

By the end of the siege there were *c.* 6,000 civilians crowded into the walled city. Filth accumulated in the streets, water supplies were restricted, and there was a serious shortage of food.[10] The passage of hundreds of soldiers bound for Ireland imposed a further strain,[11] and may have brought the plague which broke out in June 1647 and killed over 2,000.[12]

CITY GOVERNMENT, 1646–60

The purge of royalists from the corporation was made official in October 1646. No fewer than 14 of the 24 aldermen were displaced, together with four sheriff-peers and three councilmen.[13] Those dismissed became liable to sequestration and fines: Recorder Brerewood was fined £387, Thomas Thropp £177, Richard Broster £170; Sir Thomas Smith compounded at £3,350 and Sir Francis Gamull at £940. Governor Jones reported that Mayor Charles Walley had sent intelligence to the besiegers and helped to bring about the surrender; although Walley was fined £537 he soon made his peace with the victors and entered their service.[14] Among the aldermen who retained their places were three determined parliamentarians, William Edwards, Richard Leicester, and Thomas Aldersey; four others who took part in civic affairs during the siege, including Randle Holme I, seem to have been fined but not disqualified.[15] Edwards was appointed mayor and the Assembly immediately filled its vacancies. One of the two new sheriffs, Robert Sproston, had been suspended from the Assembly in 1645; two new counsel were named, one of whom succeeded John Ratcliffe (son of the puritan alderman prominent in the 1620s and 1630s), who became recorder. Eleven other aldermen were elected: nine were ex-sheriffs, seven of whom had been suspended from the governing body by the royalists in 1645.[16]

The plague epidemic of 1647–8 seriously delayed the return to normality in city government. Parliament suspended the mayoral election in 1647, appointing Robert Wright as mayor and naming the two sheriffs, arrangements confirmed in March 1648 when meetings of the Assembly resumed.[17] At sessions in

---

1 *Letter Books of Brereton*, ii, nos. 1167, 1177, 1196–8, 1229–30, 1251; Morris, *Siege of Chester*, 237–42.

2 *Letter Books of Brereton*, ii, no. 1260.

3 Ibid. nos. 1063, 1066–7, 1088, and pp. 582, 584–5, 591–2; Morris, *Siege of Chester*, 163.

4 Hist. MSS. Com. 29, *13th Rep. I, Portland*, i, p. 352.

5 Morris, *Siege of Chester*, 197; *Memorials of Civil War in Ches.* 201.   6 Johnson, 'Aspects', 318–19.

7 J. S. Morrill, 'Mutiny and Discontent in Eng. Provincial Armies, 1645–7', *Rebellion, Popular Protest, and Social Order*, ed. Slack, 193–6.

8 Hist. MSS. Com. 29, *13th Rep. I, Portland*, i, p. 352.

9 Ibid. p. 465; B.L. Harl. MS. 1944, ff. 98–9; Johnson, 'Aspects', 99, 211.

10 Above, this chapter: Demography; B.L. Harl. MS. 2135, f. 98

sqq., reworked in Morris, *Siege of Chester*, 237–43.

11 *Cal. S.P. Dom.* Addenda 1625–49, 698–9, 711; 1645–7, 532, 534, 536.

12 Above, this chapter: Demography; Morris, *Siege of Chester*, 209–10; Shrewsbury, *Hist. Bubonic Plague*, 422–3, 425; *C.J.* v. 280; *L.J.* ix. 371; C.C.A.L.S., ZAB 2, f. 84v.

13 *Acts and Ordinances of Interregnum*, ed. C. H. Firth and R. S. Rait, i. 876–9.

14 Morris, *Siege of Chester*, 8–12, 205–7; Keeler, *Long Parl.* 182–3, 341–2; *Letter Books of Brereton*, ii, pp. 82, 584.

15 Johnson, 'Aspects', 320–1; idem, 'Politics in Chester', 215–16; *J.C.A.S.* n.s. iv. 123–5; Morris, *Siege of Chester*, 12–13.

16 C.C.A.L.S., ZAB 2, ff. 78v.–81, 97; *Crisis and Order*, ed. Clark and Slack, 216–17.

17 *L.J.* ix. 490; *C.J.* v. 337, 488; C.C.A.L.S., ZAB 2, f. 82.

March and May the Assembly appointed a new clerk of the Pentice and elected four more aldermen and seven councillors to fill vacancies; three of the new aldermen were ex-sheriffs, the other a councilman suspended in 1645.[1] The reconstituted aldermanic bench included two of Brereton's wartime associates, William Edwards and Richard Bradshaw, who, along with Calvin Bruen, Edward Bradshaw, Robert Wright, Peter Leigh, and John Ratcliffe, represented a strong puritan tradition.[2] Most of the new aldermen, however, were less committed and indeed had been members of the Assembly for most of the time that the city was under royalist control.[3] Chester's governing body therefore remained tainted with royalist sympathies and included men who were apparently content to wait upon events. Parliament's abolition of the sheriff-peers as a separate group, which would have increased the influence of the aldermen, may have been ineffective in practice, as there were still sheriff-peers on the council in 1662.[4]

There were no further purges of the corporation after 1646, but it proved difficult to enforce attendance and the Assembly did not meet at all between January and July 1649.[5] Although there were many Commonwealth supporters among the city's rulers, official reluctance to enforce the new oaths and a tardy response to the Act of 1650 requiring an Engagement of fidelity to the Commonwealth indicate some lack of commitment to the new regime. In March 1650 it was reported to the Council of State that only two of the aldermen had subscribed to the Engagement, which had been attacked by Presbyterian preachers in the city as contrary to the Covenant.[6] Two months later the Council ordered the dismissal of Mayor William Crompton, a non-subscriber, but the instruction was ignored.[7] In October it was more forceful, directing the corporation to impose the oaths and the Engagement on office-holders and deploying an armed detachment from the garrison during the mayoral election. Its presence in the streets secured the displacement of the candidate who had won the contest under the normal procedures.[8] In 1651 the Council of State demanded the names of those still refusing the Engagement and

attempted unsuccessfully to fill an aldermanic vacancy with its own nominee;[9] it also forced the removal of the clerk of the Pentice, a non-Engager,[10] and of Recorder Ratcliffe, though the latter was made a counsel for the city in 1652 and was reappointed as recorder in 1657.[11] Government pressure resumed in 1653, when the mayor was ordered to take the city's charter for inspection in London by the committee for corporations, though it was eventually confirmed unchanged.[12]

The normal routine of civic administration returned after the siege and plague. In 1648 the corporation set its finances in order.[13] The recorder was involved in safeguarding the income from prisage and ensuring that the city, not the governor, received the profits from the sequestrated Dee Mills.[14] In 1649 a full audit was ordered and the rental was revised, and by 1655–6 receipts totalled £211 and expenditure only £197. The Assembly nevertheless renewed enquiries about rent arrears and repeated the attempt to draw up a full rental.[15]

The pre-war dispute between the officers of the mayor and sheriffs recurred from 1647, and finally in 1657 the Assembly abolished the right of the serjeants-at-mace to act as attorneys; in future the mayor, recorder, and sheriffs were to choose other citizens to act in that capacity.[16] Another old controversy was settled more readily in 1649, when the vice-chamberlain of the palatinate offered to issue writs circumspectly in order to avoid clashes of jurisdiction with the city.[17]

During the Protectorate Chester came under the authority of Major-General Charles Worsley, whose commissioners for the city (mostly government supporters on the bench) were careful not to challenge the city's rights. The Assembly was even in the process of electing Worsley to an aldermanship at the time of his death in 1656.[18] From the early 1650s opportunities to influence the composition of the Assembly were in any case limited by the rarity of aldermanic vacancies.[19] After Oliver Cromwell's death in 1658, however, there was more open disaffection in Chester. The corporation's encouragement of Booth's rising in August 1659 had severe but in the event only temporary consequences. The government planned to purge the Assem-

1 C.C.A.L.S., ZAB 2, ff. 82–3.
2 *Letter Books of Brereton*, ii, p. 15 and nos. 1147–8; Dore, *Civil Wars in Ches.* 68, 86; *J.C.A.S.* lxviii. 108–9; for Bradshaw: *Letter Books of Brereton*, ii, pp. 15, 310, and nos. 940, 959; *D.N.B.*
3 *Crisis and Order*, ed. Clark and Slack, 217–18.
4 *Acts and Ordinances*, i. 877; below, this chapter: The Restoration.
5 C.C.A.L.S., ZAB 2, ff. 84v., 86, 89v.; *Crisis and Order*, ed. Clark and Slack, 220.
6 *Acts and Ordinances*, ii. 2, 241–2, 325–9, 348; *Cal. S.P. Dom.* 1650, 20–1; *Crisis and Order*, ed. Clark and Slack, 220–1.
7 *Cal. S.P. Dom.* 1650, 137.
8 Ibid. 385; Morrill, *Ches. 1630–60*, 262; *Crisis and Order*, ed. Clark and Slack, 222.
9 *Cal. S.P. Dom.* 1651, 31, 316, 325, 329; C.C.A.L.S., ZAB 2, f. 96v.; Johnson, 'Politics of Chester', 222–3.

10 C.C.A.L.S., ZAB 2, ff. 93, 97; ZAF 31/6, 8.
11 Ibid. ZAB 2, ff. 97, 99, 106v., 113; ZAF 32/3; ZAF 36/6; *Cal. S.P. Dom.* 1651, 384, 391, 420.
12 C.C.A.L.S., ZML 3/347; B. L. K. Henderson, 'Commonwealth Charters', *Trans. R.H.S.* 3rd ser. vi. 156.
13 C.C.A.L.S., ZAB 2, ff. 84v., 86v., 87v.–88, 90, 92; ZAF 29/6–7.
14 Ibid. ZML 2/308–11, 313–16.
15 Ibid. ZAB 2, ff. 92v., 107, 111v.; ZAF 31/5; Johnson, 'Aspects', 92.
16 C.C.A.L.S., ZAB 2, ff. 86v.–87, 104, 115v., 118; ZAF 33/20–1; ZML 2/303; Johnson, 'Aspects', 166.
17 Johnson, 'Aspects', 178.
18 *Crisis and Order*, ed. Clark and Slack, 224; C.C.A.L.S., ZAF 35/7.
19 *Crisis and Order*, ed. Clark and Slack, 224–5, mistakenly counting 10 vacancies.

bly and give the governor special powers, and indeed discharged the mayor and sheriffs, suspended the charter, and annulled the city's independent status as a county. Those measures were, however, revoked in February 1660, and in March elections were held and a new mayor and sheriffs chosen. The Assembly had apparently not met since September 1659, but when it was convened at the end of March it was functioning normally.[1]

ECONOMY AND SOCIETY, 1646–60

War and plague left the city with social and economic difficulties from which recovery was very slow.[2] Unsettled times encouraged some to seek higher wages or practise occupations for which they were unqualified. In response the magistrates tried, apparently unsuccessfully, to regulate wages,[3] and enforced guild restrictions. Wartime disorder had weakened the city companies, which met irregularly, lost some of their meeting places (notably the Phoenix Tower), and suffered from non-payment of dues, avoidance of rules, and interlopers.[4] As early as December 1646 the corporation attempted to enforce regular enrolment of apprenticeship indentures.[5] In 1648 c. 250 freemen complained about encroachments by strangers on the privileges of freedom, and grievances were expressed then and in 1650 about the employment of outsiders by company widows.[6]

National legislation in 1647 and 1654 exempted from apprenticeship requirements those who had served the parliamentary cause,[7] but the Chester guilds still tried to defend restrictions, and some inter-guild disputes continued, as between the Saddlers and Spurriers and the Cutlers over the trade in spurs,[8] between the Joiners and the Carpenters about timber supplies, and between the Mercers and the Linen-drapers over silk wares.[9] The Mercers complained that the Innholders competed unlawfully in the distributive trades, and textile craftsmen were aggrieved by the Drapers' attempts to monopolize the sale of cloth.[10] After a lengthy agitation, wheelwrights were admitted to the Joiners, Turners, and Carvers' company in 1657, whereupon they began to interfere with the privileges of the other occupations and were excluded from the guild aldermanship and custody of the records.[11]

From 1647 to 1660 admissions to the freedom

approached an annual average of 40,[12] with 67 in 1647–8 in the immediate aftermath of the siege and plague. The leather crafts remained the largest category, and the biggest individual occupations included shoemakers, glovers, tanners, ironmongers, and tailors. During the 1650s there was a marked increase in the number of feltmakers, and in 1654 the Feltmakers' company claimed that 500 people were dependent on their work.[13] Very occasionally the corporation waived the regulations in order to attract those with particular skills: in 1653 strangers were allowed to work in the building industry on payment of 1*d.* weekly to the guild concerned, and in 1655 Thomas Hancock, a gunsmith, was permitted to work for the garrison.[14]

Adverse economic conditions continued to hamper the city's markets. During the later 1640s and in 1657 the corporation had difficulty in controlling private wholesale trading by strangers.[15] The need to safeguard food supplies was paramount, especially in view of additional demand from the garrison and troops bound for Ireland. On those grounds the corporation successfully obstructed parliamentary orders to demolish the Dee Mills and the causeway.[16] Bad harvests in 1648–9 prompted restrictions on buying corn by maltsters and brewers.[17] The epidemic of 1650, which caused cancellation of the Michaelmas fair, also led the authorities to impose constraints on corn dealers, but by then the Bakers' company had secured stricter controls on country bakers.[18]

The city's overseas trade recovered only very slowly from the war. The Continental trade in cereal exports and wine imports was beginning to improve by 1648–9, but the Irish trade remained at a low ebb: small quantities of cloth and larger cargoes of wool were exported; hides, tallow, and herring were imported, but the livestock trade had yet to revive. The Irish trade was increasingly conducted by Irish merchants from the smaller ports of the Dee estuary, and its effects on the city's fortunes therefore remained limited.[19]

Poor relief and charity collapsed during the years 1642–8: regular collection of the poor rate seems to have ceased early in the war, the house of correction outside the Northgate was deliberately demolished by the city's defenders, and a large proportion of the charitable benefactions was appropriated for the city's funds in 1642–3.[20] Only three city-wide charities

1 *Crisis and Order*, ed. Clark and Slack, 226–8; *C.J.* vii. 854; C.C.A.L.S., ZAB 2, ff. 125v.–126v.; ZAF 37C/2–4; below, this section (Military and Political Affairs, 1646–60).

2 Hist. MSS. Com. 29, *13th Rep. I, Portland*, i, pp. 352, 465–6; above, this chapter: Demography.

3 Woodward, *Men at Work*, 189; C.C.A.L.S., ZAB 2, f. 102v.

4 *J.C.A.S.* xxxix. 101.

5 C.C.A.L.S., ZAB 2, ff. 80, 84; ZAF 28/5; ZAF 29/15.

6 Ibid. ZAB 2, ff. 85–6, 93v.; ZAF 29/6, 18–19; ZAF 31/12.

7 *Acts and Ordinances*, i. 1055; ii. 1006–7.

8 C.C.A.L.S., ZAB 2, ff. 80v.–81; ZAF 28/12; Johnson, 'Aspects', 272–3; *Chester: 1900 Years of Hist.* ed. A. M. Kennett, 27.

9 C.C.A.L.S., ZAB 2, ff. 102v., 104–5; ZAF 33/22–4, 31.

10 Ibid. ZAB 2, f. 118v.; ZAF 36/29; ZAF 37A/32.

11 Johnson, 'Aspects', 267–8.

12 What follows is drawn from figures supplied by Miss S. Richardson from *Rolls of Freemen of Chester*, i; cf. Johnson, 'Aspects', 26–7.   13 C.C.A.L.S., ZAF 33/5, 16.

14 Ibid. ZAB 2, f. 102v.; ZAF 35/13–19.

15 Ibid. ZAB 2, ff. 89v.–90, 113v.–115v.; ZAF 27/18.

16 Ibid. ZML 2/307–9; *V.C.H. Ches.* v (2), Mills and Fisheries: Dee Corn Mills.

17 C.C.A.L.S., ZAB 2, ff. 88, 89v.–90; ZAF 30/7, 14.

18 Ibid. ZAB 2, ff. 94v.–95; ZAF 31/14.

19 *T.H.S.L.C.* cxxii. 39–40.

20 Johnson, 'Aspects', 92, 99, 211.

survived the war: those of Sir Thomas White, John Vernon, and Valentine Broughton.[1]

The numbers of poor increased after the siege, and in 1651 the Assembly instituted a regular monthly survey.[2] The outbreak of plague in 1654 prompted the corporation to rebuild the house of correction and 18 months later it appointed a new master with instructions to employ 60 people in making cloth.[3] In 1658 the corporation successfully petitioned Oliver Cromwell for control of the hospital of St. John at the Northgate and made plans for its reorganization.[4]

There were few signs of intellectual or artistic activity, for plays were officially proscribed and the musical traditions of the cathedral had lapsed. However, Randle Holme II sorted the corporation's records,[5] and in 1656 the engraver David King published his *Vale Royal of England*, a compilation of the writings of Cheshire antiquarians, including William Webb's material on the city.[6] Some local customs survived: the night bellman continued his rounds, on at least one occasion the mayor beat the bounds, and there was strong interest in reviving the Midsummer show.[7] Horse races were banned no later than 1654, however, and after festivities at Christmas were prohibited nationally the magistrates resolved to hold markets on Wednesdays and Saturdays irrespective of Christmas Day and other holy days.[8]

RELIGION, 1642–60

In 1642 Chester became a haven for royalist clergy; they included refugees from Ireland, one of whom, an unnamed bishop, ministered at St. Michael's in 1643–4. In 1643 John Ley's former curate William Ainsworth, who had turned royalist and taken refuge in Chester, was named as divinity lecturer at the cathedral and city preacher at St. Peter's.[9] In 1644 the governor sequestered Ley's prebend, dividing the proceeds among various clerics in the city, and the corporation gave his Friday lectureship at St. Peter's to William Seddon, a protégé of Bishop Bridgeman. John Glendal's preferments were also transferred to other clerics.[10] At first the diocesan administration continued to operate, proving wills, issuing marriage licences, and holding a ruridecanal visitation of Chester and Wirral

in 1643. The consistory court ceased to function, however, and the bishop and dean left the city in 1645. In 1646 two of the clergy, Thomas Bridge of St. Oswald's and Prebendary Edward Moreton, acted as royalist commissioners for the surrender, by the terms of which ministers were allowed to leave the city with their 'manuscripts, notes, and evidences'; among those taking advantage of the terms were the curate of St. Peter's and the vicar of St. John's.[11] Although some of the clergy remained in the city, none of those ministering there during the siege was allowed to continue in office; the 11 who were sequestered included Ainsworth of St. Peter's, Bridge of St. Oswald's, Richard Wilson of Holy Trinity, Richard Hunt of St. Mary's, Dean William Nicholls, and the surviving prebendaries and petty canons.[12]

The siege caused much damage to churches, notably St. John's and St. Mary's, and under parliamentarian control there was renewed destruction of stained glass, crosses, fonts, and other furnishings. Communion became irregular and Rogationtide ceremonies and other traditional observances ended.[13] After 1646 an attempt was made to improve clerical incomes. Capitular property was sequestered and the proceeds were redirected to the livings of the four main churches: £150 for St. Peter's, £120 for St. Oswald's, and £100 each for Holy Trinity and St. John's. Payments, however, soon fell into arrears and were never fully made up in the 1650s.[14]

After the city fell to the parliamentarians the familiar puritan preachers, John Ley, John Glendal, and Nathaniel Lancaster, resumed their ministrations at St. Peter's. Presbyterianism soon became dominant. There were new men first at St. John's, Holy Trinity, and St. Oswald's, and later at St. Mary's, but St. Bridget's, St. Martin's, and St. Olave's remained without ministers, and nobody was appointed to St. Michael's until 1650; by then the abolition of the cathedral chapter and the sale of the bishop's palace and furniture marked the collapse of the diocesan administration.[15] There was apparently no organized classis in the city, but the new clergy were all Presbyterians and signatories to the Cheshire Attestation of 1648, Ley and Lancaster being the most influential.

1 *Cal. Chester City Cl. Mins. 1603–42*, 214–19; C.C.A.L.S., ZAB 2, ff. 92, 101v.–102; ZAF 30/24; ZAF 31/10–11, 13; *V.C.H. Ches.* v (2), Charities for the Poor: Municipal.

2 C.C.A.L.S., ZAB 2, ff. 84v., 86–7, 89, 95v.; ZAF 30/4, 8; ZML 2/295A–B.

3 Ibid. ZAB 2, ff. 109, 110, 116; ZCHB 3, f. 169v.; ZML 3/376; *Cal. S.P. Dom. 1654*, 132, 168.

4 *Cal. S.P. Dom. 1656–7*, 264; *1657–8*, 226; *1659–60*, 427; *J.C.A.S.* xxviii. 191; *V.C.H. Ches.* iii. 182.

5 C.C.A.L.S., ZAB 2, ff. 105, 108v.; ZAF 34/42.

6 *Eng. County Histories*, ed. Currie and Lewis, 73–4.

7 C.C.A.L.S., ZAB 2, ff. 100–1, 119; ZAF 34/26; *V.C.H. Ches.* v (2), Plays, Sports, and Customs before 1700: City Watches and Midsummer Show.   8 C.C.A.L.S., ZML 2/297; ZML 3/379.

9 Ibid. ZAB 2, ff. 60, 66, 67v.; ZAF 26/18, 29; *Letter Books of*

Brereton, i, no. 545; *J.C.A.S.* lxviii. 113–14.

10 C.C.A.L.S., ZAB 2, f. 66; *J.C.A.S.* lxviii. 113.

11 *V.C.H. Ches.* iii. 36; *J.C.A.S.* lxviii. 114; Morris, *Siege of Chester*, 192, 195.

12 *Walker Revised*, ed. A. G. Matthews, 88, 90–4, 230; L. M. Farrall, 'Holy Trinity Ch., Chester', *J.C.A.S.* xxi. 164; ibid. lxviii. 98, 114–15.   13 *J.C.A.S.* lxviii. 115–16.

14 *Minutes of Committee for Relief of Plundered Ministers, and of Trustees for Maintenance of Ministers, 1643–54* (R.S.L.C. xxviii), 152, 193–4, 207–9, 216; *1650–60* (R.S.L.C. xxxiv), 5, 10, 34, 37–8, 43–7, 53, 70–1, 81–3, 87, 92–3, 103, 112, 140–1, 153–4, 210, 226, 317–18; C.C.A.L.S., ZAB 2, f. 92; ZAF 20/23; *Cal. S.P. Dom. 1653–4*, 122; *1657–8*, 241; *J.C.A.S.* lxviii. 117.

15 *J.C.A.S.* lxviii. 116–17; *Miscellanies*, i (R.S.L.C. xii), 48; Morris, *Siege of Chester*, 213; *V.C.H. Ches.* iii. 36, 190.

Ley, who organized ordinations and was responsible for the Attestation, became a Presbyterian publicist, president of Syon College, and a prominent member of the Westminster Assembly; Lancaster, author of an account of the siege, seems to have been the dominant influence in the city's churches until his retirement in 1659.[1]

Although Presbyterianism was clearly stronger in Chester than Independency, several well known ministers of other persuasions preached in the city, including Edmund Calamy, the pamphleteer Simeon Ashe, and Samuel Eaton. The last, who was chaplain to the parliamentarian garrison, established Chester's first Independent congregation, to which John Knowles, a Socinian, ministered briefly before his ejection; Eaton held services during the 1650s but there is no evidence of extensive support. By then the more radical sects were active, partly because the governor, Thomas Croxton, was apparently tolerant; they included an enthusiastic group of Baptists.[2] Quakerism attracted adherents through the work of Elizabeth Morgan and Richard Hickock. The Quakers made enemies by haranguing citizens, disturbing church services, and mocking those in authority. The magistrates dealt severely with them, imprisoning many in unpleasant conditions by 1654, and they again suffered harsh treatment during the mayoralty of Peter Leigh (1656–7). Nevertheless, a flourishing meeting was established in Chester, and became a base for missionary activity, pamphlet-printing, and a county fund.[3]

The sects added to the disruption of parish life and services, but by the later 1650s there were signs of returning sympathies for the Church of England. Rogationtide was again being observed at St. John's and Holy Trinity, and former royalist clergy were active in the city. Some of them certainly preached at St. John's and possibly elsewhere, and Richard Hunt, the ejected rector of St. Mary's, was reappointed to the living when it became vacant in 1655. Finally, during Sir George Booth's rising, William Cook, minister at St. Michael's, played a part in persuading the citizens to yield up the city, and he and at least one other minister prayed openly for the exiled king.[4]

MILITARY AND POLITICAL AFFAIRS, 1646–60

The parliamentarian garrison after 1646 was large and by 1648 a source of grievances.[5] By then rumours were current about Chester's uncertain political allegiance, and there were suggestions that as a precaution parliamentarian county gentry should be associated with the command of the city's militia.[6] In 1648 the deputy governor uncovered a supposed plot to betray the city to the king's forces. Nothing was proved against members of the corporation, but Brereton took the opportunity to add county gentlemen to the city's militia committee.[7] As the Scots advanced in July, the city was placed under defence, with a new company of foot and repairs to breaches in the walls.[8] Military precautions continued even after the Scots' defeat in August.[9] When the fighting in England ended in 1651 Chester became a venue for trials of royalist delinquents.[10] A garrison remained at the castle, although some munitions were transferred to the Tower of London in 1653.[11] Continuing precautions were justified at the time of John Penruddock's rising in 1655, when John Werden, a former royalist colonel, plotted to seize the castle; the small group of conspirators fled when they realized that the garrison had been strengthened.[12]

Hostilities in Ireland and Scotland involved the city authorities in organizing the passage of several thousand troops through the port in 1646–7.[13] Between 1648 and 1650 the city's officers were repeatedly asked to watch for royalists travelling between England and Ireland and to arrange for the dispatch of troops, money, guns, ammunition, clothing, and foodstuffs.[14] Involvement in organizing shipments of provisions, money, and equipment for garrisons in Ireland, Scotland, and the Channel Islands continued sporadically throughout the 1650s.[15] The corporation repeatedly but unsuccessfully sought some reduction in its con-

1 C.C.A.L.S., ZAB 2, ff. 84v., 124; ZAF 29/8; ZAF 37B/5; Morris, *Siege of Chester*, 212; Morrill, *Ches. 1630–60*, 20, 165–7, 267–8, 270; Kennett, *Loyal Chester*, 17; V.C.H. Ches. iii. 102–3; D.N.B.

2 J.C.A.S. lxviii. 117; Dore, *Civil Wars in Ches.* 70, 84–5; Morrill, *Ches. 1630–60*, 264 sqq., 275; V.C.H. Ches. iii. 103; C.C.A.L.S., ZML 3/352, 355–6, 361–2; D.N.B.

3 F. Sanders, 'Quakers in Chester under Protectorate', *J.C.A.S.* xiv. 36–76; W. C. Braithwaite, *Beginnings of Quakerism*, 125–7, 158, 168, 216, 268, 328, 388; V.C.H. Ches. iii. 103–4; Johnson, 'Aspects', 343 n.

4 S. C. Scott, 'Extracts from Churchwardens' Accts. and Vestry Mins. of St. John's, Chester', *J.C.A.S.* n.s. iii. 57; ibid. lxviii. 116–18; H. D. Roberts, *Matthew Henry and his Chapel, 1662–1900*, 27.

5 C.C.A.L.S., ZML 2/308–9.

6 Ibid. ZML 2/312, 316; Morrill, *Ches. 1630–60*, 188–9.

7 C.C.A.L.S., ZML 2/319–20; ZML 6/180; Hist. MSS. Com. 29, *13th Rep. I, Portland*, i, p. 463; *Memorials of Civil War in Ches.* 214–16; Morris, *Siege of Chester*, 211–12; Morrill, *Ches. 1630–60*, 188–9; Dore, *Civil Wars in Ches.* 71–2.

8 C.C.A.L.S., ZAB 2, f. 84v.; ZAF 29/8–9.

9 Cal. S.P. Dom. 1648–9, 183, 218; 1649–50, 229, 468, 535; 1650, 149, 301, 336; 1651, 524.

10 Ibid. 1651, 137, 196, 379, 416, 422–3, 427, 496.

11 Ibid. 1651–2, 179; 1652–3, 32, 215; 1654, 196; C.C.A.L.S., ZML 3/377.

12 Cal. S.P. Dom. 1655, 78, 597; R. N. Dore, 'Ches. Rising of 1659', *T.L.C.A.S.* lxix. 53; Morrill, *Ches. 1630–60*, 254–5.

13 Cal. S.P. Irel. 1633–47, 535–6; 1647–60, 731; Armour, 'Trade of Chester', 237 sqq.

14 Cal. S.P. Dom. Addenda 1625–49, 717; 1648–9, 48; 1649–50, 29, 107, 131, 141, 149, 160, 218, 228, 284, 296–7, 393, 495, 497, 533–4, 536, 572, 580, and *passim*.

15 e.g. ibid. 1651, 183, 520, 522, 584; 1651–2, 551, 553, 611; 1652–3, 175, 228, 271, 474, 478, 480, 513; 1654, 146, 150, 368; 1655, 340–1, 607; 1655–6, 79, 246; 1656–7, 120; 1658–9, 27; C.C.A.L.S., ZML 3/349.

sequent burdens, for instance pressing the county committee for repayment of £1,000 due for quartering troops, taking legal advice about parliamentary taxes, and petitioning in 1655 for a reduced monthly assessment.[1]

Chester's involvement with parliamentary politics was minimal,[2] and in the Interregnum the city's representation was reduced to one seat.[3] Political opinion was sharply divided by early 1659, when the second seat was restored, and there was a keenly fought contest, eventually won by supporters of the Protectorate.[4] In the summer the city became involved in the Cheshire rising headed by Sir George Booth.[5] Booth and his gentry associates colluded with members of the corporation opposed to the regime, notably Mayor Gerard Jones, Sheriff William Heywood, and Recorder Ratcliffe. Consequently, when Booth's force approached Chester on 2 August, Heywood ordered the gates to be opened and the insurgents took control

of the city, while the governor, Colonel Thomas Croxton, withdrew his small garrison into the castle. Booth's 'Declaration' was proclaimed at the High Cross. The corporation raised three companies of foot and diverted the proceeds of the monthly assessment to the city's defence. Ministers openly supported the royal cause in church services, and Chester remained in rebel hands for almost three weeks, although the governor held out in the castle against a loose blockade and maintained contact with the government. After Booth's force was defeated at Winnington bridge on 19 August, however, the rising collapsed, and the city was taken by Colonel John Lambert. The main local supporters of the rebellion were sequestered and suspended from office.[6] In the elections to the Convention of 1660 Chester returned Recorder Ratcliffe and Alderman William Ince, the latter a moderate and possibly a Presbyterian who had survived the purge of 1646.[7]

THE RESTORATION

After the reinstatement of the charter and the election of the mayor and sheriffs there was only one recorded meeting of the Assembly, on 30 March 1660, before the Restoration.[8] Amid modest jubilation the corporation sent a loyal address to the king in early May.[9] Soon afterwards the aldermen began to dismiss some of the main supporters of the previous regime, principally the Cromwellian alderman and city counsel Jonathan Ridge.[10] Between then and the autumn three aldermen resigned, including the leading puritan Calvin Bruen, three royalists purged in 1646 were restored, and Charles Stanley, earl of Derby, was newly appointed.[11]

The new Assembly sought to improve routine administration by exhorting its members to attend regularly, organizing the flow of petitions in a more orderly way, publishing a tariff of court fees, and undertaking a thorough audit.[12] In March 1661 it resolved to revive the Midsummer show, but continuing anxieties were manifest in concern for the city's defences and in the election as M.P.s in 1661 of a

former royalist along with a Presbyterian parliamentarian.[13]

The provisions of the Corporation Act evidently caused uncertainty, and the Assembly did not meet between December 1661 and June 1662.[14] In 1662 seven aldermen J.P.s and four aldermen were displaced, all but one elected since 1646. Nine sheriff-peers and 12 councilmen, including the serving treasurers, coroners, and leavelookers, were removed. Civic officials who lost their places were headed by the clerk of the Pentice, Ralph Davenport. Those permitted to remain included 10 aldermen J.P.s and one alderman, to whom were added two more restored aldermen. Five of that number had been elected since 1646; two, Robert Harvey and William Ince, had served continuously from pre-war days; and six had been among those purged in 1646. The two serving sheriffs, with a sheriff-peer and eight councilmen, continued in office; one sheriff-peer and a councillor were restored. The deputy town clerk, the eight serjeants, the crier, and the

1 Hist. MSS. Com. 29, *13th Rep. I, Portland*, i, p. 465; C.C.A.L.S., ZAB 2, f. 86; ZAF 29/8–9, 12; ZML 2/300, 304–5, 319; ZML 3/344, 365–6; *Cal. S.P. Dom.* 1655, 133; M. J. Braddick, *Parl. Taxation in 17th-Cent. Eng.* 144, 278–9.

2 *Letter Books of Brereton*, ii, p. 15 and no. 1148; *Hist. Parl., Commons, 1660–90*, iii. 315–16; *V.C.H. Ches.* ii. 114; D. Underdown, *Pride's Purge*, 372, 383; C.C.A.L.S., ZAB 2, ff. 79, 97, 99; ZAF 32/3; *Crisis and Order*, ed. Clark and Slack, 219–20.

3 *Cal. S.P. Dom.* Addenda 1625–49, 698–9; 1655, 294–5; 1655–6, 208; C.C.A.L.S., ZAB 2, f. 101v.; *V.C.H. Ches.* ii. 114; *Crisis and Order*, ed. Clark and Slack, 223–4.

4 C.C.A.L.S., ZAB 2, ff. 113, 123v.; *Crisis and Order*, ed. Clark and Slack, 225; cf. P. J. Pinckney, 'Ches. Election of 1656', *Bull. John Rylands Libr.* xlix. 390–1.

5 J. R. Jones, 'Booth's Rising of 1659', *Bull. John Rylands Libr.* xxxix. 416–43; *T.L.C.A.S.* lxix. 43–69.

6 C.C.A.L.S., ZAB 2, ff. 124v.–125; ZAF 37B/8, 10; Morrill, *Ches. 1630–60*, 307–9, 313–14; *T.L.C.A.S.* lxix. 63, 65, 67; *Crisis and Order*, ed. Clark and Slack, 225–8.

7 *Crisis and Order*, ed. Clark and Slack, 227–8; *Hist. Parl., Commons, 1660–90*, ii. 632; iii. 315–16; Dore, *Civil Wars in Ches.* 94.

8 C.C.A.L.S., ZAB 2, ff. 125v.–126v.; ZAF 3C/2–4.

9 *Cal. S.P. Dom.* 1660–1, 4; H. Taylor, 'Chester City Companies', *J.C.A.S.* n.s. v. 21; xviii. 154.

10 C.C.A.L.S., ZAB 2, ff. 106v., 127; ZAF 37C/25; Johnson, 'Aspects', 344–5.

11 C.C.A.L.S., ZAB 2, ff. 128, 130.

12 Ibid. ff. 125–31, 134, 142–3; ZAF 37C, 38A, 38B; ZML 6/185.

13 Ibid. ZAB 2, f. 132; below, this chapter: City Government and Politics, 1662–1762 (Parliamentary Representation, City Politics).

14 C.C.A.L.S., ZAB 2, ff. 133v.–134v.; ZAF 38B/2–7.

yeoman of the Pentice all held their places. Vacancies were filled by the commissioners. They promoted to aldermanic rank nine of the sheriff-peers, named 28 new councilmen, and appointed new treasurers, coroners, and leavelookers. Richard Levinge became the recorder and an alderman, and Daniel Bavand clerk of the Pentice.[1]

No further changes were imposed from outside. At the next aldermanic vacancy the place was filled in the usual way by the election of a former sheriff; at the same time the displaced recorder, John Ratcliffe, was permitted to re-enter civic service as a fee'd counsel.[2] The sheriff-peers were not restored as a distinct group: councilmen who were elected sheriff were replaced in the ranks of the Forty only when they became aldermen, left the Assembly, or died; otherwise, after the shrievalty they reverted to the position of councilman, holding the title of sheriff-peer only as a courtesy.[3] To allay any remaining uncertainties about the city's rights and privileges, however, the corporation began the quest for a charter of confirmation.[4]

Anglican worship was resumed at the cathedral after Henry Bridgeman, a son of the late bishop, became dean in June 1660. Four of the surviving pre-war prebendaries resumed their duties, and were joined in July 1660 by Thomas Mallory, a son of the late dean. Their puritan colleague John Ley had moved away and died in 1662. Only three of the petty canons returned to their posts, leaving the prebendaries with heavier duties.[5] The first two Restoration bishops, Brian Walton and Henry Ferne, died within a few months of each other before spring 1662.[6] By January 1661 a new diocesan chancellor had been appointed and the bishop's consistory court revived.[7]

During his short tenure Walton put pressure on clergy to use the Prayer Book.[8] Nevertheless, only one Presbyterian lost his living, Thomas Upton at Holy Trinity, where the pre-war vicar was restored.[9] For several months various ministers who later fell foul of the law continued to conduct worship in the forms accepted during the 1640s and 1650s, apparently without opposition. They included the incumbents of St. Michael's, St. Peter's, and St. Oswald's, and the Friday lecturer at St. Peter's; as late as June 1662 the best known of Lancashire's Presbyterians, Henry Newcome, preached at St. Peter's and Holy Trinity.[10] At first, use of the Prayer Book was resumed only at the cathedral, Holy Trinity, and St. Mary's, and perhaps St. Martin's and St. Bridget's, where one of the restored petty canons returned to his cure; in the other churches Prayer Books were purchased during the spring and summer of 1662.[11] Complete restoration of Anglican worship was made possible only by the 'Great Ejection' under the Act of Uniformity of 1662. None of the cathedral clergy was displaced, but four of the leading ministers in the city were deprived: the incumbents of St. Michael's, St. Peter's, St. Oswald's, and St. John's. At St. Peter's the Friday lecturer also resigned.[12]

RELIGION, 1662–1762

The cathedral chapter, whose finances were deteriorating in the later 17th century,[13] needed to borrow money, first for major repairs to the dilapidated cathedral and palace, and later for ordinary expenses. In 1701 it obtained a royal brief to meet some costs.[14] Episcopal visitations were infrequent and found little wrong,[15] and relations between the dean and prebendaries, who mostly came from outside Chester after 1660,[16] were generally harmonious. Occasionally, however, the chapter took exception to the behaviour of the bedesmen (who were royal nominees), disrespectful vergers, or the petty canons, the reduction in whose numbers from six to three or four restricted their availability for parochial work.[17] From the 1670s a single Sunday morning sermon was preached in the south transept (St. Oswald's parish church), to avoid having simultaneous sermons there and in the choir.[18]

The chapter remained a stronghold of the High Church in the earlier 18th century,[19] apprehensive when threatened, as in 1707, with the prospect of a bishop appointed by a Whig government.[20] It was not until the 1730s that the deaths of several long-established prebendaries gave the Whiggish bishops appointed since 1726 an opportunity to alter the

1 C.C.A.L.S., ZAB 2, ff. 135–137v.   2 Ibid. f. 139.
3 Ibid. ff. 135, 164, 176; ZAB 3, f. 19; Johnson, 'Aspects', 38–9, 41–2.
4 C.C.A.L.S., ZAB 2, f. 140; ZML 3/399–401.
5 Burne, *Chester Cath.* 127–9, 131–4; *V.C.H. Ches.* iii. 37.
6 A. Swatland, *House of Lords in Reign of Chas. II*, 276–7; J. Spurr, *Restoration Ch. of Eng. 1646–89*, 115–17; Burne, *Chester Cath.* 139–40.
7 Hemingway, *Hist. Chester*, ii. 242; *J.C.A.S.* xxviii. 192; *V.C.H. Ches.* iii. 37–8, 42; *Cal. S.P. Dom.* 1661–2, 49; Burne, *Chester Cath.* 133–4.
8 *V.C.H. Ches.* iii. 101; R. Hutton, *The Restoration*, 173.
9 *Cal. S.P. Dom.* 1660–1, 115; *J.C.A.S.* xxi. 160; lxviii. 118; *Calamy Revised*, ed. A. G. Matthews, 500.

10 *Diary of Revd. Henry Newcome* (Chetham Soc. [o.s.], xviii), 98; C.C.A.L.S., ZAB 2, f. 124; *J.C.A.S.* lxviii. 119; *Calamy Revised*, 132–3, 224–5, 250–1.
11 *J.C.A.S.* lxviii. 118.
12 Ibid. 119; *Calamy Revised*, 132–3, 224–5, 250–1, 320–1.
13 For this para. and next: *V.C.H. Ches.* iii. 190–3.
14 Burne, *Chester Cath.* 132–8, 150–1, 157, 164–5, 168–70; *J.C.A.S.* xlix. 15; *V.C.H. Ches.* iii. 37, 42, 192.
15 Burne, *Chester Cath.* 99–101, 141, 148.
16 Ibid. 120, 128–9, 131, 144, 146, 148–9, 158, 161, 177–8.
17 Ibid. 130–1, 143; *V.C.H. Ches.* iii. 191; *J.C.A.S.* lxviii. 118.
18 Burne, *Chester Cath.* 131, 136, 147–8; *V.C.H. Ches.* iii. 191.
19 Burne, *Chester Cath.* 166–210.
20 e.g. *Diary of Henry Prescott*, i. 133–6, 147, 149–50, 172–3.

chapter's ecclesiastical complexion. The chapter contained few men of any distinction, although William Smith, dean 1758–87, was a noted translator from the Greek.[1] Despite difficulties with indolent, disorderly, or incompetent organists and choirmen,[2] the canons maintained the usual round of choral services, and in the 1740s refurbished the choir, where the need for galleries in 1745 and 1749 suggests a sizeable regular congregation.[3] They also established a theological library in the newly repaired chapter house in 1728, including books bequeathed by Dean James Arderne in 1691 and others bought from a canon's widow in 1730.[4]

In the city churches the restoration of the books, vessels, and ornaments essential for Anglican worship after 1660 went slowly, through poverty at St. Olave's and St. Martin's and nonconformist sympathies at St. Oswald's and St. Peter's.[5] Most of the churches required extensive repairs or rebuilding: at St. Mary's they were not put into effect until after 1676, and in the 1690s the poor condition of St. Bridget's justified the issue of a brief to collect funds for repairs.[6] The pace of rebuilding picked up after 1700, despite continuing protestations of poverty. The ruinous parts of St. John's were repaired *c.* 1720, and towers were rebuilt at St. Peter's, St. Michael's, and Holy Trinity.[7] The erection of galleries in some of the larger churches (St. John's in 1727 and 1741, St. Mary's three times between 1703 and 1756, and Holy Trinity in 1750 and 1761)[8] suggests that church attendance rose at least in line with the gradual increase in the city's population.[9]

In some parishes clerical stipends posed a problem throughout the century after the Restoration: St. Olave's, for example, was too poor to have a minister until 1693, and even St. Oswald's was in financial straits when its outlying townships failed to pay their dues.[10] In 1675 Bishop John Pearson drew the mayor's attention to a scheme for uniting parishes in Exeter as a possible model, but the Assembly decided against the idea.[11] The reduction in the number of petty canons at the cathedral also contributed to vacancies in the smaller churches and the discontinuance of services.[12]

About 1720 only three benefices were worth over £30 a year, and some derived half or more of their income from voluntary contributions. Only two or three had houses for their clergy.[13] The best endowed, St. Mary's and Holy Trinity, were frequently held by cathedral dignitaries or aristocratic pluralists. The Wilbrahams, patrons of St. Mary's, sometimes treated it as a family benefice. At St. Peter's the minister saw his house taken over from the 1690s for the city archives. Not surprisingly some city livings were held together, such as St. Martin's with St. Bridget's until 1725, and then with St. Peter's 1739–76.[14]

Among the conforming clergy in the 1660s, the incumbents of St. Oswald's and St. Peter's allegedly neglected services, and the vicar of St. John's was accused of scandalous living.[15] The others exhibited no sign of their puritan predecessors' fervour. The limitations of the clergy partly explain the deepening religious divisions in the city, reflected also in parish disputes. At St. Olave's, for example, there were refusals to pay church rates and a lawsuit between incoming and retiring churchwardens,[16] and in 1663 at Holy Trinity disputatious parishioners destroyed the royal arms and disrupted the Prayer Book funeral service of a displaced alderman, Jonathan Ridge.[17]

The cathedral clergy who held many of the city's livings at least had dwellings in Chester, but as several simultaneously held country livings they were not likely to perform much more than the minimum of services legally required.[18] In the years before 1720 two sermons were normally preached each Sunday in the cathedral and the largest churches.[19] The cathedral was often well filled, with up to 200 people attending the sacrament.[20] The preaching at St. Martin's favourably impressed John Wesley in 1752.[21]

The Tory-dominated corporation did its part towards upholding the Church, for instance maintaining aldermanic seats in most of the parish churches for the occasions when the mayor or corporation attended in state.[22] After the dean and chapter recovered effective control of St. Oswald's in 1662, the main corporation church was St. Peter's. The corporation rebuilt its seats there in 1701,[23] provided stone from the quarry at

1 Burne, *Chester Cath.* 142, 160–1, 167, 177–8, 190–1, 197, 216–19; *D.N.B.* s.vv. Fogg, Laur.; Smith, Wm. (1711–87).

2 Burne, *Chester Cath.* 175, 179–80, 194–5, 208.

3 Ibid. 203–6. Plate 17.

4 Ibid. 159–60, 185, 188–9. Plate 18.

5 *J.C.A.S.* n.s. iii. 66–7; lxviii. 118–19; *V.C.H. Ches.* v (2), Medieval Parish Churches.

6 *V.C.H. Ches.* v (2), Medieval Parish Churches; C.C.A.L.S., ZML 4/532.

7 *V.C.H. Ches.* v (2), Medieval Parish Churches.

8 Ibid.

9 But cf. J. Wesley, *Works* (1872 edn.), iii. 457.

10 *V.C.H. Ches.* v (2), Medieval Parish Churches.

11 C.C.A.L.S., ZAB 2, f. 180; ZML 4/493.

12 *J.C.A.S.* lxviii. 118; *V.C.H. Ches.* v (2), Medieval Parish Churches: St. Bridget, St. Martin, St. Michael, St. Olave.

13 *V.C.H. Ches.* v (2), Medieval Parish Churches; cf. Gastrell,

Not. Cest. 98–120.

14 *V.C.H. Ches.* v (2), Medieval Parish Churches; TS. lists of incumbents, compiled by A. T. Thacker (copy at C.C.A.L.S.).

15 *J.C.A.S.* lxviii. 119, 122; *V.C.H. Ches.* iii. 41.

16 C.C.A.L.S., ZAB 2, f. 166; ZAF 40B/27.

17 *J.C.A.S.* xxi. 164–5; lxviii. 120.

18 Burne, *Chester Cath.* 142, 160–1, 177–8, 191, 197, 217–18; cf. *Alum. Cantab. to 1751*, i. 74 (Jn. Baldwin), 228 (Thos. Brooke); ii. 154 (Arthur Fogg), 353 (Chas. Henchman), 457 (Ric. Jackson); iii. 127 (Edw. Mainwaring); iv. 183 (Chas. Sudell); *Alum. Oxon. 1500–1714*, iii. 1687 (Ric. Wright).

19 e.g. *Diary of Henry Prescott*, i. 15, 28, 30, 91, 100, 107, 125, 181, 250, 287; ii. 317, 330, 357, 367, 446, 459; cf. ibid. i. 38, 79, 117.

20 Ibid. i. 120, 135, 152; ii. 354–5, 397, 572.

21 Wesley, *Works* (1872 edn.), ii. 269.

22 e.g. C.C.A.L.S., ZAB 3, f. 101; ZAB 4, f. 35; ZTAB 3, f. 58v.

23 Ibid. ZAB 3, ff. 94v., 106v.; cf. *Diary of Henry Prescott*, i. 36–8.

Hough Green for repairs,[1] and from 1704 contributed to the organist's salary.[2] Some ministers there were favoured with the virtually sinecure chaplaincy of St. John's hospital, which required only an occasional sermon and the consolation of condemned prisoners in the Northgate gaol.[3]

Some of the Presbyterian and Independent clergy ejected in 1662 stayed in the city and held their congregations together in difficult circumstances, aided on occasion by itinerant preachers.[4] There were also a few Baptists and Quakers, some of the latter in trouble before the end of 1660 for refusing the oath of allegiance or trying to distribute pamphlets.[5]

After Sir Geoffrey Shakerley's appointment as governor in 1663 action against conventicles became more vigorous, with arrests, fines, and imprisonment used against all the main groups.[6] A pause in the campaign, possibly because Bishop John Wilkins (1668–72) supported concessions to nonconformity,[7] was followed by renewed persecution, directed mainly against Baptists and Quakers.[8] A further respite accompanied the appointment of Bishop John Pearson (1672–86)[9] and the royal Declaration of Indulgence, under which licences were issued for meetings in private houses, mostly Presbyterian, some Independent, and a few seemingly for both. At least seven nonconformist preachers were licensed in the city, including some of those ejected in 1662: John Glendal, Ralph Hall, and William Jones as Presbyterians; Thomas Harrison as an Independent; and William Cook and John Wilson for congregations of both persuasions. The main meetings were in White Friars, Northgate Street, and Grange Lane.[10]

The number of recusants in Chester remained small, but the mayor and governor received orders to watch for suspected papist travellers. The discovery that five men arrested when passing through Chester at the time of the Popish Plot in 1678 were Roman

Catholic ex-officers from the king's army added to the hysteria, in the middle of which a captured priest, John Plessington, was executed at Boughton in July 1679.[11]

Charles II's persecution of nonconformists began again in 1682;[12] dissenting preachers were haled before the magistrates, and the Whiggish mayor, George Mainwaring, was blamed for protecting them.[13] Religious tensions were heightened by the duke of Monmouth's visit in September, when a mob damaged the cathedral, while at St. Peter's rioters hostile to the incumbent broke into the church and rang the bells.[14] The renewal of toleration under the Declaration of Indulgence of 1687 allowed the Presbyterian congregation led by Matthew Henry to establish strong roots in the city.[15]

The appointment of Bishop Thomas Cartwright (1686–9) brought to Chester an active supporter of James II, tainted for loyal Anglicans by suspicions of popish sympathies.[16] He was a vigorous diocesan administrator, holding ordinations and confirmations in the cathedral, preaching to large congregations, and monitoring the sermons given by his cathedral clergy.[17] Cartwright mixed socially with certain aldermen and especially recusant gentry, and was in frequent contact with the papal vicar-apostolic, Father John Leyburn.[18] James II's visit to Chester at the end of August 1687 was the signal for more open popish activity: the king attended service in the cathedral but also worshipped privately at the castle, where the garrison had its own Catholic chaplain; other priests were seen in the streets; and the bishop himself offered to find a chapel in the city for Roman Catholic worship.[19] Sir Thomas Grosvenor of Eaton Hall was also sympathetic to recusants, holding meetings with them at his house in the city.[20]

The nonconformists, too, relaxed their guard. William Penn himself spoke in the city during the king's

1 C.C.A.L.S., ZAB 3, ff. 163v., 213.

2 Ibid. ff. 116v.–117, 155, 251v.; ZAB 4, ff. 3, 37.

3 Ibid. ZAB 3, ff. 115, 179v., 185, 221; ZAB 4, f. 30.

4 *V.C.H. Ches.* v (2), Protestant Nonconformity: Early Presbyterians and Independents.

5 Ibid.: Baptists, Quakers; *V.C.H. Ches.* iii. 104–5; Hutton, *Restoration*, 156.

6 *V.C.H. Ches.* v (2), Protestant Nonconformity: Early Presbyterians and Independents, Baptists, Quakers.

7 Spurr, *Restoration Ch.* 57, 59, 317; Swatland, *House of Lords*, 276–7; *V.C.H. Ches.* iii. 43.

8 *V.C.H. Ches.* v (2), Protestant Nonconformity: Baptists, Quakers.

9 Spurr, *Restoration Ch.* 158, 317; *V.C.H. Ches.* iii. 44.

10 *V.C.H. Ches.* v (2), Protestant Nonconformity: Early Presbyterians and Independents; G. L. Turner, *Original Recs. of Early Nonconf.* ii. 691–2, 696–7; *Calamy Revised*, s.nn.; Roberts, *Matthew Henry*, 72–4; *J.C.A.S.* lxviii. 122; *V.C.H. Ches.* iii. 43, 105. There are no surviving returns for Chester from the religious census of 1676: *Compton Census*, ed. A. Whiteman, 631.

11 C.C.A.L.S., ZAB 2, ff. 191v., 196v.; ZML 4/495–6, 498–501, 508, 514; M. W. Sturman, *Catholicism in Chester, 1875–1975*,

11–12; *V.C.H. Ches.* iii. 88–92; P. J. Challinor, 'Restoration and Exclusion in Ches.' *Bull. John Rylands Libr.* lxiv. 369.

12 *V.C.H. Ches.* v (2), Protestant Nonconformity: Early Presbyterians and Independents, Quakers.

13 C.C.A.L.S., ZQSF 82; *Cal. S.P. Dom. 1682*, 67, 92, 107, 110, 120, 157–8.

14 *Cal. S.P. Dom. 1682*, 313–14, 342–3, 387–9, 393–4; Jan.–June 1683, 11; July–Sept. 1683, 409; Burne, *Chester Cath.* 151–3.

15 *V.C.H. Ches.* v (2), Protestant Nonconformity: Early Presbyterians and Independents.

16 F. Sanders, 'Thomas Cartwright, D.D.' *J.C.A.S.* n.s. iv. 6–7, 12–14, 18–20, 22–3; Spurr, *Restoration Ch.* 9, 89, 92; Burne, *Chester Cath.* 157; *V.C.H. Ches.* iii. 45.

17 *Diary of Dr. Thomas Cartwright* (Camd. Soc. [1st ser.], xxii), 16, 19, 21–2, 29–32, 35; Burne, *Chester Cath.* 154–5, 157; *V.C.H. Ches.* iii. 45.

18 *Diary of Thos. Cartwright*, esp. 15–19, 81; *J.C.A.S.* n.s. iv. 12; *V.C.H. Ches.* iii. 45.

19 *Diary of Thos. Cartwright*, 74–6; Burne, *Chester Cath.* 155; J. Childs, *The Army, James II, and the Glorious Revolution*, 24.

20 *Cal. S.P. Dom. 1689–90*, 238–9; Sturman, *Catholicism*, 17–18.

visit, and during the 1690s Quaker activity grew.[1] Both of the leading dissenting ministers in Chester, Matthew Henry and John Harvey, supported the address presented to James II, thanking him for the renewal of the Indulgence, but a year later Henry refused a royal invitation to suggest names for the city's re-modelled corporation, and when nominated anyway he and other dissenters declined to serve.[2] In the more favourable conditions from 1689 new places for non-conformist worship were licensed, though Henry's congregation continued to be the largest.[3] At that time the Cheshire classis was formed, with Henry and Harvey as members.[4]

The only clerical nonjuror after the Revolution was Bishop Cartwright.[5] His successor, Nicholas Stratford (1689–1707), was a High Churchman who revitalized the diocesan administration, aided the repair of the cathedral, and shared in the foundation of the Blue Coat school. He and Dean Lawrence Fogge (1692–1718) also promoted a local Society for the Reformation of Manners, and despite some opposition from both Anglicans and dissenters, secured the co-operation of Matthew Henry, a further sign of more harmonious relations between differing religious groups.[6]

Dissent remained vigorous in the early 18th century. Besides the established sects, rooms were frequently registered for worship by unidentified denominations, at least 15 between 1700 and 1710,[7] and another 14 by 1726,[8] though few thereafter.[9] Although the Quakers opened a meeting house in 1703 big enough for hundreds of people, their numbers later declined,[10] and a 'French church' briefly established in the 1710s disappeared when its Huguenot members moved on to Ireland.[11] By the 1730s Chester nonconformity was concentrated in the Presbyterian congregation, united under Matthew Henry in 1707, which was regarded with some friendliness by the minister of Holy Trinity parish, in which it stood. By 1750 strains were appear-ing between the more orthodox members and those inclined to Unitarianism, foreshadowing a schism in 1768.[12] Meanwhile dissent was revivified in the late 1740s by Methodists, attracting large and mostly respectful audiences, especially after John Wesley's first preaching in 1752.[13] Roman Catholicism, despite its relative strength in neighbouring parts of Lanca-shire, remained weak within the city. Investigations in 1741 and 1743 revealed no more than 45 Catholic householders, mostly craftsmen and journeymen.[14]

CITY GOVERNMENT AND POLITICS, 1662–1762

Three strands ran intertwined through the affairs of Chester's governing classes in the century after the Restoration. For the sake of clarity they are here separated out as military matters, parliamentary rep-resentation, and the city's own 'internal' politics, though each influenced the others and all had some effect on the city's routine government.

MILITARY AFFAIRS

Rumours of plots prevailed for some time after the Restoration. In 1661 doubts about the loyalty of the citizens led the corporation to pay for a permanent

guard of 30 men and to stockpile match, while the county militia was also placed on alert.[15] In 1662 the government stationed 60 foot soldiers in Chester, and the following year, immediately after his appointment as governor,[16] Sir Geoffrey Shakerley repaired the city's fortifications and repressed dissent.[17] The defences were further strengthened in 1671.[18] Tensions with the city authorities over financing the repairs were exacerbated in 1668 when the mayor gaoled a soldier without first informing the governor, and in the early 1670s by resistance to the impressment of sailors.[19]

The Popish Plot in 1678 led to cancellation of the

1 *V.C.H. Ches.* v (2), Protestant Nonconformity: Quakers.

2 Roberts, *Matthew Henry*, 84–6.

3 Ibid. 81–2; *V.C.H. Ches.* iii. 122; *V.C.H. Ches.* v (2), Protestant Nonconformity: esp. Early Presbyterians and Inde-pendents. Plate 36.

4 *Ches. Classis Mins. 1691–1745*, ed. A. Gordon, 6, 106, 122–3; Roberts, *Matthew Henry*, 88.

5 J. H. Overton, *The Nonjurors*, 475.

6 W. W. Taylor, 'Matthew Henry's Chapel', *J.C.A.S.* xxii. 180–2; *V.C.H. Ches.* iii. 45–6; Burne, *Chester Cath.* 170–1; C.C.A.L.S., ZAB 3, f. 80v.

7 e.g. C.C.A.L.S., ZQSF 90/3/229, 243, 245, 248, 252; ZQSF 91/2/127, 138, 149–50, 176–8, 180–1; ZQSF 91/3/274.

8 e.g. ibid. ZQSF 91/3/234–6, 267; ZQSF 92/2/136, 158; ZQSF 93/1/27, 48, 50; ZQSF 93/2/215; ZQSF 94/1/9; ZQSF 94/2/233.

9 Ibid. ZQSF 95/1/72; ZQSF 97/1/5.

10 *V.C.H. Ches.* v (2), Protestant Nonconformity: Quakers.

11 Ibid. Other Churches: Huguenots.

12 Ibid. Protestant Nonconformity: Early Presbyterians and

Independents; cf. *J.C.A.S.* xxii. 177–8.

13 *V.C.H. Ches.* v (2), Protestant Nonconformity: Method-ists (Wesleyans); cf. Wesley, *Works* (1872 edn.), ii. 267, 282–3, 384.

14 C.C.A.L.S., ZQSF 98/1/74; ZQSF 98/2/145.

15 Ibid. ZAB 2, ff. 132v., 133v., 139v.; R. L. Greaves, *Deliver us from Evil: Radical Underground in Brit. 1660–3*, 54, 65; Morrill, *Ches. 1630–60*, 326–8; *Bull. John Rylands Libr.* lxiv. 364.

16 *Cal. S.P. Dom. 1661–2*, 423, 436, 442, 452, 462, 467, 498, 565, 576; 1663–4, 248, 453; Childs, *Army*, 9; Greaves, *Deliver us*, 101, 104, 130–1; *Hist. Parl., Commons, 1660–90*, iii. 426.

17 *Cal. S.P. Dom. 1665–6*, 58, 331, 509, 533, 541, 550–1; 1666–7, 530; 1667, 37, 210, 389, 441; C.C.A.L.S., ZAF 39A/10; ZML 3/393–5; Greaves, *Deliver us*, 189; idem, *Enemies under his Feet: Radicals and Nonconformists in Brit. 1664–77*, 43, 127; *Bull. John Rylands Libr.* lxiv. 364; J. H. Hodson, *Ches. 1660–1780*, 3–5; above, this chapter: Religion, 1662–1762.

18 *Cal. S.P. Dom. 1671–2*, 8.

19 Ibid. 330–1, 363, 429–30, 535; C.C.A.L.S., ZAB 2, f. 157v.; ZML 3/424; Willan, *Eng. Coasting Trade*, 32.

Midsummer show and the Christmas watch in successive years, as well as repairs to the city walls.[1] As the crisis passed, temporary additions to the garrison were disbanded, but the Secretary of State still interfered in the appointment of the city's militia officers.[2] The visit of the duke of Monmouth in September 1682 was accompanied by searches for arms, surveillance of those deemed disaffected, a few arrests, and frequent reports to London.[3] Both the Rye House Plot in 1683[4] and the accession of James II in 1685 led to similar precautions, and in the latter year there was mob violence during the county election held in Chester.[5] Further measures followed the outbreak of Monmouth's rebellion in June 1685: the Midsummer fair was cancelled, suspects were imprisoned at the castle, and arrangements were made (in the event proving unnecessary) to send 1,000 foot from Ireland to protect the city.[6] The duke's cause evidently had some support in Chester, but there was no uprising.[7]

The garrison remained large enough to justify a new armoury in 1687 and to require billets in private houses.[8] Events in autumn 1688 emphasized Chester's military significance. Troops from Ireland, recalled by James II, began to arrive in October and were joined by others from Lancashire. Governor Peter Shakerley prepared to make a stand, but James II's flight weakened the garrison's resolve and in December Shakerley declared for William of Orange and ceded control of the castle to the Whig mayor, William Street.[9] Governors after the Revolution remained watchful,[10] and after the Lancashire Jacobite plot in 1694 more suspects were held in the castle.[11]

Chester's earlier importance as a base for military operations in Ireland was regained after the outbreak of the Irish rebellion in 1689. Troops passed through the city before embarkation from anchorages on the Dee.

There were shipments of military supplies, money, and foodstuffs, while senior military officers and State dignitaries also sailed from Chester.[12] Sick and wounded soldiers were evacuated to a temporary hospital established in the city in 1691, while prisoners of war and occasionally an alleged spy were detained there.[13] The flow of troops continued in the later 1690s.[14]

Despite its Tory inclinations and some sympathy for the Jacobites,[15] the city made no move in support of the rising of 1715. The defeat of the rebels at Preston (Lancs.) in November spared it direct involvement in military operations, although its trained bands were called up and government troops marched through. Captured Jacobites numbering up to 500 at a time were brought for temporary imprisonment at Chester, crowding the castle and the city gaol and overflowing into houses throughout the city. Initially many perished of cold, hunger, and fever because local sympathizers were prevented from assisting them.[16] Two regiments were kept at Chester for almost a year,[17] and there was some friction between civil and military authorities. The recorder, Roger Comberbach, who had shown ostentatious enthusiasm for the Hanoverians,[18] fell foul of the colonel commanding at the castle in 1715 in a dispute over jurisdiction, and was briefly placed under house arrest in humiliating circumstances before the colonel was himself removed.[19] Despite occasional fights between soldiers and citizens,[20] relations between city and garrison later improved.[21]

The initially unexpected approach of the Jacobites in 1745 caused greater alarm than in 1715. In mid November part of the county militia was brought in to garrison the city.[22] The city gates were bricked up, save for wickets at the Bridgegate and Eastgate, the walls were patrolled, cannon were mounted to com-

1 C.C.A.L.S., ZAB 2, ff. 188–92, 195v., 196v.; ZML 4/504, 506–7; *Cal. S.P. Dom.* 1678, 512.

2 *Cal. S.P. Dom.* 1679–80, 370; 1680–1, 141, 452; 1682, 166.

3 Ibid. 1682, 387–9; R. L. Greaves, *Secrets of the Kingdom: Brit. Radicals from Popish Plot to the Revolution*, 107–12, 120, 125; J. R. Western, *Eng. Militia in 18th Cent.* 62–3; above, this chapter: Religion, 1662–1762; below, this section (City Government).

4 Hodson, *Ches. 1660–1780*, 13–14.

5 *Cal. S.P. Dom.* 1684–5, 307; 1685, nos. 1060, 1062; *Hist. Parl., Commons*, 1660–90, i. 152; *V.C.H. Ches.* ii. 118.

6 C.C.A.L.S., ZAB 3, f. 2; *Cal. S.P. Dom.* 1682, 487, 537; 1685, 214, 226, 230–1, 234, 254–5; Childs, *Army*, 7.

7 C.C.A.L.S., ZQSF 83; Greaves, *Secrets*, 274, 287–8, 291; Childs, *Army*, 100; below, this section (City Politics).

8 *Cal. S.P. Dom.* 1687–9, no. 373; Childs, *Army*, 89, 113 n.; *V.C.H. Ches.* v (2), Castle: Buildings.

9 *Cal. S.P. Dom.* 1687–9, no. 2102; *By Force or by Default? The Revolution of 1688–9*, ed. E. Cruickshanks, 35–7; Childs, *Army*, 180–1, 194; *Britain in the First Age of Party, 1680–1750*, ed. C. Jones, 24; J. R. Western, *Monarchy and Revolution: Eng. State in 1680s*, 274–6; C.C.A.L.S., ZML 4/525.

10 *Cal. S.P. Dom.* 1689–90, 21, 124, 136, 233; 1690–1, 220, 232, 248, 447; 1693, 31; Western, *Monarchy and Revolution*, 302–3; C.C.A.L.S., ZAB 3, ff. 26v., 40v.

11 *Cal. S.P. Dom.* 1694–5, 230, 232–3, 271, 312; 1695, 272, 276; 1696, 245; C.C.A.L.S., ZMF 113; Western, *Eng. Militia*, 70.

12 *Cal. S.P. Dom.* 1690–1, 26 sqq., 152, 253, 273, 279, 285, 344, 381, 461, 502, and *passim*; 1691–2, 75, 85, 226, 399; 1693, 24, 213, 232, 238; C. Armour, 'Trade of Chester and State of Dee Navigation' (Lond. Univ. Ph.D. thesis, 1956), 239; C.C.A.L.S., ZAB 3, ff. 25v.–26.

13 *Cal. S.P. Dom.* 1690–1, 309, 463, 466; 1696, 82; 1697, 97.

14 Ibid. 1694–5, 34, 108, 123, 302; 1695, 240, 243, 247, 298; 1698, 79, 113, 381; 1699–1700, 101; 1702–3, 249; C.C.A.L.S., ZMF 113; ZML 4/538, 555, 566, 568, 574, 576.

15 *Diary of Henry Prescott*, i. 190; ii, pp. ix–x, 473–4, 480–1.

16 Ibid. ii. 463–4, 470–6, 479, 481–3, 485, 496, 533; J. H. E. Bennett, 'Ches. and "The Fifteen"', *J.C.A.S.* xxi. 30–46; C.C.A.L.S., ZAB 3, ff. 229v.–230; ZML 6/204.

17 *J.C.A.S.* xxi. 39, 44; cf. C.C.A.L.S., ZTAB 3, ff. 12, 20v.–21v., 30v.; *Diary of Henry Prescott*, ii. 489, 501, 547.

18 e.g. *Diary of Henry Prescott*, ii. 470, 476, 479, 481, 513.

19 Ibid. ii. 481–3; C.C.A.L.S., ZAB 3, ff. 228v.–230; ZML 6/198–205; ibid. Cowper MSS., i, pp. 264–6.

20 e.g. *Diary of Henry Prescott*, ii. 580.

21 *Letter from Freeman of Chester to Friend in Lond. on Late Election* (Lond. 1733), 17, 23–4, 26.

22 R. C. Jarvis, 'Rebellion of 1745', *T.L.C.A.S.* lvii. 49–67; C.C.A.L.S., Cowper MSS., i, pp. 277–80; cf. ibid. ZAB 4, f. 115v.

mand the bridge, and the castle defences were improved.[1] Business came to a standstill, leading citizens evacuated their families and valuables, and refugees from outside flocked within the walls, where inhabitants were directed to lay in two weeks' provisions against a siege. In the event the Jacobite army went nowhere near Chester, but the city had been involved in heavy expense and had to turn to Sir Robert Grosvenor to obtain reimbursement from the government in 1746.[2]

PARLIAMENTARY REPRESENTATION[3]

The M.P.s returned in 1661, Sir Thomas Smith, Bt., and the recorder, John Ratcliffe, upheld the city's interests in parliament but were not especially active.[4] The contested byelection on Ratcliffe's death in 1673, between Colonel Robert Werden, a courtier with local connexions, and the recorder, William Williams, involved serious disorder and accidental loss of life during the poll. Werden had a majority of 50 in a total of 1,152 votes, but his election was confirmed only in 1675, after the Commons had considered complaints about the mayor's admission of new freemen during the contest. By then the other M.P., Smith, had died, and Recorder Williams was apparently returned unopposed at the byelection. Werden was not prominent in parliamentary business, but Williams spoke frequently for the Country opposition.[5]

The byelections of 1673 and 1675 heralded a period of sharp political discord which reflected national divisions. At first the Whig and Tory factions were evenly balanced.[6] Recorder Williams was elected without a contest to the first two Exclusion parliaments in 1678 and 1679 along with the local landowner Sir Thomas Grosvenor, Bt., both men being associated with the Country opposition. By 1681 Grosvenor had become a Court supporter and probably did not seek re-election, being replaced by Colonel Roger Whitley, an opposition supporter. Anti-government opinion in Chester, hardened possibly by the city's trading difficulties, was demonstrated in 1682 by a tumultuous welcome for the duke of Monmouth. Recorder Williams tried to protect the Monmouth rioters from severe punishment and to stiffen resistance to the government's attack on the city's liberties. On the

other hand, the new charter of 1685, which Grosvenor as mayor helped obtain, strengthened royal influence within the corporation. The election of 1685 completed the Tory reaction by returning Grosvenor and Werden unopposed.[7] The election for the county seats, also held in Chester, was marked by disorder, Whig complaints of official malpractice, and corporation-supported celebrations of the Tory success.[8]

With the political tide in Chester running strongly in the Court's favour there was no public response to Monmouth's rebellion in 1685, and Williams himself became one of the main Whig collaborators with James II, though he lost both his seat in parliament and his position on the council.[9] Mistrust of the king, however, was evident during his visit in August 1687, to the extent that the governor was unable to procure a loyal address from the corporation.[10] Local Tory dominance was eventually undermined by national events in 1688 and the débâcle over the remodelling of the corporation. When Williams was reinstated along with the old corporation he was quick to re-establish his Whig credentials.[11] Nevertheless, in 1689 there was a sharp contest for the city's seats in the Convention: Whitley and the Whig alderman George Mainwaring were opposed unsuccessfully by Grosvenor and Richard Levinge, the former recorder.[12]

In the 1690s the city's political alignment was in the balance. Chester needed influential connexions to obtain a scheme for the Dee navigation, relief from heavy taxation, and a relaxation of the regulations hindering the import of cattle and hides. Economic and political issues were therefore linked as Whig and Tory groups, led respectively by Whitley and Grosvenor, vied for control of parliamentary representation. There were also differences about the rights of dissenters and the method of choosing officers and members of the Assembly, though the parliamentary franchise undisputedly rested with the freemen.[13]

In 1690 Grosvenor and Levinge were returned, and Whitley and Mainwaring complained that the mayor had wrongly created 125 new freemen during the election.[14] Levinge later turned to a career outside Chester (though he was still an alderman in 1698),[15] and in 1695 Grosvenor was re-elected along with

1 C.C.A.L.S., ZAB 4, f. 125.

2 Ibid. ff. 119, 125v.

3 A detailed treatment appears in *V.C.H. Ches.* ii. 127–35.

4 *Hist. Parl., Commons, 1660–90*, i. 152–3; iii. 315–16, 444–5; *V.C.H. Ches.* ii. 128.

5 *Hist. Parl., Commons, 1660–90*, i. 153; iii. 689–90, 731 sqq.; *Cal. S.P. Dom. 1672–3*, 505–6, 559, 587; *C.J.* ix. 342, 346; C.C.A.L.S., ZML 3/485; *V.C.H. Ches.* ii. 99–100, 128–9.

6 S. W. Baskerville, 'Establishment of Grosvenor Interest in Chester, 1710–48', *J.C.A.S.* lxiii. 61.

7 *Hist. Parl., Commons, 1660–90*, i. 153; ii. 448–9; iii. 689–90, 709–11, 731–5; M. Knights, *Politics and Opinion in Crisis, 1678–81*, 298–9; *Cal. S.P. Dom. 1682*, 280, 313–14, 342–3, 387–9; *V.C.H. Ches.* ii. 117–18, 129–30; C.C.A.L.S., ZML 4/515–16; below, this section (City Politics).

8 *V.C.H. Ches.* ii. 118; *J.C.A.S.* xxviii. 201–2; *Hist. Parl., Commons, 1660–90*, i. 152.

9 *V.C.H. Ches.* ii. 129; *Hist. Parl., Commons, 1660–90*, iii. 734; *D.N.B.*

10 *Diary of Thos. Cartwright*, 75; Childs, *Army*, 59, 131; Western, *Monarchy and Revolution*, 209; Hemingway, *Hist. Chester*, ii. 243.

11 *V.C.H. Ches.* ii. 129; below, this section (City Government).

12 *Hist. Parl., Commons, 1660–90*, i. 153–4; iii. 3–4, 709–11, 734; *V.C.H. Ches.* ii. 130.

13 *V.C.H. Ches.* ii. 100, 127–31; below, this section (City Government).

14 *V.C.H. Ches.* ii. 100; *Cal. S.P. Dom. 1700–2*, App. 547–9.

15 C.C.A.L.S., ZAB 3, f. 64v.; ZML 4/531A; *D.N.B.*

Whitley. The latter's death in 1697 left the city's Whigs in difficulties, enabling the Tories to win the election of 1698 decisively and establish a longer-term electoral ascendancy: Grosvenor was elected with Peter Shakerley, the High Tory former governor, who continued as M.P. until 1715, having been joined in 1701 (after Grosvenor's death) by another High Tory, Sir Henry Bunbury, who served in the Commons until 1727. Those two long-serving M.P.s, who worked hard for the city's interests, thus provided a measure of stability in Chester's political life in the early 18th century.[1]

CITY POLITICS

The city received its first post-Restoration charter in 1664. It confirmed Chester's liberties with minor amendments, including a standard clause making appointments to the recordership and the clerkship of the Pentice subject to royal approval.[2] Interference was minimal for many years, although in 1667 Governor Sir Geoffrey Shakerley helped to oust John Ratcliffe as recorder.[3] During 1680–1 government supporters accused the city's ruling Whigs of misconduct, including partiality in the admission of freemen.[4]

Local antagonisms were intensified by the duke of Monmouth's visit on 9 September 1682, planned earlier in the summer by Mayor George Mainwaring, Colonel Roger Whitley, and other leading Whigs. Monmouth was greeted enthusiastically by the populace and acted as godfather at the christening of the mayor's daughter. The disturbances which accompanied his visit, however, had serious consequences for the city.[5] Shakerley rightly suspected that the aldermen J.P.s would deal leniently with the rioters, and the government attempted to transfer the trial to a special commission under Sir George Jeffreys, chief justice of the palatinate of Chester, but in the end the city's quarter sessions heard the case and only two men were convicted.[6] Other Tory moves included interference by the governor's son and deputy, Peter Shakerley, in the mayoral election of 1682 to succeed Mainwaring. He persuaded some of the aldermen to support a moderate Whig, Peter Edwards, rather than Whitley,[7] but the

plan misfired when Edwards as mayor maintained the line taken by the Whig magistrates.[8]

The defence of the charter against the quo warranto proceedings begun by the privy council in July 1683, which was led by Recorder Williams and backed by an association of some 500 freemen and a vote of the grand jury, was undermined by the Assembly's failure to support Edwards's successor as mayor, William Street. Denied the use of the common seal, Street appealed under his own official seal, but the document was deemed invalid and the city's charter was overturned in 1684.[9]

A new charter was procured in 1685 through Sir Thomas Grosvenor.[10] It largely confirmed the city's constitution, also empowering the mayor to appoint a deputy, but with a clause, normal at the time, allowing the Crown to remove civic office-holders. The charter disfranchised eight men, including Recorder Williams and Aldermen Street, Mainwaring, and Whitley, and made Sir Thomas Grosvenor mayor and Sir Edward Lutwyche, a newcomer, recorder; it also named the sheriffs, the clerk of the Pentice, and 22 aldermen, of whom six were new to the Assembly, and made changes among the Forty. The new recorder resigned later in the year on becoming a judge and was succeeded by Richard Levinge, son of the earlier recorder.[11]

The charter of 1685 extended royal influence on the city's affairs.[12] In 1688 the government removed the entire Assembly and obliged the city to petition for a new charter, which named the corporation and principal officers, reserved the Crown's right to dismiss individuals, dispensed all members from the prescribed oaths, and restricted the franchise to the corporation.[13] Of the 24 aldermen named in addition to the mayor and recorder only 11 had already served as aldermen and four as sheriffs. Grosvenor and William Stanley, earl of Derby, were among those displaced. Members removed in the purge of 1685 and restored in 1688 included Mainwaring, Whitley, and Peter Edwards. The attempt to conciliate Whigs and those with nonconformist connexions was fruitless: the nominated corporation apparently never met, and in October the charters of 1685 and

1 *J.C.A.S.* lxiii. 61–71; *Hist. Parl., Commons, 1660–90*, iii. 427; *1715–54*, i. 506–7; *Diary of Thos. Cartwright*, 81; *Cal. S.P. Dom. 1689–90*, 238–9.

2 C.C.A.L.S., ZAB 2, ff. 146, 148–9; ZAF 39A/12, 14, 22; ZML 3/399–400; *J.C.A.S.* xxviii. 192–4.

3 *V.C.H. Ches.* ii. 129; iii. 104–5; *Cal. S.P. Dom. 1667*, 14, 25; *Hist. Parl., Commons, 1660–90*, iii. 731; cf. C.C.A.L.S., ZAB 2, ff. 164v., 170–1, 174v.–175; ZML 3/427.

4 *Cal. S.P. Dom. 1680–1*, 238–9, 600; *1682*, 67.

5 Ibid. *1682*, 280, 313–14, 342–3, 387–9; G. W. Keeton, *Lord Chancellor Jeffreys and the Stuart Cause*, 164–5.

6 *Cal. S.P. Dom. 1682*, 402, 406, 427, 439–40, 465, 467, 475; Keeton, *Jeffreys*, 165–9.

7 *Cal. S.P. Dom. 1682*, 449, 471–2, 480, 487, 523–4, 537; R. G. Pickavance, 'Eng. Boros. and King's Government: Study of Tory Reaction, 1681–5' (Oxf. Univ. D.Phil. thesis, 1976), 379–84.

8 C.C.A.L.S., ZAB 2, f. 197; *Cal. S.P. Dom. July–Sept. 1683*, 188, 190; Keeton, *Jeffreys*, 170–2; Pickavance, 'Eng. Boros.' 365; M. Landon, *The Triumph of the Lawyers: Their Role in Eng. Politics, 1678–89*, 138–9.

9 C.C.A.L.S., ZAB 2, f. 197v.; *Cal. S.P. Dom. 1683–4*, 165–6, 200; *1684–5*, 38–9; *J.C.A.S.* xxviii. 194–5; Keeton, *Jeffreys*, 159–60; Landon, *Lawyers*, 139–41.

10 *Hist. MSS. Com. 17, 12th Rep. VI, H.L.* ii, p. 298; *J.C.A.S.* xxviii. 200; Landon, *Lawyers*, 141.

11 C.C.A.L.S., ZAB 3, f. 1v.; ZCH 39, m. 1; *Cal. S.P. Dom. 1684–5*, 215; J. Hall, 'Royal Charters and Grants to City of Chester', *J.C.A.S.* xviii. 65, 72; xxviii. 197; Landon, *Lawyers*, 141; below, this section (City Government).

12 *Diary of Thos. Cartwright*, 75, 79; *J.C.A.S.* xxviii. 204.

13 *Cal. S.P. Dom. 1687–9*, 252, 256–7; *Hist. MSS. Com. H.L.* ii, p. 300; Western, *Monarchy and Revolution*, 211 n.; *J.C.A.S.* xxviii. 206; *E.H.R.* lv. 50–1, 54–5; C.C.A.L.S., ZCH 40, m. 1.

1688 were annulled and the city resumed its earlier privileges.[1]

In effect the charter of 1664 was confirmed, and the surviving members of the corporation of 1683–4 were reinstated, including William Street as mayor and William Williams (now knighted) as recorder. During the 1690s several of the newcomers imposed in 1685 became aldermen or sheriffs.[2] A few opponents of the Revolution of 1688–9 were also weeded out: in 1691 Thomas Simpson, an alderman for 20 years, was expelled for refusing the oaths to William and Mary, and in 1702 nine councilmen were displaced for refusing the oaths for the protestant succession.[3]

A sharp internal dispute followed about the interpretation of the electoral provisions of the 1664 charter.[4] In 1693, during Colonel Whitley's first mayoralty, Sir John Mainwaring, George Booth, and more than 400 supporters petitioned the Assembly that the Forty should be elected annually by the freemen, according to the letter of the charter, challenging the long-standing practice of co-option for life. Ignoring a counter-petition, the mayor, recorder, and aldermen J.P.s, with only two dissentients, called a citizens' meeting which elected a list nominated by the mayor. Some of the 20 ejected councilmen complained to the privy council, which left the matter to be settled in King's Bench.[5] With the re-election of Whitley as mayor in 1693, 1694, and 1695, and in the absence of the court's decision, the annual election of councilmen continued. In 1696, before leaving office, Whitley secured approval for detailed arrangements for future elections, giving freemen the right to reject serving councilmen, allowing the mayor to nominate candidates, and permitting the freemen to propose other names to be put to the vote.[6]

After Whitley had gone, however, the old system was gradually restored: in 1697 the Assembly co-opted to four aldermanic vacancies, two of them caused by the deaths of the leading Whigs Whitley and Street,[7] and in 1698 it formally abolished annual elections, restored 17 ex-councilmen, co-opted 23 others, and confirmed the existing 22 aldermen in office for life.[8]

From the 1710s the Grosvenor family repeatedly intervened in the city's affairs. Attempts to break their power were always thwarted, despite popular support and the presence within the corporation of a faction opposed to Grosvenor influence.[9] Membership of the corporation was occasionally conferred on the Grosvenors, their allies among the Cheshire gentry, and

other outside supporters, including in 1720 their steward and political agent, Robert Pigot, who served as mayor in 1723–4.[10]

From the 1720s their growing interest in monopolizing parliamentary elections led the Grosvenors to try packing the body of freemen with supporters. Normally the Assembly admitted many new freemen before an election. Some were members of the county gentry and their dependants,[11] many of whom resigned the freedom as soon as the election was over.[12] Most, however, were inhabitants of Chester and its environs, entitled to the freedom by descent or apprenticeship but unwilling or unable to take it up until the Grosvenors paid the fees. The total numbers admitted could be very large, as for example 338 by birth and 162 by apprenticeship in 1720,[13] and *c.* 450 and *c.* 175 in 1732.[14]

Mayoral elections in the early 18th century continued under the previous arrangements, the freemen choosing each 13 October between two candidates nominated by the corporation. Sometimes as many as 500 or 600 freemen voted. Occasionally the aldermen overruled their choice.[15] The fiercest contest came in the early 1730s. To protect their position the Grosvenors needed to retain the support of the mayor, whose prerogative it was to call the Assemblies at which honorary freemen could be created. The Whigs first tried to win over the mayor of 1731–2, Trafford Massie, by offering clerical preferment for his son. Shortly before the election in 1732 the Whig candidate for mayor left £100 in gold with Massie in return for a written promise to call no further Assemblies. Meanwhile sporadic disorders culminated in a clash in Bridge Street in early October between a Whig mob (allegedly reinforced with disguised soldiers, revenue officers, and Liverpool sailors) and Tory supporters who included Welsh miners. The latter came off worse, and the Whigs, suspecting that Tory aldermen were admitting more freemen after dark, broke into and wrecked the Pentice. The mayor called for dragoons from Warrington to help restore order and appointed *c.* 270 special constables. The violence shocked the faction leaders into a truce, but when polling was adjourned the Whigs, supposing that their man had won, pursued the mayor and justices into the coffee house under the Exchange and carried off the mayoral sword and mace. In fact the Tories had won by *c.* 1,100 votes to *c.* 850, perhaps in part through intimidation.[16]

1 *Cal. S.P. Dom.* 1687–9, 324; Hist. MSS. Com. *H.L.* ii, p. 300; R. R. Steele, *Tudor and Stuart Proclamations*, i, no. 3881; Keeton, *Jefferys*, 160.

2 C.C.A.L.S., ZAB 3, ff. 19–20 and *passim*; ZCH 41.

3 Ibid. ZAB 3, ff. 33, 60, 66v., 102; ZMF 113.

4 Johnson, 'Aspects', 39–42; *V.C.H. Ches.* ii. 99–100.

5 C.C.A.L.S., ZAB 3, ff. 36–40v.; ZML 4/53A.

6 Ibid. ZAB 3, ff. 46, 51v.–52, 53–4.

7 Ibid. ff. 57, 58v., 59v.–61.

8 Ibid. ff. 64, 66v.; *J.C.A.S.* xxviii. 208; lxiii. 61.

9 *J.C.A.S.* lxiii. 59–84.   10 C.C.A.L.S., ZAB 3, f. 258v.

11 e.g. ibid. f. 260; ZAB 4, ff. 52–3, 55–57v.

12 Ibid. ZAB 4, ff. 59–65.   13 Ibid. ZTAB 3, f. 62 sqq.

14 Ibid. ZTAB 4, ff. 86v.–91.

15 Ibid. ZAF 49–51; cf. *Diary of Henry Prescott*, i. 170; ii. 200, 331, 598.

16 *Letter from Freeman*, 7–12, 14–17, 20–8; C.C.A.L.S., Cowper MSS., i, pp. 270–2; cf. ibid. ZAB 4, ff. 48, 70; ZAF 52, pt. 4 (mayoral election protocol, 1732); ZCL 113A–c (depositions); ZTAB 4, ff. 91v.–92v., 107; ZTAB 5, f. 7.

In the following year, 1733, incensed by the Tories' allegedly irregular co-option of Sir Robert Grosvenor and his ally Watkin Williams Wynn as aldermen,[1] the Whigs went to law to assert the rule of election by freemen laid down in 1506; a jury of Cheshire gentlemen, however, basing themselves on a lost order of 1525, ruled that the charter's terms should be overridden by constant practice.[2] From 1734 the Tories also adjusted the method of electing the mayor and the freemen's sheriff, thenceforth entirely excluding the freemen;[3] later mayors were normally chosen in order of seniority of their membership of the Assembly. Several times the mayoralty was held by the Grosvenors or their aristocratic or gentry allies in the county, two serving successively in 1736–8, and three between 1759 and 1762. By then the next mayor but one was also being formally designated at the time of his predecessor's election. Only twice, in 1744 and 1748, did open division among the aldermen permit the freemen to vote.[4] The mayoral election day was moved under an Act of 1753 from the Friday after St. Denis (9 October) to the Friday after 20 October in order to prevent its falling within the period of the Michaelmas fair; the starting date of the latter had changed from 29 September to 10 October as a consequence of the calendar reform of 1752.[5] In 1747 the House of Commons ruled that non-resident freemen might not vote in parliamentary elections, but the ruling did not prevent them from voting in mayoral elections, and the dominance of Grosvenor supporters in the corporation was unaffected.[6]

The city had always since 1714 celebrated Hanoverian royal anniversaries,[7] and in 1745 there was little overt sympathy for the Jacobites, though two cathedral choirmen were in trouble for making disloyal speeches.[8] The corporation, which was anti-Jacobite,[9] shared in the political reconciliation of the 1750s, for example making William Pitt a freeman on his resignation as Secretary of State in 1757.[10] Thereafter it proclaimed its loyalty to the Crown whenever a British military or naval victory or a royal family occasion gave opportunity.[11]

CITY GOVERNMENT

Despite the purges of 1662 and the 1680s the Assembly usually included some very experienced aldermen.[12] Two who had served without a break since before the Civil War, Robert Harvey and William Ince the elder, remained until their deaths in 1669 and 1678. Of the new appointees in 1662 two served until the 1690s. Apparently very few men tried to avoid service in the later 17th century,[13] though reluctance may have grown in the earlier 18th, since fines for refusal were set in 1703 and increased sharply in 1741 and 1754.[14] Except when outsiders were appointed during the 1680s, the *cursus honorum* remained as before. Repeated election as mayor became exceptional, the main instance being Colonel Whitley's service for four consecutive terms from 1692 to 1696, in unusual political circumstances. Aristocratic and gentry landowners and a broad range of urban occupations continued to be represented in the Twenty-Four, and among councilmen the range was even wider. The larger distributive trades, such as mercers, drapers, chandlers, upholsterers, ironmongers, and from *c.* 1730 linendrapers, produced almost a third of all Assemblymen after 1700, brewers and innkeepers about another seventh. Apothecaries and booksellers were also over-represented. Fewer manufacturers gained a place, especially as aldermen, and the building crafts and retail food trades were almost entirely excluded. New aldermen and councillors were almost always chosen by consensus, without voting.[15]

During the 1660s and 1670s there were normally six to eight recorded meetings of the Assembly every year, but the changes in the charters disrupted that routine: there were no meetings for 13 months from February 1684,[16] or between August 1688 and January 1689, or between February and September 1689.[17] Up to seven meetings a year were again being held by 1694,[18] but from October 1695, while the conduct of elections was in dispute, the Assembly met less frequently and minutes were also kept by the mayor and aldermen J.P.s gathered in the inner Pentice. They met there five times in December 1695 alone, 45 times in 1696, and 16 times during the first four months of 1697.[19] Once

1 C.C.A.L.S., ZAB 4, f. 46v.

2 Ibid. ZCL 1A–D; ZCL 2A–E; cf. ibid. ZAB 4, ff. 48 and v., 57v.–58.   3 Ibid. ZAF 52–4.

4 Ibid. ZAF 52 sqq. (attendance lists), esp. ZAF 53, pts. 14–15 (mayoral election protocols, 1744, 1748); *V.C.H. Ches.* v (2), Lists of Mayors and Sheriffs.

5 Cattle Distemper, Vagrancy, Marshalsea Prison, etc. Act, 26 Geo. III, c. 34, s. 4, summarized in *Rep. Com. Mun. Corp.* pp. 2619–20.

6 *C.J.* xxv. 425, 497–8, 504–5; cf. *J.C.A.S.* lxiii. 83–4; C.C.A.L.S., ZAB 4, f. 123v.

7 C.C.A.L.S., ZTAB 3–5 *passim*; cf. ZAB 3, f. 137.

8 Burne, *Chester Cath.* 199–200.

9 C.C.A.L.S., ZAB 4, ff. 114v., 115v.; cf. ibid. Cowper MSS., i, p. 280.

10 Ibid. ZAB 4, f. 172v.; cf. ibid. f. 195; ZTAB 6, f. 95v.

11 Ibid. ZAB 4, ff. 177, 194, 205; *Adams's Weekly Courant,* 19 Sept. 1758, p. 3; cf. ibid. 17 Nov. 1761, p. 3; C.C.A.L.S., ZAB 4, ff. 189v., 194 and v. Drafts of addresses: ibid. ZAF 54, pt. 9; cf. *Complete Peerage,* vi. 209.

12 Para. based on *V.C.H. Ches.* v (2), Lists of Mayors and Sheriffs, and on C.C.A.L.S., ZAB 2–3 *passim*.

13 C.C.A.L.S., ZAB 2, f. 176v.; ZAB 3, ff. 110v.–111.

14 Ibid. ZAB 3, ff. 108, 110v.–111, 126, 169; ZAB 4, ff. 70, 94v.–95, 96v.–97, 160.

15 Ibid. ZAB 2–4 *passim*.

16 Ibid. ZAB 2, f. 197v.; ZAF 411–42A; ZML 4/521–2.

17 Ibid. ZAB 3, ff. 16–21; ZAF 44–5.

18 Ibid. ZAB 3, ff. 34v., 42 sqq., 46v. sqq., 51–58v.

19 Ibid. ZMF 113.

the dispute was over the Assembly again met more regularly,[1] up to 11 times a year under Queen Anne.[2] From the 1720s, however, it seldom met more than twice or thrice a year, attended by only half or two thirds of the full complement of 70 or more, with the aldermen J.P.s more assiduous than councilmen. From the late 1740s attendance was often low enough to allow sittings during the colder months to be held in the inner Pentice rather than the larger common hall at the Exchange.[3] By 1710 the mayor and aldermen J.P.s also met every Friday in the inner Pentice,[4] not as an 'inner cabinet', but rather as an administrative subcommittee to handle routine business between Assembly sessions. Its main concerns were poor-law settlement rights and the formal swearing-in of freemen.[5]

The Assembly's business during the later 17th and earlier 18th century, apart from financial matters, consisted mainly of responses to suggestions and requests made by others.[6] Much time was spent on filling vacancies and offices, guild affairs, and admissions to the freedom. From the 1670s petitions, most commonly for leases of city property or leave to enclose parts of the streets and Rows, were normally referred to small committees, rarely of more than six and at first just of aldermen but in the 18th century usually also including the mayor and recorder, and, when finance was involved, the treasurers. The committees' recommendations were almost invariably accepted by the full Assembly, which after 1700 hardly ever recorded votes, except on the level of fines for those admitted to the freedom. The quasi-parliamentary system of petition, report to the 'House', and final approval allowed for responses to difficult or unfavoured requests to be indefinitely postponed from one Assembly sitting to another without open rejection, especially in the 1750s. The Assembly also devised and enforced local regulations, in 1685 confirming a long list of bylaws.[7] From the 1690s minute-keeping was improved,[8] and arrangements were made for storing the city's records in rooms adjacent to the Pentice, where in 1762 they

were set in order by the joint town clerk, Thomas Brock.[9]

In the earlier 18th century the main activities of the city government were still the traditional ones: caring for its public buildings, dispensing justice, maintaining order, upholding economic privileges, and occasionally encouraging trade. From the 1720s the magistrates devoted much effort to checking the finances of debtors imprisoned in the Northgate gaol.[10] Their criminal business mainly concerned assaults and theft. A few of those convicted were transported to America,[11] but more, especially women, were whipped through the streets from the Northgate to the Eastgate or Bridgegate, a penalty occasionally followed by brief imprisonment in the house of correction.[12] Most offenders were simply bound over for good behaviour. In the early 1750s a short campaign was waged against begging, gambling in the Rows after dark, disorderly houses outside the Northgate,[13] and swearing.[14] In the 1710s the city still maintained a whipping post and cucking stool,[15] and a gallows at Boughton, where in 1711 the mayor had a gentleman's servant, convicted of murder, hanged in haste before influence could secure a reprieve.[16]

The Assembly had in its gift many low-ranking civic posts, such as the mayor's and sheriffs' officers, night and day bellmen, common crier, city mason, water bailiff, and keepers of the Roodee and the common hall.[17] By the early 18th century many were treated as hereditary.[18] The corporation's two senior officers remained the clerk of the Pentice (or town clerk) and recorder. Both appointments were affected by the factional politics of the later 17th century,[19] but after 1700 patronage and family connexions were more influential. William Williams, a distinguished lawyer, served as recorder from 1667 until his death in 1700, though with an interruption in the 1680s.[20] His successor, clerk of the Pentice Roger Comberbach (d. 1720), was followed by his son-in-law Thomas Mather,[21] but when Mather died in 1745 William Falconer was chosen on the recommendation of Sir Robert Grosvenor.[22] Comberbach arranged in 1712 for

---

1 Ibid. ZAB 3, ff. 61v.–68v., 75–85.
2 Rest of para. based on ibid. ZAB 3, f. 104 to end; ZAB 4, ff. 1–217; ZAF 49–54.
3 e.g. ibid. ZAB 4, ff. 123v., 127v., 132, 149v., 153v.; cf. ZTAB 6, f. 16v.
4 Ibid. ZAB 3, f. 194v.; cf. ibid. f. 256.
5 Sampled: ibid. ZMIP 16, 36, 55.
6 Para. based on ibid. ZAB 2–4 passim.
7 Ibid. ZAB 3, f. 2v. sqq.
8 Ibid. ff. 23v., 59, 72v., 75, 108v.
9 Ibid. ZAB 4, f. 200 and v.
10 e.g. ibid. ZQSF 92/2/11; ZQSF 93/1/92; ZQSF 93/2/14; ZQSF 95/1/90; ZQSF 97/1/33; ZQSF 98/2/152.
11 e.g. ibid. ZQSF 92/2/178; ZQSF 94/1/22; ZQSF 95/2/175, 238; ZQSF 96/2/119; ZQSF 98/3/191; cf. ZTAB 6, ff. 61v., 67.
12 e.g. ibid. ZQSF 90/1/150; ZQSF 92/2/122; ZQSF 93/1/97; ZQSF 93/2/192; ZQSF 96/2/102, 164; cf. ZTAB 6, f. 114.
13 Ibid. ZQSF 100/1/13; cf. ZQSF 96/2/133; Adams's Weekly Courant, 26 Mar. 1761, p. 3.

14 C.C.A.L.S., ZQSF 100/1/39–74; ZQSF 100/2/83–125; ZQSF 100/3/146–76.
15 Ibid. ZTAB 2, f. 24v.; ZTAB 4, f. 9.
16 Ibid. ZTAB 3, ff. 20v., 48v.; cf. ibid. Cowper MSS., i, pp. 262–3; Adams's Weekly Courant, 2 Dec. 1760, p. 3.
17 C.C.A.L.S., ZAB 2, ff. 143, 162v., 163v., 172, 196; ZAB 3, ff. 21, 24v.–25, 27, 30v., 33v., 34v., 52, 62v.–63; ZAF 37c–47D passim.
18 e.g. ibid. ZAB 3, ff. 136v., 143, 165v.; ZAB 4, ff. 75v., 166v.
19 Clerkship: ibid. ZAB 3, ff. 20v., 23, 31v., 81, 83; ZAF 37c/20; ZAF 38B/6; ZAF 38c/4, 19–20; ZAF 39A/19, 44; ZAF 41G/17; ZAF 45B/19; ZCH 39, m. 1; ZCH 40, m. 1; J.C.A.S. xxiii. 16.
20 C.C.A.L.S., ZAB 2, ff. 135–136v., 158, 159; ZAB 3, ff. 25v., 81; ZAF 47c/29; ZCH 39, m. 1; ZCH 40, m. 1; ZCH 41; Cal. S.P. Dom. 1667, 14, 25, 44, 51; Hist. Parl., Commons, 1660–90, iii. 731–5; Keeton, Jeffreys, 357; D.N.B.
21 C.C.A.L.S., ZAB 3, ff. 253 and v., 255v.; ZAB 4, f. 16v.; cf. ZTAB 4, f. 63; ibid. Cowper MSS., i, p. 267.
22 Ibid. ZAB 4, f. 112; ZAF 53, pt. 12 (letter May 1745).

the clerkship of the Pentice to be granted for life to his son, also Roger, then aged 19, jointly with Thomas Lloyd.[1] Lloyd had a deputy by 1735[2] and died in 1754, after which in 1757 the younger Comberbach took out a new life-grant jointly with Thomas Brock, recommended by Sir Richard Grosvenor.[3]

Taxation caused the city many difficulties during the 1660s and 1670s, beginning with demands for arrears of the post-Restoration assessments and the administration of the hearth tax.[4] By 1670 the recorder and others were accused by the farmers of the excise of conniving with the city's brewers in their opposition to it.[5] Above all, from 1665 the corporation was in dispute with the county about their respective assessments for the Royal Aid and Further Supply.[6] During the first year (1664–5) the city paid a tenth of the whole for Cheshire under protest, but in the second year it refused. The matter was complicated in 1666 when Chester and the county were separated and the city's liability was reduced to a twentieth of the total. The city's commissioners used the lower rate for the third year, but by the end of 1667 a total of £1,178 remained uncollected. After intensive lobbying of the Treasury by both parties, it was finally decided in 1670 that the city should meet about two thirds of the arrears; they were paid off by 1672, partly through borrowing.[7]

Chester's financial resources and management were mainly unchanged in the later 17th century. The corporation frequently reviewed its leases and rents.[8] Income from grazing on the Roodee was rising after 1660, to £88 in 1691,[9] but the revenue from fees for admission to the freedom varied. Those duly qualified paid an amount fixed by custom, but for others the corporation could charge what it liked: the minister of St. Peter's, for example, was admitted *gratis* in 1666, but the normal fee in the 1670s was £30 or more, and in 1693 a flexible scale was fixed, starting at £10.[10] Income from tolls, collected by the swordbearer at the shambles and the macebearer at the gates, remained a source of contention, though in 1666 Francis Talbot, earl of Shrewsbury, sold his interest in the Bridgegate

tolls and certain other rights to the corporation for the large sum of £200.[11] The tolls payable at the gates were confirmed in 1670, but there was evidently much evasion.[12]

Corporation finances were subsidized indirectly in the new collection of plate formed after the Restoration to replace that sold in the Civil War. The long-standing custom by which new aldermen and councilmen presented a piece of plate was revived, and Charles Stanley, earl of Derby, presented a mace in 1668.[13] Some plate was sold in 1685 to pay for the new charter, and in 1700 gifts of plate were commuted to cash payments towards the cost of the new Exchange.[14]

Smaller customary exactions from the mayor, sheriffs, leavelookers, other officers, and new aldermen and councillors went particularly to supplement the wages paid to the mayor's and sheriffs' attendants.[15] More important were *ad hoc* loans raised, for example, to meet arrears on the Royal Aid, repair the city walls in 1690, and build the Exchange, a project which also attracted outright gifts.[16] Whenever ordinary revenue proved inadequate, special assessments were made for particular purposes, including the renewal of the charter in 1664 and scavenging, street repair, and fire-fighting equipment in the 1670s and 1680s.[17]

Much of the revenue continued to go on salaries, wages, and fees, not least on arrears which had built up by the 1660s, due for instance to the school usher and the sons of former recorder Robert Brerewood and treasurer Randle Holme II.[18] The corporation made *ex gratia* payments to the family of another former recorder, John Ratcliffe,[19] and sent gratuities, treats, or gifts of cheeses to men of influence in London for help over the charters and the tax controversy.[20]

The regular income of the treasurers' accounts (which did not include the funds administered by the sheriffs and other office-holders) was rarely adequate.[21] In the early 1670s the Assembly therefore began closer scrutiny and audit of the accounts. Revenues, gifts, legacies, fees, and perquisites were inquired into in 1693,[22] prompted by the prospect of additional financial burdens. Hitherto the corporation had tried to

---

1 C.C.A.L.S., ZAB 3, ff. 198v.–199, 221; cf. ZAF 49D, nos. 56–9.

2 Ibid. ZAB 4, f. 69v.; cf. ibid. f. 192 and v.

3 Ibid. ff. 158v., 169–70; ZAF 54, pt. 6 (letter Jan. 1757).

4 Ibid. ZML 3/386–9, 391–2, 404–5, 469.

5 Ibid. ZMF 87/5–6, 62, 70; ZMF 88–9 *passim*; ZML 3/445–7, 454–6, 458, 470–5, 480 (references kindly supplied by M. J. Braddick).

6 M. J. Braddick, *Nerves of State: Taxation and Financing of Eng. State, 1558–1714*, 113–14, 157–8.

7 C.C.A.L.S., ZAB 2, ff. 152–77; ZML 3/406–84 *passim*; M. J. Braddick, 'Resistance to Royal Aid and Further Supply in Chester, 1664–72', *Northern Hist.* xxxiii. 108–36.

8 C.C.A.L.S., ZAB 2, ff. 167, 184, 185v., 190, 193v., 198; ZAB 3, ff. 32v., 37v., 43v.–44, 72v.

9 *Chester: 1900 Years of Hist.* ed. A. M. Kennett, 38.

10 C.C.A.L.S., ZAB 2, ff. 157, 175, 177v., 187v.; ZAB 3, f. 38.

11 Ibid. ZAB 2, ff. 138, 156, 158, 161, 188v.; ZAF 38B/23; ZML 6/189.

12 Ibid. ZAB 2, ff. 167v., 168v., 187, 188v., 190v.; ZAB 3, ff. 21v.–22, 25v.–26, 76, 82; ZAF 40D/16, 40; ZAF 40G/67; ZAF 41C/32; ZAF 45A/25; ZMF 113.

13 Ibid. ZAB 2, ff. 166, 173v., 177, 184; M. J. Groombridge, *Guide to Charters, Plate, and Insignia of City of Chester*, 45, 48–9.

14 C.C.A.L.S., ZAB 2, f. 199v.; *J.C.A.S.* xviii. 65; Groombridge, *Guide to Charters*, 48.

15 C.C.A.L.S., ZAB 2, ff. 183, 184v.–185; ZAB 3, ff. 8, 23v.

16 Ibid. ZAB 2, ff. 171, 177; ZAB 3, f. 26v.; ZAF 47A/4.

17 Ibid. ZAB 2, ff. 149, 166, 169, 172, 183, 187, 194; ZAB 3, ff. 6, 9, 10; ZAF 39A/14, 22.

18 Ibid. ZAB 2, ff. 126, 131v., 142, 143, 179v.; ZAF 38A/15; ZAF 40F/30; ZML 3/398.

19 Ibid. ZAB 2, ff. 157v., 178; ZAB 3, ff. 43v., 49, 94, 95v.

20 Ibid. ZAB 2, f. 198; ZMF 87/38; ZML 3/442–4.

21 Johnson, 'Aspects', 92–3.

22 C.C.A.L.S., ZAB 2, ff. 164, 167, 170v.–171, 178v., 184, 198; ZAB 3, f. 37v.

avoid expensive undertakings, relying on others for the new waterworks and improvements to the Dee navigation,[1] but from 1687 it faced the need to rebuild the common hall. In 1692–3 a new building was approved, costing £1,000, a sum manageable only through gifts from the king and others. Progress on building was impeded by the dispute over Assembly elections, and an additional £500 had to be raised in 1698.[2]

The corporation's income remained inelastic in the earlier 18th century.[3] The largest of the traditional revenues was rent from city property, c. £270 a year, including over £120 from lands outside the liberties. Grazing on the Roodee and the rent of the flesh shambles each usually brought in at least £100, the Roodee sometimes up to twice as much after the 1720s. Other revenues were falling: the prisage of wines, once also yielding c. £100, was halved by the 1740s, and the leavelookers' income fell sharply as traders sold more 'by order' rather than bringing their goods into Chester and paying tolls.[4] The tolls themselves, whether taken at the gates or in the markets, were increasingly challenged by outsiders and from c. 1750 led to legal expenses in their defence.[5]

When deficits arose, the treasurers were expected to meet them personally and be reimbursed later.[6] The city's debts became especially pressing in the two decades after 1700.[7] It ordered minor economies, as in 1711,[8] and resorted to other expedients. The need in 1706 to meet long overdue payments for the Exchange led it to centralize the revenues collected by officers other than the treasurers.[9] In 1711 it prohibited new leases of corporate property for more than three lives or 21 years, and began letting its shops under the Pentice at rack rent.[10] In 1712, when it appeared that even regular expenditure would exceed income, the city empowered itself to sell freehold interests in property hitherto held for fee-farm rents, giving existing lessees first refusal. Sales were stopped in 1713, after helping pay off a £350 debt.[11]

There were more expensive projects c. 1750, as the city began to consider repairing the Exchange and building a workhouse.[12] Timber on its lands was sold in bulk for £100 in 1750.[13] In 1755, on the death of the macebearer, who collected the Eastgate tolls, the corporation took over the mayor's power to name his successor, and rented the tolls to its appointee, initially the deceased incumbent's son, for £80 a year. The mayor was compensated for his loss of revenue by assigning him a capital sum to meet his expenses.[14] Other offices previously filled by the mayor were likewise taken over in 1759.[15]

The city also reorganized its debt in the 1750s. Since 1700 it had repeatedly borrowed by issuing bonds, sometimes secured on particular revenues such as the murage duties.[16] Although interest rates were reduced from 6 per cent c. 1705 to 5 per cent by the 1720s, the accumulated debt had reached over £1,000 by the late 1730s.[17] In 1740 the city arranged to pay off all such sums owing to individuals by borrowing at 4 per cent from other funds under its control, especially the St. John's hospital trust, to which by 1750 it owed c. £1,600.[18] In 1757, to pay for repairs to the Exchange and building a poor-law workhouse, it decided to raise £6,000 by issuing annuities under the tontine system. Only £4,000 came in initially, but the city itself subscribed c. £2,000.[19] Of the money raised, a quarter was used to repay the loan from St. John's hospital, but in 1758 the corporation borrowed £1,500 back again, by mortgaging the new workhouse and the shops at the Exchange.[20]

ECONOMY AND SOCIETY, 1662–1762

By 1700 Chester was on the verge of losing its dominance as a regional economic hub, as nearby towns, especially in south Lancashire, began to specialize in trade or manufacturing in a manner which suited neither Chester's traditions nor its position. Even so its markets and fairs remained important and well attended,[21] and it developed a diverse economy based mainly upon consumption and services offered to an extensive hinterland. In comparison with Liverpool, its main rival as a trading port, it had poor commun-

1 *V.C.H. Ches.* v (2), Public Utilities: Water; Water Transport: River.

2 C.C.A.L.S., ZAB 3, ff. 13, 35v.–36, 54v.–59, 62, 63, 74, 83–4, 85v.–86; ZAF 47A/4; ZML 6/195; *Cal. S.P. Dom.* 1694–5, 461, 495; *V.C.H. Ches.* v (2), Municipal Buildings: Exchange.

3 This and following paras. based on C.C.A.L.S., ZTAB 2–7.

4 Ibid. ZAB 3, f. 203; ZAB 4, ff. 115, 134v.–135v., 136v., 149v., 162, 169v.–170, 177v.

5 Ibid. ZAB 3, f. 272; ZAB 4, ff. 4, 125, 135v., 139, 151 and v., 173; ZAF 50H, no. 20.

6 e.g. ibid. ZAB 3, ff. 148, 182, 238v.–239; ZAB 4, ff. 81v., 118v., 158; cf. ZAB 4, f. 108.

7 e.g. ibid. ZAB 3, ff. 155v., 160v., 182v., 187, 191v.; ZAB 4, f. 9v.

8 Ibid. ZAB 3, f. 187v.

9 Ibid. ff. 145v.–146v., 156–7, 193v.

10 Ibid. ff. 187v., 200v.–201v.; cf. ZAB 4, ff. 58v., 65.

11 Ibid. ZAB 3, ff. 193v.–194, 202, 207v.

12 Ibid. ZAB 4, f. 174.

13 Ibid. f. 133v.; cf. ZTAB 6, s.a. 1749–50.

14 Ibid. ZAB 4, ff. 165v., 166v.; cf. ZAB 3, f. 202.

15 Ibid. ZAB 4, ff. 189v.–190.

16 e.g. ibid. ZAB 3, ff. 161, 177v., 189 and v., 224, 245v., 265v., 272v.; ZAB 4, ff. 19v., 24v., 92v.

17 e.g. ibid. ZTAB 4, ff. 9 and v., 52v., 82v., 107; ZTAB 5, ff. 6v., 62.

18 Ibid. ZAB 3, f. 255; ZAB 4, ff. 55, 89, 100v., 113, 139v., 196v.; cf. ZTAB 5, f. 88; ZTAB 6, ff. 7v., 18.

19 Ibid. ZAB 4, ff. 170–171v., 173v.–174v., 183 and v., 187v.; ZTAB 6, ff. 104–5.

20 Ibid. ZAB 4, ff. 176v., 178v., 196v.

21 e.g. *Diary of Henry Prescott*, i. 72, 117, 251; ii. 448–9.

ications. Only the London road was turnpiked before 1750,[1] and links with the hinterland were relatively bad. Salt from central Cheshire, for instance, was from 1721 carried on the newly opened Weaver navigation, bypassing Chester altogether.[2] Road access to the expanding Flintshire coal and lead mines was difficult, and their production was usually loaded at the ports along the north-east coast of Wales, nominally out-ports of Chester.[3]

MARITIME TRADE

The revival of the city's overseas commerce after 1660 was hampered by wars and privateering, and it was never large even in the best years. In 1700, for example, there were only 10 outward international sailings and 20 inward. The export of tanned calfskins to France and Spain continued on a much reduced scale, with many interruptions. Instead, lead exports expanded markedly during the 1690s, when nearly 1,800 tons, two thirds of it ore and the rest pig lead smelted in Flintshire, was shipped to the Low Countries, with smaller quantities to Spain, Portugal, and France. Exports rose again after the peace of 1713, mainly of pig lead to France, and after 1740 Portugal, with totals sometimes reaching 2,300 tons a year.[4] Miscellaneous cargoes were also shipped to French, Iberian, and Mediterranean ports.[5]

Imports of French wine were displaced in the later 17th century and the earlier 18th by Spanish and especially Portuguese products, which arrived with cargoes of fresh and dried fruits, especially oranges and raisins. The quantities of wine were small in comparison with those at other provincial ports. Other imports from the Mediterranean included modest volumes of almonds, anchovies, and skins.[6] Sugar must also have been imported, since by 1715 a Liverpool merchant had a refinery at Chester.[7] Iron imports from Spain were replaced by supplies from the Baltic, along with flax, hemp, timber, and other naval stores, a sizeable trade by 1695 which continued throughout the earlier 18th century, sometimes

through Holland.[8] Even by 1700 Chester had thus been eclipsed as a port for foreign trade, and what remained was mainly dependent on lead exports. Only a very few Chester ships went further afield, for instance in the 1720s to South Carolina for rice, tar, and pitch. In the mid 1750s and the 1770s one or two Chester merchants were in the African slave trade, mostly in partnership with Liverpool men.[9]

Coastal traffic, in contrast, doubled in both volume and shipments between 1660 and 1700, and although stagnant for much of the earlier 18th century was beginning to expand again from 1750.[10] Trade increased with all Chester's main partners (Liverpool, London, and the south-western ports), and mainly involved coal, lead, and cheese. In the earlier 18th century there was also some re-export of silk, sugar, and other luxuries.[11] Of the staples, only cheese passed through the city. Ships carrying cheese, coal, and lead frequently returned in ballast.[12]

The trade in coal grew to between 1,000 and 1,400 chaldrons a year by 1700, mainly to Lancashire, Wales, and London, but then fell in the early 18th century and did not recover until the 1750s.[13] Lead shipments grew from the 1690s because of the London Lead Company's operations in Flintshire, from 1,400–1,800 tons a year to a peak of over 5,700 tons in the later 1720s, of which four fifths went to London. By the early 1760s the total had fallen back to no more than 3,500 tons a year, of which Liverpool took the largest share. The tonnage of cheese carried, mainly to London, doubled between 1664 and 1676 and exceeded 1,000 tons in 1683 before dwindling rapidly because of French privateering after 1689.[14] From the 1710s, with the renewal of peace, the trade grew enormously under London cheesemongers who used local cheese factors to collect from all over the Cheshire plain and neighbouring counties. About 1730 there were supposedly 20 ships making three round trips each and carrying over 5,500 tons a year, though no more than 1,500 tons a year was ever registered through the port records.[15] In the 1750s there were also some shipments

1 *V.C.H. Ches.* v (2), Roads and Road Transport: Roads; cf. C.C.A.L.S., ZML 4/642, 653.

2 C. Armour, 'Trade of Chester and State of Dee Navigation' (Lond. Univ. Ph.D. thesis, 1956), 115–16, 141–4, 289; Willan, *Eng. Coasting Trade*, 102; C.C.A.L.S., ZAB 3, ff. 93v., 255; ZAF 49c/17, 34; ZML 4/639–41, 655; R. Craig, 'Some Aspects of Trade and Shipping of River Dee in 18th Cent.' *T.H.S.L.C.* cxiv. 116 and n.

3 Armour, 'Trade of Chester', 102–5, 131–40; *T.H.S.L.C.* cxiv. 103–4.

4 Armour, 'Trade of Chester', 32–3, 190–5, 258, 300; cf. *T.H.S.L.C.* cxiv. 120–3.

5 *Cal. S.P. Dom.* 1660–1, 384–5; Armour, 'Trade of Chester', 31–2, 183–4, 190–5, 209–13; C.C.A.L.S., ZCR 352.

6 Armour, 'Trade of Chester', 183–4, 196–202, 204–9; *T.H.S.L.C.* cxiv. 118; cxvi. 49–50.

7 C.C.A.L.S., ZAF 49G, no. 25; cf. *Diary of Henry Prescott*, ii. 464.

8 *T.H.S.L.C.* cxiv. 118–20; Armour, 'Trade of Chester', 50,

203–4, 210–13; C.C.A.L.S., ZCR 352, Mar. 1704; cf. *Adams's Weekly Courant*, 30 Sept. 1760, p. 4.

9 R. Craig, 'Ships and Shipbuilding in Port of Chester in 18th and Early 19th Cent.' *T.H.S.L.C.* cxvi. 45–9; Armour, 'Trade of Chester', 213–17.

10 *T.H.S.L.C.* cxiv. 111–15; Armour, 'Trade of Chester', 281.

11 *T.H.S.L.C.* cxiv. 116; C.C.A.L.S., ZAB 4, f. 97 and v.

12 Armour, 'Trade of Chester', 2–3, 280–2; Willan, *Eng. Coasting Trade*, 181.

13 Para. based, except where stated otherwise, on Armour, 'Trade of Chester', 74, 86, 121–6, 254–6, 284–92, 298–304; Willan, *Eng. Coasting Trade*, 16–17, 48–9, 67–8, 86–7, 104–5, 181.

14 C. Foster, 'Ches. Cheese', *T.H.S.L.C.* cxliv. 6, 8, 34, 37.

15 *Agrarian Hist. of Eng. and Wales*, v (2), 486–7; *T.H.S.L.C.* cxiv. 125–7; Poll Bks. 1732 (C.C.A.L.S., ZCEA 1), 1747 (printed); *Rolls of Freemen of Chester*, ii (R.S.L.C. lv), index s.vv. cheese-factor, cheese-monger; C.C.A.L.S., ZAF 50E, nos. 57–8; *C.J.* xxii. 60.

from Chester of wheat, timber,[1] and cannon made at a foundry near Wrexham.[2] Imports from London and Liverpool comprised sugar, tobacco, and other colonial products, while ships from Wales delivered wheat, barley, fish, lead, and large quantities of slates (445,000 in 1689, for example).[3]

The expansion of Chester's Irish trade from the 1650s to the early 1670s was followed after 1680 by five slack decades during which the number of sailings fell below those from Liverpool and Whitehaven (Cumb.).[4] Even then, however, Ireland was much the city's most important overseas trading partner: in the 1710s, for example, of 150–200 ships cleared for overseas voyages each year only 20–30 were for other destinations.[5] Exports from Chester were led by Welsh coal, shipped largely in Chester vessels, which amounted in 1699, for example, to as much as 7,800 chaldrons. Other exports included limited quantities of lead and iron, clothing, woollen cloth from Yorkshire and Lancashire (the latter 'cottons'), cheese and other foodstuffs, hops, and supplies for the English military expeditions.[6] The main import from Ireland was at first livestock. Government legislation began to interfere with the trade in the earlier 1660s by imposing duties on imported live cattle, followed in 1667 by a total ban. Smuggling flourished, and when the Act temporarily lapsed in 1679 the trade resumed on a large scale: in 1680 more than 12,700 head of cattle and over 41,000 sheep were imported. The ban was reimposed in 1681, forcing Chester's leather industry into a greater dependence on imported Irish skins and hides, which numbered 3,000 or more a year *c.* 1705 but became fewer in the later 1710s and did not grow again until the 1750s.[7]

In the later 17th century the city's trade with Ireland also included small-scale imports of wool, woollen cloth, linen yarn, and linen cloth.[8] Quantities of the last remained small at first despite the reduction of the city's tolls between 1707 and 1710,[9] since Irish linen merchants preferred to ship through Liverpool.[10] The

linen trade grew from the mid 1730s. Some Irish yarn was imported, but much more cloth, which doubled in quantity between 1744 and 1755 to almost 1 million yards, and trebled again by 1761. Most came directly from Ireland, some by Liverpool. All the importers did extensive business at Chester's Michaelmas fair,[11] which required a succession of ever-larger linen halls.[12] Most of those involved in the linen trade were outsiders present only during the fairs, and even in the 1730s and 1740s there were probably fewer than 15 resident linendrapers.[13]

From the 1660s the royal yachts, provided by the Royal Navy for the lord lieutenant of Ireland, plied between Dublin and the Dee anchorages, carrying officials, dispatches, and money for troops, but also taking ordinary passengers by arrangement. At first they used Dawpool (in Thurstaston) but by the 1680s had transferred to Parkgate, where from 1686 a regular packet boat service for passengers developed.[14] Parkgate remained the main port for Ireland until the first improvements to the London–Holyhead road in the 1760s.[15] As a result, many travellers passed through Chester, including the lords lieutenant of Ireland,[16] John Wesley,[17] Handel, who attempted to rehearse *Messiah* in Chester on his way to its first Dublin performance,[18] and Irish casual labourers.[19]

In Chester two anchorages were accessible to smaller vessels after 1660: the quay and warehouses across the Roodee from the Watergate, and the anchorage near the Dee Bridge and old cheese warehouse. Shipbuilding was also well established on the Roodee. Thirty ships were owned at Chester in 1672, and at least 25 (totalling 1,925 tons) in 1701, though not all were locally built. The industry seems to have expanded during the 1690s, when the company of Drawers of Dee complained that a new shipyard would encroach on the ground where they hung their fishing nets. The number of roperies on the Roodee had also grown by the 1690s.[20] Ships continued to be built on the Dee in the earlier 18th century, many intended for traders

1 *T.H.S.L.C.* cxiv. 114, 118–19.

2 Armour, 'Trade of Chester', 142; cf. *T.H.S.L.C.* cxiv. 125.

3 Cf. *Agrarian Hist. of Eng. and Wales*, v (1), 404; v (2), 273.

4 Armour, 'Trade of Chester', 78–9; R. Davis, *Rise of Eng. Shipping Ind. in 17th and 18th Cent.* 211.

5 *T.H.S.L.C.* cxiv. 109.

6 Armour, 'Trade of Chester', 32–3, 190–5, 250–4, 258–62, 300.

7 Ibid. 265–73; D. Woodward, 'Anglo-Irish Livestock Trade of 17th Cent.' *Irish Hist. Studies*, xviii. 489–523; C.C.A.L.S., ZML 4/509; R. C. Gwilliam, 'Chester Tanners and Parl. 1711–17', *J.C.A.S.* xliv. 41–9; 'Where Deva Spreads her Wizard Stream': *Trade and the Port of Chester*, ed. P. Carrington, 61–2.

8 Armour, 'Trade of Chester', 31–2, 273–4; C.C.A.L.S., ZAF 48E/4–6; ZAF 49C/24, 39.

9 C.C.A.L.S., ZAB 3, ff. 155v.–156, 182v.–183.

10 Ibid. ZAF 48E, no. 5.

11 Armour, 'Trade of Chester', 146, 275–7; cf. C.C.A.L.S., Cowper MSS., i, p. 330.

12 *V.C.H. Ches.* v (2), Fairs.

13 Poll Bks. 1732, 1747.

14 *Cal. S.P. Dom.* 1652–3, 312; *T.H.S.L.C.* lxxix. 141–74; G. W. Place, *Rise and Fall of Parkgate: Passenger Port for Irel. 1686–1815*, 1–2, 17, 61–5, 200–1, 212; Armour, 'Trade of Chester', 259.

15 Armour, 'Trade of Chester', 244–50; cf. *T.H.S.L.C.* cxiv. 104–5.

16 e.g. C.C.A.L.S., ZAB 3, ff. 152, 171v., 236, 264v.; ZAB 4, ff. 13v., 82, 120v., 173; ZTAB 2, f. 42v.; cf. *Diary of Henry Prescott*, i. 152–3, 230; ii. 314.

17 e.g. Wesley, *Works* (1872 edn.), iii. 14, 83, 107, 206, 425.

18 Burne, *Chester Cath.* 200–1.

19 C.C.A.L.S., Cowper MSS., i, pp. 255–7, 320–6.

20 Ibid. ZAB 2, ff. 178, 179v., 192; ZAB 3, ff. 15, 16, 25, 28, 47v., 49; ZAF 30/27; ZAF 47A/57–9; *Cal. S.P. Dom.* 1652–3, 511; Armour, 'Trade of Chester', 38, 40, 42, 44–5, 52–3, 187; 'Where Deva Spreads', ed. Carrington, 66–7; Place, *Parkgate*, 7; *T.H.S.L.C.* cxvi. 39–40.

elsewhere,[1] and a few shipwrights and ship's carpenters were freemen of the city.[2]

All traffic, however, was hindered by navigational hazards in the Dee, which despite repeated efforts from the 1660s were not removed until Nathaniel Kinderley's new cut along the Welsh shore was opened in 1737.[3] The reopening of the Dee did not halt Chester's relative decline as a port. About 1701 its shipowners had only 25 vessels, and in the early 1710s the total tonnage, no more than 3,400, was less than half that owned at Liverpool. By the 1730s it had fallen to *c.* 1,650 tons, barely a tenth of Liverpool's total, and in the late 1750s Chester's 1,000–1,400 tons was scarcely a twentieth of Liverpool's fleet.[4] The tonnage of all Chester's foreign and Irish trade, which in the 1710s had reached at least 9,500 tons both inward and outward, seldom exceeded 6,000 tons each way from the 1730s to the 1750s.[5]

OCCUPATIONS AND ECONOMIC REGULATION

In the later 17th century the Assembly still insisted that traders and craftsmen take up the freedom of the city before working there.[6] Between 1660 and 1699 at least 1,930 new freemen were admitted, an annual average exceeding 48. Chester's occupational structure was probably changing.[7] The proportion of new freemen in the wholesale and distributive trades fell from 24 per cent in the period 1660–74 to less than 20 per cent between 1675 and 1699, the manual crafts remained steady at about 46 per cent, and the service trades increased from 30 to 36 per cent. Markedly more professional men were being enfranchised. Occupations meeting basic needs for catering, clothing and textiles, and building amounted to about a third of all identifiable admissions: the leather crafts, with tanneries in Foregate Street and between St. John's church and the river, remained buoyant,[8] and there was steady growth in the building industry, metalworking, victualling, and the clothing and textile trades until the later 1670s. In 1679, however, the Tailors' company obstructed applications for admission, and in 1691 renewed its opposition on the

grounds that trade was poor. Feltmaking attracted fewer new freemen and attempts to revive cloth production were a failure.[9]

The corporation waived the rules for enfranchisement for a few men with desirable skills, including those of cooper, confectioner, distiller, soap boiler, musical instrument maker, watchmaker, upholsterer, periwig maker, button maker, tinplate worker, and sugar refiner.[10] Such admissions became more common in the 1690s, when a tobacco cutter, a silk weaver, a flax dresser, watchmakers, a sievemaker, a linen printer, a brassfounder, a forge smith, and a needlemaker were admitted under a new scale of fees, and several mariners and an inkhorn turner were enfranchised *gratis*.[11] Occupations in the city became much more diverse in consequence, but the corporation's policy was not always welcome to the guilds, and it overruled opposition to discretionary admissions from the Innholders, the Smiths and Pewterers, the Joiners and Carvers, and others.[12]

The basic urban trades remained numerically important after 1700:[13] of *c.* 1,000 resident craftsmen and tradesmen polled in 1732 and 1747, almost a sixth supplied food and drink, another sixth were engaged in construction, and almost a fifth in the clothing trades. There were well over 50 tailors,[14] but only a few silk weavers or dyers and barely 20 woollen weavers; the fulling mill on the Dee was converted after 1725 for making paper and snuff.[15] Fifty or more men specialized in making felt hats. Among the distributive trades the most numerous were chandlers and ironmongers. From the late 17th century several workshops made clay tobacco pipes,[16] a trade supporting *c.* 25 workmen by the 1730s. The Pembertons, who by 1700 had a ropewalk under the city's western walls, were still in business *c.* 1760,[17] and another ropemaker was established from 1733 close to the Water Tower.[18] Chester's largest specialism, occupying possibly a fifth of its skilled workers, remained leather and its products, using skins produced locally or imported from Ireland and the Mediterranean.[19] Besides tanners and curriers, there were *c.* 25 wet glovers, making leather gloves mainly in workshops between the river and the south-

1 *T.H.S.L.C.* cxvi. 55–62; Armour, 'Trade of Chester', 40–2, 45; cf. C. Fiennes, *Journeys*, ed. C. Morris, 179; C.C.A.L.S., ZAB 4, f. 144.

2 e.g. *Rolls of Freemen of Chester*, ii, index, s.vv. shipbuilder, ship-carpenter; cf. C.C.A.L.S., ZAB 4, f. 41v.; ZAF 50B, no. 31.

3 *V.C.H. Ches.* v (2), Water Transport: River.

4 Armour, 'Trade of Chester', 53; *T.H.S.L.C.* cxvi. 40–1.

5 *T.H.S.L.C.* cxiv. 106, 109.

6 e.g. C.C.A.L.S., ZAB 2, f. 182v.; ZAB 3, ff. 38, 61, 71.

7 *Rolls of Freemen of Chester*, i, pp. xv–xvi; except where otherwise stated what follows is based on figures compiled from that source by Miss S. Richardson.

8 Johnson, 'Aspects', 298; Armour, 'Trade of Chester', 34–6; *Cal. S.P. Dom.* 1666–7, 129.

9 C.C.A.L.S., ZAB 2, ff. 182v., 191v., 192v.; ZAB 3, f. 32; ZAF 46A/29; ZML 4/492; Armour, 'Trade of Chester', 36–7.

10 C.C.A.L.S., ZAB 2, ff. 151, 164v.–165, 167, 170, 171, 189; ZAF 40B/20.

11 Ibid. ZAB 3, ff. 2v., 23v.–24, 25v., 26v.–27, 34, 38, 43v., 50, 52v., 64v., 73, 74v., 78, 82v., 85v.

12 Ibid. ZAB 2, ff. 187v., 195v.–196, 197v.; ZAF 39A/35–9; ZAF 47E *passim*.

13 Rest of para. based on *Rolls of Freemen of Chester*, ii.

14 Cf. *Diary of Henry Prescott*, i. 129; ii. 313, 315, 641.

15 *V.C.H. Ches.* v (2), Mills and Fisheries: Dee Fulling Mills.

16 *Rolls of Freemen of Chester*, i. 161–2, and index s.v. pipemaker.

17 Ibid. ii, index s.v. ropier; C.C.A.L.S., ZAB 3, ff. 116, 120v.; ZAB 4, ff. 69, 91v., 214v.; ZCHB 3, f. 255v.; *Diary of Henry Prescott*, i. 292–3; *Adams's Weekly Courant*, 13 May 1761, p. 3.

18 C.C.A.L.S., ZAB 4, ff. 54v., 70, 114, 142v.

19 *T.H.S.L.C.* cxiv. 117; Armour, 'Trade of Chester', 209.

western walls.[1] Most numerous were the shoemakers, for whom a few corkcutters produced heels.

The guild system, involving active regulation by individual companies and the attempted exclusion of unfree interlopers, continued well into the 18th century;[2] until *c.* 1730 the city authorities were closely concerned with guild affairs, trying to settle internal differences and to ensure the correct enrolment of apprenticeship indentures, though the magistrates' attempts to regulate wages seem to have ended well before 1700.[3] Prolonged demarcation disputes from the 1660s to the 1690s among craftsmen in the building industry, especially joiners and carpenters, perhaps resulted from its expansion.[4] The corporation several times prevented the formation of new guilds, placing six masons in the Carpenters' company *c.* 1691, and forbidding new guilds for both pewterers and plasterers, the latter in 1705.[5] The Tanners' company was the most active in defence of its members' interests after 1700.[6] In the 1710s, in concert with tanners' guilds in London and elsewhere, it campaigned against new taxes on leather and sought to restrict the export of oak bark to Irish competitors.[7] The Butchers, presumably to limit numbers, doubled their entry charge for 'foreigners' to £20 in the 1730s, and required any member taking an apprentice also to pay £20.[8] About 1750 they still tried to enforce a traditional closing time for butchers' stalls in the shambles.[9]

Numbers of guild members were falling sharply by 1740 as the guilds turned themselves into social clubs,[10] and in most trades fewer men took up the freedom from the 1730s, except when elections were imminent: in 1732 qualified resident applicants accounted for almost three quarters of *c.* 600 freemen admitted in the three months before a mayoral election.[11]

SHOPPING

The city's fairs declined during the later 17th century then revived after 1700, partly through the growing trade in Irish linen, and partly through horse dealing, which drew purchasers from a wide area.[12] A flourishing trade in saddle, pack, and draught animals also developed in Chester's markets, and focused on the inns because innkeepers bought horses either for resale or for hiring to travellers.[13] By the later 17th century Chester had largely overcome competition from smaller markets in the region, and as late as 1677 the corporation successfully opposed a proposed market and fair at Neston.[14] Chester's role as the main regional market was enhanced by the expansion of livestock farming in the county, especially in the production of cheese, which was marketed by local cheese factors and sent through the port or overland to cheesemongers in London and elsewhere.[15] By 1700 the city was publicizing its markets and fairs in national and local newspapers.[16]

The city played an important part in the distribution of wine and especially groceries, including luxury foodstuffs imported from abroad through London or increasingly Liverpool.[17] There were, however, sporadic difficulties over the ways ordinary victuals were produced and sold. In the 1670s the tightly regulated bakers renewed their campaign to exclude country bakers from the markets.[18] The corporation was still trying to enforce the assize of bread *c.* 1710, and in 1736 reaffirmed the right of country bakers to sell in the markets at prices set by itself.[19] During the 1690s the Butchers' company tried to monopolize the cheaper standings at the new flesh shambles and seized meat sold by country butchers,[20] though by the 1720s the country butchers' right to trade was established.[21] The Fishmongers' company, too, complained about sales by unfree interlopers during the 1670s.[22]

From the 1670s Chester's development as a shopping centre led to frequent applications for leases of plots of land for building, and of shops and chambers in the Rows.[23] Imports of luxuries and a great variety of other goods from London stimulated both wholesaling and retailing, and well stocked shops began to attract more gentry, professionals, and wealthier country

1 e.g. C.C.A.L.S., ZAB 3, ff. 119, 177v., 187, 192v., 196, 207v., 255v.; ZAB 4, f. 152v.; *Diary of Henry Prescott*, ii. 534.
2 *V.C.H. Ches.* v (2), Craft Guilds: Economic Regulation; C.C.A.L.S., ZAB 3, f. 27v.; ZG 5/1; ZG 6/2–5; ZG 8/6; ZG 11/1; ZG 19/1; ZG 21/2, 4; ZG 22/1; ZG 23/4; Johnson, 'Aspects', 298; *J.C.A.S.* n.s. v. 22; xviii. 151–2; xx. 48–9, 74; xxi. 92–3, 100–5, 109–11; xxii. 66, 71–2, 74–7; *T.L.C.A.S.* lxix. 106–7.
3 C.C.A.L.S., ZAB 2, f. 134; ZAB 3, f. 29; ZMF 113; Woodward, *Men at Work*, 12, 174–7, 189, 202.
4 C.C.A.L.S., ZAB 2, ff. 150v., 158–9, 172, 192, 197; ZAF 39B/20; ZAF 40C/35; ZAF 41H/8.
5 C.C.A.L.S., ZAB 2, f. 195; ZAB 3, ff. 30, 31v., 34, 134v.; cf. ZAF 48B, nos. 76, 94.
6 e.g. ibid. ZAB 3, f. 179.
7 Ibid. ZG 21/4, petition at front; *J.C.A.S.* xliv. 41–9.
8 C.C.A.L.S., ZG 5/1, s.a. 1731–6.
9 Ibid. ZAF 53, pt. 5 (Butchers' petition).
10 *V.C.H. Ches.* v (2), Craft Guilds: Activities after 1750.
11 *Rolls of Freemen of Chester*, ii. 282–307.

12 *Cal. S.P. Dom.* 1682, 280; 1693, 177, 183; Willan, *Inland Trade*, 91, 97–8; Armour, 'Trade of Chester', 259; Hodson, *Ches. 1660–1780*, 115; *V.C.H. Ches.* v (2), Fairs.
13 *J.C.A.S.* lxii. 91–3, 98–103.
14 C.C.A.L.S., ZAB 2, f. 186; *Cal. S.P. Dom.* 1677–8, 368; Place, *Parkgate*, 243.
15 *Agrarian Hist. of Eng. and Wales*, v (1), 131, 153–4; *T.H.S.L.C.* cxliv. 5–6, 8, 19–20; Armour, 'Trade of Chester', 116, 120, 122–3.
16 e.g. C.C.A.L.S., ZAB 3, ff. 109, 110v.; ZTAB 6, f. 17v.
17 Willan, *Eng. Coasting Trade*, 104–5.
18 C.C.A.L.S., ZAB 2, f. 147; *Cal. S.P. Dom.* 1668–9, 368; 1670, 44; 1672–3, 249, 293.
19 C.C.A.L.S., ZAB 4, f. 82; ZAF 52, pt. 3 (Bakers' petition); cf. ZQSF 90/2/120, 175.
20 Ibid. ZAB 2, f. 152; ZAB 3, ff. 63v., 66v.; ZMF 113.
21 Ibid. ZG 5/1, f. 197.
22 Ibid. ZAB 3, ff. 62v.–63, 90; ZAF 40G/39; ZMF 113.
23 Ibid. ZAB 2 *passim*.

people. By 1700 the central shopping area was thus becoming more clearly defined, with the beginnings of the later separation of high-class retailers and more workaday shops in distinct areas of the city.[1] In particular Eastgate Street in the earlier 18th century was increasingly given over to high-class shops, though some older methods of retailing persisted: as late as the 1760s London milliners hired premises in the street during the fairs to put their goods on view.[2]

To accommodate visitors on business or pleasure, and especially those travelling between England and Ireland, there were many inns, mostly clustered in the main central streets and Foregate Street. In 1686 the city's 682 guest beds and stabling for 871 horses far exceeded the figures for any other place in the North-West.[3] The importance of the city's role within the region was emphasized in other ways, for example by the existence of regular coach services to London,[4] by its continuing status as a head port for customs administration, based on the customs house in Watergate Street,[5] and by the assay office set up permanently in 1700.[6]

SOCIAL CONDITIONS

In the mid 1660s Chester had 1,666 households which paid tax on 4,273 hearths,[7] a low average of 2.5 hearths a household. Two fifths of the households (671 in number) were exempt because of poverty and in all almost half (781 households) had only one or no hearth. The most modest houses, those with no more than two hearths, accounted for some two thirds of the city's dwellings and accommodated not only the very poor but also many labourers and humbler craftsmen, especially in the textile and leather industries. About a sixth of householders had three or four hearths, among them many master craftsmen, shopkeepers, butchers, bakers, small-scale dealers, and clergy. Those with five or six hearths included cathedral clergy, merchants, drapers, and medical men. Householders taxed on seven, eight, or nine hearths comprised aldermen, Sir Peter Pindar, Bt. (the collector of customs in the port), a goldsmith, the subdean Dr. William Bispham, and several merchants and ironmongers. Occupiers with 10 or 11 hearths included the former recorder John Ratcliffe and Sir Richard Grosvenor. Among householders with 12 or 13 hearths were the diocesan chancellor John Wainwright and the castle governor

Sir Geoffrey Shakerley. Lady Calveley (Mary, widow of Sir Hugh Calveley of Lea)[8] and Lady Kilmorey (Eleanor, widow of Robert Needham, Viscount Kilmorey)[9] each had 16 hearths and the bishop's palace 17, as did two inns. The two largest establishments in the city, with 20 and 33 hearths, were also inns. Some five per cent of families were headed by armigerous or professional people, but the town houses of the gentry were still mostly modest, as many of them containing only two, three, or four hearths as had thirteen or more. There was some social segregation: many of the poorer sort dwelt in the outer wards, the cathedral clergy around the precinct, tanners mainly in St. Giles's ward, and exchequer officials, lawyers, and gentry in Bridge Street and Watergate Street.

In the later 17th century the Assembly was often anxious lest vagrants be attracted to Chester and add to the numbers of its poor. In the 1660s it ordered the constables to make monthly reports on 'undersettlers' to the magistrates,[10] but thereafter left the aldermen, sitting as J.P.s in the inner Pentice, to deal with vagrants and supervise the regular relief provided by parish officers. In the 1690s the magistrates occasionally made supplementary payments, for instance to shipwrecked seamen and indigent travellers with passes.[11] The able-bodied poor were sent to the house of correction, which caused the authorities many difficulties. There was already dissatisfaction with the master, John Barker, in 1660 when the Weavers' company claimed that it could put more poor people to work than the 60 whom he employed. The Assembly eventually removed him in 1670.[12] In 1675 a weaver and a woolcomber came from Norwich to employ the poor in a new manufactory, with unknown success, and the objective of providing work and correction together was still being pursued in 1698, in a scheme to set the poor to work in silk weaving.[13]

Until the new house of industry was opened in 1759 the poor were maintained by their own parishes, some of which founded poorhouses, including St. John's c. 1730 and St. Oswald's by 1750.[14] The law of settlement was, however, handled centrally for the whole city by the magistrates sitting in the inner Pentice, with individual settlement rights formally certified by quarter sessions to the relevant parish.[15] By the 1740s the city also paid centrally for the removal

1 *T.H.S.L.C.* cxliv. 18, 33; S. I. Mitchell, 'Retailing in 18th-and Early 19th-Cent. Ches.' *T.H.S.L.C.* cxxx. 45–6.

2 e.g. *Adams's Weekly Courant*, 9 June 1747, p. 4; 27 Sept. 1748, p. 3; 8–15 Apr. 1755, p. 3; 17–24 June 1755, p. 3; 26 June 1758, p. 3; 17 June 1760, p. 2; 7 Oct. 1760, pp. 2–3.

3 P.R.O., WO 30/48, ff. 21v.–22v., 25–27v., and *passim*.

4 J. Ogilby, *Britannia*, 41, 46; Place, *Parkgate*, 8, 140, 231; Armour, 'Trade of Chester', 243; C.C.A.L.S., ZAF 39A/35–9; *Cal. S.P. Dom.* 1666–7, 129; 1691–2, 495.

5 Armour, 'Trade of Chester', 44–5, 155, 157, 160, 162–3; C.C.A.L.S., ZAF 48E/52.

6 *V.C.H. Ches.* v (2), Craft Guilds: Economic Regulation.

7 Rest of this para. and next based on 'Hearth Tax Returns for

City of Chester, 1664–5', *Miscellanies*, v (R.S.L.C. lii), 3–83 and tables derived from the latter kindly supplied by Mr. N. J. Alldridge; cf. E. J. D. Morrison, 'Hearth Tax in Chester', *J.C.A.S.* xxxvi. 31–43.   8 Ormerod, *Hist. Ches.* ii. 769.

9 *Complete Peerage*, vii. 261.

10 C.C.A.L.S., ZAB 2, ff. 126, 156v.

11 Ibid. ZAB 3, f. 42; ZMF 113.

12 Ibid. ZAB 2, ff. 125v., 130v., 143, 150, 153v., 166v.–167, 183v., 197; ZAF 38C/13, 40.

13 Ibid. ZAB 2, ff. 182v., 184A; ZAF 47A/9; ZML 4/492.

14 R. V. H. Burne, 'Treatment of Poor in 18th Cent. in Chester', *J.C.A.S.* lii. 33–48; idem, *Chester Cath.* 210–16.

15 e.g. C.C.A.L.S., ZMIP 16, 36, 55; ZQSF 94–8.

of vagrants, sometimes through the master of the house of correction.[1]

Public poor relief was augmented after 1660 by new privately endowed charities, several of which used John Vernon's of 1617 as a model. They were mainly under corporation control and provided bread, clothing, shelter, or assistance, but in the main only for freemen and their families. The endowments virtually dried up after 1700 and even bequests for parochial charities diminished after 1720. Members of the wealthiest nonconformist congregation, the Presbyterians, had their own charities.[2] Pensions and places in the corporation's almshouses were granted according to lists drawn up for the Assembly,[3] and by the 1750s potential almsmen were paying for their names to be included.[4] Newer types of charitable giving were exemplified by the foundation of the Blue Coat schools for boys (1700) and girls (1720),[5] and by Peter Cotton's bequest in 1716 of £100 for medical relief for the poor and £50 for the distribution of devotional books in rotation among the poor of each parish.[6]

CHESTER AS A COUNTY RESORT

The cultural life of Chester in the century after the Restoration reflected its growing importance as a social centre for the gentry of the surrounding area and as a place where many leisured families resided. One sign was the very early establishment of freemasonry: the 'Society' of which Randle Holme III (1627–1700) was a member *c.* 1673 was evidently one of the first permanent lodges in England. At that date he was the only gentleman involved, his 25 companions being mostly well-off employers, notably in the building trades. By 1725 the city had three separate lodges, more than in any other provincial town, who met at the Sun, Spread Eagle, and Castle and Falcon inns. Membership had shifted decisively towards country gentlemen, members of the urban élite, and army officers from the garrison. The master of the Sun lodge, Colonel Francis Columbine, was the first Provincial Grand Master in the country.[7]

Initially there was little increase in cultural interests

or literary habits, though enough business for stationers and perhaps bookbinding and basic printing.[8] In 1668 Peter Bodvile claimed to have the only bookshop in the city, but there were certainly others by 1685, when John Minshull and his son had a stock valued at £1,000.[9] Randle Holme III maintained the family tradition as a deputy herald and heraldic painter and was probably involved in printing and publishing, notably his own large-scale but uncompleted *Academy of Armory*. His son, Randle Holme IV (1659–1707), continued the heraldic work and was responsible for supplementing, arranging, and partly indexing the antiquarian and genealogical collections made by his forebears. The collections were dispersed after his death, but some 270 volumes were bought by Edward Harley, earl of Oxford, and thus passed with the Harleian manuscripts into national ownership in 1753.[10] The main scholarly writers in Chester were clergymen: Dean James Arderne as a controversialist; Bishop John Pearson in theology and patristics; and the Presbyterian minister Matthew Henry on hymns, catechism, prayer, and biblical studies. Henry's brother-in-law John Tylston (1663–99), a nonconformist physician who spent some time in Chester, published on medical experiments, while the eminent mathematician John Wilkins was bishop of Chester 1668–72 and the astronomer Edmund Halley was deputy comptroller of the Chester mint during its brief existence 1696–8.[11]

In the earlier 18th century there were usually at least two booksellers, handling the scholarly libraries of deceased local clergy and gentlemen.[12] From the early 1710s one or two worked their own presses, producing mostly sermons and other religious and educational works. One also began to print books in Welsh.[13] William Cooke started a local newspaper in 1721, rivalled from 1732 and then driven out of business by another, later the *Chester Courant*, founded by Roger Adams (d. 1741) and continued by his widow Elizabeth and her successors into the late 18th century.[14]

After 1660 Chester silversmiths found a good local

---

1 e.g. ibid. ZTAB 5, ff. 54, 62v., 79v., 87, 105; ZTAB 6, ff. 8, 27; cf. ZAB 4, ff. 188v.–189.

2 Ibid. ZAB 2, f. 129; ZAB 3, ff. 24, 27v.; ZCHB 3, ff. 188–189v., 227, 229; ZML 6/190; *V.C.H. Ches.* v (2), Charities for the Poor.

3 C.C.A.L.S., ZAF 47–54 *passim*.

4 Ibid. ZAB 4, f. 161v.   5 *V.C.H. Ches.* v (2), Education.

6 *31st Rep. Com. Char.* 365; cf. C.C.A.L.S., ZAB 3, ff. 238v.–239; ZTAB 6, f. 13v.

7 D. Stevenson, *Origins of Freemasonry: Scotland's Century, 1590–1710*, 225, 229; D. Knoop and G. P. Jones, *Genesis of Freemasonry*, 15, 132–3, 139–40, 144–5, 150–2, 155; R. H. Gough Smallwood, *Early Freemasonry in Chester and Col. Francis Columbine* [Chester, 1937], reprinted from *Trans. Quatuor Coronati Lodge*, l. 77–91. This para. was contributed by Dr. C. P. Lewis.

8 C.C.A.L.S., ZAB 2, f. 185; ZAF 37A/26; ZCHB 3, f. 245v.;

D. Nuttall, 'Hist. of Printing in Chester', *J.C.A.S.* liv. 40–2.

9 C.C.A.L.S., ZAB 2, ff. 162v., 187v.; ZAF 42A/25; *Diary of Dr. Thomas Cartwright* (Camd. Soc. [1st ser.], xxii), 34.

10 *J.C.A.S.* n.s. iv. 137–53, 157–60, 163–70; liv. 41–51; *Complete Peerage*, x. 267–8.

11 Burne, *Chester Cath.* 140–1; D. Harley, 'Good Physician and Godly Doctor: John Tylston of Chester', *17th Cent.* ix. 93 sqq., 102, 108; *New Hist. of Royal Mint*, ed. C. E. Challis, 396; *D.N.B.*

12 R. Stewart-Brown, 'Stationers, Booksellers, and Printers of Chester to *c.* 1800', *T.H.S.L.C.* lxxxiii. 109–11, 122–4, 128, 132–9, 142–3; *Diary of Henry Prescott*, ii. 347; *Adams's Weekly Courant*, 22–9 Nov. 1757, p. 3; 4 Apr. 1758, p. 3; 6 Oct. 1761, p. 2.

13 *J.C.A.S.* liv. 51–9; cf. M. Parry, 'Chester Welsh Printing', ibid. xxi. 57–8, 67.

14 Ibid. liv. 53–7; *V.C.H. Ches.* v (2), Newspapers.

demand for their work,[1] but painters were few. In 1671–2 the royal arms and pictures of Justice and Prudence were drawn for the portmote court by Elnathan Rowlandson, apparently a local man,[2] and about 1715 a miniature painter planned to move from Liverpool to Chester, where there were no competitors.[3] Campanology flourished among a select group of gentry, following the foundation in 1686 of the Gentlemen Bellringers of St. John's by Mayor Edward Oulton and others.[4] In the field of orthodox music, there was a musical instrument maker in Chester by 1670, the tradition of religious music was revived at the cathedral from 1660 under Dean Henry Bridgeman, and the four city waits, a paid ensemble with their own livery, performed at public celebrations and civic ceremonies.[5]

In reaction to the rigours of the Interregnum the traditional civic ceremonies enjoyed a brief revival after 1660 before succumbing to a fear of disorder and the growth of a new puritanical spirit. The Christmas watch and the Midsummer show were both in effect abandoned in 1678.[6] Less elaborate forms of ceremonial continued, such as civic processions to church services and occasional beatings of the bounds.[7] Public rejoicing, with bellringing, pageantry, and drinking, accompanied the arrival of a new charter, news of military victories, and the foundation of the Chester mint.[8] The Assembly also marked the reception of William III and the arrival of notables such as Bishop Cartwright, a Secretary of State, and the lords lieutenant and lords justice of Ireland.[9]

All those entertainments attracted people from elsewhere. Visitors were also drawn by cathedral services, diocesan administration, county parliamentary elections, the palatinate law courts, the fairs, markets, shops, inns, and alehouses,[10] and increasingly by the specialized services offered by teachers of writing and dancing, physicians and surgeons, vintners, watch-

makers, cabinetmakers, tobacconists, and many others.[11] From the 1690s, for example, several surgeons and usually two or three physicians practised in the city.[12] Chester was more and more a magnet for country gentry. Mayors gave venison feasts where country gentlemen sat down with prominent citizens, and many private occasions of wining, dining, and merrymaking allowed the mingling of lawyers, cathedral dignitaries, civic families, county figures, and urban gentry.[13] After the abolition of the Midsummer show the greatest annual attraction was the horse races held on St. George's Day, which were closely supervised by the Assembly.[14] Other outdoor amenities included archery and bowls, promenading on the city walls (as enjoyed by Ralph Thoresby and Celia Fiennes), and gardens in the open spaces on the west side of the city.[15]

All those attractions were enhanced in the earlier 18th century. The walls were increasingly used for recreation by visitors and residents alike after the city had them repaired and flagged from 1707. They became a favoured promenade, for example, of the deputy diocesan registrar Henry Prescott in his declining years.[16] By the 1720s the city had over 20 inns and public houses, where Prescott and his friends met for convivial purposes either as members of clubs or informally.[17] Leading establishments included the White Talbot in Eastgate Street, extensively rebuilt from the 1710s by its owners, the Talbot dukes and earls of Shrewsbury,[18] the ancient Blossoms in Foregate Street, rebuilt c. 1718,[19] and the White Bear in Bridge Street, rebuilt c. 1747.[20] In the 1740s there were almost 60 public houses and at least as many licensed beer-sellers.[21]

From c. 1700 the newly built Exchange had on its ground floor a coffee house, where newsletters and gazettes from London were available,[22] and there was

1 *J.C.A.S.* liii. 1–189; M. H. Ridgway, *Chester Silver, 1727–1837*.

2 C.C.A.L.S., ZAB 2, ff. 176v., 197.

3 Ibid. ZAB 3, f. 225v.

4 J. W. Clarke, 'Chester Scholars or Gentlemen Bellringers of St. John's', *J.C.A.S.* xl. 55–7.

5 C.C.A.L.S., ZAB 2, ff. 157v., 175v.; ZAF 40B/20.

6 *V.C.H. Ches.* v (2), Plays, Sports, and Customs before 1700: City Watches and Midsummer Show.

7 C.C.A.L.S., ZAB 2, f. 181; ZAB 3, ff. 5v., 91; *V.C.H. Ches.* v (2), Local Government Boundaries: The Medieval Liberties.

8 C.C.A.L.S., ZMF 113; *J.C.A.S.* xxviii. 200; *New Hist. Mint*, ed. Challis, 385–6; Hodson, *Ches. 1660–1780*, 104.

9 C.C.A.L.S., ZAB 3, ff. 25v.–26, 92; *Cal. S.P. Dom. 1695*, 195; 1697, 173, 179; *Diary of Thos. Cartwright*, 74–5; Childs, *Army*, 100; Hodson, *Ches. 1660–1780*, 104.

10 C.C.A.L.S., ZAB 3, f. 40v.; ZMF 113; *V.C.H. Ches.* ii. 56–8; P. Clark, *Eng. Alehouse*, 53; above, this section (Shopping).

11 C.C.A.L.S., ZAB 3, ff. 23v.–24, 26v.–27v., 43v., 69; ZAF 39B/25; ZAF 48E/91; ZQSF 87 (1695–6); *Chetham Miscellanies*, iii (Chetham Soc. N.S. lxxiii), 37–8, 56, 58; *Autobiography of Mrs. Alice Thornton* (Surtees Soc. lxii), 31.

12 e.g. C.C.A.L.S., ZAF 50H, no. 9; *Diary of Henry Prescott*, i. 104; ii. 358; *Adams's Weekly Courant*, 12 Apr. 1748, p. 4; *Rolls of Freemen of Chester*, ii, index s.v. chirurgeon.

13 e.g. *Cal. S.P. Dom. 1682*, 280; *Diary of Revd. Henry Newcome* (Chetham Soc. [o.s.], xviii), 98–9; *Diary of Thos. Cartwright*, 15–19, 22–3, 26–7, 78.

14 *V.C.H. Ches.* v (2), Chester Races.

15 C.C.A.L.S., ZAB 2, ff. 146, 185v., 197; ZAB 3, f. 78; ZQSF 88 (1698); *Chester: Contemporary Descriptions*, ed. D. M. Palliser, 16–17.

16 *Diary of Henry Prescott*, i. 2–3, 68, 129–30, 280, and *passim*; ii. 568 and *passim*; *Contemporary Descriptions*, ed. Palliser, 18, 22–3; D. Defoe, *Tour thro' Whole Island of G.B.* (Everyman edn.), ii. 69; Wesley, *Works* (1872 edn.), ii. 268; *V.C.H. Ches.* v (2), City Walls and Gates: Medieval and Later.

17 *Diary of Henry Prescott*, i. 2–3, 22, 42, 74, 101, 112, 118, 123, 125, 166, 173, 257, 276, and *passim*; ii. 344–5, 368, 395, 478, 565–6, 689, and *passim*.

18 C.C.A.L.S., ZAB 3, ff. 221–2; ZAB 4, f. 26 and v.

19 Ibid. ZAB 3, f. 241v.

20 *Adams's Weekly Courant*, 24 Mar. 1747, p. 4.

21 C.C.A.L.S., ZQRL 3, ff. 29v.–32v., 38v.–42v., 52–56v., 66v.–70, and at f. 80.

22 e.g. *Diary of Henry Prescott*, i. 12, 31, 38, 53, 93, 100, and *passim*; ii. 336, 344, 349, 376, and *passim*; cf. C.C.A.L.S., ZTAB 2, f. 4v.

another on Castle Lane by 1708, perhaps that later called the Countess.[1] In the 1750s there was another coffee house at the Red Dog, on Eastgate Street.[2] From the 1710s the city's two or three dancing masters staged public balls once a year, usually at Christmas, in the common hall at the Exchange, either with or without official permission.[3] By the mid 1740s Booth Mansion north of Watergate Street also accommodated assembly rooms, which as 'Mr. Eaton's Great Room' gave space in the 1750s for such diversions as rope dancing, fire eating, and a learned dog. It closed in 1758.[4] By 1710 a public cold bath was open at Boughton.[5] Chester's principal attractions for outsiders were the races and the fairs, especially the Midsummer fair, where entertainments were put on by the 1710s.[6] Some county gentry also came in for the assize sessions held in spring and autumn and from 1760 the theatrical season extended into the period of the assizes.[7]

Chester in 1660 had few public services,[8] but from the 1680s the corporation took more interest in the city's sanitary condition and appearance, perhaps aware of their importance to residents and visitors alike. Detailed arrangements were made for disposing of rubbish and cleaning the Rows and main streets,[9] the city pavior was instructed to keep pavements in good repair, and citizens were required to hang lights at their doors.[10]

The pace of civic improvement picked up in the 1690s with improvements to the water supply[11] and the start of work on the Exchange, an intentionally handsome building, coherently designed.[12] For some time the Assembly had been controlling encroachments on the main streets, in an attempt to secure even, uniform frontages, especially in the Rows.[13] Street repair and cleaning had long been the responsibility of householders. In 1712 the macebearer was made liable for streets alongside the city's own property,[14] and by the late 1720s the grand juries responsible for enforcing all such duties increasingly expected the city's treasurers to do the repairs.[15] About 1760 a foot passage was made at the Northgate, partly to save children from being run over.[16] As well as the city streets and the carriageways of the roads approaching Chester,[17] the corporation maintained the Cop, planned in 1706 and completed in 1710, an embankment which protected the Roodee from flooding.[18] Better measures for fire protection were taken in 1709,[19] and street lamps were provided at the Exchange and the Pentice in 1708.[20] Such official measures to improve the environment and the face of the city were, like the earlier traditional ceremonies and observances, a means of promoting a sense of civic dignity and pride, and giving Chester an aspect in keeping with its standing as a cathedral city and county capital.

1 *Diary of Henry Prescott*, i. 190, 287; ii. 426.
2 e.g. *Adams's Weekly Courant*, 22–9 Sept. 1757, p. 4; 8 Jan. 1760, p. 3.
3 *Rolls of Freemen of Chester*, ii. 226; C.C.A.L.S., ZAB 3, ff. 157, 249v.–250, 268, 271; ZAB 4, ff. 4, 20v.
4 Lavaux, *Plan of Chester*; *Adams's Weekly Courant*, 15–22 Apr. 1755, p. 3; 22–9 Sept. 1755, p. 3; 31 Jan. 1758, p. 4; 26 Dec. 1758, p. 3.
5 *Diary of Henry Prescott*, ii. 320, 322.
6 Ibid. i. 40, 45, 143, 280; ii. 363–4, 384, 572, 630.
7 e.g. *Adams's Weekly Courant*, 22 July 1760, p. 3; 29 July 1760, p. 3; 19 Aug. 1760, p. 2; 26 Aug. 1760, p. 3; 9 Sept. 1760, p. 3.
8 *V.C.H. Ches.* v (2), Law and Order: Fire Service; Public Utilities: Water.
9 C.C.A.L.S., ZAB 3, ff. 10, 33, 58, 84v.–85; ZMF 113; ZML 4/577.

10 Ibid. ZAB 3, ff. 6, 37v., 45–7.
11 *V.C.H. Ches.* v (2), Public Utilities: Water.
12 Ibid. Municipal Buildings: Exchange. Plate 25.
13 C.C.A.L.S., ZAB 2, ff. 171, 174v., 192v., 194v.; ZAF 41B/30, 33, 53, 69; *V.C.H. Ches.* v (2), The Rows: Rebuilding and Enclosure.
14 C.C.A.L.S., ZAB 3, f. 191v.
15 Ibid. ZQSF 90–100; cf. ZML 4/577.
16 Ibid. ZAB 4, f. 191v.
17 e.g. ibid. ZAB 3, ff. 118, 163v., 188v.–189, 201–2, 244v.–245, 270v.; ZAB 4, ff. 7v., 16v., 18, 103, 158, 179, 183v.; ZTAB 2–6 *passim*.
18 Ibid. ZAB 3, ff. 141, 144, 176, 179v., 182; *Diary of Henry Prescott*, i. 268–70, 272.
19 *V.C.H. Ches.* v (2), Law and Order: Fire Service.
20 C.C.A.L.S., ZAB 3, ff. 128v., 131; ZCHB 3, f. 259v.

LATE GEORGIAN AND VICTORIAN CHESTER 1762–1914

IN THE 1760s Chester was still a regional capital despite the rise of Liverpool and Manchester. It dominated the economy of the western half of Cheshire and north-east Wales, and provided a focus for the leisured classes of a much larger area.[1] On the other hand, its traditional manufactures were already in decline, its maritime trade was as good as dead, and its politics were completely overshadowed by the Grosvenors of Eaton Hall. The creation of new institutions of local government in 1757 and 1762 and repeated but unsuccessful challenges to the Grosvenor interest from the 1770s were not harbingers of renewed vitality, but political reform at a national level in the 1830s freed municipal politics from Grosvenor influence and was followed shortly by thirty years of railway-led industrialization and population growth. The boom faltered after 1870, but Chester was able by 1914 to reposition itself as a county town, historic cathedral city, and tourist centre which provided a wide range of shops and other services for a still sizeable hinterland.

CITY GOVERNMENT AND POLITICS

CITY GOVERNMENT, 1762–1835

The long-standing institutions of civic administration which operated in the earlier 18th century – the Assembly and its informal inner circle – were supplemented in 1762 by two new bodies, a board of poor-law guardians and an improvement commission.[2] Although both were modern institutions of local government, and although Chester was relatively early among provincial towns in acquiring them, neither marked a radical departure, not least because their memberships overlapped with that of the Assembly, though members of the latter apparently took little part in the affairs of the board of guardians.[3] The influence of the Assembly's leading figures was nevertheless reinforced rather than undermined by the new bodies, and the Assembly continued to govern the city, by and large, in wholly traditional ways, as an oligarchy tied to the political interest of the Grosvenor family of Eaton Hall.[4]

THE ASSEMBLY

The outward forms of city government re-established after the upheaval of the mid 1690s[5] continued with little alteration until 1835. The corporation or Assembly of 24 aldermen and 40 common councilmen filled vacancies by co-option, and elected from among its ranks the mayor, recorder, sheriffs, and lesser officials. The exclusion of any real participation by the large number of freemen was defended at law several times at great expense and amid increasing political turmoil.[6]

On average two or three new councilmen were recruited each year to fill places vacated by death, promotion to alderman, or the occasional resignation.[7] A few refused office and were fined £50,[8] and in 1775 an attorney claimed exemption and was discharged.[9] In all there were some 200 new Assemblymen during the period, drawn mainly from a widening circle of

---

1 For social and cultural activities in this period, *V.C.H. Ches.* v (2), esp. Craft Guilds: Activities after 1750; Leisure and Culture, *passim.*

2 Thanks are offered to Mrs. Joy Campbell, who provided additional references for the whole section on city government and politics, esp. from local newspapers, and to Dr. M. F. Cragoe, who commented on a draft.

3 Below, this section (Poor Law).

4 Below, this chapter: Politics, 1762–1835.

5 Above, Early Modern Chester: City Government and Politics, 1662–1762 (City Politics, City Government).

6 *Rep. Com. Mun. Corp.* pp. 2619–23; below, this chapter: Politics, 1762–1835.

7 This para. and next based on C.C.A.L.S., ZAB 4–6.

8 Ibid. ZAB 5, p. 458; *Rep. Com. Mun. Corp.* p. 2626.

9 C.C.A.L.S., ZAB 4, f. 310v.

well-to-do commercial and mercantile occupations. About half were merchants or retailers in the wealthier trades, notably grocers, druggists, wine merchants, and linendrapers. Among manufacturers only the leather trades were well represented, and as in earlier periods very few members of the corporation were involved in the building trades, food retailing, or clothing manufacture. More new councilmen were styled gentleman or esquire than followed any single occupation. The Grosvenors and their landed allies, especially the Williams-Wynns of Wynnstay (under their former name of Williams long prominent in Assembly affairs), were regularly admitted. Few of the few industrialists active in the city joined the Assembly, which was at least as accommodating to new professions, recruiting, for example, the printer John Monk and the architect Joseph Turner in the 1770s and the newspaper proprietor and businessman John Fletcher in 1810. Surgeons sat on the Assembly throughout the period, lawyers (other than the recorder) occasionally. The first clergyman was elected in 1809: Charles Mytton, rector of the Grosvenors' home parish of Eccleston and a prominent political supporter of theirs.[1]

The Assembly was apparently more socially selective in choosing aldermen. With an average of only one or two vacancies a year, perhaps as many as half of all councilmen were never promoted, most commonly because they died before serving sufficiently long on the Assembly for their turn to come round, typically between 12 and 19 years. With very few exceptions councilmen were promoted to the aldermanic bench in strict order of seniority. Rapid promotion, however, was offered to allies of the Grosvenors such as Henry Vigars and Sir Watkin Williams-Wynn, 4th Bt. Proportionately more of the gentlemen and merchants and fewer of the shopkeepers and tradesmen became aldermen, though that may have been because less wealthy men were elected to the Assembly later in life. A few councilmen refused election as aldermen and were fined £100.

The mayor was nominally chosen at a meeting of freemen on the Friday after 20 October, from two candidates (always aldermen) whose names were put forward by the Assembly after an elaborate series of meetings and votes.[2] In practice, except during the political strife after 1807,[3] the Assembly almost always nominated the two most senior aldermen who had not already been mayor, and the longer serving of those

was almost invariably chosen as mayor at a thinly attended meeting of the freemen. Throughout the period the gap between election as alderman and election as mayor was very short, about two years on average. Virtually all serving aldermen had thus been mayor already, and presumably councilmen were allowed to proceed as aldermen in rough order of seniority on the basis of their willingness, competence, and political acceptability to serve as mayor soon afterwards. Mayors also had to be wealthy, since their allowance, which fluctuated between 100 and 200 guineas, fell far short of the expenses of the office, reckoned in the 1830s to be at least £400 a year.[4] A high proportion of all councilmen nevertheless eventually served as mayor: of the 100 Assemblymen appointed between 1762 and 1798 no fewer than 54 became aldermen, of whom 40 served as mayor. If an Assemblyman lived for twenty years after his first appointment he was thus almost certain to become mayor. From 1803 the mayor was empowered to appoint a deputy to act in his place in case of illness or other incapacity; the deputy was always a former mayor.[5]

The full Assembly met infrequently and irregularly, averaging only three sessions a year and on dozens of occasions allowing more than six months to pass between meetings, a pattern established in the 1720s.[6] Attendance was supposedly enforced by a small fine,[7] by 1835 not exacted in living memory.[8] Business normally began with the election of aldermen and common councilmen and proceeded through the appointment of almspeople to the corporation-controlled charities, admissions to the freedom of the city, listing potential recipients of charities, hearing petitions and appointing committees of inquiry, receiving committee reports and making orders, and ending with miscellaneous other business. From 1801 apprenticeship indentures were registered as the final item.[9]

The corporation was largely reactive rather than forward-looking in its attitude to the city, though it seems to have had a clear and unwavering view about what sort of place it wished Chester to be, and in pursuit of that it was capable of putting aside both narrow interests and tradition. Much time was spent in preventing encroachments on the streets and Rows,[10] largely by commercial interests very similar to those of most Assemblymen, while the Pentice, for centuries the

---

1 *Hist. of Contested Election in Chester, 1812, with Papers, Squibs, Songs, &c.* (1812, publ. J. Monk), 18, 23; *Rep. of Proc. and Evidence before Cttee. of H.C. upon Late Controverted Election for Chester* (1819, publ. J. Gorton), 23, 47–8, 176, 178–84; Ormerod, *Hist. Ches.* ii. 831; iii. 731, 735.

2 *Rep. Com. Mun. Corp.* pp. 2619–20; for the date: Cattle Distemper, Vagrancy, Marshalsea Prison, etc. Act, 1753, 26 Geo. II, c. 34, s. 4.

3 Below, this chapter: Politics, 1762–1835.

4 C.C.A.L.S., ZAB 4, ff. 249v.–250; ZAB 5, pp. 99, 107, 224,

323; *Rep. Com. Mun. Corp.* p. 2620.

5 Hemingway, *Hist. Chester*, i. 274–7; *Rep. Com. Mun. Corp.* p. 2620; C.C.A.L.S., ZAB 5, p. 211.

6 C.C.A.L.S., ZAB 4–6, *passim*; above, Early Modern Chester: City Government and Politics, 1662–1762 (City Government).

7 C.C.A.L.S., ZAB 5, pp. 154–5.

8 *Rep. Com. Mun. Corp.* p. 2626.

9 C.C.A.L.S., ZAB 5, pp. 161–2 and later.

10 Para. based on ibid. ZAB 4–5, *passim*; cf. *V.C.H. Ches.* v (2), The Rows: Rebuilding and Enclosure.

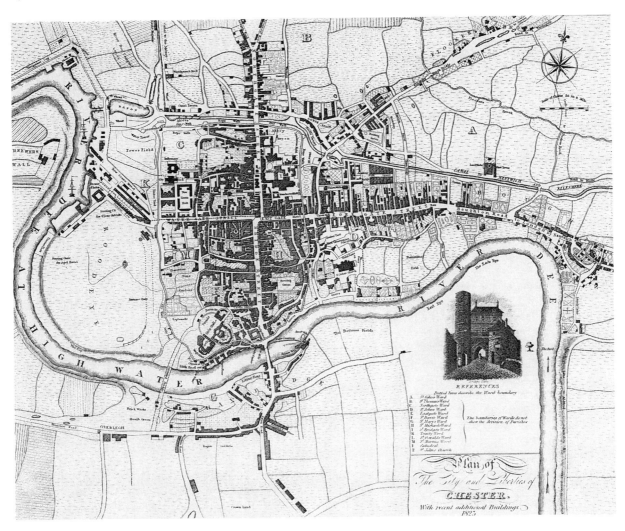

FIG. 7. *Chester, 1823*

seat of civic government and as such a highly charged symbol of corporate activity, was removed in the interests of street improvements in two stages in 1781 and 1803.[1] Concern for the seemliness of the town must have been prompted at least in part by a recognition of its importance to well-bred residents and visitors. The corporation thus kept the walls in good repair, rebuilt the four ramshackle medieval gates in the classical style between 1768 and 1810 with financial help from the Grosvenors,[2] and removed public conveniences from the walls in 1772.[3] It laid new pavements for pedestrians along the roads from the Water Tower to the riverside embankment (probably a fashionable promenade) and from the city to Flookersbrook in the 1770s, and paid a city pavior to keep other footways in repair.[4] It provided clocks at the New Linenhall and the work-

house in 1781,[5] supplementing those at the Exchange and the Pentice.[6]

When others took an initiative of which the corporation approved it was co-operative, for example with the promoters of a proposed foundling hospital in 1762 and with Dr. John Haygarth's census of inhabitants in 1775.[7] It also worked with turnpike trustees and neighbouring townships to maintain roads in the outlying parts of the liberties.[8] In other respects, however, the Assembly was timid. Strongly in favour of the intended canal to Nantwich and beyond, and indeed a heavy investor through the Owen Jones charity in the company's shares, it took fright at the possible effects of the canal on the physical fabric of the city and became querulous in its dealings with the company, no doubt in part because its investment never paid a dividend.[9] Water supply was left to private

1 *V.C.H. Ches.* v (2), Municipal Buildings: Pentice.
2 Ibid. City Walls and Gates. Plates 19–24.
3 C.C.A.L.S., ZAB 4, f. 294.
4 Ibid. ff. 289v., 291v., 323v.   5 Ibid. ff. 340, 343.
6 Ibid. ZTAV 2/43, pt. 1, acct. for winding clocks.

7 Ibid. ZAB 4, ff. 206 and v., 305v.
8 e.g. ibid. f. 287v.; ZAB 5, p. 369.
9 Ibid. ZAB 4, ff. 287v., 297 sqq.; *Rep. Com. Mun. Corp.* p. 2628; *V.C.H. Ches.* v (2), Water Transport: Canals; Charities for the Poor: Municipal.

commercial interests.[1] Pushing forward large projects not directly connected with its existing responsibilities, such as the building of a new bridge in the late 1810s, was beyond its capacity.[2]

The only significant area in which the Assembly innovated was in relation to the retail and wholesale trades, and even there in the 1760s and 1770s it saw its role in purely traditional terms, acting through the mayor (as *ex officio* clerk of the markets) against illicit manipulation of the retail markets, and regulating weights and measures for fresh produce,[3] while at the same time leaving the promotion of the linen trade to private enterprise.[4] In the 1820s, however, the corporation started new specialist fairs for livestock and cheese and undertook a comprehensive rebuilding of the markets in Northgate Street.[5]

The Assembly delegated many matters to *ad hoc* committees, not least the petitions submitted to it on a great range of topics, especially those concerning corporation property or encroachments on the streets and Rows.[6] Some such committees dealt with diverse business; one which sat in 1774, for example, considered improvements to Bridgegate and Northgate, drew up new regulations for the city waits, and reviewed the leases of the corporation's warehouses in Skinners Lane and on the Roodee.[7] As the Assembly seems normally to have ratified their decisions without much further discussion, the committees were often dealing with policy as much as its implementation. Greater formality was observed after committee meetings were minuted from 1805.[8] In the same year the Assembly established a finance committee, also called the city lands committee, chaired by the mayor, which sat more or less continuously until 1835. In pursuit of its initial remit to enquire into the corporation's financial state, it drew up a new rental in 1805–6; thereafter it was largely concerned with routine management of the city's property and with street repairs,[9] but also made recommendations to the Assembly about financial policy.[10]

The other forum for day-to-day administration was a regular meeting of the mayor and a few senior aldermen, which had a history stretching back into the early 17th century.[11] The meetings took place in the inner Pentice until it was demolished in 1803, when they were transferred to the Exchange, though the name of 'inner Pentice' was retained for the meeting until 1816. The mayor almost always attended, the

recorder occasionally, and the aldermen in small numbers, rarely more than three or four and often only one. As the mayor was inevitably new to the bench, the presence of an alderman of many years' standing was normal and indeed almost essential. Meetings became more frequent over the period, from once or twice a week in the 1750s, when Saturday was the most common day, to every other day or even daily in the 1810s.[12]

The inner Pentice functioned in at least two different capacities without differentiating its business.[13] On the one hand, since the mayor, recorder, and those aldermen who had already been mayor were the city's magistrates,[14] it served as Chester's petty sessions. As such it heard matters to do with poor-law administration, including settlement and bastardy cases, but also cases of assault, theft, and drunkenness, infringements of the licensing laws, and other minor offences reported by the city's watchmen and constables or by private citizens. By 1835 the J.P.s sat daily as police magistrates, and twice a week as petty sessions, four or five normally attending out of the 15 then qualified.[15] The inner Pentice also administered corporation business of the most routine sort, such as the admission of freemen and the swearing-in of new Assemblymen, acting as a kind of standing committee. The two functions overlapped when the inner Pentice enforced laws which defended the corporation's interests and practices, such as apprenticeship regulations and the collection of tolls.

The mayor and magistrates also continued to meet in a more private capacity, under the name of the court of aldermen or meeting of magistrates. As such they acted as a steering committee and policy-making body for the Assembly, considering matters which might have been initiated by the Assembly, one of its committees, or the mayor. They minuted their decisions from 1813 and over the following twenty years dealt both with uncontentious business, such as the arrangements for proclaiming George IV's accession, and with topics of great political sensitivity, like docking the salary due to Alderman William Seller, a leading opponent of the Grosvenors.[16]

Some of the more formal civic traditions were in decline during the later 18th century. The mayor was still attended in public by the swordbearer, carrying the civic sword point up;[17] lords lieutenant of Ireland passing through Chester in the 1760s were still treated

1 *V.C.H. Ches.* v (2), Public Utilities: Water.
2 *J.C.A.S.* xlv. 43–5.
3 C.C.A.L.S., ZAB 4, ff. 229v., 235v., 282v., 300v.–301, 308v.; ibid. ZMBB; ZTCC 61.   4 *V.C.H. Ches.* v (2), Fairs.
5 Ibid.   6 e.g. C.C.A.L.S., ZAB 4, ff. 250v., 336.
7 Ibid. ff. 304v.–305, 308.
8 Ibid. ZAC 1, esp. ff. 53v.–56, 60, 61, 62–4, 68, 103–4, 107v., 109–110v., 113v.–114.
9 Ibid. esp. ff. 1 and v., 13, 14, 24v., 70v.–71, 115, 119v., 128v.–132.   10 e.g. ibid. ZAB 5, pp. 284, 349–50.
11 Above, Early Modern Chester: City Government, 1550–

1642 (The Assembly); City Government and Politics, 1662–1762 (City Government).
12 C.C.A.L.S., ZMIP 55–79; ZMF 113, 158, 168, 171–3, 175–88, 191–8.
13 Para. based, except where stated otherwise, on ibid.
14 *Rep. Com. Mun. Corp.* p. 2620.   15 Ibid. p. 2625.
16 C.C.A.L.S., ZAC 1, ff. 30–1, 49, 53, 61, 64v.–65, 69v.–70, 75, 77v., 106v.–107, 114v.–115, 116, 118v., 121v.–123v.; for Seller: below, this chapter: Politics, 1762–1835.
17 Hemingway, *Hist. Chester*, i. 244; *Rep. Com. Mun. Corp.* p. 2622.

by the corporation;[1] and there was still an annual civic dinner for which the city cook was paid 10 guineas.[2] Other observances, however, were allowed to lapse or were ended,[3] notably the civic bull bait on the mayoral election day, official corporate attendance at the races,[4] and the mayor's feast, abolished in 1797.[5] Public days of rejoicing other than the king's birthday were dropped in 1783,[6] but their place was taken for a time by the large-scale civic celebrations which followed naval victories during the Revolutionary and Napoleonic wars and the peace treaties of 1801 and 1814, and accompanied visits to Chester by war heroes. Thanksgiving day in 1814 was especially lavish: a regatta, dinners, the ringing of the cathedral bells for the first time in sixty years, and a grand procession of almost every organization of consequence in the city, led by the corporation.[7] The Assembly was also still capable of standing on its dignity in small matters: in 1774 it took offence when the assize judges ordered a thief to be whipped through the streets, contrary to city custom.[8]

THE OFFICERS

The mayor, as chief magistrate, remained the key figure in the government of Chester before 1835, though the importance of the town clerk was growing steadily, not least in view of his enhanced role in financial administration.[9] Town clerks were appointed for life by the corporation and acted at one and the same time as clerks to the Assembly, the city courts, the magistrates, and the improvement commission.[10] In the 1820s the commissioners for the new bridge made the town clerk their solicitor too.[11] Only five men held the office during the period, two of them for thirty years or more: Thomas Brock 1757–85, William Hall (who had been Brock's deputy for 20 years) 1785–95, George Whitley 1795–9, William Richards 1799–1817, and

John Finchett (after 1824 Finchett-Maddock) 1817–57.[12] They were all attorneys who also had a private practice in the town.[13]

Among the elected officers the recorder retained the formal primacy which the office had long enjoyed. He acted as a J.P. and in the portmote and crownmote courts for a salary of £105 a year,[14] but also informally as a source of legal advice to the Assembly, for which he might be paid additional fees. He was always a barrister of some years' standing,[15] and had to be an alderman, so that at each vacancy the man chosen was admitted as a freeman (if not one already) and promoted through the rank of councilman.[16] The recordership had ceased to be politically contentious in the earlier 18th century,[17] but in the one-party administration of the later 18th century and the early 19th recorders had to be both politically acceptable and well connected locally. Thus the longest serving, Robert Townsend (1754–87), was from a gentry family settled at Christleton just outside the city;[18] the forebears of Thomas Cowper (1787–8) had held high civic office since the 16th century;[19] Foster Bower (1788–95), a brilliant barrister on the Chester circuit, came from a more recent Chester merchant family on his mother's side;[20] Hugh Leycester (1795–1814) was from a very old Cheshire house;[21] and the father of David Francis Jones (1814–20) was a Flintshire lawyer settled in the city.[22] Of those, Leycester was a Tory M.P. and Jones tried to become one. In the early 19th century connexions in Chester were apparently less needed, and the last two recorders elected by the Assembly before 1835 were, by comparison, outsiders: Samuel Yate Benyon (1820–2), a law officer of the duchy of Lancaster, came from a family of Shrewsbury burgesses,[23] and Richard Tyrwhitt (1822–36) from a dispersed but well connected gentry family also linked to Shropshire.[24]

1 C.C.A.L.S., ZAB 4, ff. 213v., 235, 253.

2 *Rep. Com. Mun. Corp.* p. 2628.

3 Cf. R. Sweet, *Writing of Urban Histories in 18th-Cent. Eng.* 260 n.

4 *V.C.H. Ches.* v (2), Chester Races; Sport after 1700: Other Sports (Bull and Bear Baiting).

5 Hemingway, *Hist. Chester,* ii. 254.

6 C.C.A.L.S., ZAB 4, f. 352v.

7 Hemingway, *Hist. Chester,* ii. 254–5, 258, 260–2, 267–8.

8 C.C.A.L.S., ZAB 4, ff. 306–7.

9 Below, this section (Finance).

10 *Rep. Com. Mun. Corp.* p. 2621.

11 *J.C.A.S.* xlv. 46.

12 C.C.A.L.S., ZAB 4, ff. 169 and v., 218v.; ZAB 5, pp. 1–2, 11, 95, 136, 389–90; Hemingway, *Hist. Chester,* i. 241; Ormerod, *Hist. Ches.* i. 223; *Trial at Large of Quo Warranto, King vs. Amery and Monk* (1786, publ. J. Fletcher), 16; *Lond. Gaz.* 6 Mar. 1824, p. 370.

13 C.C.A.L.S., ZTCP 5–7 *passim;* ZTCP 8/75–270.

14 *Rep. Com. Mun. Corp.* p. 2620.

15 Ibid.; the assertion is borne out by the careers of those mentioned in this para.

16 C.C.A.L.S., ZAB 5, pp. 17, 26, 86, 335–6, 453, 464.

17 Above, Early Modern Chester: City Government and Politics, 1662–1762 (Parliamentary Representation, City Politics).

18 *Reg. of Admissions to Middle Temple,* i. 317; Ormerod, *Hist. Ches.* ii. 780; *Rolls of Freemen of Chester,* ii (R.S.L.C. lv), 280.

19 *Reg. of Admissions to Middle Temple,* i. 363; Ormerod, *Hist. Ches.* i. 374–6; *Rolls of Freemen of Chester,* ii. 357.

20 *Cal. Inner Temple Recs.* v. 184; *Gent. Mag.* lxv (1), pp. 257–8; Ormerod, *Hist. Ches.* iii. 779, 787; *Rolls of Freemen of Chester,* ii. 232, 345, 355, for his mother's family, the Marsdens.

21 *Reg. of Admissions to Middle Temple,* i. 370; *Middle Temple Bench Bk.* (2nd edn.), 194–5; *Hist. Parl., Commons, 1790–1820,* iv. 435–6.

22 *Gent. Mag.* n.s. xxiv. 537–8; *Rolls of Freemen of Chester,* ii. 407; Ormerod, *Hist. Ches.* iii. 261; C.C.A.L.S., ZTCC 131.

23 *Black Bks. of Lincoln's Inn,* iv. 141, 160, 239; R. Somerville, *Office-Holders in Duchy of Lancaster,* 53, 97; *Alum. Cantab. 1752–1900,* i. 240; *Shrewsbury Burgess Roll,* ed. H. E. Forrest, 23.

24 Foster, *Baronetage* (1882), 622–3; J. Burke, *Hist. of Commoners* (1823), i. 583–7; *Gent. Mag.* cvi (1), p. 334; *Law List* (1805), 39; (1820), 40; and later edns.; *Hist. Parl., Commons, 1790–1820,* iv. 324; E. Foss, *Judges of Eng. 1066–1870,* 379.

The most important of the corporation's ordinary elected offices was the double shrievalty.[1] Within a few years of appointment to the Assembly it was normal for a councilman to serve as sheriff for a year, usually in order of seniority,[2] though gentlemen were not expected to take up a position which involved much routine judicial administration. In theory one sheriff was elected by the Assembly and the other by a meeting of the freemen, but in practice it was normal to select the next two most recently appointed councilmen who had not already served. No sheriff ever served more than one term. In 1771, 1804, and regularly after 1809 the second shrievalty was hotly contested between the corporation and its opponents, and several times non-members of the Assembly were elected.[3] Apart from regular attendance in the city courts and until 1823 management of the gaol,[4] the sheriffs were required to execute criminals condemned to death anywhere in Cheshire. There were 68 such public executions between 1768 and 1829, of which perhaps only a tenth arose from felonies committed in the city. Hangings (and in 1763 a burning at the stake)[5] took place at Boughton until 1801 and then at the city gaol. The requirement to conduct county executions was disputed by the sheriffs in 1834 after the abolition of palatine jurisdiction but was reiterated by Act of Parliament in 1835 and remained in force until 1867.[6]

Other offices filled by members of the Assembly were less demanding. That of leavelooker was normally the first to be undertaken by a new councilman, before serving as sheriff. It was possible to refuse service on payment of a fine set at £50 in 1771.[7] The duties were confined to collecting the income from tolls at the gates, enforcing the freedom of the city on those who wished to trade, and fining the recalcitrant. Tolls were payable until 1835, but after repeated attempts to enforce entry to the freedom the Assembly gave up trying to collect 'leavelookerage money' in 1816. A decision of the exchequer court of the palatinate in 1825 definitively abolished the right to take such dues.[8]

The two murengers, who directed the corporation's expenditure on the walls, gates, and streets, continued to be chosen from among the most senior aldermen

and normally continued in office in successive years.[9] The coroners, also two in number, were until 1784 sometimes chosen by the mayor from among fairly junior councilmen and sometimes from new aldermen, and several served for periods of five years or more. After 1784, however, when the office was combined with that of treasurer, it was nearly always held by recently elected aldermen for two years only. The coroners' jurisdiction covered the Dee estuary as well as the city liberties.[10]

The lesser appointed corporation offices, not held by Assemblymen, were those of swordbearer, macebearer, four serjeants-at-mace, four ministers of the Pentice court, the yeoman of the Pentice, and the crier. At first some were so lucrative because of the income from tolls and other sources as to attract keen bidding when they fell vacant: the office of swordbearer was sold for £682 10s. in 1776 and that of yeoman for £380 in 1779.[11] By the 1830s, however, the tolls had fallen away and the Assembly had withdrawn most of the traditional perquisites of office, such as the breakfast and dinner provided for the yeoman and other officers every Saturday and Sunday,[12] and they had become purely salaried positions with mostly ceremonial duties.[13] The corporation also had on its payroll a dozen or so caretakers, cleaners, market supervisors, and other functionaries, ranging in status from the beadle and the mayor's porter to the winder of the Exchange clock.[14]

FINANCE

The corporation's finances were notionally entrusted to two treasurers, elected each year from within the Assembly and after 1784 also serving as coroners. It was the rule for the senior coroner and treasurer to act single-handed, his junior operating only as a deputy during any incapacity, and for the junior to succeed as senior coroner and treasurer in the following year.[15] From 1763, however, the town clerk was made directly responsible for the receipt of all corporation income and the payment of all its expenditure, in effect becoming the city's executive treasurer, paid at the rate of 2½ per cent of its income, raised by 1835 to 5 per cent. Non-routine financial matters remained the responsibility of the senior treasurer. By 1804 the

1 Para. based on pattern of careers reconstructed from C.C.A.L.S., ZAB 4–6 *passim*; *V.C.H. Ches.* v (2), Lists of Mayors and Sheriffs.

2 Cf. *Trial, King vs. Amery and Monk*, 29.

3 Below, this chapter: Politics, 1762–1835.

4 *V.C.H. Ches.* v (2), Law Courts; Law and Order: Municipal Prisons (Northgate Gaol, New City Gaol).

5 C.C.A.L.S., ZAB 4, f. 215; cf. L. Radzinowicz, *Hist. of Eng. Criminal Law from 1750*, i. 209–13.

6 *V.C.H. Ches.* ii. 59–60; Hemingway, *Hist. Chester*, ii. 296–9; *Rep. Com. Mun. Corp.* p. 2621; 3 *Sheaf*, xi, p. 80; C.C.A.L.S., ZAB 4, f. 305v.   7 C.C.A.L.S., ZAB 4, f. 286.

8 Ibid. ff. 244–5, 249v., 277, 297v., 352v.; ZAB 5, pp. 90, 116,

161–2, 170, 179, 375; *Rep. Com. Mun. Corp.* p. 2621.

9 C.C.A.L.S., ZMUV 4/1–421; cf. ZAB 5, pp. 29, 41.

10 Ibid. TS. cal. of ZQCI 23–9 compared with career patterns reconstructed from ZAB 4–5 *passim*; below, this section (Finance); *Rep. Com. Mun. Corp.* pp. 2615–16; *Trial, King vs. Amery and Monk*, 28.

11 C.C.A.L.S., ZAB 4, ff. 316–18, 335 and v.

12 Ibid. ff. 312v.–313.

13 *Rep. Com. Mun. Corp.* p. 2622.

14 Salaries itemized in C.C.A.L.S., ZTAB 8–10 *passim*; ibid. ZAB 4, f. 310; ZAB 5, pp. 51, 57–8, 62, 154, 197, 207, 210–11, 221, 323, 354, 428, 469.

15 Ibid. ZAB 5, pp. 29, 41; *Rep. Com. Mun. Corp.* p. 2621.

accounts were drawn up entirely by the town clerk's office, though the treasurers were supposed to examine and sign them.[1]

The biggest of the Assembly's regular sources of income was the rental of its property, which amounted to £1,000 in 1775 and had grown to £1,500 fifty years later,[2] largely by raising rents after a searching enquiry in 1798.[3] Within the liberties the corporate estate included shops, houses, and chief rents, besides the Roodee and Hough Green; outside the city there were farms and tithes in Hope and Shordley and land at Iscoyd (all Flints.) and Guilden Sutton. The other large item was income from the markets, which grew from £92 to £527 between 1775 and 1825, and doubled again to over £1,000 after the markets were rebuilt in 1827. Income from tolls at the gates, by contrast, was at best stagnant as it became increasingly difficult to enforce payment.[4] Those at the Eastgate were in the hands of the macebearer, who paid the corporation £60 or £80 a year for them in the 1760s.[5] The Watergate tolls came into the city's hands only in the 1770s, but the Northgate had long been in the custody of the sheriffs,[6] and the Assembly built a new tollkeeper's house there in 1817.[7] In 1831–2 those three gates brought in less than £80 between them, whereas the Bridgegate tolls had been leased in 1824 at £200 a year to the trustees of the intended new bridge.[8] Leys on the Roodee were let for £291 in 1775, £460 in 1825, and £388 in 1831.

There were other minor and less reliable sources of income. The corporation's weighing machine in Bridge Street, used mainly by coal merchants, was never very profitable after the River Dee Co. installed its own machine in 1769; the corporation's was moved to the Bars in 1805.[9] Revenue from the tax on imported wine, the prisage, levied at a flat rate per cargo, grew from £56 in 1775 to £270 in 1825 but plummeted after Liverpool stopped charging duty on wine c. 1830.[10] The duty on bricks made on corporation-owned waste ground at Hough Green fluctuated greatly though could be as high as £100 a year. Those qualified to become freemen of the city by birth paid £2 12s. and those by apprenticeship £3 12s., but of those sums the corporation received only 3s. 4d. and £1 3s. 4d. respectively, significant sums only when very large numbers of freemen were admitted during a contested parliamentary election. On the other hand, unqualified

persons wishing to trade in the city had to pay £10 or £20 to be made freemen, and fifty or sixty might be admitted in a single year. In 1825, however, the corporation's right to insist on unfree traders' taking up the freedom was overturned at law, and fees for admission by purchase ceased.[11]

The total regular income was £1,678 in 1775 (of which 60 per cent came from rents) and £3,133 in 1825 (50 per cent from rents). Even though many rents ran into arrears after 1780,[12] it was enough for normal recurrent expenditure, much of which went on salaries and fees to the city's officials and functionaries and on workmen's wages and tradesmen's bills for repairing and maintaining public buildings. It was not enough to pay for any extraordinary item, like the new city gaol and house of correction built in 1808, the market halls put up in the 1820s (both of which cost several thousand pounds), or the heavy legal fees incurred in defending corporate privileges and the Assembly's method of conducting elections. In such circumstances the Assembly resorted to a variety of expedients, nearly always with consequences for its future liquidity. In 1757 it had raised £6,000 by selling annuities under the tontine system, committing itself to relatively modest payments but over a potentially lengthy period:[13] the last annuitant was still being paid in 1840.[14] More commonly it borrowed money from the city charities against the security of the corporate estate. The main lender was the Owen Jones charity, whose trustees (not coincidentally) were the mayor and sheriffs: £500 in 1762 to finance a prosecution over the Bridgegate tolls;[15] £800 in 1799 to cover a shortfall in the accounts after the Assembly had given the government £500 for the war effort;[16] £1,700 in 1815 for reasons unspecified.[17] By the 1830s the charity had advanced the corporation £10,640, much of it for purposes which were apparently not recorded. The annual interest charge by then was £425 12s. A further annual payment of £80 to the trustees of the Blue Coat school was believed to represent interest on another loan secured by mortgage, but no record had been kept beyond 'the tradition of the town clerk's office'.[18] In the mid 1820s the new markets were paid for by allowing tenants who owed chief rents to redeem them and by outright sales of land.[19] Between 1800 and 1835 at least 96 properties were sold.[20] There were further complications over the municipal charities, for which separate accounts had

---

1 C.C.A.L.S., ZAB 4, ff. 215v.–216; *Rep. Com. Mun. Corp.* pp. 2621, 2629; *Rep. of Finance Cttee. as to Charities* (1839), 11 (copy in C.C.A.L.S., ZCR 600/1).

2 Rest of section based, except where stated otherwise, on C.C.A.L.S., ZTAB 8–10; *Rep. Com. Mun. Corp.* pp. 2626–7.

3 C.C.A.L.S., ZAB 5, pp. 110, 119.

4 Ibid. ZAB 4, ff. 206v.–207, 217, 226, 234, 279v., 287 and v., 294.   5 Ibid. ff. 225, 249v.–250.

6 *V.C.H. Ches.* v (2), City Walls and Gates: Medieval and Later.

7 C.C.A.L.S., ZAB 5, p. 385.   8 Ibid. pp. 480–1.

9 Ibid. ZAB 4, ff. 248v., 260, 268 and v., 281; ZAB 5, pp. 149, 234.

10 *Rep. Com. Mun. Corp.* p. 2628.   11 Ibid. p. 2623.

12 C.C.A.L.S., ZCCB 1, printed rep. of 1836 at pp. 38–9 (p. 8).

13 Ibid. ZTAA; Hist. MSS. Com. 7, Pt. 1, *8th Rep. I, Chester,* pp. 401–2.

14 C.C.A.L.S., ZCCB 1, pp. 203, 224, 242.

15 Ibid. ZAB 4, ff. 206v.–207.

16 Ibid. ZAB 5, pp. 107, 127–8.   17 Ibid. p. 386.

18 *Rep. Com. Mun. Corp.* pp. 2629–30.

19 Ibid.; C.C.A.L.S., ZTAB 10, ff. 131v.–132v.

20 C.C.A.L.S., ZCCB 1, printed rep. of 1836 at pp. 38–9 (p. 8).

never been kept: in some cases the corporation had evidently spent the charity's capital endowment, while remaining liable for annual payments which amounted to some £250; in others it was drawing income from surviving charitable endowments but failing to spend the full revenue on the objects of the charity.[1] Perhaps because the accounts were known to be irregular they were left unsigned and perhaps unaudited from 1812 until the Municipal Corporations Act loomed in 1834.[2] In 1835 the corporation hastily put its affairs (though not the charities') in order and balanced its books by selling property, cutting salaries, and economizing even on the cost of the assize judges' lodgings.[3]

POOR LAW

In 1757 all the city parishes, several of which had their own poorhouses, combined in an agreement to send their poor to a new workhouse, to be built at corporation expense in Paradise Row on the north-west side of the Roodee. The new building, three-storeyed and of brick round a central courtyard, was completed in 1759,[4] and 200 poor were admitted immediately.[5] A small building for pauper lunatics was added in 1819 and an infants' school in 1823.[6] The workhouse served the rural townships which belonged to city parishes as well as the city itself, as had earlier parochial arrangements.

Under the Chester Improvement Act of 1762 the workhouse passed under the control of a board of guardians of the poor for the city, who comprised the mayor, recorder, and aldermen J.P.s together with representatives elected by the vestries of the nine parishes: twelve from each of St. John's, St. Mary's, and St. Oswald's; eight from each of St. Peter's, Holy Trinity, St. Bridget's, and St. Michael's; and three from each of St. Martin's and St. Olave's.[7] By the 1830s members of the corporation seldom attended.[8] The Assembly at first hoped to save three quarters of what was spent on poor relief,[9] but the annual cost of running the workhouse reached over £8,000 in the years of worst distress around 1820, apportioned among the parishes in proportion to the number of their poor relieved, so that separate parish poor rates continued to be levied and collected by the church-wardens and overseers of each parish. The Act thus did

not, as elsewhere, equalize poor rates across the city.[10] In the 1830s an outside observer thought the rates 'not very heavy' for a town of Chester's size and condition.[11] The workhouse also housed the poor of the extra-parochial districts of Abbey Court and St. John's Hospital, who had previously been relieved respectively by the dean and chapter out of the cathedral revenues and by the Assembly out of the income from the hospital,[12] in both cases without any local overseers or rates. The cathedral precinct remained exempt from poor rates in 1835.[13]

IMPROVEMENT COMMISSION

The 1762 Improvement Act also set up an improvement or police commission for Chester, made up of the mayor, recorder, J.P.s, and six inhabitants from each ward, the last elected by owners and occupiers whose property was rated as worth at least £10 a year.[14] The commission, which was chaired by the mayor and met in the inner Pentice, set up a night watch, supervised by the ward constables,[15] and a fire brigade, and took charge of street lighting and cleansing. Its finances came from a rate limited to 1s. in the pound, which was gathered for the commission by the land-tax collectors.[16]

The improvement commission was remodelled under an Act of 1803, steered through parliament by Chester's M.P.s and the recorder, who was also an M.P.[17] Thereafter it comprised the mayor, recorder, and J.P.s, the dean and chapter, and 120 named individuals, who were to fill vacancies by co-option.[18] The usual progression in the method of appointing improvement commissions from co-option to election was thus reversed in Chester's case.[19] Rates for lighting and policing the city were still limited to 1s. in the pound, with the further restriction that no property was to have a rateable value of more than £70 except for the Dee Mills, which were to be rated as worth £100.

Despite the wide membership of the improvement commission, its direction was in practice left to few hands. Meetings took place about once a month with usually ten or a dozen commissioners present and often chaired by the mayor,[20] but of the 65 com-

1 *Rep. Com. Mun. Corp.* pp. 2629–30; *V.C.H. Ches.* v (2), Charities for the Poor: Municipal.

2 C.C.A.L.S., ZTAB 9; but cf. ibid. ZAB 5, p. 373.

3 Ibid. ZAB 6, pp. 59–61.

4 R. V. H. Burne, 'Treatment of Poor in 18th Cent. in Chester', *J.C.A.S.* lii. 44–8; C. P. Lewis, 'Building Chester's First Workhouse', *Ches. Hist.* xxxviii. 50–4.

5 Hemingway, *Hist. Chester*, ii. 248.

6 Ibid. 193; C.C.A.L.S., ZAB 5, pp. 427, 438.

7 Rest of para. based on Hemingway, *Hist. Chester*, ii. 192–5; 2 Geo. III, c. 45.

8 *Rep. Com. Mun. Corp.* pp. 2625–6.   9 *C.J.* xxix. 56.

10 S. and B. Webb, *Eng. Local Government: Statutory Authorities for Special Purposes*, 114–16.

11 *Rep. Com. Mun. Corp.* p. 2631.

12 *C.J.* xxix. 92.

13 *Rep. Com. Mun. Corp.* p. 2616.

14 Para. based, except where stated otherwise, on 2 Geo. III, c. 45.

15 Cf. C.C.A.L.S., ZTRI 1; *V.C.H. Ches.* v (2), Law and Order: Policing.

16 Cf. C.C.A.L.S., ZCAS 2.

17 *C.J.* lviii. 159–60, 226, 453; *Hist. Parl., Commons, 1790–1820*, iii. 706; iv. 116, 435; *Chester Chron.* 17 Sept. 1802; cf. C.C.A.L.S., ZTCC 82.

18 Rest of para. based, except where stated otherwise, on Chester Improvement Act, 1803, 43 Geo. III, c. 47 (Local and Personal).

19 Webb, *Eng. Local Government: Statutory Authorities*, 244.

20 C.C.A.L.S., ZTRI 2–3 *passim*.

missioners who attended at least one meeting during 1811, for example, 32 attended only once and 22 only twice or thrice. Meetings in that year were dominated by two aldermen, Rowland Jones and John Wright, attending 16 and 17 times respectively; both men had been mayor in the 1790s and between them had 74 years' experience on the Assembly.[1]

The new commissioners continued to supervise policing and fire precautions,[2] but took on other responsibilities as well, notably in the field of civic improvements. They provided lighting in all the main streets, lanes, and Rows from 1804,[3] began macadamizing the surfaces in 1824,[4] and ordered the first official street names to be put up in 1830.[5] At the same time much closer attention was paid both to the cleanliness of the streets and to the removal of obstructions such as frontages projecting from commercial premises and posts in front of private houses, attending even to shop signs, barbers' poles, and bootscrapers.[6]

For all its activity, by the 1830s the deficiencies of the improvement commission had long been apparent: the maximum rate collectable did not provide enough income to undertake desirable improvements, and the two biggest industrial enterprises in Chester, the lead-works and the Dee Mills, were woefully under-rated because of the cap on rateable values. The loan capital which it was empowered to borrow, only £1,000, was soon spent on rainwater culverts in the main streets, and attempts to obtain a new Act had foundered on a lack of consensus about what was required.[7]

POLITICS, 1762–1835

THE STRUCTURE OF POLITICS

The politics of the municipal corporation were tightly bound up with control of the city's two seats in parliament,[8] and so were under the pervasive influence of the Grosvenors of Eaton Hall, in the persons of Richard, Lord and from 1784 Earl Grosvenor, and his son Robert, the second earl.[9] Their chief object until 1829 was to have the nomination of both M.P.s, for which the electorate was the entire body of resident freemen, numbering perhaps 1,500 until the 1810s and 1,700 in the 1820s, about a quarter of adult males.[10] The Grosvenors thus needed to dominate the Assembly, which regulated the admission of new freemen and enjoyed extensive patronage in the city, and whose chief officers conducted parliamentary elections. It thus suited the Grosvenors that the Assembly maintained its oligarchic ways.[11]

Many Cestrians, whether voters or not, aligned themselves wholeheartedly with the Grosvenor interest, offering political deference in return for due regard by the Grosvenors to their obligations to the city.[12] From 1750 to 1782 Grosvenor political interests were managed by their estate steward at Eaton, Henry Vigars, who joined the Assembly in 1767 and was elected alderman in 1770 and mayor the following year.[13] In later elections practical leadership for the Grosvenor party came from within the city. The general election campaign of 1818, for example, was masterminded by John Fletcher, owner of the *Chester Chronicle*. Although in the later 1780s and the 1790s he had been a bitter opponent of the corporation, Fletcher had switched sides when Earl Grosvenor joined the Whigs in 1807 and became a councilman in 1810, alderman in 1825, and mayor twice.[14]

At its most effective the Grosvenor political machine

1 Ibid. ZTRI 2, ff. 162–71; careers from ibid. ZAB 4, ff. 288v., 316v.; ZAB 5, pp. 42, 67; *V.C.H. Ches.* v (2), Lists of Mayors and Sheriffs.

2 e.g. C.C.A.L.S., ZTRI 2, ff. 10v.–11, 14v.–19, 249, 338, 341, 389v.–396.   3 Ibid. ff. 2–7v.

4 Ibid. f. 337v.   5 Ibid. ZTRI 3, f. 7.

6 Ibid. ZTRI 2–3 *passim*, e.g. ZTRI 2, ff. 126, 304v.–305.

7 Hemingway, *Hist. Chester*, i. 277–8; *V.C.H. Ches.* v (2), Public Utilities: Sewerage.

8 Parl. representation is treated in *V.C.H. Ches.* ii. 133–8; *Hist. Parl., Commons*, 1754–90, i. 221; 1790–1820, ii. 37–40; F. O'Gorman, 'General Election of 1784 in Chester', *J.C.A.S.* lvii. 41–50.

9 Section largely based on Hemingway, *Hist. Chester*, ii. 400–32, and copies of following at Institute of Hist. Research, Lond., bound as *Chester Poll Bks. and Election Pamphlets, 1747–1827* (3 vols.): *Alphabetical List of Freemen of Chester who Polled at General Election, with Papers and Songs* (1784, publ. J. Monk); *Sketch of Political Hist. of Chester* (1790, publ. J. Fletcher); *Colln. of Papers Relative to Electioneering Interests in Chester* (1807, publ. J. Hemingway); *Letter to John Egerton, M.P. for Chester* (1807, publ. J. Hemingway); *Compilation of Papers Relating to Election for City Officers in 1809 and Parl. Representation of Chester* (1810, publ. J. Monk); *Hist. of Contested Election in Chester, 1812, with Papers, Squibs, Songs, &c.* (1812, publ.

J. Monk); *Political Hist. of Chester* (1814, publ. W. C. Jones); *Hist. of Contested Election in Chester, 1818, with Papers, Squibs, Songs, &c.;* also *Poll-Bk.* (1818, publ. M. Monk); *Poll-Bk. for Sheriff, with Concise Hist. and Papers* (1818, publ. M. Monk); *Poll-Bk. for Mayor and Sheriff, with Squibs, Addresses, and Other Papers, and Brief Narrative of Election* (1819, publ. M. Galway); original colln. of newspaper cuttings, election ephemera, and MS. materials with printed title-page *Colln. of Material Facts Connected with Contest for Representatives of Chester in Parl.* (1820, publ. M. Monk); *Narrative of Proceedings at Contest for Representation of Chester, 1826, with Squibs and Papers;* also *Poll Bk.* (1826, publ. M. Monk).

10 *Hist. Parl., Commons*, 1754–90, i. 221; 1790–1820, ii. 37; F. O'Gorman, *Voters, Patrons, and Parties*, 180 n., 190; *J.C.A.S.* lvii. 48.

11 Above, this chapter: City Government, 1762–1835 (The Assembly).

12 O'Gorman, *Voters, Patrons, and Parties*, 43–4.

13 Ibid. 81; *Rolls of Freemen of Chester*, ii. 315; C.C.A.L.S., ZAB 4, ff. 254, 272v., 288v.

14 *Trial at Large of Quo Warranto, King vs. Amery and Monk* (1786, publ. J. Fletcher); *Sketch of Political Hist.* (1790); *Compilation Relating to Election for City Officers, 1809*, 29–41, 85–8; *Hist. Contested Election, 1812*, 18; *Rep. of Proc. and Evidence*

was vigilant for every opportunity to influence voters in Chester,[1] and willing to spend heavily: perhaps £4,000 a year between elections and far more during them. In 1784 the Grosvenors spent £24,000 in all, of which £15,000 went on drink and £1,600 on yellow ribbons and cockades (their opponents sported blue and red). In 1812 the total came to £23,000.[2] Treating, generosity to the poor at times when food was dear, paying admission fees for freemen, offering well paid employment during elections, and sponsoring public works were all part of the currency; when the machine moved up a gear in the 1810s and 1820s there was coercion and outright bribery.[3]

Among the levers at the Grosvenors' disposal was the ownership of houses and cottages in Chester. From before 1784 they were also lessees of Crown property in the city. Tenants could be offered favourable terms in return for guaranteed support, or pressurized by the threat of higher rents or eviction.[4] The already extensive Grosvenor rental was enlarged between 1810 and 1822 by buying up dozens of houses and shops, both within the walls and in Handbridge.[5]

Hostility to untrammelled aristocratic influence in Chester was led by men drawn from the city's mercantile and manufacturing interests, but was also linked to county families. It employed the rhetoric of civic freedom and Independence, rejecting the undertones of servility implied by the acceptance of Grosvenor patronage.[6] In parliamentary elections the Independents conceded that the Grosvenors had the right to nominate to one of the seats, but for both self-interested and ideological reasons sought to widen access to office in the Assembly. In particular their demand was for elections to the mayoralty and the second, 'popular' shrievalty to be conducted under the strict terms of the charter of 1506, which gave the decisive vote to the freemen, whereas the Assembly wished to retain the nomination of both offices, basing its claims on the disputed charter of Charles II and long-established custom. Opposition to the corpora-

tion, which grew in significance by the end of the period, also flowed from the simple fact that it had excluded opponents of the Grosvenors since the early 18th century. By the 1830s critics were citing the lack of accountability for corporate expenditure (especially that undertaken in defence of its own unacceptable practices); the failure to attend to Chester's commercial facilities; and partiality along political lines in the management of the municipal charities, admissions to the freedom, and the issue of licences to sell drink. The improvement commission was also alleged to have been run on one-party lines.[7]

In contested parliamentary elections from 1784 to 1826 between two fifths and half of the voters gave at least one vote to candidates who articulated those views.[8] Nevertheless over the whole period more than half supported the Grosvenor interest. The Grosvenor candidates were favoured by more of both the wealthiest freemen (gentlemen, professionals, merchants, and industrialists) and the poorest (unskilled and semi-skilled labourers), whereas retailers and craftsmen were on the whole more likely to back the Independents.[9] Individual occupations occasionally voted heavily one way or the other. In the 1818 election for popular sheriff, for example, the tobacco interest, chandlers, skinners, shoemakers, tailors, carpenters and joiners, and plasterers were strongly against the corporation candidate, whereas the shipbuilding trades, plumbers, and painters voted fairly solidly for him.[10] Political allegiances did not necessarily last for life: some 11 per cent of voters changed sides between 1820 and 1826,[11] including one of the Independents' former leaders, the silversmith John Walker.[12]

The city had almost no tradition of radicalism. Tom Paine was burnt in effigy at the Cross in 1793,[13] and the radical *Chester Guardian* established in 1817 folded for lack of support in 1823,[14] the year in which Henry Hunt, making a private visit to Chester, was hoaxed and subjected to vulgar abuse by Whig members of a drinking club, the King's Arms Kitchen.[15]

---

before Cttee. of H.C. upon Late Controverted Election for Chester (1819, publ. J. Gorton), esp. 23–4, 30–1, 41–3, 139; C.C.A.L.S., ZAB 5, p. 288; ZAB 6, p. 1; *V.C.H. Ches.* v (2), Lists of Mayors and Sheriffs.

1 *V.C.H. Ches.* ii. 134; C.C.A.L.S., ZCR 60/8/16 (formerly ZCR 74/328/IX); [F. O'Gorman], 'Decline of Unreformed Politics: Chester 1784–1826' (TS. at C.H.H., cited by kind permission of author), esp. 25.

2 *V.C.H. Ches.* ii. 134, 136; O'Gorman, *Voters, Patrons, and Parties*, 147; colours: e.g. *Compilation Relating to Election for City Officers, 1809*, 106; cf. G. Huxley, *Victorian Duke*, 202.

3 *V.C.H. Ches.* ii. 137; O'Gorman, *Voters, Patrons, and Parties*, 48, 52–3; [O'Gorman], 'Decline of Unreformed Politics', 5; *Hist. Contested Election, 1812*, p. vi.

4 [O'Gorman], 'Decline of Unreformed Politics', 10; *Poole's Dir. Chester* [1791–2], 19; *Compilation Relating to Election for City Officers, 1809*, pp. iv–v.

5 C.C.A.L.S., TS. cat. of Grosvenor MSS. at Eaton Hall, Estate Plan 27; Estate Bks. 89, 669; Recs. Returned to Eaton Estate Office, 1980: 1/C2/2; 2/C2/1; 2/V/3–4; 3/Z/4; 3/Z/6; 5/V/13; 5/Y/7; 6/B2/4; 6/Z/2; 7/B2/5; 7/V/6; 7/V/8; 7/Z/1; 7/Z/5;

8/A2/1–2; 8/A2/4; 8/C2/3.

6 O'Gorman, *Voters, Patrons, and Parties*, 20–1, 259–62; *Letter to Freemen of Chester* (1818, publ. J. Gorton): copy in I.H.R. *Chester Poll Bks. and Election Pamphlets*, iii; cf. R. Sweet, 'Freemen and Independence in Eng. Boro. Politics, c. 1770–1830', *Past and Present*, clxi. 84–115, esp. 92, 99–101, 105.

7 *Rep. Com. Mun. Corp.* pp. 2630–2.

8 O'Gorman, *Voters, Patrons, and Parties*, 275 n.

9 Ibid. 203–4, 220, 282.

10 Based on analysis of *Poll-Bk. for Sheriff* (1818).

11 O'Gorman, *Voters, Patrons, and Parties*, 380.

12 *Compilation Relating to Election for City Officers, 1809*, 8, 17–19; *Hist. Contested Election, 1818*, 50–3 and contemporary pencil attribution to Walker in copy in I.H.R. *Chester Poll Bks. and Election Pamphlets*, ii; *Colln. of Material Facts* (1820), 13–15, 67, 78–81; *Narrative, 1826*, 60, 63, 66–7, 84–5.

13 Hemingway, *Hist. Chester*, ii. 253.

14 Ibid. ii. 264; H. Hughes, *Chronicle of Chester*, 84.

15 Undated cutting [after 1 Aug. 1823] from *Chester Guardian* pasted into *Narrative, 1826* at pp. 60–1 in copy in I.H.R. *Chester Poll Bks. and Election Pamphlets*, iii.

Issues which were believed to affect the prosperity of Chester occasionally intruded into local politics: in 1771 the Assembly's initially lukewarm attitude to the proposed canal was said to have angered mercantile interests,[1] and after 1805 the merits of a plan to deepen the Dee channel so as to allow larger ships to reach Chester had political repercussions.[2] There was also an undercurrent of hostility to Catholicism which repeatedly attached itself to the Independent cause on the grounds that the second Earl Grosvenor was sympathetic to limited measures of Catholic emancipation.[3] In the 1810s the issue seems to have brought at least parts of the clerical establishment into the Independent camp.[4] Generally there were no clear-cut divisions along religious lines. In 1812 a Grosvenor song lampooned the Presbyterians among the Independent party,[5] but in the late 18th century the Grosvenors had successfully cultivated local Methodists and Congregationalists.[6] In 1817 it was said that some freemen who normally supported the corporation objected to its nomination of a dissenter as mayor.[7] Mainly, however, politics in Chester were about access to office in the Assembly and the extent of Grosvenor influence. The Independents' watchwords were 'Freedom of Election' and 'No Bribery'.[8] Connexions between local rivalries and national political groupings were emphasized more after 1815 with the foundation of a Tory King and Constitution Club in 1817 and a Whig Club in 1820.[9]

The house of Eaton's parliamentary candidates were immediate members of the family with only two exceptions, both from the Cheshire gentry, Richard Wilbraham Bootle serving as M.P. 1761–90, and Sir Richard Brooke, Bt., standing unsuccessfully in 1812. Against them the Independents mostly fielded men from county families, notably the Egertons of Oulton, who had been active in Cheshire politics earlier in the 18th century.[10] The leaders of the Independents within the city were successively a merchant, Ralph Eddowes,[11] a gentleman, Roger Barnston of Forest House, Foregate Street,[12] and a brewer, Alderman William Seller.[13] Other prominent supporters included members of the Wrench family, owners of the Dee Mills.[14]

THE COURSE OF POLITICS

Grosvenor control of both seats in parliament was not openly opposed between 1747 and 1784,[15] but in 1771 the canal issue encouraged the Independents to put up a merchant against the corporation's nominee as second sheriff, though he was defeated in a poll of the freemen.[16] In 1784 the Independents challenged the Grosvenors at the parliamentary hustings in April and the Assembly election in October, in both of which they were outmanoeuvred and beaten.[17] John Fletcher, editor of the Whig *Chester Chronicle*, was gaoled for libelling Recorder Townsend;[18] and the Independents brought quo warranto proceedings against two Assemblymen who had been appointed in the usual manner. The House of Lords in 1790 found against the corporation's customary practices and for the validity of the charter of 1506, but negated the Independent victory by failing to award Ralph Eddowes his costs of some £2,000, whereupon he left Chester for the United States. In any case the corporation took the advice of the recorder and simply ignored the Lords' ruling.[19]

1 *Sketch of Political Hist.* (1790), p. xv; *Colln. of Papers* (1807), 58; Hemingway, *Hist. Chester*, ii. 400.

2 *Compilation Relating to Election for City Officers*, 1809, 10–14, 38–41; *Hist. Contested Election, 1818*, pp. vii–viii; *V.C.H. Ches.* v (2), Water Transport: Canals.

3 e.g. *Colln. of Papers* (1807), 43–7; *Compilation Relating to Election for City Officers*, 1809, 112; *Hist. Contested Election, 1812*, pp. xxiv–xxv; *Narrative, 1826*, 33–4, and poster bound after pollbk. in copy in I.H.R. *Chester Poll Bks. and Election Pamphlets*, i; Hemingway, *Hist. Chester*, ii. 285.

4 *Compilation Relating to Election for City Officers*, 1809, 98–106; *Colln. of Material Facts* (1820), 73–7; *Narrative, 1826*, 24; cf. J. Le Neve, *Fasti Ecclesiae Anglicanae*, ed. T. D. Hardy, iii. 272; Ormerod, *Hist. Ches.* i. 340, 344; ii. 371, 564; *Alum. Cantab. 1752–1900*, vi. 346, s.n. Ward, Peploe. Cf. G. Huxley, *Lady Elizabeth and the Grosvenors*, 84.

5 *Hist. Contested Election, 1812*, 47–8; cf. O'Gorman, *Voters, Patrons, and Parties*, 362.

6 C.C.A.L.S., ZCR 60/8/16; cf. voting record of those named in *Alphabetical List of Freemen* (1784), 13, 15, 22.

7 Hemingway, *Hist. Chester*, ii. 414.

8 e.g. *Narrative, 1826*, 22.

9 O'Gorman, *Voters, Patrons, and Parties*, 332, 352–3; Hemingway, *Hist. Chester*, ii. 263, 269.

10 *Hist. Parl., Commons, 1754–90*, ii. 557–9; iii. 638–9; 1790–1820, iii. 676, 706–7; iv. 114–17; Egertons: Ormerod, *Hist. Ches.* ii. 222; G.E.C. *Baronetage*, i. 109–10; *V.C.H. Ches.* ii. 125.

11 *Trial, King vs. Amery and Monk*, p. [i]; *Sketch of Political Hist.* (1790), p. xvi (MS. attribution of authorship to Eddowes in copy in I.H.R. *Chester Poll Bks. and Election Pamphlets*, i);

12 *Colln. of Papers* (1807), 17–18, 47–8, 51–4; *Compilation Relating to Election for City Officers*, 1809, 74–7, 93, 98–9, 106; *Hist. Contested Election, 1818*, 1–2, 11, 30, 34; *Colln. of Material Facts* (1820), 71, 77; *Narrative, 1826*, pp. [iii], 53–4, 97–8, 104; Hemingway, *Hist. Chester*, i. 422–3; ii. 263, 268; Ormerod, *Hist. Ches.* ii. 747–8.

13 *Rolls of Freemen of Chester*, ii. 382; C.C.A.L.S., ZAB 5, pp. 53, 236; *Colln. of Papers* (1807), 17–18; *Hist. Contested Election, 1818*, 34; *Colln. of Material Facts* (1820), 4.

14 *Compilation Relating to Election for City Officers*, 1809, 17–19, 98–9; *Hist. Contested Election, 1812*, 35; *V.C.H. Ches.* v (2), Mills and Fisheries: Dee Corn Mills.

15 *Hist. Parl., Commons, 1754–90*, i. 221; cf. *J.C.A.S.* lvii. 41 n.; Ormerod, *Hist. Ches.* i. 726; *Rolls of Freemen of Chester*, ii. 363–8.

16 Hemingway, *Hist. Chester*, 400; *Trial, King vs. Amery and Monk*, 28, 32, 99; *Sketch of Political Hist.* (1790), p. xv; cf. *Rolls of Freemen of Chester*, ii. 371–3.

17 *J.C.A.S.* lvii. 44–50; Hughes, *Chronicle of Chester*, 48–57; Hemingway, *Hist. Chester*, ii. 401–2.

18 Hughes, *Chronicle of Chester*, 62–3, 66–74.

19 Ibid. 63–4, 74–5; *Trial, King vs. Amery and Monk*; *Sketch of Political Hist.* (1790); *Compilation Relating to Election for City Officers*, 1809, 4, 8–9; *Political Hist. of Chester* (1814), 22–3; C.C.A.L.S., ZAB 5, pp. 9–10, 16, 44–5, 63–4, 81; *L.J.* xxxviii. 405, 441, 537, 547, 596–7; xxxix. 16, 31–3, 253, 272, 403, 522–3, 651, 753–4; *Hist. Parl., Commons, 1790–1820*, ii. 37; Hemingway, *Hist. Chester*, ii. 254, 402–5.

The Grosvenor candidates were again unopposed at parliamentary elections between 1790 and 1806,[1] but in October 1804 the Independents were able to turn to their advantage an incident the previous December in which a member of the Royal Chester volunteer corps had been press-ganged but then sprung from Northgate gaol after rioting by the volunteers. The Independents, whose leaders Roger Barnston and E. O. Wrench commanded the newly formed corps, nominated as second sheriff John Williamson, father-in-law of one of the volunteers tried after the riot; the Assembly gave way and indeed in the following year elected Williamson to the corporation, where he soon became a firm supporter of the regime.[2]

The Grosvenor interest's worst crisis came in the general election of 1807. At the last minute Earl Grosvenor forced his cousin, the former M.P. Richard Erle Drax Grosvenor, to stand down over his opposition to Catholic emancipation, without consulting his supporters in Chester or the corporation, which was said to support Drax Grosvenor's line. The Independents, already busy exploiting what they alleged was the earl's growing high-handedness towards the city, persuaded John Egerton to stand and Grosvenor backed down, leaving Egerton to be returned unopposed.[3] The date was commemorated in song as 'The Glorious Sixth of May', an Independent rallying cry for the next twenty years.[4]

The election ushered in a period of bitter political conflict which lasted until 1829. Earl Grosvenor immediately signalled his determination to resume unfettered control by taking his turn as mayor in 1807–8, thereby snubbing his strongest opponent within the corporation, Alderman William Seller, whose turn as mayor it would otherwise have been.[5] Meanwhile the corporation turned Egerton's supporters out of tenancies on the Crown estate.[6]

The four parliamentary elections until 1826 were accompanied by extensive bribery, intimidation, and disorder,[7] and at elections the city was flooded with Grosvenor's country tenants and with labourers engaged on the rebuilding of Eaton Hall. Several hundred new freemen might be admitted each time.

Canvassing was often rowdy. Polling took place over anything between eight and twelve days at hustings set up in front of the Exchange, and involved the whole community, not only the freemen. The custom in Chester was for each side alternately to bring up a tally of ten voters, gathered together by a district 'captain' in a public house, conveyed in carriages to tally-rooms at the Exchange or in nearby pubs, and escorted by a band of musicians which might be seventy strong. After voting, the freemen were issued with tickets valid for dinner and two gallons of beer back at their starting point. As many as 100 or 140 men voted each day, numbers on each side remaining very close until one party began to run out of support. The first Grosvenor candidate – until 1818 the earl's cousin Thomas Grosvenor and thereafter his son Richard, Viscount Belgrave – normally led the poll comfortably; the real contest was between the second of Grosvenor's men and the main Independent. The Independents always put up a second candidate in an attempt to prevent their supporters from splitting their votes with the Grosvenors, but never had a realistic hope of securing both seats. Egerton (from 1815 Sir John Grey Egerton, Bt.; d. 1825) continued to carry the Independent flag. He was successful in 1812 but, hampered by his support for the suspension of *habeas corpus* (an issue which divided his supporters), was heavily defeated in 1818. In 1820 he ran General Thomas Grosvenor a very close second, as did his brother General C. B. Egerton in 1826. Grosvenor victories were celebrated by elaborate parades through the streets, accompanied by stage-managed cheering and further treating of supporters.[8]

The conflict was exacerbated by the personal and business rivalry of the editors of the two Chester newspapers, the Whig *Chronicle* and the Tory *Courant*, which had changed sides in municipal terms in the wake of Earl Grosvenor's switch to the Whigs in 1807 and thereafter traded insults at every opportunity.[9] It also spilled over into Chester's social life, with rival balls being organized along political lines after 1808, and near riots taking place at the Theatre Royal in 1810 when the officers of the volunteer corps arranged

1 *Hist. Parl., Commons, 1790–1820*, ii. 37.

2 *Political Hist. of Chester* (1814), 24; C. Emsley, *Brit. Society and the French Wars, 1793–1815*, 100, citing P.R.O., HO 42/78; Hemingway, *Hist. Chester*, i. 422–3; ii. 256–9; *Return of Effective Strength of Volunteer Corps of Cavalry, Infantry, and Artillery in G.B., Mar. 1806*, H.C. 59, pp. 60–1 (1806), x; F. Simpson, *The Old Chester Volunteers and their Colour* (priv. print. 1911: copy at C.H.H.); C.C.A.L.S., ZCR 115/1; ZCR 115/3; ZTCC 89, 95–112; cf. J. Edmonds, 'Events at Theatre Royal, Chester, 1807–10', *Ches. Hist.* xxxviii. 60; *Rolls of Freemen of Chester*, ii. 405, 408; C.C.A.L.S., ZAB 4, f. 285v.; ZAB 5, pp. 37, 166, 218.

3 *Hist. Parl., Commons, 1790–1820*, ii. 37–8; iii. 706–7; iv. 115–17; *Colln. of Papers* (1807), 9–18; *Hist. Contested Election, 1818*, pp. ii–iii; Hughes, *Chronicle of Chester*, 79.

4 *Compilation Relating to Election for City Officers, 1809*, 57–9, 63, 107–9; *Hist. Contested Election, 1818*, 60–1; *Narrative,*

1826, 20; *Ches. Hist.* xxxviii. 62–8.

5 *Colln. of Papers* (1807), 19–25, 29–47, 49, 51–60; *Compilation Relating to Election for City Officers, 1809*, 2–3, 29–30; *Letter to J. Egerton* (1807), 2–4; O'Gorman, *Voters, Patrons, and Parties*, 254.

6 [O'Gorman], 'Decline of Unreformed Politics', 15.

7 Para. based on *Hist. Contested Election, 1812*; *Hist. Contested Election, 1818*; *Rep. Cttee. on Election for Chester* (1819); *Colln. of Material Facts* (1820); *Rep. of H.C. on Chester Petition, 1820* (1820, publ. M. Monk); *Narrative, 1826*; O'Gorman, *Voters, Patrons, and Parties*, 136 n., 169 n.; Huxley, *Lady Elizabeth and the Grosvenors*, 84–5.

8 Flier reproduced in [I. Callister], *The Chester Grosvenor [Hotel]: A Hist.* (copy at C.H.H.).

9 Hughes, *Chronicle of Chester*, 80–3; *Compilation Relating to Election for City Officers, 1809*, 31–8.

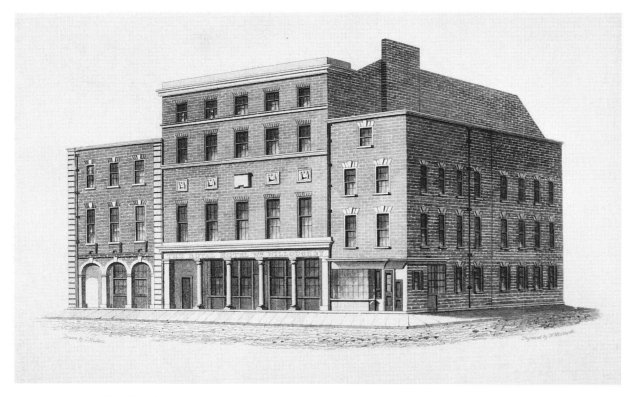

FIG. 8. *The Royal Hotel*

concerts at which 'The Glorious Sixth of May' was to be sung.[1] The Independents' political headquarters in Chester from 1784 were at the Royal Hotel in Eastgate Street, but they were forced from there in 1815 when Earl Grosvenor bought it, and from 1818 used the Albion Hotel in Lower Bridge Street.[2]

In strictly municipal politics, the few Independents on the Assembly were sidelined by the pro-Grosvenor majority as their turn for promotion to sheriff, alderman, or mayor came round. In 1809, amid rowdy scenes at the Exchange, their nomination of Seller as mayor was simply ignored, while a poll for second sheriff went against their nominee.[3] The Independents continued to try to force the issue of popular elections by legal means,[4] and in 1813 a mayor who had fallen out with his colleagues went over to the Independents, allowed them to propose a full list of 64 Assemblymen (a list which included many sitting Assemblymen but also 28 new faces), and swore in Seller as mayor, while simultaneously the recorder was swearing in the old corporation's nom-

inee. Briefly, and to the delight of Chester's wits, the city had two corporations,[5] but the courts settled the matter in favour of the old guard on the grounds of minor procedural irregularities in the 'popular' election.[6]

Seller and his supporters continued to press their case. In 1817 he was nominated by the aldermen as one of their two candidates for mayor, and came out ahead of his rival in a poll of the freemen, but the corporation exercised its right of selection and excluded him again.[7] In 1818 the Independents ran a candidate for second sheriff against the corporation's nominee, an unpopular tobacconist satirized as the 'Dandy Snuffmonger', and got him in with an easy majority,[8] but the following year the mayoral and shrieval elections both went in favour of the corporation's candidates. To the Independents' disgust, the new mayor was the turncoat John Williamson.[9] The Independents had their revenge by citing him for corruption after the general election of 1820 (during which he had gone into hiding in order to

1 *Compilation Relating to Election for City Officers, 1809*, 44–7, 57–9, 63, 74–7; Hemingway, *Hist. Chester*, ii. 408–9; *Ches. Hist.* xxxviii. 61–6.
2 *V.C.H. Ches.* v (2), Places of Entertainment: Assembly Rooms.
3 *Compilation Relating to Election for City Officers, 1809*, 1–9, 15–19, 22–9; Hemingway, *Hist. Chester*, ii. 407–8.
4 C.C.A.L.S., ZAB 5, p. 309; *Rep. Com. Mun. Corp.* p. 2623.
5 Hemingway, *Hist. Chester*, ii. 412–14; *Political Hist. of*

Chester (1814), 25–56; ibid. 26 compared with appointments of Assemblymen in C.C.A.L.S., ZAB 4–5; *Poll-Bk. for Mayor and Sheriff* (1819), 13.
6 *Hist. Parl., Commons*, 1790–1820, ii. 39; Ormerod, *Hist. Ches.* i. 205; *Chester Chron.* 1 Apr. 1814.
7 Hemingway, *Hist. Chester*, ii. 414–15; *Hist. Parl., Commons*, 1790–1820, ii. 39.
8 Hemingway, *Hist. Chester*, ii. 418; *Poll-Bk. for Sheriff* (1818).   9 *Poll-Bk. for Mayor and Sheriff* (1819).

avoid admitting any of their supporters as freemen): he was found guilty, fined £1,000, and gaoled for six months.[1]

Mayor Williamson's conduct during the election seems to have thrown the corporation into disarray, and in October 1820 the aldermen finally allowed William Seller to take his turn as mayor and named as sheriff William Cross, the twice-defeated Independent candidate for the office.[2] In 1821 Seller as mayor conducted a full election of the Assembly by the freemen which produced a more thoroughgoing clear-out of the old Assembly than in 1813, but still not a complete one. His illness, however, prevented him from swearing in the new members on the appointed day and the old corporation continued regardless, electing a new mayor and sheriffs under its usual system. From 1822 the second shrievalty became the main focus of contention between the corporation and its opponents, after the Assembly's nominee declined to stand when the Independents put up Edward Ducker, a former supporter of the Grosvenors who had switched sides.[3] In 1823 and 1824 the Independent candidate was twice beaten in a poll of the freemen. The Independents then challenged the validity of the appointment of George Harrison as mayor in 1824 through quo warranto proceedings, obtained a judgement against him, and had him turned out of office. In 1825 an Independent supporter, William Bevin,[4] was elected second sheriff without a contest, but he died in office[5] and was succeeded by Simeon Leet, who was an Assemblyman but not strongly partisan and whose declaration of impartiality at the start of the bitterly fought general election of 1826 was greeted with 'immense cheering'.[6] In 1827 the Independents brought further quo warranto proceedings against leading members of the Grosvenor party in the Assembly, including the mayor, John Larden, and the second sheriff, Gabriel Roberts, who were forced from office.[7] John Fletcher,

the Revd. Charles Mytton, and John Walker also had to resign their places, though Walker and Fletcher were back within a year as soon as new vacancies arose.[8] The Independents followed up their success by nominating four successive 'popular' sheriffs without a contest.[9] Although the sequence was then broken, it resumed in 1833 and 1834.[10] The Independent sheriffs were not members of the corporation when elected, and only one was afterwards recruited.[11] The normal succession to the mayoralty was also suspended in 1826 but resumed in 1830.[12]

Meanwhile Earl Grosvenor had taken the heat out of parliamentary politics by his announcement in 1829 that he would no longer seek to nominate both of the city's M.P.s.[13] The enormous expense of conducting elections may not have mattered to a man of his vast and growing wealth – he was the fourth richest man in England even before he began developing the Belgravia estate in London after 1826[14] – but the violence and acrimony which attended the general elections of 1820 and 1826 were seen, and rightly, as damaging his interests and influence. An Egerton thus sat for the city amicably alongside a Grosvenor in 1830–1.[15]

The Independents resumed their attack on the corporation with new quo warranto proceedings in 1829 against the mayor of 1821–2 and an alderman and three councilmen elected since 1822, but the case was abandoned after the Court of Great Sessions was abolished in 1830.[16]

Another effect of Earl Grosvenor's changed policy was to allow local politics in Chester to realign along the national division between reformers and conservatives. Whereas in December 1830 an attempt to put up a reformist parliamentary candidate in a byelection against Robert Grosvenor failed ignominiously, at the 1831 general election Sir Philip Egerton was dropped by his supporters in Chester for having voted against the Reform Bill, and they brought in the failed

1 *Colln. of Material Facts* (1820), 79, 87–92.

2 Para. based, except where stated otherwise, on Hemingway, *Hist. Chester*, ii. 421–4; *V.C.H. Ches.* v (2), Lists of Mayors and Sheriffs.

3 *Hist. Contested Election, 1812*, 54; *Hist. Contested Election, 1818*, 88; *Poll-Bk. for Sheriff* (1818), 13; *Poll-Bk. for Mayor and Sheriff* (1819), 31; *Colln. of Material Facts* (1820), 30; *Narrative, 1826*, 15–16; ibid. poll bk. p. 6.

4 *Hist. Contested Election, 1812*, 50; *Hist. Contested Election, 1818*, 84; *Poll-Bk. for Sheriff* (1818), 10; *Poll-Bk. for Mayor and Sheriff* (1819), 27; *Colln. of Material Facts* (1820), 26.

5 C.C.A.L.S., ZAB 6, p. 4.

6 Ibid. ZAB 5, p. 459; *Hist. Contested Election, 1812* (did not vote); *Hist. Contested Election, 1818* (did not vote); *Poll-Bk. for Sheriff* (1818) (did not vote); *Poll-Bk. for Mayor and Sheriff* (1819), 42; *Colln. of Material Facts* (1820), 55; *Narrative, 1826*, 17.

7 C.C.A.L.S., ZAB 6, pp. 9–10; for Larden: *Hist. Contested Election, 1812*, 18; *Narrative, 1826*, 15.

8 C.C.A.L.S., ZAB 6, pp. 8–10, 19.

9 Edw. Titley, Geo. Allender, Thos. Whittakers, and Sam. Witter in: *Hist. Contested Election, 1812*, 49, 68, 70; *Political Hist.*

of *Chester* (1814), 26; *Hist. Contested Election, 1818*, 83, 105; *Poll-Bk. for Sheriff* (1818), 9, 28–9; *Rep. Cttee. on Election for Chester* (1819), 13–14; *Poll-Bk. for Mayor and Sheriff* (1819), 26, 50–1; *Colln. of Material Facts* (1820), 25, 42–4; *Narrative, 1826*, 115; ibid. poll bk. pp. 1, 23, 25. Cf. Ric. Phillpot, who did not vote in those elections.

10 References to Jos. Ridgway and Jn. Kearsley in: *Compilation Relating to Election for City Officers, 1809*, 8; *Hist. Contested Election, 1812*, 61, 67; *Hist. Contested Election, 1818*, 96, 101; *Poll-Bk. for Sheriff* (1818), 20, 26; *Poll-Bk. for Mayor and Sheriff* (1819), 41, 47; *Colln. of Material Facts* (1820), 40, 50; *Narrative, 1826*, 15–16; ibid. poll bk. pp. 14, 20.

11 C.C.A.L.S., ZAB 6, p. 35 (Whittakers).

12 Ibid. ZAB 5–6; *V.C.H. Ches.* v (2), Lists of Mayors and Sheriffs.

13 Hemingway, *Hist. Chester*, ii. 428–9; Hughes, *Chronicle of Chester*, 87; cf. *Narrative, 1826*, 97–8.

14 *Hist. Parl., Commons, 1790–1820*, iv. 115–16; Huxley, *Lady Elizabeth and the Grosvenors*, 2, 7–8.

15 G. L. Fenwick, *Hist. of Ancient City of Chester*, 399.

16 Hemingway, *Hist. Chester*, ii. 424; *Rep. Com. Mun. Corp.* p. 2623; 11 Geo. IV & 1 Wm. IV, c. 70, ss. 14, 39.

candidate of the previous year, Foster Cunliffe Offley, to run unopposed alongside Grosvenor.[1]

The earl's changed policy also opened up the Assembly to supporters of the opposing party. Recruitment of councilmen remained partisan with one exception until October 1829,[2] but from 1830 the corporation began to co-opt Independents (mostly not the most prominent ones) as well as some men who had previously taken little or no part in politics, such as the banker William Wardell.[3]

By then the tide in Chester was moving swiftly towards support for municipal reform.[4] The usual succession to the mayoralty was again suspended in 1831, the office being held in turn by two former mayors;[5] the Assembly discontinued official attendance at church on election day and appointed a committee to report on the municipal charities and the state of its finances. In light of the report it declared that there was nothing to hide in the accounts but ordered strict economies in expenditure.[6] In 1833 some 2,400 residents petitioned parliament for reform of elections to the Assembly,[7] and in 1834 the Assembly declined to join in plans being made by other municipal corporations to resist the intended reform.[8]

CITY GOVERNMENT, 1835–1914

THE REFORMS OF THE 1830S

Under the Municipal Corporations Act of 1835 Chester became a municipal borough governed by a corporation of 30 councillors and 10 aldermen.[9] Its boundaries were extended to match those of the slightly larger parliamentary constituency created in 1832,[10] and it was divided into five wards, each with six councillors.[11] As elsewhere, the latter were elected for three-year terms, two places falling vacant in each ward each year. Aldermen were elected by the councillors for six-year terms, half standing down every three years. The mayor was chosen by the full council on 9 November each year. As a county of itself, the corporation was permitted to appoint a sheriff and a coroner, but was thwarted in its desire to nominate an undersheriff so as to retain the traditional double shrievalty.[12]

The police powers of the improvement commission were transferred to the city council by the 1835 Act,[13] but the commission at first kept charge of the fire service and street lighting and cleansing.[14] There was some confusion over street repairs: the extent of the old corporation's liability had never been clear, the improvement commission maintained some streets, though not to widespread public satisfaction,[15] and it was uncertain after 1835 whether the council was allowed to apply the rates to that purpose. The matter was resolved in 1837, when, using a provision of the 1835 Act, the improvement commission dissolved itself and transferred its powers to the council.[16]

In 1836 the Crown reconfirmed the city's separate quarter sessions and appointed a recorder to replace the old corporation's nominee, who had died early in the year.[17]

Other local government bodies, unchanged during the 1830s, were the bridge commissioners[18] and the poor-law guardians: in the latter case, the union of Chester parishes established in 1762 was not affected by the Poor Law Amendment Act of 1834.[19]

At first, with duties enlarged only by the addition of policing and street repairs, the council managed with committees for finance, watch (i.e. police), paving, city lands, repairs and lettings, and markets, the last three merging in 1838 as the corporate estate committee.[20] Much council business in the very early years was similar to that conducted before 1835, not least because the city's gownsmen and almshouses remained under corporation control until the Municipal Charities Trustees were formed as a separate body in 1837.[21] The council was also active in attempting to

1 Hemingway, *Hist. Chester*, i. 430; Huxley, *Lady Elizabeth and the Grosvenors*, 94; for Offley: G.E.C. *Baronetage*, v. 111–12; *Gent. Mag.* cii (1), 477; 8 *Parl. Deb.* 3rd ser. 434–6; 11 *Parl. Deb.* 3rd ser. 501.

2 C.C.A.L.S., ZAB 6, pp. 9, 15, 19, 24; cf. their votes in *Poll-Bk. for Mayor and Sheriff* (1819), 28, 34, 38–9, 47; *Narrative, 1826*, poll bk. pp. 3, 8, 10, 12, 19–21, 25.

3 C.C.A.L.S., ZAB 6, pp. 35, 39, 45, 49, 56, 58; cf. their votes in *Poll-Bk. for Mayor and Sheriff* (1819), 36, 39, 51; *Colln. of Material Facts* (1820), 18; *Narrative, 1826*, 115; ibid. poll bk. pp. 2, 4, 6, 11, 25.

4 Huxley, *Lady Elizabeth and the Grosvenors*, 99.

5 *V.C.H. Ches.* v (2), Lists of Mayors and Sheriffs.

6 C.C.A.L.S., ZAB 6, pp. 48–9, 59–61.

7 *Rep. Com. Mun. Corp.* p. 2630; *C.J.* lxxxviii. 40; 15 *Parl. Deb.* 3rd ser. 634.

8 C.C.A.L.S., ZAB 6, pp. 54–5.

9 Para. based, except where stated otherwise, on 5 & 6 Wm. IV, c. 76, esp. ss. 31, 61–2, sched. A.

10 *V.C.H. Ches.* v (2), Local Government Boundaries: Modern Boundary Extensions.

11 Ibid.: Ward Boundaries; *Lond. Gaz.* 7 Dec. 1835, pp. 2314–23; cf. *Chester City Cl. Mins. 1906/7*, 610–11, 706–7.

12 T. W. Scragg, 'Chester City Council, Old and New' (Liverpool Univ. B.Phil. thesis, 1971: copy at C.H.H.), 28–9.

13 5 & 6 Wm. IV, c. 76, s. 76; *V.C.H. Ches.* v (2), Law and Order: Policing.

14 C.C.A.L.S., ZTRI 3, ff. 76–77v., 85v., 100–102v., 118v., 122.

15 *Chester Chron.* 1 Jan. 1836.

16 C.C.A.L.S., ZTRI 3, ff. 122–9.

17 Ibid. ZCH 43; *Chester Courant*, 2 Feb. 1836.

18 *V.C.H. Ches.* v (2), Roads and Road Transport: Bridges and Other River Crossings (Grosvenor Bridge).

19 4 & 5 Wm. IV, c. 76, s. 29; *V.C.H. Ches.* ii. 75.

20 *Archives and Records*, ed. Kennett, 44–51.

21 *V.C.H. Ches.* v (2), Charities for the Poor: Municipal; Scragg, 'Chester City Council, Old and New', 34; C.C.A.L.S., ZAB 6.

recover corporation property leased on disadvantageous terms by the Assembly, in fending off the Crown's claim to part of the Roodee,[1] and in taking immediate steps to repair the streets.[2] Rather more significant for continuity was the reappointment as town clerk of John Finchett-Maddock.[3] Whether symbolically or simply from a distaste for unnecessary expense, he had the new council's proceedings minuted in the old Assembly Book.[4]

The most obvious change in 1836 was financial. The finance committee's estimate for its first year was for an outlay of nearly £6,500, but the traditional sources of income (rents and other revenues due to the old corporation) produced just under £4,000, leaving almost £2,500 (38 per cent of the total) to be found from the rates.[5] Escalating expenditure and static non-rate income briefly took the proportion to over 50 per cent in the early 1840s.[6]

COUNCIL POLICIES AND ACTIVITIES

The expanding scope of local government in Chester between 1835 and 1914 largely followed the national pattern and was driven as much by the changes in what central government required of urban local authorities as by the aspirations of Chester's councillors and aldermen.

The first extension in the council's activities was effected under a local Improvement Act of 1845, which gave it powers similar to those exercised a little later by local boards of health.[7] The Act was prompted in part by the need for additional borrowing powers so that the corporation could provide the services which had fallen to it on taking over from the improvement commission. The commissioners had borrowed only £1,000 and their rating powers were tightly constrained;[8] the Act allowed the council to borrow £10,000 and to raise an improvement rate of up to 9*d.* in the pound and a lamp rate (to pay for the fire service and street cleansing as well as lighting) of up to 6*d.* in the pound,[9] both of them additional to the borough rate. The council set up an improvement committee in 1846 to implement its new executive powers and take over the role of the paving committee. At first progress was slow, except in the greater effectiveness with which it pursued existing policies in minor matters such as obliging property owners to keep the steps giving access to the Rows in repair.[10]

The more important business of improving the sewerage system was delayed by the corporation's parsimony and by the incompetence and corruption of its first engineer: work on the main streets was not completed until 1854 and much had to be redone in the 1870s.[11] The council was more energetic in providing better facilities for the markets, another reason for obtaining the Act, but it took time to implement its new powers to buy land and replace inadequate buildings: the cattle market was improved in 1850 but a new building for the main retail markets opened only in 1863.[12]

Although the council thus began putting into place measures similar to those required under the Public Health Act of 1848 it did not adopt the Act itself, partly on grounds of cost and partly through a dislike of central government intervention in its affairs. On the other hand, faced with an influx of poor Irish migrants during the Potato Famine of the later 1840s, and with deteriorating social conditions in parts of the city, it used powers available under the Nuisances Removal and Diseases Prevention Act of 1848, through a new sanitary committee on which representatives of the poor-law guardians also sat. Although the committee relied on persuasion rather than compulsion in its relations with property owners, it took the lead, in advance of legislation in 1851, in inspecting the common lodging houses where many of the poorest Cestrians lived, and was credited with averting many deaths during the cholera epidemic of 1848–9.[13]

The council could also be forceful when it did not have to spend ratepayers' money, notably over shortcomings in the supply of water and gas by private companies.[14] From 1835 it repeatedly sought improvements to the water supply, while baulking at the cost of buying out the company. The sanitary committee was much concerned with water purity and with the inadequacy of the supply to the mainly working-class district of Handbridge. A water supply committee was set up in 1852 with a brief to consider taking over the company: it pressed for filtration, an extension of the mains, and a constant supply, and by threats and cajoling eventually pushed the company into action in the later 1850s.[15] The Chester Gas Light Company was of concern mainly because it provided street lighting. Again, the council was eager to complain about the service but unwilling to

1 *Chester Chron.* 12, 19 Feb., 8 July, 12 Aug., 30 Sept., 9 Dec. 1836. 2 Ibid. 5 Feb., 2 Sept. 1836.

3 Scragg, 'Chester City Council, Old and New', 28.

4 C.C.A.L.S., ZAB 6, p. 63.

5 *Chester Chron.* 20 May, 26 Aug., 2, 30 Sept., 25 Oct., 30 Dec. 1836; C.C.A.L.S., ZCCB 1, p. 49.

6 C.C.A.L.S., ZCCB 1, pp. 203, 224, 242.

7 Para. based, except where stated otherwise, on Chester Improvement Act, 1845, 8 & 9 Vic. c. 15 (Local and Personal).

8 Above, this chapter: City Government, 1762–1835 (Improvement Commission).

9 8 & 9 Vic. c. 15 (Local and Personal), ss. 26, 271, 273.

10 *Archives and Records*, ed. Kennett, 47; *V.C.H. Ches.* v (2), The Rows: Rebuilding and Enclosure.

11 *V.C.H. Ches.* v (2), Public Utilities: Sewerage.

12 Ibid.: Markets; 8 & 9 Vic. c. 15, ss. 41–2.

13 M. Glazier, 'Common Lodging Houses in Chester, 1841–71', *Victorian Chester*, ed. R. Swift, 53–83, esp. 60–4; J. Perry, 'Cholera and Public Health Reform in Early Victorian Chester', ibid. 119–47, esp. 131–4, 140; Nuisances Removal and Diseases Prevention Act, 11 & 12 Vic. c. 123; Common Lodging Houses Act, 14 & 15 Vic. c. 28.

14 Cf. *Business Hist.* xix. 142–8.

15 *V.C.H. Ches.* v (2), Public Utilities: Water.

provide its own; in 1851 it backed a rival new company by renting a site to its promoter and giving him the street-lighting contract, but was outwitted when the new company re-established a monopoly.[1]

Other issues concerned with public health were handled whenever possible at a distance, though there were occasional signs of more direct involvement. A much needed new public cemetery was provided by a private company in 1848 but the mayor was an *ex officio* director and part of the land had belonged to the corporation.[2] In the same year the council facilitated a private initiative to provide a public baths and wash-house by leasing a suitable plot and making a grant; more remarkably, when the promoters ran into financial difficulties, the council took over the baths in 1850 (albeit on a split vote) and in so doing became only the eighth local authority in the country to adopt the 1846 Baths and Wash-houses Act.[3] The powers obtained under the 1845 Act to buy land as places of public recreation were never exercised, though Chester acquired an early public park in 1867 when the Grosvenor family donated the site of what became Grosvenor Park, paid for it to be laid out, and provided an endowment towards its upkeep.[4]

The council's unsystematic approach to public health policy and its implementation was exemplified by the establishment of no fewer than five separate committees dealing with interconnected aspects between 1848 and 1852.[5] Only when the Public Health Act of 1872 made Chester an urban sanitary authority and required it to appoint a medical officer of health was a wider-ranging unitary public health committee formed.[6] The first medical officer of health, appointed in 1873, also acted for adjoining districts in west Cheshire.[7]

The council was more successful in its reluctance to spend public money on education. The extra school places required after the 1870 Education Act were provided by voluntary efforts rather than through a school board. After 1877, conforming with national legislation, it appointed a school attendance officer and committee.[8] A minor educational initiative was to acquire the Mechanics' Institution library and

museum in 1875–6;[9] Chester thus adopted the Free Libraries Acts well ahead of many towns of similar size and character.[10]

The Chester union became a regular poor-law union in 1869 and was enlarged by the addition of 43 rural townships in 1871.[11] The guardians built a new workhouse in Hoole Lane in 1877–8 to accommodate the larger numbers,[12] and the old workhouse on the Roodee then reverted to the corporation, which rented it for commercial use, latterly as a jam factory, before selling it in 1900.[13] The city was made into a single civil parish in 1885 so that poor rates could be equalized between the parishes and to save on the costs of collection.[14]

The Chester Improvement Act of 1884 marked a further increase in the council's powers,[15] notably in its capacity to borrow £15,000 towards buying out the bridge commissioners' interest in the Dee and Grosvenor Bridges and abolishing the tolls, and £35,000 for future street improvements. For the first time it was able to issue stock as well as raise mortgages against its rate income.[16] Otherwise the new powers were mainly regulatory: for acquiring closed burial grounds, controlling infectious diseases, and passing bylaws to limit advertising hoardings, for example. It was also permitted to enforce more stringent building regulations, lease the Roodee for public entertainments, and control pleasure boating on the river as far upstream as Aldford, well beyond the city boundary.[17]

Chester became a county borough in 1889.[18] Its boundaries were those delimited in 1835, and apart from minor adjustments in 1898 remained the same until the 1930s,[19] leaving the city on the eve of the First World War as the second smallest county borough in England and Wales (after Canterbury).[20] In 1898–9 the council applied in vain to extend its boundaries into both Cheshire and Flintshire,[21] and negotiations in 1905–6 about incorporating Hoole into the city also failed, ostensibly over the period during which Hoole's rates would be capped.[22] In 1914 the city thus excluded significant parts of the built-up area, notably the heavy industries in Saltney and the important residential suburb of Hoole. Saltney, which had a population of

1 *V.C.H. Ches.* v (2), Public Utilities: Gas.
2 Ibid.: Cemeteries. Plate 41.
3 Ibid.: Baths and Wash-Houses.
4 8 & 9 Vic. c. 15 (Local and Personal), s. 44; *V.C.H. Ches.* v (2), Open Spaces and Parks: Public Parks.
5 *Archives and Records*, ed. Kennett, 44–5, 50–1, 54.
6 Ibid. 46–7; 35 & 36 Vic. c. 79, esp. ss. 3–4, 10.
7 *Chester Chron.* 11 Jan., 14 July 1873.
8 *V.C.H. Ches.* v (2), Education: 1870–1902.
9 Ibid. Libraries; Museums.
10 *Municipal Corporations Companion* (1879), 372; *Municipal Year Bk.* (1909), 706–8.
11 *V.C.H. Ches.* ii. 75–6.
12 *Archives and Records*, ed. Kennett, 80; *V.C.H. Ches.* v (2), Medical Services: City Hospital.
13 *Chester City Cl. Mins. 1899/1900*, 34, 38, 424, 430, 475,

479–80; *Chester City Cl. Abstract of Accts. 1902/3*, 42 (copy in C.C.A.L.S., ZDTR 5/28).
14 Chester Improvement Act, 1884, 47 & 48 Vic. c. 239 (Local), preamble, s. 11.
15 Para. based on ibid. *passim.*
16 Ibid. ss. 13–75, 108–28.
17 Ibid. ss. 84–107, 129–40, 146, 148, 150, 168, 171–80, 188.
18 *V.C.H. Ches.* ii. 79; Local Government Act, 1888, 51 & 52 Vic. c. 41, s. 31, sched. 3.
19 *V.C.H. Ches.* v (2), Local Government Boundaries: Modern Boundary Extensions.
20 e.g. *Municipal Year Bk.* (1909), 959–60.
21 C.C.A.L.S., ZCA 5; *Chester Chron.* 21 Jan. 1899.
22 *Chester City Cl. Mins. 1904/5*, 1008, 1050–1; *1905/6*, 37, 377–9, 748, 953–4, 1055–8, 1062–3; *1906/7*, 6; cf. *1907/8*, 580; *Chester Chron.* 2 Nov. 1895, p. 2; 7 Jan. 1911.

perhaps 2,000 in 1911, was merely a township and civil parish,[1] but Hoole acquired its own local board in 1864 under the provisions of the 1858 Local Government Act. The built-up part of the township became an urban sanitary district under the 1872 Public Health Act and an urban district in 1894; by 1914 it had a population of almost 6,000.[2] The local board's main activities were sewerage works in the 1860s, the organization of street lighting and cleansing, and building new offices for itself in Westminster Road in 1893.[3] The urban district council, which was divided into two wards each electing six councillors,[4] was initially preoccupied with laying out new residential streets,[5] but built a fire station for a volunteer brigade in 1898[6] and opened a small public park in 1904.[7]

At the end of the 19th century Chester city council was still largely reactive, unwilling to commit itself to major new initiatives except when compelled by central government. For example, it acquired powers to supply electricity in 1890 largely to forestall private suppliers, then, like many other towns, delayed making use of them for years;[8] it opened a recreation ground in Handbridge in 1892 only when the duke of Westminster paid for it;[9] and it undertook a much needed reform of the race meeting in 1893 only to outflank those who wished to abolish it altogether.[10] After 1900, however, the council was more interventionist, partly because national legislation compelled it to be, but partly by choice. As a county borough, Chester became a local education authority in 1902, and educational provision immediately became its most onerous and expensive duty.[11] It spent heavily on a new public baths opened in 1901,[12] bought the horse-drawn tramway, electrified the system, and extended it between 1901 and 1906,[13] and opened discussions on taking over the privately funded Grosvenor Museum in 1904.[14] The council's most far-sighted visions were often shaped in committee or by its salaried officers. As early as 1905, for example,

the tramways committee wanted to start a motor-bus service which would have been one of the earliest municipal services in the country, though the full council vetoed the idea;[15] while in Sydney Britton, appointed in 1904, the council took into its service one of the most innovative municipal electrical engineers of his generation. Among his early projects was the hydroelectric power station opened at the Dee Bridge in 1913 on the site of the Dee Mills which the council had earlier bought and demolished.[16]

The council also began cautiously providing public housing at a time when few towns of similar size and status were doing so. It set up a housing committee in 1899 and used the legislation of 1890–1900 to build 12 cottages at Tower Road near the canal basin in 1904. Plans for 28 more were first approved in 1906 but delayed by the First World War.[17] Smallholdings were laid out at Lache in 1911–13 under the 1908 Act.[18]

The growing complexity of local government was recognized in 1902 when the council reorganized its committee structure, set out the duties of its chief officers, and determined on a fuller record of its business.[19] The council and committee minutes had been printed since 1896 and were henceforth indexed too.[20] From 1903 the town clerk was a full-time salaried official.[21]

The council's increasing activity in the early 20th century was exemplified by its efforts to attract visitors. It had already acquired good and early public parks and recreation areas with a minimum of its own expenditure.[22] From small beginnings in 1900, by 1906 it was advertising widely and distributing 10,000 copies of an annual illustrated handbook.[23] The work was thought sufficiently important by 1905 to justify a separate advertising committee,[24] which co-opted three representatives of the Chester Traders' Association.[25] Its budget was limited by the lack of powers to spend rate income on advertising, but the council set aside £100 a year from the issue of

1 *Census*, 1861, 177; 1871, 526; 1881, 523; 1891, 458; 1901, *Flints.* 8, 10; 1911, 411, 475.

2 *V.C.H. Ches.* ii. 77, 79, 218, 227; *Archives and Records*, ed. Kennett, 83–4.

3 C.C.A.L.S., ZTRH H1/24, 44–5. Detail of local government in Hoole is reserved for treatment elsewhere in the V.C.H.

4 *Kelly's Dir. Ches.* (1910), 365.

5 C.C.A.L.S., ZTRH 81.

6 Ibid. pp. 282, 401, 439.

7 *V.C.H. Ches.* v (2), Open Spaces and Parks: Public Parks.

8 Ibid. Public Utilities: Electricity; cf. *Business Hist.* xix. 156.

9 *V.C.H. Ches.* v (2), Open Spaces and Parks: Public Parks.

10 Ibid. Chester Races.   11 Ibid. Education: 1903–18.

12 Ibid. Public Utilities: Baths and Wash-Houses.

13 Ibid.: Local Public Transport.

14 Ibid. Museums.

15 *Chester City Cl. Mins. 1904/5*, 483–93, 599–601, 765–6; *1905/6*, 638–9, 801, 917, 1010–12; *1906/7*, 109, 464–5.

16 *V.C.H. Ches.* v (2), Mills and Fisheries: Dee Corn Mills; Public Utilities: Electricity.

17 *Chester City Cl. Mins. 1905/6*, 950–2, 1038–41; *Chester City*

Cl. Abstracts of Accts. 1904/5 and later (copies in C.C.A.L.S., ZDTR 5/30–40); *Municipal Year Bk.* (1909), 616–22, 625; Housing of the Working Classes Acts, 1890, 53 & 54 Vic. c. 70; 1894, 57 & 58 Vic. c. 55; 1900, 63 & 64 Vic. c. 59.

18 *Chester City Cl. Abstracts of Accts. 1911/12* to *1913/14*; Small Holdings and Allotments Act, 1908, 8 Edw. VII, c. 36.

19 *Chester City Cl. Mins. 1901/2*, 727, 829–30, 882–9.

20 Ibid. *1896/7* and later.

21 *Archives and Records*, ed. Kennett, 36–7.

22 *V.C.H. Ches.* v (2), Open Spaces and Parks: The Groves, Public Parks.

23 *Chester City Cl. Mins. 1899/1900*, 537, 541; *passim* to *1913/14*, via indexed refs. s.v. advertising, e.g. *1902/3*, 276, 279, 296, 372, 469, 488; *1903/4*, 141–2, 246–8, 259, 562; *1904/5*, 226, 402–3, 405, 572–3, 650–3, 1018–20; *1905/6*, 539–40; *1913/14*, 402, 600.

24 Ibid. *1904/5*, 256; *1905/6*, 23.

25 Ibid. *1905/6*, 130, 343, 441–6; *1913/14*, 258–9, 401. For membership of C.T.A. compare ibid. *1905/6*, 441–6, 806 (names of reps.) with *Kelly's Dir. Ches.* (1906), 251 (Geo. Day), 257 (Rob. Knowles), 261 (A. O. Roberts).

boating licences, and the Traders' Association contributed too.[1]

The council also showed itself increasingly responsive to local lobbying for often quite minor improvements to the city centre, above all in matters where the impression made on visitors was either a real issue or could be invoked. Thus in 1902 it referred unauthorized city guides to the chief constable on the grounds that they were a nuisance to visitors, and in 1904 provided waste baskets in Grosvenor Park and the Groves, in both cases following up requests from residents.[2] At around the same time, and for similar motives, it concerned itself with the location of urinals and the discouragement of spitting.[3]

By 1914 local government in Chester was thus far more complex and wide-ranging than it had been in 1835. The council's committee structure had burgeoned with its responsibilities,[4] and its paid staff had grown in numbers, the salary bill for the core staff rising from under £700 a year in the 1850s to c. £2,500 in 1914.[5] Because Chester was so small a town, however, the scale of local government was rather limited. In 1906 the city employed only 630 people, the fourth lowest total of all the county boroughs, of whom a mere 59 were clerical staff. Per head of population its workforce was commensurate with those of several other resorts and small county towns.[6] Although small, the council embraced modernity in office practice, buying its first typewriter apparently in 1903, and by 1905 installing typewriters and duplicating machines in its main departments.[7]

FINANCE

Until the 1860s the corporation's finances were relatively stable.[8] In the 1850s annual income was in the order of £10,000 to £12,000, of which about £1,500 came from rents, £1,200 from market tolls, £2,000–£3,500 from the borough rate, between £1,500 and £3,250 from the watch rate, and smaller sums from a great variety of other sources. The largest fixed items of expenditure were the police force (up to £2,000 a year), the city gaol (usually about £1,600), and servicing the council's debt (normally about £1,100). They remained the largest recurrent annual costs until the 1870s. From 1853 to 1872, for instance, the gaol always cost over £1,300 a year, occasionally over £2,000, towards which only a few hundred pounds a year was ever recovered from the sale of prisoners' labour in oakum-picking and stone-breaking.

Capital projects which required borrowing were few before the 1860s. Apart from the £10,000 borrowed under the 1845 Improvement Act,[9] the only sums raised were £900 in 1852 to buy the baths, £2,446 in 1853 to extend the cattle market, and £800 in 1856 for repairs to the Exchange. From the 1860s, however, ever-larger sums were borrowed for capital works. The biggest items were £11,000 in 1863 for a new market hall, £35,000 in 1867 and 1870 for a new town hall after the Exchange was destroyed by fire (the balance of the cost coming from insurance), and £50,000 over the period 1873–9 for sewerage works. Even the smaller amounts spent on buying up property for extending the markets were large by earlier standards, so that by the time of the 1884 Improvement Act the council had raised a little over £120,000 in loans.[10] Of £101,000 outstanding in 1878–9, the main source was public works loans, accounting for 46 per cent; private individuals had advanced 30 per cent, the governors of the Chester infirmary 11 per cent, and the trustees of the Owen Jones charity 10 per cent.[11] The Act itself sanctioned loans of a further £50,000,[12] and allowed the corporation to create £150,000 of 3½ per cent stock, mostly redeemable in 40 years; by 1891–2 over £136,000 of stock had been issued.[13]

The total borrowed over the period 1884–1914 was over £1½ million. By far the largest object of capital expenditure in that period was electricity generation and supply, for which £143,000 was borrowed between 1895 and 1913, together with the electric tramway system, which required another £82,000.[14] Street improvements took £64,000 and sewerage schemes £88,000, principally for the new sewage works in Sealand. £64,000 was spent on school buildings between 1902 and 1914, and other building works required about as much: £21,000 for the isolation hospital, £19,000 for the swimming baths, £8,000 to buy and then replace the fire station, £13,000 on

---

1 *Chester City Cl. Mins.* 1904/5, 402–3; 1905/6, 343, 713–15.

2 Ibid. 1901/2, 675; 1903/4, 792, 804–5, 866.

3 e.g. ibid. 1901/2, 631–2; 1903/4, 612–13, 684; 1904/5, 194–5, 512–13, 1060.

4 *Archives and Records*, ed. Kennett, 44–56.

5 *Chester City Cl. Abstracts of Accts.* 1853/4 to 1914/15, passim.

6 *Municipal Year Bk.* (1909), 959–60, compared with pop. figs.: ibid. 9–207; cf. Bath, Blackpool, Bournemouth, Brighton, Exeter, Hastings, Ipswich, Lincoln, and Southport.

7 *Chester City Cl. Mins.* 1903/4, 150; 1904/5, 171, 232, 252, 258, 669, 685, 836.

8 Section based on printed *Chester City Cl. Abstracts of Accts.* [under various titles] from 1853/4 to 1914/15: copies (sometimes multiple) in C.C.A.L.S., ZCCF 1 (pts. 3–5); ZDTR 5/1–40. No similar accts. before 1853/4 have been traced, nor those for 1858/9, 1864/5, 1867/8, or 1868/9. The financial year began on 1 Sept. until 1880/1 and on 26 Mar. from 1882/3; an acct. for the period 1 Sept. 1881 to 25 Mar. 1882 bridges the gap. The only copy of the accts. for 1861/2 is defective.

9 8 & 9 Vic. c. 15 (Local and Personal), s. 26.

10 Chester Improvement Act, 1884, 47 & 48 Vic. c. 239 (Local), 7th sched.

11 *Chester City Cl. Abstract of Accts.* 1878/9.

12 47 & 48 Vic. c. 239 (Local), 7th sched.

13 *Chester City Cl. Abstract of Accts.* 1884/5, 38–9; in later years entered under Chester Corp. Loans Fund.

14 Para. based on ibid. 1881/2 to 1913/14, Borough Fund Capital Accts. passim; ibid. 1902/3 and 1913/14, Borrowings on Stock and Mortgage Accts. Figures rounded to nearest £1,000.

repairs and improvements to the town hall, and £5,000 on the market buildings.

Revenue expenditure continued to rise throughout the period from the 1860s, not least as the council took on a greater range of tasks. Almost every service that it already provided in the 1850s cost far more by 1914. Taking 1853–4 as a base, street repairs and related works, for example, cost three times as much, the police force four and a half times, street lighting almost six times, and the fire brigade over eight times, all during a period free of price inflation. The services newly provided by the corporation – whether voluntarily or imposed by central government – inevitably added further to its expenditure, and on an increasing scale. The new public markets, for example, cost on average £662 a year to run before they were enlarged in 1882, and £1,062 afterwards. Average annual expenditure on the parks was £325 before the 1890s and £582 after 1900; on the swimming baths under £150 before the new baths were opened in 1901 but over ten times as much later. The public health committee was spending *c.* £700 a year between 1884 and 1892 but *c.* £1,400 between 1892 and 1914, while the annual running costs of the sewage works grew from £1,400 to £5,200 after they were enlarged in 1900–5. Even one-off costs were higher: the 1884 Improvement Act cost the corporation under £1,200, the 1896 Chester Corporation Act over £7,600. At the same time the rising tide of capital expenditure added inexorably to the cost of servicing the council's debt, from under £2,000 in a typical year before 1866 to over £7,000 *c.* 1900.

After *c.* 1900 the council's expenditure was growing even more sharply. The isolation hospital opened in 1898, for instance, incurred a net average running cost (after taking into account charges for patients from other local authorities) of £1,889 between 1900 and 1914. By far the largest new item, however, was the cost of schools after 1902. By the earlier 1910s the council was spending on average £13,838 a year, representing in 1913–14 some 46 per cent of a total education budget of £30,000, the balance coming from Board of Education grants and other outside sources.

The council's income other than the rates was inelastic. Traditional sources carried over from before 1835 were far outstripped by the rising cost of providing services. Rents from the corporation's land and houses in particular were scarcely higher in 1914 than they had been in the 1820s, while the public markets, profitable as they were, brought in only three times the revenue of the 1850s on the eve of the First World War, and the Roodee generated only £2,000 a year by 1914, though that was almost ten times what it had made in the 1850s.

Ratepayers bore the brunt of the increase in council expenditure. In cash terms the main borough rate produced *c.* £2,000 in 1853–4 but almost £38,000 in 1913–14; as a proportion of expenditure from the main account it needed to cover only about a third in the 1850s and 1860s, 60 per cent from the 1870s to the 1890s, and almost three quarters by 1914. The total sum raised from all the rates was stable in the range £21,000–£23,000 a year in the period 1878–92, then jumped by stages to twice that level in 1903–7. From 1908 it was rising year on year and had reached £57,000 by 1914. Ratepayers were normally required to pay between 2s. 9d. and 3s. 4d. in the pound between the 1870s and 1897 but thereafter saw a huge increase which took the rate over 4s. every year after 1902 and to almost 6s. by 1914. The rate was made up of four components, of which the three smaller parts other than the borough rate were a watch rate for the police force (3d. in the pound 1876–1904, then 4d.), a lamp rate for lighting and cleansing the streets and for the fire brigade (always the maximum permissible of 6d. in the pound except for 1884), and from 1876 a library rate of 1d. in the pound.

The corporation's two large new enterprises, electricity and tramways, were both remunerative. The revenue accounts of the electricity department showed a surplus over the period 1896–1914 of £155,000. Although most of it had to be spent on servicing the debt incurred in setting up the business, £23,000 was available for sinking and reserve funds, £10,000 for new capital expenditure, £8,000 for repairs, and £7,000 to subsidize the rates.[1] The tramways, which began working in 1903, were less profitable, but of a total working surplus before 1914 of £49,000, £7,000 remained as the net balance after paying interest and creating a sinking fund.[2] Those sums went only a little way towards offsetting the council's expenditure in other areas, and in 1907–8, for example, neither business produced as big a surplus as the markets.[3] The total subsidy to the rates from Chester's municipal trading was nevertheless as much as 5¼d. in the pound in 1908–9, about the middle of the range for those towns where a profit was made, when many others were losing money on similar enterprises.[4]

1 *Chester City Cl. Abstract of Accts. 1913/14.*
2 Ibid. *1903/4* to *1913/14*, Tramways Accts.
3 *Municipal Year Bk.* (1909), 494, 553, 689.
4 Ibid. 895–6.

POLITICS, 1835–1914

The two-member constituency, at first solidly Liberal and still much influenced by the Grosvenors, was riddled with bribery until 1880, votes being freely bought for beer by both parties. There was a further source of corruption. Although freemen retained their parliamentary votes until 1918 and were a significant proportion of the electorate before 1867, many were too poor to qualify under the £10 householder franchise, and party agents on both sides paid admittance fees and a day's wages when they took up the freedom. There were almost 1,000 freemen voters in 1880 and still over 700 in 1914.[1]

By abandoning their hotly disputed claim to both seats in 1829, the Grosvenor family strengthened a widely acknowledged right to one of them, which was unchallenged by Liberal factions and Tories alike.[2] Lord Robert Grosvenor sat from 1832 to 1847, when he was replaced at an uncontested byelection by his nephew Hugh, Earl Grosvenor. The latter remained M.P. until he succeeded his father as marquess of Westminster in 1869, when in another uncontested byelection he was followed by his cousin Norman Grosvenor. The family's first partner at Chester was the lawyer John Jervis, knighted as attorney-general in 1846, who left the Commons in 1850. He was succeeded by W. O. Stanley, son of Lord Stanley of Alderley, who sat until 1857, when he was replaced by a local businessman, the Radical Enoch Salisbury.[3] The Conservatives did not always bother to fight Chester and when they did (in 1837, 1850, and 1857) they were beaten heavily, receiving only 350–800 votes to the Liberals' 1,000–1,300 from an electorate which grew slowly from 2,000 in 1832 to 2,500 in 1865. The Chester Tories had a chance only when the Liberals fell into disarray in 1859, Salisbury being defeated for the second seat by a popular local man, Philip Humberston, who had the support of Whigs unwilling to give their second vote to a Radical.[4] A worse Liberal split took place in 1865, when the Whig and Radical factions each ran a candidate alongside Earl Grosvenor. The Conservative, Chester-born H. C.

Raikes, nevertheless came fourth after vigorous interventions for the Whig, W. H. Gladstone, by his father, the chancellor of the exchequer, against the normal understanding that cabinet ministers did not campaign outside their own constituencies.[5]

The 1867 Reform Act more than doubled the electorate to some 6,000, adding more natural Conservatives than Liberals among the newly enfranchised working men, though also boosting support for Earl Grosvenor. Of the two candidates who stood in both 1865 and 1868 the earl put on 900 votes, but Raikes added 1,600. Again in 1868 the second Liberal vote was divided between Salisbury and a Whig, and Raikes got in. The Radical vote had been falling as a share of the total: from 38 per cent in 1857 to 28 per cent in 1859 and 1865 and only 21 per cent in 1868. Although in 1859 Salisbury drew some support from across the social spectrum, more of his voters were qualified as freemen than as £10 householders, and well over half were small shopkeepers, tradesmen, and labourers.[6] In 1868 he made special efforts to target Welsh-speaking electors,[7] but the new votes of railway servants probably largely went to Raikes in 1868,[8] and it is doubtful that any second Liberal candidate could have beaten him. Raikes later claimed that he failed to head the poll only because his party agents were so fearful of the consequences for Chester of displacing Earl Grosvenor that late in the day they instructed their supporters not to plump for Raikes but to give their second vote to the earl.[9]

Raikes also improved the party's organization in Chester, using the existing Constitutional Society to spawn a Constitutional Friendly Society in 1873 as a front for channelling private funds into an annual treat for Conservative supporters. In September 1879 the Friendly Society sent some 2,287 trippers to the seaside at Rhyl.[10] He was probably also behind the large and successful branch of the Primrose League established in the 1880s.[11]

The Grosvenors withdrew from the seat in 1874, when the Liberal candidates were the senior party politician J. G. Dodson and one of the local leaders, Sir Thomas Frost, but in 1880 they came back, partnering Dodson with the first duke of Westmin-

---

1 *Rep. Com. Corrupt Practices in Chester* [C. 2824], pp. v, xii, xvi–xvii, H.C. (1881), xl; *City of Chester Year Bk.* (1903 and later edns.).

2 Results and biographical details in this para. based on *Brit. Parl. Election Results, 1832–85*, ed. F. W. S. Craig (1989), 86–7; *Who's Who of Brit. M.P.s*, i. 157, 170–1, 204, 211–12, 339–40, 361.

3 Below, this section (Municipal Politics).

4 H. St. J. Raikes, *Life and Letters of Henry Cecil Raikes*, 46; *Browns and Chester*, ed. H. D. Willcock, 144.

5 *Gladstone Diaries*, ed. M. R. D. Foot and H. C. G. Matthew, vi. 348, 351, 357, 359, 369; Raikes, *Life and Letters*,

pp. xiii, 47–52.

6 *Brit. Parl. Election Results, 1832–85*, 86–7; J. R. Vincent, *Pollbks.: How Victorians Voted*, 95–6.

7 Welsh-language election posters etc. in Cardiff Univ., Salisbury Libr. Archive, Salisbury MSS.: inf. from Dr. M. F. Cragoe.

8 Raikes, *Life and Letters*, 69, 156.

9 Ibid. 70; H. J. Hanham, *Elections and Party Management: Politics in the Time of Disraeli and Gladstone*, 80.

10 C. O'Leary, *Elimination of Corrupt Practices in Brit. Elections, 1868–1911*, 136; *Rep. Com. Corrupt Practices in Chester*, pp. xi, 78–9.

11 M. Pugh, *The Tories and the People, 1880–1915*, 18, 243.

ster's nephew Beilby Lawley. In 1874 Raikes, who was building up a strong local following, cleverly chose to run alone and won narrowly.[1] The local Liberal party determined to organize better for the 1880 election through a Liberal Association established in 1879; on the model of those elsewhere, it comprised a large representative (but nominal) ruling body, the '300', and a small executive committee. Sir Thomas Frost was its president, but the key figures were two of the vice-presidents, Enoch Salisbury and A. O. Walker, and William Brown, who was chairman and treasurer of the finance committee.[2]

Extensive treating and bribery were undertaken by both parties in 1880 in a campaign also marked by mob violence in the streets, directed especially against an Independent candidate. Salisbury, Walker, and the candidates resigned from the Liberal Association in order to conduct it more discreetly.[3] The result of the election was a comprehensive Liberal victory.[4] The Conservatives immediately petitioned against the result; after a short hearing in Chester had uncovered much evidence of corruption, the M.P.s were unseated and the matter was referred to a Royal Commission which exonerated the candidates but imposed a seven-year disqualification from voting on 914 individuals who had given or received bribes or treats. Chester was left unrepresented in parliament until 1885.[5]

The redistribution of 1885 left Chester with one seat, for which the electorate grew steadily from 6,300 to 8,100 by 1910.[6] National issues played an increasingly important part in the city's parliamentary elections,[7] especially the immediate matter of Irish Home Rule, over which the duke of Westminster broke decisively with Gladstone and the Liberal party. Both Gladstone and the duke were influential in Chester,[8] and Home Rule had many supporters in the city,[9] but Grosvenor's weight may have been critical. In 1885 the Liberal-Radical, an Anglo-Irish Home Ruler, beat the Conservative by 300 votes,[10] but the following year the duke refused to endorse the new member, Walter Foster, lent transport to the Conservatives during the

election, and made two powerful Unionist speeches in Chester.[11] Partly as a result, the Conservative, Robert Yerburgh, won by a narrow margin. Both Gladstone and the Liberal leadership in the county bitterly condemned the duke's 'interference', which they believed had cost them the seat.[12] Chester was thereafter a relatively safe Conservative constituency: Yerburgh won it in 1892, 1895 (unopposed), and 1900, and was defeated only in the Liberal landslide of 1906, regaining and then holding it in the two elections of 1910. The number of Conservative voters grew from 2,400 in 1885 to almost 4,000 in the very high turnout of January 1910; the Liberals mustered 2,400–2,700 in elections between 1885 and 1900 and 3,500–3,700 in 1906 and 1910.

MUNICIPAL POLITICS

The Grosvenor family's direct influence over the corporation was broken by the Municipal Corporations Act of 1835 and the first council elections at the end of the year. More revealing than the success of only 5 Tories against 35 Liberals[13] was the pattern of former political allegiances. Twelve of the 40 had voted against the Grosvenor candidates in the 1826 general election and a further six had split their votes, which amounted to the same thing. There were only six out-and-out Grosvenor supporters. A large group, who had not voted at all in 1826, had presumably been uncommitted in the earlier struggles.[14] They included some of the larger businessmen new to the council, several of whom served for many years, such as E. S. Walker of the leadworks and the banker William Wardell.[15] There were thus many new faces in the council chamber. The only man with long service was the banker Thomas Dixon, a councilman since 1811 and an alderman since 1827, who received the largest number of votes in any of the wards and, with Walker, headed the new list of aldermen. Another seven had entered the old corporation between 1823 and 1830, five of them in the Grosvenor camp, though they only just secured their places in 1835. They were balanced by five of the Independents who had served as sheriff since 1822.

1 Raikes, *Life and Letters*, 83–4; *Brit. Parl. Election Results, 1832–85*, 86–7, 639; *Who's Who of Brit. M.P.s*, i. 112, 229; ii. 295–6.

2 C.C.A.L.S., ZCR 159/1; *Rep. Com. Corrupt Practices in Chester*, pp. v–vi; O'Leary, *Elimination of Corrupt Practices*, 136; *Browns and Chester*, 144–5, 148–9.

3 *Rep. Com. Corrupt Practices in Chester*, pp. xiii–xviii; O'Leary, *Elimination of Corrupt Practices*, 136–9; Raikes, *Life and Letters*, 136–54.

4 *Brit. Parl. Election Results, 1832–85*, 86–7.

5 *Notes on Trial of Chester Election Petition*, H.C. 301 (1880 Sess. 2), lvii; *Rep. Com. Corrupt Practices in Chester*, esp. pp. xiii–xviii; Corrupt Practices (Suspension of Elections) Acts, 1881, 44 & 45 Vic. c. 42; 1882, 45 & 46 Vic. c. 68; 1883, 46 & 47 Vic. c. 46; 1884, 47 & 48 Vic. c. 78; Raikes, *Life and Letters*, 225–6.

6 *Brit. Parl. Election Results, 1885–1918*, ed. F. W. S. Craig (1989), 96.

7 e.g. H. Bolitho, *Alfred Mond, First Lord Melchett*, 121–6.

8 Gladstone: *Gladstone Diaries*, indexed refs. to Chester, esp. vi. 635; viii. 385; ix. 437; xii. 265; xiii. 36, 244; Raikes, *Life and Letters*, 136–7; the duke: G. Huxley, *Victorian Duke: Life of Hugh Lupus Grosvenor, First Duke of Westminster, passim*.

9 S. E. Koss, *Sir John Brunner: Radical Plutocrat, 1842–1919*, 81.

10 Results and biographical details in rest of para. based on *Brit. Parl. Election Results, 1885–1918*, 96; *Who's Who of Brit. M.P.s*, ii. 126, 384–5.

11 Huxley, *Victorian Duke*, 160–5.

12 Koss, *Brunner*, 74–5, 81, 86, 102.

13 *Chester Chron.* 1 Jan. 1836.

14 Comparing C.C.A.L.S., ZAB 6, pp. 63, 69, with poll bk. in *Narrative of Proceedings at Contest for Representation of Chester, 1826*.

15 Rest of para. based on C.C.A.L.S., ZAB 6 *passim*, esp. pp. 63, 65–6, 69, 169.

The first mayoral election was contested, and Dixon as Grosvenor candidate lost to a former Independent,[1] but was elected unopposed the following November.

There was initially a high turnover of councillors and aldermen: of those elected to the first council only 16 still sat in 1841.[2] At no time was the council dominated by a single economic interest. Rather it represented the diverse sectors of the city's economy. Professional men and the biggest shopkeepers and merchants were always well to the fore, and became more numerous by 1914; smaller retailers and craftsmen retained a presence; the drink trade was present throughout; and there were normally a few large manufacturers and industrialists.[3]

The size of the municipal electorate fluctuated from year to year but in general grew with the rise in population from 1,400–1,800 in the 1840s to 3,500–4,000 in the 1860s, then leapt to over 6,400 when the residency qualification was reduced to 12 months in 1869. Thereafter, as the population increased more slowly, it crept up to 7,400 in 1914. Those figures represented about 9 per cent of all inhabitants before 1869 and 18 per cent afterwards.[4] There were thus considerably more municipal voters than parliamentary ones before 1867, but afterwards up to 1,000 fewer.

Even in the heightened party politics of the period after 1880 only about half of ward elections were contested, either because one party was impregnably dominant or because the parties tacitly or openly agreed to divide the representation. Byelections were contested more often than the main November elections. The turn-out reached 76 per cent in the exceptional year of 1893, when all five wards were contested.[5]

Party political divisions on the council mattered little before the 1870s,[6] but local issues were often highly contentious, personal rivalries were involved, and corruption was extensive. By the 1850s election managers, known locally as 'Bashi-Bazouks', were said to be able to return any candidate for a price, mainly by treating voters in the pubs. A later chief constable attributed the corruptibility of the electorate in part to

widespread apathy about council elections.[7] Certainly in 1856 it was evidently normal to bribe voters with drink.[8] In the same decade a Whig caucus was based at no. 86 Watergate Street, the premises of William Shone, who as collector of the improvement rate held the only complete list of ratepayers eligible to be registered as burgess voters.[9]

The Whig caucus excluded the Radical wing of the Liberal party, but Radical politics in Chester were galvanized by the arrival of Enoch Salisbury in connexion with the new gas company in the early 1850s. A self-made Welsh businessman and barrister and a teetotal Congregationalist of advanced Radical views, he was a contentious figure for over twenty years, both in politics and in his business dealings.[10] A public split between Whigs and Radicals seemed likely as early as 1852 but was averted apparently by a rallying call to their common political principles.[11] In 1857, however, Salisbury denounced the caucus, and went on to disrupt the Liberal machine over the four general elections to 1868, then briefly united the factions in a short-lived Liberal Association (which he himself called a 'dead-alive thing'), and finally joined the council for the first time in 1873.[12]

In the meantime a variety of local issues which cut across party and even factional lines had come and gone. In the later 1830s and the 1840s, a time of economic stagnation, there were bitter disputes over whether the council should back those who wished to bring new industries to the city. Most plans which required the release of council-owned land were turned down, with the exception of direct railway access, over which a pro-railway lobby won the day. The chairman of the Chester and Crewe Railway Co., John Uniacke, who lived in Chester, was brought on to the council in 1838 and was immediately voted in as mayor, serving for the crucial two years while the lines to Crewe and Birkenhead were opened. Industrial development faded as an issue as the local economy revived in the 1850s.[13] In the 1840s and 1850s the council was instead preoccupied with stabilizing its finances, extending its powers, and improving public health. In the 1860s attention turned, still in a non-partisan

1 *Chester Chron.* 8 Jan. 1836.

2 C.C.A.L.S., ZAB 6, pp. 168–9, 247–8, 307–8, 310–12, 314–15, 368–70, 411–13, 452–3, 456.

3 Based on membership in 1835–6, 1859–61, 1881, and 1898–1900: ibid. pp. 63, 69; *White's Dir. Ches.* (1860), 75, 1012; *Chester Chron.* 5 Nov. 1881, p. 5; *Chester City Cl. Mins.* 1897/8, 571; 1898/9, 2; 1899/1900, 2, 284, 337, 339, 397, 453, 514; 1900/1, 2, 132, 189; *City of Chester Year Bk.* (1903), 30–3; cf. *Victorian Chester*, ed. R. Swift, 28.

4 C.C.A.L.S., TS. lists of classes ZCEB and ZCEC; *City of Chester Year Bk.* (1903 and later edns.); *V.C.H. Ches.* v (2), Population.

5 *Chester Chron.* 6 Nov. 1880, p. 5; 5 Nov. 1881, p. 5; 4 Nov. 1882, p. 7; 3 Nov. 1883, p. 5; 8 Nov. 1884, p. 2; 7 Nov. 1885, p. 5; 6 Nov. 1886, p. 7; 5 Nov. 1887, p. 7; 3 Nov. 1888, p. 8; 4 Nov. 1893, p. 8; *City of Chester Year Bk.* (1905), 123–41; (1914), 181–

8; (1921), 241–2.

6 W. Farish, *Autobiography of William Farish* (1889, reprint. 1996), 114.

7 *Rep. Com. Corrupt Practices in Chester*, p. xvii; Fenwick, *Hist. Chester*, 413; cf. *O.E.D.* s.v. Bashi-Bazouk.

8 Farish, *Autobiography*, 102.

9 *Browns and Chester*, 143.

10 Ibid.; *Chester Chron.* 1 Nov. 1890, p. 8; Cardiff Univ., Salisbury Libr. Archive, TS. list of Salisbury MSS.

11 Election poster reproduced in *Browns and Chester*, facing p. 152.

12 Ibid. 144; *Rep. Com. Corrupt Practices in Chester*, pp. 76–7; *Chester Chron.* 1 Nov. 1890, p. 8.

13 *Victorian Chester*, ed. Swift, 19–24, 47 n.; *Chester Chron.* 20 Jan. 1837; C.C.A.L.S., ZAB 6, pp. 307, 368, 453; Ormerod, *Hist. Ches.* i. 304; iii. 79, 81.

way, to street improvements and reforming the police and fire brigade.[1] Cross-party co-operation among the élite was exemplified by the establishment of the Grosvenor Club in 1866, which drew its early membership from the leaders of both parties and indeed from non-party figures; the first two presidents were the Whig Earl Grosvenor and the former Tory M.P. Philip Humberston.[2]

Other issues began to come to the fore in council elections during the 1850s and 1860s. One of the longest-lived was temperance, in the movement for which a leading part was taken by William Farish, a self-educated working man and former Chartist who prospered in business after settling in Chester in 1850. Chester's numerous and varied nonconformist chapels provided a firm basis for the movement. Farish polled 100 votes as a temperance candidate in St. Oswald's ward in 1856, and, after a publicity coup when the mayor refused to hold a public temperance meeting, he and a colleague defeated two liquor merchants in the same ward in 1860. Unopposed in 1863 and 1866, and sheriff in 1868–9, he was then harrassed by the drink interests within his own party, who unsuccessfully ran a brewer against him in 1869, prevented his election as mayor in 1873, held him back from promotion to alderman, and actively excluded him from the Chester Liberal Association in 1879. Temperance had some powerful friends, however, including the duke of Westminster, and Farish served as mayor in 1877–8, but attempts from 1876 to obtain pledges from voters to support only temperance candidates were undone in the beer-sodden election of 1880.[3] Temperance was afterwards mostly overshadowed by party politics.[4] The Irish voters of Boughton may have formed another special interest group: the popular Tory W. H. Churton, who occupied one of the ward's seats 1871–80 and 1882–95 certainly credited his success in part to their support.[5]

Most municipal elections were fought on party lines after 1868,[6] but it was not until the 1880s that party allegiance dominated the conduct of council business. Many issues were already being decided on party lines when Farish stood down from the council in 1881; on returning in 1887 he found the chamber transformed into a wholly party-political arena.[7] On some matters of local importance, such as education after 1866, the natural fault lines in any case lay between the parties,[8] but other issues could still cut across them. Party differences were laid aside in some wards in 1882,

for example, over the Improvement Bill: in Boughton one Tory and one Liberal hostile to the Bill were returned with much cross-party voting.[9]

The corrupt parliamentary election of 1880 also affected municipal politics. Its immediate impact was to boost the Liberals, who had a net gain of five seats in the four wards contested in November that year. One Liberal supporter boasted 'We've fought 'em with beer and licked 'em, and now we've fought 'em without beer and licked 'em.'[10] The main issue now became the domination of the mayoralty by William and Charles Brown.[11] Their uncles had been prominent councillors after 1835, and from the 1870s the huge success of their department store gave them the leisure and the money to secure great influence within the Liberal party and the council. Both brothers were scheduled for bribery at the 1880 election, but before the Royal Commission reported, Charles was nominated as mayor and beat off a challenge from a fellow Liberal but a non-briber, nominated by the Tories. He was mayor again for two terms in 1883–5 when no-one else was willing to serve at a time of much pressing business over the Improvement Bill and the abolition of the bridge tolls. After only a year's interval William was elected mayor in 1886, then re-elected the following year in order to carry through the public library extension, his gift to the town. Only two years passed before Charles was again made mayor in 1890. Opposition to the brothers' 'perpetual mayordom' was not limited to those with scruples about handing over the office to men struck off the parliamentary register for bribery.[12] Even the Liberal *Chester Chronicle* had misgivings. There was, moreover, unpleasant squabbling in 1891 between Charles Brown as mayor and the bishop and dean, and allegations in 1892 that he wished to serve yet again because he hoped to be knighted if still in office when the Royal Agricultural Show came to Chester during the ensuing year. Particular resentment was voiced at the way that both Charles and William had turned the mayoralty into almost a full-time job and spent their own money lavishly on public projects, making it difficult for men with business or professional responsibilities, or less money, to aspire to the position.

After the 1881 municipal elections the Liberals had 28 seats and the Tories 11, with 1 Independent.[13] More important than the Browns as an influence on party strength in the council was the secession of the Liberal Unionists in 1886, which was led by the head of the

1 Above, this chapter: City Government, 1835–1914 (Council Policies and Activities); Farish, *Autobiography*, 128–30.
2 F. A. Latham, *Hist. of Grosvenor Club* (copy at C.H.H.).
3 Farish, *Autobiography*, passim, esp. 90, 102, 111, 130, 145–6, 155, 169–70, 187–8; D. A. Hamer, *The Politics of Electoral Pressure*, 213, 224.
4 But cf. *Chester Chron.* 8 Nov. 1884, p. 2.
5 3 *Sheaf*, xviii, p. 90; *Chester Chron.* 6 Nov. 1880, p. 5; 4 Nov. 1882, p. 7; 7 Nov. 1885, p. 5; 3 Nov. 1888, p. 8; 31 Oct. 1891, p. 2; 3 Nov. 1894, p. 8; *City of Chester Year Bk.* (1903), 118.

6 Fenwick, *Hist. Chester*, 413.
7 Farish, *Autobiography*, 194–5.
8 Ibid. 150–1; *Browns and Chester*, 149.
9 *Chester Chron.* 4 Nov. 1882, pp. 5, 7.
10 Ibid. 6 Nov. 1880, p. 5.
11 Rest of para. based on *Browns and Chester*, esp. 143–5, 148–9, 154–67, 225; *V.C.H. Ches.* v (2), Lists of Mayors and Sheriffs.
12 Farish, *Autobiography*, 195.
13 *Chester Chron.* 5 Nov. 1881, p. 5.

other great local dynasty, Sir Thomas Frost, partner with his brothers in F. A. Frost and Sons, a highly successful milling business. The Frost brothers had already been mayor almost as often as the Browns, Thomas being knighted when the prince of Wales visited Chester to open the new town hall in 1869, and serving a further two terms in 1881–3.[1] Among the councillors the Unionist converts included George Bird, perhaps the most prominent working-class Liberal, who when he came up for re-election in St. Mary's ward in 1888 stood as a Liberal Unionist with full Conservative support and beat two Liberals. By 1889 four aldermen and three councillors sat as Liberal Unionists, but some of them never took the Tory whip and in any case the Liberals at first still commanded a clear majority.[2] Feeling was heightened by the public split between the duke of Westminster and Gladstone and by rallies on both sides.[3]

The tide of council election results ran steadily against the Liberals in the early 1890s. The only two wards contested in 1890, for example, both saw a prominent Liberal, William Farish in St. Oswald's and the staunch Home Ruler Henry Stolterfoth in St. Mary's, pushed into third place by new candidates, closet Conservatives standing as Independents.[4] The Conservatives and Unionists finally achieved a majority on the council in 1894,[5] which they reinforced in 1895 by purging two Liberal aldermen, also claiming a majority on all the committees.[6]

Chester was the sort of town 'rich in strong-minded, single, and affluent ladies' who pioneered women's involvement in local politics in the late 19th century.[7] After 1869, when women were allowed to vote in municipal elections,[8] the temperance leader William Farish made special efforts to cultivate their support, and claimed in that year to have had the votes of 47 of the 60 women on the electoral roll for his ward.[9] When he sought to return to the council in 1887 he was nominated solely by women voters,[10] who were especially numerous in his ward (St. Oswald's) and Boughton.[11] Conservative women of the Primrose League were active canvassers in the 1886 municipal

elections.[12] Women were voted on to the board of guardians in the 1880s but the only woman who stood for the council after it became possible in 1907 was very poorly supported in Trinity ward in 1912.[13] The new education committee co-opted the headmistress of the Queen's school (Beatrice Clay) and the manager of the Anglican public elementary schools' foundation (Rachael Joyce) in 1904.[14]

There were only small beginnings for the Labour movement in Chester before 1914. A branch of the Independent Labour Party – apparently not a very vigorous one – existed by 1896,[15] and the Chester Socialist Society opened a meeting room between 1906 and 1910.[16] The United Trades and Labour Council put up its secretary William Carr in St. Oswald's ward at a byelection in 1894, on a platform which included council housing, an eight-hour day for corporation employees, electric lighting, and a new public baths. He polled 466 votes to the Tory's 610. In 1900 he took second place in the ward as an overtly Labour candidate, beating a sitting Liberal, and the next year a colleague joined him in Boughton, both men remaining on the council in 1914.[17]

At the other extreme of Chester's political spectrum a Ratepayers' Association was formed soon before 1904 and lobbied against all increases in council expenditure, whether on teachers' salaries, mayoral expenses, subsidized rents for the handful of council house tenants, or the employment of a lady sanitary inspector; its secretary in 1904 was an estate agent, Beresford Adams.[18]

THE FENIAN PLOT OF 1867

On 11 February 1867 an audacious plot by the Liverpool Fenians against Chester castle was put into action.[19] The plan was to infiltrate Chester with up to 2,000 men from all over the North of England under the command of Irish American officers who had military experience in the American Civil War, led by John McCafferty. After night fell, the few armed with revolvers were to seize 300 unguarded rifles stored for the Volunteers at the old cockpit near the city walls.

1 *Chester Chron.* 3 Nov. 1888, p. 2; *V.C.H. Ches.* v (2), Lists of Mayors and Sheriffs; *Mayors of Eng. and Wales, 1902,* ed. F. A. Barnes, 162–3; Farish, *Autobiography,* 130–1.

2 *Chester Chron.* 4 Nov. 1882, p. 7; 3 Nov. 1888, p. 8; 8 Nov. 1890, p. 7; 31 Oct. 1891, p. 2.

3 Ibid. 3 Nov. 1888, p. 2.

4 Ibid. 8 Nov. 1890, p. 7.

5 Ibid. 3 Nov. 1894, p. 8; 2 Nov. 1895, p. 8; 9 Nov. 1895, p. 7; not 1895 as in Fenwick, *Hist. Chester,* 413.

6 *Chester Chron.* 2 Nov. 1895, p. 8; 9 Nov. 1895, pp. 7–8.

7 P. Hollis, *Ladies Elect: Women in Eng. Local Government, 1865–1914,* 239.

8 Municipal Corporation Elections Act, 32 & 33 Vic. c. 55, s. 9.

9 Farish, *Autobiography,* 145–6.   10 Ibid. 195.

11 *Chester Chron.* 4 Nov. 1882, p. 7.

12 Ibid. 6 Nov. 1886, p. 7.

13 Hollis, *Ladies Elect,* 239, 398 n.; *City of Chester Year Bk.*

(1915), 235–42.

14 *Chester City Cl. Mins.* 1904/5, 6–7, 27–8.

15 C.C.A.L.S., ZCR 470/7 (MS. by J. Ernest Jones, 'My Experience with the Clarion Women's Van' [dated 1896 by ref. on p. 38 to death of Caroline Martyn: *Dictionary of Labour Biography,* viii. 158–9]), esp. pp. 2, 43, 45.

16 *Kelly's Dir. Ches.* (1906), 228; (1910), 233; (1914), 238.

17 *Chester Chron.* 14 July 1894, pp. 1, 3; 31 Oct. 1896, p. 6; 3 Nov. 1900, p. 8; 9 Nov. 1901, p. 2; *City of Chester Year Bk.* (1903), 116, 124–5; (1904), 130–2; (1915), 234–5, 237–8, 240–1.

18 *Chester City Cl. Mins.* 1903/4, 460–1, 564; 1904/5, 1055–6; 1905/6, 1038; 1907/8, 575; for Adams: *Kelly's Dir. Ches.* (1902), 225.

19 Section based on R. W. Durdley, 'Fenians in Chester, 1867: Prelude and Aftermath' (TS., 1994, at C.H.H.); P. Quinlivan and P. Rose, *Fenians in Eng. 1865–72,* 16–28; J. Newsinger, *Fenianism in Mid-Victorian Brit.* 53–4; Fenwick, *Hist. Chester,* 249–53.

The Fenians would then use those arms to storm the castle, which was garrisoned by only 60 regular soldiers of the 54th Regiment and where there were kept almost 10,000 rifles and 900,000 rounds of ammunition. Other gangs of Fenians were to isolate the city by cutting the telegraph wires and sabotaging railway lines. The main force was to commandeer a train, load the arms, and take them at gunpoint to Holyhead. There they would hijack a steamer and head for Wexford to raise rebellion in Ireland. Rumour, never substantiated, added that the waterworks was to be sabotaged, the town set on fire, and the shops looted.

The plan, however, was betrayed on the night of 10 February by a police informer among the leadership at Liverpool, John Carr alias Corydon. When the Americans (Corydon among them) reached Chester the following morning, they found that the authorities had been forewarned by the Liverpool police. The city's chief constable, the deputy mayor, the Volunteers' Major Philip Humberston, and the head constable of the county police had already moved the Volunteers' rifles to the greater safety of the castle,

mustered the police, militia, and Volunteers, and brought another 70 regular soldiers from Manchester.

Although the Fenian officers slipped out of Chester and made frantic efforts to turn back their men, an estimated 1,300 Fenians reached Chester by evening, in small parties from Manchester, Preston, Halifax, Leeds, and elsewhere. Overnight they abandoned what weapons they had and made off, but the emergency went on through the night. Five hundred Household troops arrived by train from London the next morning in time for a tumultuous reception and breakfast at the hotels. Only one arrest was made. The *Manchester Guardian* joked that 'the excitement seemed to be welcomed by many as an agreeable relief to the oppressive monotony of ordinary Chester life', and even in Chester it was the topic of satire.[1] It may have fomented anti-Irish feeling in the city, even though only a handful of the resident Irish population had been involved in the plot, and certainly helped to turn the duke of Westminster, who as lord lieutenant was commander of the militia and Volunteers, against granting Home Rule.[2]

ECONOMY AND SOCIETY

In 1762 Chester was still a regional metropolis despite the decline of its port over the previous 150 years.[3] By 1914 it had sunk to being a medium-sized market town, albeit one with some industry, a wide catchment area, significant administrative functions, and social pretensions which reflected its long history and architectural merits.

Chester was located in a region of early and rapid industrialization which encompassed the north Wales coalfield to the west and south-west, the chemical industries of the Cheshire saltfield 15 miles to the east, and industrial south Lancashire and the port of Liverpool only slightly further away to the north. Dynamic growth in the region, however, was reflected only weakly in Chester itself. For reasons discussed later it suffered disadvantages in comparison with areas near by. Industrial entrepreneurs had better places in the region in which to invest, a characteristic which set Chester apart from other old but more isolated cities, such as York and Lincoln, which experienced considerable industrial growth. Although Chester did not grow significantly as an industrial town, it adapted rather successfully during the industrial revolution to its relatively disadvantaged situation, though was left increasingly vulnerable to trends in its hinterland. The coming of the railway was the only major boost,

stimulating a boom in the mid 19th century. Other than that, the city was beset by difficulties which the gloss of town-centre rebuilding tended to obscure.

Population growth and migration reflected the main trends in Chester's development. In 1774 a survey by Dr. John Haygarth, physician to the infirmary, revealed a population of 14,713. By 1801, including the suburbs, it had grown to 16,095, an increase of 9.4 per cent in 27 years.[4] That was slow in relation to the rate across Britain, and suggests that many people were migrating away from Chester. The picture after 1801 is clearer, the city and its suburbs trebling their population by 1911. The increase was less than that of the immediately surrounding region of Cheshire, Flintshire, and Denbighshire, though the trend was not uniform over time (Table 7). The pattern of migration amplifies the picture.[5] From 1801 to 1841 more people left Chester than settled there except in the decade 1811–21. Between 1841 and 1871 there was sustained migration to the city, but after 1871 the flow reversed, and was staunched only in part during the 1890s. Although the actual population always grew because of natural increase, Chester was evidently finding it difficult to adapt economically for most of the period.

Demographic and other evidence examined later suggests that Chester's economic and social history

---

1 *Ensign Smith: His Affair at Chester with the Fenians* (undated printed cartoon bk., copy in Chester Public Libr., pamphlet box 35).
2 Huxley, *Victorian Duke*, 158.

3 C. Armour, 'Trade of Chester and State of Dee Navigation' (Lond. Univ. Ph.D. thesis, 1956), *passim*.
4 *V.C.H. Ches.* v (2), Population.
5 Below, this chapter, Appendix.

TABLE 7: *The population of Chester in its regional context, 1801–1911*

Decade	Population at end of decade	Percentage increase	Percentage increase in region	Chester's increase relative to region
1801–11	17,344	7.8	15.8	0.5
1811–21	21,516	24.1	18.7	1.3
1821–31	23,029	7.0	19.3	0.4
1831–41	25,039	8.7	15.5	0.6
1841–51	29,216	16.7	12.0	1.4
1851–61	34,209	17.1	9.6	1.8
1861–71	39,757	16.2	9.8	1.7
1871–81	42,246	6.3	12.1	0.5
1881–91	44,002	4.2	10.5	0.4
1891–1901	47,975	9.0	10.9	0.8
1901–11	50,220	4.7	13.7	0.3

Notes: Population is that of Chester, associated extra-parochial places, and Great Boughton, Hoole, Upton, Newton, and Bache townships. The region is defined as Cheshire, Flintshire, and Denbighshire. In the final column, 1.0 = same as region.
Source: Census, 1801–1911.

TABLE 8: *Adult males employed in retail trades and handicrafts, 1831*

Sector	No.	No.	%	%
Retail Trades		509		20.2
Retail/Wholesale		30		1.2
Processing Trades		171		6.8
Brewing	86		3.4	
Clothing	8		0.3	
Leather	77		3.1	
Crafts		1,524		60.5
Metal	179		7.1	
Leather	281		11.1	
Clothing	171		6.8	
Wood	343		13.6	
Building	332		13.2	
Fine Crafts	99		3.9	
Maritime	81		3.2	
Miscellaneous	38		1.5	
Innkeeping and Transport		211		8.4
Miscellaneous		74		2.9
Total		2,519		100.0

Note: Arithmetical corrections have been made to the figures.
Source: M. J. Kingman, 'Chester, 1801–61' (Leic. Univ. M.A. thesis, [1970]), 18.

between 1762 and 1914 can be divided into three periods: the demise of the traditional economy between 1762 and 1840, a reorientation and economic boom 1841–70, and finally a period when the limits of reorientation were revealed between 1871 and 1914.

THE ECONOMY, 1762–1840: THE DEMISE OF OLD CHESTER

Between 1762 and 1840 key elements of Chester's traditional economy withered and finally died, and the city struggled to find new roles. Previously important manufacturing trades vanished and were replaced only in part by new industries. The port declined so drastically that by 1840 Chester's wharves were of little importance, and the city also suffered problems with its road and canal traffic. The Irish linen trade reached its zenith and then disappeared rapidly, and the traditional fairs and markets were undermined by changes in the patterns of distribution. By the 1830s Chester was heavily dependent on its role as a retailing, social, and administrative centre.[1]

INDUSTRY AND TRANSPORT

From 1831 census data begin to shed light on the city's occupational structure (Table 8). In the pre-industrial economy the distinction between making and selling

goods was blurred, but most of Chester's manufacturing workers were employed in the traditional trades of clothing, wood, metalworking, and building which could be found in all similar towns and cities. By the late 18th century the manufacturing trades more distinctive to Chester were in decline or nearly extinct. The city's historian Joseph Hemingway, former editor of both local newspapers, observed in 1831 that skin-dressing and tanning had 'greatly declined', while glovemaking had 'chiefly migrated to Worcester'.[2] By 1810 the manufacture of clay tobacco pipes, which had been exported in great quantities as late as the 1770s, was also 'in a diminished state', and in 1831 employed only eight men.[3] Clockmaking declined in the late 18th and early 19th century.[4] The Napoleonic Wars provided some stimulus to shipbuilding, but the industry was modest.[5] Between 1814 and 1826 as many as 133 vessels were built and registered at Chester, with an

1 *Georgian Chester*, ed. A. M. Kennett, 9, 15–19, 31–2, 36.
2 Hemingway, *Hist. Chester*, ii. 331–2.
3 Ibid. ii. 333; M. J. Kingman, 'Chester, 1801–61' (Leic. Univ. M.A. thesis, [1970]), 14; G. C. Spence, 'Notes on Clay Tobacco

Pipes and Clay Pipe Makers in Ches.' *T.L.C.A.S.* lvi. 45.
4 [C.] N. Moore, *Chester Clocks and Clockmakers*, 4.
5 R. Craig, 'Shipping and Shipbuilding in Port of Chester in 18th and Early 19th Cent.' *T.H.S.L.C.* cxvi. 59.

average size of 126 tons.[1] Only one shipyard was in operation by 1831;[2] although it built some large vessels, the staple product from 1820 to 1850 was Mersey flats.[3] The related activity of ropemaking survived throughout the 19th century, but only 42 men worked in the trade in 1831, and the important ropewalk of Jonathan Whittle and Sons closed in 1834.[4] By 1840 most of Chester's traditional industries had thus disappeared or were of limited economic significance.

Milling occupied the middle ground between the traditional and modern sectors and was still growing in importance. At the Dee Mills there were five distinct units in the early 19th century and tenancies tended to be granted separately for each, a disincentive to modernization.[5] In 1828 the proprietors of the Ellesmere and Chester Canal took a lease over two and most of a third, subject to a stipulation preventing the introduction of steam engines.[6] Although the restrictive clause was probably a response to the fire of 1819 which gutted the whole premises,[7] it further hindered modernization. The fire also forced T. A. & J. Frost to relocate their milling business to a disused cotton mill in Steam Mill Street, a move which was the springboard for Frosts' emergence as Chester's premier milling concern.[8]

Brewing grew significantly from 1800. In the late 18th century there were three large breweries, the Seller family's in Foregate Street, the Whittle family's Lion Brewery in Pepper Street, and one in King Street. Two smaller concerns stood in Foregate Street. After 1800 breweries were started in Lower Bridge Street and Northgate Street, and by 1831 the latter was an extensive business in the hands of the Eaton family.[9] The liberal provisions of the Beerhouse Act of 1830 produced a rapid increase in the number of beerhouses in Chester during the 1830s, and the total number of licensed premises reached at least 230 by 1840. The number of breweries grew too, from 10 in 1834 to 15 in 1840, but the new arrivals seem to have been small enterprises behind public houses, offering little competition to the established firms.[10] Growth in Chester's breweries seems largely to have reflected a rise in local demand rather than any wider factors, and it was dominated by old-established families.

In the late 18th and early 19th century Chester was not a propitious place in which to establish new industries. It was not on a coalfield, and water power was restricted to the weir on the Dee, which was affected by the tide. The hinterland was mainly rural and was poorly served by transport. There seems also to have been a lack of enterprise on the part of Cestrians, and the residual power of the city guilds may have restrained development.[11] It was observed in 1814 that 'corporate privileges are not often calculated to foster commerce, and in this city, although we mark the infancy of several manufactures, few arrive at maturity'.[12] The influence of the guilds did not ebb as quickly as in other towns, due mainly to their subvention by the Owen Jones charity. Their final decay came about in part because of restrictions on membership imposed in order to maximize existing members' benefits from the charity,[13] but their authority was destroyed finally in 1825 when an unsuccessful case was brought against a tanner for trading when not a freeman.[14]

Among the new industries, there were two cotton mills, but both had closed by 1847 and little is known about either.[15] A pottery was established c. 1757 but it was unable to keep up with developments in Staffordshire and had closed by 1776.[16] The city's ironfounders mainly made small-scale products for rural consumers.[17] The exception was the Flookersbrook foundry, set up in 1803 by Cole, Whittle & Co., a firm which was later transformed into Chester's most important engineering concern.[18]

Lead was the only other modern manufacturing industry to be established successfully between 1762 and 1840. In 1800 Walkers, Maltby & Co. set up a leadworks on the banks of the Chester and Nantwich canal. The proprietors were not freemen of Chester and the business was initially in jeopardy from a reassertion of old restrictions, which it was able to evade because some of the owners were freemen of the City of London.[19] The works made white and red lead for paints, and had a shot tower. By 1812 a rolling mill for sheet lead and machines for drawing lead pipe had been added. The site was convenient for manufacturing lead products from ores mined, smelted, and refined in north Wales and Spain, and

1 Kingman, 'Chester, 1801–61', 12. The port of Chester covered the whole of the Dee estuary.
2 Hemingway, *Hist. Chester*, ii. 332.
3 *Chester and River Dee*, ed. A. Kennett, 14–15.
4 3 *Sheaf*, xxvi, pp. 56–8, 72, 80.
5 *V.C.H. Ches.* v (2), Mills and Fisheries: Dee Corn Mills.
6 C.C.A.L.S., ZCHD 12, agreement 1828.
7 F. Simpson, 'River Dee', *J.C.A.S.* xiv. 85–111.
8 G. L. Fenwick, *Hist. of Ancient City of Chester*, 477.
9 *Broster's Dir. Chester* (1782); *Wardle and Bentham's Commercial Guide* (1814/15); *Pigot's Commercial Dir.* (1818–20, 1822); 3 *Sheaf*, xxxviii, pp. 49–50; Chester Northgate Brewery Co. Ltd., *Guide to Chester and District* [c. 1930], 33; N. Barber, *Where Have All the Breweries Gone? Dir. of Brit. Brewery Companies* [c. 1980], 6; Hemingway, *Hist. Chester*, ii. 19.

10 S. G. Checkland, *Rise of Industrial Society in Eng.* 234; *Parry's Dir. Chester* (1840).
11 Armour, 'Trade of Chester and Dee Navigation', 32–44.
12 *Wardle and Bentham's Commercial Guide* (1814/15).
13 *V.C.H. Ches.* v (2), Craft Guilds: Activities after 1750.
14 Fenwick, *Hist. Chester*, 247.
15 Ibid. 477; *Chester Courant*, 14 July 1847.
16 L. and M. Hillis, 'Chester White Ware Manufactory', *Jnl. Northern Ceramic Soc.* iv. 43.
17 B. Bracegirdle, *Engineering in Chester: 200 Years of Progress*, 36.
18 Ibid. 17; *Short Hist. of [Chester] Hydraulic Engineering Co. Ltd. since its Incorporation in 1874*, 1 (copy at C.H.H.).
19 M. H. O. Hoddinott, *Site Development Hist. of Chester Leadworks, 1800–1990* (copy in C.C.A.L.S., ZCR 586/37).

their onward distribution to the industrial Midlands and North-West.[1]

An important aspect of the growth of the leadworks was thus the availability of water transport, but the history of Chester's maritime and waterway links between 1762 and 1840 was otherwise one of unful-filled potential and eventual decline. By 1800 the port of Chester had already fallen hopelessly behind Liver-pool in serving the North-West and Midlands, and Chester's own wharves were eclipsed by the Dee out-ports. Foreign trade dwindled, and most of Chester's shipping was involved in the Irish and coasting trades.[2] The most important commodity in the early 19th century was cheese.[3] The River Dee Company failed to maintain an adequate navigable channel to Chester, but even if it had, it is questionable whether any significant challenge to Liverpool could have been mounted, not least because the city lacked a merchant community with enterprise and overseas links.[4] The opening in 1777 of the Trent and Mersey Canal together with continued improvements to the river Weaver channelled inland trade from the Potteries and mid Cheshire decisively towards the Mersey and Liver-pool.[5] Chester counter-attacked with the Chester and Nantwich canal, opened in 1779, but it was thwarted from linking with the Trent and Mersey, and the canal was a dead end unable to serve the industrial areas which were its goal.[6] Only with the opening of the various sections of the Ellesmere Canal between 1795 and 1805 did Chester have satisfactory inland water-way links,[7] but by then the city's wharves had become merely an intermediate point on the route to Ellesmere Port and the Mersey. The failure to complete a direct link between Chester and the Denbighshire coalfield may have helped to prevent the growth of industry in the city using cheap Welsh coal and iron. The opening of the Birmingham and Liverpool Junction Canal in 1835, together with the long-sought connexion to the Trent and Mersey at Middlewich in 1833, finally placed Chester on the trunk canal system,[8] but by then any chance of the city's becoming a nodal point for water transport had passed.

Chester's role on the road network was initially rather healthier, but it deteriorated after 1800. The coaching and carrying trade was centred on the city's many inns, the years 1775–1832 being regarded as the 'golden age of coaching from Chester'.[9] Most of the

TABLE 9: *Coaching services from Chester, 1781–1829*

Destination	Number of coaches leaving Chester each week			
	1781	1795	1814–15	1828–9
London	2	20	10	20
Holyhead	6	7	7	14
Warrington	7			
Birmingham		3		
Bristol		3		
Liverpool		7	28	63
Preston Brook		6		
Parkgate		6		3
Shrewsbury			14	28
Manchester			20	35
Oswestry			6	7
Denbigh			3	
Holywell			6	
Newtown				7
Wrexham				7
Hereford				7
Macclesfield				3
Barmouth				3
Rhyl				3
Total	15	52	94	200

Source: Willshaw, 'Inns', 62.

main roads to the city were turnpiked between 1743 and 1787,[10] improving connexions with the hinter-land, particularly north-east Wales, but in the early 19th century long-distance services dwindled in relation to regional ones. Chester lost its rank as a nationally important coaching town with the rise of Liverpool and the progressive rerouting of Irish traffic through Shrewsbury after 1808 (Table 9).[11] Telford's improvements to the Shrewsbury–Holyhead road were largely complete by 1818,[12] and the last through Royal Mail service from Chester to London was abandoned in 1829.[13] The growing importance of road transport nationally after 1800 nevertheless enhanced Chester's regional importance both as a coaching centre and, though the evidence is more limited, for goods carriage: the city was served by a number of long-distance fly waggon services by 1823, and had a

1 Associated Lead Manufacturers Ltd., 'Chester Works' (TS. 1957 in Chester City Libr.), 1; *Mins. relating to Messrs. Samuel Walker & Co., Rotherham, Iron Founders and Steel Refiners, 1741–1829, and Messrs. Walkers, Parker & Co., Lead Manufacturers, 1788–1893*, ed. A. H. John, 35–54.

2 Armour, 'Trade of Chester and Dee Navigation', 307.

3 *Chester and Dee*, ed. Kennett, 11–12.

4 Armour, 'Trade of Chester and Dee Navigation', 31; *T.H.S.L.C.* cxvi. 45.

5 C. Hadfield, *Canals of W. Midlands* (1985), 42; *V.C.H. Ches.* v (2), Water Transport: Canals.

6 Hadfield, *Canals of W. Mids.* 42–5; E. A. Shearing, 'Chester

Canal Projects', *Jnl. Rly. and Canal Hist. Soc.* xxviii. 98–104, 146–54.

7 Ellesmere Canal Proprietors, *Rep. to General Assembly, 27 Nov. 1805* (copy at C.H.H.); Hadfield, *Canals of W. Mids.* 2–45, 166–79.

8 Hadfield, *Canals of W. Mids.* 181–9.

9 E. M. Willshaw, 'Inns of Chester, 1775–1832' (Leic. Univ. M.A. thesis, 1979: copy at C.H.H.), 7.

10 *V.C.H. Ches.* v (2), Roads and Road Transport: Roads.

11 Willshaw, 'Inns', 59–60.

12 W. Albert, *Turnpike Road System in Eng. 1663–1840*, 145.

13 Willshaw, 'Inns', 60.

comprehensive network of carrying services to its local hinterland.[1]

RETAILING AND SERVICES

Changes in Chester's significance for transport had a counterpart in its reorientation as a service centre. Its importance in national trade declined greatly, but its local role in west Cheshire and north-east Wales was strengthened with the development of more modern forms of retailing.[2] In the 1760s and 1770s Chester's fairs were dominated by the Irish linen trade but were also the focus for wholesale and retail traders of many types.[3] Imports of Irish linen cloth reached their peak between 1761 and the early 1770s,[4] and a new linen hall was opened in 1778. The linen trade had declined steeply by 1814, however, and had disappeared by 1830. Its demise was due to competition from Liverpool, the penetration of the Irish manufacturing areas by English merchants, and an increase in orders placed directly with Irish manufacturers.[5] It also reflected the decline of the rural Irish linen industry centred on Dublin and its shift north to factories around Belfast, a move resulting in turn from the competition of machine-spun English and Scottish yarns and substitution by cheap cotton goods.[6] In other words, a traditional Chester trade was destroyed as an indirect result of industrialization elsewhere in Britain. The fairs retained some importance for other goods until well into the 19th century, though the building of new trading halls in 1809 and 1815 may have represented an ultimately abortive attempt to sustain the fairs in the face of more modern modes of retailing.[7] The livestock and food markets remained significant in themselves and as a source of income for the city corporation. The new flesh shambles built in 1827 for over £4,000, for example, was yielding a rental of over £660 a year by 1832.[8]

Retailing from permanent shops grew rapidly in importance in the early 19th century. Although many retailers were also craft producers, by 1815 there were also specialist town-centre retailers whose skills were commercial rather than manufacturing.[9] Their shops were of increasingly modern appearance, notably through the introduction of glass windows to display their wares. Hemingway dated the beginning of the change to the late 1780s and observed that Chester's

shops were 'equal in elegance to those of Manchester or Liverpool', claiming that 'there is at least one in Eastgate Row, that of Messrs. William and Henry Brown, silk mercers and milliners . . . which would not suffer by a comparison with the magnificence of Regent-street'.[10] Browns, Chester's leading retailer throughout the 19th century, expanded and diversified between 1791 and 1828.[11] Increased investment in retailing produced more specialized businesses and changes in their spatial distribution. Higher-grade and luxury shops were tending to locate on the south side of Eastgate Street, especially on the Row, and more heterogeneous businesses on the north side. Watergate Street was associated with craft activities, while butchers were moving away to Cow Lane (later Frodsham Street).[12]

The number of businesses grew rapidly in the first third of the 19th century (Table 10), accompanied by changes in the business structure. In 1781 food and drink concerns formed 48 per cent of the total, rising by 1834 to 56 per cent. The increase suggests that food and drink were bought less from the markets and fairs and more from fixed shops. That is confirmed by a fall in the number of people per retail food outlet from 187:1 in 1797 to 113:1 in 1840.[13] The growth in other types of business was less marked, but in all except the luxury trades the rise in their number between 1781 and 1834 was greater in proportion than the rise in population.

The increasing importance of shops was paralleled by the development of other service activities. Local banking became established, though it was risky. Thomas & Hesketh's Bank became insolvent in 1793 and Rowton and Morhall's lasted for only a few years until its failure in 1810,[14] but Owen Williams established the Chester Old Bank in 1792 and it survived to become Chester's premier bank for much of the 19th century. It was joined in 1813 by Dixon & Co., which had strong Liverpool connexions. William Wardell joined the bank from Liverpool in 1829 and remained a leading figure in the commercial and political life of Chester until his death in 1864.[15] The Chester Savings Bank was established in 1817.[16] The city reached its peak as a printing and publishing centre at the end of the 18th century, but although the trade continued to expand in numbers, the trend was towards more

1 Ibid. 77–9.

2 S. I. Mitchell, 'Urban Markets and Retail Distribution, 1730–1815, with Particular Reference to Macclesfield, Stockport, and Chester' (Oxf. Univ. D.Phil. thesis, 1974), 281.

3 Ibid. 40.

4 Armour, 'Trade of Chester and Dee Navigation', 221, 276.

5 Ibid. 277; Mitchell, 'Urban Markets', 45–8; *V.C.H. Ches.* v (2), Fairs.

6 G. O'Tuathaigh, *Irel. before the Famine, 1798–1848*, 125.

7 Mitchell, 'Urban Markets', 52.

8 T. W. Scragg, 'Chester City Council, Old and New' (Liverpool Univ. B.Phil. thesis, 1971: copy at C.H.H.), 14.

9 Mitchell, 'Urban Markets', pp. v–vi.

10 Hemingway, *Hist. Chester*, i. 388. Plate 32.

11 *Browns and Chester*, ed. H. D. Willcock, 18, 35–7.

12 Mitchell, 'Urban Markets', 270–7.

13 Ibid. table 8.7 (1797), table 7 (1840), counting 'provision dealers' and 'grocers'.

14 M. Dawes and C. N. Ward-Perkins, *Country Banks of England and Wales: Private Provincial Banks and Bankers, 1688–1953*, ii. 153–5; *Chester, Wrexham & N. Wales Trustee Savings Bank, 1817–1967: 150th Annual Rep.* (copy at C.H.H.).

15 Dawes and Ward-Perkins, *Country Banks*, ii. 154–5; Hemingway, *Hist. Chester*, i. 415; Fenwick, *Hist. Chester*, 511–14; C.C.A.L.S., ZCR 4.

16 *Chester T.S.B. 1817–1967*, 1; C.C.A.L.S., ZCR 566.

TABLE 10: *Chester retailers, 1781 and 1834*

Type of business	1781	1834
Food and Drink	**218**	**494**
Provision Dealers and Bakers	41	143
Grocery Trades	28	30
Butchers	15	33
Wine and Spirit Dealers	13	25
Brewers and Allied Trades	10	27
Inns, Alehouses, and Eating Houses	98	195
Miscellaneous	13	41
Textiles and Clothing	**111**	**174**
Mercers and Drapers	26	28
Clothes Accessories	38	36
Clothes Shops	–	11
Tailors	19	25
Hatters	6	18
Footwear	22	48
Miscellaneous	–	8
Household Goods	**39**	**75**
Glass and China Dealers	2	7
Furniture Dealers	10	26
Metal Dealers	10	15
Candle, Soap, and Oil Dealers	7	11
Druggists	7	15
Miscellaneous	–	1
Luxuries	**18**	**19**
Watchmakers and Clockmakers	11	10
Goldsmiths and Silversmiths	5	6
Miscellaneous	2	3
Other Trades	**73**	**125**
Printers and Book Trades	8	33
Tobacconists	2	7
Apothecaries	3	–
Building Trades	40	69
Merchants	14	3
Bankers	1	3
Pawnbrokers	3	10
Total	**457**	**887**

Notes: Excludes 70 butchers attending the market in 1834. Businesses operating in more than one field are counted for each, so that the table overstates the total number of separate businesses.
Source: Mitchell, 'Urban Markets', table 8.7.

jobbing local printers who often produced poor quality work.[1] Chester's second local newspaper, the *Chronicle*, was started in 1775, and despite severe difficulties in its early years, after 1800 it became a successful rival to the older *Courant*.[2] Chester's hotels and inns also formed a distinct and sizeable economic

sector. As early as 1781 there were *c.* 140 licensed premises in the city.[3] The inns and hotels carried out a range of functions beyond providing accommodation, sustenance, and transport. The main hotels, notably the Blossoms and the Talbot, were centres of social and political life. The Talbot was sold in 1787 and its premises merged with the new and grander Royal Hotel built next door in 1784 and later acquired by Earl Grosvenor.[4] The inns were used for sales of property, luxury goods, horses, and agricultural produce. Medical and administrative activities also took place on their premises, and they were sometimes centres of small-scale production by craft workers occupying outbuildings in their yards.[5] The inns and hotels continued to derive trade from Chester's position as county town, garrison town, and bishopric, roles little changed in the period 1762–1840, though Chester was especially significant as a garrison town and recruiting centre during wartime, the 1798 Irish rebellion, and the period of heightened radical activity in the industrial areas after 1815.[6]

CHESTER AND ITS REGION

It seems likely that Chester's regional sphere of influence expanded in the early 19th century at the expense of other towns. The city already dominated west Cheshire and adjacent areas of north-east Wales, and Chester traders had customers over a catchment area bounded by Warrington, Macclesfield, Nantwich, Shrewsbury, and Denbigh. The city's newspapers circulated even more widely.[7]

Though Chester's administrative functions remained and its commercial services were modernized and expanded, the demise of the port and traditional manufactures left a large hole in the city's economy after 1800. The only exception to its stagnation was the decade 1811–21, noticed by Hemingway as one of rapid growth which he fully expected to have continued to his time of writing in 1830–1. In the late additions and corrections to his book, however, he reported the actual results of the 1831 census, but made no comment on the slackening of growth which they revealed.[8]

The reason for the sudden spurt in the 1810s may lie in the agricultural economy of the hinterland. Inclosure in Cheshire was limited by comparison with other parts of England, and only small and gradual changes took place in farming practice.[9] Even so, farming in the county was affected by the Napoleonic Wars and their aftermath. During the wars prices for farm products were high, and both landlords and tenants enjoyed a period of prosperity which presumably

1 D. Nuttall, 'Hist. of Printing in Chester', *J.C.A.S.* liv. 67–74.
2 Hughes, *Chronicle of Chester*.   3 Willshaw, 'Inns', 7.
4 [I. Callister], *The Chester Grosvenor [Hotel]: A Hist.* 4–9; *Blossoms Hotel, Chester*, 18 (copies of both at C.H.H.).
5 Willshaw, 'Inns', 23–44.

6 *Georgian Chester*, ed. Kennett, 12–13.
7 Mitchell, 'Urban Markets', 216–19.
8 Hemingway, *Hist. Chester*, ii. 223–4, 441–2.
9 C. S. Davies, *Agric. Hist. of Ches. 1750–1850* (Chetham Soc. 3rd ser. x), 107.

increased their consumption of the goods and services provided by Chester. In contrast the labourers suffered, and the inclosure of commons and waste in Cheshire may have pushed significant numbers from the land with little option but to migrate to the towns.[1] Chester is likely to have received its share.

Chester's marked growth between 1811 and 1821 thus probably reflected on the one hand increased prosperity in the service sector brought about by sharply rising purchasing power in the rural hinterland, and, on the other, migration to the city brought about by distress among the rural poor. Some probably found jobs in the growing service sector, and some at the expanding leadworks. After the wars ended, however, agriculture nationally fell into depression, and although Cheshire farming was not hit as severely as

elsewhere (thanks to rapid urbanization across the North-West), the price of wool, cattle, and horses dropped heavily at the fair of 1816 and local land rents fell sharply.[2] Purchasing power in the hinterland probably declined, which may explain why the city's population growth slowed down during the 1820s.

By 1840 Chester's older and wider trade connexions had withered and it had been forced into a diminished role servicing the local region. Modest new industries had appeared in the leadworks, steam milling, and ironfounding, but the heavy reliance on providing services for the hinterland implied a dependence on its fortunes and the need for improved transport connexions. From 1840 the railways provided the means by which that could be achieved.

THE ECONOMY, 1841–70: REORIENTATION AND BOOM

From 1841 Chester enjoyed thirty boom years. The main evidence is the extent of migration to the city, but prosperity was reflected also in a large rise in the number of businesses and in the amount of rebuilding in the city centre. The arrival of the railways reasserted Chester's importance for transport and consolidated its function as a service centre for the region. A limited growth in manufacturing further diversified the economy.

CHESTER AND ITS REGION

The railway age in Chester began in 1840 with the opening of lines to Birkenhead and Crewe. In the next thirty years others were opened which fed traffic from Shrewsbury, Bangor and Holyhead, Wrexham and Ruabon, Oswestry and Welshpool, Mold, Warrington, Rhyl and Denbigh, Llangollen and Corwen, and Wirral.[3] By 1870 the city was a focal point in the regional rail network. At first its connexions to north and central Wales and the Marches were better than those to the east. Although the lines to Crewe and Warrington were opened comparatively early, no others into south and central Cheshire appeared before 1870. The early rail network thus reinforced Chester's service function for Wales but possibly weakened it in relation to the parts of Cheshire for which there was better rail access to Manchester, Warrington, Crewe, the Potteries, or Shrewsbury.

Estimating the effect of the railways on Chester is not easy. The most obvious impact was as employers. There were 311 people, all men, working on the

railways in Chester in 1851 and the number had risen to 499 by 1861, all but five of whom were men.[4] That represented at least 5.2 per cent of the male labour force, and it is likely that the census understated railway employment.[5] By 1861 the London and North Western and Great Western Railways were the two biggest employers in the city. About 100 porters were working at Chester General station,[6] and there were at least 76 railway labourers in the city.[7] The majority, both skilled and unskilled, had been born outside either Chester or Cheshire, and many railway workers seem initially to have come from an existing national pool of labour rather than being local men newly trained.[8] Such migrant workers added new spending power to the Chester economy even though many were unskilled and relatively poorly paid.

By improving Chester's links with its hinterland, the railways enhanced prospects for at least some retailers. Although surviving business records are biased towards middle- and upper-class account customers and probably tend to overstate the city's regional influence, they do provide some evidence of the distribution of Chester's trade. The evidence can be linked to trends in the wider region, and for that purpose the city's hinterland can be divided into four main zones: Wales, subdivided into industrial Flintshire, the Denbighshire coalfield, the north Wales coastal resorts, and the rest of north and mid Wales; Ellesmere Port and Wirral; the rest of Cheshire; and elsewhere in the British Isles (Tables 11–12).

The proportion of Chester's trade from north and

1 Ibid. 58–74; M. E. Turner, 'Parl. Enclosures: Gains and Losses', *Refresh: Recent Findings of Research in Econ. and Social Hist.* iii; P. Hudson, *Industrial Revolution*, 75.
2 Davies, *Agric. Hist. Ches.* 99; R. E. Porter, 'Agric. Change in Ches. during 19th Cent.' (Liverpool Univ. Ph.D. thesis, 1974), 135 and fig. 14.
3 *V.C.H. Ches.* v (2), Railways.

4 *Census,* 1861, *Occupations,* pp. 649, 651, 653.
5 G. R. Hawke, *Rlys. and Econ. Growth in Eng. and Wales, 1840–70,* 262–3.
6 *Chester Chron.* 10 Aug. 1861.
7 *Census,* 1861, *Occupations,* p. 651.
8 G. Davies, 'Impact of Rlys. on Chester, 1837–70' (Chester Coll. B.Ed. essay, 1981), 11–12.

TABLE 11: *Source of account custom at Chester shops, 1844–1910*

Year Shop	(No.)	Chester and suburbs	Probably Chester	North and mid Wales	Ellesmere Port and Wirral	Elsewhere in Cheshire	Elsewhere
1844 Butt & Co.	(482)	46.5	29.7	10.8	0.2	12.2	0.6
1854 Butt & Co.	(365)	44.7	15.3	21.6	3.6	14.3	0.6
1864 Butt & Co.	(1,032)	51.6	5.9	17.9	2.0	21.5	1.0
1874 Butt & Co.	(1,006)	63.7	4.0	8.6	5.1	15.5	3.2
1884 Butt & Co.	(2,309)	60.7	2.3	16.9	5.6	12.2	2.4
1895 Hendersons	(499)	66.1	–	10.2	3.4	15.0	5.2
1900 Butt & Co.	(770)	48.2	–	17.1	4.9	22.6	7.1
1910 Thos. Welsby	(362)	65.8	–	8.3	4.1	16.6	5.3

Notes: The total numbers for Butt & Co. (jewellers) are transactions, the figures for 1900 being for Jan.–Apr. only; the total numbers for Hendersons Ltd. (furnishers) and Thomas Welsby & Co. (wine merchants) are customers.
Sources: C.C.A.L.S., ZCR 92 (Butt & Co.); ZCR 95 (Thos. Welsby); ZCR 558 (Hendersons Ltd.).

TABLE 12: *Source of Welsh account custom at Chester shops, 1844–1910*

Year Shop	(No.)	Industrial Flintshire	Denbighshire coalfield	North coast resorts	Elsewhere
1844 Butt & Co.	(52)	92.3	–	–	7.7
1854 Butt & Co.	(79)	62.0	8.9	1.3	27.9
1864 Butt & Co.	(185)	50.3	21.6	2.2	26.0
1874 Butt & Co.	(82)	45.1	35.4	3.7	15.9
1884 Butt & Co.	(390)	42.9	26.4	16.0	14.7
1895 Hendersons	(51)	37.5	22.9	6.3	33.3
1900 Butt & Co.	(132)	48.5	12.1	11.4	28.0
1910 Thos. Welsby	(30)	43.3	6.7	30.0	20.0

Notes: The total numbers for Butt & Co. (jewellers) are transactions, the figures for 1900 being for Jan.–Apr. only; the total numbers for Hendersons Ltd. (furnishers) and Thomas Welsby & Co. (wine merchants) are customers.
Sources: C.C.A.L.S., ZCR 92 (Butt & Co.); ZCR 95 (Thos. Welsby); ZCR 558 (Hendersons Ltd.).

mid Wales seems to have grown markedly with the opening of the railways to Shrewsbury and Holyhead, and its balance also shifted. Before the arrival of the railway, industrial Flintshire seems to have dominated the Welsh trade, and it continued to be the most important source, though its relative significance declined. Industry in the county was past its peak and the population of upland Flintshire fell during the 1840s and 1850s. Only the coastal lowland grew consistently, although Hawarden, Buckley, Hope, and Treuddyn revived somewhat in the 1850s and 1860s.[1] Trends overall in industrial Flintshire were thus not propitious for Chester.

The railway to Wrexham and Ruabon gave the Denbighshire coalfield a new lease of life,[2] and seems to have brought Chester an infusion of trade. By the 1870s the Denbighshire trade was beginning to rival that from Flintshire. There was much migration into the area, the population rising by 65 per cent between 1841 and 1871. The danger for Chester was that Wrexham was becoming a significant centre in its own right,[3] while the railways also enhanced the drawing power of Shrewsbury and even Oswestry.

Chester's trade from the resorts of the north Wales coast seems to have been small, though growing. Limited development of sea bathing at Prestatyn, Rhyl, Abergele, Colwyn Bay, and Llandudno pre-dated the railway, but even after its opening such development was modest before 1871.[4] Rural north Wales enjoyed a period of considerable prosperity between 1850 and 1880, and the railways seem to have increased Chester's trade from that area.[5]

In rural Cheshire developments in agriculture evidently worked strongly in Chester's favour, and trade from there apparently grew in both absolute and relative terms. The county was surrounded by growing urban areas to the north, south-east, and west, and the agricultural economy during the 19th century became closely tied to supplying the demands of a vast urban market.[6] Changes in farming to accommodate those demands reached a crucial phase around mid century, the key being improved accessibility to markets brought about by the expanding rail network. Cheese became relatively less important but its sale price seems to have risen from the 1830s to a peak c. 1860. Liquid milk increasingly replaced cheese from the 1840s, and market garden produce was also more important in the Chester area, though some of the development pre-dated the railway. Farm productivity improved, rents rose, and rent arrears fell. All the indicators suggest an increasingly prosperous rural economy.

Chester's position as the main regional centre in west Cheshire was strengthened by the closure of other local produce markets. Neston, Malpas, Over, and Frodsham disappeared between 1834 and 1860, though the failure of the last was attributed to Warrington rather than Chester.[7] Tarporley followed after 1860. The effect was to give Chester a wider monopoly, though the benefits were increasingly offset by the growth of farm-gate sales direct to middlemen.[8]

Although Chester's rural hinterland became generally more prosperous, wealth was not evenly distributed. Prospects for farm labourers probably worsened as farms became more capital-intensive and as liquid milk became more important at the expense of crops demanding more, if seasonal, labour. Farm labourers were forced off the land, and in Cheshire as a whole their number fell by 17.1 per cent between 1851 and 1871. Many people left the area east and south-east of Chester, where the population stagnated at c. 17,000.[9] The boom in Chester probably created some unskilled jobs for such rural migrants.

The railway into Wirral seems to have increased the peninsula's significance in Chester's trade. The city's influence, however, evidently reached no further than a line running from Parkgate to Eastham. Beyond that the pull of Liverpool and the growing commercial weight of Birkenhead were too strong.[10] The railways also brought more long-distance tourists and customers to Chester, but although the trade from outside the immediate hinterland grew, it remained a relatively small proportion of the total.

RETAILING AND SERVICES

Chester's booming economy in the early railway age offered new opportunities to its shops and other services. Between 1840 and 1878 the number of businesses rose by 46 per cent (Table 13). There were also changes in the balance between sectors. Suppliers of the basic needs of food and clothing fell from 63 per cent of the total to 53 per cent, while those associated with the growth and broadening of consumer spending power increased in importance. The household goods trades, including consumer durables such as furniture, rose to 9 per cent of businesses, while the number of people offering financial, professional, and sales services nearly trebled. The last feature indicates how Chester's role as a service centre was being strengthened. The number of accountants, solicitors, auctioneers, and property agents increased markedly, and there was a dramatic rise in the number of insurance agents. Chester's role as a printing and publishing

1 A. H. Dodd, *Industrial Revolution in N. Wales* (1971), esp. chapters 5–8; *Jnl. Flints. Hist. Soc.* xxv. 62–97; xxvi. 144–69.

2 Dodd, *Ind. Revolution in N. Wales*, 151.

3 W. T. R. Pryce, 'Social and Econ. Structure of NE. Wales, 1750–1890' (Lanchester Poly., Coventry, Ph.D. thesis, 1971), 115.

4 D. A. Halsall, 'Chester and Holyhead Rly. and its Branches: Geographical Perspective' (Liverpool Univ. Ph.D. thesis, 1976), 83.

5 *Trans. Denb. Hist. Soc.* vi. 78.

6 Rest of para. based on Porter, 'Agric. Change in Ches.' 18–21, 27, 41–2, 135, 202–5, 207, 227, 258, 262, 314, fig. 14.

7 Ibid. 13, 130, 303; *White's Dir. Ches.* (1860), 249.

8 R. E. Porter, 'Marketing of Agric. Produce in Ches. during 19th Cent.' *T.H.S.L.C.* cxxvi. 149.

9 *Census,* 1851–1911.

10 *White's Dir. Ches.* (1860), 571.

TABLE 13: *Chester businesses, 1840, 1878, and 1906*

Business categories	1840	1878	1906
Food, Drink, and Tobacco	610	772	783
	41%	36%	38%
Corn Millers, Maltsters, and Dealers	36	25	15
Shopkeepers, Provision Dealers, and Grocers	221	359	334
Butchers, Fishmongers, and Fried Fish Dealers	57	77	93
Wine and Spirit Dealers	30	19	15
Brewers	15	10	1
Inns, Beer Retailers, Hotels, and Eating Houses	230	237	224
Tobacco and Snuff Manufacturers	–	7	5
Tobacconists and Newsagents	7	25	48
Miscellaneous	14	13	48
Textiles, Clothing, and Dress	331	370	320
	22%	17%	16%
Mercers and Drapers	30	65	44
Clothes Dealers and Outfitters	9	11	24
Tailors, Dressmakers, and Milliners	108	148	95
Hatters and Hosiers	30	51	27
Boot and Shoe Makers, Shops, and Repairers	107	59	76
Hairdressers and Perfumers	25	17	41
Miscellaneous	22	19	13
Household Goods	100	191	176
	7%	9%	9%
Glass, China, and Cutlery Dealers	11	18	15
Furniture Dealers	12	10	24
Hardware Dealers and Ironmongers	18	35	26
Tallow, Oil, Candle, and Soap Dealers	10	18	8
Coal Merchants	9	28	47
Druggists and Chemists	14	25	26
Miscellaneous Household Goods Retailers	4	5	6
Other Household Goods Manufacturers	22	52	24
Printing, Books, and Specialist Trades	81	134	142
	6%	6%	7%
Bookbinders	11	8	7
Printers and Publishers	17	30	24
Booksellers and Stationers	18	35	31
Watchmakers, Jewellers, and Goldsmiths	17	16	20
Antique Furniture Dealers	–	–	4
Artists	5	6	6
Art Furnisher	–	–	1
Art Metal Workers	–	–	3
Bird Dealers	–	1	3
Dealers in Works of Art	–	1	3
Designer, Draughtsman, and Illuminator	–	1	–
Fishing Tackle Dealers	–	3	–
Gunmakers and Gunsmiths	3	–	2
Heraldic Stationer	–	–	1
Music and Musical Instrument Sellers	6	2	5
Organ Builders	–	1	2
Photographers	–	7	13
Pianoforte Makers and Tuners	3	5	7
Picture Cleaner and Restorer	–	–	1
Picture Frame Makers	1	7	7
Plaster Figure Maker	–	1	–
Sculptors	–	1	1
Taxidermists	–	1	1
Toy Dealers	–	8	–
Finance, Professional, Sales, and Service	114	338	320
	8%	16%	16%
Banking Companies	4	6	12
Pawnbrokers	7	6	7
Accountants	5	19	24
Solicitors and Barristers	26	41	56
Stockbrokers	–	2	3
Auctioneers	4	8	15
Insurance Agents and Companies	23	119	38
House and Estate Agents	4	42	18
Building Societies	–	–	4
Agents and Commercial Travellers	13	57	39
Company Head and Local Offices	–	–	18
Medical Professions	27	27	74
Servants' Registry Offices	1	7	10
Bill Posters	–	4	2
Building and Construction	122	224	168
	8%	10%	8%
Building Trades	102	154	134
Architects, Surveyors, and Civil Engineers	10	30	24
Builders' Merchants and Timber Merchants	10	40	10
Road and Water Transport	67	80	99
	5%	4%	5%
Carters, Cab Owners, Coach Owners, and Stables	14	38	38
Horse Transport Construction and Repair	44	24	31
Cycle Dealers and Makers	–	–	14
Motor Vehicle Dealers, Makers, and Repairers	–	–	5
Water Transport Businesses	9	18	11
Miscellaneous Manufactures	61	54	28
	4%	3%	1%
Boot Tree and Last Maker	–	1	–
Brass Founders	2	6	2
Braziers and Tinplate Workers	12	14	6
Manufacturing Chemists	3	3	–
Coopers	7	3	1
Electrical Engineers	–	–	5
General, Mechanical, and Hydraulic Engineers	–	8	7
Filter Manufacturer	1	–	–
Ironfounders	4	6	1
Lead Manufacturer	1	1	1
Nail Makers	8	–	–
Oil Sheet Maker	–	–	1
Roman Cement and Plaster of Paris Manufacturer	1	–	–
Rope and Twine Manufacturers	7	2	1
Surgical Instrument Maker	–	1	1
Tanners	7	2	–
Whitesmiths and Bellhangers	8	7	2
Total Businesses	1,479	2,163	2,036

Notes: Tobacco and snuff manufacturers not listed separately in 1840.

Sources: *Parry's Dir. Chester* (1840); *Cassey's Dir. Chester* (1878); *Kelly's Dir. Ches.* (1906).

centre was enhanced and new trades emerged, including such specialists as seven photographers, a bird dealer, an art dealer, and a taxidermist.

There was also growth in the size and turnover of individual businesses. Browns was highly successful, buying further premises in 1856 and opening a new building in Eastgate Street in 1858. In the 1860s the firm diversified into furniture and furnishing fabrics, for which the premises were enlarged again in 1869 and a furniture factory was opened in Newgate Street.[1] The deposits of the Chester Savings Bank increased by 15 per cent between 1847 and 1867, and the bank's success was expressed in its new premises in Grosvenor Street, opened in 1853.[2] Chester's most luxurious hotel, the Grosvenor, was built on the site of the old Royal Hotel between 1863 and 1866.[3] The rebuilding of other city-centre premises also testified to the city's economic vitality.[4] Part of the boom in all those areas can be attributed to the tourists and other visitors whom the railways brought to the city in increasing numbers.[5]

INDUSTRY

Manufacturing and craft employment remained a very important element of Chester's economy in the mid 19th century (Tables 14–15). While service employment, especially domestic service, predominated for women, for men the largest sector was manufacturing and craft employment. Such jobs increased in importance during Chester's boom. Though the trend between 1841 and 1871 was rather uneven (due in part to the unreliability of the 1841 figures), between 1851 and 1861 the proportion of males employed in manufacturing and crafts rose from 28.5 per cent to 31.5 per cent and the actual numbers by a fifth from 2,490 to 2,991, covering all the main trades. Mid 19th-century Chester thus provides clear evidence that the industrial revolution did not destroy local, small-scale craft and workshop production even in a region which was in the forefront of industrialization; for a time, indeed, it increased.

Some traditional handicraft activities grew during the mid 19th century, a reflection of the growing population and an increased demand which could not, as yet, be satisfied fully by factory products made in the industrial centres. The most important trades were tailoring and shoemaking. Both occupied a blurred area between retailing and manufacturing, since many tailors and shoemakers sold what they made directly to the public. Many, on the other hand, were probably outworkers working either for middlemen wholesalers or directly for retailers (Table 16).[6] For every one shoemaker and tailor in business on his own account, there were thus several others working as family members or outworkers.

Certain other trades in the traditional sector also showed a modest increase in employment from 1851 to 1871 but others declined, probably as victims of the increasing centralization and mechanization of production aided by the railways. Tanning, for example, retained barely a foothold, the number of tanneries dropping from seven to two. The closure of at least two was probably linked to their poor location behind the shops and businesses of Foregate Street and Brook Street.[7] Chester's breweries reached their peak and then began to decline. The brewery in Lower Bridge Street closed c. 1858,[8] and a fall in the number of public-house breweries was due probably to growing competition from the larger firms. The Eaton family sold the Northgate brewery in 1864 to a partnership which developed it into the city's predominant brewing concern.[9]

Steam milling along the canal side expanded, peaking in the late 19th century. Milton Street (Cestrian) Mill was erected in the 1850s,[10] and Albion Mill in Seller Street by John Wiseman in 1868–9.[11] The expansion reflected agricultural prosperity and the economies of scale in large steam-powered plants located alongside cheap water transport.[12] The Dee Mills were becoming outmoded by those developments, but were rebuilt after a fire in 1847.[13]

Modest growth in manufacturing related to road transport was offset by the end of shipbuilding in Chester. The Roodee (or River Dee) yard changed hands twice in the 1850s. The final occupier, Cox and Miller of Liverpool, provided a dramatic finale between 1857 and 1869 by launching a succession of large iron sailing ships from the yard. The slump of the late 1860s ended the shipbuilding boom, however, and in 1869 the yard was closed. The site was used for the new gasworks.[14]

The leadworks continued to grow and prosper. Additions were made to the white lead stacks between 1840 and 1871 which made it into a very large plant, and acetic acid production for the white lead process began in 1844. By 1870 there were eight retorts. The site was enlarged in 1854 to over 16 acres, and a sheet mill was transferred to Chester from Bagillt (Flints.) in 1855.[15]

1 *Browns and Chester*, esp. 81–4.

2 *Chester T.S.B., 1817–1967.*

3 [Callister], *Chester Grosvenor*, 10.

4 Below, Topography, 900–1914: Victorian and Edwardian (City Centre).

5 e.g. R. M. Bevan, *The Roodee: 450 Years of Racing in Chester*, 30.

6 *Jnl. Staffs. Ind. Arch. Soc.* x. 37; A. Fox, *Hist. of Nat. Union of Boot and Shoe Operatives, 1874–1957*, 21–6; *Northants. Past and Present*, vi (3), 151–9.

7 *White's Dir. Ches.* (1860); O.S. Map 1/2,500, Ches.

XXXVIII.11 (1875 and later edns.).

8 C.C.A.L.S., ZCR 56/1–2.

9 C.H.H., Z 37: photocopy of Chester Northgate Brewery Co. min. bk. 1877–81; *Archives and Records*, ed. Kennett, 105.

10 *Bagshaw's Dir. Ches.* (1850); *White's Dir. Ches.* (1860).

11 Fenwick, *Hist. Chester*, 478.

12 *Econ. H.R.* 2nd ser. xliii. 420.

13 1 *Sheaf*, ii, p. 242.

14 *Chester and Dee*, ed. Kennett, 15.

15 Hoddinott, *Leadworks*, 1, 15, 37, 82.

TABLE 14: *Employment structure, 1841–1911*

A. MALES

Occupational class	1841 %	1851 %	1861 %	1871 %	1901 %	1911 %
Agriculture and Fishing	5.4	12.4	10.3	8.1	4.0	4.5
Mining and Quarrying	0.1	1.0	1.4	0.7	0.2	0.2
Building and Construction	9.6	11.0	11.8	14.4	13.1	10.7
Manufacturing and Crafts	31.9	28.5	31.5	30.4	26.5	26.1
Transport	4.0	9.3	10.0	8.9	16.8	16.6
Dealing and Shopkeeping	12.6	14.0	14.4	12.2	12.4	14.1
Finance and Insurance	2.3	1.1	1.4	2.9	6.1	6.2
Public Service and Professional	7.2	10.5	7.0	8.2	9.2	10.4
Domestic Service	4.3	2.5	2.5	2.7	2.3	3.3
Labourers (Unspecified)	14.7	7.0	8.1	9.3	6.2	4.4
Propertied and Independent	3.1	1.2	0.6	0.8	2.7	3.0
Indefinite	4.8	1.5	1.0	1.4	0.7	0.6
Total Employed	6,752	8,750	9,506	8,925	12,000	12,604

B. FEMALES

Occupational class	1841 %	1851 %	1861 %	1871 %	1901 %	1911 %
Agriculture and Fishing	0.2	0.5	1.3	1.5	0.6	0.5
Mining and Quarrying	–	–	–	–	–	–
Building and Construction	–	–	–	0.1	0.1	0.1
Manufacturing and Crafts	14.2	21.1	23.1	21.8	21.8	17.5
Transport	–	0.3	0.1	0.2	0.7	0.6
Dealing and Shopkeeping	6.6	10.4	9.4	15.4	12.5	19.3
Finance and Insurance	–	–	–	0.1	1.0	2.1
Public Service and Professional	2.3	3.6	4.3	6.4	7.8	8.5
Domestic Service	49.0	52.2	50.7	44.9	44.6	42.3
Labourers (Unspecified)	0.2	0.2	0.1	0.1	0.1	–
Propertied and Independent	20.6	7.3	6.9	9.5	10.7	8.7
Indefinite	7.0	4.5	4.2	0.1	0.2	0.4
Total Employed	3,237	4,420	5,230	3,818	5,758	6,017

C. TOTAL WORKING POPULATION

Occupational class	1841 %	1851 %	1861 %	1871 %	1901 %	1911 %
Agriculture and Fishing	3.7	8.4	7.1	6.1	2.9	3.2
Mining and Quarrying	0.1	0.6	0.9	0.5	0.1	0.1
Building and Construction	6.5	7.3	7.6	10.1	8.9	7.2
Manufacturing and Crafts	26.1	26.0	28.5	27.8	25.0	23.3
Transport	2.7	6.3	6.5	6.3	11.6	11.5
Dealing and Shopkeeping	10.7	12.8	12.6	13.2	12.4	15.8
Finance and Insurance	1.6	0.7	0.9	2.0	4.4	4.9
Public Service and Professional	5.6	8.2	6.0	7.7	8.7	9.7
Domestic Service	18.8	19.2	19.6	15.4	16.0	15.9
Labourers (Unspecified)	10.1	4.7	5.3	6.6	4.2	3.0
Propertied and Independent	8.8	3.2	2.8	3.4	5.3	4.8
Indefinite	5.5	2.5	2.1	1.0	0.6	0.6
Total Employed	9,989	13,170	14,736	12,743	17,758	18,621

Note: 1841 includes all employed regardless of age, but there are flaws in the Census occupation data; 1851 and 1861 include all employed regardless of age; 1871 includes employed people aged 20 and over; 1901 and 1911 include employed people aged 10 and over.

Source: *Census*, 1841–71, 1901–11, *Occupations*, Chester.

TABLE 15: *Adult manufacturing employment, 1851–1911, by 1911 Census classifications*

Sector	Males			Females			Total		
	1851	1871	1911	1851	1871	1911	1851	1871	1911
A. Traditional and Handicraft Sector									
Precious Metals, Jewels, Watches, etc.	29	66	75	5	11	1	34	77	76
Cabinet Makers and Upholsterers	123	136	131	20	32	18	143	154	149
Other Furniture Workers	18	19	45	0	0	3	18	19	48
Wood and Bark	172	187	63	3	0	1	175	187	64
Skins and Leather	68	71	5	0	3	1	68	74	6
Hair and Feathers	22	11	23	0	1	1	22	12	24
Tailors, Milliners, and Dressmakers	229	252	250	498	528	530	727	780	780
Shirt Makers	0	0	1	63	100	21	63	100	22
Footwear	376	444	147	64	61	10	440	505	157
Other Dress	33	17	3	13	5	5	46	22	8
Bread etc.	118	162	110	17	6	4	135	168	114
Other Food and Drink	51	82	94	0	0	10	51	82	104
Tobacco Manufacturers (incl. Pipes)	19	47	68	3	13	83	22	60	151
Spirituous Drinks	75	63	20	0	3	0	75	66	20
Bookbinders and Paper	41	22	8	0	7	9	41	29	17
Printers and Lithographers	64	66	134	0	2	4	64	68	138
Total	1,438	1,645	1,177	686	772	701	2,124	2,434	1,878
	68%	61%	43%	98%	93%	97%	75%	69%	54%
B. Transport-Related Crafts									
Ships and Boats	44	69	94	0	0	0	44	69	94
Cycles and Motor Cars	0	0	49	0	0	1	0	0	50
Other Vehicle Workers	107	137	180	0	0	0	107	137	180
Blacksmiths and Strikers	105	133	115	1	0	0	106	133	115
Saddlery and Harness	31	29	33	2	1	1	33	30	34
Total	287	368	471	3	1	2	290	370	473
	14%	14%	17%	0%	0%	0%	10%	10%	14%
C. Metals and Other Modern Manufactures									
Iron, Steel, etc.	58	144	44	0	0	0	58	144	44
General Engineering and Machine Making	129	262	185	0	0	0	129	262	185
Tools, Dies, and Miscellaneous (incl. Leadworks)	130	204	567	6	38	5	136	242	572
Electrical Apparatus	0	0	139	0	0	0	0	0	139
Bricks, Cement, etc.	4	1	28	0	4	1	4	5	29
Oil, Grease, and Soap	28	28	81	0	2	0	28	30	81
Chemicals	17	16	40	0	1	5	17	17	45
Textiles	33	44	8	8	16	7	41	60	15
Total	399	699	1,092	14	61	18	417	735	1,110
	19%	26%	40%	2%	7%	3%	15%	21%	32%
Total	2,124	2,712	2,740	703	834	721	2,831	3,546	3,461
D. Other General and Undefined Workers possibly in Manufacturing									
General Labourers	541	830	507	7	4	0	548	834	507
Engine Drivers (not Transport)	0	2	68	0	0	0	0	2	68
Others	2	24	70	0	27	17	2	51	87
Total	543	905	645	7	31	17	550	936	662

Source: Census, 1851, 1871, 1911, *Occupations*, Chester.

TABLE 16: *Self-employed and employees in shoemaking and tailoring, 1860–1*

Employment type	Shoemakers	Tailors
Total	689	290
Self-employed and middlemen	91	59
Employees and outworkers	598	231
Employees per self-employed	6.6	3.9

Sources: Total: *Census, 1861, Occupations,* Chester; Self-employed and middlemen: *White's Dir. Ches.* (1860); Employees and outworkers calculated by deducting self-employed and middlemen from total.

The railways could have helped the development of new industries in Chester by reducing the cost of raw materials and making access to markets cheaper or faster. Although there is some evidence for such railway-led industrialization, especially in the emergence of Saltney as an industrial suburb, the city's manufacturing base remained limited. The engineering sector grew most, and the numbers employed in metalworking increased greatly between 1851 and 1871, particularly in the more modern trades. Older metal trades, such as nailmaking and whitesmithing, declined, presumably due to competition from elsewhere, but engineers, machine makers, mechanics, and iron manufacturers leapt in numbers. In 1850 there were only three engineering enterprises.[1] One was Edward and Bryan Johnson, successors to Cole, Whittle & Co. at the Flookersbrook foundry. By the 1860s the firm had diversified into general engineering, machining, and boilermaking, and E. B. Ellington entered the partnership, bringing expertise in hydraulic engineering.[2]

The other two engineering firms operating in 1850 appear to have had contrasting fortunes. John Gray & Co., Roodee Iron Works, had disappeared by 1860,[3] but it is unclear whether it was swallowed up by the revived shipyard or was too poorly located to make efficient use of rail transport. The foundry in Crook Street had changed hands by 1860 but survived as a back-street enterprise beyond 1870. More significantly, by 1860 five new firms had emerged and by 1870 a further three, making eleven in all.[4] The new foundries and engineering firms were located in two main areas. The first lay between the canal and the railway around Brook Street, Egerton Street, and George Street, where the most important businesses were E. & B. Johnson, James Mowle, and James Rigg. None was actually on the canal side itself or had direct rail access, and most occupied restricted sites hemmed in by housing which limited their possibility for expansion. The two railway wagon repair shops in the same area were linked of necessity to the railway. The London and North Western Railway had a cramped works between Francis Street and City Road, to which rail access involved crossing the station approach road at street level.[5] The Birmingham Wagon Co.'s works occupied a better and more spacious site between Black Diamond Street and the Brook Street bridge. The company's main works was in Smethwick near Birmingham, and the branch in Chester maintained wagons leased to the railway companies and private operators.[6]

The new industrial zone at Saltney was related directly to the arrival of the railway. Though administratively it was only partly within Chester, geographically and economically Saltney was an extension of the city. It developed rapidly into the city's most vibrant industrial area in the mid 19th century and made a large contribution to diversifying Chester's economic base. The trigger for its growth was the opening by the Shrewsbury and Chester Railway in 1846 of a wharf on the Dee adjacent to the railway junction with the Chester and Holyhead line.[7] Industrial development began in 1847 with the establishment of Henry Wood & Co.'s anchor, chain, and general engineering works. The firm had been founded in Stourbridge (Worcs.) in 1786. The Saltney works, on Boundary Lane, had both a railway siding and access to Saltney wharf. A number of other firms followed Wood's to Saltney. Lloyd's Cambrian Chain and Anchor Testing Co., symbiotically related to Woods, was set up next door in 1866.[8] By 1870 three oil refineries were in operation, of which the largest was the Flintshire Oil & Cannel Co. at St. David's Oil Works. The others were E. S. Rogers & Co.'s British Oil Works and the Dee Mineral Oil Co., set up in 1869. They mostly processed crude oil produced from cannel coal in the Flintshire coalfield, and were part of an industry which boomed locally from 1858 to the 1880s.[9] The Sal Ammonionic works was operating in Saltney as early as 1843, and in 1856 Proctor and Ryland moved there from Birmingham and opened a bone manure works on the riverside.[10] The railway also brought industry to Saltney on its own account. The Shrewsbury and Chester Railway established its locomotive and carriage works there in 1847, and after the company was acquired by the Great Western in 1854, the latter moved its standard-gauge carriage and wagon works from Wolverhampton to Saltney.[11] The Victoria Waggon Co. was also operating

1 *Bagshaw's Dir. Ches.* (1850).

2 Bracegirdle, *Engineering in Chester*, 34–6 (dating Ellington's arrival 1869); *Short Hist. Hydraulic Engineering Co.* 1 (probably more reliable date of 1850s).   3 *White's Dir. Ches.* (1860).

4 Ibid.; *P. & G. Dir. Chester* (1870).

5 O.S. Map 1/2,500, Ches. XXXVIII.11 (1875 edn.).

6 J. Simmons, *Rly. in Town and Country, 1830–1914*, 126; cf. *V.C.H. Staffs.* xvii. 112.

7 *Saltney and Saltney Ferry: Third Illustrated Hist.* (1992), 12.

8 Flints. R.O., NT/1(a); NT/903; *Saltney and Saltney Ferry: Short Illustrated Hist.* ed. B. D. Clark (1988); *Saltney and Saltney Ferry: Second Illustrated Hist.* ed. B. D. Clark (1989), 11; G. Lloyd, *Notes on Henry Wood & Co. Ltd.* (1964).

9 *Jnl. Flints. Hist. Soc.* xxv. 166–9; xxvi. 151; Flints. R.O., NT/1(a); ibid. D/BC/3419; Dodd, *Ind. Revolution in N. Wales.*

10 *Jnl. Flints. Hist. Soc.* xxvi. 148; Flints. R.O., NT/1(a).

11 R. Christiansen, *Regional Hist. of Rlys. of G.B., VII: W. Midlands*, 98; C. H. Ellis, *Brit. Rly. Hist. 1830–76*, 198–207.

at Saltney by 1860, though it had closed by 1870. Furthermore the goods yards at Mold Junction became the main concentration and distribution point for roofing slates from the north Wales quarries.[1] Saltney's population grew from 554 in 1841 to 1,901 in 1871 as a result of the area's industrial development.[2]

The mid 19th century was Chester's most successful period between 1762 and 1914. Much of the success can be attributed to the arrival of the railway, which created direct employment and strengthened links with the hinterland and beyond. The service economy prospered, and there was growth and diversification in manufacturing. By 1870 the city had managed to reorientate to a significant degree after the demise of many of its traditional functions in the eighty years before 1840. The limitations of the reorientation were, however, revealed after 1871.

THE ECONOMY, 1871–1914: THE LIMITS OF REORIENTATION

Chester's mid-century boom was not sustained after 1871. The importance of manufacturing diminished because the development of new industry did not offset a steep decline in craft production and a slackening of Saltney's rate of growth. The fairs effectively disappeared and the regional role of Chester's markets dwindled. Shopping continued to grow, and many businesses, though not all, did well. The central shopping district was more intensively developed. Chester's significance for transport, administration, health, and other services was enhanced. The overall picture was thus mixed. The city continued its reorientation in late Victorian and Edwardian times, but with less obvious success than in the thirty years before 1870.

The growth rate of Chester's population fell sharply after 1871 to only half that of the region.[3] There were two periods of very low growth separated by a somewhat faster interlude in the 1890s, but even then Chester was below the regional average. The migration of people away from the city after 1871 probably exceeded the inflow which had occurred during the mid-century boom.[4]

Although migration out of Chester suggests weaknesses in the city's economy, the picture is complicated by growing emigration from the British Isles as a whole.[5] Overseas emigration probably formed a large part of the migration from Chester, and was mainly the result of national and international factors rather than local ones (Table 17).[6] If such emigration is discounted the result is a more positive picture of Chester's fortunes. Even so, the period 1871–91 seems to have been one of relative depression for the city, and although improvement took place in the 1890s it was not sustained after 1900.

INDUSTRY

By 1900 the division between manufacturing and retailing was more ingrained in the economy and a much higher proportion of goods was produced in large factories and workshops, distributed by the railways, and sold by specialist retailers.[7] The trend undermined Chester's handicraft producers. The number of manufacturing workers in Chester actually fell between 1871 and 1911, mainly through a large reduction in the already limited number of women employed in manufacturing. Male jobs remained almost static.[8]

In 1871 as many as 93 per cent of women workers in manufacturing worked in the traditional sector, rising to 97 per cent by 1911. The decline of traditional crafts thus had a disproportionate impact on women, particularly in the case of shirt-making, an occupation almost monopolized by them which fell away sharply in the period. Dressmaking and millinery remained the main manufacturing jobs for women in 1911, with little change in the numbers employed after 1871. At both dates much of the employment was outwork for Chester shops and private customers, but Browns directly employed 150 in their own dressmaking workroom in the 1870s.[9] The continued importance of dressmaking and millinery in Chester reflects the fact that the production of women's and children's outer garments was still not dominated by large specialist firms in 1914.[10]

Only tobacco and snuff-making provided a significantly growing number of jobs for women. In 1910 there were five manufacturers in Chester, two of which were large concerns, W. T. Davies & Sons of Canal Street and Thomas Nicholls & Co. of Deeside Mills, Handbridge.[11] The former, established in 1860, was

1 *Saltney: 2nd Illus. Hist.* ed. Clark, 7.
2 *Census*, 1851–71 (Saltney township).
3 Above, Table 7.
4 Below, Table 25.
5 *Econ. Hist. of Brit. since 1700*, ed. R. Floud and D. McCloskey, ii. 159–60.
6 D. Baines, *Emigration from Europe, 1815–1930*, 21–30.
7 D. Davis, *Hist. of Shopping*, chapter 12; D. Alexander,

Retailing in Eng. during the Industrial Revolution, 12–18; *Shopkeepers and Master Artisans in 19th-Cent. Europe*, ed. G. Crossick and H.-G. Haupt, 12–13.
8 Above, Table 15, on which following paras. based.
9 *Browns and Chester*, 209.
10 Davis, *Hist. Shopping*, 293.
11 *Kelly's Dir. Ches.* (1910); Bracegirdle, *Engineering in Chester*, 14.

TABLE 17: *Estimates of overseas emigration and net migration, 1851–1911*

Decade	Estimated total city migration	Overseas emigration estimate 1	Regional migration estimate 1	Overseas emigration estimate 2	Regional migration estimate 2
1851–60	+ 1,913	− 718	+ 2,631		
1861–70	+ 1,636	− 629	+ 2,265	− 1,184	+ 2,820
1871–80	− 2,454	− 1,038	− 1,416	− 712	− 1,742
1881–90	− 2,842	− 1,538	− 1,304	− 1,580	− 1,262
1891–1900	− 453	− 1,017	+ 564	− 616	+ 163
1901–10	− 2,713	− 1,688	− 1,025		

For notes and sources see Appendix, below, pp. 204–5.

already in the ownership of Imperial Tobacco, an example of national firms strengthening their direct involvement in the local economy.

Although the number of male manufacturing workers remained almost static between 1871 and 1911, there was a great change in the work they did. The proportion employed in the traditional and handicraft sector dropped from 61 per cent to 43 per cent. The most dramatic fall was in shoemaking. As the footwear trade became more concentrated in specialist towns like Stafford, Northampton, and Leicester, and as mechanized factory production progressively eliminated hand-work,[1] so shoemaking as domestic outwork declined in Chester. Attempts were made to move to factory production there, notably by William Collinson and his various partners. He traded from premises in Watergate Street from the mid 1840s, and later opened a shop in Eastgate Row South. Between 1864 and 1866 he also started a large new factory at the canal bridge on City Road, housing 'vast amounts of machinery' and employing 250 hands who turned out 2,000–3,000 pairs of boots a week.[2] Collinson did not, however, stay in manufacturing. Around 1875 the factory was taken over by Alfred Bostock & Co., a Stafford shoe firm, but by 1892 Bostocks had left and the premises were occupied by a rope and twine manufacturer. Another member of the same Stafford family, Edwin Bostock, opened a small shoe factory in King Street in the 1860s, but it closed between 1902 and 1906. Factory production of footwear thus failed to establish itself in Chester,[3] and by 1911 the number of male shoemakers had dropped to a third of the 1871 level. Very few women remained in the trade.

Milling reached its zenith in the late 19th century, but decline thereafter was rapid and by 1914 Chester's mills were a shadow of their former prosperity. Two structural changes eroded the industry's base locally: increasing imports of hard foreign wheat from c. 1860 and the development of roller milling from the 1870s.[4] Chester's mills, which were wrongly located and not big enough, were ill-fitted to respond to the challenge. F. A. Frost and Sons was the city's most successful firm. It installed the first Simon automated roller mill in the country in 1881,[5] and by 1889 had switched over completely to roller milling.[6] Around 100 workers were employed in 1892,[7] and in 1904 the mill was 'equal to anything in the country'.[8] The firm switched to milling imported hard wheat brought by river and canal from Birkenhead and Liverpool,[9] but the need for transhipment exposed the disadvantage of the site in Chester, and in 1910 Frosts opened new mills at Ellesmere Port on the Manchester Ship Canal served directly by ocean-going ships. By 1913 they had stopped milling in Chester, and the premises were abandoned soon after Frosts' amalgamation with Spillers in 1920.[10] Frosts' mill thus closed because the firm adapted successfully to changing conditions in the industry.

In contrast the demolition of the Dee Mills in 1910 resulted from a clear failure to respond to such changes. After 1864 William Johnson, who had entered the mills as a boy in the 1830s, gradually increased his share of the mills, acquiring almost complete control in 1885.[11] Although 'the Miller of Dee' became wealthy and an alderman of the city, he was regarded as 'plodding',[12] and did little to modernize the mills. By

1 Fox, *Hist. Nat. Union Boot and Shoe Operatives*, 12–13, 137, 260.

2 H. Mackay, *Stranger's Handbook of Chester* (1867), 28; *Chester Chron.* 4 Dec. 1869.

3 *Slater's Dir. Ches.* (1848, 1856, 1882–3); *Bagshaw's Dir. Ches.* (1850); *White's Dir. Ches.* (1860); *Morris's Dir. Ches.* (1864, 1874); *P. & G. Dir. Chester* (1870–1); *Kelly's Dir. Ches.* (1892, 1896, 1902).

4 *Slater's Dir. Ches.* (1848, 1856, 1882–3); *Bagshaw's Dir. Ches.* (1850); *White's Dir. Ches.* (1860); *Morris's Dir. Ches.* (1864, 1874); *P. & G. Dir. Chester* (1870–1); *Kelly's Dir. Ches.*

(1892, 1896, 1902, 1906, 1910, 1914); *Econ. H.R.* 2nd ser. xliii. 423–5.   5 *Econ. H.R.* 2nd ser. xliii. 427.

6 *Chester Chron.* 24 Mar. 1894.

7 *Chester in 1892* (Robinson, Son and Pike: copy at C.H.H.), 32.

8 *Chester Chron.* 24 Sept. 1904.   9 Ibid. 14 July 1894.

10 P. J. Aspinall and D. M. Hudson, *Ellesmere Port: The Making of an Industrial Boro.* 78.

11 C.C.A.L.S., ZCHD 12, deeds dated 3 Mar. 1864, 26 Mar. 1864, 24 June 1864, 20 July 1870, 4 May 1872, 29 Apr. 1885, 30 May 1885.   12 *Chester Chron.* 24 Mar. 1894, obituary.

1892 their value was declining rapidly,[1] and after Johnson's death in 1894 and a fire which gutted one of the five units, they were put up for sale and bought by the city council in 1895 for the relatively small sum of £7,000.[2] The city wanted them in connexion with an abortive scheme to improve Chester's water supply, and it is clear that it would have closed them immediately if it had been technically necessary, further evidence that they were already of little economic significance. In the event the city council leased the four remaining units to William Gregg.[3] Limited modernization must have been carried out as they contained some roller milling machinery by 1903, when the new tenants, Messrs. T. Wright and S. Robinson of Liverpool, sought replacements of a higher grade.[4] Wright and Robinson may have taken over the lease to acquire reserve capacity for their mills in Liverpool, and no further modernization was in fact carried out. They quit the premises in 1908, after which the Dee Mills remained empty until 1910, when they were demolished.[5]

The fate of Chester's other milling firms varied, but all were in decline by 1914. John Wiseman & Co. grew rapidly in the 1870s but declined as steeply less than forty years later. Although the firm's Albion Mill in Seller Street was presumably built with millstones,[6] by 1892 it was fitted with the latest roller machinery and employed between 50 and 60 workers.[7] Wiseman also operated Milton Street (or Cestrian) Mill from c. 1869, but the owner's death in the 1900s seems to have coincided with a sharp contraction of the business. By 1910 Cestrian Mill had been leased to Griffiths Bros. for use as a warehouse and by 1913 Albion Mill was mainly producing animal feedstuffs, having fallen heavily in value.[8]

Some Chester corn and provender merchants also undertook milling. Bowling Green Mill, Milton Street, was a small concern operated in 1871 by the Chester Provender and Carting Co.[9] It continued as such into the 1920s. Griffiths Bros. became Chester's largest firm of corn merchants in the late 19th century. The firm was founded in Lower Bridge Street, perhaps in the 1850s, and c. 1873 expanded into premises on Queen's Wharf vacated by the Chester Provender and Carting Co. The increasing import of foreign wheat led it to open an office in Liverpool c. 1874.[10] The Queen's Wharf premises were greatly extended in the 1870s and

again in 1912, but they were used mainly as warehouses and the amount of milling on site seems to have been limited. In 1902 the firm was milling provender, but at Mickle Trafford watermill rather than in Chester.[11] Some other corn merchants also appear to have done some milling on a small scale. The last surviving mill in Chester proved to be Upton windmill, operated by Edward Dean and his son from the 1870s to the 1930s. They had installed an auxiliary steam engine by 1892.[12] By 1914 milling in Chester was thus a dying industry, though its final demise took place after 1918.

In the 19th century Chester became a centre for market gardening, plant nurseries, and seed merchants. As early as 1837 Chester market gardens were supplying Liverpool,[13] and the coming of the railways allowed some Chester firms to expand greatly. The trade increased in importance right up to 1914 and maintained its position until the 1930s. The city's location at the geographical centre of the British Isles, together with its good rail connexions and mild climate, made it an ideal place to serve the national market.[14] The Dickson family, established in Chester by 1820, was pre-eminent in the trade, F. & A. Dickson operating at Upton nurseries and James Dickson & Sons at Newton. The two enterprises merged in the 1880s, when the grounds under cultivation extended to over 400 acres. It was one of the largest businesses of its type in the country. By the late 19th century the firm supplied all types of bedding plants and trees, together with farm and garden seeds, garden tools, and agricultural implements, and undertook commissions to design gardens for country houses.[15] Other large nurseries were operated by Samuel Dobie and John Kirk in the Vicars Cross area, F. W. Dutton at Queen's Park, McHattie & Co. at Overleigh, and Alexander McLean at Upton.[16] In 1883 James Hunter established a farm seed business in Chester, attracted to the city solely by its location. Hunter was a leading advocate of the need for scientific testing of seeds and his firm was the first to offer a guarantee of purity, genuineness, and germination rate. Operating from premises in Foregate Street, by 1913 it had become one of the leading farm seed suppliers in the country.[17] In 1911 at least 413 people living in the city, together with an unknown number from outside, worked in nurseries or related businesses, double the number in 1861.[18]

Brewing, on the other hand, almost disappeared

1 C.C.A.L.S., ZTRP 2; ZTRP 14.
2 Ibid. ZCB 5, 10 Apr. 1895; ZCCB 39, pp. 86–7.
3 Ibid. ZCCB 59, p. 299.   4 Ibid. p. 834.
5 Ibid. 17 June 1908, p. 674; 15 Dec. 1909, ratified 26 Jan. 1910.
6 Fenwick, *Hist. Chester*, 478.   7 *Chester in 1892*, 32.
8 C.C.A.L.S., ZTRP 54; C.H.H., Chester Arch. Soc. oral hist. transcripts, no. 18 (Miss Elsie Green).
9 *P. & G. Dir. Chester* (1871).
10 *Morris's Dir. Ches.* (1874).
11 *Kelly's Dir. Ches.* (1902).   12 Ibid. (1892).
13 Porter, 'Agric. Change in Ches.' 226–7; cf. R. Desmond,

Dictionary of Brit. and Irish Botanists and Horticulturalists (1994), 2, 62, 245, 380, 592, 725.
14 Inf. from Mr. P. Hunter, Hunters of Chester Ltd., 1991.
15 *Chester Chron.* 25 Oct. 1879, 10 May 1884, 21 Jan. 1899; *Chester in 1892*, 34; Desmond, *Dict. Brit. and Irish Botanists and Horticulturalists*, 206–7; E. Hubbard, *Buildings of Wales: Clwyd*, 205, 453.
16 *Kelly's Dir. Ches.* (1910); O.S. Map 1/2,500, Ches. XXXVIII.11 (1899 edn.).
17 Inf. from Mr. Hunter; *Hunter's Jnl.* i (Autumn 1915) (Hunter's of Chester Ltd., Oulton Park).
18 *Census*, 1861, 1911, *Occupations*.

from Chester in the late 19th century, and by 1909 only one concern was left. The decline was due to the elimination of public-house breweries and the concentration of ownership among the commercial brewery companies. In 1871 there were 13 breweries in Chester, of which seven appear to have been pub breweries.[1] All the latter had ceased operation by 1892. Of the commercial breweries, the three biggest were Edward Russell Seller & Co. in Foregate Street, the Lion Brewery in Pepper Street, and the Chester Northgate Brewery. The Seller family continued in ownership until the 1880s, but in 1889 the concern was sold to the Albion Brewery Co. of Wigan and the brewery closed shortly afterwards.[2] Between 1871 and 1892 the Lion Brewery passed through at least four hands[3] before being acquired by Thomas Montgomery. His business was incorporated as the Chester Lion Brewery Co. Ltd. in 1896, but was taken over by Bent's Brewery of Liverpool in 1902. The brewery was closed soon afterwards.[4] The Northgate Brewery was the only Chester brewery to survive beyond 1914. By 1891 the company owned 21 tied houses in Chester and numerous others within a radius of 15 miles from the city.[5]

The history of brewing illustrates a wider transition in the economy from small-scale production to business concentration and industrialized methods. The trend weakened the city's manufacturing base and was only partly offset by developments in the limited number of modern industrial concerns. Between 1871 and 1911, for example, the number of workers aged over 20 in metal manufacturing increased from 735 to 1,110, a rise of 53 per cent. Nationally, however, the increase was around 130 per cent.[6] The successful firms were those able to take advantage of new national or regional markets. The leadworks went through a difficult period, though by 1900 was probably at the zenith of its development. It continued to specialize in white lead production, which by 1890 took up over half the operational site. The production of lead shot also remained important, and Chester benefited from the decline of the firm's Bagillt works as the increasing import of overseas lead undercut ore produced, smelted, and refined in north Wales. The transfer of lead milling to Chester was completed in 1909, and shortly before the First World War the decision was taken to open a new lead refining plant. Finally, in 1929 the smelter was moved from Bagillt to Chester

and the north Wales works closed completely. The production of acetic acid for the white lead process was, however, closed down before 1900 because synthetic acid could be bought in more cheaply.[7] The Chester works also suffered from more fundamental problems. In the 1880s the Walkers Parker partnership was destroyed by an acrimonious dispute between two of the partners, one of whom was manager of the Chester works. In 1889 the new limited company of Walkers, Parker & Co. bought out the partners' assets and took over the Chester works.[8] The change came at a time when trading conditions in the lead industry were difficult, and the new concern's financial performance was poor throughout the 1890s.[9] Parts of the site were sold to improve the financial position. Though no overall figures are available, it seems likely that employment grew only slowly between 1880 and 1914 before expanding dramatically during the First World War because of the firm's importance for arms production.[10]

The engineering sector in Chester in the late 19th century was very volatile. During the national economic boom of the early 1870s the number of firms increased from 11 in 1870 to 16 in 1876.[11] By then the boom was over, and in 1878 the Chester engineering trade was in depression. Wage cuts were imposed at Hydraulic Engineering, and the Northgate Iron Works in Victoria Road went into liquidation.[12] Conditions remained difficult during the 1880s, and in 1889 Arthur Rigg's Victoria Engine Works failed.[13] Though the number of firms rose again in the 1890s and 1900s, particularly with the growth of electrical engineering, many lasted only a short time, and only three Chester engineering firms survived the whole period to 1914: Hydraulic Engineering, Henry Lanceley & Co., and Samuel Taylor Parry.[14]

The engineering business of Edward and Bryan Johnson was renamed the Hydraulic Engineering Co. in 1874. The decision to specialize in hydraulic machinery proved sound as demand expanded in the late 19th century. The firm opened offices in London, Paris, and Brussels, and developed a significant export trade.[15] Hydraulic Engineering became a large employer, with 200 workers in Chester in 1879 and between 300 and 400 by 1892. The works was expanded and modernized and as early as 1879 a new erecting shop was lighted by electricity.[16] It remained, however, on the cramped site between

1 *P. & G. Dir. Chester* (1871); O.S. Map 1/2,500, Ches. XXXVIII.15 (1874 edn.).

2 Barber, *Dir. of Breweries*, 6; *Kelly's Dir. Ches.* (1892, 1896).

3 *P. & G. Dir. Chester* (1871); C.C.A.L.S., ZD/JWW 341; *Kelly's Dir. Ches.* (1878, 1892); Barber, *Dir. of Breweries*, 6.

4 *Chester Chron.* 30 Sept. 1899; Barber, *Dir. of Breweries*, 6.

5 C.H.H., Z 37: photocopy of Chester Northgate Brewery Co. min. bk. 1877–81; *Chester Chron.* 7 Mar. 1891.

6 Above, Table 15; B. R. Mitchell and P. Deane, *Abstract of Brit. Hist. Statistics*, labour force table 1.

7 Hoddinott, *Leadworks*, 15, 37, 61, 68, 82.

8 *Mins. of Walkers, Parker & Co.* ed. John, 49–54.

9 *Chester Chron.* 17 Mar. 1894, 12 Mar. 1904; Hoddinott, *Leadworks*, 7.

10 C.C.A.L.S., ZCR 586/9.

11 *P. & G. Dir. Chester* (1870, 1876); *Morris's Dir. Ches.* (1874).

12 *Chester Chron.* 4 Jan. 1879.   13 Ibid. 14, 28 Feb. 1891.

14 *P. & G. Dir. Chester* (1870–1, 1876); *Morris's Dir. Ches.* (1874); *Slater's Dir. Ches.* (1882–3); *Kelly's Dir. Ches.* (1892, 1902, 1914).

15 *Chester in 1892*, 24–7; C.C.A.L.S., ZCR 256/13.

Egerton and Charles Streets, partly bisected by the latter. There was no direct rail access and the removal of large equipment must have been difficult.[1] The failure to move to a more convenient site suggests a certain lack of enterprise during the firm's most successful period.

Henry Lanceley, Son & Co. was more typical of engineering firms in Chester. It grew modestly in the late 19th century by exploiting opportunities in the region. Founded *c.* 1869, the firm started in a small way in George Street but after a move to larger premises in the same street, in the mid 1880s it took over a former tannery in Brook Street and converted it into the Providence Foundry and Engineering Works.[2] In 1881 Lanceleys' business was largely concerned with satisfying the jobbing engineering requirements of other Chester enterprises, but it dealt with an extremely wide range of customers, and activities ranged from repairing mangles to supplying complete steam engines and boilers. By 1909 the volume of business had almost doubled and about half was from outside the city. In the 1900s Lanceleys benefited from the growth of John Summers's steelworks at Shotton and the sheet metal industry at Ellesmere Port, but the firm also carried out contracts along the north Wales coast, in the north-east Wales coalfield, and in the rural areas south-east and east of Chester. Even so, with a turnover of under £10,000 in 1908–9, it was a relatively small enterprise.[3]

The firm of Samuel Taylor Parry was even smaller, but was unique in Chester engineering by surviving from the 18th century to 1914 and beyond. A jobbing engineering business, Parrys occupied premises in Princess Street throughout the period and also operated the foundry in Crook Street before 1855 and again between 1876 and the early 1890s. By 1896 the firm had diversified into electrical engineering, and it played an important role in the early provision of electric lighting in Chester.[4]

Hughes and Lancaster was one engineering firm which found Chester an unsuitable place for expansion. Founded in 1865, it established a works in City Road to exploit the increasing demand for water and sewerage machinery, but the premises were too small and impossible to enlarge. In 1892 the firm moved to Acrefair near Ruabon.[5] Its disappearance was ultimately counterbalanced by the founding in 1900 of Brookhirst, another engineering firm which exploited new market potential, in its case in electrical switch-

gear. Neither of the original partners, John A. Hirst and Percy Shelley Brook, was a Cestrian, and the firm's location in the city was due solely to Hirst's view that Chester was a better place to live than his native Manchester and would provide 'gentle and pleasing conditions' for his workers. The original premises in Northgate Street were soon outgrown and a new works was built in 1906 at Newry Park off Brook Lane. Such was the firm's success that the works had to be expanded within two years, and it was extended again in 1915 and 1917.[6]

Two other metalworking firms established before 1914 added to the manufacturing base. Williams Bros. began *c.* 1859 as a timber business in the Kaleyards, but later switched to making metal windows and relocated to Victoria Road. The firm of Williams and Williams was founded in 1910 and also made metal window frames, at premises in the old engineering works on the corner of Victoria Road and George Street. It later became a company of national significance.[7]

In Saltney there were no major new developments in the main industries established before 1871, and by 1914 some decline had set in.[8] The visual contrast with Chester was startling. In 1884 it was reported that 'Saltney presents the appearance of a miniature "Black Country"; unusually high chimneys soar into the sky and the atmosphere is impregnated with thick heavy smoke. Large works abound on all sides [and] the place is alive with all the signs of industrial activity.'[9]

Between 1873 and 1910 Saltney's pioneer firm, Henry Wood & Co., may have trebled in size,[10] due partly to the closure of works elsewhere. By 1892 the works was said to be 'the largest and most complete in the kingdom [for producing] all descriptions of chains, cables and anchors and crane chains for collieries and lifting purposes'. The firm became a limited company in 1899.[11] Other activities also expanded, notably railway wagon and carriage repair, and in 1890 the L.N.W.R. opened the Mold Junction engine shed, housing 40 locomotives, which employed *c.* 200 workers in 1899.[12]

Saltney's oil industry seems to have peaked in the 1870s. The largest concern, the St. David's Works belonging to the Flintshire Oil and Cannel Co., was forced into liquidation in 1884 after the collapse of the cannel industry.[13] The site was later annexed by its neighbour, the Dee Oil Co. By 1884 that firm

1 *Chester Chron.* 8 Nov. 1879.
2 O.S. Map 1/2,500, Ches. XXXVIII.11 (1899 edn.).
3 *Chester Chron.* 4 Dec. 1909, obituary of R. H. Lanceley.
4 Ibid. 5 Jan. 1884, advert; C.C.A.L.S., ZCR 77/1–2.
5 C.C.A.L.S., ZCR 210/3; ZCR 210/6.
6 *Trans. Denb. Hist. Soc.* viii. 112–13; C. J. Williams, *Industry in Clwyd: Illustrated Hist.* 74; *Chester in 1892*, 27–9.
7 C.C.A.L.S., ZCR 420/2: 'Perfect Control: Outline Hist. of Brookhirst Switchgear of Chester'.

8 Bracegirdle, *Engineering in Chester*, 55, 60.
9 Flints. R.O., G/A/160/21(4) VAL; G/A/159/123; G/A/160/15 VAL.
10 *Chester Chron.* 5 July 1884.
11 Flints. R.O., G/A/160/21(4) VAL; G/A/159/123; G/A/160/15 VAL.
12 Ibid. NT/903; NT/1(a), p. 30.
13 Ibid. D/DM/1064/1; *Saltney: Short Illus. Hist.* ed. Clark.
14 Flints. R.O., D/BC/3419.

employed 300 workers producing candles and a varied range of oils,[1] but in 1913 the refinery was closed and all operations moved to Bootle (Lancs.).[2] Rogers' British Oil Works, Saltney's third refinery, had closed by 1890,[3] but the chemical industry remained important. The bone manure works of Proctor and Ryland was taken over c. 1894 by Edward Webb and Sons, seed merchants of Stourbridge, who expanded the plant to such an extent that by 1910 it was Saltney's second largest business.[4]

By the 1890s Saltney's port was in terminal decline. In the 1880s the G.W.R., owners of the wharf, put up stiff resistance to the Manchester, Sheffield, and Lincolnshire Railway's bridge over the Dee at Queensferry. When completed in 1889 it had to be provided with an opening span to allow access to Saltney and Chester.[5] Though the G.W.R. persevered at Saltney, by 1904 there was little traffic, and in 1913 the wharf was taken over by J. Crichton & Co. Ltd. to become a shipyard building small coasting vessels.[6] By 1914 Saltney had thus lost its oil refineries but benefited from the continuing growth of its other firms and from Crichton's modest revival of shipbuilding.

Shipbuilding did not return to Chester itself after the 1869 closure, and boatbuilding firms in the city were very small. William Roberts's yard, building river pleasure craft, operated at the Groves until c. 1906 when it moved to the Dee branch canal basin. The Shropshire Union Canal Co. built narrowboats and Mersey flats at Tower Wharf until 1913 and the yard was taken over by J. H. Taylor & Sons in 1917.[7]

Motor manufacturing was confined to a few cars made by George Crosland-Taylor between 1906 and 1910 using parts imported from France. Five cars were produced bearing the Crosville name, but only two appear to have been built in Chester. From 1910 the firm concentrated on running buses.[8]

Between 1871 and 1914 the limited expansion of modern industries in Chester thus brought a somewhat greater integration with the international industrial economy. By 1914 the city had three engineering firms, Hydraulic Engineering, Henry Wood, and Brookhirst, which were leaders in their fields and, together with the leadworks, gave the city a more significant national role in manufacturing than is commonly perceived. That growth did not, however, offset the decline of the local craft sector brought about by better communications and factory production elsewhere. The opening of the Hawarden Bridge (or Shotton)

steelworks on Deeside in 1896 proved to be the most important industrial development in the Chester region in the late 19th century.[9] That fact, together with the rapid growth of industry in Ellesmere Port, confirmed that other localities near by were more attractive than Chester itself to major industrial investors.

RETAILING AND SERVICES

The faltering of Chester's industrial development increased its reliance on shops and services. Evidence on shopping after 1871 is limited and somewhat contradictory, but it suggests that despite the continued improvement in the quality of Chester's shops, the sector did not grow much. Employment in shops, services, and transport rose from 26 per cent of the working population in 1861 to 42 per cent in 1911, when nationally only 35 per cent of the labour force worked in service employments.[10] Although Chester already had a large service sector in the early 1870s, it did not grow particularly quickly before 1914, and certainly less rapidly than in the country as a whole, by 58 per cent between 1871 and 1911 compared with a national rate of 69 per cent (Table 18).[11] Services in nearby towns grew faster, though from a lower base, and some trade was diverted from Chester to Wrexham and, to a much lesser extent, Ellesmere Port, Northwich, and Crewe. Chester's own service sector was influenced by six factors: structural and cyclical trends in the national economy; developments in the city's hinterland; local transport; purchasing power within Chester; changes in manufacturing, wholesaling, and retailing; and trends in other public and private services.

The general rise in the standard of living which occurred during the later 19th century was probably the main factor behind growth in Chester's shops and services.[12] Despite wide disparities in wealth and income, there was more money in the local economy which could be spent on goods and services. Although the total number of businesses fell slightly between 1878 and 1906 for reasons discussed below, their diversity increased.[13] Specialist trades such as those concerned with picture restoration, heraldic stationery, and antique furniture found a niche, and the number of photographers, jewellers, and music shops grew. Over the 18 years from 1892 to 1910 the gross estimated rental for poor-rate purposes of the central shopping streets rose by 18 per cent.[14]

---

1 *Chester Chron.* 5 July 1884.
2 *Saltney: 3rd Illus. Hist.* 18.
3 Flints. R.O., G/A/159/123.
4 Ibid. NT/1(a); G/A/159/123; G/A/160/15 VAL.
5 *Chester Chron.* 2 Feb. 1889.
6 Ibid. 14 Apr. 1894, 16 Feb. 1904; *Saltney: Short Illus. Hist.* ed. Clark; *Chester and Dee,* ed. Kennett, 15, 29–32.
7 *Chester and Dee,* ed. Kennett, 15; *Chester Chron.* 25 Apr. 1874, 14 July 1894; C.C.A.L.S., ZCR 366. Plate 45.

8 W. J. Crosland-Taylor, *Crosville: The Sowing and the Harvest* (1948), 2–11.   9 *Jnl. Flints. Hist. Soc.* xxv. 102.
10 Above, Table 14; *Econ. Hist. Brit.* ed. Floud and McCloskey, ii, table 1.4.
11 P. Deane and W. A. Cole, *Brit. Econ. Growth, 1688–1959* (1967), table 31.
12 *Econ. Hist. Brit.* ed. Floud and McCloskey, ii. 121–43.
13 Above, Table 13.
14 C.C.A.L.S., ZTRP 14; ZTRP 48.

Overall growth was, however, modulated by cyclical trends in the national economy. The generally depressed period between 1873 and the 1890s seems to have hit Chester's most prestigious shop, Brown, Holmes & Co., where sales in real terms stagnated after 1870, and there were some particularly bad years, notably 1871–2 and between 1879 and 1884.[1] Both of Chester's private banks were badly affected by the banking crisis of 1878, itself a reflection of the depression; Dixon & Co. was forced into amalgamation with Parr's Bank, and although the Chester Old Bank, Williams & Co., survived, it remained weak during the 1880s.[2] The severe depression of 1879 led to a reduction of wages in the Chester engineering trade, and the cheese market of that year was described as 'the deadest for 30 years'. The impact of recession was noted again in 1894 and 1904.[3]

Periods of national recession weakened the economy of both Chester and its hinterland, and structural changes in the latter also tended to limit the growth of the city's service sector. Some 10–15 per cent of the city's trade seems consistently to have come from north and mid Wales, and the largest group of Welsh customers, 45 per cent, lived in industrial Flintshire.[4] Unfortunately for Chester, much of that area was in decline during the late 19th century, and even the establishment of Shotton steelworks in 1896 was only partial compensation.[5]

Chester's importance as a service centre for the Denbighshire coalfield seems to have declined after 1871. That, too, was unfortunate for the city since the industrial zone around Wrexham and Ruabon had continued to grow after 1850.[6] The problem for Chester was that Wrexham itself became an important shopping centre which even began to poach trade from Buckley and Connah's Quay in Flintshire after the Wrexham, Mold, and Connah's Quay Railway was opened in 1866. The extension of the line across the Dee to Bidston and Chester Northgate in 1889–90 may have benefited Wrexham as much as Chester.[7] Butt & Co. of Chester opened a shop in Wrexham c. 1895,[8] showing the town's rising significance and resulting in a sharp decline in patronage of the Chester shop by Denbighshire customers. Chester did benefit, however, from the growth of the north Wales coastal resorts, and by the 1900s trade from that area may have rivalled that from Denbighshire. The city also continued to draw custom from rural north and central Wales.

Chester's trade from Wirral and Ellesmere Port, however, remained relatively insignificant, amounting to only 4–5 per cent of the total from a district which by 1911 accounted for 28 per cent of the hinterland population.[9] Wirral customers mainly came to Chester from places near by, and a line from Parkgate to Eastham still seems to have marked the limit of significant trade. Birkenhead emerged as a distinct rival to Chester, and Liverpool's hold on the area was strengthened by the opening of the Mersey railway tunnel in 1886.[10] Only the rapid growth of Ellesmere Port in the thirty years before 1914 worked to Chester's advantage, though even there the city's drawing power was weakened by the lack of a direct rail link, a problem remedied in 1910 by the bus service established by Crosville.[11] Ellesmere Port's population exceeded 10,000 in 1911 and was heavily skewed towards industrial workers, but 182 shops had been opened there by 1914.[12]

Around 15 per cent of Chester's trade between 1871 and 1914 may consistently have come from the areas of Cheshire to its east and south-east. Access was improved by the opening of the Tattenhall Junction to Whitchurch (Salop.) railway line in 1872 and the Cheshire Lines route to Northwich in 1875.[13] They seem to have strengthened Chester's hold over its south-eastern hinterland and opened up the Northwich area more effectively. The frontier of significant trade evidently ran roughly along the southern boundary of the county as far as Whitchurch and then north along the mid-Cheshire ridge to Frodsham, with some coming from Nantwich and the Cheshire salt towns, notably Northwich.[14] That area declined somewhat in the late 19th century, principally because the cheese trade was depressed by large-scale imports of American cheese. Even though farmers responded by switching more to liquid milk,[15] there continued to be heavy migration out of the area and the population was static.[16] Thus although the rural area remained relatively prosperous and an effective market for Chester's goods and services, there were limits to the amount of trade it offered. Similarly, the Cheshire salt towns were in difficulties after 1870, when the market for salt became glutted and prices fell. Even the creation of the Salt Union in 1888 did little to improve matters, and production fell in the 1890s and 1900s.[17] As with industrial Flintshire, a significant part of Chester's

1 Ibid. ZCR 658/3 (adjusting figures for inflation).

2 Ibid. ZCR 4/2–3; Dawes and Ward-Perkins, *Country Banks*, ii. 154–5; *Econ. H.R.* 2nd ser. xlii. 507.

3 *Chester Chron.* 4 Jan., 1 Mar. 1879, Feb.–Mar. 1894 *passim*, Feb.–Apr. 1904 *passim*.

4 Above, Tables 11–12.

5 *Jnl. Flints. Hist. Soc.* xxv. 103; xxvi. 144–69; xxvii. 101–6.

6 *Trans. Denb. Hist. Soc.* vi. 67–96; vii. 38–66; viii. 95–113; ix. 146–73.

7 Pryce, 'Social and Econ. Structure of NE. Wales', 102–11; J. I. C. Boyd, *Wrexham, Mold and Connah's Quay Rly.* 134, 214, 271–92.   8 C.C.A.L.S., ZCR 92/232.

9 Above, Tables 11–12, on which this and next para. based.

10 G. O. Holt, *Regional Hist. of Rlys. of G.B., X: NW.* 42.

11 Crosland-Taylor, *Crosville* (1948), 5–6.

12 Aspinall and Hudson, *Ellesmere Port*, 54.

13 Christiansen, *Regional Hist. of Rlys.: W. Mids.* 181, 183–4.

14 Derived from mapping of data in Table 11.

15 Porter, 'Agric. Change in Ches.' 136, 202, 210; *Chester Chron.* 9 Aug. 1879, 2 Feb. 1889, 21 July 1894.

16 *Census,* 1871–1911.

17 *Scientific Survey of Merseyside,* ed. W. Smith, 253; *Chester Chron.* 20 Jan. 1894; A. F. Calvert, *Hist. of the Salt Union;* *T.H.S.L.C.* cxvii. 59–82.

TABLE 18: *Service, administrative, and professional employment, 1871–1911* (*adults, by 1911 Census classifications*)

Employment category	1871 Males	1871 Females	1911 Males	1911 Females
I. Central and Local Government				
National Government	148	–	200	28
Local Government	18	4	132	5
Total	166	4	332	33
II. Defence of the Country				
Army	149	–	138	–
Navy	4	–	2	–
Total	153	–	140	–
III. Professional Occupations and their Subordinate Services				
Clergymen, Priests, and Ministers	60	–	50	–
Other Religious	12	22	26	5
Barristers and Solicitors	46	–	58	–
Law Clerks	57	–	71	–
Physicians, Surgeons, etc.	40	–	33	1
Midwives, Sick Nurses, etc.	–	7	–	134
Other Medical	–	34	20	4
Teaching	80	153	83	222
Literary, Scientific, and Political	1	1	28	2
Engineers and Surveyors	12	–	23	–
Art, Music, Drama, etc.	40	25	133	63
Total	348	242	525	431
IV. Domestic Offices or Services				
Domestic Indoor Service in Hotels etc.	60	63	15	107
Other Domestic Indoor Service	59	1,407	21	1,319
Domestic Outdoor Service	75	–	161	–
Hospitals, Institutions, etc.	3	26	28	55
Day Girls and Day Servants	–	–	–	4
Charwomen	–	162	–	176
Laundry Workers etc.	–	4	10	160
Others	4	3	83	56
Total	201	1,665	290	1,877
V. Commercial Occupations				
Merchants, Agents, and Accountants	98	–	210	10
Commercial or Business Clerks	148	4	306	71
Dealers in Money and Insurance	28	–	139	1
Total	274	4	655	82
VI. Conveyance of Men, Goods, and Messages				
Railway	377	1	690	8
Road	148	2	525	6
Maritime, River, and Canal	168	3	183	2
Docks, Harbours, etc.	5	–	10	–
Messengers, Porters, and Watchmen	90	1	132	–
Others	9	–	63	10
Total	797	7	1,603	26

TABLE 18 (*continued*)

Employment category	1871 Males	1871 Females	1911 Males	1911 Females
IX–XI, XIII–XX. Dealers in Manufactured Commodities				
Mines and Quarries	48	3	39	2
Metals, Machines, Implements, etc.	30	1	65	8
Jewels, Watches, etc.	14	6	23	12
Wood, Furniture, etc.	50	44	63	6
Brick, Cement, Pottery, and Glass	8	5	9	5
Chemicals, Oil, Soap, etc.	57	–	50	6
Skins, Leather, Hair, etc.	85	–	9	1
Stationers, Newsagents, etc.	35	6	62	37
Drapers and Other Textiles	24	32	97	106
Dealers in Dress	12	34	84	51
Milksellers	25	19	23	18
Butchers and Meat Salesmen	116	37	117	16
Bakers and Confectioners (Dealers)	162	24	171	81
Grocers	115	75	168	61
Other Food Dealers	47	–	139	62
Tobacconists	44	10	32	14
Eating and Lodging House Keepers	8	87	36	177
Innkeepers, Hotel Keepers, and Publicans	119	50	131	112
Cellarmen and Bar Staff	1	–	67	32
Waiters	n/a	n/a	43	45
Others in Inn Service etc.	n/a	n/a	25	10
Wine and Spirit Merchants and Agents	32	2	16	2
Shopkeepers, Dealers, and Pawnbrokers	49	79	83	78
Hawkers and Street Sellers	51	45	51	14
Newsvendors (Street)	–	–	12	–
Total	1,047	559	1,615	956
XXI. Gas, Water, Electricity, and Sanitary Service				
Gas, Water, and Electricity	34	–	121	–
Sanitary Service	4	–	26	–
Total	38	–	147	–
Total in Service Occupations	3,024	2,481	5,307	3,406
XXII–XXIII. Others and without Specified Occupation				
General Labourers	830	1	507	–
Other Unspecified	122	–	70	17
Retired, Pensioners, and Private Means	38	302	377	521

Note: n/a: not applicable.
Source: Census, 1871, 1911, *Occupations*.

catchment area was relatively depressed. It thus seems that although the general rise in the standard of living in the late 19th century greatly boosted Chester's trade, unfavourable trends in the hinterland may have limited the benefit which it derived in comparison with other more prosperous areas.

By 1871 the railways were fundamental to Chester's links with its hinterland and had great economic significance within the city. The facilities were much expanded in the later 19th century,[1] and work on railway projects provided many jobs in construction. In addition, the railways' most direct effect continued to be as employers. Railway workers aged over 20 increased from 378 in 1871 to 698 in 1911,[2] when there were another 80 aged under 20. An estimated 200 platform staff alone worked at Chester General at the time of the 1911 railway strike,[3] and men were also employed in the three wagon repair shops in Chester and the two at Saltney. Much railway work was unskilled and quite poorly paid, though it was relatively secure.[4] The railways were also purchasers of local goods and services. In 1909, for example, Thomas Welsby & Co. had the contract to supply beers, wines, and spirits to the L.N.W.R. refreshment rooms at Chester General.[5] The centralized management of the railway companies, however, meant that large orders were placed from head office, and Chester had few manufacturing firms strong enough to compete except for the Hydraulic Engineering Co., which supplied railway cranes and other heavy equipment.[6] By 1910 five motor engineers operated in the city,[7] and in 1911 the transport sector as a whole accounted for 17 per cent of male employment.[8]

The prosperity of Chester's shops and services depended to a large extent on custom from the city itself. Demand from outside enabled it to support a larger range than its own population would have justified, but perhaps 60–65 per cent of Chester's trade came from residents of the city and its suburbs.[9] Chester's restricted manufacturing base must therefore have weakened the local service economy, since the city was deficient in both an industrial middle class and a skilled working class, two groups with significant purchasing power in the late Victorian economy.[10] Furthermore, the presence of dying manufactures alongside extensive transport and service employment meant that low-paid and vulnerable workers were probably over-represented among Cestrians. Their

demand for goods and services was doubtless relatively weak and volatile.

Chester did benefit in the later 19th century, however, from the purchasing power of two other groups. Improved railway connexions allowed commercial people from Liverpool, Manchester, and other towns to choose the city as an elegant place of residence, though it is difficult to estimate their numbers.[11] In 1899 Hoole was described as a 'commercial nest' because so many of its residents travelled to Liverpool and elsewhere each day, and it was asserted that only four of 75 occupiers in Hoole Road derived their living from Chester.[12] Chester also attracted a growing *rentier* class living off inherited wealth and investment income, who perhaps formed 5 per cent of the population by the Edwardian period. Their purchasing power was undoubtedly significant, particularly in Chester's more elegant shops.[13] Finally, there were visitors and tourists. Day excursions were run to the city from early in the railway era, though day trippers probably did not spend much. There is evidence, however, that purchases by better-off clients from outside Chester increased in the later 19th century and may have formed 5–6 per cent of the total trade of its shops.[14] While some such customers were undoubtedly short-stay visitors, Chester shops could also build up a circle of loyal clients from outside the region through initial visits to the city or by recommendation from existing customers. Thomas Welsby, for example, had customers as far afield as Shaftesbury (Dors.), Lowestoft (Suff.), and Anascaul (co. Kerry). The business also supplied wines and spirits for the wardrooms of naval vessels.[15] Brown, Holmes & Co. also sent goods in bulk to customers outside Chester, though after 1870 the trade was increasingly dominated by orders from hotels.[16] Such trade was largely independent of any weaknesses in the local and regional economy and was an important bonus for Chester.

In the late 19th century most of Chester's shops became modern retail businesses. One symptom was the increasingly diverse and sophisticated range of suppliers used by shopkeepers, as the retail sector became integrated completely into the industrial economy. Goods purchased locally from individual craft producers or fairs were superseded by direct supplies from industrial producers or commercial wholesalers.[17] The relationship depended on efficient distribution by the railways and the Post Office.[18] In certain cases shopowners participated directly in industrial enter-

1 Christiansen, *Regional Hist. of Rlys.: W. Mids.* 168–86; Holt, *Regional Hist. of Rlys.: NW.* 44–50, 84–5.
2 *Census*, 1871, 1911, *Occupations*.
3 *Chester Chron.* 19 Aug. 1911.
4 P. S. Bagwell, *The Railwaymen: Hist. of Nat. Union of Railwaymen*, i. 262; F. McKenna, *Rly. Workers, 1840–1970*, chapter 2.   5 C.C.A.L.S., ZCR 95/2.
6 Ibid. ZCR 256/13.   7 *Kelly's Dir. Ches.* (1910).
8 Above, Table 14.   9 Above, Table 11.
10 *Econ. Hist. Brit.* ed. Floud and McCloskey, ii. 123–43.
11 G. A. Audsley, *Stranger's Handbk. to Chester* (1891), 3.

12 *Chester Chron.* 21 Jan. 1899.
13 Above, Table 14; sources for Table 11.
14 Above, Table 11.
15 C.C.A.L.S., ZCR 95/9.
16 Ibid. ZCR 658/2.
17 Davis, *Hist. Shopping*, 276–302; Alexander, *Retailing*, 12–18; A. Adburgham, *Shops and Shopping, 1800–1914* (1981), esp. 137–48, 215–26; P. Mathias, *Retailing Revolution*, pt. 1; *Shopkeepers and Master Artisans*, ed. Crossick and Haupt, 62–94.
18 T. C. Barker and C. I. Savage, *Econ. Hist. of Transport in Brit.* 118.

TABLE 19: *T. G. Burrell & Co., location of suppliers, 1883–90*

North-West and north Wales	No. of suppliers	Elsewhere	No. of suppliers
Manchester	36	London	20
Stockport	6	Leicester	8
Liverpool	3	Birmingham	4
Rochdale	1	Leeds	4
Bolton	1	Glasgow	3
Bury	1	Wakefield	3
Carlisle	1	Paisley	2
Bowdon (Ches.)	1	Bradford	2
Radcliffe (Lancs.)	1	Nottingham	2
Preston	1	Redditch	1
Littleborough	1	Worcester	1
Hebden Bridge	1	Kettering	1
Leek	1	Reading	1
Hanley (Staffs.)	1	Bath	1
Machynlleth	1	Sheffield	1
		Belper	1
Unknown	9	Wigton	1
		Kilmarnock	1
		Belfast	1
Total	66 (53%)	Total	58 (47%)

Note: 'Unknown' might include Chester-based suppliers, though cross-checking with contemporary directories revealed no proven cases.
Source: C.C.A.L.S., ZCR 529/16.

prises in order to control supplies to their retail outlets. In 1874 William Brown of Brown, Holmes & Co. became chairman of the North Wales Flannel Manufacturing Co., a newly floated firm which took over two woollen mills at Holywell (Flints.) employing 170 workers.[1] Flannel sales at Brown, Holmes & Co. rose from 3.7 per cent of total sales in 1871 to 5.0 per cent in 1883, a period when Welsh flannel was generally out of fashion.[2] The success of the Chester Co-operative Society, founded in 1884, similarly depended in part on the Co-operative Wholesale Society's ownership of factories producing goods for member societies.[3] Most other shops depended on outside suppliers for their stock, and the larger shops seem to have dealt directly with producers and importers. Between 1883 and 1890 T. G. Burrell's drapery and clothing business purchased goods from 124 different suppliers, none apparently based in Chester. Firms in the industrial areas and London predominated (Table 19). Small shops, especially grocers, probably became dependent on tied contracts with wholesale suppliers from outside the city.[4]

Department and chain stores were increasingly represented in Chester's shopping centre after 1871, though smaller local businesses continued to be im-

portant. The Brown family remained Chester's premier shopowners until 1907, but the period seems to have been one of transition for the firm.[5] Until 1907 the two main sides of the business, clothing and house furnishings, were run separately. The clothing store, which traded as Brown, Holmes & Co. between 1874 and 1894, seems to have marked time between 1870 and the early 1890s. The firm diversified into new lines such as tennis costumes and cycling clothes for women in the 1890s, and advertised more aggressively. The shop was more successful after *c.* 1890, but the potential for further growth was restricted by the firm's orientation towards a wealthy clientele limited in size. In 1907 the two businesses were combined and turned into a limited company, Brown & Co. (Chester) Ltd., an event which also ended Brown family representation on the board. More significantly, the firm started to aim at a broader custom. In 1909 both the drapery and furniture departments were renovated and in 1914 Browns was clearly Chester's leading modern department store.

Browns' monopoly had been broken in the late 19th century, however, by the growth of three other stores which exploited the increased spending power of the middle classes and to a lesser extent working people.

1 *Browns and Chester*, 102–6; *Jnl. Flints. Hist. Soc.* xxvi. 155.
2 Adburgham, *Shops and Shopping*, 195–6.
3 C.C.A.L.S., ZCR 294.

4 *Shopkeepers and Master Artisans*, ed. Crossick and Haupt, 64.
5 Para. based on *Browns and Chester*, 99–114, 180–3; C.C.A.L.S., ZCR 658/3.

Richard Jones's drapery business was founded in Watergate Street in the 1850s, and expanded into larger premises in Bridge Street in the 1860s.[1] It diversified into furnishings and grew rapidly from the 1890s, and in 1900 opened a new clothing shop in Eastgate Street, by which time it was second only to Browns in importance (Tables 20–2). The growth of the Chester Co-operative Society was even more rapid. The first shop was a grocery in Black Diamond Street which opened in 1884. The society moved into the city centre in the 1890s, and by 1905 the Foregate Street premises had developed into a large department store.[2] Burrells was also a newcomer to the city. Thomas Gaze Burrell, a Norfolk man working in London, was advised in 1877 that Chester 'was growing in importance as a shopping centre and would be an ideal place to start a business'. He bought an existing haberdashery shop at no. 32 Foregate Street and renamed it the 'Little Wonder'. By 1890 he had opened men's, women's, and children's clothing shops and in 1899 expanded into furnishings.[3] Burrells, however, represented a transitional form of business in that different activities were carried out in separate premises acquired as the firm expanded.

The growth of Chester's large stores may have undermined older specialist businesses, particularly those in clothing and furniture. Established firms like Beckett & Co., William Garnett, Elias Williams, and Samuel Hamley seem to have been in relative or actual decline by the 1900s, and were also challenged by younger, more vigorous businesses such as Hendersons in Bridge Street, founded in 1890.[4] The grocery trade also changed greatly between 1890 and 1914. Although the number of grocers was little altered, new shops were dispersed in the suburbs and the number of city-centre grocers fell.[5] The chain stores of Liptons, Home & Colonial, Maypole, and Pegrams established branches in Chester, and their branded, packaged goods started to supplant the shop-blended and shop-packed provisions typical of the older and often more exclusive retailers.[6] By 1910 there were *c.* 20 chain stores in the city, including Boots, Marks & Spencer, and Hepworths,[7] but Chester remained a shopping centre dominated by local businesses which, though often biased towards a wealthy and socially select clientele, increasingly broadened their appeal to other income groups.

The growth and modernization of Chester's shops meant that the traditional fairs and markets both declined and changed in nature.[8] The rise of corporate wholesalers and direct purchases from factories made the fairs in their original form largely redundant by 1900. The sale of livestock continued, but pressure from shopkeepers forced the fairs from the main streets into specialized auction marts. The horse fair in Foregate Street was the last street fair to survive, but a combination of trader pressure and the new trams expelled it *c.* 1880.[9] Chester's importance as a livestock market seems to have declined relative to railway-connected marts, notably that established at Crewe in 1874, which aimed particularly to deflect trade in Irish and foreign cattle from Liverpool and Birkenhead to the Holyhead route. Chester could have pursued the same policy, but there is no evidence that it did.[10] Chester's livestock market remained pre-eminent in west Cheshire, but the growth of auctions at Tattenhall Road and Beeston Castle stations suggests that it was not totally secure even within the immediate area.[11] Although relocated to the Gorse Stacks in 1884 with high hopes of restoring its former wider dominance, it was still not served by rail, and really needed a fresh start in a new location.[12]

Chester's corn and cheese markets also had problems in the late 19th century. With the growth of overseas imports and the onset of agricultural depression *c.* 1874, cereal growing for the market declined in west Cheshire and prices fell steeply. Wheat sold at 56*s.* 8*d.* a quarter in Cheshire markets in 1871 but only 26*s.* 4*d.* in 1893.[13] That fact, together with the growth of large corn merchants like Griffiths Bros., reduced the role for Chester's corn exchange, though weekly dealing continued and was well attended by farmers in the 1900s.[14] Chester's cheese fairs remained important, but until the 1890s trade was very depressed. Only 100–150 tons was offered for sale in 1879, and the market was 'a bitter experience for every farmer present'.[15] Undercutting by imported American cheese was blamed, as again in 1889.[16] Trade had improved somewhat by 1894, but there were poor prices again in 1898 'partly because the working classes left off cheese in summer in favour of tinned fruits, meats etc.', an indication of changed habits helped, in part, by the modernization of the grocery trade in Chester.[17] The trade picked up again in the 1900s, and the 1911 Chester dairy show, held in the market hall, took place in boom conditions.[18] Throughout the late 19th century Chester's pre-eminence in the regional cheese trade was, however, under challenge from the market at Whitchurch, established in the 1860s and more convenient for many farmers in south-west Cheshire. Chester responded by increasing the frequency of its cheese fairs, but by the 1900s they were held in rotation

1 *White's Dir. Ches.* (1860); C.C.A.L.S., ZCR 310.

2 C.C.A.L.S., ZCR 294.

3 Ibid. ZCR 529/61: hist. survey in *Chester Chron.* 23 Sept. 1977.   4 Below, Tables 20–2; C.C.A.L.S., ZCR 558.

5 *Kelly's Dir. Ches.* (1902, 1910).

6 *Chester in 1892,* 43–4.   7 *Kelly's Dir. Ches.* (1910).

8 *V.C.H. Ches.* v (2), Markets; Fairs.

9 *Chester Chron.* 28 June 1879, 28 June 1884.

10 *T.H.S.L.C.* cxxvi. 146.

11 *Chester Chron.* 27 Apr. 1889.   12 Ibid. 28 June 1884.

13 Ibid. 5 May 1894; Porter, 'Agric. Change in Ches.' 232.

14 *Kelly's Dir. Ches.* (1902, 1910).

15 *Chester Chron.* 1 Mar. 1879.

16 Ibid. 2 Feb. 1889.

17 Ibid. 25 Mar. 1899, Ches. Dairy Farmers' Assoc. A.G.M.

18 Ibid. 14 Oct. 1911.

TABLE 20: *Chester's largest businesses, 1890–2*

Business (name as listed in rate books)	Gross estimated rental £
Walkers, Parker & Co., Leadworks	2,027
Dee Oil Co., Saltney (oil refiners; three works)	1,887
F. A. Frost & Sons, Steam Mill St. (millers)	1,785
Hydraulic Engineering Co., Charles St.	750
Grosvenor Hotel	730
Henry Wood & Co., Saltney (chain and anchor manufacturers)	657
William Johnson, Dee Mills (miller)	620
John Wiseman, Albion and Cestrian Mills (miller)	547
Birmingham Wagon Co., Black Diamond St. (railway wagon works)	450
Parr's Bank, Eastgate St.	400
Brown, Holmes & Co. (silk mercers, linen drapers, etc.)	400
Proctor & Ryland, Saltney (bone manure works)	370
William Roberts, Blossoms Hotel	338
W. & F. Brown & Co. (cabinetmakers and upholsterers)	330
Mowle & Meacock, Egerton St. (engineers and founders)	298
Joseph Beckett & Co., Eastgate St. (silk mercers)	280
William Garnett & Son, Bridge St. (cabinet makers)	250
Thomas Wood & Sons, Bridge St. (ironmongers)	250
Richard Jones, Bridge St. (draper and furnisher)	243
George Oliver, Eastgate St. and Northgate St. (boot and shoe supplier)	240
James Tomkinson (Chester Old Bank), Foregate St.	230
Alice Maude Sykes, Northgate St. (wine merchant)	230
Alfred Parks, Bridge St. (silk mercer)	230
Adam Richardson, Bridge St. (piano and music warehouse)	220
Dickson's Ltd., Eastgate St. (seed merchants etc.)	225
Chester Northgate Brewery, Northgate St.	218
Griffiths Bros., Canal Side (corn merchants)	207
Elias Williams, Foregate St. (draper and milliner)	200
Henry William Richards, Bridge St. (tailor and hatter)	200
Samuel Hamley ('Madame Hamley'), Bridge St. (costumier)	200

Sources: C.C.A.L.S., ZTRP 14; Flints. R.O., G/A/159/123.

TABLE 21: *Chester's largest businesses, 1910*

Business (name as listed in rate books)	Gross estimated rental £
Walkers, Parker & Co. Ltd., Leadworks	2,054
Dee Oil Co., Saltney (oil refiners)	1,772
F. A. Frost & Sons, Steam Mill St. (millers)	1,488
Hydraulic Engineering Co., Charles St.	1,475
Edward Webb & Sons, Saltney (Proctor & Ryland bone manure works)	1,435
Grosvenor Hotel	1,250
Henry Wood & Co., Saltney (chain and anchor manufacturers)	1,232
Brown & Co., Eastgate St. (furnishings and drapery)	1,200
Richard Jones Ltd., Eastgate St. and Bridge St. (drapers and furnishers)	818
Chester Northgate Brewery Co. (malt kilns and brewery)	698
Blossoms Hotel	650
Birmingham Wagon Co., Black Diamond St. (railway wagon works)	500
Dickson's Ltd., Eastgate St. (seed merchants)	500
F. J. Denson & Sons, Northgate St. (outfitters)	490
Parr's Bank Ltd., Eastgate St.	450
Lloyd's Bank, Old Bank Buildings, Foregate St.	400
Chester Co-operative Society, Foregate St. (department store)	360
William Sykes, Northgate St. (wine merchant)	350
Chester City Council, Dee Mills (closed)	323
Cambrian Testing Co., Saltney (chain and anchor testers)	322
J. A. Lawton & Co., Northgate St. (coachbuilders)	320
Boots Cash Chemists Ltd., Eastgate St.	310
Joseph Beckett & Co., Eastgate St. (silk mercers)	300
Grosvenor Motor Co., Eastgate St.	300
North & South Wales Bank, Eastgate St.	285
Thomas Wood & Sons, Bridge St. (ironmongers and engineers)	250
Bank of Liverpool, Eastgate St.	242
W. Garnett & Son, Bridge St. (cabinet makers)	240
Bradleys, Foregate St. and Brook St.	240
Bolland & Son, Eastgate St. (confectioners)	230
Charles Wiseman, Albion Mill (miller)	229
Chester & North Wales Newspaper Co., Bridge St.	220
J. E. Brassey & Co., Foregate St. and St. John St. (ironmongers etc.)	210
Brook Hirst & Co. Ltd., Brook Lane (switchgear manufacturers)	200
Griffiths Bros., Canal Side (corn merchants)	200

Source: C.C.A.L.S., ZTRP 48; Flints. R.O., G/A/160/15.

TABLE 22: *Business trends, 1890–2 to 1910*

Businesses gaining rank

Edward Webb & Sons, Saltney (former Proctor & Ryland bone manure works)
Chester Northgate Brewery, Northgate St.
Cambrian Testing Co., Saltney (chain and anchor testers)
J. A. Lawton & Co., Northgate St. (coachbuilders)
Brook Hirst & Co. Ltd., Brook Lane (switchgear manufacturers)
Dickson's Ltd., Eastgate St. (seed merchants etc.)
Richard Jones, Bridge St. (draper and furnisher)
Alice Maude Sykes, Northgate St. (wine merchant)
F. J. Denson & Sons, Northgate St. (outfitters)
Chester Co-operative Society, Foregate St. (department store)
Boots Cash Chemists Ltd., Eastgate St.
Grosvenor Motor Co., Eastgate St. [new in 1910]
William Roberts, Blossoms Hotel
Parr's Bank, Eastgate St.
Bank of Liverpool, Eastgate St.
James Tomkinson (Chester Old Bank), Foregate St. [Lloyd's Bank after 1897]
Chester & North Wales Newspaper Co., Bridge St.

Businesses maintaining rank

Walkers, Parker & Co., Leadworks
Dee Oil Co., Saltney (oil refiners)
F. A. Frost & Sons, Steam Mill St. (millers)
Hydraulic Engineering Co., Charles St.
Grosvenor Hotel
Brown & Co. Ltd., Eastgate St. (combined businesses)

Businesses losing rank

Henry Wood & Co., Saltney (chain and anchor manufacturers)
William Johnson, Dee Mills (miller) [closed 1908]
John Wiseman, Albion Mill (miller)
Birmingham Wagon Co., Black Diamond St. (railway wagon works)
Mowle & Meacock, Egerton St. (engineers and founders) [closed by 1910]
Joseph Beckett & Co., Eastgate St. (silk mercers)
William Garnett & Son, Bridge St. (cabinet makers)
Thomas Wood & Sons, Bridge St. (ironmongers)
George Oliver, Eastgate St. and Northgate St. (boot and shoe supplier)
Alfred Parks, Bridge St. (silk mercer) [closed by 1910]
Adam Richardson, Bridge St. (piano and music warehouse)
Griffiths Bros., Canal Side (corn merchants)
Elias Williams, Foregate St. (draper and milliner) [closed by 1910]
Henry William Richards, Bridge St. (tailor and hatter) [closed by 1910]
Samuel Hamley ('Madame Hamley'), Bridge St. (costumier)

Sources: As Tables 20–1.

with those at Nantwich and Whitchurch, illustrating Chester's loss of influence over the trade.[1]

Trends in wholesaling and retailing in the later 19th century confirmed the final transformation of Chester's general market into a permanent outlet for goods sold to the public rather than a periodic one whose main customers were other traders. As the general standard of living rose there were changes in the balance of traders in the market hall (Table 23). Butchers were always dominant but their sharp decline in numbers between 1896 and 1910 was almost certainly caused by the growth of private butchers' shops, the Co-op, and chain butchers. The larger number of specialist fruiterers reflected the increasing importance in the diet of fruit, much of it imported, while the distinct growth in stalls catering for specialist and leisure needs also suggests some rise in the standard of living.

Chester's importance as a centre for other tertiary activities increased only modestly. By 1910 six commercial banks operated in the city, but all were members of national or regional concerns.[2] Chester's last independent bank, Williams & Co., was forced into a takeover by Lloyd's in 1897 following the auditors' severe criticism of its liquidity and management.[3] The Chester Savings Bank amalgamated with others in Wrexham, Frodsham, Knutsford, Mold, and Nantwich between 1906 and 1912, and Chester became the head office.[4] Five building societies were based in the city by 1902, but there were interconnexions between them, and rationalization had brought the number down to two by 1910.[5] The number of people working in commercial and professional jobs approximately doubled between 1871 and 1911.[6]

The significance of Chester's administrative functions in the period 1871–1914 is difficult to assess. The effect overall must have been to strengthen links with the hinterland, particularly those parts of Cheshire which were otherwise more liable to look to Manchester, Liverpool, or the Potteries. The placing of the county council's headquarters in Chester in 1889, despite its marginal location, was important for maintaining the city's stature and drawing power. Before 1914 the number of officers employed directly in government by the county, city, and rural district councils was, nevertheless, quite modest. Only 137 people were recorded in such employment in 1911, though to them must be added local authority service employees such as tramwaymen, teachers, policemen, and utility workers, as well as the employees of the Chester poor-law union.[7] The continuing presence of the courts and various central government offices also helped maintain the city's role, though the gaol was closed in 1872.[8]

1 *T.H.S.L.C.* cxxvi. 142–3.
2 *Kelly's Dir. Ches.* (1910).
3 C.C.A.L.S., ZCR 4/6.
4 Ibid. ZCR 566.
5 *Kelly's Dir. Ches.* (1902, 1910).
6 Above, Table 18.
7 Ibid.
8 *V.C.H. Ches.* v (2), Law and Order: Municipal Prisons (New City Gaol).

Trade	1878	1896	1910
Butchers	19	40	24
Fruiterers	1	2	8
Greengrocers	16	11	6
Florists	2	5	5
Market Gardeners and Nurserymen	1	–	5
Confectioners and Bakers	1	3	5
Potato Dealers	2	2	4
Fishmongers	3	2	4
Booksellers	–	–	2
Grocers and Provision Dealers	3	5	2
Bazaars	–	1	2
Refreshment Rooms and Cocoa House	1	1	1
Draper	–	–	1
Fent Dealer (fabric remnants)	–	–	1
Basket Dealer	1	1	1
Lace Dealer	–	–	1
Bird Dealer	–	–	1
Earthenware Dealers	2	2	1
Hatter and Rabbit Dealer	1	–	–
Fishmonger and Game Dealer	1	–	–
Brush Maker	1	–	–
Total	55	75	74

Source: *Kelly's Dir. Ches.* (1878, 1896, 1910).

Chester was confirmed as the main medical centre in the area, though the impact on employment was still limited. The infirmary served much of west Cheshire and north-east Wales, but in 1890 employed only 24 nurses, rising to 52 in 1911. The workhouse hospital performed a similar function for a smaller area around the city, while *c.* 1910 the county lunatic asylum at Bache had over 1,000 patients.[1]

The military presence became more significant in the late 19th century. Under the Cardwell reforms of 1872–3 the castle barracks became the headquarters depot of the 22nd (Cheshire) Regiment and, though the garrison rarely exceeded 300, Chester was the training centre for new recruits to the regiment. In 1881 the militia and volunteers were re-formed into battalions attached to the Cheshires' regimental district at the castle, though some also had training depots elsewhere in the city.[2] Chester was also the headquarters of Western Command.[3] The other ranks formed a continually shifting element in the city's population, and were largely divorced from it, but many officers were based there for longer periods, and their custom in local shops, together with that of the officers' messes, was significant. Many seem to have stayed on in Chester after retirement.[4]

Chester's continuing role as an administrative, ecclesiastical, and military centre may to some extent have helped offset its economic weaknesses in the late 19th century. The city's social and political sphere of influence was wider than its purely economic one, but the two were interrelated in that élite groups attracted to the city because of its social role spent money there and so helped support some of its tertiary economy. The race meetings performed a similar function on a mass basis. 'Once a year at least our streets are thronged with sightseers', claimed the *Chester Chronicle* in 1889, estimating that not less than 100,000 had attended the Chester Cup meeting that year.[5] The real economic impact of such popular invasions was nevertheless probably limited.

In 1914 Chester remained the leading centre for west Cheshire and north-east Wales. Many of its traditional functions had withered away over the previous 150 years, but the city had adapted to change and retained a modest prosperity through the development of some new industries, the growth of shops and services, and the strengthening of its attraction as a place to live. There were, nevertheless, weaknesses. Its manufacturing base remained limited and was dominated by obsolescent industries. Its services were overshadowed by the regional metropolises of Liverpool and Manchester, and local rivals had emerged to poach some trade. The increasingly service-based economy was vulnerable to national economic fluctuations and to structural changes in the region. Chester in the period 1762–1914 exhibited the symptoms of a difficult adjustment to the demands of a changing but increasingly integrated regional and national economy, and it is clear that the city had declined greatly in relation to other centres in north-west England.[6]

SOCIAL CHARACTER

Evidence for the origins of the city's population and workforce is scanty before 1851. In the 18th century the most obvious newcomers were those participating in Chester's fashionable social scene. A well established winter season attracted landed families from their estates to town houses in Chester, and the May races

1 Ibid. Medical Services.

2 *22nd (Ches.) Regiment: Tercentenary, 1689–1989,* 25, 30; M. Roper, *Recs. of War Office,* 252–3.

3 C. P. Dryland, 'Headquarters, Western Command: Hist. Survey', 5–7 (TS., 1971, at C.H.H.).

4 C.C.A.L.S., ZCR 92; ZCR 95; ZCR 558; ZCR 658.

5 *Chester Chron.* 11 May 1889.

6 J. Herson, 'Victorian Chester', *Victorian Chester: Essays in Social Hist. 1830–1900,* ed. R. Swift; *Scientific Survey of Merseyside,* ed. Smith, 286.

and assizes were highlights of the calendar, but social activities for such people continued throughout the year.[1] The city also drew permanent settlers from Cheshire, Wales, and Ireland. There were small waves of Irish migrants around 1730 and 1748,[2] but the numbers seem to have declined in the later 18th century despite the importance of the Irish linen trade. Because of its location Chester was always likely to receive many Irish people at times of heightened migration to Britain,[3] and new influxes occurred from 1798 to 1808 and in the 1820s. The main Irish district in the city throughout the 19th century was around Steven Street in Boughton,[4] but Irish people were always to be found elsewhere in Chester, and were not confined in a ghetto.[5] In 1834 they were reportedly employed mainly in farm work and roadmaking.[6]

Chester's social character was influenced by its historic traditions and even more strongly by its economic base. Hemingway concluded in 1831 that the absence of factories 'and the crowds of the lowest rabble they engender' gave the city an unusually large resident gentry, though they tended not to be remarkable for their opulence. The middling ranks had to make their money slowly and carefully and were characterized by 'solidity'. The poor formed a smaller proportion than in manufacturing or commercial towns and were mainly employed in domestic service.[7] The corollary was a social structure polarized between a prosperous bourgeoisie and a working class overdependent on unskilled and often casual jobs in the service sector or in decaying manufactures. Chester's economy gave only limited opportunity for a skilled working class to emerge, although the development of more modern manufactures in the mid 19th century widened the social base somewhat.

Where people lived was determined to some extent by occupation and status as well as by housing type and cost. In the early 19th century the rich, the middle classes, and the poor often lived in close proximity, but there were also areas of distinct segregation, for example the tobacco pipe makers of Love Lane and the watchmakers of Gloverstone.[8] Even before 1800, however, such residential traditions were disappearing along with the trades they reflected. In 1831 Hemingway offered a summary of Chester's social geography, identifying Eastgate Row as an area of particular elegance and commenting favourably upon Queen Street, Egerton Street, Stanley Place, Nicholas Street, Paradise Row, and Liverpool Road.[9] The

environs of Frodsham Street, Love Street, Steam Mill Street, Watergate Street, Northgate Street, Commonhall Street, Cuppin Street, Pepper Street, and Lower Bridge Street were all of inferior grade or worse, while Handbridge as a whole was dismissed as 'almost exclusively inhabited by the lower orders'.[10]

Although Chester's population doubled between 1841 and 1911, its social character changed little. The city was polarized between a middle- and upper-class population whose income came from land, agriculture, trade, and, increasingly, inherited wealth, and a working class employed in declining manufactures or in unskilled and casual jobs in the service sector. The distinctive economic base meant that Chester lacked both a significant class of industrial capitalists and a sizeable skilled working class employed in modern industries.[11]

Natural increase ensured that Chester's population rose continuously, but between 1841 and 1871 and again in the 1890s it was augmented by migration. Large numbers of Irish people came to Chester during the Famine, in 1851 forming 7.3 per cent of the population. The Irish were, nevertheless, a minority among the newcomers to Chester. In 1851 over 30 per cent of the city's population had come from the surrounding counties and another 20 per cent from further afield in Great Britain. The proportions had not altered greatly by 1911.[12] There seems to have been some correlation between geographical origin and the type of job undertaken after arrival in Chester. The city did not attract many unskilled workers from beyond its immediate region, apart from the Irish, since for such people it was not worth coming from afar to enter an already overcrowded labour market. Not all the Irish were unskilled: in 1861 only half of those living within the walls were labourers, the rest being spread across other occupations.[13] Female domestic servants were a large unskilled group of mainly local origin, about 85 per cent of a sample in 1881 having been born in Cheshire, Flintshire, or Denbighshire. At the other extreme, nearly 40 per cent of skilled male workers had been born outside that area. For some employers, recruitment beyond the city may have been a necessity, given the limited skills of the local workforce. Most of the skilled engineers at the Hydraulic Engineering Co. in 1881 had been recruited from firms outside Chester. Labourers, on the other hand, were predominantly local in origin. The size of the firm's labour force fluctuated rapidly and markedly,

---

1 *Georgian Chester*, ed. Kennett, 36–9. Plate 43.

2 M. W. Sturman, *Catholicism in Chester, 1875–1975*, 25.

3 A. Redford, *Labour Migration in Eng. 1800–50*, chapter 8.

4 Sturman, *Catholicism in Chester*, 53.

5 K. Jeffes, 'The Irish in Early Victorian Chester', *Victorian Chester*, ed. Swift, 85–117.

6 *1st Rep. Royal Com. on Poorer Classes in Irel., App. G: Rep. State of Irish Poor in G.B.* H.C. 41, p. 515 (1836), xxxiv.

7 Hemingway, *Hist. Chester*, ii. 341, 346.

8 Ibid. i. 421–2; Moore, *Chester Clocks and Clockmakers*, 3.

9 Hemingway, *Hist. Chester*, i. 388, 420, 426; ii. 11–12, 23.

10 Ibid. i. 421, 428; ii. 4–9, 22, 25–6, 31, 35.

11 Above, this chapter: The Economy, 1841–70; The Economy, 1871–1914.

12 *Census*, 1851, 1911, *Birthplaces*.

13 Rest of section based, except where stated otherwise, on C. Hargreaves, 'Social Areas within Walls of Chester, 1861', *J.C.A.S.* lxv. 69–75; P.R.O., RG 11/3554–3561.

reflecting the volatility of demand in the engineering industry.[1] Long-term job security was largely unknown in Victorian Chester, even for skilled workers, but in that the city was not unusual.

Chester's restricted size in the later 19th century gave it great social variety over very small areas. Where people lived was, nevertheless, conditioned to some extent by the jobs they did, and there were distinct variations in the occupational structure of different parts of the city. Within the walls the inhabitants of the main streets and Rows still included a strong proprietorial and professional element, but most of the intramural population were artisans, unskilled, or engaged in shop work. In 1861 there were still sizeable enclaves within the walls, particularly on the western side, which were inhabited by the wealthy élite, and it could be said of the cathedral precinct that 'much of the city's life lapped against but did not enter this area'. The better off, however, were tending to desert the city centre by then, and shopowners increasingly abandoned accommodation over their premises to live in the more salubrious suburbs. Eastgate Street and Bridge Street continued to be affluent, but Northgate Street, Watergate Street, Whitefriars, King Street, St. Martin's Fields, Grosvenor Street, and Nicholas Street,

among others, were more mixed, and behind many of the frontages lurked the huddled, impoverished occupants of the courts. Much the same mixture was found in Foregate Street and Boughton. Indeed, the central core of the city as a whole continued to be characterized by social diversity, and although shopkeepers, shopworkers, and others in commerce formed the largest single class of residents, building workers also seem to have favoured the city centre, perhaps because of the mass of cheap courtyard housing. North of the canal, and especially in Newtown near the railway station, transport and manufacturing workers predominated, each making up nearly a quarter of the labour force. The streets around Garden Lane and Cheyney Road tended to be of low social status, but beyond the fork of Liverpool and Parkgate Roads lay a wedge of generally high-status residents and their servants. South of the Dee the influence of Saltney meant that manufacturing workers, labourers, and others working in industry made up over 40 per cent of the workforce, concentrated in Saltney itself and Handbridge. The genteel suburbs of Queen's Park, Hough Green, and Curzon Park were home to upper-middle class and professional residents whose obtrusive properties belied their quite small numbers.

TRADE UNIONISM

By the late 19th century a significant number of Chester workers were joining trade unions, doubtless partly in response to the poor and often insecure working conditions which they faced. Although Cestrians played little role in the development of the union movement nationally before 1914, worker organization was not absent from the city. Its origins can be traced in the later 18th century, when workers in some of the traditional trades were already participating in proto-trade unions. In 1777 Chester hatters were involved in a national organization of journeymen and joined with colleagues elsewhere in unsuccessfully petitioning parliament against a Bill promoted by the employers to remove limitations on the number of apprentices which each master might take.[2] Craftsmen in the city's building industry also seem to have had a tradition of organization. There was a branch of the Operative Stonemasons in the city in 1833, and in 1867 they were involved in a nine-month strike on the town hall building site.[3] Chester plumbers took part in the establishment of the United Operative Plumbers' Association in 1865.[4] In 1894 there was a strike of joiners and carpenters over rules of work,[5] and in 1899

bricklayers' labourers went on strike, gaining support for their demands from the *Chester Chronicle*.[6] The national explosion of industrial unrest and trade unionism in the early 1870s also found some expression in Chester. The city's rail workers were represented at the foundation meeting of the Amalgamated Society of Railway Servants in 1872,[7] and formed a local branch in 1874.[8] Some Chester shoemakers attended the meeting at which the footware riveters seceded from the Amalgamated Cordwainers' Association in 1873 to form their own union, although the Chester men chose to remain with the older craft association, an indication perhaps of the technical backwardness of the trade locally.[9] In 1874 there was a wage strike of planters at F. & A. Dickson's nurseries.[10]

In 1871 the Chester Trades Council included bakers, bricklayers, cabinetmakers, coachbuilders, engineers, ironfounders, joiners, masons, plasterers, railway servants, tailors, tobacconists, and the chain and anchorsmiths of Saltney. The number of affiliated members was around 600, almost 7 per cent of the adult male labour force,[11] and including workers both

1 C.C.A.L.S., ZCR 256/4/1.
2 S. and B. Webb, *Hist. Trade Unionism, 1666–1920*, 28, 52–3.
3 R. W. Postgate, *The Builders' Hist.* 70, 262–4; Harris, *Chester*, 57–8.   4 Postgate, *Builders' Hist.* 232.
5 *Chester Chron.* 2, 9, 16, 23, 30 June 1894.

6 Ibid. 24 June 1899.
7 Bagwell, *Railwaymen*, i. 60.
8 *Chester Chron.* 28 Mar. 1874.
9 Fox, *Hist. Nat. Union Boot and Shoe Operatives*, 8.
10 *Chester Chron.* 14 Mar. 1874.
11 Ibid. 20 June 1874; above, Table 14.

in traditional crafts and in the newer industries. Union organization probably weakened in Chester in the later 1870s, as it did nationally,[1] and the trades council seems to have fallen into abeyance. In 1879 wage reductions were imposed in the Chester engineering trade, and there was an unsuccessful strike at the Hydraulic Engineering Co. over the introduction of piecework.[2] The national upsurge of New Unionism in 1889 does not seem to have found any immediate local response, but the trades council was refounded in 1894,[3] and in 1904 attempts were made to organize tramwaymen, cabmen, and women tailors.[4] A majority of Chester railway workers took part in the 1911 national strike even though most of the strikers still belonged to no union, but workers at the General passenger station mostly stayed at work.[5] In the same

year there was a strike of apprentices at the electrical engineering firm of Brookhirst.[6]

It seems clear that trade unionism in Chester before 1914 was typical of that in many provincial market towns. Only a minority of workers ever joined a trade union, and union bargaining power in most sectors was weak and fluctuating. Apart from the railways, the service sector remained almost totally unorganized and the weak manufacturing base meant that there was never a significant 'labour aristocracy' in Chester to play a formative role in developing the labour movement locally. There were, nevertheless, surges in both militancy and union membership at favourable times, and Chester shared, albeit rather weakly, in the trend towards greater worker organization which characterized the years before 1914.

RELIGION

Despite being a cathedral city and a magnet for the region's Anglican establishment, Chester was fertile ground for religious nonconformity from the later 18th century.[7] The growing strength of dissenters was not much due to continuity with earlier traditions. Old Dissent had largely withered away by 1750, leaving only small groups of Baptists and Quakers besides the larger Matthew Henry congregation. The last was riven by doctrinal factionalism and in the 1760s the orthodox Congregationalists seceded, leaving the chapel in the hands of Unitarians.

From the 1770s, however, the Congregationalists were growing rapidly in strength and respectability. Methodism, too, had taken hold in the 1740s and continued to widen its appeal, not least through John Wesley's frequent visits to Chester on his journeys between England and Ireland. By 1800 it had probably overtaken the older sects. The Church of England, in contrast, was at quite a low ebb. Between 1752 and 1828 eight bishops served Chester in rapid succession, several being driven to seek preferment elsewhere because the see was so poorly endowed. The cathedral was also still hampered by poor finances. Musically it improved, housing a series of music festivals between 1772 and 1829, but by the 1820s its liturgical standards appear to have been dismal. Among the parish churches, the main alternative to Methodist and Congregationalist enthusiasm was at St. Peter's, where there were daily services in 1778.[8] Some of the city's dissenters had a high social profile and in the later 18th century their leaders were thought worth cultivating

for their influence over freemen voters in parliamentary elections.[9]

In contrast to Anglican torpor, Dissent in Chester was greatly boosted by the religious revival of the late 18th century. The main development apart from the growth of Methodism was the secession from the Congregationalists in the 1790s of the evangelical Philip Oliver, who had earlier been driven from the Anglican communion by Bishop Cleaver. He soon forged links with Calvinistic Methodism and formed a small connexion in the Chester area. In the same decade the city witnessed a Particular Baptist revival, and the more liberal Methodists in the chapel at Trinity Lane split from the Wesleyan mainstream at the Octagon to form one of the first branches of the Methodist New Connexion.

The greater diversity of worship on offer by 1800 must have been fuelled in part by the increasing number of migrants to Chester. In particular, Roman Catholicism in the city was almost exclusively an Irish phenomenon. The first purpose-built chapel was opened in 1799 and numbers rose slowly before the Famine and rapidly afterwards, reaching an estimated 2,000 by 1889. By then there were some prominent Catholic families of English origin in the city, including partners in the legal firm of Hostage, Tatlock, and Hostage, and the Tophams, best known as clerks of the Chester and Aintree racecourses.[10] For the large number of newcomers from Wales, the equivalent national church was what became the Presbyterian Church of Wales, which sprang locally from Philip

1 J. Lovell, *Brit. Trade Unions, 1875–1933*, 9–19.
2 *Chester Chron.* 4 Jan., 19 Apr. 1879.
3 *Bull. Soc. for Study of Labour Hist.* xxix. 43.
4 *Chester Chron.* 25 June 1904.
5 Ibid. 19, 26 Aug. 1911.   6 Ibid. 2 Sept. 1911.
7 Except where stated otherwise, what follows is based on the fuller treatment in *V.C.H. Ches.* v (2), Medieval Parish Churches;

Modern Parish Churches; Roman Catholicism; Protestant Nonconformity; Other Churches.
8 *V.C.H. Ches.* iii. 58, 61, 192; A. T. Thacker, *Chester Cath.: Music and Musicians* (Chester, [1981]), 15–16; *V.C.H. Ches.* v (2), Cathedral Music and Music Festivals.
9 Above, this chapter: Politics, 1762–1835.
10 Sturman, *Catholicism in Chester*, 56–9. Plate 38.

Oliver's connexion. From the early 19th century there were separate chapels for services in Welsh and English, the former being the largest Welsh-speaking congregation in the city in 1854.[1] By then all the other main denominations represented in Chester except the Primitive Methodists provided Welsh-language chapels or services, starting with the Wesleyans before 1804 and the Church of England from 1826, and spreading to the Congregationalists and Baptists probably in the 1840s, when migration to the city from north-east Wales began to quicken pace.[2]

The Evangelical movement began to affect the Established Church in Chester during the episcopacy of J. B. Sumner (1828–48).[3] Its stronghold was St. Peter's, where an incumbent appointed by Sumner, Charles Taylor, built on firm Low Church traditions. In 1845 he helped to form the Chester City Mission, the first of several interdenominational or undenominational evangelical missions in the city. An important role in the City Mission was played by the local banker and councillor William Wardell.

Tractarianism was held back in Chester by the hostility of Sumner and his successor, John Graham (1848–65), but gained a hold under William Jacobson (1865–84) and William Stubbs (1884–9).[4] Holy Trinity, where the advowson was owned by the earls of Derby, was High Church from the 1860s, at St. Thomas's the dean and chapter appointed an Anglo-Catholic vicar in 1909, and High Church services were introduced at St. John's in 1915. The other parish churches were moderate in their Anglicanism. Four besides St. Peter's had the bishop as patron, while the advowsons of St. John's and St. Mary's belonged to the Grosvenors from 1810 and 1819 respectively. Both the latter served parishes with a large working-class population, and both saw missionary efforts in working-class districts in the later 19th century. The diversity of churchmanship represented in Chester as a whole, and the moderation of most of the parishes, probably explain why an anti-ritualist Protestant Episcopal Church founded in the 1880s made little headway. The cathedral itself played a more prominent role from the time of Dean Howson (1867–85), who began Sunday services in the nave and permitted the revival of the music festivals in 1879.[5]

By 1851, in the midst of an economic boom and with heavy inwards migration from Cheshire, Wales, Ireland, and elsewhere, levels of religious worship in the city were relatively low.[6] Probably not much more than two fifths of the population went to church or chapel on Census Sunday,[7] rather fewer than in most medium-sized county towns and resorts but more than in industrial towns and cities.[8] A little more than half of worshippers were Anglicans. Attendance at Anglican morning service, amounting to 15 per cent of the population, was comparable with that in other county towns of Chester's size but less than in cathedral cities such as Exeter, Oxford, and Worcester.[9]

The largest nonconformist denominations in 1851 were the Wesleyans and the Congregationalists, whose best attended services drew 1,000 and 900 people respectively, to the Anglicans' 4,250. Their total attendance perhaps amounted to 1,500 and 1,300. Roman Catholics were in fourth place, with perhaps 700–800 worshippers, while the Primitive Methodists and the Calvinistic Methodists each probably had over 300 attenders in total, the Methodist New Connexion over 200, and the Particular Baptists and Unitarians over 100. There were also small or very small congregations of English Presbyterians, Quakers, Scotch Baptists, and unsectarian Christians (the last probably a branch of the Church of Christ).

The various nonconformist churches appealed to different social constituencies. In the 1790s the Methodists at the Octagon chapel were believed by their rivals at Trinity Lane to be reluctant to force a breach with the Church of England because they thought it would undermine their social standing among their Anglican neighbours.[10] The Unitarians were regarded as 'highly respectable' as early as 1822, and later included several of Chester's wealthiest business and manufacturing families. The Frosts (millers), Moulsons (tobacco manufacturers), Woods (chain and anchor makers), Brasseys (ironmongers), and Johnsons (Hydraulic Engineering Co.) were all long-standing members, and Sir John Brunner of Brunner, Mond & Co. was a trustee in 1900.[11] They and the small English Presbyterian church offered no free sittings in their chapels in 1851.[12] The Catholic Apostolic Church established later may have had a similar appeal. The Wesleyans, Calvinistic Methodists, Methodist New Connexion, Particular Baptists, and Congregationalists each had about a third of their sittings free in 1851, broadly in line with Anglican provision, whereas well over half the seats in the Primitive Methodist chapel were free.[13]

1 G. Borrow, *Wild Wales*, ed. D. Jones, 25.
2 For migration trends: above, this chapter: The Economy, 1841–70.
3 *V.C.H. Ches.* iii. 60, 63.   4 Ibid. iii. 67, 69.
5 Ibid. iii. 70, 74, 194.
6 This para. and next based on *Census, 1851, Religious Worship*, p. cclv.
7 Calculated by adding for each denomination the attendance for the best attended service, half that of the next best, and a third that of the third best.

8 Cf. *Census*, 1851, *Religious Worship*, pp. cclii–cclxxii.
9 Ibid.
10 *Hist. Methodist Ch. in G.B.* ed. R. Davies and G. Rupp, i. 309.
11 *J.C.A.S.* xxii. 192–4; H. D. Roberts, *Matthew Henry and his Chapel, 1662–1900*, 225; *Trans. Unitarian Hist. Soc.* v. 191.
12 Rest of para. based on *Census*, 1851, *Religious Worship*, p. cclv.
13 No figs. were returned for the chapel of Lady Huntingdon's connexion.

There was clearly an appetite for grass-roots working-class revivalism in Chester throughout the 19th century, from the Primitive Methodists in the 1820s to the Salvation Army in the 1880s. Small congregations of Scotch Baptists and Brethren appeared in mid century, the former helping to launch the Church of Christ, an evangelical sect with strong Chester associations. Most strikingly, a Mormon service on Census Sunday in 1851 drew 250 people, a very large number for a city of Chester's size.[1]

The Church of England, the Wesleyans, and the Congregationalists, as the three strongest denominations in Chester, were best placed to respond effectively to the challenges of population growth and suburban dispersal. In the city centre the Anglicans retrenched by closing churches in 1839 and 1842 and by reorganizing the parishes in 1882. They were also quick to build new churches in the suburbs, starting in Boughton and Newtown in the 1830s and extending to Hoole and Saltney in the 1850s and north Chester and Handbridge in the 1880s. The Wesleyans and Congregationalists started building suburban chapels in the 1850s, each eventually having four or five. The Calvinistic Methodists and the Church of Christ concentrated on Saltney, the Baptists on Hoole and Newtown, and the Primitive Methodists on Hoole and Boughton. The more mixed residential areas of Hoole and Boughton were thus the ones best served for variety, whereas working-class Newtown and Saltney each had an Anglican church, a Wesleyan chapel, and one or two others.

All the principal chapels except the Quakers and Unitarians joined forces to form the Chester Evangelical Free Church Council in 1897. Its main activities before 1914 were campaigns against the races (specifically gambling) and Sabbath-breakers, and an ambitious plan to divide the city into nonconformist 'parishes' for a common missionary effort.[2]

The main nonconformist groups may have peaked before 1900. Membership of the Wesleyan Methodist circuit fell from 588 in 1883 to 429 in 1910 and a mission to Hoole collapsed in the 1890s.[3] In contrast, fringe groups were proliferating between 1900 and 1914: a second Mormon missionary effort was begun, the Brethren fragmented, and for the first time there appeared small groups of Swedenborgians, Spiritualists (of two varieties), and Christian Scientists.

APPENDIX: MIGRATION TRENDS IN THE CHESTER REGION, 1801–1911

This appendix outlines the methods used to derive estimates for net migration trends in the Chester region over the period 1801–1911. Estimates before 1851 (Table 24) are more tentative in view of the lack of statistics for births and deaths within the region. The natural increase of population in Cheshire between 1801 and 1831 has been estimated as 12.7 per 1,000.[4] That rate was applied to the population of Chester and its suburbs, subtracting the actual population increase to calculate an estimate for net migration in each decade.

Estimates for the period 1851–1911 (Table 25) have been derived from data for Chester registration district, which covered more than the city and its suburbs, including the rural hinterland, the Deeside industrial belt, and part of Ellesmere Port. The registration district was standardized on its 1871 boundaries, excluding Ellesmere Port, and the natural increase of population was calculated from the number of births and deaths recorded in the decennial census, allowing for possible under-registration.[5] For each decade the natural increase was apportioned *pro rata* between Chester and other parts of the registration district, and the figure for Chester was then subtracted from the actual decennial population change to calculate the net migration balance for Chester.

Emigration overseas probably formed a large element in migration trends from the Chester area after 1850, and two methods have been used to estimate its extent (Table 17). Estimate 1 involved using the figures for net emigration from England and Wales as a whole,[6] reducing the gross figures of emigrants by 39 per cent to allow for those who returned from overseas.[7] Overseas emigration from Chester was estimated by applying the national rate each decade *pro rata* to the population of the city and its suburbs at the start of the decade and subtracting the result from the estimate of overall net migration. The residual balance of regional migration for Chester and suburbs thus omits emigrants overseas.

Estimate 2 is an alternative and probably sounder estimate of emigration from Chester, based on more detailed figures of emigrants by county of birth.[8] The estimate for Chester is based on the average for those

---

1 *Census*, 1851, *Religious Worship*, pp. cclii–cclxxii.

2 C.C.A.L.S., ZCR 55(2)/141; ZCR 572/1–3.

3 Ibid. ZCR 55/21, no. [2]; ZCR 55/33.

4 Deane and Cole, *Brit. Econ. Growth*, table 29.

5 Using multipliers in E. A. Wrigley and R. S. Schofield, *Population Hist. of Eng. 1541–1871*, 636 (table A8.5).

6 N. H. Carrier and J. R. Jeffery, *External Migration*, 92–3, table C(1).

7 D. Baines, *Migration in a Mature Economy: Emigration and Internal Migration in Eng. and Wales, 1861–1900*, 131 and n.

8 Ibid. chapter 4 and app. I.

TABLE 24: *Estimated net migration, Chester and suburbs, 1801–51*

Decade	Estimated population at end of decade by natural increase	Actual population at end of decade	Estimated net migration
1791–1801		16,095	
1801–11	18,258	17,344	− 915
1811–21	19,679	21,516	+ 1,837
1821–31	24,408	23,029	− 1,379
1831–41	26,128	25,039	− 1,089
1841–51	28,406	29,216	+ 810

Source: See text.

TABLE 25: *Estimated net migration, Chester region and Chester, 1851–1911*

Decade	Estimated natural increase, Chester registration district	Estimated net migration, Chester registration district	Estimated net migration, Chester and suburbs
1851–61	+ 5,702	+ 564	+ 1,913
1861–71	+ 7,081	+ 1,552	+ 1,636
1871–81	+ 8,781	− 5,696	− 2,454
1881–91	+ 8,161	− 5,105	− 2,842
1891–1901	+ 7,485	− 4,457	− 453
1901–11	+ 8,799	− 799	− 2,713

Note: Using 1871 boundaries for registration district, excluding Ellesmere Port.
Source: See text.

born in Cheshire, Denbighshire, and Flintshire, which themselves varied markedly.

The two estimates differ but show similar trends.

Although they must therefore be used with caution, they suggest the possible significance of overseas emigrants within Chester's wider migration pattern.

TOPOGRAPHY 900–1914

EARLY MEDIEVAL, 900–1230

Although Roman buildings survived and were perhaps occupied for at least part of the period between the 5th century and the 10th, settlement can be traced only in Lower Bridge Street, outside the walls of the former fortress. Æthelflæd's reconstruction of the defences, however, evidently encouraged fresh building in timber within the Roman enceinte.[1] The reoccupation seems to have advanced from the south: throughout the early Middle Ages occupation was densest in the area between the river Dee and the city's main east–west axis, along Eastgate Street and Watergate Street. Further north, part at least of the area between Northgate Street and Eastgate Street was occupied by St. Werburgh's minster and its precinct, while the north-western quarter seems to have remained largely derelict after the abandonment of the Roman buildings.[2]

TOPOGRAPHICAL EFFECTS OF THE ROMAN REMAINS

The relationship of the Roman fortress to the medieval street plan is complex.[3] Most obviously, the four main gates and the streets to which they gave access had Roman origins. Eastgate, Watergate, and Bridge Streets correspond almost exactly to their Roman counterparts, the *via principalis* and the *via praetoria*, although in places later street frontages encroached upon them. The development of Northgate Street was less straightforward. In the Roman plan north–south thoroughfares ran east and west of the headquarters building (*principia*) and of a large courtyarded building immediately behind it, before uniting to form the *via decumana*. In the early Middle Ages, however, a new main axis ran north from the intersection of Watergate Street and Bridge Street; passing initially over the eastern part of the *principia*, presumably by then ruined or demolished, it then traversed the remains of the eastern wing of the courtyarded building, before passing over levelled barracks to reach the Northgate. In the middle of the street there was an open area, formed from the courtyard of the building behind the *principia* and later the site of St. Werburgh's fair and a market. Such evidence suggests that the location of

Chester's four main streets was determined as much by the need for direct routes between the Roman gates as by the continued use of Roman thoroughfares. The relatively limited continuity between the Roman and early medieval street plans is further indicated by the abandonment of many of the fortress's lesser roads.[4]

The remains of the fortress's buildings left a lasting impression on the city's physical character.[5] In late Anglo-Saxon times, for example, a sunken-floored hut was built within a roofless but still largely intact Roman building north of Princess Street.[6] Other major structures, including the *principia*, the elliptical building, and the legionary bathhouse, survived at least in part until the 12th century, and even as late as the 14th Ranulph Higden could refer to 'foundations made from enormous stones, established . . . by the labour of the Romans'.[7] Above all, the siting of several parish churches was determined by Roman buildings or their remains. St. Peter's, for example, was raised several feet above street level on the foundations of the Roman *principia*, while St. Michael's, St. Bridget's, Holy Trinity, and perhaps St. Chad's were built into or abutting the defences of the legionary fortress, and St. Martin's was next to the south-west angle tower.[8]

Almost certainly the accumulation of collapsed Roman materials caused a steep rise in ground level on either side of the main thoroughfares, a feature which contributed to the formation of the Rows.[9] The largest Roman buildings were particularly difficult to clear and obstructed the development of later streets. The *principia*, for example, survived in sufficient bulk to ensure that Northgate Street did not, as would seem natural, continue Bridge Street but deviated slightly to the east. The legionary baths, much of which remained until their clearance in the 1960s, prevented the development of streets leading off the east side of Bridge Street and the south side of Eastgate Street.[10]

The Roman walls and gates, including those which later disappeared, exerted a particularly strong influence. The medieval Eastgate, for example, was formed from the north portal of its Roman predecessor, which survived until 1768. Several early streets, moreover,

---

1 Above, Early Medieval Chester: Sub-Roman and Early English Chester, The 10th-Century Refortification.

2 Cf. below, this section (Layout of the City).

3 For the fortress, above, Roman Chester. See map, above, p. 36.

4 S. Ward and others, *Excavations at Chester: Saxon Occupation within Roman Fortress*, 121–2.

5 What follows depends largely upon T. J. Strickland, 'Survival of Roman Chester', Ward and others, *Excavations at Chester: Saxon Occupation*, 5–17; Strickland, 'Roman Heritage of Chester:

Survival of Buildings of *Deva* after Roman Period', *J.C.A.S.* lxvii. 17–36.

6 *Medieval Arch.* xxvii. 170; Ward and others, *Excavations at Chester: Saxon Occupation*, 12.

7 R. Higden, *Polychronicon* (Rolls Ser.), ii. 76.

8 *V.C.H. Ches.* v (2), Medieval Parish Churches: Holy Trinity, St. Bridget, St. Martin, St. Michael, St. Peter; *J.C.A.S.* lv. 48.

9 *V.C.H. Ches.* v (2), The Rows: Origin and Early Development.

10 *J.C.A.S.* lxvii. 20–1, 29–30.

followed the line of the Roman defences. Thus the south and west walls of the legionary fortress were by 1200 skirted on the outside by Pepper Street, Cuppin Street, Nicholas Street, and Linenhall Street, and on the inside by White Friars, Weaver Street, and Trinity Street, which ran roughly along the line of the Roman *intervallum* road. Water Tower Street occupied a similar position in relation to the north wall. A similar feature at Abbey Green, later abandoned, replaced a Roman road over which soil had accumulated.[1]

Extramural Roman streets and buildings also left their mark. Lower Bridge Street perpetuated the line of the *via praetoria* from the south gate of the legionary fortress to the bridge over the Dee, while other streets continued the *via decumana* and the *via principalis* through the north, east, and west gates. Roman buildings remained standing west of the fortress until they were robbed or demolished by the Franciscans and Dominicans in the 13th century. To the east, the amphitheatre remained a notable feature, skirted by the road issuing from the Newgate and leading to St. John's church.[2]

LAYOUT OF THE CITY

By the mid 11th century Chester contained *c.* 500 houses or more,[3] concentrated along Watergate, Eastgate, and Bridge Streets. Those thoroughfares therefore probably presented quite an urban appearance, crowded with properties laid out on long strips stretching back from narrow frontages to afford the maximum number of citizens access to the street.[4] That was certainly the arrangement in the post-Conquest city, and there is little to imply that it was the result of recent planning: neither the 12th- and 13th-century holdings in the main streets nor the undercrofts built upon them were particularly uniform in size.[5] On the other hand there are indications that beneath that diversity there lurked a degree of planning at an earlier phase. Especially suggestive is the frequency with which measurements involving a unit of 11 feet occur in the frontages along the main thoroughfares: some 45 frontages measured about 55 feet each and another 14 about 66 feet. Such relatively wide plots clearly predated the irregularly sized undercrofts of the 12th and 13th centuries, and may have originated in the Anglo-Saxon period.[6]

It seems unlikely, therefore, that the Normans

replanned the core of Chester. Even the apparent discontinuity between the late Anglo-Saxon structures found in Lower Bridge Street and the later street pattern may be explained by interpreting the huts there as standing to the rear of plots fronting the main thoroughfare. Replanning is apparent only in the northern part of the medieval walled town, for instance in the comparatively undeveloped area around Princess Street, where the Anglo-Saxon timber structures were not aligned with the later plots fronting Northgate Street or Princess Street.[7]

If the Normans did not replan Chester as a whole, their impact was nevertheless great. In particular, the building of a motte and bailey castle south-west of the legionary fortress probably entailed much destruction, and was associated with the enlargement of the walled area to its full medieval extent. By the 1070s the west and south walls of the Roman fortress were already perhaps disappearing; the protection afforded by extending the north and east walls to the river would have rendered them unnecessary. The building of churches at or near the west and south gates also suggests that the latter were disused. At all events, Shipgate in the southern riverside wall existed by the 1120s, and by the 1190s both St. Mary on the Hill and the Benedictine nunnery were within the walled enclosure.[8]

The castle and the area around it became an important focus in the Anglo-Norman town. The castle itself was the scene of much building activity in the 12th century. Originally relatively small, with a bailey co-extensive with the present inner ward, by the 13th century it had been greatly enlarged, and the earliest buildings, presumably of wood, had been replaced in stone.[9] Also highly conspicuous were the residences of the earl's senior officials. Earl Ranulph III's chancellor, Peter the clerk, for example, built a house at the corner of Lower Bridge Street and Castle Street, later known as the Stone Hall, which included an undercroft and presumably a large first-floor hall.[10] It provides a good instance of the quite grand urban buildings put up by such men, especially under Ranulph III, when the city and shire were central to the earl's grandiose territorial ambitions.[11]

A dominant feature of the early town was its two ecclesiastical precincts, upon which the Normans also had a considerable impact. At St. John's, the enhancement of its status to that of cathedral, although

1 Ibid. 21–3; D. J. P. Mason, *Excavations at Chester: 26–42 Lower Bridge St.* 36–9; Ward and others, *Excavations at Chester: Saxon Occupation,* 122.

2 Below, this chapter: Later Medieval (Street Plan within the Walls).

3 *V.C.H. Ches.* v (2), Population. See map, above, p. 36.

4 Cf. Winchester: *Winchester in the Early Middle Ages,* ed. M. Biddle, 454–5, 458.

5 *V.C.H. Ches.* v (2), The Rows: Physical Form (Burgage Plots, Undercrofts).

6 Pers. comm. Dr. R. Harris (Dept. of Arch., Univ. of

Reading), based on O.S. Map 1/500, Ches. XXXVIII.11.17 (1875 edn.); *Rows of Chester,* ed. A. Brown, 14–15.

7 Ward and others, *Excavations at Chester: Saxon Occupation,* 64.

8 Lucian, *De Laude Cestrie,* 27, 63; *J.C.A.S.* lxiv. 23–31; *V.C.H. Ches.* v (2), City Walls and Gates: Medieval and Later; Castle: Buildings.

9 *V.C.H. Ches.* v (2), Castle: Buildings.

10 *Charters of A.-N. Earls,* no. 282; B.L. Add. Ch. 50177.

11 A. T. Thacker, 'The Earls and their Earldom', *J.C.A.S.* lxxi. 14–19.

temporary, inaugurated a new building programme. The work, however, proceeded very slowly, presumably because of shortage of funds, and interest in the building revived only in the early 13th century, when important local officials like the justice of Chester, Philip of Orby, were establishing chantries there. In the 12th century the area around St. John's still formed a distinct quarter, the bishop's borough, which included the 'basilica' or minster of St. Mary, the parochial chapel of St. James, a hermitage, and residences assigned to the bishop and archdeacon.[1]

Nothing is known of the Anglo-Saxon church and precinct of St. Werburgh's. The existence of a bone-working industry appropriate to an early minster, housed in late Anglo-Saxon workshops at Abbey Green near the Northgate, might suggest that the early precinct occupied almost the whole north-east quarter of the Roman fortress.[2] In the 1090s, however, the minster's successor, the new Benedictine abbey, acquired from Earl Hugh I an area between the church and the Northgate.[3] The refoundation entailed much building activity, almost certainly planned before 1092. The work, which was evidently well advanced by the 1120s, probably continued spasmodically throughout the 12th century. It was accompanied by the enclosure of the precinct and by the establishment outside the Northgate of a graveyard with a chapel dedicated to St. Thomas Becket.[4]

By the late 12th century the basic outlines of the medieval city were established. The defences which surrounded Chester had reached their full extent.[5] To the south lay the harbour and to the west the Roodee was a broad expanse of tidal meadow.[6] Within the walls there was a market place where the main streets intersected, at the Cross, and further open space used for markets and fairs west of the abbey precinct.[7] In the south-west, around the castle, lay a prosperous quarter favoured by the earl's retainers.[8] Elsewhere, however, there was probably much open land. In the north-west quarter of the Roman enceinte the abandonment was such that the fortress plan was lost, and by the 12th century one or two new streets wandered over the foundations of demolished barrack blocks.[9] The area remained relatively open throughout the Middle Ages.[10] Further west, between the Roman and medieval

west walls, there was more open ground, occupied partly by the religious communities established there between the 1150s and the 1230s, and partly by the area known throughout the Middle Ages as the Crofts.[11]

Within the medieval walls a new street plan was emerging by the 12th century. Besides Northgate Street and the roads which followed the Roman defences, innovations included westward extensions of the fortress's surviving lesser thoroughfares across the additional area enclosed by the medieval defences at City Walls Road and Bedward Row.[12] Fleshmongers Lane (later Newgate Street) connected St. Werburgh's with St. John's, running from Eastgate Street across the line of the Roman south wall to Newgate; Barn Lane (later King Street) led to the abbey's grange; and Parsons Lane (later Princess Street) ran westwards from the abbey gate. Claverton Lane (later Duke Street) apparently housed burgesses of Claverton living in the city by 1086, while Gerrards Lane (later Crook Street), a Roman road reused by the Anglo-Saxons, seems to have been extended northwards to Princess Street.[13]

Beyond the landward walls lay suburbs. Outside the Northgate much of the area near the walls must have been taken up by the hospital of St. John. Further out lay the abbey's graveyard and chapel. Although there were already some houses, the area cannot have been heavily built over, since in the 13th century fields lay next to the graveyard.[14] There had probably been more building to the east, both in the area of the bishop's borough around St. John's, and further north along what by the 13th century was known as Foregate Street, the extramural continuation of Eastgate Street.[15] In the later 12th century there were evidently three roads running eastwards from the town, one carrying straight on to Christleton, a second going south-east along the right bank of the Dee to Aldford, and a third leading north-east.[16] At the city limits the hospital of St. Giles had already been established.[17]

To the south, across the river, lay the suburb of Handbridge, divided in 1086 into three small manors. The area was largely agricultural: the manors were assessed at 3 carucates and contained land for eleven oxen worked by seven bordars.[18] By the 12th century the site of mills and fisheries,[19] in the early 13th it also

---

1 *V.C.H. Ches.* v (2), Collegiate Church of St. John; R. Gem, 'Romanesque Archit. in Chester *c.* 1075–1117', *Medieval Arch., Art, and Archit. at Chester*, ed. A. Thacker, 38–43.

2 *J.C.A.S.* lxiii. 31; Ward and others, *Excavations at Chester: Saxon Occupation*, 83–4, 92–3.

3 *Cart. Chester Abbey*, i, p. 55.

4 Ibid. i, pp. 55, 132; ii, p. 274; *Medieval Arch., Art, and Archit. at Chester*, ed. Thacker, 31–8, 41–3.

5 *J.C.A.S.* lxiv. 23–31.

6 Lucian, *De Laude Cestrie*, 24, 46.

7 Ibid. 24–8, 46–7; *Cart. Chester Abbey*, i, pp. 25, 251; ii, p. 268; *Charters of A.-N. Earls*, no. 231.

8 *J.C.A.S.* lxiv. 23–31.

9 Ward and others, *Excavations at Chester: Saxon Occupation*,

13, 122–3.

10 Below, this chapter: Later Medieval (Street Plan within the Walls).   11 *J.C.A.S.* lv. 32–3.

12 Mason, *Excavations at Chester: Lower Bridge St.* 39.

13 *P.N. Ches.* v (1:i), 9, 11, 13, 16–17, 26; Ward and others, *Excavations at Chester: Saxon Occupation*, 21, 122–3.

14 *Cart. Chester Abbey*, i, p. 40; ii, pp. 274, 352; *Charters of A.-N. Earls*, p. 14.

15 *P.N. Ches.* v (1:i), 75–6.

16 Lucian, *De Laude Cestrie*, 63–4.

17 *V.C.H. Ches.* iii. 178.

18 Ibid. i. 356, 358 (nos. 183, 211, 218).

19 *V.C.H. Ches.* v (2), Mills and Fisheries: Dee Corn Mills, Dee Fisheries.

contained a settlement at Newbold, somewhere to the east of Dee Bridge.[1]

The buildings of the city burned twice, in 1140 and disastrously in 1180,[2] an indication that they were largely of wood. There were, however, stone churches at St. Werburgh's, St. John's, and St. Michael's, and the castle acquired stone towers and walls in the 12th century and the early 13th.[3] In addition some large

houses were also of stone, such as those of Peter the clerk and perhaps Winebald the sheriff, the latter standing in the market place.[4] The only surviving material evidence for a secular building of the period is, however, the undercroft of no. 37 Watergate Street, the walls of which pre-dated the insertion of its late 13th-century stone vault.[5]

LATER MEDIEVAL, 1230–1550

STREET PLAN WITHIN THE WALLS

The essential elements of the city's topography were well established by the early 13th century. Its dominant feature remained the four principal streets whose intensive development was illustrated by their incorporation of the unique first-storey walkways known as the Rows,[6] and by the fact that until the 16th century they were used as the basis for the administrative divisions of the city.[7] The north–south axis, comprising Northgate Street, Bridge Street, and Lower Bridge Street, intersected with that running east–west, Eastgate Street and Watergate Street, in the area in front of St. Peter's known by the 14th century as the Cross. The Cross was the social and commercial heart of the city, the site of the Pentice, High Cross, and pillory, and the focus of the markets.[8]

Although it is clear that other streets besides those forming the main axes were also in use in late Anglo-Saxon and Norman times, most were recorded only in the 13th century. By the mid 14th century at the latest the intramural area had attained the layout which was described in detail in a survey transcribed into the city's first Assembly Book c. 1570 and allegedly copied from a certain record 'in writing in a table', dating from the time of Edward III.[9] That layout survived largely unaltered until the 19th century.

Eastgate Street, a broad thoroughfare, especially where it opened out into the market area at the

Cross, formed an obvious starting point for the survey. It contained numerous shops, and in the 13th and 14th centuries the premises of leading merchants and many of the city's bakers and goldsmiths.[10] At its north-western corner it included the Buttershops, which by the late 13th or early 14th century had probably developed into a free-standing structure on the site of the original stalls.[11] Further east was the abbot of Chester's stone hall which in the later 13th century was leased to Sir John Orby.[12] By then a number of streets extended northwards to the graveyard which lay south of the abbey church. The westernmost, Leen Lane, took its name from a merchant family which owned property in it in the 13th century.[13] Later blocked, in the 14th and 15th centuries it gave access to St. Oswald's vicarage and St. Giles's bakehouse.[14] Immediately east of Leen Lane lay Godstall Lane, mentioned in the survey but one of the few intramural thoroughfares not otherwise recorded until the 15th century.[15] Further east still lay St. Werburgh Lane, in being by the 13th century[16] and later the site of a large stone building, perhaps the abbot's hall.[17]

By the 1270s the south side of Eastgate Street was dominated by the corn market and its associated shops and malt kilns.[18] In the 17th century the frontage still included 'a great stone building' with five arches and 'a long broad pair of stairs' known as the Honey Stairs.[19] Because development behind was hampered by the collapsed remains of the Roman legionary bathhouse

1 B.L. Add. Ch. 72201–2; *P.N. Ches.* v (1:i), 57–8.
2 Lucian, *De Laude Cestrie*, 55; *Ann. Cest.* 20–1, 28–9.
3 *V.C.H. Ches.* v (2), Collegiate Church of St. John; Medieval Parish Churches: St. Michael; Cathedral and Close: Abbey Church to 1541; Castle: Buildings.
4 *Facsimiles of Early Ches. Charters*, ed. G. Barraclough, pp. 34–6; *Charters of A.-N. Earls*, nos. 13, 282.
5 *J.C.A.S.* lxix. 140.
6 *V.C.H. Ches.* v (2), The Rows: Origin.
7 Above, Later Medieval Chester: City Government, 1230–1350 (Serjeants); City Government and Politics, 1350–1550 (Emergence of the Assembly; City Government, 1430–1506).
8 *P.N. Ches.* v (1:i), 12; Morris, *Chester*, 250–1; C.C.A.L.S., ZCHD 2/1; B.L. Harl. MS. 2158, ff. 31v., 36v. See map above, p. 36.
9 C.C.A.L.S., ZAB 1, ff. 34v.–35v., 55 (modern fol.); Morris, *Chester*, 255–7; datable to mayoralty of Ric. Dutton (1567–8 or 1573–4): *V.C.H. Ches.* v (2), Lists of Mayors and Sheriffs.
10 C.C.A.L.S., ZMR 3, m. 7; ibid. ZD/HT 18–19; B.L. Add. Ch.

75195; *J.C.A.S.* xxii. 119–28, 130.
11 *Ches. Chamb. Accts.* 74; *Cal. of Deeds and Papers of Moore Fam.* (R.S.L.C. lxvii), no. 993; 3 *Sheaf*, xxxvi, pp. 3, 33; B.L. Add. Ch. 75161.
12 *Cart. Chester Abbey*, ii, p. 340; 3 *Sheaf*, xx, p. 69; *J.C.A.S.* xxxvii. 81.
13 Morris, *Chester*, 255; *P.N. Ches.* v (1:i), 15; *J.C.A.S.* n.s. ii. 166; x. 26; xxii. 127–9; 3 *Sheaf*, xxxvi, p. 32; B.L. Harl. MS. 2061, f. 15v.; C.C.A.L.S., ZMR 3, m. 7.
14 B.L. Add. Ch. 50141, 50217; *J.C.A.S.* n.s. ii. 166–8; xxii. 127–9; 3 *Sheaf*, xxxvi, p. 32.
15 *P.N. Ches.* v (1:i), 13–14; Morris, *Chester*, 255; *Sel. R. Chester City Cts.* 85; *J.C.A.S.* xxii. 126–41; cf. B.L. Harl. MS. 7568, f. 156v.
16 *P.N. Ches.* v (1:i), 19; *Cart. Chester Abbey*, ii, p. 343; *J.C.A.S.* n.s. ii. 172; x. 27–8; Morris, *Chester*, 255; C.C.A.L.S., ZD/HT 20.   17 B.L. Harl. MS. 7568, f. 156v.
18 P.R.O., WALE 29/122, 272; C.C.A.L.S., ZD/HT 26.
19 B.L. Harl. MS. 7568, ff. 154v., 158.

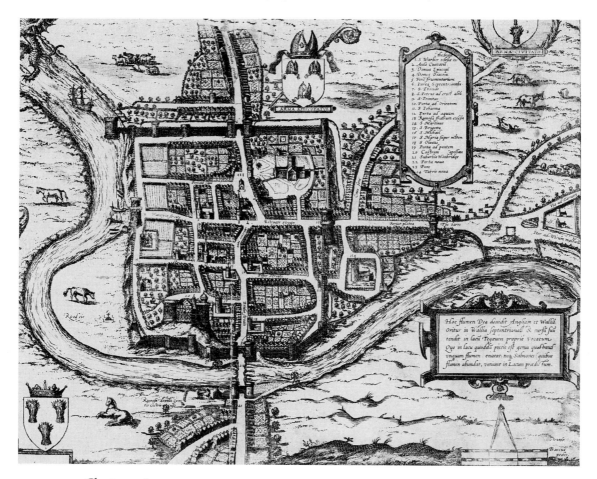

FIG. 9. *Chester, 1580*

only one throughfare opened from that side: Flesh-mongers Lane (later Newgate Street) lay east of the baths near the east wall, and ran south to Wolfeldgate (later Newgate). In existence by the earlier 12th century, in the 14th and 15th it contained shops.[1]

Bridge Street, like Eastgate Street, was a major thoroughfare filled with shops. It also had important merchant houses, such as Godwit Hall, between Commonhall Street and White Friars,[2] and Stone Place near St. Bridget's church, which in the early 15th century belonged to Roger of Derby and which probably survived in 2000 as nos. 48–52.[3] The southern termination of the street, the site of the former gate of the Roman fortress, was marked by the churches of St. Michael and St. Bridget. Later known as the Two Churches, it was spanned by an arch marking the junction with Lower Bridge Street.[4] Behind the eastern side of the street, development was blocked by the

collapsed bathhouse, and as a result Pepper Street – which ran south of the ruins – was the only thoroughfare to extend eastwards to the city walls. Though first recorded in the 13th century, it followed the line of the southern wall of the legionary fortress and was presumably no later in date than Wolfeldgate to which it led.[5] Probably, as the name Pepper Street suggests, the location of the city's spicers,[6] by the mid 14th century it contained shops and a large corner house known as the Black Hall, at the junction with Bridge Street.[7] On the south side of the street lay Daresbury Hall, which in the 13th century belonged to the mayors Walter de Livet and Ranulph of Daresbury.[8]

Street development was more complex on the west side of Bridge Street, which by the mid 13th century was the location of the commercial quarter known as the selds.[9] Three streets led off westwards along roughly parallel courses. The northernmost, Commonhall Lane

1 *P.N. Ches.* v (1:i), 13; *Cart. Chester Abbey*, i, pp. 243–4, 276; *J.C.A.S.* n.s. x. 36–7, 51–2; P.R.O., SC 6/784/5, m. 5; B.L. Add. Ch. 72317, 72319.

2 3 *Sheaf*, xix, p. 83; xliii, pp. 10–11; B.L. Harl. MS. 7568, f. 134; C.C.A.L.S., DBA 35.

3 *J.C.A.S.* xlv. 30; Morris, *Chester*, 50–1; *Rows of Chester*, ed. Brown, 164.

4 B.L. Harl. MS. 7568, f. 136v.; Hemingway, *Hist. Chester*, ii. 26.

5 *P.N. Ches.* v (1:i), 17; *Cal. Ches. Ct. R.* pp. 161, 204–5; *Ches.*

Chamb. Accts. 74; *Cart. Chester Abbey*, ii, p. 339; 3 *Sheaf*, lvi, p. 72; B.L. Add. Ch. 72269; C.C.A.L.S., DVE 1/CI/14.

6 *J.C.A.S.* lv. 45.

7 P.R.O., CHES 29/60, m. 12; J.R.U.L.M., Arley Deeds, box 25, nos. 13–14; B.L. Harl. MS. 7568, f. 134v.; 3 *Sheaf*, xix, p. 83.

8 C.C.A.L.S., ZCR 469/542; *Cart. Chester Abbey*, ii, p. 339.

9 Above, Later Medieval Chester: Economy and Society, 1230–1350 (Trades and Industries); *V.C.H. Ches.* v (2), The Rows: Physical Form (Selds).

(later Street), also known as Moothall, Normans, or John Norman's Lane, extended west to Berward or Alban Lane (later Weaver Street) and presumably provided access to the common hall which lay behind the selds from the mid 13th century.[1] Its other names almost certainly recall John son of Norman, who held land in Alban Lane in the earlier 13th century, and suggest that the lane pre-dated the common hall.[2] In the early 16th century it became the site of almshouses founded by Sir Thomas Smith.[3]

Further south, Fulcards Lane (later White Friars) existed by 1200.[4] In the mid 13th century it became known as Alexander Harre's Lane after an important citizen who is almost certainly to be identified with Alexander the clerk, son of Earl Ranulph III's nurse Wymark.[5] Alexander owned a chapel, houses, and a garden to the north, in or near Pierpoint Lane.[6] By then the area may have been a fashionable place to live, for another grandee, Ranulph the chamberlain, owned a stone chamber in Alexander Harre's Lane by c. 1240.[7] In the later 13th century the Carmelites established an extensive precinct north of the lane, bounded by Alban Lane on the west, Commonhall Lane to the north, and the rear of the properties fronting Bridge Street on the east.[8] Its impact upon the area is reflected in a further change of name from Alexander Harre's Lane to White Friars Lane.[9]

Between Commonhall Lane and White Friars Lane lay Pierpoint Lane, named after the family of Pierrepont which in the 13th century produced a sheriff of the city and an abbess of the Benedictine nunnery.[10] A lane leading from Bridge Street to the land of Robert Pierrepont was in being by the time of Abbot Birchills (1291–1323) and probably by the 1290s; it is to be identified with that named after an unidentified sheriff Richard, where in the later 13th century the Arneway family owned property including a chapel (probably that which earlier belonged to Alexander Harre).[11] The lane also appears in the Assembly Book survey where it was described as 'the way some time to the common hall', an indication that it probably extended no further west than that building.[12]

Almost certainly only the easternmost ends of the streets just described were densely built up in the Middle Ages. Much of Alban Lane, for example, was occupied by gardens in the late 13th and earlier 14th century, while the western end of White Friars Lane was the site of a barn.[13] The layout was regular and gridded; the streets followed parallel courses and, except for Pierpoint Lane, terminated to the west either in St. Nicholas Lane (later Nicholas Street) or in Alban Lane, both of which ran south from Watergate Street. It is difficult to assess the antiquity of the plan. Though several of the streets bore the names of 13th-century inhabitants or buildings, it cannot be assumed that they originated then. Many thoroughfares changed their name or had more than one name concurrently, and the predominance of 13th-century nomenclature may merely reflect better documentation in that period. At least one element in the plan, Fulcards Lane, dated from before 1200.

Lower Bridge Street extended from the Two Churches south to the river. It too contained important houses, most notably the mansion which in the late 13th century belonged to Richard the engineer and which lay beside St. Olave's church, perhaps originally its chapel.[14] Further south the street seems to have had an agricultural character; the principal messuage of the Dunfoul family was located close to the Bridgegate, complete with shops, dovecot, orchard, and barns, while near by was a property known as 'the earl's byre'.[15] Two lanes led off eastwards. St. Olave's Lane, a minor way beside the church in being before 1272, terminated at some uncertain point to the north-east and was later described as 'waste . . . without any house but one'.[16] Further south, Claverton Lane (later Duke Street) extended to the city walls.[17] Probably the site of the eight 11th-century burgages within the city dependent upon Claverton manor,[18] it later included a messuage known in the 1340s as Earl Ranulph's forge.[19] By the late 13th century part of its northern side was occupied by the south front and barn of the town house of Richard the engineer.[20] Behind the three main frontages of Pepper Street, Lower Bridge Street, and Claverton Lane lay gardens, extending to the walls and still undeveloped in the late 18th century.[21] To the south, however, in the area between Claverton Lane and the river, there had

1 B.L. Add. Ch. 50058, 50089–99, 50117–18, 50152, 72207; C.C.A.L.S., ZD/HT 46; P.R.O., SC 6/771/5, m. 14; *Ches. Chamb. Accts.* 74–5; 3 *Sheaf,* xxviii, p. 79.

2 *J.C.A.S.* lv. 35; *P.N. Ches.* v (1:i), 16; B.L. Add. Ch. 49979.

3 *V.C.H. Ches.* iii. 183–4. Plate 30.

4 *Cart. Chester Abbey,* ii, pp. 277–8.

5 *P.N. Ches.* v (1:i), 9; *J.C.A.S.* N.S. x. 47; 3 *Sheaf,* xxxiii, pp. 81, 85; xliii, p. 10; B.L. Add. Ch. 72224; C.C.A.L.S., DBA 35; ibid. ZD/HT 1; Eaton Hall, CH 45.

6 *Cart. Chester Abbey,* ii, pp. 467, 469.

7 B.L. Add. Ch. 72224.

8 *J.C.A.S.* xxxi. 7–9.

9 *P.N. Ches.* v (1:i), 21.

10 *V.C.H. Ches.* v (2), Lists of Mayors and Sheriffs; *V.C.H. Ches.* iii. 150.

11 *Cart. Chester Abbey,* ii, pp. 467, 469.

12 Morris, *Chester,* 256; B.L. Harl. MS. 7568, f. 143.

13 *P.N. Ches.* v (1:i), 8–9, 20; C.C.A.L.S., DVE 1/CI/2–6, 13.

14 B.L. Harl. MS. 7568, f. 134; 3 *Sheaf,* xix, pp. 72–3; *Hist. of King's Works,* ed. H. M. Colvin, i. 468.

15 Eaton Hall, MS. 321; P.R.O., SC 6/784/5, m. 5; B.L. Add. Ch. 75137.

16 *Cat. Anct. D.* iii, C 3659; 3 *Sheaf,* xxiii, p. 49; B.L. Harl. MS. 7568, f. 137v.

17 3 *Sheaf,* xxxiii, pp. 73, 98; *Ches. Chamb. Accts.* 74; *Talbot Deeds, 1200–1682* (R.S.L.C. ciii), p. 18; *Cal. Ches. Ct. R.* pp. 155, 163; B.L. Add. Ch. 72238, 75143.

18 *V.C.H. Ches.* i. 367 (no. 332).

19 B.L. Add. Ch. 75151.

20 *Cal. Ches. Ct. R.* p. 204.

21 *J.C.A.S.* lv. 49–50.

been rather more building, and by the later 14th century a minor thoroughfare known as Capel Lane linked Claverton Lane with the Capelgate.[1] Outside the city wall lay houses[2] and fisheries with stalls in the King's Pool, the deeper part of the river Dee below the causeway; the causeway itself was at least as old as the Dee Mills, which lay at its western end on the north bank and were in existence by the 1090s.[3]

South of St. Bridget's church, Lower Bridge Street intersected with Cuppin Lane, first recorded in the mid 13th century and extending as far west as St. Nicholas Lane.[4] It contained shops by the mid 14th century.[5] The area to the south, between Cuppin Lane and the castle, was perhaps relatively densely occupied, its residents including senior officials of the earl. Castle Lane, on the same axis as the streets further north, connected the castle and nunnery with Lower Bridge Street and was presumably in being by the late 11th century.[6] In the 14th century, when it contained shops and carpenters' premises,[7] it was still dominated by the Stone Hall, the large mansion with hall, undercrofts, and stables built by Peter the clerk which lay in the north-eastern angle of the intersection with Lower Bridge Street, at the point known as Castle Lane End, and which had passed to Peter's descendants, the Thornton family.[8] Castle and Cuppin Lanes were connected by Bunce Lane,[9] named after a family which had land in the area in the 13th century, and which in 1243 produced a sheriff of the city.[10] To the south-west, in front of the castle's outer gatehouse, there was an irregular open area known by the 13th century as Gloverstone, which like the castle itself lay outside the city liberties,[11] and which was crossed by a roadway leading to the castle gate, constructed over demolished houses in 1295.[12] The eponymous stone which marked the limit of the city's jurisdiction, a great slab of blue or grey marble, stood in front of the gatehouse until the late 18th century.[13]

The area south of Castle Lane seems to have been the

scene of much building in the 13th and 14th centuries. From Gloverstone, St. Mary Lane (later St. Mary's Hill) followed the boundary of the churchyard of St. Mary on the Hill steeply down to Ship Lane (later Shipgate Street).[14] In the late 14th century it contained a large mansion known as the Bultinghouse, the property of Hugh de Holes.[15] Ship Lane itself connected the Shipgate with Lower Bridge Street and was certainly in existence by c. 1290.[16] A modest thoroughfare, described merely as 'a way for a horse and a man', it was the site of the residence of the rich citizen Philip the clerk in the early 13th century and thereafter of property belonging to the Bruyn family and later to the Troutbecks, serjeants of the Bridgegate. An alternative name, Rabys Lane, derived from the family who held the serjeanty of Bridgegate in the 14th century.[17] Just outside the walls at the west end of the causeway, on the west side of the Dee Bridge, were the Dee Mills, near which lay houses, barns, and other property belonging to the city's fishermen.[18] Along the riverside itself, Skinners Lane contained industrial buildings known in the late 14th century as the Mustard Houses, by the mid 16th as the Glovers Houses, and c. 1700 as the Skinners Houses.[19]

Watergate Street, on its way to the medieval Watergate, crossed the line of the former western wall of the legionary fortress at the point marked from the late 12th century by Holy Trinity church.[20] Like the other principal thoroughfares it contained shops and town houses belonging to important citizens.[21] At its eastern end were the fishboards and the shambles.[22] Because Commonhall Lane, south of and parallel to Watergate Street, was densely built up, the only thoroughfares to join Watergate Street from the south lay well towards its western end: Alban Lane along a line just inside the former west wall of the Roman fortress,[23] and St. Nicholas Lane just outside. The latter was named from the Dominican friary's chapel of St. Nicholas[24] and extended to the junction

1 *J.C.A.S.* xxii. 123; *P.N. Ches.* v (1:i), 11.

2 e.g. B.L. Add. Ch. 72223.

3 *P.N. Ches.* v (1:i), 46, 48; *V.C.H. Ches.* v (2), Mills and Fisheries: Dee Corn Mills.

4 *Charters of A.-N. Earls*, p. 281; *Coucher Bk. or Chartulary of Whalley Abbey*, ii (Chetham Soc. [o.s.], xi), pp. 347–8; *J.C.A.S.* n.s. x. 40; *Cart. Chester Abbey*, i, p. 210.

5 Eaton Hall, MS. 321.

6 *P.N. Ches.* v (1:i), 11; B.L. Add. Ch. 75142, 75145, 75171; *Coucher Bk. Whalley Abbey*, ii, pp. 345–6; *Cart. Chester Abbey*, i, p. 256; *Ches. Chamb. Accts.* 74.

7 *Cat. Anct. D.* vi, C 5270; B.L. Add. Ch. 75171.

8 *P.N. Ches.* v (1:i), 11; Morris, *Chester*, 51; Ormerod, *Hist. Ches.* ii. 14–15; B.L. Harl. MS. 7568, f. 139 (quoted 3 *Sheaf*, xx, pp. 52–3); ibid. Add. Ch. 50177; P.R.O., SC 6/784/7.

9 C.C.A.L.S., DVE 1/CI/20; 3 *Sheaf*, lvi, pp. 72–3.

10 *P.N. Ches.* v (1:i), 10–11; *Coucher Bk. Whalley Abbey*, ii, pp. 345–8; Eaton Hall, CH 45, 53; B.L. Add. Ch. 72233; *V.C.H. Ches.* v (2), Lists of Mayors and Sheriffs.

11 B.L. Add. Ch. 49971; *Coucher Bk. Whalley Abbey*, ii, pp. 343–5; *P.N. Ches.* v (1:i), 44–5; *J.C.A.S.* lv. 43.

12 *Cal. Close*, 1288–96, 422; *Ches. in Pipe R.* 160.

13 *J.C.A.S.* n.s. v. 175–206; lv. 43; 1 *Sheaf*, i, pp. 268–9; Morris, *Chester*, 108–10.

14 Morris, *Chester*, 256.   15 B.L. Add. Ch. 75178.

16 Ibid. Add. Ch. 72233, 75148, 75154, 75156–7, 75180, 75182, 75184; *P.N. Ches.* v (1:i), 18–20, 34; *Talbot Deeds*, pp. 22, 27.

17 B.L. Add. Ch. 75148, 75151, 75156–7, 75162, 75168–70, 75173, 75180, 75182, 75184; C.C.A.L.S., DVE 1/CII/16; Morris, *Chester*, 256; Ormerod, *Hist. Ches.* i. 356.

18 B.L. Add. Ch. 75142.

19 *P.N. Ches.* v (1:i), 46, 49–50; *J.C.A.S.* lv. 43; 37 *D.K.R.* App. II, p. 370; Morris, *Chester*, 297; B.L. Add. Ch. 75142; ibid. Harl. MS. 7568, f. 165v.; C.C.A.L.S., ZAB 3, ff. 2v., 196; ZCCH 2/8; ZCCH 2/10.

20 *V.C.H. Ches.* v (2), Medieval Parish Churches.

21 C.C.A.L.S., ZMR 3, m. 12; B.L. Add. Ch. 50032; P.R.O., SC 6/784/5, m. 5; *J.C.A.S.* n.s. x. 41–2.

22 *V.C.H. Ches.* v (2), Markets: General Produce Markets.

23 *J.C.A.S.* n.s. x. 23; lv. 34–6; 3 *Sheaf*, lvi, pp. 23–4, 61–2, 68, 82, 88, 96; C.C.A.L.S., DVE 1/CI/2–6, 13, 36.

24 *P.N. Ches.* v (1:i), 10, 15; Morris, *Chester*, 256; 3 *Sheaf*, xliii, p. 11; C.C.A.L.S., DBA 35; B.L. Add. Ch. 72324.

with White Friars Lane where the church of St. Martin marked the south-western corner of the Roman fortress.[1] Its line was continued to the south by Nuns Lane, the site of the Benedictine nunnery from the mid 12th century.[2]

Four lanes led off the north side of Watergate Street. The most easterly, Goss Lane on the western side of the Roman *principia*, existed by the early 13th century. Its northern termination is uncertain but it seems likely that it joined the east–west arm of Crook Lane (probably on the line of Hamilton Place).[3] At the intersection with Watergate Street was the large property known in the 13th century as the 'Erbereyert' (the 'shelter yard'), leased from Stanlow abbey by the Saracen family with other land in the lane.[4] Further west lay the other, north–south arm of Crook Lane, also called Gerrards Lane (later Crook Street), which by the early 13th century ran northwards to Parsons Lane (later Princess Street).[5] Beyond that, immediately east of Holy Trinity church and on the line of the inner side of the west wall of the legionary fortress, was Trinity Lane.[6] Another lane followed the other side of the wall, running northwards to St. Werburgh's grange in the north-western corner of the city and eventually meeting the western end of Barn Lane (later King Street).[7] In being by the earlier 13th century, it was known by the mid 14th as Crofts Lane (later Linenhall Street).[8]

Northgate Street extended from the Cross to the Northgate. Its southern end, where it passed over the east side of the *principia*, was very narrow, lined on the west side by shops and eventually also the back Pentice, which abutted the east end of St. Peter's church, and on the east by the frontage of an important mansion.[9] Further north it opened out into a broad space in front of the abbey gateway, the site of St. Werburgh's fair.[10] The northern two thirds of the eastern side of the street was followed by the precinct wall of St. Werburgh's, against which by the late 13th century abutted small shops and houses owned by the abbey.[11] No other features, except the two abbey gateways, the gate into the abbey's graveyard, and, from the mid 14th century, the chapel of St. Nicholas, enlivened that part of the

street. No thoroughfare is known to have run east-wards, although it seems likely that there was a lane on the southern side of the graveyard wall, along and continuing the line of Music Hall Passage.

Almost certainly the western side of Northgate Street was lined with buildings for much of its length.[12] Three lanes led off westwards. The southernmost, immediately north of the remains of the Roman *principia*, was an arm of Crook Lane, in existence by the 13th century. It joined Gerrards Lane, to which the name Crook Lane was also applied.[13] To the north two streets extended west beyond the former legionary fortress to Crofts Lane. Parsons Lane, described in the early 13th century as 'the lane opposite the abbey gate',[14] crossed over Roman foundations and owed its name to the fact that in the 13th century the vicar of St. Oswald's had a house there. In the 14th century it also contained shops.[15] Further north Barn Lane, which also wandered over Roman foundations, by the 13th century gave access to the abbey's grange and in 1366 contained another barn with an orchard, belonging to the Erneys family.[16] By the 16th century Ox Lane ran north from Barn Lane to join another lane running alongside the city wall; neither contained any houses, passing only through crofts, orchards, and gardens.[17]

Much of the area on either side of Northgate Street north of the abbey gatehouse was still relatively open in the mid 14th century. To the east lay the abbey precinct and graveyard, and to the west the sparse network of minor lanes just described. Although none of those lanes was recorded before the 13th century it seems likely that the topography of the area had changed little from the Norman or even the late Anglo-Saxon period and was still dominated by barns, orchards, and ox stalls.

The whole area between the western wall of the legionary fortress and the medieval west wall was also largely undeveloped. After the mid 12th century much of it was gradually occupied by religious communities. The first to be established, the Benedictine nunnery, lay in the south-west corner of the medieval city, near the castle.[18] Immediately to the north was the Dominican

1 *V.C.H. Ches.* v (2), Medieval Parish Churches.

2 B.L. Harl. MS. 7568, f. 140; *P.N. Ches.* v (1:i), 16; Morris, *Chester*, 256.

3 *J.C.A.S.* lv. 40; cf. an indictment of 1686 for stopping up an ancient way that led from Goss Lane to Northgate Street: C.C.A.L.S., ZAB 3, f. 8v.

4 *P.N. Ches.* v (1:i), 14, 41; *J.C.A.S.* n.s. x. 41–2; lv. 42; *Cal. Deeds Moore Fam.* nos. 1021, 1036; 3 *Sheaf*, xxviii, p. 83; *Coucher Bk. Whalley Abbey*, ii, pp. 340–1; B.L. Add. Ch. 50032.

5 B.L. Add. Ch. 49980, 50089, 50143; *J.C.A.S.* n.s. x. 20; *Ches. Chamb. Accts.* 73; *P.N. Ches.* v (1:i), 12–13.

6 *P.N. Ches.* v (1:i), 20; *J.C.A.S.* n.s. x. 35; B.L. Add. Ch. 50013, 50059, 50175.

7 B.L. Add. Ch. 49985, 50059; 3 *Sheaf*, xxviii, pp. 59–60.

8 B.L. Add. Ch. 50202; *Cal. Deeds Moore Fam.* no. 1009; *P.N. Ches.* v (1:i), 12.

9 *V.C.H. Ches.* v (2), Municipal Buildings: Pentice; The Rows: Origin and Early Development.

10 *V.C.H. Ches.* v (2), Fairs.

11 *Cart. Chester Abbey*, i, p. 213; *Cal. Ches. Ct. R.* pp. 155–6; *Cal. Pat.* 1272–81, 104–5.

12 Cf. B.L. Add. Ch. 50020, 50028, 50054, 50068; *Cart. Chester Abbey*, i, pp. 237–42.

13 *P.N. Ches.* v (1:i), 12; *J.C.A.S.* lv. 39–40; B.L. Add. Ch. 49980, 50089.

14 *P.N. Ches.* v (1:i), 16–17; *J.C.A.S.* lv. 36–7; *Cart. Chester Abbey*, i, p. 242; ii, p. 345; 3 *Sheaf*, xxxvii, p. 35; B.L. Add. Ch. 50143.

15 *J.C.A.S.* lxvii. 39–41; Burne, *Monks*, 46; *Cart. Chester Abbey*, i, p. 119.

16 *P.N. Ches.* v (1:i), 9, 16–17; *Cal. Ches. Ct. R.* p. 198; *J.C.A.S.* n.s. x. 22; B.L. Add. Ch. 49985, 50059, 50185.

17 *P.N. Ches.* v (1:i), 16, 66; *King's Vale Royal* [ii], 23; B.L. Harl. MS. 7568, f. 150v.

18 For dates and sites of religious houses: *V.C.H. Ches.* v (2), Sites and Remains of Medieval Religious Houses.

friary, established in the 1230s in a precinct bounded by St. Nicholas Lane to the east, Watergate Street to the north, and, by the mid 14th century, Arderne (later Walls or Black Friars) Lane to the south.[1] On the north side of Watergate Street lay the Franciscan friary, also founded in the 1230s, with a precinct bounded to the east by Crofts Lane and to the north by Little Parsons or Dog Lane (on or near the line of Bedward Row).[2]

The north-western corner of the intramural area, known as the Crofts and bounded by Crofts Lane to the east and Little Parsons Lane to the south, continued to be occupied mostly by gardens throughout the Middle Ages.[3] The principal buildings included St. Werburgh's barn, in being by the 13th century and probably situated near the junction of Barn Lane and Crofts Lane, and St. Chad's chapel, which from the mid 13th century lay on the north side of Little Parsons Lane at the intersection with Crofts Lane.[4] By the early 14th century a lane crossed the Crofts winding northwards from the east end of St. Chad's to a postern in the north wall of the city by Bonewaldesthorne Tower.[5] In the early 15th century the area was the site of some poor quality housing and shops.[6]

Clearly much of the intramural area remained relatively undeveloped. The collapsed remains of the two greatest Roman buildings, the *principia* and the bathhouse, continued to inhibit street development near by, and there was room for the large precincts of the friars and for areas in the north-west and south-east corners of the city which contained little but crofts, orchards, and gardens throughout the later Middle Ages. Urban activity was intense only in the southern part of Northgate Street, Eastgate Street, Watergate Street, Bridge Street with the adjacent parts of the lanes on its western side, and perhaps Lower Bridge Street.

EXTRAMURAL AND SUBURBAN DEVELOPMENT

There was early and dense extramural settlement outside the Eastgate along Foregate Street, the principal landward approach to the city.[7] There, beyond the town ditch, lay properties, occasionally termed burgages, which by the late 13th century housed inns, large shops, goldsmiths' premises, and smithies.[8] The group of 15 shops with gardens held by the bishop, and later leased to the Egerton family, affords some indication of the intensive nature of development,[9] which by the early 14th century led to encroachment on the street near the Eastgate in the form of what were later termed 'piazzas', colonnaded walkways produced by buildings oversailing the pavement, their first storeys brought forward on posts.[10] Further east, buildings presumably straggled along the street at least to the Bars and perhaps as far as the leper hospital by the city boundary at Boughton.[11] They included the residences of prominent families, such as the descendants of the 13th-century mayor Richard the clerk, who had land near Cow Lane (later Frodsham Street),[12] and the Payns, who produced two sheriffs of the city in the late 13th century and whose holdings were concentrated near the Bars.[13]

Outside the Eastgate, streets led off both north and south. Cow Lane extended northwards, with the Kaleyards – the walled monastic garden of St. Werburgh's – on its western side, and barns, shops, and gardens to the east.[14] It formed the route by which the citizens' cattle could be driven to and from the common known as Henwald's Lowe (later the Gorse Stacks) just outside the north-east corner of the walled city.[15] On the far side of the common the road was continued by a way perhaps called the Greenway (later Brook Street), which led off in a north-easterly direction to the city boundary at Flooker's brook, beyond which were the town field of Newton and the common pasture of Hoole heath.[16] From Henwald's Lowe another thoroughfare, Bag Lane (later George Street), ran west beside the town ditch to intersect with Upper Northgate Street opposite St. John's hospital. In the earlier 13th century it contained houses belonging to the abbot of Chester, demolished during the siege of 1264; later there was a quarry alongside.[17]

Elsewhere in the large north-eastern segment of the liberties bounded by Upper Northgate Street, Foregate

1 *P.N. Ches.* v (1:i), 9; *J.C.A.S.* lv. 39; Morris, *Chester,* 256; C.C.A.L.S., DVE 1/CI/37.

2 *P.N. Ches.* v (1:i), 9, 12, 17; *J.C.A.S.* lv. 36–9; Morris, *Chester,* 256.

3 *P.N. Ches.* v (1:i), 40–1; *Ches. Chamb. Accts.* 74–5; *Cart. Chester Abbey,* ii, pp. 467–8; P.R.O., SC 6/771/5, m. 4; B.L. Add. Ch. 50202, 72211.

4 *P.N. Ches.* v (1:i), 9, 40; *J.C.A.S.* lv. 30–9; 3 *Sheaf,* xxviii, pp. 59–60; *Cart. Chester Abbey,* ii, pp. 346, 468; B.L. Add. Ch. 49985, 50059, 72277.

5 *J.C.A.S.* lv. 38; 3 *Sheaf,* xxxiii, p. 117; xl, pp. 1–2.

6 C.C.A.L.S., ZMR 75, m. 1; ZMR 81, m. 1; ZMR 98. Thanks are due to Dr. J. Laughton for the references.

7 C.C.A.L.S., ZD/HT 1, 30–1; 3 *Sheaf,* xxxiii, p. 71; *Ches. Chamb. Accts.* 74; *Cal. Ches. Ct. R.* p. 153; *Cal. Deeds Moore Fam.* no. 998.

8 e.g. B.L. Add. Ch. 50053, 50078, 50099, 50134; P.R.O., WALE 29/333; C.C.A.L.S., ZMR 35; 3 *Sheaf,* xxxvi, p. 16; *Cal.*

Inq. Misc. i, p. 477; *Ches. Chamb. Accts.* 74; *J.C.A.S.* n.s. iv. 178–85.

9 *Cat. Anct. D.* iii, C 3291; 3 *Sheaf,* xxiii, p. 49.

10 *Sel. R. Chester City Cts.* 118.

11 *P.N. Ches.* v (1:i), 79–80; Morris, *Chester,* 255; *Cat. Anct. D.* iii, C 3684; vi, C 4636.

12 *J.C.A.S.* n.s. iv. 179–80; *Sel. R. Chester City Cts.* 102–3.

13 P.R.O., C 146/3653, 3682, 4044, 5512, 6335, 6339, 6341; *Cal. Ches. Ct. R.* p. 195; cf. C.C.A.L.S., ZMR 5, m. 4d.

14 P.R.O., WALE 29/138; SC 6/784/5, m. 5; Eaton Hall, MS. 321; C.C.A.L.S., ZD/HT 18, 31; *Cal. Ches. Ct. R.* pp. 165, 171.

15 *P.N. Ches.* v (1:i), 65–6, 68–9.

16 Ibid. iv. 130, 146–8; v (1:i), 66, 74; Ormerod, *Hist. Ches.* ii. 813; *Cal. Ches. Ct. R.* p. 188; *J.C.A.S.* n.s. x. 35–6, 43–7; B.L. Add. Ch. 50035, 50188; J.R.U.L.M., Arley Deeds, box 1, no. 53; P.R.O., CHES 19/1, m. 27; CHES 25/1, m. 3.

17 *P.N. Ches.* v (1:i), 65–6; *Ann. Cest.* 86, 88; *Cart. Chester Abbey,* i, p. 213; ii, pp. 349–50; C.C.A.L.S., ZCHD 7/1; B.L. Harl. MS. 7568, f. 182.

Street, and Flooker's brook, there were only fields and gardens. East of Cow Lane and behind the tenements fronting Foregate Street were Dene field (the field of the dean and chapter of St. John's)[1] and North field, in which, near the city, lay the Justing Croft, presumably the site of civic tournaments in the later Middle Ages.[2] Further east, the land between the line of the later Queen Street and Hoole Lane was occupied by Herkin's Well field.[3] The area between Brook Street and Upper Northgate Street, north-east of the city, was also wholly agricultural. The greater part comprised the Town field (also called Chester field),[4] the western boundary of which was formed by Windmill or Besom Lane (later Victoria Road), in the 13th century a path which gave access to the abbot of Chester's windmill and extended to Wallfurlong, land belonging to the abbot next to Flooker's brook.[5] Between Windmill Lane and Upper Northgate Street lay crofts or gardens.[6]

Southwards from Foregate Street St. John's Lane led off beside the town ditch. Also called Ironmonger Lane, it gave access to Wolfeldgate and by its continuation, known from the 13th century as Souters Lode, to a landing place beside the river. An important thoroughfare, by the 16th century dignified with the appellation 'street', it intersected with Little St. John Lane which continued south-eastwards to St. John's church. Together the two streets, the site of the city tanneries, probably comprised 'Bishop's Street', in which the bishop of Coventry and Lichfield claimed a liberty in 1499.[7] They were evidently therefore within the 'bishop's borough', which certainly extended to Foregate Street.[8]

Little St. John Lane continued eastwards along the graveyard wall of St. John's as Vicars Lane, on the north side of which were the houses of the college's vicars and petty canons.[9] To the south, forming the core of the bishop's borough, the precinct of St. John's contained, in addition to the collegiate church itself, houses for the bishop and archdeacon, the chapel of St. James, and, from the late 14th century, the oratory and offices of the confraternity of St. Anne and a small

oratory probably associated with a hermitage.[10] Further east, the area between Foregate Street and the river remained fields, reached from the north in the late 14th century by Love Lane, whose 15th-century residents appropriately included a brothel keeper,[11] and crossed by Barkers Lane (later Union Street), a continuation of Vicars Lane whose early name again records the presence of tanners in the area.[12] At the Bars, Payns Lode (later Dee Lane), named after the shrieval family, extended south to the river,[13] and beyond it lay more fields, occupying most if not all of the narrow area above the Dee reaching eastwards to the city limits.

The other main area of early suburban development was south of the river at Handbridge. The core of the settlement lay along the high street of Handbridge and its southern continuation, Claverton Way (later Eaton Road), which ran through Netherleigh to cross the creek marking the city boundary at Heronbridge.[14] From the high street Newbold or Bottoms Lane led off eastwards towards the Earl's Eye, passing through Newbold town field and the hamlet of Newbold, where tofts and crofts were held by millers and fishermen in the early 13th century.[15] On the west side of the high street there was a minor way leading towards Kettle's Croft (later Edgar's Field) known as Green Lane (later Greenway Street), and further south the way to Overleigh.[16] At Overleigh by the mid 13th century Bromfield Way (later Wrexham Road) ran almost directly south, and Kinnerton (later Lache) Lane south-west to Lache Hall at the boundary of the liberty.[17] To the west the Hollow Way ran through Hough Green, a common marked by a cross, and continued to Saltney. There the boundary was marked from the late 15th century by a bridge with stone foundations and a timber superstructure known as the Blackpool or Stoop Bridge.[18] Beyond lay marshes where the citizens had common pasture in the earlier 13th century.[19] North of Hough Green and within the liberties, in a peninsula of land between the marshes and the Dee, was Brewer's Hall, an estate held by the serjeants of the Eastgate from 1286.[20]

Beside the river east of Dee Bridge, the area at the

1 P.R.O., WALE 29/17, 138; B.L. Add. Ch. 50053, 50078, 50135, 75190; C.C.A.L.S., DBA 35; 3 *Sheaf*, xxxvi, pp. 2–3; xlii, no. 8940; *Cat. Anct. D.* iii, C 3356.

2 *P.N. Ches.* v (1:i), 73; cf. P.R.O., WALE 29/19, 109.

3 *P.N. Ches.* v (1:i), 74; 1 *Sheaf*, ii, pp. 376–7.

4 *P.N. Ches.* v (1:i), 74; B.L. Add. Ch. 50138, 72304, 75166, 75171; P.R.O., WALE 29/138.

5 *P.N. Ches.* v (1:i), 67, 74–5; *Cart. Chester Abbey*, ii, pp. 349–50, 357; B.L. Harl. MS. 7568, f. 182.

6 C.C.A.L.S., EDD 12/1, 4.

7 *P.N. Ches.* v (1:i), 76–7; Morris, *Chester*, 255; *J.C.A.S.* n.s. x. 35; lv. 42, 47; 3 *Sheaf*, xxx, pp. 6, 114; xxxvi, p. 20; *Cart. Chester Abbey*, ii, p. 273; B.L. Add. Ch. 49984, 50102, 50105, 50135, 50143, 72248–9, 72257–8, 72265–6, 72283; C.C.A.L.S., ZD/HT 37.   8 e.g. 36 *D.K.R.* App. II, p. 91.

9 *P.N. Ches.* v (1:i), 78; Morris, *Chester*, 255; B.L. Harl. MS. 2073, f. 98; Harl. MS. 7568, f. 176.

10 *V.C.H. Ches.* v (2), Collegiate Church of St. John.

11 *P.N. Ches.* v (1:i), 76; Morris, *Chester*, 49, 255.

12 Morris, *Chester*, 255; *P.N. Ches.* v (1:i), 78; B.L. Harl. MS. 7568, f. 176.

13 *P.N. Ches.* v (1:i), 75; Morris, *Chester*, 255; *Cat. Anct. D.* iii, C 3653, 3682; vi, C 4636; B.L. Harl. MS. 7568, f. 176v.

14 *P.N. Ches.* v (1:i), 52–6; B.L. Add. Ch. 72268; C.C.A.L.S., EDT 96/2.

15 *P.N. Ches.* v (1:i), 48, 57–8, 61; C.C.A.L.S., EDT 96/2; B.L. Add. Ch. 72199, 72201–2, 72204, 72213, 72217, 72226, 72229, 72279–80.

16 *P.N. Ches.* v (1:i), 49; C.C.A.L.S., EDT 96/2; B.L. Add. Ch. 75140; P.R.O., CHES 29/11, m. 4d.

17 *P.N. Ches.* iv. 159; v (1:i), 56–8; Morris, *Chester*, 497; C.C.A.L.S., EDT 96/2.

18 *P.N. Ches.* v (1:i), 56; B.L. Harl. MS. 7568, ff. 130, 160v., 210.   19 *Close R.* 1247–51, 237, 347, 419–20.

20 B.L. Harl. MS. 7568, f. 210v.; *P.N. Ches.* v (1:i), 50; Ormerod, *Hist. Ches.* i. 373.

eastern end of the causeway was occupied in the mid 14th century by the fulling mills, their tenter frames, and, in the early 15th century, a quarry.[1] A hermitage stood between the river and the quarry.[2] Beyond Newbold lay the great expanse of meadow known in the 12th century as King's Hay and by 1285 as the Earl's Eye.[3] The area west of the bridge was also relatively undeveloped.

South of Handbridge was the town field of Handbridge or Claverton 'in Chester', reaching as far as the Grey or Great ditch which defined the southern edge of the liberties.[4] Beyond the ditch, in the township of Claverton itself, there were further open fields, where the religious communities and leading citizens of Chester also owned land.[5]

Outside the Northgate lay the smallest of the city's suburbs. Apart from the hospital of St. John, whose precinct occupied a narrow strip of land extending westwards from the gate outside the town ditch, most of the area belonged to the monks of St. Werburgh's. In the 1280s and 1290s the abbot was indicted in the county court for raising a court there for his tenants and for obstructing the highway with a bakehouse.[6] The suburb's main axis lay along Upper Northgate Street, the road north into Wirral, which from early times forked to form Bache Way (later Liverpool Road) running north, and Mollington Lane (later Parkgate Road) running north-west.[7] In the 13th century a lane also led off west from Upper Northgate Street beside St. John's hospital. It soon divided, one branch continuing alongside the town ditch to the Dee on the line of the later Canal Street[8] and the other leading off north-westwards along the later Garden Lane to the anchorage of Portpool, which lay at the city boundary, Finchett's Gutter. The growing significance of Portpool Way perhaps reflected the shift in seaborne traffic from the ancient harbour near the Dee Bridge to the anchorages downstream from the Watergate, but even so the lane's status remained uncertain as late as the 1290s, when the abbot, claiming it was his 'proper soil', levied tolls on those using it, and even ploughed it up.[9]

The Northgate suburb also contained a stone cross[10] and buildings belonging to the abbey, of which the most important were St. Thomas's chapel with its

graveyard, at the fork terminating Upper Northgate Street, and the abbey's tithe barn on Mollington Lane.[11] The land on either side of Upper Northgate Street, from Portpool to Windmill Lane, formed gardens, mostly the property of Chester abbey and including the Battle Croft, whose name implies that it was the site of judicial battle in the Middle Ages.[12] Beyond lay open fields extending to the northern limits.[13] Outside the liberty was Bache, which contained the abbot's mill[14] and further fields in which the abbey and a number of important local citizens had holdings.[15] A little to the west Mollington Lane was carried over Bache brook into the township of Blacon by a stone bridge.[16]

The west side of the city was occupied at its northern end by the harbour, protected from 1322 by the New or Water Tower; further south was the Roodee, a meadow marked since the 13th century by a stone cross and used for both recreation and grazing.[17] At its southern end, near the Benedictine nunnery but outside the city walls, lay a quarry and crofts, across which the nuns had a right of way to the Roodee and the river.[18]

Much of the land within the city liberties remained agricultural throughout the Middle Ages. In areas such as those to the north and east of Bag Lane and Cow Lane the fields reached almost to the city walls. Within the walls, although the principal streets were highly developed, Chester retained a distinctly agricultural flavour. Even c. 1350, at the end of a century which had seen intensive economic activity, rustic buildings such as barns and byres were scattered through its streets. With the advent of economic depression in the 15th century the settled area probably shrank and many plots in the heart of the city were apparently unoccupied.[19]

BUILDING ACTIVITY, 1230–1400

The local building stone was the soft and friable red sandstone which gave the early name of 'Redcliff' to the suburb near St. John's church and which was quarried at a number of sites within the city limits, near the Northgate, the Roodee, and the fulling mills.[20] Although by the 13th century it was being used for the castle, walls, gates, churches, and some important domestic and commercial buildings, stone

1 *P.N. Ches.* v (1:i), 47–8; P.R.O., SC 6/790/5, m. 4.

2 *V.C.H. Ches.* v (2), Medieval Chapels: St. James (Handbridge).

3 *P.N. Ches.* v (1:i), 46–7.

4 Ibid. 60–1; B.L. Add. Ch. 50114, 72307; C.C.A.L.S., EDT 96/2.

5 B.L. Add. Ch. 72205, 72219, 72246, 72252, 72254, 72268, 75142; P.R.O., CHES 29/1; *J.C.A.S.* n.s. x. 33, 41; *P.N. Ches.* iv. 161–2; v (1:i), 53.

6 *Cal. Ches. Ct. R.* p. 159; *Cal. Inq. Misc.* i, pp. 127–8.

7 *P.N. Ches.* v (1:i), 66, 70, 72; B.L. Harl. MS. 7568, f. 182v.

8 *P.N. Ches.* v (1:i), 65.

9 Ibid. i. 23–4; iv. 170; v (1:i), 68, 70–2; Ormerod, *Hist. Ches.* i. 372; ii. 385; *Cal. Ches. Ct. R.* p. 204; *Cart. Chester Abbey*, ii, p. 352; 3 *Sheaf*, lvi, p. 6; C.C.A.L.S., DVE 1/CI/39.

10 *Cal. Ches. Ct. R.* p. 163.

11 *P.N. Ches.* v (1:i), 70.

12 Ibid. 40, 74; C.C.A.L.S., DVE 1/CI/39; EDD 12/1, 4; *Cart. Chester Abbey*, ii, p. 374; *Cal. Deeds Moore Fam.* no. 1015.

13 C.C.A.L.S., EDD 12/1, 4; *Cart. Chester Abbey*, ii, p. 352.

14 *P.N. Ches.* iv. 144; v (1:i), 68, 72; 3 *Sheaf*, xxxiii, pp. 116–17.

15 P.R.O., WALE 29/246, 249–52, 255–6, 258.

16 *P.N. Ches.* v (1:i), 70.

17 *V.C.H. Ches.* v (2), City Walls and Gates: Gates, Posterns, and Towers (Water Tower); Open Spaces and Parks: Roodee.

18 *J.C.A.S.* xiii. 103–4; *Cal. Pat.* 1399–1401, 301.

19 e.g. C.C.A.L.S., ZCHD 2/3–7; P.R.O., SC 6/784/5, m. 5.

20 Above, this section (Extramural and Suburban Development).

was sufficiently unusual to attract notice and special nomenclature.[1] Most of Chester's secular buildings were probably of mixed construction. While the party walls which divided properties along the principal streets were generally of stone, at least at the level of the undercrofts, the vanished superstructures were almost certainly timber-framed.[2] Outside the main streets timber framing was probably even more prevalent.

In the earlier 13th century timber was widely available from the earl's forests in Cheshire and from north Wales. The region's resources were, however, exploited heavily by Edward I for his military and building campaigns,[3] and thereafter timber of the size and quality required for the structural members of a major building was much scarcer. By the mid 14th century the grant of mature trees for building purposes became a mark of the Black Prince's special favour.[4]

Building activity was most intense in Chester from the early 13th to the mid 14th century. To that period belonged the eastern limb and south transept of the abbey church, the chapel of St. Nicholas, the main claustral buildings and gatehouse of St. Werburgh's, the rebuilding of the castle, the gates, the more important towers on the walls, the initial building schemes for the friaries, and considerable work at St. John's, St. Peter's, and possibly other parish churches.[5] The city's growing prosperity also affected domestic and commercial buildings, especially in the four main streets. From the mid 13th century there is evidence of the subdivision of undercrofts and selds and of an increasingly intensive use of the street frontages, with the appearance of numerous groups of small shops often crammed on a single plot at Row level.[6] Several major town houses were clearly built between *c.* 1200 and 1330.[7]

Building activity on a considerable scale in the city centre in the earlier 14th century is suggested by William of Doncaster's grant to Richard of Wheatley in 1310 of a strip of land adjoining Richard's property in Northgate Street, almost certainly near St. Peter's church.[8] The strip was of curious dimensions. In length 15 royal ells (*c.* 17 metres) and in breadth 2 ells (*c.* 2 metres) at the rear but only ¼ ell (0.3 metres) at the street end, it allowed some minor adjustment of the boundary between the two properties; in fact, there long remained a kink in the boundaries of the plots further north which perhaps represented an irregular-

ity like that which Richard and William were seeking to eliminate.[9] Such an insignificant alteration in plot size implies either that there were as yet no stout party walls on the site, or that the rebuilding was on a scale sufficient to justify the effort required in removing them. The latter is perhaps more plausible. The deed expressly mentioned that the rear end of the strip lay towards Wheatley's stone-built solar, and it may well be that having erected such a substantial structure Wheatley intended to complete the work with an elaborate new street frontage.[10] Certainly the Wheatley family still had shops in Ironmongers' Row in the 1330s.[11]

The more important building work of the period, produced under the patronage of the royal earl or his principal officials, was of high quality. At St. Werburgh's, for example, the chapter house and perhaps other claustral buildings, including the refectory, were built by masons who had worked on St. Chad's chapel at Lichfield in the 1220s or 1230s.[12] The choir, the pioneering design of which was probably by Edward I's Savoyard masons, was closely related to other work done for the court in the 1270s.[13] Similarities in the profiles and mouldings of columns and arches suggest, moreover, that the teams which worked on Edward's Welsh castles, the greatest building project of the time, were also employed upon the abbey church and other buildings including the gateway. A further phase, which focused on the enlargement of the south transept, also produced the shrine of St. Werburg, an outstanding member of a group of structures inspired by Henry III's tribute to Edward the Confessor at Westminster Abbey.[14]

The royal presence provided the abbey's workshop with a powerful aesthetic stimulus and perhaps some financial assistance in the form of timber from the earl's forests and the relaxation of certain dues. On the other hand, the king's need for craftsmen meant that from time to time the abbey's workforce was requisitioned and taken off into Wales.[15] Even so, the workshop remained the dominant enterprise of its kind in Chester and undoubtedly left its mark on other buildings within the city. At St. John's a major reconstruction of the east end in the mid 14th century was related to contemporary work in the south transept at the abbey.[16] At St. Peter's the continuous wave mouldings in the tower arch were also a product of the team responsible for the crossing and the eastern bays of the

1 Below, this subsection, for the Stone Seld and other bldgs.

2 *Rows of Chester*, ed. Brown, 33–54.

3 *King's Works*, i. 396.

4 *V.C.H. Ches.* ii. 176.

5 For details: *V.C.H. Ches.* v (2), Medieval Parish Churches; Cathedral and Close; Castle; City Walls and Gates; Sites and Remains of Medieval Religious Houses.

6 *V.C.H. Ches.* v (2), The Rows.

7 Below, this subsection.   8 C.C.A.L.S., ZD/HT 6.

9 O.S. Map 1/500, Ches. XXXVIII.11.17 (1875 edn.).

10 C.C.A.L.S., ZD/HT 6; *J.C.A.S.* N.S. vi. 55.

11 C.C.A.L.S., ZMR 30, m. 5.

12 *V.C.H. Ches.* v (2), Cathedral and Close: Monastic Buildings to 1541.

13 J. Bony, *Eng. Decorated Style*, 14, 76; V. Jansen, 'Superposed Wall Passages and Triforium Elevation of St. Werburgh's, Chester', *Jnl. Soc. Archit. Historians*, xxxviii. 223–43.

14 *Jnl. Brit. Arch. Assoc.* cxxix. 15–34. Plate 6.

15 *V.C.H. Ches.* v (2), Cathedral and Close: Abbey Church to 1541.

16 J. M. Maddison, 'Decorated Archit. in NW. Midlands' (Manchester Univ. Ph.D. thesis, 1978), 265–6.

nave of the abbey church.[1] Almost certainly, too, the castle was the scene of large projects under both Henry III and Edward I. Although virtually nothing now survives, the exceptional quality of the paintings in the Agricola Tower is indicative of the ambitious nature of the work executed there under royal patronage.[2] There also in the late 13th and early 14th century the Welsh castles probably provided a paradigm. Certainly the city's Edwardian Eastgate appears to have been closely related to them.[3]

The pattern of activity was rather different at the friaries, where relatively simple buildings of the 13th century were aggrandized in the 14th. The Dominicans, for example, greatly enlarged their single-celled church in the early 14th century and further altered it by the early 15th. Important work was also going on at the Carmelite friary in the 1350s and 1360s.[4] While such activity is evidence that the Black Death did not bring building entirely to a halt in Chester, most of the major projects evidently lapsed around that time. Work at the castle almost ceased, while at the abbey there was apparently a hiatus until the patronage of Richard II brought a fruitful, if brief, new spell of building which included the completion of the crossing, the construction of the choir stalls, and perhaps some work on the nave.[5]

The period before *c.* 1350 also saw the production of the city's main stone-built domestic and commercial buildings. As well as the stone house of Peter the clerk, there was a stone chamber in White Friars Lane belonging to the chamberlain Ranulph of Oxford in the 1240s, a stone hall in Eastgate Street belonging to the abbot of Chester in the later 13th century, and Richard of Wheatley's stone solar set back from Northgate Street in the early 14th century.[6] The houses of wealthy and important figures such as Richard the engineer and William of Doncaster were presumably also built largely of stone, as was at least one of the selds in Bridge Street, where the designation the Stone Seld remained current until well into the 15th century. The five surviving stone-vaulted undercrofts dating from the mid 13th to the early 14th century may represent the remains of such buildings.[7] More fragmentary survivals, including corbels and doorways, were also mostly earlier than the mid 14th century.[8]

More plentiful at the time, though now much scarcer because of their less durable nature, were timber structures, which survive mostly at undercroft level in the four main streets. The arcades which supported the floors above the wider undercrofts, such as those at nos. 22 and 28–34 Watergate Street, 11 Bridge Street, and 12 Watergate Street (demolished 1985), are especially numerous, but arch-braced beams performing a similar function are also to be found at, for example, nos. 38–42 Watergate Street.[9] Other survivals include the massive joists which ceiled the undercrofts and which might, as at the eastern house of Booth Mansion (nos. 28–34 Watergate Street) and at nos. 12 Watergate Street and 36 Bridge Street, support a layer of rubble or sand into which the stone-flagged floors above were embedded.[10] At higher levels much less survives. A 14th-century beam at no. 17 Watergate Street (Leche House) provides the only evidence of a timber frontage on the main streets, and a doorway in the eastern house of Booth Mansion is the only example of internal timberwork. Medieval timber roofs are also extremely rare, though one particularly elaborate 13th-century example survives at no. 6 Lower Bridge Street (the Falcon), reused in a later undercroft. Another timber element within the city's medieval buildings which has now disappeared is the 'porches' on the main thoroughfares, probably light structures added to the street frontages to protect their entrances from rain.

Of the city's commercial buildings, the most distinctive were the selds: substantial, long, narrow market halls, raised over undercrofts and in some instances stone-built. They were concentrated in a single quarter, between the Cross and the common hall on the west side of Bridge Street, and were fronted by a Row.[11]

Dwellings varied greatly in size and status from the simplest accommodation, no more than one or two rooms, to merchants' houses with spacious halls. Although nothing is known of the humbler structures, the appearance and layout of the bigger domestic buildings may be reconstructed. Pares or Paris Hall, for example, the home of Richard the engineer in Lower Bridge Street, was stone-built and had a high tower.[12] The Bultinghouse next to St. Mary on the Hill, in 1390 the town house of the wealthy local landowner Hugh de Holes, included several 'lower rooms' next to the kitchen, and a principal chamber, a barn, and stables, which Hugh reserved when letting the rest to a local skinner.[13] In 1369 the Black Hall in Pepper Street was

1 *V.C.H. Ches.* v (2), Medieval Parish Churches: St. Peter; Cathedral and Close: Abbey Church to 1541.
2 S. Cather, D. Park, and R. Pender, 'Henry III's Wall Paintings at Chester Cast.' *Medieval Arch., Art, and Archit. at Chester*, ed. A. Thacker, 170–89.
3 *J.C.A.S.* lix. 47.
4 *V.C.H. Ches.* v (2), Sites and Remains of Medieval Religious Houses.
5 *V.C.H. Ches.* v (2), Cathedral and Close: Abbey Church to 1541; Castle: Buildings.
6 B.L. Add. Ch. 72224; *Cart. Chester Abbey*, ii, p. 340; C.C.A.L.S., ZD/HT 6.

7 i.e. nos. 11, 21, and 37 Watergate St., 28 Eastgate St., and 12 Bridge St.; cf. evidence for stone vaulting at nos. 28–34 and 63–5 Watergate St., 12 and 17 Eastgate St., and 27 Northgate St.: *Rows of Chester*, ed. Brown, 38–40; *J.C.A.S.* xlv. 12, 22–3. Plate 33.
8 Rest of subsection largely based on *Rows of Chester*, ed. Brown, 40–2.
9 S. Ward, *Excavations at Chester: 12 Watergate St.* 36–7.
10 Ibid.
11 *V.C.H. Ches.* v (2), The Rows: Physical Form (Selds).
12 3 *Sheaf*, xix, pp. 72–3; *Sel. R. Chester City Cts.* 114–15.
13 B.L. Add. Ch. 75178.

the subject of a similar agreement, in which the owner retained the stables and the principal apartments, the stone and painted chambers.[1] Other examples included a house in Bridge Street with a chapel, dovecot, and garden,[2] and a major structure near the river, perhaps the former residence of the Dunfouls, which when it was taken down in the 1380s comprised chambers, sub-chambers, a kitchen, gatehouse, and hall.[3]

The bigger houses occupied plots with wide street frontages and were on the main thoroughfares, often on corner sites at junctions with side streets, where there was more wall space for windows and hence better lighting. They included nos. 38–42 Watergate Street, 48–52 Bridge Street, and 6 Lower Bridge Street. In their fully achieved form they were all largely the product of building work carried out in the early to mid 14th century. The house at nos. 38–42 Watergate Street, for example, was rebuilt almost entirely at that time. Others retained more of the preceding structures; in one instance, nos. 48–52 Bridge Street, at least two earlier houses may have been reconstructed as a single unit, retaining the stone façade of one of them.[4]

Such houses combined commercial and domestic use. On the first floor they incorporated a large hall, which might be over 12 metres long and 8 wide and which lay parallel to the street, running across as many as three undercrofts. Set back behind shops, usually quite small lock-ups numbering up to five,[5] and reached from the Row,[6] the hall terminated in a screens passage, beyond which lay the service bay usually with a spacious solar above it. The service bay generally overlooked the side lane, which provided both extra window space and easy access to the rear of the plot with its scatter of kitchens, outbuildings, and stables. The lock-up shops may have had modest premises over the Row, such as the solars above the Buttershops mentioned in 1361.[7] The Row walkway formed an integral part of the structure from the start, encouraging the development of a compact main block focused on the hall and backing on to a yard. The dominance of the Row is illustrated by the fact that, perhaps unexpectedly, there is no evidence for steps providing access from street to Row walkway opposite the screens passage. It is clear that in their earliest phase such houses were entered by an inconvenient route at either end of the frontage.[8]

The more standard courtyard plan, seen for example in town houses in Norwich and King's Lynn, was incompatible with the extended two-tiered street fronts characteristic of the main thoroughfares, and hence was rare in Chester. The only building possibly of that type within the main streets is nos. 14–16 Northgate Street, which included a courtyard with an extensive domestic range to the rear.[9]

The largest houses such as those just described were never the norm even in the main streets. Much more common were houses whose halls, constructed over only one or two undercrofts, lay at right angles to the street, behind shops fronting the Row walkway. They generally had timber superstructures of which little remains, although one unusually lavish stone-built example survived in 2000 as the eastern house of nos. 28–34 Watergate Street (Booth Mansion), with a hall measuring some 8.5 by 6.8 metres and two sizeable shops in front. As with the grander houses, the service areas were included in outbuildings lying in yards to the rear. Though most of the standing evidence has been destroyed by post-medieval development and by demolition during slum clearance in the 1930s, excavations at nos. 32–4 Watergate Street have revealed the stone footings of a variety of such structures.[10]

BUILDING ACTIVITY, 1400–1550

Throughout the earlier 15th century there was little building in Chester, apparently the result of increasing impoverishment. The citizens' pleas for a reduced fee farm, initiated in the 1440s, reached a peak in 1484, when they claimed that the 'greater part' of their city was 'wasted, desolate, ruinous, and scantily inhabited'. While such jeremiads doubtless involved much exaggeration,[11] the impression remains that in the earlier 15th century the fabric of Chester was in decay. The only significant enterprise which can be ascribed with certainty to the period was at St. Mary on the Hill, where the Troutbeck chapel was added in 1433 and the south aisle was remodelled almost contemporaneously, both probably through the action of a single wealthy family.[12] There may also have been a major remodelling of the Dominican friary shortly after 1400.[13] Otherwise building work was restricted to repairs, usually to timber-framed private houses and often making use of beams and posts from demolished buildings.[14]

Activity had resumed by 1467 with fresh work at the Dominican friary, where the church was extensively but incompletely remodelled in the late 15th and early

1 J.R.U.L.M., Arley Deeds, box 25, nos. 13–14; cf. B.L. Harl. MS. 7568, f. 134v.

2 J.R.U.L.M., Arley Deeds, box 25, no. 16.

3 C.C.A.L.S., ZMR 52, m. 1. Thanks are due to Dr. Laughton for supplying the reference.

4 Detailed descriptions in *Rows of Chester*, ed. Brown, 164, 166–7, 184.

5 e.g. at nos. 48–52 Bridge Street and 38–42 Watergate Street.

6 *V.C.H. Ches.* v (2), The Rows: Origin and Early Development.

7 B.L. Add. Ch. 75161.

8 Pers. comm. Dr. R. Harris (Dept. of Arch., Univ. of Reading).

9 *Rows of Chester*, ed. Brown, 176–7.

10 Pers. comm. S. W. Ward (Chester Arch.).

11 Morris, *Chester*, 520, 523.

12 *V.C.H. Ches.* v (2), Medieval Parish Churches.

13 Ibid. Sites and Remains of Medieval Religious Houses.

14 e.g. P.R.O., SC 6/784/5, m. 5; SC 6/796/6, m. 9; SC 11/890, m. 1; B.L. Harl. MS. 2158, f. 211; C.C.A.L.S., ZMR 52, m. 1; *Rows of Chester*, ed. Brown, 63–75. Thanks are due to Dr. Laughton for the MS. references.

16th century.[1] More significant were the building campaigns at St. Werburgh's between the 1480s and the 1520s, which included the addition of a new chancel to the parochial chapel of St. Oswald, and substantial work on the nave, choir aisles, and cloisters, part of an intended replacement of all the conventual buildings.[2] Other ecclesiastical projects of the period included an ambitious north-west tower at St. John's, begun *c.* 1518;[3] the remaking of the steeple and main body of St. Mary's in the 1490s and early 1500s; the addition of two northern aisles to St. Peter's in the 1530s; a new chancel for St. Michael's in the 1490s;[4] and new cloisters for the nunnery in the 1520s.[5] Much of the work was supported by citizens, who, at least until the Dissolution, were clearly willing to spend fairly lavishly on their favourite ecclesiastical institutions.[6] Never of more than provincial significance, the work was generally of a lower quality than that of the 13th and 14th centuries, and in some instances, such as the clerestory of the abbey nave, notably austere.

The citizens were equally involved in the renewal of their public buildings, for which they obtained timber from their own estates or local religious houses, rather than the Crown's forests and parks.[7] A major project was the reconstruction of the Pentice in the 1460s and 1497.[8] In 1508 Roger Smith, a former sheriff, left money to convert his property in Commonhall Lane into almshouses, a bequest quickly augmented by the corporation, which converted the nearby common hall into a chapel for the new establishment.[9] A new common hall, probably envisaged from 1511, was eventually obtained in 1546 with the extensive refitting of the abandoned chapel of St. Nicholas.[10]

One or two important timber-framed domestic buildings were also built during the period, most notably Leche House (no. 17 Watergate Street), which probably dates from *c.* 1500 and provides a late example of a town house with a large hall over an undercroft and at right angles to the street. The only other significant structure surviving from the period is the timber-framed upper portion of the rear wing of nos. 48–50 Lower Bridge Street (the Old King's Head), which stretched west along Castle Lane above the remains of the Thorntons' stone-built mansion.[11]

EARLY MODERN AND GEORGIAN, 1550–1840

STREET PLAN

Within the walls, there was little development in the city's layout until the early 19th century.[12] Chester remained densely built up in Watergate, Eastgate, Bridge, Northgate, and Newgate Streets, with a loose grid of lanes west of Bridge Street and large areas of gardens elsewhere. The expanding population was accommodated mainly by infilling or by building on back land rather than by the creation of new streets.

By the early 17th century the town was surrounded by suburbs to the north, east, and south. The largest lay outside the Eastgate, where Foregate Street was continuously built up as far as Boughton, and where Cow Lane (later Frodsham Street) and the Gorse Stacks to the north, and St. John's Lane and Vicars Lane to the south were also lined with houses. In Handbridge there

was housing along the main street, Greenway Street, and Overleigh Road. Outside the Northgate, where over thirty houses and several bakehouses and barns were burnt in 1564 or 1565, building extended mainly along Upper Northgate Street. Even to the west, where there was least development, there was building outside the Watergate on the edge of the Roodee.[13] The suburbs contained concentrations of gentlemen's houses and inns, the latter most notably in Foregate Street.[14] After the destruction caused by the Civil War siege of Chester the suburbs were slowly rebuilt, but do not appear to have expanded much beyond their mid 17th-century limits before 1745.[15]

Apart from the introduction of minor roads servicing developments on the Greyfriars and Blackfriars sites,[16] the layout of the intramural streets remained largely unaltered even in the later 18th century.[17] Major

---

1 B.L. Harl. MS. 2176, f. 27 and v.; *J.C.A.S.* xxxix. 48; S. W. Ward, *Excavations at Chester: Lesser Medieval Religious Houses,* 69–71.

2 *V.C.H. Ches.* v (2), Cathedral and Close: Abbey Church to 1541, Monastic Buildings to 1541.

3 Ibid. Collegiate Church of St. John.

4 Ibid. Medieval Parish Churches.

5 Ibid. Sites and Remains of Medieval Religious Houses.

6 Above, Later Medieval Chester: Religion.

7 e.g. C.C.A.L.S., ZMUR 1/3; B.L. Harl. MS. 2158, ff. 210v.–211.

8 *V.C.H. Ches.* v (2), Municipal Buildings: Pentice.

9 *V.C.H. Ches.* iii. 183–4; *V.C.H. Ches.* v (2), Sites and Remains of Medieval Religious Houses: Hospital of St. Ursula.

10 *V.C.H. Ches.* v (2), Municipal Buildings: Common Hall.

11 *Rows of Chester,* ed. Brown, 168, 178–9.

12 Maps used in this section include Wm. Smith's map of Chester (1580): B.L. Harl. MS. 1046, f. 172 (printed in Morris, *Chester,* facing p. 256); G. Braun and F. Hohenberg, *Civitates Orbis Terrarum,* iii (1588), no. 3; J. Speed, *Theatre of Empire of G.B.* (1611), plan of Chester; Lavaux, *Plan of Chester.*

13 *King's Vale Royal* [i], 85; Morris, *Chester,* 278; *Chester: 1900 Years of Hist.* ed. A. M. Kennett, 40–1; C. Armour, 'Trade of Chester and State of Dee Navigation, 1600–1800' (Lond. Univ. Ph.D. thesis, 1956), 44; *J.C.A.S.* xxv. 204.

14 e.g. *King's Vale Royal* [ii], 15; *J.C.A.S.* xxv. 10; xxvii. 24–36; *Cal. of Lancs. and Ches. Exchequer Depositions* (R.S.L.C. xi), 119–20; C.C.A.L.S., ZAB 2, f. 109v.; ZCHB 3.

15 Lavaux, *Plan of Chester.*

16 Below, this section (Residential Development, 1760–1840).

17 J. Hunter, *Plan of Chester* (1789).

change came only in 1829 when Grosvenor Street was built to link the new Grosvenor Bridge with the town centre; cutting diagonally through the existing street plan and isolating the eastern end of Cuppin Street and Bunce Lane, it entailed the destruction of St. Bridget's church. Castle Esplanade (formerly Nuns Road), which joined the new street in front of the castle, was improved into a 'fine spacious way' at the same time.[1]

There was still much open space within the walls. Despite building along Nicholas Street and White Friars, the sites of the nunnery and the Carmelite and Dominican friaries remained almost undeveloped. There were also some 2 acres of gardens in the south-east of the intramural area, in the 18th century known as Hamilton's Park[2] and in 1818 converted into lawns, flower gardens, and a bowling green for the Albion Hotel.[3]

The suburbs expanded modestly in the later 18th and early 19th century and several new streets were laid out. Outside the Watergate, Crane Street and Paradise Row were created in the 1760s. From the 1770s development was especially concentrated north of Foregate Street, beginning with Queen Street and expanding later to include Bold Square and Seller and Egerton Streets before 1820. By the 1830s Milton Street and Leadworks Lane connected Brook Street with the canal side and the leadworks in Boughton. By then, too, a cluster of streets had been laid out north-east of the walled city south of St. Anne Street, in what was to become Newtown.[4]

BUILDING ACTIVITY, 1550–1640

The period saw a great deal of building in the city centre as rising prosperity led to a widespread desire to replace long neglected and increasingly dilapidated medieval structures.[5] The new work, still largely in timber, often involved fundamental reconstruction rather than mere refacing or repair, but nevertheless in the four main streets the Row walkways were retained.[6] Rebuilding was accompanied by encroachment on the street, usually in the form of oversailing upper storeys supported on posts to create arcaded walkways at ground level; such development occurred especially in association with Row buildings in Bridge Street and Eastgate Street, but also in Foregate Street

and the northern part of Northgate Street. They were occasionally termed Rows despite the dissimilarity with the traditional form.[7] Major building projects included the corporation's complete reconstruction of the Buttershops at the Cross in 1592–3; henceforth known as the New Buildings, they included shops, chambers, and undercrofts.[8] In 1633 a new customs house was established in Watergate Street, replacing the office formerly in the castle.[9] Much of the new building, however, even when it included shops, was primarily domestic. In Northgate Street, at the junction with Parsons Lane (later Princess Street), the sheriff, Thomas Whitby, replaced two decayed tenements with a new timber-framed house, jettied over the pavement on five posts; of some pretension, it contained much glass and wainscot panelling and numerous decorative features including painted chimney-pieces and coats of arms.[10] In Watergate Street there was another grand new house, built by Alderman John Aldersey in 1603, probably on the north side at the junction with Trinity Street.[11] Other new work near by included the western half of the two tenements which in 2000 formed no. 41 Watergate Street (Bishop Lloyd's House), with its elaborately carved timber-framed and gabled frontage and decoratively plastered large rooms over the Row;[12] also remodelled was no. 17 (Leche House), with an enlarged great chamber over the Row and a new private chamber and gallery overlooking the courtyard at the back.[13] Further west on the same street, Stanley Palace, a timber-framed building with three gables at right angles to the street, was built in the north-east corner of the former Dominican precinct.[14] In Bridge Street new building included Lamb Row, immediately south of St. Bridget's church, a deeply jettied late 16th-century timber-framed building with large cusped brackets supporting the oversailing storey;[15] Tudor House (nos. 29–31 Lower Bridge Street), early 17th-century and four-storeyed, with a large second-floor street chamber; and the main range of the Old King's Head (nos. 48–52 Lower Bridge Street), probably rebuilt in the later 16th century.[16] In Eastgate Street largely intact houses from 1610 and 1643 survived in 2000 at no. 22 and no. 9 Row level (the Boot Inn).[17]

---

1 J. W. Clarke, 'Bldg. of Grosvenor Bridge', *J.C.A.S.* xlv. 45–9; Hemingway, *Hist. Chester*, ii. 11; *P.N. Ches.* v (1:i), 16.

2 Hunter, *Plan of Chester* (1789).

3 J. Wood, *Map of Chester* (1833); Hemingway, *Hist. Chester*, ii. 32; *Georgian Chester*, ed. A. M. Kennett, 38–9.

4 J. H. Hanshall, *Hist. of Co. Palatine of Chester*, map facing p. 13; Wood, *Map of Chester* (1833); *P.N. Ches.* v (1:i), 66; Hemingway, *Hist. Chester*, i. 425–6. See map, above, p. 148.

5 What follows depends heavily upon *Rows of Chester*, ed. Brown, 77–94.

6 *King's Vale Royal* [ii], 19.

7 e.g. C.C.A.L.S., ZTAR 1/8; ZTAR 2/23, m. 2d.; *J.C.A.S.* lxx. 103; *Rows of Chester*, ed. Brown, 1, 3; Hemingway, *Hist. Chester*, i. 424.

8 K. M. Matthews and others, *Excavations at Chester: 3–15*

Eastgate St. 34–5; C.C.A.L.S., ZAB 1, ff. 238, 240; ZAP 2, nos. 10–11; ZCHD 3/8; ZML 5/119.

9 Armour, 'Trade of Chester', 12.

10 *J.C.A.S.* lxx. 99–132.

11 C.C.A.L.S., ZQSF 53, nos. 6, 77; ibid. WS 1605 and WC 1606, Jn. Aldersey; 3 *Sheaf*, xxxii, p. 68.

12 *J.C.A.S.* n.s. vi. 245–8; lxix. 140.

13 Ibid. xxi. 5–22; lxix. 138–9.

14 *V.C.H. Ches.* v (2), Sites and Remains of Medieval Religious Houses: Dominican Friary.

15 Hanshall, *Hist. Co. Palatine*, 255, 287; *Rows of Chester*, ed. Brown, 29, 153; P. Boughton, *Picturesque Chester*, nos. 53, 119, 146. But cf. *J.C.A.S.* n.s. iv. 122, 126–7, 156–7. It collapsed in 1821: Hemingway, *Hist. Chester*, ii. 30–1. Plate 31.

16 *Rows of Chester*, ed. Brown, 165, 168.

17 Ibid. 170, 172.

Outside the four main streets and Foregate Street there was less development. Minor streets largely built up by the late 16th century included King Street, Princess Street, Commonhall Street, White Friars, Cuppin Street, Bunce Street, and Pepper Street.[1] Elsewhere, mansions were built into the remains of the nunnery and on the western part of the Carmelite site in the mid 16th century, and on the site of the Carmelite church in 1597.[2] The chapel of St. Thomas outside the Northgate had been replaced by a house known as Green Hall (later Jollye's Hall) by *c.* 1580.[3]

The larger new houses had numerous rooms. Within the Rows they might include undercrofts containing shops or offices, a hall or parlour and shops on the first floor, and a great or 'street' chamber generally on the second floor over the Row walkway together with other rooms over the hall.[4] The great chamber supplanted the hall as the principal living space, and in some instances the hall was subdivided.[5] Enclosure of the stallboards on the street side of the Row to form small shops, which darkened the walkway and the rooms behind and created conditions favourable to anti-social behaviour,[6] led to the development of private quarters around courtyards at the back of the buildings together with kitchens, cisterns, privies, and stables.[7]

The handsome timbered façades of the new buildings, well exemplified by those of the Falcon (no. 6 Lower Bridge Street) and Bishop Lloyd's House with its carved frieze, added to the attractions of the city, the streets of which were deemed 'very fair and beautiful' in the 1620s.[8] Other civic improvements included the establishment in the 1580s of a cistern at the Cross to store water brought from Boughton, and in 1605 of a waterworks housed in a tower on the Bridgegate to draw water from the Dee.[9] There was also renewed attention to paving and cleansing the streets. In the late Middle Ages the responsibility of the murengers, by the 16th century maintenance of the pavement devolved directly upon the citizens.[10] By 1567 in the main streets the paved area formed a causeway down the middle of the highway with drainage channels on either side crossed periodically by iron gratings to provide access to the frontages, a system apparently extended there-

after to the lesser streets.[11] The Assembly also rehoused the markets, removing some to Northgate Street in the later 16th century to be near the new common hall. A new corn market was built there in 1556 and replaced in 1576, to be joined in 1582 by the former shire hall re-erected as a shambles. The former corn market was moved to the quarry outside the Northgate where it became the house of correction.[12]

Despite such improvements, in other areas the fabric of the city was neglected. The city walls were so decayed that parts had collapsed and they had become generally dangerous to walk upon; repairs were undertaken only with the prospect of civil war in the early 1640s.[13] Equally deleterious to the environment was the state of the monastic precincts after the Dissolution. Although St. Werburgh's survived largely unaltered until the Civil War,[14] and the outer court of the nunnery was made into a mansion, in most cases the buildings suffered neglect or demolition. The destruction in 1597 of the Carmelite church and steeple, a notable landmark, altered the skyline of the city, already changed by the collapse of the north-west tower of St. John's in the 1570s. In the west, prolonged neglect of the other two friaries, the loss or decay of the nunnery church, and the generally poor condition of the castle meant that much of the western section of the city was derelict.[15]

EFFECTS OF THE SIEGE AND INTERREGNUM

In the early 1640s the prospect of civil war brought with it a refurbishment of the city walls and gates, and in 1643 earthen fortifications were built to protect the northern and eastern suburbs, the latter being much altered as the siege progressed.[16] The siege entailed much damage, especially in the suburbs. Indeed in 1648 the citizens claimed that a quarter of the city had been burnt.[17] Initially, destruction was the work of the defenders, who cleared large numbers of suburban buildings which they feared might threaten their new fortifications.[18] Further damage was later inflicted by the parliamentarian forces, and by 1646 large parts of the eastern suburbs had been burnt: at Boughton,

1 Smith's map of Chester (1580); Braun and Hohenberg, *Civitates*, iii, no. 3; Speed, *Theatre of Empire of G.B.* plan of Chester.

2 *J.C.A.S.* xxxi. 33, 36, 39–40; *V.C.H. Ches.* v (2), Sites and Remains of Medieval Religious Houses: Benedictine Nunnery, Carmelite Friary.

3 Braun and Hohenberg, *Civitates*, iii, no. 3; Speed, *Theatre of Empire of G.B.* plan of Chester; *King's Vale Royal* [i], 39; *P.N. Ches.* v (1:i), 69.

4 e.g. B.L. Harl. MS. 2022, ff. 140–1; cf. *King's Vale Royal* [ii], 19.

5 e.g. nos. 38–42 Watergate Street: *J.C.A.S.* lxix. 142–3.

6 *V.C.H. Ches.* v (2), The Rows: Rebuilding and Enclosure.

7 e.g. B.L. Harl. MS. 2022, ff. 140–1.

8 *King's Vale Royal* [ii], 19–20.

9 *V.C.H. Ches.* v (2), Public Utilities: Water.

10 e.g. C.C.A.L.S., ZAB 1, ff. 179v., 264; ZQSF 40/22–7; *King's*

Vale Royal [i], 85; Morris, *Chester*, 260–1, 264–74; *Cal. Chester City Cl. Mins. 1603–42*, 117–18.

11 Morris, *Chester*, 266–7.

12 *V.C.H. Ches.* v (2), Markets.

13 Ibid. City Walls and Gates: Medieval and Later.

14 A. T. Thacker, 'Re-use of Monastic Bldgs. at Chester, 1540–1640', *T.H.S.L.C.* cxlv. 21–43.

15 *V.C.H. Ches.* v (2), Castle: Buildings; Sites and Remains of Medieval Religious Houses.

16 S. Ward, *Excavations at Chester: Civil War Siegeworks, 1642–6*, passim.

17 *J.C.A.S.* xxv. 211.

18 Rest of para. and next based on S. Porter, *Destruction in Eng. Civil Wars*, 45, 50–1, 68, 85–6; Ormerod, *Hist. Ches.* i. 373–4; *J.C.A.S.* xxv. 203–8, 219, 222–4, 226, 233–4; B.L. Harl. MS. 1944, ff. 98v.–99; Harl. MS. 2135, ff. 40–1; Harl. MS. 2155, ff. 108–26; C.C.A.L.S., ZAF 26; ZAF 34.

around the Bars, and along Foregate Street, Cow Lane, and St. John's Lane. St. John's church was severely damaged, and Lord Cholmondeley's house in the churchyard and St. Giles's hospital at Boughton were razed. The northern suburbs were entirely burnt. Losses there included St. John's hospital, the house of correction, the great windmill, and Jollye's Hall. In Handbridge the high street and the surrounding lanes and buildings were destroyed, including the fulling mills, Overleigh Hall, and Brewer's Hall. Immediately outside the walls, the buildings beyond the Watergate on the Roodee and the Glovers Houses near the Shipgate were all taken down. In all perhaps 300 or 350 houses were lost.

Within the walls, the citizens destroyed Sir William Brereton's house at the former nunnery when hostilities broke out. The besiegers wrought much harm by firing cannon into the city: the water tower on the Bridgegate was demolished and the houses of Eastgate Street and the eastern half of Watergate Street were greatly damaged. After the city was taken, the bishop's palace was sacked, the interior of the cathedral wrecked, and St. Mary's deprived of its stained glass. The defences themselves suffered heavily: major breaches were made in the north and east walls, and the Eastgate was probably partly demolished.

Reconstruction after 1646 proceeded at best unevenly. The water supply had clearly been disrupted and in 1652 the cistern at the Cross was partly demolished;[1] the walls remained breached, with a large section between Eastgate and Newgate razed; the suburbs continued derelict.[2] In 1655 the receipts of the new municipal rental were only a fifth of what they had been before the siege.[3] By then, however, building activity seems to have been increasing, and new buildings and workshops were being erected on the waste land outside the Eastgate.[4] In 1653 the Assembly permitted citizens to employ 'foreigners' after complaints that local building workers had been exacting high wages,[5] while in 1654 the pressures were such that members of the Joiners' company claimed that their monopoly over the buying and selling of timber had been infringed.[6] Clay-pits were established in Cow Lane and elsewhere, and there was still a great demand for bricks in 1658 when the Assembly attempted to control digging for clay on the city's land.[7] By then there was much building within the walls and in Handbridge.[8]

BUILDING ACTIVITY, 1660–1760

Reconstruction continued after the Restoration, although hampered by economic stagnation. In 1660 the Assembly ordered repairs to various public buildings, including the common hall, the Northgate, and Dee Bridge.[9] Work also began immediately on the bishop's palace and the prebendaries' houses, and new buildings were put up within the cathedral precinct on what were to become Abbey Green and Abbey Street and, eventually, in Abbey Court.[10] Repairs and reconstruction of the parish churches, the fabric of which seems to have been long neglected, were begun only in the late 1660s and continued into the early 18th century. Major rebuildings included the spire of St. Peter's in 1669, the south side of Holy Trinity in 1678, the chancel of St. Michael's about the same time, the whole of St. Bridget's *c.* 1690, and the Troutbeck chapel at St. Mary's in 1693.[11]

Within the walls, several town houses were put up in the later 17th century. Early signs of such activity survive at nos. 22–6 Bridge Street (the Dutch Houses), timber-framed with two storeys above the Row adorned with twisted columns, and no. 1 White Friars, altered in 1658, when an elaborate jetty with a carved fascia board and pargeting was added to a house already of high status.[12] The largest concentration of smart town houses was in Lower Bridge Street, where the Row walkway was enclosed and converted to domestic use, a process initiated in 1643 by Sir Richard Grosvenor at no. 6 (the Falcon). By the early 18th century the Row was largely enclosed throughout the street.[13] One of the first of the new mansions was the earl of Shrewsbury's town house at no. 94 (the Bear and Billet), which had a jettied timber-framed frontage with full-width bracketed windows to the principal floors, all beneath a single wide gable. Others followed, most notably nos. 16–24 (Bridge House), a stuccoed brick building of five bays adorned with two tiers of pilasters, erected *c.* 1676 for Lady Mary Calveley; no. 51, built in 1700 and of three bays with a brick façade and an elaborate doorcase; and no. 84 (Shipgate House), a brick building of the late 17th or early 18th century, handsomely refronted in the mid 18th.[14] By the early 18th century the street had few if any shops and had become grandly residential.

By 1745 there were town houses for the gentry elsewhere within the walls, in Northgate Street, King Street, Watergate Street, the Blackfriars precinct, Castle

1 C.C.A.L.S., ZAB 2, f. 99v.

2 *J.C.A.S.* xxv. 206–14.

3 C.C.A.L.S., ZTAR 3/52; Johnson, 'Aspects', 91–2. Thanks are due to Mr. N. J. Alldridge (Paris) for these references.

4 C.C.A.L.S., ZAF 34.

5 Ibid. ZAB 2, f. 102v.   6 Ibid. f. 105.

7 Ibid. f. 122v.; ZAF 34, nos. 33–4; ZAF 37A, no. 12. Thanks are due to Mr. Alldridge for these references.

8 Ibid. ZQSF 78.

9 Ibid. ZAB 2, ff. 125v.–126v.; ZAF 3C, nos. 2–4.

10 *V.C.H. Ches.* v (2), Cathedral and Close: Precinct from 1541.

11 Ibid. Medieval Parish Churches.

12 *J.C.A.S.* lxix. 97–111.

13 *V.C.H. Ches.* v (2), The Rows: Rebuilding and Enclosure.

14 *Rows of Chester*, ed. Brown, 101–4, 166–7, 169–70.

Street, Fleshmongers Lane (later Newgate Street), Pepper Street, and Cuppin Street. Genteel early 18th-century rebuilding was especially conspicuous in Watergate Street, and included no. 11, comprising four storeys and three bays of brick dating from 1744, with a Tuscan colonnade at Row level and a late 17th-century dwelling to the rear; no. 39, early 18th-century and of painted ashlar; nos. 63/5–7, a substantial early 18th-century house of which only the stone and stucco façade with its colonnade survived in 2000; no. 26, four storeys, *c.* 1720; nos. 28–34, remodelled in 1700 to make Booth Mansion, with an impressive brick frontage of eight bays gently angled towards the Cross and adorned with a Tuscan colonnade at Row level and an elaborate cornice; and no. 68, dating from 1729 with a rusticated stone ground floor.[1] Further south, most of Castle Street was also early Georgian; notable houses included nos. 15–17, which had two gables with pineapples and was originally perhaps one town house of seven bays (1685), no. 23 (front of *c.* 1720), no. 25 (*c.* 1700), and nos. 22–4 (mid 18th century). In between, White Friars, a rather less grand redevelopment, was begun in the 1720s.[2]

Most of the new houses occupied sites fronting the street. A notable exception was Lion House, an early 18th-century brick house set behind Leche House in Watergate Street and reached by an alley.[3] By 1745 a large house belonging to Edward Morgan had apparently been erected further west, also south of Watergate Street.[4] Occasionally rebuilding was limited to a fashionable brick façade, a process which gathered momentum in the 18th century. Early examples include Gamul House (nos. 52–8 Lower Bridge Street), dating from *c.* 1700, the four-storeyed early 18th-century front of no. 21 Watergate Street, and no. 23 Castle Street (*c.* 1720).[5]

By the earlier 18th century many of the grander town houses were located in the suburbs to the south and east. In Handbridge, Overleigh Hall was rebuilt following its acquisition by the Cowper family after the Restoration.[6] Just outside the walls on part of the Roman amphitheatre stood Dee House, a brick building of three storeys and five bays dating from *c.* 1700 and belonging to the Comberbach family.[7] Near by in Vicars Lane was the vicarage house of St. John's (later the Grosvenor Club), also of three storeys and five bays, with a rusticated doorway (*c.* 1740). In the Groves lay the ecclesiastical property known as the Archdeacon's House, leased by Bishop Peploe to his daughter in 1741 and rebuilt a few years later with a main south front of five bays and three storeys in style resembling houses shortly to be built on the north side of Abbey Square. Just to the north-west the bishop added a second house with a front of similar proportions, enlarged westwards in 1754 by a canted bay behind which there was a new dining room with rococo plasterwork.[8] There was an especial concentration of gentlemen's houses along Foregate Street. Notable examples included those of the Wettenhalls on the north side and of Sir John Werden and the Walley and Egerton families on the south, the last two near the Bars.[9]

Early to mid 18th-century work at Chester was quite distinctive, in brick and generally with rusticated quoins and window heads, bracketed or dentilled cornices, and wide plat bands above the window voussoirs. Some earlier examples have moulded cornices and window architraves, while in the Rows the first-floor walkway was commonly lit by a Tuscan colonnade opening on to the street.

By 1700 the city authorities were seeking to beautify Chester and improve its amenities. An important element in their programme was the provision of better accommodation for the council: in the 1690s the common hall was replaced by a handsome new Exchange, and in 1704 the south side of the Pentice was rebuilt in brick.[10] In 1715–17 the corporation co-operated with private subscribers in replacing the former hospital of St. John outside the Northgate. The new building comprised a main east-facing block of five bays recessed between short wings. It was of red brick with stone dressings and the windows of the principal floor had semi-elliptical heads.[11] A further public building, an infirmary paid for by public subscription, was completed in 1761; built around a small courtyard, it had an entrance front of thirteen bays with a central block of seven, the middle three canted forward to form a first-floor bay window on Tuscan columns.[12] The earliest purpose-built nonconformist chapels, Presbyterian (later Unitarian) in 1700 and Quaker in 1703, were plain brick boxes hidden away with small burial grounds behind minor streets, respectively off Trinity Street and Cow Lane.[13]

In addition to new public buildings, in 1707–8 the corporation restored and levelled the walls to provide an agreeable pathway around the city.[14] They were

---

1 *Rows of Chester*, ed. Brown, 177–8, 180–1, 183–5.

2 Dates 1685 and 1720s (various) on houses.

3 *Rows of Chester*, ed. Brown, 179.

4 Lavaux, *Plan of Chester*.

5 *Rows of Chester*, ed. Brown, 112, 168–9, 179; *J.C.A.S.* lxix. 138–43.

6 Ormerod, *Hist. Ches.* i. 374.

7 R. Cleary and others, *Dee House, Chester: Evaluation* (copy at C.H.H.), 6.

8 C.C.A.L.S., EEC 99070–3; *J.C.A.S.* xxxvii. 71; Lavaux, *Plan*

of Chester; dated rainwater head.

9 Lavaux, *Plan of Chester*; Hemingway, *Hist. Chester*, i. 424.

10 *V.C.H. Ches.* v (2), Municipal Buildings: Exchange, Pentice.

11 Ibid. Sites and Remains of Medieval Religious Houses: Hospital of St. John.

12 Ibid. Medical Services: Chester Royal Infirmary.

13 Ibid. Protestant Nonconformity: Early Presbyterians and Independents, Quakers.

14 Ibid. City Walls and Gates: Medieval and Later.

connected with the Groves, also used as a public walk in the early 18th century, by the Recorder's Steps, built by the corporation in 1720.[1] The Groves themselves were enhanced with an avenue in 1726, and by 1745 public walks along the riverside extended past a bowling green to a point half way between Souters and Dee Lanes.[2] The Roodee was also improved and between 1706 and 1710 was protected from flooding by a bank known as the Cop.[3] Thereafter corporation land was developed by lessees at its northern end, close to wharves on the new channel of the Dee.[4] By the 1740s timber yards and ship repairing facilities occupied the area between the Watergate and the river.[5] In 1759 the Chester poor-law union workhouse was established south of the wharves, approached by a new road from outside the Watergate (later Paradise Row).[6]

By the mid 18th century the pace of residential development was increasing. The tone was set by Abbey Court (later Abbey Square), where the bishop and prebendaries had their houses. In the 1750s Robert Taylor designed a reconstruction of the ruined palace, the single-storeyed entrance front of which occupied the south side of Abbey Court. The west and north sides of the square were also rebuilt, in a succession of speculative developments, to provide improved housing for the prebendaries and other members of the cathedral establishment, and a new linen hall was built south-west of the cathedral.[7]

The style evolved in the houses in Abbey Square, which were generally of three storeys, of brick with stone quoins, a solid parapet, and elaborate doorcases, was largely followed in other developments in the third quarter of the 18th century, especially on the east side of Northgate Street (on cathedral land backing on the precinct wall), along King Street, in White Friars, on the north side of Pepper Street (demolished), and in Newgate Street (largely demolished).[8]

The period also saw some imposing suburban houses, including Egerton House in Upper Northgate Street, a large building of seven bays and three storeys with an interrupted balustrade, built c. 1760.[9] Grandest of all was Forest House, in Foregate Street at the junction with Love Lane (Fig. 10). Built probably by Sir Robert Taylor[10] for Trafford Barnston in 1759, it was three storeys high above a semi-basement and

stood behind a forecourt flanked by low service buildings. To its south, as with the other larger houses on the south side of Foregate Street, there was a garden which ran back to paddocks on the high ground above the river.[11]

PUBLIC, COMMERCIAL, AND INDUSTRIAL BUILDINGS, 1760–1840

The main civic buildings continued to be concentrated in Northgate Street,[12] the only exception, the Pentice, being reduced in size in 1781 and demolished entirely in 1803.[13] The area around the Cross was also opened up and modernized by the removal of the stocks and pillory in 1800.[14] With the demolition of the old Northgate, in 1807–8 a new gaol was built, in a curious juxtaposition of land uses, between the infirmary and the rear of elegant Stanley Place.[15] In 1827 new market buildings were put up north and south of the Exchange to replace the dilapidated structures removed in 1812.[16] Between 1768 and 1810 the corporation was also responsible for renewing the four main city gates as elegant single arches spanning the street, thereby maintaining the pedestrian walkway along the walls while offering better access to traffic.[17]

A major project, transforming the south-western corner of the intramural area, was the rebuilding of the outer bailey of the castle between 1788 and 1813 under the auspices of the county authorities. The new work, forming the grandest ensemble of neo-classical public buildings in Britain, was the masterpiece of the architect Thomas Harrison and earned him his sobriquet 'of Chester'. It caused Harrison to establish his practice in the city, to which he moved in 1795 and where he remained until his death in 1829.[18] Harrison's buildings comprised a main range containing a new shire hall and grand jury room, and northern and southern wings occupied by the armoury and barracks of the castle garrison. They were disposed around a large new parade ground, entered from the north-west by a remarkable pillared 'propylaeum' containing two lodges. Behind, on the side towards the river, lay Harrison's 'panoptic' county prison with its rugged rusticated walls, completed with the main block in 1800.[19] In 1830 the castle precinct was enlarged to the south, entailing the diversion of a portion of the city

1 C.C.A.L.S., ZAB 3, ff. 258v., 259v.

2 Ibid. ZAB 4, f. 6; Lavaux, *Plan of Chester*. Frontispiece.

3 C.C.A.L.S., ZAB 3, ff. 141, 144, 176, 178, 179v., 182 and v.; *Diary of Henry Prescott*, i. 265–70, 272.

4 *V.C.H. Ches.* v (2), Water Transport: River.

5 Lavaux, *Plan of Chester*; C.C.A.L.S., ZAB 4, ff. 98–9, 101v.

6 Hemingway, *Hist. Chester*, ii. 192–3; C.C.A.L.S., ZAB 4, ff. 170–171v., 173v.–174v., 183 and v.; ZCHD 9/46.

7 *V.C.H. Ches.* v (2), Cathedral and Close: Precinct from 1541.

8 For demolished bldgs.: C.H.H., Chester Photographic Survey.

9 Ibid.

10 Windows evidently in his manner.

11 Hemingway, *Hist. Chester*, i. 423; C.C.A.L.S., ZAB 4,

ff. 177v.–178; ZCHD 4/74–5; ZCR 39/85.

12 Lavaux, *Plan of Chester*.

13 *V.C.H. Ches.* v (2), Municipal Buildings: Pentice.

14 C.C.A.L.S., ZAB 5, p. 145; *Browns and Chester*, ed. H. D. Willcock, 64.

15 *V.C.H. Ches.* v (2), Law and Order: Municipal Prisons. Plate 34.

16 Ibid. Markets: General Produce Markets.

17 Ibid. City Walls and Gates: Gates, Posterns, and Towers (Eastgate, Northgate, Watergate, Bridgegate). Plates 19–24.

18 H. Colvin, *Biographical Dictionary of Brit. Architects* (1995), 466–70; M. A. R. Ockrim, 'Thos. Harrison and Rebldg. of Chester Cast.' *J.C.A.S.* lxvi. 57–67.

19 *V.C.H. Ches.* v (2), Castle: Buildings, County Gaol. Plates 28–9.

FIG. 10. *Forest House*

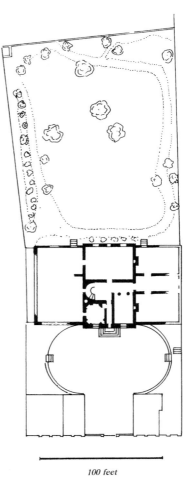

100 feet

walls and the removal of the western part of Skinners Lane and the warehouses and noisome acid works sited there.[1] By then work had begun on another major public project, Harrison's Grosvenor Bridge, which when completed in 1833 constituted the largest stone arch in the world.[2]

Several important commercial buildings were put up to serve the cloth fairs of the later 18th century. They included the New Linenhall, a large rectangular brick building comprising small shops around a courtyard and erected in 1778 on the eastern half of the Greyfriars site.[3] The lane leading to the Crofts, Lower Lane, was renamed Linenhall Street and perhaps remodelled.[4] In the early 19th century similar structures of brick with galleried courtyards were built on either side of Foregate Street: the Union Hall (1809) to the south and Commercial Hall (1815) to the north.[5] A further venture, managed by a committee on behalf of the proprietors, was the Commercial News Room (in 2000

the City Club), built in 1808 on the site of the Sun Inn next to St. Peter's church in Northgate Street. Designed by Thomas Harrison in a neo-classical style, it was of brick with an ashlar front of three bays, adorned with Ionic columns carrying a pediment, and with a rusticated ground arcade behind which a walkway was inserted in the 1960s. Inside there was a fine neo-classical news room.[6]

Despite the cutting of a canal through Chester in the 1770s and the 1790s, in part on the line of the old town ditch immediately outside the north wall,[7] new industry left only a limited imprint on the city's fabric. By the early 19th century there was some industrial building around the Gorse Stacks, including a needle factory and a foundry.[8] The Dee Mills, although by then in terminal decline, still dominated the riverside around Dee Bridge; five storeys high and with numerous iron-framed windows, they formed an impressive but starkly utilitarian complex.[9] By the canal, the Steam Mill, which originated

1 *V.C.H. Ches.* v (2), City Walls and Gates: Medieval and Later; Hemingway, *Hist. Chester*, i. 366–7. Plate 44.

2 *V.C.H. Ches.* v (2), Roads and Road Transport: Bridges and Other River Crossings (Grosvenor Bridge).

3 Ibid. Fairs.

4 *P.N. Ches.* v (1:i), 15; Lavaux, *Plan of Chester*.

5 *V.C.H. Ches.* v (2), Fairs.

6 *Rows of Chester*, ed. Brown, 174; Hemingway, *Hist. Chester*, ii. 188–9.

7 *V.C.H. Ches.* v (2), Water Transport: Canals.

8 Hanshall, *Hist. Co. Palatine*, map facing p. 13.

9 T. E. Ward, *Chester As It Was* (1980); K. Goulborn and G. Jackson, *Chester: Portrait in Old Picture Postcards*, i (1987), 77.

in the late 18th century as a cotton mill but was used as a corn mill from 1819,[1] probably occupied a low four-storeyed building still surviving in 2000. Another major enterprise initiated in the period was the leadworks, established in 1800 on a large site on the north bank of the canal; the shot tower, still a Chester landmark in the 1990s, dated from its earliest years.[2] The Flookersbrook foundry in Charles Street, which originated in 1803, added to the industrial character of the area north-east of the city centre.[3]

To the west of the walled city the New Crane Wharf on the river Dee, with its large warehouses and harbour master's house, was mostly developed by 1772 and remained largely intact into the 1990s.[4] From 1804 further industrial development was spreading along the riverside edge of the Roodee south of the workhouse of 1759: shipbuilding yards and an iron foundry before 1815, and a paper mill by the 1830s.[5] At Tower Wharf on the canal, warehouses, a hotel, and a dry dock were built shortly after the opening of the Ellesmere Canal's Wirral branch in 1795. Much of the site survived in 2000.[6]

NEW CHURCHES AND CHAPELS, 1760–1840

Repairs to some of the parish churches made a visual impact on the city, in particular the reconstruction of the south side of St. Peter's after the removal of the Pentice in 1803, and the removal of the spires of St. Peter's in 1780 and Holy Trinity in 1811. Old St. Bridget's, by then very decayed, was demolished in 1829 and replaced by a neo-classical church opposite the castle in the angle between Grosvenor Street and Castle Esplanade. New churches were built in the growing suburbs of Boughton in 1830 and Newtown in 1838.[7]

Non-Anglican places of worship were also opened in areas of expanding population. In Queen Street, for example, a Congregationalist chapel opened in 1777 and a Roman Catholic church in 1799. Notable non-conformist chapels serving relatively well-to-do neighbourhoods included the Octagon chapel opened in 1765 north of Foregate Street near the Bars, the Wesleyan chapel in St. John Street designed by Thomas Harrison in 1811, and the Methodist New Connexion chapel opened in Pepper Street in 1835.[8] Less prestigious denominations built smaller, architec-

turally undistinguished chapels in inconspicuous locations, such as the Particular Baptists in Hamilton Place (1806), the Primitive Methodists in Steam Mill Street (1823), and the Scotch Baptists in Pepper Street (1827), or made do with converted buildings.[9]

RESIDENTIAL DEVELOPMENT, 1760–1840

Although the centre of Chester bears much evidence of later 18th-century rebuilding, completely new housing was limited to a few speculative developments, and the city had no substantial Georgian suburbs. In the earlier 19th century population growth provoked rather more rebuilding and Chester's housing stock expanded by over half between 1801 and 1841.[10] Much building took the form of infill on sites within the existing urban framework; small or medium-sized cottage property predominated. Such developments included the courts and, like the leadworks, detracted from the city's character.[11]

The best housing within the intramural area in the later 18th century was in the cathedral precinct and on the Greyfriars and Blackfriars sites. At the cathedral, work continued after the completion of Abbey Square, in Abbey Green in the 1760s and 1770s and Abbey Street until the 1820s.[12] The Greyfriars site was developed after its sale by the Stanleys in 1775. The principal houses, which were on the western half of the site, comprised two opposing red-brick terraces, three storeys high, on either side of Stanley Place, and similar dwellings at Watergate Flags on the Watergate Street frontage.[13] The project also entailed the laying out of Stanley Street and probably of City Walls Road, which extended by 1789 from Watergate Street to the northern edge of the site.[14]

The Stanleys, together with the architect Joseph Turner, were also involved in development on the Blackfriars site, where in the 1780s a substantial brick terrace, designed by Turner, was erected fronting the western side of Nicholas Street.[15] Behind, between the gardens of the terrace and an earlier house belonging to Sir Richard Brooke, a service road known originally as Brooke's Street and later as Nicholas Street Mews was set out. Further development included the reconstruction of Brooke's house in 1820 by the architect Thomas Harrison for Henry Potts, the county treasurer.[16] By

1 Hunter, *Plan of Chester* (1789); above, Late Georgian and Victorian Chester: Economy and Society (The Economy, 1762–1840).
2 M. H. O. Hoddinott, *Site Development Hist. of Chester Leadworks, 1800–1990* (copy in C.C.A.L.S., ZCR 586/37).
3 Above, Late Georgian and Victorian Chester: Economy and Society (The Economy, 1762–1840).
4 *Chester and River Dee*, ed. A. Kennett, 12; *Chester Guide* (1782), 28; Chester Action Programme Partnership, *Strategies and Action*, sections 2/13, 3/5 (copy at C.H.H.).
5 C.C.A.L.S., ZCHD 9/74, 79–80; Wood, *Map of Chester* (1833).
6 Chester Action Programme, *Update*, iii (Oct. 1994), 1 (copy at C.H.H.); *V.C.H. Ches.* v (2), Water Transport: Canals. Plate 47.

7 *V.C.H. Ches.* v (2), Medieval Parish Churches: Holy Trinity, St. Bridget, St. Peter; Modern Parish Churches: Christ Church, St. Paul. Plate 27 for St. Bridget's.
8 Ibid. Roman Catholicism; Protestant Nonconformity: Congregationalists, Methodists (Wesleyans, Methodist New Connexion). Plates 37–9.   9 Ibid. Protestant Nonconformity.
10 *Census*, 1801–41.
11 Below, this section (The Courts).
12 *V.C.H. Ches.* v (2), Cathedral and Close: Precinct from 1541.
13 Ibid. Sites and Remains of Medieval Religious Houses: Franciscan Friary.   14 Hunter, *Plan of Chester* (1789).
15 Para. based on details in *V.C.H. Ches.* v (2), Sites and Remains of Medieval Religious Houses: Dominican Friary.
16 Colvin, *Biog. Dict.* (1995), 469.

the late 18th century Smith's Walk (later Grey Friars) had been laid out to the south to provide access to the large house which had long existed in the south-west corner of the precinct.[1]

Other late Georgian work within the city centre included further development in King Street (relatively genteel), White Friars, and Pepper Street (distinctly modest).[2] Within the Rows there was a good deal of rebuilding in the late 18th and early 19th century, mostly in brick, often rubbed, and adorned with continuous cills forming strings. Many houses or façades of the period survive in Bridge Street, Watergate Street, the south side of Eastgate Street, and the east side of Northgate Street.[3]

By the later 18th century the intensified development of sites within the old city centre led to its desertion by Chester's wealthiest inhabitants. Gamul House in Lower Bridge Street, for example, had ceased to be a private residence by the 1760s and was occupied by a dancing academy and a boarding school; by 1831 the house and its outbuildings were divided into inferior dwellings.[4] Stanley Palace, which in the mid 18th century was occupied by the Hesketh family and frequented by the gentry during race week, was by the 1830s in the possession of two builders and described as 'decayed'.[5]

Although the periphery, including Foregate Street, continued to include some large houses in the later 18th century,[6] much of the suburban building around Chester between 1760 and 1840 was relatively modest. One of the earliest and best developments was outside the Watergate on corporation land, where a new road was laid out in 1763 and building leases were available from 1766 onwards. The corporation was concerned that the houses should be of a uniform appearance and in 1769 laid down minimum standards for materials and design.[7] The new houses, which were in Crane Street and on the north side of Paradise Row, were described as among the most pleasant in the city in 1831.[8] Although an attempt to extend housing northwards on to Tower field came to nothing, perhaps because it was found that some of the existing houses were liable to occasional flooding, new commercial development on the river bank was actively encouraged.[9]

Outside the Northgate, Upper Northgate Street was already by the 1770s lined with houses, some of them of size and quality, as far as the junction of Parkgate and Liverpool Roads.[10] West of Parkgate Road in the 1830s

the land remained open on either side of the former Portpool Way, renamed Cottage Street (later Garden Lane),[11] but by 1830 middle-class housing was beginning to spread over the dean and chapter's land along Liverpool Road, including a short early 19th-century terrace named Abbots Grange, and a few large villas such as Abbot's Hayes and Abbotsfield, both later demolished.[12] Further east much of the new building was terraced cottages. To the south of St. Anne Street, for example, where a few early 19th-century houses survived in 2000 amid later redevelopment, streets of small terraced houses were built by local investors, notably Thomas Clare, a builder of Oulton Place who was elected to the council in 1836.[13] By 1831 the area, then known as Newtown, contained over 500 houses.[14] There had also been scattered housing and commercial development along the north bank of the canal and Brook Street in the later 18th century,[15] and in the early 19th century terraces of small houses were built off the north side of George Street and around the bowling green behind the Bowling Green Inn at the Gorse Stacks.[16]

Although the land between the south bank of the canal and the gardens to the north of Foregate Street was still fields in the 1770s,[17] development started there before 1800. Queen Street was the first to be built up, by John Chamberlaine and Roger Rogerson after 1778,[18] but the earliest planned development was Bold Square, built c. 1814 by Thomas Lunt, a foundry owner and builder, and comprising two terraces of small houses facing each other across a strip of garden. Lunt also erected Union Bridge across the canal at his own expense and on the north bank built much of Egerton Street (c. 1820), which included a terrace on the west side and five pairs of slightly larger semi-detached houses on the east. South of the bridge, Seller Street was developed in 1818–19 by the brewery owner Alderman William Seller.[19]

To the south of Foregate Street, St. John Street, in the early 19th century 'dark, narrow, and incommodious', was improved after the building of the Wesleyan chapel in 1811, and by 1831 contained 'many genteel residences'. Further east in Boughton, near the site of St. Paul's church, Richmond Terrace was an imposing late Georgian development, and nos. 125–7 Boughton an early 19th-century one, of three storeys with a balcony carried on coupled Tuscan columns. To the south, on the high ground above the river, Thomas

1 *P.N. Ches.* v (1:i), 20; Hunter, *Plan of Chester* (1789).
2 Hemingway, *Hist. Chester*, ii. 20, 31.
3 *Rows of Chester*, ed. Brown, 156–64, 171–4, 176–85.
4 Hemingway, *Hist. Chester*, ii. 32–3.
5 Ibid. ii. 9.   6 Ibid. i. 423.
7 C.C.A.L.S., ZAB 4, ff. 217v.–218, 243 and v., 267.
8 Hemingway, *Hist. Chester*, ii. 12.
9 C.C.A.L.S., ZAB 4, ff. 320v., 357v.–358; ZAB 5, p. 98.
10 P. P. Burdett, *Map of Ches.* (1777).
11 Wood, *Map of Chester* (1833).
12 Hemingway, *Hist. Chester*, ii. 22–3; *P.N. Ches.* v (1:i), 72;

C.C.A.L.S., EDE, unsorted leases, 1754.
13 C.C.A.L.S., ZAB 6, pp. 169, 836, 868–70; ZTRP 2, pp. 320–3, 332–4, 361–2.
14 Hemingway, *Hist. Chester*, i. 421.
15 Burdett, *Map of Ches.* (1777); Hunter, *Plan of Chester* (1789).
16 Hanshall, *Hist. Co. Palatine*, map facing p. 13.
17 Burdett, *Map of Ches.* (1777).
18 *Georgian Chester*, ed. Kennett, 45; Hemingway, *Hist. Chester*, i. 420.
19 Hemingway, *Hist. Chester*, i. 425–6.

Harrison designed Dee Hills, a two-storeyed stuccoed villa, for Robert Baxter in 1814.[1]

South of the river, Handbridge contained mostly working-class housing by the early 19th century,[2] though still including Netherleigh, the moated mansion of the Cotgreave family on Eaton Road. Further out on Eaton Road was Greenbank, an impressive neo-classical house with a stuccoed front of two storeys and seven bays, built by Alderman J. S. Rogers in 1820.[3] Over to the west, Overleigh Hall, the home of the Cowper family, was purchased from their heir and demolished by the 2nd Earl Grosvenor *c.* 1830.[4]

THE COURTS

The growing subdivision of once grand town houses and the insertion of small dwellings into much of the available space, and especially into back gardens, gave rise in the city centre to slum courts[5] which came to pose a problem as severe as that in the region's industrial towns.[6] At the time of their greatest extent in the 1860s and 1870s, Chester had 178 courts lacking effective street frontage, generally with access only by a passage through other property. Although it is difficult to date precisely, such housing was probably built mostly between the earlier 18th century and the 1840s. Within the walls much dated from before 1789.[7] Building took place in back yards and gardens between Watergate Street and Commonhall Street,

behind Shoemakers' Row in Northgate Street, and in Lower Bridge and Castle Streets. In the 1790s and more especially in the early 19th century courts were built further from the main streets, for example north of Watergate Street off Goss, Crook, Trinity, and Princess Streets. A further group behind St. Olave and Duke Streets also seems to date from that period.[8] Within the walls only the north-eastern quarter had few courts, their development being inhibited by the cathedral precinct and the commercial value of sites along and behind Eastgate Street. Beyond the walls an extensive network of courts also developed on both sides of Foregate Street, and in the 19th century more were built in Boughton and behind Upper Northgate Street, and a few in Newtown. The largest number of later courts outside the city centre was in Handbridge.[9]

Court building reflected the surge in the city's population after 1800 and continued until effectively prohibited by the 1845 Chester Improvement Act. The owners of courts increased accommodation, particularly for migrants, by packing more people into existing properties, by subdividing the buildings, and by inserting new dwellings into the remaining open spaces. The population of the intramural parishes of St. Olave's, St. Michael's, and St Peter's, each with much court housing, peaked in 1821 and declined somewhat thereafter as the number of migrants faded and some residents found better accommodation elsewhere in the city.[10]

VICTORIAN AND EDWARDIAN, 1840–1914

Chester's appearance in 1914 had been largely determined by the new building and reconstruction of the previous seventy years. By then a remarkable modern commercial centre had been created, clothed in the antiquarian styles of the vernacular revival. There had also been considerable, if much less distinctive, suburban development, and on the rural fringes there was a scatter of middle-class villas and, towards the end of the period, terraced housing produced by speculative builders.

THE CITY CENTRE

The city centre was transformed between 1840 and 1914 by improvements to the street plan, the erection of a number of large public buildings, and above all by the rebuilding of many commercial

premises in the half-timbered styles of the vernacular revival.

To the south of the city the most significant alteration to the street plan was the building of Castle Drive in 1901 to provide an elegant link around the south side of the castle between Grosvenor Road and the Bridgegate.[11] In the south-east of the intramural area a small group of new streets was built on the former gardens of the Albion Hotel: Albion Place, Albion Street, and Volunteer Street were laid out in the mid 1860s[12] and Steele Street was added in the 1880s, partly on the site of Roberts' and Wilkinson's Courts.[13] All four streets had terraced working-class housing. The centrepiece of the area was the new Volunteer Drill Hall, erected by public subscription in 1869 at a cost of £2,500. Built of red sandstone in an 'Edwardian

1 Hemingway, *Hist. Chester*, i. 380, 415, 429.

2 Ormerod, *Hist. Ches.* i. 374; cf. below, this section (The Courts).

3 Hemingway, *Hist. Chester*, ii. 230–1; inf. sheet from W. Ches. Coll., Greenbank; date on bldg.

4 Ormerod, *Hist. Ches.* i. 374.

5 This subsection was contributed by Dr. J. Herson.

6 *Chester Chron.* 27 Dec. 1879. Plates 48–9, 51–2.

7 Hunter, *Plan of Chester* (1789); C.C.A.L.S., ZCR 574; O.S. Map 1/500, Ches. XXXVIII.11.17 (1875 edn.).

8 Wood, *Map of Chester* (1833).

9 Hunter, *Plan of Chester* (1789); Wood, *Map of Chester* (1833).

10 *V.C.H. Ches.* ii. 210–11; 8 & 9 Vic. c. 15 (Local and Personal), s. 64.

11 *Chester City Cl. Mins. 1901/2*, 37; *Browns and Chester*, 170.

12 R. K. Morriss, *Bldgs. of Chester*, 98; C.H.H., Perm. Corr. Howell: Drill Hall, 1981.

13 O.S. Map 1/2,500, Ches. XXXVIII.11 (1875, 1899 edns.).

FIG. 11. *An area of courtyard housing in the city centre, 1875*

castellated' style, it was for the use of the Chester Artillery and Rifle Volunteers. An extension of the building through to Duke Street in the 1900s resulted in the demolition of almshouses and two courts.[1] Only the front elevation survived in 2000.

St. Werburgh Street was converted after 1845 from a 'narrow and incommodious' street, 'occupied principally by deformed masses of unseemly buildings',[2] into a fitting approach to the cathedral. Its improvement began with the demolition of the old linen hall, by then dilapidated and used for warehousing and workshops.[3] Between 1867 and 1874 the dean and

1 C.H.H., Perm. Corr. Howell; *Kelly's Dir. Ches.* (1896), 191.
2 Hemingway, *Hist. Chester*, i. 411.

3 Ibid.; C.C.A.L.S., EDD 12/4; ibid. ZCCB 48; J. M'Gahey, [*Bird's Eye View of*] *Chester c. 1855* (reprinted 1971).

chapter and their lessee completely redeveloped the property opposite the cathedral,[1] while the entrance from Northgate Street was enlarged by demolition on the south side and setting back the frontage of the new King's school building of 1876 on the north side.[2] The transformation of St. Werburgh Street was completed in the mid 1890s by the widening of its southern end and the erection of John Douglas's spectacular range of half-timbered buildings on the eastern side.[3]

Major changes were made to central Northgate Street in the 1860s. In 1863 a new public market with an ornate baroque façade was opened adjacent to the site of the Exchange.[4] The building of the market coincided with the destruction of the Exchange by fire in 1862, and a competition was held for designs for a new town hall. It was won by W. H. Lynn (1829–1915) of Belfast, and his building, in 13th-century Gothic style with a central tower, steeply pitched tiled roofs, and corner turrets, was completed in 1869.[5]

In the west of the intramural area there were two notable developments. A barracks for the Cheshire Militia was built in the 1860s on the west side of Castle Esplanade on the site of the nunnery, an area which had remained largely undeveloped since the 17th century.[6] The Queen's school was built in 1882 on the site of the old city gaol in City Walls Road. Designed by E. A. Ould, a pupil of John Douglas, it was in 'Tudor Gothic' style with patterned brickwork.[7]

The formation of the Chester Archaeological Society in 1849 created a forum through which half-timbered vernacular revival styles of architecture were promoted in Chester.[8] An anonymous author in the society's *Journal* argued in 1857 for the retention of 'ancient landmarks', the restoration of old houses, and the erection of new ones 'after the same distinguishing type'.[9] The vernacular revival made its impact through the extensive rebuilding of city-centre premises between the 1850s and 1914, a process reflecting growth in Chester's service economy during the period. The rebuilding, bringing a distinctive style of architecture which established Chester's urban identity and accounted substantially for its popularity as a tourist destination in the 20th century, occurred in four main phases. The first, from 1850 to 1865, was clearly the result of Chester's mid-century economic boom. There was then a short flurry of activity c. 1873, linked possibly to the national economic upturn of the early 1870s. A third phase lasted from 1888 to 1902 and can be explained by Chester's somewhat improved

economic performance around the 1890s. A final spurt after 1909 was cut short by the First World War. Redevelopment was concentrated almost entirely in Eastgate and Bridge Streets in the first two phases but later spread to Northgate and Foregate Streets.[10] Watergate and Lower Bridge Streets, on the other hand, declined increasingly into picturesque decrepitude.[11]

The half-timbered revival in Chester was pioneered by the architect Thomas Mainwaring Penson (1818–64). His first building in the style was erected in 1852 in Eastgate Street and he was also responsible for the expansion of Browns' shop in 1857–8, a scheme which produced adjacent buildings of wildly differing styles, one proto-vernacular revival and the other 13th-century Gothic. In the earliest phase the half-timbered style was not universal, and was breached most notably by George Williams's classical stone building for the Chester Bank at the corner of Eastgate and St. Werburgh Streets. Williams and Penson, as well as James Harrison (1814–66) and to some extent Edward Hodkinson, were nevertheless instrumental in initiating the revival style in Chester, but in their work the styling lacked depth, the timbering was insubstantial, and the detailing was devoid of historical accuracy.[12]

The next generation of architects adopted a more scholarly and disciplined approach. The dominating figures were John Douglas (1830–1911) and Thomas Meakin Lockwood (1830–1900), but others, including H. W. Beswick, James Strong, W. M. Boden, and Thomas Edwards, were also active. The work of Lockwood, a local man much patronized by the Grosvenors, was perhaps best exemplified at the Cross. In 1888 he was responsible for one of the best known groups of vernacular revival buildings in Chester, no. 1 Bridge Street, on the eastern corner of Eastgate and Bridge Streets, and in 1892 he designed those on the opposite corner, between Bridge and Watergate Streets, a more eclectic composition with renaissance and baroque elements in stone and brick interwoven with half-timbering.[13]

An even more distinguished contribution was made by another architect much employed by the Grosvenors. John Douglas was perhaps the most successful exponent of the vernacular revival in Chester.[14] His work had a strong sense of craftsmanship and sensitivity to materials, exemplified by his best buildings in the city such as the east side of St. Werburgh Street (1895–9), Shoemakers' Row in Northgate Street

1 C.C.A.L.S., EDD 10/7/17; E. Hubbard, *Work of John Douglas*, 243–4; Harris, *Chester*, 55–6.

2 O.S. Map 1/2,500, Ches. XXXVIII.11 (1875, 1899 edns.); Harris, *Chester*, 67–8.

3 Hubbard, *Work of John Douglas*, 189–92.

4 *V.C.H. Ches.* v (2), Markets: General Produce Markets.

5 Ibid. Municipal Buildings: Exchange, Town Hall. Plate 26.

6 Harris, *Chester*, 114.   7 *V.C.H. Ches.* iii. 233.

8 What follows depends upon *Rows of Chester*, ed. Brown, 114–15, 124; *J.C.A.S.* [o.s.], i. 1–14.

9 *J.C.A.S.* [o.s.], i. 463–4; *Rows of Chester*, ed. Brown, 114.

10 Above, Late Georgian and Victorian Chester: Economy and Society (The Economy, 1841–70; The Economy, 1871–1914); *Rows of Chester*, ed. Brown, 114–30; *Chester Chron.* 9 May 1874; 18 Nov., 16 Dec. 1911; K. Goulborn and G. Jackson, *Chester: Portrait in Old Picture Postcards*, i (1987); ii (1988).

11 Ward, *Chester As It Was* (1980), 8–11, 19–20.

12 *Rows of Chester*, ed. Brown, 114, 117.

13 Ibid. 118–21. Plate 50.

14 Hubbard, *Work of John Douglas*, esp. 23–6.

(1899), and no. 38 Bridge Street.[1] Not all of Douglas's many buildings in Chester were in half-timbered style. Notable exceptions were the Grosvenor Club and North and South Wales Bank, Eastgate Street (1881–3), and the Cheshire county constabulary building, Foregate Street (1884), both of brick in a style derived from late medieval Flanders.[2] Equally distinguished, though modest in scale, was a terrace of houses in Bath Street dating from 1903 and built of sandstone with conical-roofed turrets. They combined with the Prudential Assurance building on Foregate Street, also of 1903, to produce an attractively irregular townscape.[3]

Besides new building, there was much 'restoration' of earlier half-timbered building in the city centre. James Harrison, for example, reconstructed God's Providence House, Watergate Street, in a fashion later found highly unsatisfactory by local antiquarians. T. M. Lockwood was responsible for the restoration of Bishop Lloyd's House (no. 41 Watergate Street) in 1899–1900, in the course of which major alterations were made to the façade and detailing. For its date it was nevertheless a reasonably sensitive piece of work which retained some notable interior features. The conservation movement in 19th-century Chester was still at a rudimentary stage and extensive archaeological remains were destroyed during redevelopment, often without being properly recorded.[4]

The vernacular revival in Chester was not without its critics, and the architect W. T. Lockwood made a determined, though ultimately unsuccessful stand against it. In 1910 he was responsible for the most controversial building erected in Chester for half a century, the St. Michael's Row development in Bridge Street for the duke of Westminster. The dramatic four-storeyed frontage, dubbed immediately 'the White City', utilized white and gold faience tiling and provoked a storm of hostility so severe that the duke bowed to the pressure and in 1911 ordered the whole façade to be demolished and replaced in half-timbered style. The resultant structure apparently appeased contemporary critics. By 1914 the vernacular revival had run its course in Chester, but by then the Victorian redevelopment of Eastgate Street, Northgate Street, and Bridge Street had transformed a nucleus of modest domestic brick and timber buildings into a shopping centre of metropolitan appeal.[5]

The rebuilding described above served to accentuate the contrast between the prosperous parts of the urban core and other areas of more limited growth or even decline.[6] Rating evidence for the later 19th century shows that Eastgate Street retained its place as the commercial heart of Chester and that Bridge

FIG. 12. *North and South Wales Bank and Grosvenor Club*

Street, Foregate Street, and Northgate Street also prospered. In each of the last three streets the number of separate premises diminished as small businesses were squeezed out by the expansion of bigger and more successful shops. Elsewhere the situation was quite different. Lower Bridge Street and Watergate Street experienced economic decline as property became increasingly subdivided, a process reflecting colonization by small, often marginal businesses needing cheap premises. In Frodsham Street development seems to have intensified as an offshoot from the central area because its location served customers from working-class suburbs in the north of the city. Overall, however, Chester's central area saw little absolute expansion in the 19th century. City Road, laid out in the 1860s to provide more convenient access to the railway station, would have been a natural line of growth if the commercial centre had been expanding, yet it developed only slowly and

1 Hubbard, *Work of John Douglas*, 166–7, 189–92, 196, 268–9, 272–3; *Rows of Chester*, ed. Brown, 121–4. Plate 53.
2 Hubbard, *Work of John Douglas*, 120–3, 251, 254.
3 Ibid. 192–3, 273.
4 *Rows of Chester*, ed. Brown, 115–16, 120; pers. comm. P. de

Figueiredo, conservation officer for Chester, Nov. 1994.
5 *Rows of Chester*, ed. Brown, 125–30.
6 Para. based on sources cited and arguments rehearsed above, Late Georgian and Victorian Chester: Economy and Society (The Economy, 1871–1914).

included few shops.[1] Landowners and developers preferred to invest in the old established core. The Grosvenors in particular had acquired much land in the city centre in the previous 150 years and were very active in the redevelopment of sites and buildings there between 1850 and 1914. In Bridge Street, for example, they were not only the biggest owners of both sites and buildings but their holdings were in the higher-value properties. The Grosvenor development of the St. Michael's Row arcade in 1910–11 markedly expanded Bridge Street's commercial area, though only half the shops had been let by July 1913.[2]

The attractiveness of the city centre for shopping and social intercourse was enhanced by the 1845 Chester Improvement Act, which gave the council stronger powers to repair and drain streets and set minimum road widths. It also clarified responsibilities for maintaining the Rows and footpaths.[3] With the opening of the public market building in 1863, markets and fairs were removed from the streets,[4] and other disreputable inheritances from the past were suppressed, such as the mug market in St. Werburgh Street.[5] The fortunes of Northgate Street were improved by the removal of the flesh shambles and the erection of the new town hall. Those changes allowed the creation of Market or Town Hall Square as a more formal incident in the progression of the street.[6] Its northern end was enhanced in 1911 by the erection of the fire station, designed by James Strong in half-timbered style.[7]

INDUSTRIAL BUILDINGS

Although Chester's industrial base remained relatively modest after 1840,[8] the city nevertheless developed areas with a Victorian industrial and urban character grafted rather incongruously on to the ancient core. Indeed, the city centre became ringed on its western, northern, and north-eastern sides by areas of industry, housing, and railways little different from those in the region's younger manufacturing cities and towns, while Saltney, straddling the Flintshire border, was Chester's own 'miniature Black Country'.[9]

The Gorse Stacks and Brook Street area was the main industrial centre on the edge of the older urban core, with foundries, engineering works, saw mills, tanneries, and a chemical works.[10] After 1875 the site of the Flookersbrook Foundry was occupied by the Hydraulic Engineering Co.; in the following thirty years, as the

firm attained its greatest prosperity, extensions were built backing on to Egerton Street. The Egerton Iron and Brass Foundry, operated by James Mowle & Co. in 1871 and Mowle and Meacock by 1892,[11] lay between Crewe Street and Albert Street, but had been demolished by 1910 when Egerton Street school was built on the site.[12] The Providence Iron and Brass Foundry of H. Lanceley and Son, founded in George Street around 1869, moved later to a group of mostly single-storeyed buildings on the west side of Brook Street previously used by a tannery. Egerton Street Saw Mill was a three-storeyed range incorporating offices at the street end and works with an arcaded ground floor at the rear, probably built in the mid 19th century; by 1906 it was occupied by paint manufacturers.[13]

In City Road the shoe factory of Collinson, Gilbert, & Co. was built between 1864 and 1866 as a four-storeyed building with elevations of ten bays and closely spaced windows to the north and east, in a style redolent of the early 19th century. At the northern end of the area lay extensive railway wagon works on both sides of Brook Street adjacent to General station.

In the later 19th century the view from Frodsham Street Bridge eastwards along the canal was dominated by the leadworks and a line of corn mills and related premises. Furthest east, the leadworks covered a large area by 1873 and had its own gas works and railway sidings.[14] The proprietor's house had extensive gardens on the west which were built over with terraced housing in the 1890s and 1900s. Further west again was Frosts' Steam Mill, a tall and dominating presence on the south bank of the canal. The mill acquired additional buildings in the later 19th century, at first on the west side of Steam Mill Street and then on the east side, the two parts being connected by a high-level bridge. The eastern additions, which were of three or more dates and had decorative architectural elevations to the north, were almost complete by 1873. The final additions appear to have been a south-east extension, demolished by 2000, and an office building of 1891 to the south-west.[15] Further west in Seller Street lay the Albion Mill. Founded in 1868–9, it included a long four-storeyed building of red brick with iron window frames. Nearer to the city centre was the Milton Street Mill (in 2000 the Chester Mill Hotel), the oldest part of which, with a tall chimney, was built in the 1850s. By 1873 a narrower six-storeyed block had been added to the west. Finally, nearest Frodsham Street Bridge lay

1 Harris, *Chester*, 167–70.
2 C.C.A.L.S., ZTRP 54, 2 May 1913; Eaton Hall, Estate Plan 26, Estate Bks. 2–186, 979–1071.
3 8 & 9 Vic. c. 15 (Local and Personal), esp. ss. 50–84, 96–107.
4 *V.C.H. Ches.* v (2), Markets: General Produce Markets.
5 *Chester Chron.* 15 Aug. 1874.
6 Harris, *Chester*, 57–60.
7 Ibid. 87; *Rows of Chester*, ed. Brown, 123.
8 Economic trends and individual industries and firms are discussed above, Late Georgian and Victorian Chester: Economy

and Society (The Economy, 1841–70; The Economy, 1871–1914).
9 *Chester Chron.* 5 July 1884.
10 Para. based on Hanshall, *Hist. Co. Palatine*, map facing p. 13; O.S. Map 1/2,500, Ches. XXXVIII.11 (1875, 1899 edns.).
11 *P. & G. Dir. Chester* (1871), 60; *Kelly's Dir. Ches.* (1892), 223.
12 *V.C.H. Ches.* v (2), Education: List of Schools.
13 C.C.A.L.S., ZTRP 42.
14 Para. based on O.S. Map 1/2,500, Ches. XXXVIII.11 (1875, 1899, 1911 edns.).
15 Date on bldg.

the Queen's Wharf premises of Griffiths Brothers which seem to have originated in the mid 19th century. They were expanded in the 1870s and again in 1912, and their gaunt five-storeyed buildings, with small iron-framed windows and loading gantries spanning the canal towpath, were a striking feature of the area.

The coming of the railway drastically altered the layout and physical appearance of the north and west side of Chester after 1840.[1] Two temporary stations of 1840 on each side of Brook Street were replaced in 1847–8 by an ornate Italianate building, still standing in 2000, which had a central two-storeyed range of fifteen bays between squat towers at the ends. The opening of Northgate station in 1875 represented a wasteful duplication of facilities. The building itself was dominated by a plain two-bay train shed incongruously open at the city end despite the fact that the station was a terminus.[2] The large, relatively undeveloped area of land absorbed by the railways formed a barrier which inhibited expansion in that direction.

CHURCHES AND CHAPELS

The city's ecclesiastical buildings were transformed in the Victorian period, not least the cathedral, to which George Gilbert Scott gave a wholly new external appearance, Gothic but clearly of the 19th century, between 1868 and 1876.[3] Its precinct was also much altered in the 1870s and 1880s, while St. John's was changed in appearance by the tidying of its ruinous east end in the 1870s and the collapse of its tower in 1881.

The most prestigious new churches and chapels, whichever denomination was responsible, were all Gothic in style, though sometimes eclectically so, and often built or faced in stone. In the city centre the Anglicans began the process of Gothicization with the complete rebuilding of St. Michael's in 1849–51 and Holy Trinity in 1864–9, and completed it towards the end of the period by demolishing neo-classical St. Bridget's in 1892. Already by the 1860s they were being emulated by the English Presbyterians in Newgate Street (1860), the Welsh Presbyterians in St. John Street (1866), and more modestly by the Primitive Methodists' first church in George Street (1863). In the following decade, city-centre churches in a variety of Gothic idioms were erected by the Roman Catholics (St. Francis, Grosvenor Street, 1873–5), the Congregationalists (Upper Northgate Street, 1875), and the Welsh Congregationalists (Albion Street, 1870).

Similar churches were put up in the wealthier new suburbs at much the same time. North of the centre the Anglicans built St. Thomas of Canterbury in Parkgate Road in 1869–72, and the Catholic Apostolics a church near by in Lorne Street in 1868; to the east, Roman Catholic St. Werburgh's (1873–5) and a Baptist church

(1880) dominated Grosvenor Park Road, while the Wesleyans built in City Road (1873); in Handbridge, St. Mary's (1887) was the most imposing of all the new churches and there was also a Congregational church of 1880. In the outer suburbs the Church of England built wholly Gothic new churches in Upton (1853–4), Hoole (1867), and Saltney (1893), while plainer churches with Gothic detailing were put up by the Wesleyans at Hough Green (1856), the Congregationalists and Primitive Methodists in the Tarvin Road/Christleton Road triangle (1873 and 1884), and the Primitive Methodists in Hoole (1903).

Two existing churches were Gothicized towards the end of the period: Christ Church, Newtown, in 1893–1900 (by John Douglas) and the Methodist chapel in St. John Street in 1906. Among the larger new buildings the only ones not in Gothic style were perhaps significantly both completed for Welsh congregations: the neo-classical Presbyterian Church of Wales in City Road (1865), replacing the demolished Octagon chapel, and the neo-Romanesque Wesleyan church in Queen Street (1884). John Douglas's remodelling of St. Paul's, Boughton, was in his own characteristic vernacular revival style.

Among the smaller and less wealthy denominations, and in purely working-class districts, chapel-building was much more modest. Examples of plain brick boxes included the Welsh Congregationalist chapel of 1860 in Back Brook Street and the Ebenezer Strict Baptist chapel of 1882 in Milton Street. Several were later swept away in favour of larger Gothic structures, or given up to other users as the congregations which built them became more established. The mission chapels, which existed in some numbers as different denominations evangelized new areas, were commonly temporary structures of corrugated iron. Two that survived, both Congregational, were those in Walker Street, Hoole (1894), and Whipcord Lane (1909). Brethren, Mormons, Swedenborgians, Spiritualists, Christian Scientists, Jews, and others worshipped in converted premises without making much impact on Chester's fabric before 1914.

RESIDENTIAL DEVELOPMENT

The 1840s saw a decline in the rate of house building in Chester, in line with national trends. In the 1850s, however, the city's housing stock increased by a fifth, the sharpest rise in the whole of the 19th century, a deviation from the national pattern stimulated by local prosperity. The 1860s witnessed much house building but a sharp decline set in after 1871 and lasted until the 1890s, perhaps a response to the city's economic downturn in the same period. The relative upsurge of the 1890s was not fully sustained after 1901 and house

1 Para. based on details given in *V.C.H. Ches.* v (2), Railways.
2 S. Nichols, *Chester in Old Photographs* (1993), 84; P. Bolger, *Ches. Lines Cttee.: Illustrated Hist.*
3 This section was contributed by C. P. Lewis, based on

details given in *V.C.H. Ches.* v (2), Medieval Parish Churches; Modern Parish Churches; Roman Catholicism; Protestant Non-conformity; Other Churches; Cathedral and Close: Cathedral Church from 1541. Plates 15–16 for the cathedral.

completions virtually ceased in Chester between 1909 and 1919, a reflection of the national picture but in an extreme form.[1]

The Courts. Chester's mid-century boom brought another wave of migrants crowding into the courts, the population of which probably reached its maximum in the 1860s, when they housed *c.* 5,500 people or 17 per cent of the city's population.[2] By the late 1870s the 'core of rottenness' which they represented was becoming the subject of debate. Although the appalling conditions of court dwellers concerned middle-class observers, the courts were also feared as 'foul and filthy dens, the resorts of thieves, prostitutes, and drunkards'.[3] Action to clear them was, nevertheless, intermittent before 1914. The establishment of the public health committee in 1872 and the appointment of a medical officer of health in 1873 presaged some activity, and a further impetus was given in 1892 by the formation of the Chester Cottage Improvement Co., in which the duke of Westminster took a leading role.[4] Although by 1894 twenty courts containing 186 houses had been cleared, five closed, and nine improved, the remainder were further overcrowded through the rehousing of those displaced, probably over 1,000 people.[5] By 1908 a further thirty courts, containing 166 houses, had been removed, while eight had been replaced by new housing.[6]

Although action to clear slum courts was taken under the 1875 Public Health Act and later legislation, the most powerful motive for their removal was the potential of their sites for commercial redevelopment. Those in St. Olave Street were an exception, replaced by new housing and a school.[7] Most of the other courts removed from within the walls and around Foregate Street succumbed to commercial development, including those behind Shoemakers' Row in Northgate Street (1899–1902),[8] and Allen's Court at the Bars (1910); Valentine's Court in Northgate Street was replaced by a new fire station in 1911.[9] Relatively few disappeared from the south-western quadrant inside the walls, an indication of the area's depressed character in the 19th century. In Handbridge, courts were cleared from Grosvenor land to make way for St. Mary's church (1887) and new housing in Hugh Street.[10] Even so, in 1912 some 2,636 people still lived in the 660 court houses which remained, and their death rate was 23.9 per 1,000, compared with a city average of 15.2.[11]

The Suburbs.[12] Chester's suburban development between 1840 and 1914 was very piecemeal and in many areas building took place over a long period. The city's revived prosperity prompted a building boom until the early 1870s, mainly of modest terraced housing for artisans and the lower middle classes and of villas for the wealthy. The economic downturn thereafter limited the growth of exclusive suburbs, however, and some schemes begun in mid century developed only slowly in late Victorian and Edwardian times. Although smaller houses continued to be built, they were supplemented by areas of larger terraced housing for the more prosperous middle classes, including people travelling to work in neighbouring towns and cities.

The constraints imposed by the river Dee and its meadows meant that most suburban development took place in an arc to the north, north-east, and east of the walls or across the river at Handbridge, Queen's Park, Curzon Park, and Saltney. The northern suburbs were predominantly of terraced housing while those to the south and east of the river generally contained more spacious properties. The following account traces their development in approximately chronological order, examining first those started in the mid 19th century and secondly those whose main growth was later.

In the eastern suburbs, the most significant change was the laying out of City Road from the railway station to the Bars in the early 1860s. Although intended as a grand approach to Chester, it came to be lined with hotels, two chapels, a theatre, and miscellaneous commercial buildings; development was slow and the overall effect somewhat unimpressive.[13] Near by lay the main residential development on the already crowded northern side of Foregate Street: Parker's Buildings, a three-storeyed range of workers' flats put up by the Northern Counties Housing Association in 1890, from designs by John Douglas, on the site of Seller & Co.'s brewery.[14]

On the southern side of Foregate Street the paddocks on the high ground above the river were preserved as an open area by the laying out of Grosvenor Park between 1867 and 1874.[15] On their northern edge and

1 *Census*, 1841–1911; J. P. Lewis, *Building Cycles and Britain's Growth*, 62, 66–70, 106–41, 205–10; C.C.A.L.S., ZDH 2/5 (1919).

2 C.C.A.L.S., ZDH 2/4–5 (1910, 1911, 1912, 1919); D. R. Savage, 'Working Class Standards of Living in Chester, 1870–1914' (Durham Univ. B.A. dissertation, 1990: copy at C.H.H.), 40–2; *Chester Chron.* 29 Nov. to 27 Dec. 1879; 10 Feb. 1894.

3 *Chester Chron.* 29 Nov. 1879.

4 Savage, 'Working Class Standards of Living', 40; G. Huxley, *Victorian Duke: Life of Hugh Lupus Grosvenor, First Duke of Westminster*, 146.

5 *Chester Chron.* 10 Feb. 1894.

6 C.C.A.L.S., ZDH 2/4 (1908).

7 O.S. Map 1/2,500, Ches. XXXVIII.11 (1875, 1899 edns.); *Chester Chron.* 27 Dec. 1879.

8 *Rows of Chester*, ed. Brown, 120–3.

9 C.C.A.L.S., ZDH 2/4 (1911); Harris, *Chester*, 87.

10 Harris, *Chester*, 148.

11 C.C.A.L.S., ZDH 2/5 (1912).

12 Section based, except where stated otherwise, on O.S. Map 1/2,500, Ches. XXXVIII.11, 14–15 (1875, 1899, 1911 edns.); above, Late Georgian and Victorian Chester: Economy and Society. See map, below, p. 240.

13 Harris, *Chester*, 167–70.

14 Hubbard, *Work of John Douglas*, 166–7, 258.

15 *V.C.H. Ches.* v (2), Open Spaces and Parks: Public Parks.

on the gardens behind the Foregate Street frontage, smaller houses were put up, including to the west of Love Street a small estate of 1898–1900 belonging to the Chester Cottage Improvement Co. The main developments, however, were further east, where Grosvenor Park Road was built in the early 1870s to provide access to the new park, and Bath Street was cut in 1901 to link up with Union Street and the new swimming baths. Both contained terraces by John Douglas.[1] South of the park, by the river, the Groves were improved in the early 1880s and the 1900s to become one of Chester's leading tourist attractions.[2] From 1867 they included the bishop's palace, established in the Archdeacon's House at the foot of Souters Lane; the house was extended to include a Gothic chapel and three additional bays to the west in the style of the original building.[3] East of Grosvenor Park, Dee Hills, an estate of 10 acres, was by the 1850s being broken up by its owner, William Titherington of Liverpool, who was responsible at the eastern end for Sandown Terrace, three large Italianate houses, and at the south-west corner for Deva Terrace, a prominent group of smaller, plainer houses on the river bank. In 1873 Dee Hills still had extensive grounds with pleasure gardens above the river and a tree-lined drive from the Bars, flanked by paddocks to the north and kitchen gardens to the south-east. Land was being sold for building in the 1880s and by the end of the century the terraces of Beaconsfield Street had been built over the northern part of the paddocks, and larger houses lined the drive, now named Dee Hills Park. One of the largest was the four-storeyed Uffington House, designed by E. A. Ould for Thomas Hughes in 1885.[4] By 1892 Dee Hills House and the remaining gardens had been sold to the government and the house was being used as the residence of the Army's district commander.[5]

Newtown was the most extensive suburb to develop north of the walled city before 1870. When the railway arrived in 1840 the area north of St. Anne Street was largely fields and kitchen gardens,[6] but Trafford, Gloucester, and Cornwall Streets had been laid out before 1833.[7] In Newtown small terraced houses were built without front or back gardens but after 1845 with individual yards and back access. Employment on the railways was undoubtedly part of the reason for the rapid development of the area, though the railway companies apparently did not themselves provide

workers' housing. Further working-class terraces were built east of Brook Street, where development was restricted by the L.N.W.R. wagon repair works and the laying out of City Road in the early 1860s. The area between Egerton Street and City Road was covered with terraced housing by the early 1870s, after which it spread east of City Road on to the leadworks garden, sold off for building in the 1890s.[8]

More exclusive suburbs began to develop after 1840 along Liverpool Road to the north of the city and at Queen's Park and Curzon Park south of the river. Most of the land on either side of the Parkgate and Liverpool roads as far as the Bache boundary belonged to the dean and chapter and was known as the Bailiwick estate. After 1845, as a consequence of the Cathedrals Act of 1840, it passed to the Ecclesiastical Commissioners, who began to sell building plots on which covenants controlled the value and nature of development.[9] It became an attractive area for suburban villas, and development before the early 1870s was almost exclusively of substantial houses set in large gardens. The area became a rival to the leafy suburbs south of the Dee and largely retained that character until 1914. Its bisection in 1890 by the Northgate–Shotton railway and Liverpool Road station,[10] however, led to some undermining of its status, and building east of Liverpool Road and north of Brook Lane between 1890 and 1914 was mainly of terraces and semi-detached houses.[11]

South of the river Chester's mid-century prosperity encouraged the promotion of two exclusive suburbs, Curzon Park and Queen's Park. Although access had been improved by the opening of Grosvenor Bridge in 1832, it was the advent of the Chester–Saltney railway which prompted Earl Howe to develop Curzon Park in the mid 1840s on land formerly farmed from Brewer's Hall between Hough Green and the river.[12] It was hoped that Liverpool merchants would be attracted to the estate,[13] but most of the early householders were Chester merchants or professional men.[14] The first house, Highfield, was built in 1847, and by 1851 there was a line of nine large detached houses along the top of the river cliff, from where they had extensive views across the city. Three others had been built near the entrance to the estate.[15] South of Curzon Park a strip of land in corporation ownership ran along the north side of Hough Green from the Curzon Park entrance to Saltney, and after 1850 it was auctioned in individual plots. Building was rapid, and by 1861 a

1 Harris, *Chester*, 159–60; Hubbard, *Work of John Douglas*, 193–4, 250, 273.

2 Harris, *Chester*, 145; Goulborn and Jackson, *Chester in Old Postcards*, i (1987), 76; *V.C.H. Ches.* v (2), Open Spaces and Parks: The Groves.

3 *J.C.A.S.* xxxvii. 71.

4 Pevsner, *Ches.* 173.

5 *Kelly's Dir. Ches.* (1892), 190, 198.

6 Hughes, *Stranger's Handbk.* (1856), 10; Hanshall, *Hist. Co. Palatine*, map facing p. 13.

7 Wood, *Map of Chester* (1833).

8 Hoddinott, *Leadworks*, 6–7.

9 C.C.A.L.S., EDD 12/4; ibid. ZD/PB 1; ZD/PB 16.

10 *V.C.H. Ches.* v (2), Railways.

11 O.S. Map 1/2,500, Ches. XXXVIII.7, 11 (1899, 1911 edns.).

12 N. T. Thomas, 'Curzon Park', 11–12 (unpubl. material generously made available by the author).

13 *Chester Courant*, 27 Sept. 1846.

14 R. Scott, 'Victorian Suburb: Development of Hough Green, Chester' (Chester Coll. dissertation for Diploma in Landscape Design, 1982), 20.

15 P.R.O., HO 107/2171, f. 850.

line of thirty smaller detached and semi-detached villas stretched for half a mile along the road.[1] Development of the intervening wedge of land in Curzon Park was much slower. Some houses were built on Park Road (later Curzon Park South) after 1870, and by 1914 the eastern end of the wedge was largely developed,[2] but the western end remained empty. The early years of the 20th century also saw the building of large detached houses south of Hough Green along the tree-lined Westminster Avenue, and of terraced housing on the southern edge of Handbridge. Late in 1913 the council appointed Patrick Abercrombie as planner for its first large estate of working-class housing, south of Hough Green on an estate initially named Buddicom Park from its previous owner, Mr. H. Buddicom, but the realization of the scheme had to wait until after the war.[3]

Suburban development at Saltney contrasted greatly with that close by in Hough Green and Curzon Park. Following the arrival of the railway and Henry Wood's anchor works in 1846–7,[4] small terraced houses were built adjacent to the railway north and south of Chester Street and on both sides of the county boundary. The names of Wood Street and Cable, Anchor, and Chainmaker Rows reflected Wood's ownership of much of the property.[5]

East of Dee Bridge a suspension bridge was opened in 1852 to serve a residential development at Queen's Park which was promoted by Enoch Gerrard.[6] Building there was slow, however, and only four villas and two semi-detached pairs had been built by 1873. By 1910 the total had still reached only 17, and although a further 10 houses had been built on St. George's Crescent to the south,[7] the experience there and at Curzon Park suggests that the demand for exclusive property in Chester was smaller than the number of sites on offer. On the southern edge of Queen's Park some smaller semi-detached houses had appeared in the mid 19th century around Victoria Pathway. Elsewhere, a few villas were built east of the river on Dee Banks, including a pair completed in 1869 by John Douglas.[8] Further infilling occurred in the area *c.* 1897, including two more houses by Douglas,[9] and in 1896 he built a large house, Walmoor Hill, for his own use, dramatically exploiting the steeply sloping site above the river.[10]

After 1870 the most extensive area of terraced housing built within the city boundary lay between Sealand and Parkgate Roads. The district was bisected by the canal. The eastern part, between the canal and Parkgate Road, was known as Garden Lane from the road which ran diagonally across it from near the Blue Coat School towards Blacon. Before 1860 it was little developed except for isolated buildings along the banks of the canal, on Garden Lane itself, and a substantial terrace in Lorne Street,[11] but by 1873 small terraced houses had been built along part of Garden Lane, in Garden Terrace, and on Orchard Street. The main development took place between then and 1898, by which time most of the land south of Cheyney Road was built up, with larger terraced houses towards the east, where the land rose quite steeply to Parkgate Road, and smaller houses lower down.

West of the canal, Whipcord Lane ran along the bottom of another steep rise which commanded extensive views towards the Welsh hills and on which two pairs of large houses had been built in the mid 19th century. A small estate of two-storeyed red-brick terraced houses was built in the late 1870s and 1880s towards its southern end, between Whipcord Lane and Sealand Road. The largest and earliest were on Sealand Road,[12] and after them Gladstone Avenue and Catherine Street were built before the central Vernon Road, which took the name of the developer, William Vernon, a builder and contractor of Upper Northgate Street.[13] The completion of the area west of the canal waited until the 1890s, when the narrow Upper Cambrian Road was extended northwards, behind Whipcord Lane and parallel to the canal, and terraced houses were built in Granville and Gladstone Roads. Larger properties were erected at the same time on the adjacent part of Whipcord Lane. At the south end of the area a terrace of twelve houses facing Crane Wharf was put up by the Chester Cottage Improvement Co. probably in 1895. They were the model for Chester's first council houses which were built near by on the south side of Tower Road in 1901–4.[14]

At the other end of the city, many terraces were built at Boughton in the late 19th century. Proximity to the river, and, for some, fine southerly views across the valley, were probably the reason for the building earlier of a number of large and middling houses in the area. By *c.* 1850 the north side of the road for some distance east of Hoole Lane was almost continuously built up, partly with detached houses in grounds and partly with short terraces. Further out many of the houses on the road frontages were smaller but behind them were detached houses and small villas set in orchards and

1 Scott, 'Hough Green', 20, 30.   2 Ibid. 17.
3 *Chester City Cl. Mins. 1912/13*, 740–1; *1913/14*, 108–9 and later indexed refs. to Housing.
4 Above, Late Georgian and Victorian Chester: Economy and Society (The Economy, 1841–70).
5 *Saltney and Saltney Ferry: Third Illustrated Hist.* (1992), 1, 6–11.
6 Hughes, *Stranger's Handbk.* (1856), 39.
7 *Kelly's Dir. Ches.* (1910).

8 Hubbard, *Work of John Douglas*, 5.
9 Ibid. 268; datestone on no. 9 Dee Banks.
10 Hubbard, *Work of John Douglas*, 7–8.
11 *White's Dir. Ches.* (1860), 131.
12 Datestone, 1878.
13 *Chester City Cl. Mins. 1898/9*, 541; *Kelly's Dir. Ches.* (1896), 236.
14 Above, Late Georgian and Victorian Chester: City Government, 1835–1914 (Council Policies and Activities).

gardens. The character of the area, affected since 1800 by the proximity of the leadworks, was further undermined in the mid 1860s by the construction of the water company's reservoir, filter beds, and water tower.[1] The nature of development changed thereafter. Terraces of smaller houses were built before 1873 off Spital Walk between Boughton and the canal but the main development of similar property on the north side of Tarvin Road and between there and Christleton Road occurred in streets built between 1873 and 1908. North of the canal a cramped site at Station View, hemmed in by the canal, the leadworks, and the railway, was densely built up in stages until the 1900s, partly to house railway and canal workers.

In the later 19th century Chester's suburbs were extended into Hoole, north-east of the railway station and outside the city boundary. There had already been some development of villas and smaller houses north of Hoole Road in Flookersbrook, but the arrival of the railway in 1840 produced a Victorian suburb of considerable diversity and with an ambiguous relationship to the city as a whole. Development began in the 1850s, and from a nucleus around Faulkner Street areas of relatively modest terraced housing spread south-westwards in the late 19th century towards the L.N.W.R. goods yard and across Hoole Road towards the G.W.R. goods and engine sheds. Higher-quality development extended in the opposite direction, especially after Charles Brown helped to push through the Flookersbrook Improvement Act of 1876; housing in that area catered both for Chester's own middle classes and for those travelling by train to work elsewhere.[2]

1 *V.C.H. Ches.* v (2), Public Utilities: Water.

2 *Browns and Chester*, 168–9.

TWENTIETH-CENTURY CHESTER 1914–2000

CENTRAL government became increasingly involved in the administration of Chester after 1914. Its involvement was the creative force which determined the direction and level of social and environmental change. Small towns such as Chester tended to suffer from the 'politics of the rates', which meant that local politics were reactive, not dynamic. Most ratepayers were concerned primarily with keeping rates low, with the result that local government alone was unable to fund the creation of a healthy, beautiful, or culturally stimulating urban environment. In particular, the problems and opportunities associated with Chester's special status as a historic city would not have been addressed without funding from central government. It was difficult at first to persuade Chester city council of the need to preserve the city's historic environment, because conservation cost money, and the preservation of old buildings or archaeological sites could interfere with more obviously profitable commercial developments. For many years the dilemma was presented to Cestrians as a choice between incompatible opposites rather than as a unique opportunity. They were asked whether Chester was to become 'a dead museum piece rather than a living, dynamic city', not how they could capitalize on the survival of the physical evidence of its past. The prevailing attitude before the 1960s can be summed up by the mayor's declaration in 1955 that 'we are not a lot of old fogies living on our traditions'.[1]

The difficulty in nurturing civic pride was compounded because many Cestrians lived in suburbs outside the county borough; although they were provided with services by the city council they paid rates to the county. The city within the walls alone retained some coherence, but the dominance of retailing interests there made it difficult to provide an effective cultural focus for the urban area as a whole. The problem was highlighted after 1974, when the county borough was merged with the outlying suburbs and an extensive rural area as one local authority. By then, however, Chester had begun to benefit from recon-

ciling environmental enhancement with economic self-interest, through a growing recognition at all levels that the location of new businesses and the encouragement of tourists and shoppers depended on the attractiveness of the built environment.

Meanwhile the city's economic base had been transformed, in part through the development of its long-standing role as a regional centre.[2] In 1914 Chester was an old-fashioned and declining county town, with a stagnant population, moribund traditional craft industries, and some mid-Victorian heavy engineering. Although it attracted a few modern factories between the First and Second World Wars, the rising prosperity and growing suburbs of that period depended as much on industrial employment elsewhere in the region and on the provision of services, including high-quality shopping, for people living beyond the city. Those developments were qualified by severe national economic difficulties and by the fact that until the 1950s the city centre was disfigured by slum housing and semi-derelict areas such as Lower Bridge Street and Watergate Street. From the 1960s, however, Chester's economic fortunes and physical appearance were revived in tandem by the consolidation and then the massive extension of the city's importance as a shopping centre, by the accumulation of other types of service jobs, especially in the public and financial sectors, and by the rise of tourism. Economic growth was accompanied by a pioneering and highly successful conservation of the city centre's historic fabric in the wake of the Insall Report of 1968. Although parts of the city, notably the largest council estate, Blacon, were blighted by all the characteristics of late 20th-century social deprivation, Chester as a whole was very prosperous. By the 1980s it was widely regarded as 'the Surrey of the North',[3] and it was symptomatic of Chester's image at the end of the 20th century that in 1995 a glamorous new television soap opera, *Hollyoaks*, was set in a fictional suburb modelled on Handbridge and filmed in and around the city.[4]

1 *Ches. Observer*, 28 May 1955; C.C.A.L.S., ZCA 11.
2 This para. was contributed by C. P. Lewis.
3 e.g. *The Times*, 19 Oct. 1989.
4 *Independent on Sunday*, 22 Oct. 1995, p. 5.

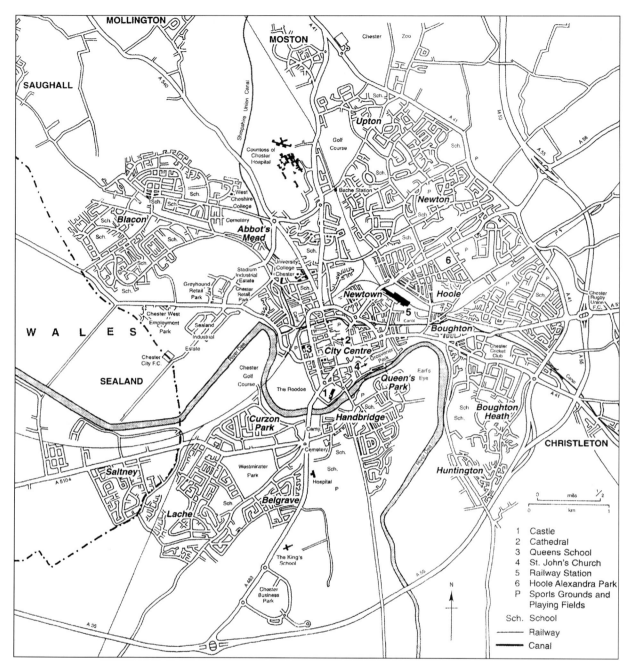

FIG. 13. *Chester, 2000*

CHESTER AND THE FIRST WORLD WAR

The 1st Battalion of the Cheshire Regiment, in Ireland when war was declared, was sent straight to France to fight at Mons. Within three weeks there were 800 casualties among the 1,000-strong battalion, and hospital trains full of the wounded began to arrive at Chester. The city was then the headquarters of Western Command and the principal recruiting centre for Cheshire; troops were enlisted and trained in camps within or around the city and mass meetings were held at the town hall to persuade men to volunteer for military service.[1] The Army requisitioned the Roodee for training, and from 1915 the races were discontinued.[2] Normal political activity was also suspended. In 1916 the city's Unionist M.P. resigned, and his

1 F. W. Longbottom, *Chester in Gt. War; Images of Eng.: Ches. Regiment,* comp. R. Barr (2000), 34–5.

2 *Ches. Observer,* 8 Aug. 1914; R. J. Barr, '1st Battalion, 22nd

(Ches.) Regiment and Military Disaster at Mons', *Ches. Hist.* xxxv. 78–88; *Chester City Cl. Mins. 1913/14,* 665–6, 745; *1914/15,* 68, 206, 311, 340–2; *1915/16,* 117, 227.

replacement, Sir Owen Philipps, took his seat without a contest.[1] The mayor, John Frost, remained in office for six successive years from 1913, and was knighted in 1918 for his services to the city.[2]

Because so many men joined the armed services, industry was soon short of labour, and men were sought from the surrounding districts, especially for the large new munitions factory built by the government in 1915 at Queensferry (Flints.).[3] By 1917 some 3,000 munitions workers had come to live in the already overcrowded city.[4] Although the government encouraged women to take work, the corporation was reluctant to employ them, using them only as lamp-lighters and tram conductors, and dismissing its female employees in 1919.[5] Working women were blamed for the rise in the infantile death rate to an all-time recorded high of 106.9 per 1,000 live births in 1916, although it was acknowledged that overcrowded living conditions were partly responsible.[6] Inflation was a further cause of hardship, particularly to those reliant on poor-law relief or Army allowances. By early 1916 the board of poor-law guardians thought that there had been a 40 per cent increase in the cost of living since the war began. The reasons were little understood, and food price rises were blamed on profiteers.[7] The presence of many troops and the greater freedom for women led to some relaxation in socially acceptable standards of behaviour. There was no support for prohibition, but licensing restrictions were introduced.[8] For fear of air raids the street lights were extinguished at night, the blackout being blamed for the 'disgraceful conduct of young girls in the Rows'.[9]

Men and women not directly engaged in war work were drawn into voluntary activities such as entertaining servicemen and auxiliary nursing of war wounded in the military hospitals which were set up in the workhouse, at Sealand, and in private residences, including Eaton Hall.[10] There were many fund-raising events, and several voluntary organizations came together as the Council of Social Welfare. Much of the work fell upon women.[11] The most important organization for men was the Chester Volunteer Regiment, a home-guard unit given official recognition in 1915 and active until the end of the war.[12]

In 1918 American soldiers began to arrive in the city and baseball matches were held to make them feel welcome. Despite the onset of the 'Spanish' influenza epidemic, peace was celebrated 'exuberantly', with huge bonfires.[13] Mayor Frost placed a roll of honour in the town hall for the 771 Chester citizens killed in action, and Dean Bennett successfully urged the donation of memorial stained-glass windows to the cathedral. The council chose as the official war memorial a red sandstone cross designed by Royson and Crossley, an Oxford firm with strong Chester connexions.[14] There was some difficulty in raising sufficient funds by public subscription, but in 1922 the cross was erected on a site south of the cathedral, facing St. Werburgh Street. It was unveiled by two mothers, one of whom had lost three of her four sons, and the other, four of six.[15] Remembrance Day services were held there or inside the cathedral until 1929, after which they took place outside the town hall.[16] The honorary freedom of the city was accepted by Sir David Beattie, Sir Douglas Haig, and Lloyd George, but President Wilson declined.[17]

THE ECONOMY, 1918–39

In 1919 the medical officer of health described Chester as 'chiefly residential', though he also noted the presence of industry within and just outside the city limits.[18] The city's dependence on visitors, whether shoppers or tourists, was highlighted in 1920 by the *Daily Despatch*, which described Chester as 'a trip town' with 'more shops than houses', and claimed

that it served Wirral, Staffordshire, Shropshire, and south Lancashire.[19] Although the description was exaggerated, Chester's prosperity certainly depended heavily on the wealth and diversity of a large agricultural and industrial hinterland and on its ability to attract those living there to its shops, markets, and financial services. Railway communications were good,

1 *Brit. Parl. Election Results, 1885–1918*, ed. F. W. S. Craig (1989), 96.

2 Burke, *Peerage* (1931), 2683.

3 *Ches. Observer*, 26 June 1915; cf. ibid. 20 Aug. 1921.

4 Ibid. 4 Aug. 1917.

5 Ibid. 18 Dec. 1915; 21 Jan. 1917; *Chester City Cl. Mins. 1914/15*, 317, 569; *1918/19*, 424–6, 440.

6 *Annual Rep. of Medical Officer of Health* (1916): copies in C.C.A.L.S., ZDH 2/5, and bound with copy of *Chester City Cl. Mins. 1915/16* at C.H.H.; *Ches. Observer*, 20 Sept. 1916.

7 *Ches. Observer*, 9 Sept. 1916.

8 Ibid. 8 Aug., 5 Sept. 1914.

9 Ibid. 12 Feb. 1916; 26 Jan. 1918.

10 Ibid. 27 Jan., 17 Mar. 1917; *Chester City Cl. Mins. 1914/15*, 441.

11 *Ches. Observer*, 30 Jan. 1915.

12 Ibid. 9 Jan. 1915; 6 Dec. 1918.

13 Ibid. 26 Oct., 16 Nov. 1918; *Annual Rep. of M.O.H.* (1919); Longbottom, *Chester in Gt. War*, 22; cf. *Chester City Cl. Mins. 1918/19*, 53, 252, 285, 319, 344, 355–6.

14 *Ches. Observer*, 18 Oct. 1919; 9 Apr. 1921; A. Bruce, 'Oxford War Memorial: Thomas Rayson and Chester Connection', *Oxoniensia*, lvi. 155–68.

15 *Ches. Observer*, 21 Jan. 1921; 27 May 1922.

16 Ibid. 16 Nov. 1929.

17 Longbottom, *Chester in Gt. War*, 24, 27; *Chester City Cl. Mins. 1918/19*, 170–1.

18 *Annual Rep. of M.O.H.* (1919).

19 *Ches. Observer*, 13 Mar. 1920; cf. C.C.A.L.S., ZCLB 19, brief.

providing links with industrial south Lancashire, the Midlands, and north Wales.[1] The railway companies were also the main employers of male labour, with a workforce of 1,160 men in the city in 1921.[2] Several main roads also converged on Chester, and although the railway was still an important factor in locating industry within the city, as well as for carrying people to work outside it, trains became less significant as the use of motor vehicles increased. The General Strike in 1926 heightened people's perceptions of the trend and perhaps encouraged its intensification.[3]

By 1939 commercial use of the canal had ended and Chester had long ceased to be a busy seaport, though Crane Wharf was occasionally visited by seagoing ships until the 1940s. The Dee remained important to the region because of the docks at Connah's Quay and Mostyn and the wharf at Shotton steelworks, all in Flintshire, but Chester did not support any of the many schemes for improving navigation. The council opposed anything which it thought would attract further manufacturing industry to the city or diminish its attractions for visitors and shoppers.[4] It also resisted flood prevention schemes which might have necessitated the loss of its hydroelectricity works at the weir.[5]

The service sector created much employment in the city, notably in transport and the retail trades, but also in hotels and catering, domestic service, the professions, and public administration.[6] Between the World Wars half of all jobs for men, and three quarters or more of those for women, were in services. For men, the largest single area was transport (17–18 per cent of all men's jobs), followed by shops and financial services (rising to 13 per cent in 1931). Female employment was concentrated in domestic service (40 per cent) and shop work (15–17 per cent). The most important areas of expansion, for men and women alike, were in retailing and office work. That included employment in the public sector, which was reinforced by the county council's decision in the early 1930s to remain in Chester, where a new county hall adjoining the castle was begun shortly before the Second World War.[7] There were also economic benefits from remaining a cathedral city and a military town with a large

staff of officers at Western Command.[8] Chester's prestige in educational matters was preserved when Bishop Geoffrey Fisher saved Chester Diocesan Training College from closure in 1933.[9]

With its good rail communications and favourable labour situation, Chester also had advantages for manufacturing. The firm of Pratt Levick & Co., which made precision-ground instruments, gave as a further reason for setting up in Chester the fact that it was 'a nice place to live', an early indication of awareness of the wider urban environment. There were factories within the county borough, in a belt stretching from Boughton in the east, across the north of the city, to Saltney in the west,[10] and the manufacturing sector, including the building trades, employed over 7,000 men and 1,000 women between the World Wars, accounting for over 45 per cent of men's jobs and *c.* 15 per cent of women's.[11] Metal workers in a wide variety of trades were more numerous than any other group, largely because by 1921 Shotton steelworks employed over 1,000 of the city's residents.[12] The foremost of several engineering firms within the county borough was Williams and Williams, makers of metal window frames and other products, who employed 1,200 in 1939. The council became increasingly uneasy about the impact of its factory on the environment, and created difficulties when the firm wished to expand on its existing site at Grange Road, off Brook Lane.[13]

Advised on planning and land use by Patrick Abercrombie, professor of civic design at the University of Liverpool, the city council adhered to a policy of concentrating on Chester's residential, commercial, and recreational roles, while hoping that the city would profit from the growth of industry outside its boundaries.[14] The hope was realistic: in 1921 over 3,000 Cestrians already worked outside Chester,[15] and the uncongested riverside sites on Deeside and at Ellesmere Port were ideal for the very large manufacturing and processing plants typical of much early 20th-century industrial development. The council's development and advertising committee gave a lukewarm welcome to enquiries from industry about

1 *V.C.H. Ches.* v (2), Railways.

2 *Census*, 1921, *Industry*, pp. 338–82, esp. 370.

3 *Chester Chron.* 15 May 1926.

4 J. Herson, 'Canals, Rlys. and Demise of Port of Chester', *'Where Deva Spreads her Wizard Stream': Trade and Port of Chester*, ed. P. Carrington, 85–6; *Chester Canal Boat Rally, 1972*, 20 (copy at C.H.H.); *Chester and River Dee*, ed. A. M. Kennett, 11.

5 C.C.A.L.S., ZCCB 41, p. 323; *Ches. Observer*, 31 Jan. 1914.

6 Para. based on *Census*, 1921, *Ches.* pp. 58–73 (Chester), 77 (Hoole); 1921, *Industry*, pp. 338–82; 1931, *Occupations*, pp. 170–85; 1931, *Industries*, pp. 23–31 (Chester), 187 (Hoole).

7 *V.C.H. Ches.* ii. 84; *Ches. Observer*, 10 Jan. 1931; 22 Oct. 1932.

8 C. P. Dryland, 'Headquarters, Western Command: Hist. Survey, 1971' (TS. at C.H.H.).

9 *Ches. Observer*, 17 Dec. 1932; *V.C.H. Ches.* v (2), Education: Chester College.

10 Above, Late Georgian and Victorian Chester: Economy and Society; cf. J. T. Scott, 'Geographical and Hist. Factors Associated with Industries and Occupations of Chester', *Geography*, xxxvi. 53, 55; quotation from B. Bracegirdle, *Engineering in Chester: 200 Years of Progress*.

11 Para. based on *Census*, 1921, *Ches.* pp. 58–73 (Chester), 77 (Hoole); 1921, *Industry*, pp. 338–82; 1931, *Occupations*, pp. 170–85; 1931, *Industries*, pp. 23–31 (Chester), 187 (Hoole).

12 Inferred from *Census*, 1921, *Workplaces*, 32 (Hawarden R.D.).

13 *Ches. Observer*, 10 Jan. 1920; 14 Mar. 1936; 20 May 1939.

14 e.g. P. Abercrombie, S. Kelly, and T. Fyfe, *Deeside Regional Planning Scheme: Rep. for Joint Cttee.* (1923).

15 *Census*, 1921, *Workplaces*, 2, 32.

opportunities within the city. Its main activity was co-operation with the Chamber of Trade and the railway companies in placing advertisements devised to attract day trippers.[1]

The most important test of Chester's resolve to put environmental factors before industrial growth came in 1919. The opportunity presented then demonstrates the city's potential to attract a large heavy industrial firm. A syndicate bought 30 acres at Curzon Park in order to construct a steelworks employing 4,000–5,000 at a time when the city had 1,000 unemployed. Abercrombie advised the corporation that industry in Curzon Park would be 'destructive to the health and amenities of the city and would pollute the surrounding residential areas', and after heated debate the proposal was rejected, a decision which led to a protest meeting reportedly attended by 3,000 people.[2] The council then quickly designated Curzon Park a residential zone and so prevented any reversal of the decision. The syndicate disposed of the land to two councillors who sold it to the borough on the grounds that it would be needed for council houses. Roads and sewers were laid but eventually the land was sold in lots for private housing.[3] The syndicate was offered an alternative site at Sealand Road, where the council wished to see industrial development, but turned it down on the grounds that it was unhealthy, too low-lying for a heavy industrial site, too near the sewage works, and had poor access.[4]

Chester did not suffer from serious labour unrest during the troubled years after 1918. The national railway strike of 1919, which locally affected 1,500 men, was said to be orderly and free of violence.[5] The city was also mostly peaceful during the General Strike of 1926.[6]

Because so many male Cestrians were employed in large factories, albeit outside the city boundaries, Chester was profoundly affected by the difficulties experienced by manufacturing industry between the wars. Despite high unemployment and reduced business in the shops, it was recognized locally that conditions would have been much worse if there had not been so much service employment in the city.[7] By the late 1930s the number of tourists was increasing. They included day trippers, holiday-makers, and foreign visitors, among whom Americans were especially numerous.[8] Responding to complaints that visitors were being harassed and exploited by unqualified self-appointed guides, the council initiated a scheme for training official personnel.[9] The increase in day trippers, for whom the Little Roodee was laid out as an omnibus park, highlighted the potential of the Dee as a tourist attraction. Pleasure boating was on the increase from 1920, and after 1934 the corporation organized one or sometimes two weeks of illuminations each August.[10] In 1937 an historical pageant was staged with over 6,000 participants,[11] and in 1938 there was talk of reviving the Chester mystery plays.[12] By then provision for tourism had become an acknowledged public service.

LOCAL GOVERNMENT AND POLITICS, 1918–39

Parliamentary Elections. In 1918 the Boundary Commission extended the Chester constituency to cover Hoole urban district and Chester rural district as well as the county borough, while retaining the name City of Chester and keeping the city sheriff as the returning officer.[13] The Conservatives dominated the constituency between the wars, usually winning over half the votes cast. Sir Owen Philipps was succeeded as M.P. in 1922 by Sir Charles Cayzer, Bt., who served until his death in 1940. The Liberals were in second place at each general election apart from 1922, but were well behind except in 1929. The Labour Party fielded a candidate for the first time in 1918 and from the 1920s

mustered between 4,500 and 6,500 votes.[14] An attempt to establish a Chester branch of the British Union of Fascists in 1934 failed when the organizer could find no one to rent him a hall for a meeting to be addressed by Sir Oswald Mosley.[15]

Municipal Politics.[16] Municipal politics were also dominated by the Conservatives, who remained the majority party on the council. The two main parties generally chose the mayor alternately and invited him to serve a second successive term. Aldermen, usually former mayors, were appointed by the council, and held office until resignation or death. The Labour

1 *Chester City Cl. Mins. 1918/19* to *1923/4*, by indexed refs. to Development and Advertising Cttee.

2 Ibid. *1918/19*, 488, 552–3; *1919/20*, 47, 51–2, 137–40, 189–90, 213, 216–17; *Ches. Observer*, 8 Nov. 1919; 31 Jan. 1920.

3 *Chester City Cl. Mins. 1919/20*, 652, 670, 690, 713; *1920/1*, 61–2; later years by indexed refs. to Curzon Park; *Ches. Observer*, 23 June 1923.

4 *Ches. Observer*, 31 Jan., 6 Mar. 1920.

5 Ibid. 18 Oct. 1919.

6 *Chester Chron.* 15 May 1926; cf. 18 Sept. 1926.

7 *Annual Rep. of M.O.H.* (1936): copies in C.C.A.L.S., ZDH

4/3, and bound with *Chester City Cl. Mins. 1936/7* at C.H.H.

8 *Ches. Observer*, 11 Aug. 1934; 17 Aug. 1935.

9 Ibid. 8 Sept. 1934.

10 Ibid. 10 Aug. 1935; 3 July 1937; *Chester Riverside Study* [1972], section FR4B.

11 *Ches. Observer*, 3 July 1937.

12 Ibid. 16 Apr. 1938.

13 Ibid. 9, 30 June, 25 Aug., 6 Sept. 1917; *V.C.H. Ches.* ii. 141.

14 *Brit. Parl. Election Results, 1918–49*, ed. F. W. S. Craig, 302.

15 *Ches. Observer*, 12 May 1934.

16 Para. based on *City of Chester Year Bks.* (1921–39) (copies at C.H.H.) and local press.

Party made little headway. Until the collapse of the coalition government in 1922, there was a pact between Tories and Liberals not to compete with one another in local elections. Afterwards, out of a total council membership of 40 (44 after 1936), the Conservatives usually had between 16 and 19 seats, and the Liberals between 10 and 14. Until 1919 the only representative of organized labour was not a candidate of the official Labour Party; thereafter, there were usually between seven and nine official Labour councillors, although in 1928, their worst year, they shrank to three. Even so, in 1930 Labour took its turn in choosing the mayor, as well as aldermen in proportion to the number of its councillors, an arrangement which often caused dissension. A mayor's purse of £250 was first granted in 1925 after a highly respected councillor turned down the mayoralty on financial grounds. The first female councillor was Mrs. Phyllis Brown, from the department store family, who was elected as a Liberal in 1920. In 1933 she became the first female alderman and in 1939 the first female mayor. Another prominent woman councillor was Labour's Mrs. Kate Clarke, first a candidate in 1920, elected to the council in 1929, the first female sheriff in 1937, and mayor 1939–40.[1]

The most influential council official was the town clerk, the universally respected and often outspoken J. H. Dickson, who served from 1903 to 1939 and was also closely involved with the work of the Council of Social Welfare and the Royal Infirmary.[2] Also notable was Charles Greenwood, who made a significant contribution to town planning and conservation during his long period as city engineer and surveyor (1922–53).[3]

Because Labour was relatively weak in Chester, the question whether responsibility for social and environmental reform was to be public or private was debated on its merits rather than on party-political lines. Opponents of public provision could not, as elsewhere, denigrate and often defeat proposals merely by asserting that they were advocated on impractical ideological grounds by a profligate Labour Party. The chief exponent of publicly owned utilities before the First World War had been a Conservative, B. C. Roberts,[4] but after his death in 1923 there was little enthusiasm for public enterprise, apart from the purchase of the Overleigh cemetery in 1933 after complaints about its upkeep.[5]

The burden of the rates was largely borne by householders and retailers. Unusually for a town of Chester's size, shopkeepers were poorly represented on the corporation: in 1925 the mayor claimed that they paid three quarters of the rates but formed only a third of the council.[6] The Chester Chamber of Trade, inaugurated in 1921, periodically exhorted its members to obtain greater representation but recognized that they disliked being 'politically labelled' and apparently relied on householders to keep down the rates. An additional weapon in the battle for 'economy' was the threat to call an electors' meeting under the Borough Funds Acts. A short-lived ratepayers' association was formed in the late 1930s under the pressure of rapidly rising rates.[7] Its absence earlier may well have reflected satisfaction with the council: finance committee chairmen could boast that rates in Chester were much lower than the national average for county boroughs. As elsewhere, the rates increased because of central government initiatives rather than local ones. Health and education were the main spending areas. In 1939 2s. 9d. out of Chester's total rate of 13s. 3d. in the pound was spent on public health, largely on the City Hospital. Education cost almost as much, and public assistance was third, at 1s. 9d. Housing and town planning together cost the ratepayers only 6¼d.[8]

Public Services. The corporation's chief assets in offsetting the rates were its public and livestock markets. It also had an income from letting the Roodee for the race meeting and for pasture during the rest of the year.[9] Neither the electricity works nor the tram system made any significant contribution. Electricity was from 1913 provided by a hydroelectric generating station, cost-effective but of limited capacity, built on the site of the Dee Mills.[10] After the acquisition in 1922 of the government-owned power station at Queensferry, the area supplied was extended beyond the city, and by 1930 the municipal undertaking supplied an area of 144 square miles around Chester. Costs were kept down by avoiding investment in modernization, and the long-overdue transfer to alternating current in 1930 increased electricity bills by 33 per cent. By 1939, however, the enterprise was in profit again, and able to reduce its prices.[11]

Chester's municipally owned transport system illustrates the pressures brought by private interests able to harness ratepayers' anger at utilities which burdened the rates. The tram system was not financially self-supporting between the World Wars, partly because of the debt incurred when the council bought and electrified it,[12] and partly because the tramways committee

---

1 *Chester City Cl. Mins.* 1920/1, 7; 1932/3, 589; *Ches. Observer*, 6 Nov. 1920, p. 6.

2 e.g. *Ches. Observer*, 30 Sept. 1933; 3 June 1939.

3 *Chester City Cl. Mins.* 1953/4, pp. 161, 183.

4 *Ches. Observer*, 2 June 1923, p. 4.

5 Ibid. 26 Sept., 19 Dec. 1931; *V.C.H. Ches.* v (2), Public Utilities: Cemeteries.   6 *Ches. Observer*, 12 Dec. 1925.

7 Ibid.; C.C.A.L.S., ZCA 9.

8 *Ches. Observer*, 3 Dec. 1938; C.C.A.L.S., ZDTR 5/66.

9 e.g. C.C.A.L.S., ZCLB 19; ZDTR 5/56; *Ches. Observer*, 13 Aug. 1938; 30 Sept. 1939.

10 *Ches. Observer*, 31 Oct. 1914; *V.C.H. Ches.* v (2), Public Utilities: Electricity.

11 *Ches. Observer*, 31 July 1915; 21 Oct., 30 Dec. 1922; 28 June, 11 Oct. 1930; 8 July 1933; 5 May 1934; 29 July 1939.

12 Ibid. 15 Apr. 1933; C.C.A.L.S., ZCLB 19.

was responsible for street repairs. In 1928, rather than renovate the system, which needed new cars and tracks, the council converted to motor buses which it proposed to run on routes extending over a 10-mile radius from the city centre. The move was vigorously opposed, and a campaign was mounted to abandon the city routes to the privately owned Crosville Bus Company, whose proprietor, Claude Crosland-Taylor, was a member of the council. The council compromised and agreed to reduce the corporation's bus routes to a radius of three miles from the centre, sufficient to serve the built-up areas outside the borough boundary at Newton, Hoole, and Great Boughton.[1] Although the first corporation buses appeared in 1930, there was continuing pressure to sell or lease the routes to Crosville. The transport committee claimed that it ran at a profit and had contributed greatly to reducing traffic jams in the city; by 1936 it was indeed profitable, but still financing the tramway debt incurred in 1903.[2]

Among the privately owned utilities, the Gas Company provoked little public comment and was evidently adequate for the city's needs. The water supply, however, remained an issue, because dirty water contributed to Chester's poor health record, a fact not publicly acknowledged. From 1914, the corporation made several attempts to buy the Water Company, which had failed to provide sedimentation tanks and still relied on the less effective method of sand filtration to purify the supply.[3] In 1928, after the failure of yet another attempt at purchase,[4] the chairman of the public health committee admitted publicly that the

standard of water was unsatisfactory. Its quality was in fact deteriorating. From 1928 the Water Company briefly chlorinated the supply, before beginning extensive improvements, virtually complete by 1933.[5] In 1932 the corporation opened a new sewage works costing over £100,000.[6] Those improvements were complemented by the establishment of the Dee Catchment Board to control pollution on the river as a whole. By 1939 the river, which had hitherto been seriously polluted, was considered relatively clean.[7]

Borough Extension.[8] The council had difficulty in finding land for development within the borough boundaries, and sometimes had to buy sites for housing in the surrounding rural districts. In such areas the cost of roads, electricity, sewerage, and other services laid on by the borough could not be recovered because the rates went to the county. The population within the city boundary rose very slowly, and Chester, one of the smallest county boroughs, was in danger of losing its independent status. The incorporation of the built-up areas outside the boundary into the county borough thus became extremely desirable.[9] In 1932 the council planned a large extension into both Cheshire and Flintshire, but dropped the proposal when it became clear that a parliamentary Bill would be vigorously contested by Cheshire county council and that the government would not allow the borough to extend across the Welsh border.[10] In 1936, however, the county agreed to surrender Blacon, the built-up part of Newton, and a part of Hoole which included the City Hospital and the railway station.[11]

TOWN PLANNING AND THE BUILT ENVIRONMENT, 1918–39

The council's commitment to providing municipal housing led it to accept the principle of urban regulation through town planning. In 1917 it commissioned Professor Patrick Abercrombie to consult with the city engineer on the preparation of a town planning scheme, necessary for the development of the Buddicom housing estate and to regulate land use,[12] and

from 1918 began to set up such a scheme. By 1919 it had resolved to develop Chester as 'a residential town, a shopping and business centre, a social meeting ground, a recreational resort and a focus for artistic effort'.[13]

Permission was sought to extend the planning zone to include areas outside the municipal boundaries,

1 *Ches. Observer*, 13, 27 Oct. 1928; 26 Jan. 1929; C.C.A.L.S., ZCLB 19, mins. of evidence and supplementary brief.

2 *Ches. Observer*, 14 Feb. 1931; 30 Jan. 1932; 15 Apr. 1933; 30 May 1936; *Chester City Cl. Transport Undertaking, Statement of Accts. 1936/7*: copy bound with *Chester City Cl. Mins. 1936/7* at C.H.H.

3 *Ches. Observer*, 25 Sept. 1920.

4 Ibid. 29 Sept. 1923; 12 Jan. 1929; *Chester City Cl. Mins. 1926/7*, 678, 714, 809; *1927/8*, 50, 217, 251, 272, 461, 509–10, 602, 777; *1928/9*, 78, 132, 170, 172.

5 *Annual Reps. of M.O.H.* (1928, 1933): copies in C.C.A.L.S., ZDH 4/2–3, and bound with *Chester City Cl. Mins. 1928/9* and *1933/4*.

6 *Ches. Observer*, 26 Mar., 15 Apr. 1932.

7 Ibid. 3 Jan., 21 Mar. 1931; *Annual Rep. of M.O.H.* (1939): copies in C.C.A.L.S., ZCCF 9/17; ZDH 4/3; and bound with *Chester City Cl. Mins. 1939/40*.

8 Para. largely based on C.C.A.L.S., ZCA 7.

9 e.g. *Ches. Observer*, 13 Nov. 1926; *Chester Chron.* 2 Jan., 26 Mar. 1932.

10 *Ches. Observer*, 9 Jan. 1932; *Chester City Cl. Mins. 1931/2*, 84, 214, 336.

11 *V.C.H. Ches.* v (2), Local Government Boundaries: Modern Boundary Extensions; *Ches. Observer*, 28 Sept., 5 Oct. 1935.

12 *Ches. Observer*, 27 Oct. 1917; C.C.A.L.S., ZCLC 5, proof of evidence.

13 C.C.A.L.S., ZCA 9, statement to Sir John Maude; *Chester City Cl. Mins. 1918/19*, 15, 55, 283–4, 468, 488.

notably Hoole urban district, parts of Chester and Tarvin rural districts, and Hawarden rural district (Flints.), on the grounds that they were inextricably linked with the city's economy.[1] Regional planning was needed to build a ring-road and so relieve the city's traffic congestion, and to improve the Dee by preventing flooding, deepening the channel, and reclaiming land for industrial development. The Ministry of Health set up a joint committee of local authorities in 1920, and in 1923 approved the Deeside Regional Planning Scheme, but Chester was allowed to include in its own plan only those parts of Hoole and the rural districts which were already built up.[2]

Little positive action came out of Chester's early planning initiatives except the designation of areas of the city as residential, commercial, recreational, or industrial; by 1926, maps showing 'zoning' had been prepared, confining shops to the city centre and excluding them from residential areas.[3] A further attempt by the council to control development over land outside the borough boundaries, in the wake of new town-planning legislation in 1928, was unsuccessful.[4]

A preliminary planning scheme, approved by the government by 1933, contained little that would prevent environmentally destructive building projects within the borough. Despite growing local concern about environmental damage to the historic city,[5] constructive proposals for its development were slow to emerge. In 1940 a draft development scheme confined itself to generalities, except for a proposal to develop high-value land in the city centre made available by the clearance of the Princess Street slums. Further planning was then abandoned because of the war.[6] In 1941 Chester was described by one embittered citizen as an example of 'unplanned, greedy development at its worst', its streets 'airless, narrow, overhung, traffic-bound, bottle-necked alleys' fronting 'an agglomeration of slums'.[7]

Traffic.   The most serious threat to Chester's environment was motorized traffic, the volume of which was increasing rapidly. By 1914 the number of vehicles had grown to the point that the coroner thought that a speed limit of 10 miles an hour ought to be imposed.[8] On bank holidays there were frequently long queues of traffic attempting the journey through the city centre to the seaside resorts of north Wales. Local traffic also

increased because of the concentration of commercial and business premises at the heart of the city. Traffic on the main roads doubled between 1925 and 1928.[9] Modest measures to ameliorate traffic problems included the introduction of pedestrian crossings and traffic lights at the Dee Bridge in 1934. Traders, however, successfully resisted all attempts to restrict parking in the city centre, or to introduce one-way traffic systems.[10]

By 1920 it was recognized that the only effective remedy was to build an outer ring-road to divert through traffic away from the city centre altogether. Such a solution was expensive and required the co-operation of Cheshire and Flintshire county councils, on whose territory much of the new road would run.[11] Even so, by 1924 a complete route had been mapped, controversially cutting across the avenue leading from Overleigh to Eaton Hall, the home of the duke of Westminster. A start was made on the Flintshire section in 1929, when the government provided 75 per cent of the cost, but in 1931 the financial crisis halted the project. In 1935 work was resumed on the same terms. Hopes of a rapid conclusion were, however, dashed by the outbreak of war.[12]

By the early 1920s there was an additional proposal, attributed to the town clerk, for an eastern inner bypass to relieve traffic congestion at the Cross by cutting across the grounds of Dee House to connect Vicars Lane with Pepper Street. In 1926 the Ministry of Transport agreed to find a third of the cost.[13] Work had begun when archaeological investigations revealed the remains of the Roman amphitheatre in the path of the proposed road. Reluctantly the city council's improvement committee was forced by central government to change the route so that it followed the curve of the amphitheatre's outer wall along a widened Little St. John Street. Controversy over the route and the design of the new gateway cut in the city wall, and the effect of the Depression on government funding, delayed completion of the scheme until 1938.[14]

The City Centre.   The taste for mock half-timbered buildings persisted in Chester well into the 1920s, even though they were going out of fashion in most other town centres.[15] Not all Chester's buildings of that kind were of poor quality, notwithstanding the comments made in 1929 by the dean of Chester's son, Francis Bennett, who deplored the replacement of 'decent,

---

1 *Ches. Observer*, 20 Mar. 1920; 3 June 1923; C.C.A.L.S., ZCLC 5, proof of evidence.

2 Abercrombie, Kelly, and Fyfe, *Deeside Regional Planning Scheme*; *Ches. Observer*, 20 Mar. 1920; 30 June 1923; C.C.A.L.S., ZCLB 19, mins. of evidence.

3 *Chester Chron.* 9 Oct. 1926.

4 C.C.A.L.S., ZCLB 19, mins. of proceedings.

5 e.g. *Ches. Observer*, 19 Oct. 1929.

6 C.C.A.L.S., ZCA 11, replies to questionnaire; C. Greenwood, *Chester: Plan for Redevelopment* [1945], 24.

7 *Ches. Observer*, 4 Oct. 1941.

8 Ibid. 14 Feb. 1914; cf. 14 Mar. 1936.

9 *Chester City Cl. Mins.* 1927/8, 699, 717, 793–4.

10 Ibid. *1924/5* and later years by indexed refs. to Traffic; *Ches. Observer*, 1 Feb. 1930; 28 Apr., 1 Dec. 1934; 27 June 1936; 18 Sept. 1937.

11 *Ches. Observer*, 3 Dec. 1921.

12 Ibid. 4 June 1932; 27 Apr. 1935; 12 Mar. 1938; 3 June 1939; *Chester City Cl. Mins.* 1931/2, 71–2, 78, 201, 205–6, 328.

13 *Ches. Observer*, 20, 27 Feb. 1932.

14 P.R.O., WORK 14/263; below, this section (Archaeology).

15 Pevsner, *Ches.* 39.

honest Georgian' by 'wretched, ill-designed black and white'.[1] For example, the Manchester and District Bank (later Royal Bank of Scotland) at the corner of Foregate Street and Frodsham Street was built to a well detailed design of 1921 by Francis Jones.[2] Nor did all new buildings in the centre conform to the black-and-white idiom. Several national chain stores built shops in their own house styles at the east end of the town centre, including the neo-Georgian Marks & Spencer, designed in 1932 by Norman Jones and Leonard Rigby of Manchester, and the cautiously Art Deco premises of Montague Burton, designed by Harry Wilson of Leeds in 1928, both in Foregate Street.[3] Many shops received alterations, such as the steel-framed third storey added to Browns in Eastgate Street by Forbes and Tate of London in 1929,[4] and during the mid 1930s the centre was transformed at street and Row level by dozens of new shop fronts.[5] The most unashamedly modern buildings were the cinemas built on prominent sites in the main streets, particularly the Odeon, designed by Harry Weedon and opened in 1936, which was un- avoidable in the view down Northgate Street.[6] The Regal, designed in the same year by the A.B.C.'s architects in a more subdued Art Deco style, filled the corner of Foregate Street and Love Lane.[7] Only a few new buildings, such as Maxwell Ayrton's St. Werburgh Row of 1935 in St. Werburgh Street, were designed in a manner consciously sympathetic with their surroundings.[8]

The corporation's town planning not only failed to ensure that most new buildings enhanced the environ- ment, but also made low cost rather than quality the motivation in its own projects. The council's attitude was apparent in 1929 in the controversy about the design of a new gate in the walls to connect with Pepper Street. The Chester Archaeological Society spearheaded a campaign, supported by the Society for the Protection of Ancient Buildings, for a sympath- etically designed gateway and for keeping the land surrounding it as public open space. Its case was that 'the city's greatest asset, even in a narrow financial sense, is its historic character'.[9] It is unlikely that the council, whose improvement committee had initially wanted a simple postern gate,[10] would have heeded such admonitions had the walls and gates not been scheduled under the Ancient Monuments Act of 1913.[11] The Office of Works, whose permission was necessary to breach the walls, pressed the council to

commission a design for the new gate from Walter Tapper, president of the Royal Institute of British Architects. Tapper's original plan, a large gateway with posterns, gardens outside the walls, and a large piazza within, was rejected by the improvement com- mittee as much too expensive, and work started on the road before the matter was resolved. Renewed pressure from the Office of Works ensured that Tapper was consulted on two further occasions, the last in 1935.[12] Although he died before giving his advice, his son Michael produced a design for a gate with simplified medieval references which was officially opened in 1938 as the Newgate.[13] The largest public building planned in Chester between the wars, the neo-Georgian extension to County Hall designed in 1938 by the county architect E. Mainwaring Parkes and completed after 1945, was a meagre affair unworthy of its historic site and riverside setting.[14]

Conservation. The city's existing reputation for neglecting or destroying its historic architecture was reinforced after 1918.[15] Not only were Georgian build- ings replaced, but genuine timber-framed houses were allowed to fall into disrepair. The council delayed, for example, over the restoration of Stanley Palace, pur- chased by the Archaeological Society but then sold to the earl of Derby, who presented it to the city in 1928. When work eventually began in 1932, it was greatly criticized as overzealous and undertaken at the behest of 'council reactionaries'.[16] There were also allegations that Chester's 'meagreness of civic pride' led it to neglect the walls, described as 'squalid and depressing' and unfit to be open to the public.[17]

Throughout the 1920s and 1930s the revivified Archaeological Society lobbied the council hard on conservation issues,[18] but government intervention was the principal means of preserving the city's historic fabric. Indeed in 1927 a local inspector of ancient monuments, reporting that the walls were in disrepair, commented that 'the city will do nothing worth doing unless it has to, and no one but the Office of Works can protect what remains from decay'.[19] Although the Dee Bridge and by 1938 the amphitheatre were also sched- uled, many historic buildings remained neglected. The problem was of great concern to Greenwood, the city surveyor, who in 1933 sought to make a list of those worthy of preservation.[20]

One seriously endangered historic building was the

1 *Ches. Observer*, 19 Oct. 1929.
2 P. Boughton, *Picturesque Chester*, no. 161.
3 C.C.A.L.S., ZDS 3/165, 307.
4 Ibid. ZDS 3/206.
5 Ibid. ZDS 3/244–842 *passim*.
6 Boughton, *Picturesque Chester*, no. 155.
7 C.C.A.L.S., ZDS 3/551.   8 Pevsner, *Ches.* 163.
9 *Ches. Observer*, 4 Jan. 1930; *J.C.A.S.* xxx. 92–3.
10 *Chester City Cl. Mins.* 1928/9, 323.
11 Ibid. *1914/15*, 138–9, 207.
12 Ibid. *1928/9*, 383–4, 464, 471, 516–17, 539, 589; *1933/4*,

770, 776, 843–4, 884–5; *1934/5*, 228–9, 632–3, 687, 787, 877, 1028; *Ches. Observer*, 14 Dec. 1929; 22 Nov. 1930; 28 Feb. 1931; 28 July 1934; P.R.O., WORK 14/264.
13 *Ches. Observer*, 2 May 1936; 8 Sept. 1938; T. Ward, *Chester in Camera* (1985), 13.
14 Boughton, *Picturesque Chester*, no. 118.
15 e.g. *Ches. Observer*, 5 Dec. 1925.
16 Ibid. 6 June 1936.   17 Ibid. 19 Oct. 1929.
18 A. G. Crosby, *Chester Arch. Soc. 1849–1999*, 69–72, 80–2.
19 P.R.O., WORK 14/263.
20 Ibid. WORK 14/645.

Blue Bell Inn in Northgate Street, which dated from the mid 15th century and was reputed the oldest domestic building in the city. In 1930 it was bought by the improvement committee for demolition as part of a plan to widen Northgate Street.[1] Abandoned for six years, it fell into serious decay despite protests from the Chester branch of the Council for the Preservation of Rural England, the Chester Archaeological Society, and the duke of Westminster. Eventually the Office of Works intervened, asking the council to reconsider, and pointing out that the plan to widen Northgate Street was impracticable since the Northgate itself was a scheduled monument.[2] Although the council was thus prevented from destroying the Blue Bell it refused to spend money preserving it and the building remained unrepaired in 1939.[3]

The state of the Watergate Street Rows also caused anxiety and public debate, and in 1938 the council bought several buildings apparently in order to preserve them. By then the improvement committee, which declared that 'we depend very largely on our antiquities for our prosperity', may have had a change of heart about the city's historic buildings.[4] Local conservationists, mindful of its past record, remained sceptical.[5]

Archaeology. The controversy over the design of the Newgate coincided with an even more contentious issue, the fate of the Roman amphitheatre. Interest in Roman Chester had already been stimulated by the excavation of Roman barrack blocks in Deanery Fields by Robert Newstead, curator of the Chester Archaeological Society's collections and the dominant figure in the city's archaeology between the wars. It was greatly heightened by the accidental discovery of the amphitheatre in 1929 in the grounds of Dee House. Excavation in 1930–1 by Newstead and J. P. Droop, professor of classical archaeology at Liverpool University, was financed by the Archaeological Society and made a pioneering contribution to Roman archaeology in Chester.[6] The improvement committee, some of whose members attempted to deny that the remains were those of an amphitheatre, nevertheless continued

with its original plan to build a road across the site. The Office of Works responded by offering to pay the costs of excavation and preservation. Together with the Ministry of Transport, which was providing financial support for the road, it insisted that the road should be diverted round the amphitheatre, arguing that it would be a unique addition to the city's attractions and result in 'a large and permanent increase in the number of visitors'.[7]

The council, which owned only the land needed for the road, refused to buy the rest of the site. A campaign was mounted to raise sufficient private funding to buy it, but national and international interest was greater than in Chester, partly perhaps because there was little to see above ground. An Epstein sculpture, *Genesis*, was lent to the Grosvenor Museum to help raise money, and Mussolini sent his good wishes for the project to the Archaeological Society. By 1934 the society had collected sufficient funds to buy St. John's House on the northern half of the site, which could therefore be excavated. The rest, perhaps better preserved because the ground level was higher there, was to remain buried in the grounds of Dee House.[8] There matters rested until after the war.

Open Spaces. In 1919 Chester had high levels of environmental pollution more usually associated with industrial towns, largely caused by smoke from closely packed domestic chimneys and perhaps by emissions from the gas works.[9] Although there was some improvement in the 1930s, mainly because of slum clearance in the city centre, such conditions made the need for public open spaces particularly important. There were, however, only 186 acres of open space, well short of the 518 acres required by the accepted standards of the day. The shortage was worse than it seemed, for some of the existing space was not laid out for recreation and the total included the Roodee, which was not always available to the public, and Earl's Eye or the Meadows, which was subject to serious flooding. In 1929 the city acquired 64½ acres of the Meadows, but shrank from the expense of providing drainage and access.[10]

HOUSING AND SUBURBAN DEVELOPMENT, 1918–39

In 1914 most working-class Cestrians lived in 19th-century terraced housing with tiny back sculleries, outside lavatories, small back yards, and front doors

opening on to the street. In the city centre, conditions in the courts of Princess Street, Goss Street, and Crook Street remained below that standard into the 1930s.[11]

1 *Ches. Observer*, 22 Mar. 1930.
2 Ibid. 30 May 1936; *Chester City Cl. Mins.* 1935/6, 613–14, 700–1, 913–14; 1936/7, 62–3; P.R.O., WORK 14/604.
3 *Ches. Observer*, 18 Mar. 1939.
4 Ibid. 3 Apr. 1938; P.R.O., WORK 14/1309.
5 *Ches. Observer*, 19 Feb. 1944.
6 Ibid. 27 Sept. 1930; 30 May 1931; R. Newstead and J. P. Droop, 'Roman Amphitheatre at Chester', *J.C.A.S.* xxix. 5–40.

7 *Chester City Cl. Mins.* 1931/2, 71, 169, 206, 329–30, 394–5, 427–8, 1004, 1070; P.R.O., WORK 14/263, 476, 813.
8 Crosby, *Chester Arch. Soc.* 80–3; *Ches. Observer*, 2 Apr., 24 Sept., 26 Nov. 1932; 1 Feb. 1934; P.R.O., WORK 14/264.
9 *Annual Rep. of M.O.H.* (1919).
10 *V.C.H. Ches.* v (2), Open Spaces and Parks: The Meadows; *Ches. Observer*, 18 Dec. 1937.
11 Plate 52.

In Princess Street alone there were 224 houses, of which 140 were damp and 120 verminous; 103 shared lavatories, 118 had no suitable washing accommodation, and 108 lacked a sink or internal water supply. In one sublet house in Crook Street lived seven separate families, 39 people in all.[1]

By the early 20th century the corporation had accepted the principle that it should provide housing as long as it did not become a charge on the rates. Encouraged by the success of its first small estate of 12 houses at Tower Road in 1904,[2] the council commissioned Professor Abercrombie to design a garden suburb for the 13-acre Buddicom estate at Lache.[3] Abercrombie planned what was initially called the Buddicom Park estate in 1914, and work began in 1919 to a revised layout; by then it formed part of an enlarged scheme to provide Chester with 800 houses, drawn up in response to the Addison Act of that year which inaugurated the government's national housing programme.[4] Abercrombie preferred formal layouts and house designs, against the prevailing taste for the picturesque garden-suburb style.[5] Consequently, the first phase of the estate was centred on an oval of houses lining Sunbury and Abingdon Crescents and facing a central green, which was enclosed by a rectangle of streets bounded on the east by the estate's straight spine road, Cliveden Road. The housing committee favoured local architects, from whom Abercrombie chose James Strong, who designed terraced and semi-detached houses in early 19th-century urban-cottage style; they were built of pink brick, with diapering in the manner of 19th-century Grosvenor estate buildings.[6] The 138 houses approved in 1919 were occupied by 1921, and by 1922 only 24 houses were needed to complete the estate.[7] The housing was extended after 1924, when the city surveyor drew up plans and it was decided to sell off surplus land for private housing,[8] but completion was delayed until after the Heath Lane estate was completed in 1926.[9] The later houses along Cliveden Road and east of it, probably designed after Strong died in 1921, were different in style, their brick detailing inspired by 17th-century Dutch architecture.

Abercrombie was also responsible for a similar layout at the centre of the Boughton Heath estate off Heath Lane, Great Boughton, planned in 1920,[10] based on a central rectangular green facing outward to Neville, Westward, and Kingsley Roads. The cottage-style brick houses, designed by the city surveyor, were similar to the later houses at Buddicom Park. Specifications were approved in 1923 for 212 houses, to be built in blocks of four, six, and eight, mostly without separate parlours and bathrooms;[11] the first 16 were finished in 1924 and those in Neville Road and Heath Lane in 1926.[12] The green was linked to the east, off Marian Drive, to a similar layout, not built until after 1945. The large central open space was later partly built over. The same type of layout was planned in 1926 by the city surveyor between Meadows Lane and Appleyards Lane on the Handbridge estate, which had, in contrast, a picturesque mix of houses laid out in classic garden-suburb fashion round a large informal green at Watling Crescent.[13] The Handbridge estate had the greatest variety of house types, ranging from variants of the last ones built at Buddicom Park to a plain hipped-roofed kind along Meadows Lane.

The Lache estate, a southward extension of Buddicom Park begun in 1931,[14] also followed the government's recommended garden-suburb layout with houses set obliquely at road junctions and round a green at the junction of Clover Lane and Sycamore Drive. Some corner terraces had central passages leading to an open space at the back, originally shared in common but later divided up.

The very high cost of the earliest post-war housing schemes led the council to consider concrete construction as a cheaper option as early as 1920–1.[15] Experimental methods were examined again in 1925 when members of the housing committee inspected demonstration houses at the Empire Exhibition and made site visits, but attempts failed to persuade contractors to build trial houses on the Telford All-Steel, Triangular-block, and Univers poured-concrete systems at Bottoms Lane, Handbridge. Eventually Universal agreed to allow six Univers houses to be built by licensed contractors.[16] Inflated building costs were reflected in high rents, since the council was determined to minimize the charge on the rates.[17] Even the rents for later houses built at Lache in the 1930s were relatively high.[18]

The city's council houses provided working people with improved living conditions. They were larger than most 19th-century terraced houses, free from damp, and had more bedrooms, better cooking and laundry facilities, internal plumbing, and small gardens.[19] They were also more spaciously laid out, conforming to the government standard of 12 houses an acre. However, not only were council houses more expensive to rent,

1 *Chester City Cl. Mins.* *1934/5*, 35–41, 160–201; *Ches. Observer*, 2 Mar. 1935.

2 *Ches. Observer*, 2 Apr. 1927.

3 Ibid. 31 Jan. 1914.

4 Ibid. 31 Jan. 1919; *Chester City Cl. Mins.* *1918/19*, 32–4, 56, 89, 196, 334–5, 377, 390–2, 458–61, 485.

5 M. Swenarton, *Homes Fit for Heroes*, 64.

6 *Chester City Cl. Mins.* *1918/19*, 56, 196, 360, 392.

7 Ibid. *1918/19*, 300, 495, 695.   8 Ibid. *1924/5*, 170.

9 Ibid. *1925/6*, 82, 343.   10 Ibid. *1920/1*, 94, 96.

11 Ibid. *1922/3*, 85, 431, 492.

12 Ibid. *1924/5*, 170; *1925/6*, 817.

13 Ibid. *1925/6*, 637. Plates 59–60.

14 Ibid. *1929/30* and later years, by indexed refs. to Lache Housing Estate (to *1931/2*) and Housing: Lache Estate (from *1932/3*), esp. *1930/1*, 505.

15 Ibid. *1920/1*, 240.

16 Ibid. *1924/5*, 705; *1925/6*, 803.

17 *Ches. Observer*, 28 July 1928.

18 Ibid. 30 July 1932.   19 C.C.A.L.S., ZCR 204/1.

their tenants also incurred higher costs in travelling to work from the suburbs. The new estates, all of which lay south of the city centre, were socially uniform and segregated from the city by a belt of privately owned houses in established suburbs. Men found their homes little more than dormitories,[1] while mothers of young children were isolated, and there were no play areas.[2] Residents of the Lache estate campaigned continuously for facilities such as a public house or a fish and chip shop, which the council was reluctant to allow.[3]

While Chester's municipal housing met a great need among relatively well paid workers, it was too expensive to alleviate the plight of the poor. Indeed, in 1929 a councillor criticized the corporation for becoming a speculative builder, 'hoping to make money but not meeting the difficulty that was still rampant'.[4]

Although the council, prompted by government initiatives, maintained a continuous building programme between the World Wars, there were never enough new houses to reduce the waiting lists, and overcrowding remained a serious problem. By 1928 it had completed 725 houses and had 417 more under construction, figures which included 235 built privately in Curzon Park and Handbridge with the aid of corporation mortgages supported by government subsidy.[5] Flats were provided for old people in Hoole Lane and Heath Lane. By 1939 the council had built 1,628 houses and flats, besides 206 taken over from Hoole urban district council in 1936.[6]

In 1928 the council appointed its first housing manager, a woman graduate trained on a system devised by Octavia Hill, which Chester was only the third local authority to adopt.[7] It continued to appoint female housing managers until the 1970s because the housing committee thought it easier for women to deal with social problems.[8] There remained unhealthy courts in all the wards, but the council resisted building cheap blocks of flats to replace them because it was 'not prepared to put people in barracks'.[9] In 1924, when the government began to encourage slum clearance, 59 back-to-back houses were pulled down in Handbridge, and replaced by a row of shops. Although the government paid half the cost, there was no rent subsidy for the evicted tenants.[10] Other small-scale demolition schemes followed,[11] but an effective general slum clearance did not start until the 1930s.

In 1935, after the government had offered large

financial inducements to persuade councils to carry out slum clearance, Chester produced a report which showed that 902 houses, inhabited by 4,117 people, were in need of demolition, and considerably more of extensive renovation. The first clearance area to be dealt with, and the only scheme completed before 1939, was near the town hall, in Princess, Crook, and Goss Streets. Their dreadful condition did not deter vociferous objections to demolition, but clearance was encouraged by the possibility of a lucrative redevelopment of the site.[12] During the 1930s over 1,000 tenants from the demolished houses were rehoused on the Lache estate. The new tenants were thought to have settled down well and 'standards of housekeeping improved'.[13] Opposition to the Princess Street clearance at the public inquiry in 1935 probably deterred the council from embarking on further schemes, and all such plans were abandoned at the outbreak of war, leaving at least two thirds of Chester's slums intact.[14]

Most private houses built in Chester between the wars were inexpensive. Speculative builders and contractors included George Austin, who built round Stocks Lane in Great Boughton,[15] Enoch Kennerley and Sons,[16] Thomas B. Gorst and Sons, active at Blacon and in Sealand Road,[17] Henry and A. H. Moorcroft,[18] A. Bornstein,[19] and H. V. Basil Thorington, responsible for many houses of a slightly superior type in Curzon Park.[20] Many houses were designed by Chester-based architects, among whom John H. Davies and Sons, Richard B. and Arthur R. Keane, Arthur J. Hayton, and Douglas, Minshull & Co. (later Douglas, Minshull, and Muspratt) were particularly prolific. Some developers, for example Thorington, supplied their own designs. A few architects and builders came from Liverpool, such as Brown and Sanders, and O. Williams and Sutcliffe,[21] or further afield.

All the designs were conservative, and materials were restricted to brick and render, with a minimum of tile-hanging, half-timbering, and other decorative finishes. The simple character of much of the private housing and its proximity to similar council housing gave visual cohesion, or in some places monotony, to many of the outer suburbs, for example at Lache, where private houses of c. 1930 faced contemporary council houses across Circular Drive.[22]

Semi-detached pairs and small detached houses were built on individual plots or on small parcels of land as

1   *Ches. Observer*, 3 Nov. 1934.
2   C.C.A.L.S., ZDHO 1.
3   *Ches. Observer*, frequent refs. throughout 1930s.
4   Ibid. 28 Oct. 1929.
5   Ibid. 28 July 1928; C.C.A.L.S., ZCA 9, statement to Sir John Maude.
6   C.C.A.L.S., ZCA 11, replies to questionnaire; ZDTR 5/92, tables 10, 12.
7   Ibid. ZCA 9; *Ches. Observer*, 29 Jan. 1928.
8   C.C.A.L.S., TS. list of class ZDHO.
9   *Ches. Observer*, 16 July 1919; 2 Mar. 1929.
10   Ibid. 26 July 1924; C.C.A.L.S., ZCLB 19, brief.

11   *Ches. Observer*, 11 Dec. 1926; 26 Feb. 1927.
12   Ibid. 2 Mar. 1935; C.C.A.L.S., ZDHO 24.
13   C.C.A.L.S., ZDHO 1.
14   Ibid. ZCA 9; *Ches. Observer*, 2 Mar. 1940. Plates 48–9, 51–2.
15   C.C.A.L.S., ZDS 3/1, 54–5, 145, 188.
16   Ibid. ZDS 3/141, 155, 215.
17   Ibid. ZDS 3/16, 19, 585, 670, 690, 715, 768.
18   Ibid. ZDS 3/74, 109, 134, 305, 405, 770, 778, 788.
19   Ibid. ZDS 3/770.
20   Ibid. ZDS 3/112, 136, 149, 231, 237–9, 243, 252, 266.
21   Ibid. ZDS 3/25, 33.
22   Ibid. ZDS 3/259.

ribbon-development by arterial roads, for example *c.* 1937–9 along Sealand Road.[1] Larger concentrations were built with the aid of corporation mortgages on land sold off by the council as surplus to requirements for public housing, particularly at Lache, Handbridge, and on the 52 acres at Curzon Park which the council had bought in 1925.[2] Between 1925 and 1931 several different developers built groups of semi-detached houses in roads laid out at the west end of the last area.[3] Elsewhere from the mid 1920s existing suburbs were enlarged by the addition of mainly inexpensive houses. At Newton they were built first at the south end of Newton Lane and in and off Brook Lane in 1932–3,[4] and later on Kingsway.[5] Cheap houses were developed along Stocks Lane, Heath Lane, and Christleton Road,[6] and in 1939 permission was granted for a cinema (never finished) and a neo-Georgian shopping parade to serve them.[7] House-builders were also active east of the Lache council estate in Lache Lane from the mid 1920s[8] and near Bache station between 1935 and 1939. At Blacon, groups of houses sprang up in the late 1930s along Highfield Road, St. Chad's Road, and Saughall Road,[9] all near the station, and permission was granted

in 1936 and 1939 for over 150 more at Blacon Point.[10] In the south-east corner of Hoole, housing begun just before 1914 was continued after 1918, while at Handbridge houses spread along Brown's Lane near the cemetery.

Speculative houses of higher quality, detached and semi-detached and still Edwardian in style, were built from 1935 on a limited grid of roads between the Lache council estate and Lache Lane, including Lache Park Avenue and Marlston Avenue; further east in Queen's Park detached houses were built in Bottoms Lane *c.* 1927,[11] St. George's Crescent, and Victoria Crescent. Small pockets of land on and just off Parkgate and Liverpool Roads, north of the centre, were developed with tight closes, for example Abbots Grange of 1929,[12] some houses being built in the former gardens of larger houses, as at Abbots Park. Building in Curzon Park continued until the early 1950s, though after 1933 the pattern of development changed slightly as more plots were developed individually; the building of houses for individual clients seems to have reached a peak throughout Chester in 1936–7.[13]

SOCIETY AND CULTURE, 1918–39

Social Change. In the early 1930s a social survey of working families in Chester concluded, in line with national findings, that the factors which contributed most to their well-being, after wage and rent levels, were the strength of character of parents, their health, and the number of dependent children. In the sample of 13 families, the average size of family was seven. Of 12 surviving fathers, six were suffering from disabilities incurred during the First World War. None of the families had a 'clean bill of health'. Only one had a wireless and eight never went to the cinema or theatre. The diets of all were adjudged seriously deficient in green vegetables, fruit, fish, and dairy produce. One family had no milk at all; another lived almost entirely on bread and margarine. Overall, however, the medical officer of health believed that an increase in the weight and height of local school children since Edwardian times, also in line with national trends, was attributable to better nutrition.[14]

Dean Tubbs also noticed signs of social improvement. In 1937 he remarked on the smarter appearance of the city's young men and women, which he attrib-

uted to higher earnings, department stores, and the influence of the cinema.[15] Even so, there remained much poverty, partly because of high levels of long-term unemployment. The plight of the poor could not be ignored since the city's worst slums lay at its heart, just behind Town Hall Square. Little was done to remedy serious overcrowding there until the 1930s, when the city started to move slum dwellers to less visible housing estates in the suburbs. People from the clearance areas who could not afford council-house rents moved into formerly respectable neighbourhoods, where single rooms were sublet to whole families, so creating new areas of overcrowding. The results were evident in a complaint of 1937 that people in Watergate Street, Crane Street, Stanley Place, and Paradise Row stood in doorways with shawls over their heads, their children screaming, rolling iron hoops, and kicking footballs in the streets, or sitting in doorways. Such conditions, visible alike to shoppers and to tourists walking the city walls, were held to devalue Chester's attractiveness.[16]

In 1915 several charitable relief agencies merged to

1 Ibid. ZDS 3/19, 24, 670, 715, 803.
2 *Chester City Cl. Mins.* 1924/5, 615–17.
3 e.g. C.C.A.L.S., ZDS 3/109, 111–12, 129, 134, 136, 231, 238–9, 243, 287, 290, 295–6, 298.
4 Ibid. ZDS 3/305, 379/2.
5 Ibid. ZDS 3/17, 599.
6 Ibid. ZDS 3/1, 9, 54–5, 145, 188, 405, 475, 558, 748.
7 Ibid. ZDS 3/788.
8 Ibid. ZDS 3/33, 312.

9 Ibid. ZDS 3/25, 730.
10 Ibid. ZDS 3/561, 585, 770.
11 Ibid. ZDS 3/137.
12 Ibid. ZDS 3/5.
13 Ibid. ZDS 3/356–842 *passim.*
14 Ibid. ZCR 204/1; *Annual Reps. of M.O.H* (1938 and other years).
15 *Ches. Observer*, 18 Sept. 1937.
16 Ibid. 24 July 1937.

form the Chester Council of Social Welfare, membership of which included eight councillors and four employers. Its objectives were to relieve distress and focus public opinion; it organized mother and baby clinics, general advice agencies, and a juvenile welfare department, and advised on financial and housing matters. Chester was divided into four districts, each with its own visitor who reported to a local committee. Recommendations for action were sent from there to a central committee which administered the funds.[1]

The problem of unemployment varied in severity at different times. Male unemployment leapt from 500–600 before 1914 to a level never below 1,200, and in 1931 it stood at 3,600. In the following year 22 per cent of 'responsible' council-house tenants were unemployed, partly through problems at the Shotton steelworks and the slump in the building trade. Short-time working affected many more. Unemployment benefits were deemed sufficient to cover current expenses, though with a shortage of food, but did not allow for boots and clothing. Mothers went out to work if they could.[2] For those unemployed not covered by national insurance the only recourse was the poor law. The union workhouse at Hoole, placed under the council's control in 1930, served the sick and the destitute in one building. The city had no mental hospital and sent most of its mentally ill and insane wherever costs were lowest, for instance Middlesbrough, Cardiff, and Worcester, but made increasing attempts to place them nearer the city in the county council's mental hospital at Upton.[3]

The reforms of 1929–30 transferred the workhouse, later renamed the City Hospital, from the poor-law guardians to the management of the corporation's public assistance committee.[4] Although there were bitter exchanges between the committee and the unemployed, the city's social survey team found little demand for radical social and economic change. As unemployment rose and the government imposed the means test, the city's unemployed organized themselves into an association and held public meetings to protest. In 1932 the Labour members of the public assistance committee resigned.[5] The extent of unemployment during the 1930s Depression undermined local voluntary efforts such as the opening in 1933 of a recreational centre and canteen in the Blue Coat School, and the provision of allotments and residential holidays.[6] In 1937, when the national economy was beginning to recover, 20 per cent of council-house tenants were still

unemployed and a further 20 per cent lived on wages of less than £2 a week.[7]

Health.[8] Army service led to an increase in the incidence of tuberculosis during the First World War. Advanced cases were taken to a T.B. pavilion established at the isolation hospital at Sealand Road in 1915; others were treated at the sanatorium which Chester shared with Cheshire. By then the council's commitment to slum clearance allowed the medical officer of health to speak publicly about the connexion between bad housing and poor health. He demonstrated that in 1914 the average death rate in Chester was 15.7 per thousand people but in the slum courts reached 27.3 per thousand. The ward with the highest death rate, St. Oswald's, had the worst overcrowding. In 1919 some 300 houses were recorded as unfit for human habitation, and a further 150 as needing repair, but those figures were probably a gross underestimate, since in 1933 over 1,000 houses were recommended for demolition. Overcrowding and poor sanitation encouraged the spread of tuberculosis and diphtheria. By then most zygomatic diseases had begun to retreat, but diphtheria remained intractable. Between 1930 and 1942, when immunization was voluntary, there were 1,269 cases and 83 deaths in Chester. After compulsory vaccination was introduced in 1942, deaths from diphtheria ceased. While the overall death rate in Chester was not much higher than the national average, it always exceeded that for small towns, the category in which the city was classed. The infantile death rate gave especial cause for concern. Before 1914 it had reached 106 per thousand live births, and although after 1916 it never again exceeded 100, it still remained high, often reaching the upper 70s.

Legislation making medical officers of health responsible for maternal and child welfare entailed Chester's officer in close co-operation with voluntary agencies. Since 1909 there had been a Ladies Health Society which organized a baby clinic to help and advise mothers in need. During the war the government encouraged the council to provide better premises, and the clinic began weekly inspections of babies from poor families.[9] The Local Government Board also required the council's health visitors to spend more time in maternity and infant welfare work.[10]

From 1925 an eight-bed maternity hospital was run by the Chester Benevolent Institution. By 1934 it was thought overcrowded, but by then the City Hospital

1 *Ches. Observer*, 16 Feb. 1929; 26 Nov. 1932; C.C.A.L.S., ZCR 164, *passim*.
2 C.C.A.L.S., ZCR 164/62–4; *Ches. Observer*, 26 Nov. 1932.
3 *Chester City Cl. Mins. 1914/15* to *1939/40*, by indexed refs. to Mental Deficiency Act (to *1930/1*) and Mental Treatment; *Ches. Observer*, 30 Sept. 1933.
4 *Ches. Observer*, 6 Apr. 1930; 19 Dec. 1931.
5 Ibid. 23, 30 Jan. 1932.
6 Ibid. 7 Dec. 1929; 28 Jan. 1933; 26 Jan. 1935; C.C.A.L.S.,

ZCR 164/62–4.
7 C.C.A.L.S., ZDHO 1.
8 Para. based on *Annual Reps. of M.O.H.* (1914–45): copies in C.C.A.L.S., ZDH 2/5 (1914–20); ZDH 4/2–4 (1921–45); ZCR 388/1 (1930); ZCCF 9/15–45 (1937–42, 1944–5); and bound with copies of *Chester City Cl. Mins. 1914/15* to *1929/30, 1931/2* to *1937/8*, and *1939/40* at C.H.H. (1914–29, 1931–7, and 1939).
9 *Ches. Observer*, 6 Feb., 13 Nov. 1915.
10 *Annual Rep. of M.O.H.* (1915).

also dealt with maternity cases. The latter provided 36 specialized maternity beds in 1936 but failed to appoint a resident gynaecologist, obstetrician, or specialist nursing staff. Shortly afterwards, in 1938, the Institution's maternity hospital closed.[1]

Although children's health had improved since Edwardian times, there was still malnutrition in Chester. In 1929, out of a school population of 6,000, 80 had rickets and 77 anaemia. The council stopped providing milk during the period 1921–30 when the government grant was reduced, and there were no school meals before 1937. In the latter year 134 cases of malnutrition were reported out of a school population of 5,500. Ninety children were then given meals at a number of centres; by 1939 eighty children were being fed at Lache council school alone.[2]

Culture and Leisure.[3] A massive growth in cinema attendance contributed to the decline in theatre and music hall as popular recreations. The family-owned Royalty Theatre survived in the 1930s survived only through the introduction of summer repertory catering in part for visitors to Chester.[4] The Music Hall became a cinema in 1920, after playing host to both Jennie Lind and Nellie Melba; it converted to talkies in 1929, the first in Chester.[5] Cinemas increased both in number (to seven in 1939) and capacity, and their standards of comfort and decoration improved.[6]

Chester's social year was punctuated by the horse races and the County Agricultural Show, held on the Roodee in May and August respectively; in 1925 the Royal Agricultural Show was held in Chester and was visited by George V.[7] Football was becoming an important spectator sport and enthusiasm increased when Chester were elected to the Football League in 1931; a new stand was built at the club's stadium in Sealand Road.[8] Informal popular recreations included ice-skating when the Dee froze above the weir, as in February 1929.[9]

The council's contribution to the city's cultural life was limited. In 1928 the central library in St. John Street lacked open access and was condemned as 'everything a library should not be';[10] although enlarged in 1929, it remained unsatisfactory.[11] There was no public art gallery. The collections in the Grosvenor Museum passed to the council only in 1938, even though it controlled the building from 1915.[12] Despite frequent campaigning by the Music Society, there was no large concert hall, and a building acquired for the purpose in 1927 was eventually used as council offices.[13]

It was left to the cathedral to provide a cultural focus for the city, the only place apart from the Gaumont cinema where large concerts could be held in reasonable comfort and with satisfactory acoustics. Until 1920 the cathedral had been rather remote from the life of the city, but thereafter the new dean, Frank Bennett, began to change it into 'the diocesan town hall'. Bennett abolished the entry fee, made himself accessible to visitors as well as those needing help and counsel, and turned the medieval monastic refectory into a public space. He also persuaded the bishop to move from his comparatively remote palace by the Dee to the former deanery in the close.[14]

CHESTER AND THE SECOND WORLD WAR

Throughout the later 1930s preparations were made locally for the resumption of war. R.A.F. Sealand was established at Queensferry in 1933 as a flying training school, and during the war supported front-line squadrons by repairing engines, instruments, armaments, and wireless telegraphy equipment.[15] More significantly for the local workforce, by 1938 there were two large aircraft factories near Chester: de Havilland at Broughton and Vickers-Armstrong near Hawarden, both in Flintshire.[16] In 1936 the council established an air-raid precautions committee, which began to

train wardens and build shelters; the first council approval for a shelter, for 200 people, was given in April 1939.[17] In 1938 an imposing classical headquarters was opened for the Army's Western Command in Queen's Park, on land bought from the corporation.[18]

When Chester's M.P. died in 1940 the Tory nominee, Basil Nield, took his seat without a contest.[19] By then council politics had become muted; there were no ward elections and W. Matthews Jones served as mayor from 1940 until the end of the war.[20] Although its own

1 Ibid. (1934); *Ches. Observer,* 28 June 1936; *V.C.H. Ches.* v (2), Medical Services: Maternity Care.

2 *Annual Reps. of M.O.H.* (1929–31); *Ches. Observer,* 1 May 1937; 23 Mar. 1939.

3 For fuller details, *V.C.H. Ches.* v (2), Leisure and Culture.

4 *Ches. Observer,* 9 Jan. 1932.   5 Ibid. 9 Oct. 1920.

6 *V.C.H. Ches.* v (2), Places of Entertainment: Cinemas.

7 *Ches. Observer,* 11 July 1925.

8 Ibid. 15 Aug. 1931; *V.C.H. Ches.* v (2), Sport after 1700: Association Football.

9 Ward, *Chester in Camera,* 4.

10 *Ches. Observer,* 23 June 1928.

11 Ibid. 12 Oct. 1929; *Chester City Cl. Mins.* 1928/9, 42, 607–8.

12 *Ches. Observer,* 6 Nov. 1915; 18 Sept. 1937.

13 Ibid. 16 Apr. 1923; 2 Aug. 1924; 1 Oct. 1927.

14 A. Bruce, *The Cath. 'Open and Free': Dean Bennett of Chester.*

15 *Ches. Observer,* 12 Aug. 1933; *Chester Chron.* Jan. 1997 supplement on 'Bygone Chester'.

16 *Ches. Observer,* 19 Nov. 1938; 3 Feb. 1940.

17 C.C.A.L.S., ZDS 3/800.

18 *Ches. Observer,* 28 Mar. 1936; 6 Feb. 1937; 2 Apr., 25 June 1938.   19 Ibid. 24 Feb. 1940.

20 *V.C.H. Ches.* v (2), Lists of Mayors and Sheriffs.

affairs were generally slack, the council had to carry out numerous detailed government directives.[1]

Many local manufacturing firms turned to war production. There was soon full employment and, as in the First World War, a need to recruit labour from outside the area.[2] Poverty on the Lache council estate was alleviated when many of its residents were taken on by the aircraft factories.[3] Women were also needed, and in 1942 the government paid to establish three day nurseries.[4] Much of the women's effort was focused on the Women's Voluntary Service, set up in 1939.[5] An early task was to find homes for large numbers of children evacuated from Liverpool when war was declared. The number of evacuees exceeded that of the local school population, and the only way of teaching them was to alternate on a half-day basis. Cestrians were appalled by the poverty of the children sent to them 'unclothed, diseased, and lousy'. One local teacher evidently concluded that 'preventable poverty' was incompatible with the liberty for which the war was being fought.[6]

The government intervened to protect health, for instance through compulsory vaccination for diphtheria in 1942. Rationing of basic foods, which began early in the war, helped to ensure that food shortages did not cause serious malnutrition, and food supplements were distributed to expectant mothers at baby clinics. The government, however, could do little to improve overcrowded living conditions made worse by the large number of incoming munitions workers. Death rates in Chester, especially that of infants, remained high during the war.[7]

The war emancipated some women from home, husbands, and child care, and clergymen deplored the relaxation of moral standards.[8] Cultural life flourished through municipal concerts, plays, and debates staged for war workers and troops, including the many Americans stationed in and around Chester. Courses were run by the Workers' Educational Association, Trinity College of Music, and the Grosvenor Museum.[9]

The early years of the war were the most dangerous for civilians, although a succession of air raids from late 1940 to early 1941 did little damage. Throughout the war there were 232 alerts: 44 high-explosive bombs and three incendiaries were dropped on the city. On each of the worst occasions, 28 November 1940 and 1 July 1941, three people were killed and three seriously injured.[10] The Home Guard was established for local defence in 1940, but by 1943 the threat of invasion had passed and in 1944 it was disbanded. By then road signs had been re-erected and the Roodee reseeded for sheep pasture. Rocket attacks on London brought fresh evacuees to the Chester area.[11] In 1945 victories in Europe and the Far East were celebrated in May and August by services of thanksgiving at the cathedral, dancing in Town Hall Square, bonfires, and street parties.[12] In the ensuing flush of optimism, post-war priorities for Chester included improved housing, education, and town planning, and the restoration of Watergate Street Rows. By then German prisoners of war were already preparing the site at Blacon for the first post-war council housing estate.[13]

THE ECONOMY, 1945–74

After the war Chester's prosperity remained broadly based.[14] In the early 1950s the city still had some old-established manufacturing concerns like the lead-works and two tobacco companies, alongside newer, larger, and more modern enterprises such as Brookhirst Electrical Switchgear and two makers of metal window frames, Williams and Williams of the Reliance Works and Rustproof Metal Windows Ltd. of Saltney. Whereas the last three firms employed over 3,500 workers between them in 1951, the first three had only 500. In the same year there were some 2,000 railwaymen and 1,000 employees at Crosville Motor Services, the regional bus company based in Chester.

Much employment was generated by the city's role as the regional centre for most of west Cheshire and parts of north Wales. Farmers used its agricultural suppliers and financial services, and shoppers came in from a wide area. Retail sales per head of population in the county borough were far higher in 1950 than for any other town or city in an area stretching as far as Liverpool, Manchester, and Shrewsbury; they were higher, too, than in comparable county and resort towns elsewhere in the country, in part because of the revival of the tourist trade after the war, and its later expansion. Retailers employed over 5,000 people, and retail-type services such as catering and garages

1 *Chester City Cl. Mins.* 1938/9 to 1944/5, passim.
2 *Ches. Observer,* 13 Feb. 1940.
3 C.C.A.L.S., ZDHO 1.
4 *Ches. Observer,* 26 July 1941; 28 Mar. 1942.
5 Ibid. 1 Apr. 1939.
6 Ibid. 30 Sept. 1939; 2 Mar. 1940.
7 Ibid. 21 Mar. 1942; *Annual Reps. of M.O.H.* (1939–45).
8 e.g. *Ches. Observer,* 23 Oct. 1943.
9 Ibid. 14 July 1945.   10 Ibid. 7 Oct. 1944.

11 Ibid. 17 Apr. 1943; 1 Jan., 15 July, 9 Dec. 1944; *Images of Eng.: Ches. Regiment,* comp. Barr, 82.
12 *Ches. Observer,* 12 May, 18 Aug. 1945.
13 Ibid. 22 Sept. 1945.
14 Para. based on *Census,* 1951, *Industries,* pp. 17–18, 122; *Occupations,* pp. 168–75, 360–1; Board of Trade, *Census of Distribution,* 1950, i, p. 107 and figs. calculated from data at pp. 2–11; *Geography,* xxxvi. 51–5; *Scientific Survey of Merseyside,* ed. W. Smith, 283–4.

another 2,000. The premier department store, Browns of Eastgate Street, had a staff of over 600. Other services were also very important. The proportion of the workforce engaged in local and central government administration (the latter including the Inland Revenue and the headquarters of the Army's Western Command)[1] and banking was regarded as 'extraordinarily high': over 3,000 and 800 people respectively in 1951. There were also 1,000 Post Office and telecommunications workers. Although many city-centre workers lived in the suburbs outside the borough boundary, or further afield, the city also provided a great deal of labour for industry in the wider region, especially in aircraft manufacturing at Broughton, at the Shotton steelworks, and in the chemical industry, mostly at Ellesmere Port.

Between 1951 and 1971 the workforce increased from 30,000 to 37,000, but only because more women came into full- or part-time employment.[2] By 1971, indeed, women formed 46 per cent of the city's workers. The character of employment in Chester also changed markedly. Jobs in manufacturing fell sharply for men in the 1960s and for women throughout the period. Whereas manufacturing and construction had employed 32 per cent of men and 19 per cent of women in 1951, twenty years later they accounted for only 24 per cent and 6 per cent respectively. The decline was mainly due to the loss of jobs in engineering: Brookhirst Igranic Ltd. (formerly Brookhirst Switchgear) closed down at the end of the 1960s, while Williams and Williams, the city's largest industrial concern, was in difficulties almost throughout the decade.[3] Altogether, by 1971 there were some 2,500 fewer manufacturing jobs in the city than in 1951, two thirds of them for men. On the other hand the industrial sector in the wider region grew significantly and offered many opportunities for residents of Chester: in 1971 there were some 12,000 jobs at Vauxhall Motors in Ellesmere Port, 10,000 in oil refining and chemicals in the same town, 12,000 at the Shotton steelworks, and 4,000 at each of Hawker Siddeley in Broughton and Courtaulds man-made fibres at Flint.[4] Within the city the corporation provided a site for light industry at Sealand industrial estate in 1949, initially covering 30 acres and later extended. Eleven businesses were located there in 1960, and by 1974 it had 70 firms employing up to 2,000 people, but mostly in distribution and services rather than manufacturing.[5]

As the importance of manufacturing to the city's economy declined, so that of services grew, despite setbacks in certain areas such as the collapse of railway employment in the 1960s, from over 2,000 jobs in 1951 to significantly fewer than 1,000 in 1971. Services as a whole, including public utilities, transport, shops, financial services, public administration, hospitals, schools, hotels, and catering, already provided three in every five men's jobs and four in every five women's in Chester in 1951, much the same proportions as before the war; by 1971 the proportions had risen to 75 per cent of male employment and 90 per cent of female.[6]

Retailing was relatively stable.[7] The number of shops remained about the same at over 850, though as supermarkets became established there were fewer food shops and more selling clothes, household goods, and other non-food items. By 1971 far more jobs in shops were part-time and taken by women, and there had been a decisive shift in the relative significance of independently owned outlets and multiples: during the 1960s the share of sales in the former fell from 90 per cent to 45 per cent. By 1971 Chester had almost 1 million square feet of shopping space, most of it in the city centre. The city was absolutely the most important shopping centre in the region, with three times as much retail space as Ellesmere Port, a town of similar size, and more than Birkenhead, which had twice Chester's population. It placed Chester on a par with considerably larger county towns such as Oxford, Cambridge, and Exeter. Sales in 1971 ran at about £640 per resident, far outstripping other towns in the region and similar towns elsewhere in England, though not by as much as in 1950.

Elsewhere in the service sector, numbers employed in hotels and catering fell in the 1950s and 1960s, but nearly every other type of job became more numerous. There were 1,000 more jobs in banks, insurance companies, and other financial services in 1971 than in 1951, and 4,500 more in education, medicine, the law, and other professions: both areas of employment had more than doubled in size. The Post Office (which still ran the telephone system in 1971) had 400 more employees in 1971 than in 1951, the regional electricity board, Manweb, nearly 1,000 more, local and central government some 1,400 more.[8] In financial services, the most notable success was the rise of North West Securities under the management of Sydney Jones

1 C. P. Dryland, 'Headquarters, Western Command: Hist. Survey, 1971' (TS. at C.H.H.).

2 Para. based on *Census*, 1951, *Industries*, pp. 17–18, 122; 1961, *Occupations and Industries: Ches.* pp. 16–20, 22–4; 1971, *Econ. Activity: Ches.* pp. 29–34. Figs. for 1961 and 1971 were based on a 10 per cent sample.

3 *Kelly's Dir. Chester* (1969), 325; (1970), 327; e.g. *Chester Chron.* 13 Jan. 1962, p. 18; 3 Oct. 1964, p. 8.

4 *Census*, 1971, *Econ. Activity: Ches.* pp. 41–2; *Flints.* pp. 8–13.

5 C.C.A.L.S., ZDS 3/1282; *Kelly's Dir. Chester* (1954), 19;

(1960), 19–20; (1974), 168, 221, 236, 322; *Greater Chester District Plan: Technical Rep.* (1977), pp. 41–2.

6 *Census*, 1951, *Industries*, pp. 17–18, 122; 1961, *Occupations and Industries: Ches.* pp. 16–20, 22–4; 1971, *Econ. Activity: Ches.* pp. 29–34.

7 Para. based on Board of Trade, *Census of Distribution*, 1950, i, p. 107; 1961, p. 11/20; 1971, p. 11/65; for comparisons with other towns: 1950, i, pp. 2–11; 1971, pp. 12/38–72.

8 *Census*, 1951, *Industries*, pp. 17–18, 122; 1961, *Occupations and Industries: Ches.* pp. 16–20, 22–4; 1971, *Econ. Activity: Ches.* pp. 29–34.

(1948–79) to become a leading finance house. The company was established in Chester in 1948 as a subsidiary of a Colwyn Bay motor dealership set up to provide loans for buying cars. Expansion and diversification into industrial loans accelerated after it was bought by the Bank of Scotland in 1958. A small new head office opened in Newgate Street in 1956 and was replaced by a large one, of eight storeys, in City Road in 1963 (at the time the largest commercial building in Chester), as the company took over others and established branches nationwide. In the mid 1970s it began providing loans and other personal financial services in alliance with car manufacturers and high-street retailers, including Marks & Spencer and C & A.[1]

The rise in service employment depended very largely on Chester's position as a regional centre, whether of long standing, as for the Post Office, or newly chosen, as for the nationalized Manweb. The latter began building a new headquarters in Sealand Road in 1968 in a large group of buildings designed by Stroud, Nellis, and Partners dominated by a seven-storeyed **Y**-plan block.[2] Although Western Command disappeared as an organizational unit of the Army in 1972, its buildings were reopened as the Army Pay and Records Office in 1975.[3]

Chester's workforce was increasingly supplied from outside the city. Commuters into the county borough accounted for 37 per cent of the total employed by 1961, rising to 51 per cent by 1971, though many of them lived in the suburbs immediately beyond the county borough boundary, especially Upton and Saltney. At the same time there was a daily flow of commuters who travelled from Chester to work elsewhere, especially in the industrial plants of Ellesmere Port and Deeside: 23 per cent of the employed residents of the county borough worked outside its boundaries in 1961, 31 per cent in 1971. By the latter year there were thus large movements of workers both into and out of Chester, amounting to 18,000 and 8,500 people respectively.[4] They were signs of a healthy local economy. The city's wealth was reflected in the fact that although it was one of the smallest county boroughs, nationally ranking 74th out of 79 in population, it was seventh in rateable value per head, the joint highest (with Blackpool) in the North-West.[5] Until the

national economy began to falter in the mid 1960s Chester's unemployment rates were among the lowest in the country. In the 1950s employment was so buoyant that vacancies had to be filled from outside the area. In 1962 the Chester employment exchange area, which included parts of Tarvin and Chester rural districts and Hawarden rural district in Flintshire, had an unemployment rate of only 1.1 per cent, compared with 2.1 per cent nationally and 2.8 per cent in the North-West region.[6] Nevertheless, the dependence on a few large industrial plants for jobs in manufacturing made Chester very vulnerable in the recession of the mid 1970s.[7]

The importance of tourism to the city's prosperity was more fully appreciated in the 1960s. Tourists included day trippers, overnight visitors on their way to resorts in north Wales, and foreigners for whom Chester was the country's third most important tourist destination, after London and Stratford on Avon. The number of hotel bedrooms grew from 700 in 1960 to 1,300 twenty years later. Visitors were drawn by the antiquity of the city and by the shops in the Rows, whose character after 1947 was preserved by planning legislation. The river was also popular: motor boats were available for hire from the Groves after 1945, and by 1970 annual licences were being issued for over 650 vessels, including privately owned ones, more than three times as many as in 1950; three quarters of boat owners lived outside Chester. In 1964 the city's attitude to tourism could still be condemned as 'passive and uncertain': the council had no publicity officer or tourist information bureau, and had done nothing to develop potential attractions such as the river frontage. Only ten years later, in a rather different economic and political climate, the council had admitted past failings and was budgeting £10,000 a year to promote tourism.[8]

The notion that a university might be an economic asset emerged more slowly. When the government planned to build several new universities, the county council took the initiative and in 1961 invited Chester to send representatives to its working party. A site was identified but proposals made to the University Grants Committee were rejected in 1964.[9] Chester College remained a relatively small but expanding teacher-training institution.[10]

1 [P. Holland], *Memories of Chester* (Halifax, 1997), [10–15].

2 Pevsner, *Ches.* 172.

3 Dryland, 'Headquarters, Western Command'; *Chester Riverside Study*, section FR5L.

4 *Census*, 1961, *Workplaces*, pp. 5–6, 67; 1971, *Workplaces*, pp. 3, 30, 143 (both years based on 10 per cent sample).

5 C.C.A.L.S., ZCA 11, replies to questionnaire; *Rep. of Royal Com. on Local Government in Eng.* I [Cmnd. 4040], pp. 332, 335–6, 338–40.

6 C.C.A.L.S., ZCA 11.

7 *Ches. Observer*, 22 Jan. 1965; *Greater Chester District Plan: Technical Rep.* (1977), pp. 30–44.

8 Chester Junior Chamber of Commerce, *Rep. on Tourism* (1964); *Ches. Observer*, 15 Nov. 1974; *Chester Riverside Study*, sections FR3E, FR4B, FR4C; Chester City Cl. Econ. and Tourism Development Unit, *Chester Tourism 2000* (copy in Chester Public Libr. ref. colln.), 23.

9 Chester City Cl. Mins. 1961/2, pp. 152–3, 175; 1963/4, pp. 792, 899–900; 1964/5, p. 968.

10 *V.C.H. Ches.* v (2), Education: Chester College.

LOCAL GOVERNMENT AND POLITICS, 1945–74

Politics and Services. In 1946 Chester's parliamentary constituency was extended further into the surrounding rural districts. The Conservatives won all the elections in the period with majorities ranging from 2,800 to 11,000 and normally taking over half the vote. Labour was always in second place, usually polling around a third of the vote. The Liberals came a poor third when they stood, and failed to put up a candidate in 1951 and 1959.[1]

In local elections, too, Labour made significant gains and replaced the Liberals as the second party. The three parties had virtually equal representation in 1945, but thereafter the Conservatives gained at the Liberals' expense. When Conservative fortunes were low the Liberal vote tended to recover, and except in the mid 1960s was generally high enough to prevent Labour from achieving an overall majority. There was little serious animosity between the three parties; local politics were still the politics of the rates, and Labour was forced to adopt the same call for 'economy' as its rivals.[2]

The functions performed by the county borough were reduced by the post-war Labour government. Chester's police force was merged with the county's in 1949, although the city still contributed to its costs and was the location of the county headquarters (in Foregate Street until 1964).[3] Chester retained its own fire service until 1974.[4] With the loss of the profitable municipal electricity undertaking through nationalization in 1948,[5] the corporation's chief remaining assets were its estates, markets, and share of the profits of the race meeting. The municipal transport undertaking, which made large profits during the war, thereafter fluctuated between profits as high as £7,500 in 1959 and deficits of almost £3,000 in 1957 and 1958. In 1972 there was a surplus in the revenue account of £21,000.[6]

For a while after 1945 both main political parties believed in the need for more public spending, underpinned by central government support. As a result the council became increasingly dependent upon centrally provided rate-support grants. Although national legislation removed some heavy burdens of health and welfare from the council's remit, the rates still rose, in particular to pay for educational reform. As early as 1955 the total capital spending programme, the greater part of which was for new schools and the refurbish-

ment of older ones, had reached an unprecedented £1¼ million. In 1963 the education committee's budget alone cost the ratepayers over £1 million. The second largest spending committee, the improvement committee, took up less than a third of that even though it had built new ambulance and fire stations, a crematorium, sewage works, roads, and housing. In the later 1960s capital expenditure continued to grow, for instance on the inner ring-road and the cattle market and abattoir at Saltney.

While the council was expected to provide a higher standard and range of public services, the large increases in rates to pay for them were very unpopular.[7] By the early 1970s the council was left with little scope for independent action, accompanied by an inflexible rate bill which depended almost entirely on factors outside its control, such as the size of government grants, national interest rates, and salaries and wages negotiated nationally. Central government's contribution to the council's expenditure rose from a quarter of the total in 1952 to three fifths by 1972. Most of it was for education and housing.[8]

In the 1960s Chester spent less per head on services than the average county borough. In 1962, for example, it underspent the national average by 2 per cent on education, 32 per cent on health, 10 per cent on welfare, and 2 per cent on childrens' services.[9] Its parsimony was the cause of civic pride, even though it had probably been achieved at the expense of quality of service.[10] One of the council's objectives was to keep the rates of city-centre shops as low as possible, and when the government took over responsibility for valuation in 1955 shopkeepers found that their rates increased by up to 200 per cent.[11]

Chester was more successful than any other borough in the North-West in increasing its rateable value. The growth was mainly due to shops and offices. From 1952 to 1972 the contribution of industry as a percentage of the total rose from 3 per cent to 4.2 per cent whereas the share of shops and other commercial premises increased from 25 per cent to 38 per cent. The wish to maximize revenue determined the council's attitude towards the commercial redevelopment of the city centre, perhaps without sufficient consideration for environmental factors or the needs of Cestrians.

1 *Brit. Parl. Election Results, 1918–49*, ed. F. W. S. Craig, 302; *1950–73*, ed. Craig (1983), 336.

2 e.g. *Ches. Observer*, 25 Mar. 1966.

3 *V.C.H. Ches.* v (2), Law and Order: Policing; *Kelly's Dir. Ches.* (1923), 239; *Kelly's Dir. Chester* (1958), 55; below, this chapter: Town Planning and the Built Environment, 1945–74 (City Centre Redevelopment).

4 *V.C.H. Ches.* v (2), Law and Order: Fire Service.

5 Ibid. Public Utilities: Electricity.

6 Financial details in this para. and rest of section based on C.C.A.L.S., ZDTR 5/72–94.

7 e.g. *Ches. Observer*, 9 Mar. 1963.

8 Ibid. 15 Mar. 1973.

9 C.C.A.L.S., ZCA 11.

10 *Ches. Observer*, 25 Mar. 1966.

11 Ibid. 25 Feb. 1956.

The small size of a county borough such as Chester could lead to organizational inefficiency and a tendency to reactive, short-term decision making. In 1968 the town clerk noted the absence of a policy-making committee,[1] a problem compounded by the increased volume of council business.[2]

Borough Extension.[3]   Chester could perhaps have increased its revenues more if it had been able to extend its boundaries to include those areas of the surrounding rural districts which had become suburbs and for which the county borough provided most of the services. They included both council and private estates, many of whose residents worked in Deeside or Ellesmere Port. Attempts at widening its boundaries,

however, usually encountered strong opposition from Cheshire county council. As one of the smallest county boroughs, there was thus a genuine possibility that Chester would lose its independent status. In 1951 its population was under 50,000 and even after it absorbed Hoole urban district in 1954 it was still less than the 60,000 thought to be sufficient to guarantee the retention of county-borough status. In 1962 the council unsuccessfully sought a further extension which would have brought under its control not only the suburban housing estates but also Saltney and Sealand as potential industrial areas. In 1971 Chester's population exceeded 60,000, but by then 100,000 was considered a more realistic figure to guarantee independence.

TOWN PLANNING AND THE BUILT ENVIRONMENT, 1945–74

The town-planning proposals made by Chester immediately after the Second World War extended beyond the county borough's boundaries, but in 1947 legislation made the county council the planning authority for the rural areas and outer suburbs, confining the city's responsibilities within its own boundaries. After that the city could prepare a development plan only for the central clearance area, approved by the government in 1952.[4] In 1957, with government approval, the county drew up plans for a green belt, roughly following the line of the projected outer ring-road. The intention was to restrict further building in rural areas and to prevent urban sprawl from spreading all the way to Ellesmere Port, but in Chester it was seen as designed to prevent a successful submission for a borough extension.[5] Despite protests that the green belt had been drawn too tightly,[6] together with the shortage of building land and the continuing difficulty of balancing economic growth with environmental considerations, the planning restrictions in fact proved to be the key to prosperity. City centre shops clearly attracted visitors in part because of their historic environment, and conservation was vital to their success. The main developments in planning, rebuilding, and conservation did not really begin until after 1960, but by 1974 the appearance of much of the city centre within and just beyond the walls had changed radically, while new suburbs had spread far to the west and north of the older built-up area.

Traffic and Road Planning.   A major element in the council's plans was the completion of inner and outer ring-roads, since it was acknowledged that the solution of the traffic problem would determine whether Chester remained a regional centre.[7] The outer ring-road remained incomplete, notably south of the city, where a new bridge across the Dee was urgently needed. The inner ring-road had its origins in the widening of Little St. John Street in 1938. In 1962, after abandoning a proposal to widen Northgate Street,[8] the council adopted a scheme which connected Little St. John Street, Pepper Street, and Grosvenor Street to a new roundabout north of the castle and then ran north along a widened Nicholas Street and Linenhall Street, to swing eastwards outside the walls on an elevated viaduct and then descend southwards across the site of the cattle market at the Gorse Stacks to join Foregate Street at the junction with City Road. Although the planned route connected with Grosvenor Bridge, which already took far too much traffic, the government endorsed the scheme and paid three quarters of its construction costs of £1.2 million.[9] The north-western section was opened in 1966,[10] and the entire road had been completed by 1972. Although it improved traffic flow, its impact on the environment caused concern. The northern city wall was breached to make the austere St. Martin's Gate, designed by the city engineer and surveyor, A. H. F. Jiggens, in consultation with G. Grenfell Baines and with approval from the Royal Fine Arts Commission.[11] St. Martin's

1 *Ches. Observer*, 22 Nov. 1968.   2 Ibid. 14 May 1971.
3 Para. based on ibid. 29 Sept. 1945; 27 July 1946; 31 Aug. 1957; C.C.A.L.S., ZCA 9, 11; *V.C.H. Ches.* v (2), Population.
4 C.C.A.L.S., ZCA 9, statement to Sir John Maude.
5 Ibid. ZCA 11, notes on counter-observations.
6 e.g. *Ches. Observer*, 31 Aug. 1957.
7 e.g. D. W. Insall, *Chester: A Study in Conservation* (H.M.S.O.

1968), 39–59; cf. [Holland], *Memories of Chester*, [20–1].
8 Greenwood, *Chester*, 36–47; *Ches. Observer*, 30 Sept. 1950; 7 Apr. 1951; 7 Apr. 1962.
9 *Ches. Observer*, 11 Feb. 1961; 9 June 1962.
10 Ibid. 29 Apr. 1966.
11 *Chester City Cl. Mins.* 1962/3, pp. 218, 349, 558–9, 840, 921; Boughton, *Picturesque Chester*, no. 86.

church was sacrificed, along with Georgian houses on the east side of Nicholas Street, and Egerton House on Upper Northgate Street, regarded by one observer as among the city's best Georgian buildings.[1] In addition the viaduct was thought obtrusive,[2] the way in which the new road separated the city centre from the Dee was widely condemned, and there were doubts about the impact of the concrete multi-storey car parks built as part of the scheme.[3] The removal of the cattle market from the Gorse Stacks to a new site at Sealand Road in 1970, however, was a distinct environmental improvement, as the movement of cattle between it and the railway station had previously held up traffic, inconvenienced pedestrians, and discouraged tourists.[4]

An extensive one-way system within the city had been planned in 1950 but was opposed by traders who feared that it would affect sales. A very limited scheme, in Foregate Street alone, was begun in 1966.[5] With the inner ring-road and car parks in place, further one-way routes were introduced in 1971,[6] and vehicular access to the central streets around the Cross was restricted from 1972–3.[7]

City Centre Redevelopment.   Immediately west of the town hall was a large tract of derelict land from which substandard housing had been cleared in the 1930s. In 1945 the city engineer and surveyor, Charles Greenwood, presented a redevelopment plan which attempted to reconcile economic and cultural considerations. As well as council offices and a replacement for the Victorian public market, which no longer complied with hygiene regulations, the plan included a civic centre with a new central library, a museum and art gallery, and a concert hall. A scheme based on Greenwood's plan was approved by the government in 1952 but not put into effect.[8] In 1958 the council added a bus exchange to its requirements,[9] and in 1960 invited private developers to submit schemes. The brief was for an extension to the town hall, a general market with associated car parks, and sites for private development. The council appointed G. Grenfell Baines as its planning consultant, and in 1961, on his recommendation that it was 'sound and imaginative town planning expressed in good modern architecture', accepted a scheme, the Forum, by Michael Lyell & Associates.[10] Although the city, which owned the land,

was freed from the costs of development, it ceded the bulk of the profits to private enterprise.[11] The Forum was closely associated with the inner ring-road, which was planned to run along the western edge of the site and from which car parking under the market hall, and the new bus station, were reached.

Grenfell Baines produced planning guidelines for the whole city centre in 1964,[12] but the first phase of Lyell's scheme, the market hall, was delayed until 1967 because of archaeological work.[13] Only the market hall retained the boxy design of Lyell's original scheme; the final phase, which included council offices and a shopping mall and was delayed by excavation until 1969–72, was characterized by the Brutalist brick-clad forms made fashionable in the early 1960s by the architect James Stirling. It had council offices boldly cantilevered over the Northgate Street entrance to the shopping mall, and was widely hated from the start.[14] Office blocks were built speculatively near by, north of Hunter Street, but no attempt was made to integrate them with the Forum.

Multi-level planning similar to the Forum's was used by the Grosvenor-Laing property company for the Grosvenor Centre on 3½ acres owned by the Grosvenor estate between Bridge Street, Eastgate Street, Pepper Street, and Newgate Street. The last was blocked by the multi-storey car park and department store at the centre of the scheme. The design of 1963, by Sir Percy Thomas and Son, was an early example of the tendency in historic towns to hide bulky new shopping centres behind existing buildings. It left the Rows almost intact, including a new block along Eastgate Street, separately designed Row-fashion by Gordon Jeeves in 1962 for Central & District Properties.[15] The new buildings were exposed only to the rear, where a multi-storey car park faced the Newgate and Newgate Street, and on Pepper Street, which received a long concrete-clad façade. The scheme incorporated the early 20th-century St. Michael's Row and the Grosvenor Hotel, which was lavishly refurbished and extended, while providing 60 new shops, as well as office and conference facilities. It took only two years to complete, compared with the 12-year gestation of the Forum, and when opened in 1964, it was estimated that it would contribute £100,000 to the rates.[16] On a smaller scale but similar in planning approach was Mercia Square (1970) in Frodsham Street.

1 D. Bethell, *Portrait of Chester*, 53.

2 e.g. letters in *Ches. Observer*, 29 Apr. 1966; 8 Jan. 1971.

3 Ibid. 12 Feb. 1970; 4 Feb. 1972.

4 *Chester City Cl. Mins. 1969/70*, p. 892.

5 Ibid. *1950/1*, pp. 228–35, 287–9; *Ches. Observer*, 1 June 1957; 29 Apr. 1966.

6 *Chester City Cl. Mins. 1972/3*, pp. 62, 659–60, 715–16, 763; *Ches. Observer*, 29 Apr. 1966; 29 Jan. 1972; *Town Planning Rev.* xlvi. 394.

7 *Greater Chester District Plan: Technical Rep.* (1977), p. 62.

8 Greenwood, *Chester*; *Ches. Observer*, 28 Sept. 1946; 3 May 1958; 18 Dec. 1964.

9 *Ches. Observer*, 3 May 1958.

10 *Architect and Building News*, 8 Mar. 1961, pp. 308–9; *Architects' Jnl.* 22 May 1963, p. 1070.

11 *Ches. Observer*, 26 July 1958.

12 Ibid. 19 May 1967; G. Grenfell Baines, *Chester: Plan for Central Area* (1964).

13 *Chester City Cl. Mins. 1965/6*, p. 124.

14 *Chester Chron.* 6 Dec. 1968; *Ches. Observer*, 27 Oct. 1972.

15 C.C.A.L.S., ZDLC 3/14; *Architects' Jnl.* 22 May 1963, pp. 1070–1; *More Memories of Chester*, ed. E. Pierce Jones (2000), 88–9.

16 *Ches. Observer*, 4 Dec. 1964.

A handful of relatively small, cautiously modern commercial buildings invaded sensitive sites, for example that built in 1963 in Northgate Street,[1] and another of higher quality in Watergate Street. The most prominently sited and uncompromisingly modern new building was the eight-storeyed county police headquarters, designed in 1964 by the county architect, Edgar Taberner, for a site dominating the entrance to the city from the Grosvenor Bridge, formerly occupied by the militia barracks.[2]

By the mid 1960s the area within the walls was virtually devoid of residents and consequently free of serious smoke pollution. To enliven the centre, which at night was virtually empty and prey to vandals,[3] planners began to advocate the provision of new residential accommodation.[4] Depopulation entailed a reorganization of the city's Anglican parishes and the redundancy of several city churches in 1972.[5] The Methodists rationalized their circuits in 1963 and closed city-centre chapels in Hunter Street and George Street in 1967 and 1970. Among the other main denominations, the Congregationalists did not rebuild their chapel in Queen Street after it was destroyed by fire in 1963, and left the Upper Northgate Street chapel in 1967, while the Baptists abandoned Grosvenor Park Road in 1974. The Unitarians replaced the Matthew Henry chapel, a victim of the inner-city redevelopment scheme in 1962, with a chapel in Blacon. All the main denominations and many of the smaller groups, however, retained a presence in the city centre in 1974.[6]

In 1962 the Civic Trust, founded in 1959 to heighten public awareness of Chester's character, history, and civic design, initiated a plan to improve the appearance of the main streets. Owners and traders were persuaded to finance the refurbishment of their properties to an overall design, and to remove or replace unsightly signs. The council paid the fees of an architect to prepare the design and oversee its execution. In 1966 the first scheme, for Bridge Street, was judged a success, and Eastgate Street then received similar treatment.[7] The radical transformation of the city centre during the 1960s, however, exposed the conflict between growth and environmental quality, and heightened tensions between those who opposed change and those who sought it.[8]

Conservation.   Many Cestrians considered the historic city to be essentially medieval, which is perhaps why they had countenanced the loss of Georgian and Victorian buildings and continued to prefer a fake half-timbered version of the Domestic Revival style. The council did little to preserve Chester's genuine historic buildings, and by the 1940s much of the Rows was in very poor repair, and Lower Bridge Street could be described as 'verging on a slum'.[9] In 1955 property in Watergate Street, bought by the council to protect it, was destroyed on the grounds that it had deteriorated beyond repair.[10] The Gap, as it became known, was a constant embarrassment to the council, which organized a competition for an infill design in 1963, won by Herbert J. Rowse & Harker;[11] their block of shops and offices, designed as a Row in a contemporary idiom with flat-roofed cantilevered bays and exposed concrete, remained unfinished until the late 1960s.[12] Successive councils had proved unwilling to spend money on conservation.[13] In 1959, for example, the corporation announced that the Blue Bell Inn in Northgate Street was too expensive to repair and would be pulled down. The ensuing campaign ended when the government refused to permit demolition, and the corporation had to spend £2,500 on preserving the building.[14]

By 1966 opinion was changing; the council was persuaded to abandon plans to destroy Georgian houses in Queen Street,[15] and agreed to renovate the Nine Houses in Park Street rather than demolish them.[16] Even so, it is doubtful whether conservation on a serious scale could have begun without extensive help from national funds.[17] In 1966 Richard Crossman, minister of housing and local government, commissioned a pilot study of four towns of special historic importance, including Chester, to elicit what special problems such places faced in relation to their modern development. The study led to the formulation of a national policy on conservation which had extremely important consequences for many historic towns and cities.[18] The report of Chester's consultant, Donald Insall, was a watershed in the history of conservation in the city. The content and status of his report, with the weight of central government behind it, changed the council's attitude. The crucial factor was the availability of central government funds for conserva-

1 *Chester Chron.* 30 Mar. 1963.
2 Pevsner, *Ches.* 158; *Ches. Observer,* 16 Feb., 4 Oct. 1963.
3 e.g. *Ches. Observer,* 3 Nov. 1962.
4 e.g. ibid. 6 Dec. 1974.
5 *V.C.H. Ches.* v (2), Medieval Parish Churches; Modern Parish Churches.
6 Ibid. Protestant Nonconformity; Other Churches.
7 *Ches. Observer,* 25 Aug. 1962; 22 July 1966; Crosby, *Chester Arch. Soc.* 37.
8 Inf. from Mr. P. de Figueiredo, former conservation officer, Chester City Cl.; cf. *Ches. Observer,* 29 May 1964; 7 June 1966; 29 June 1973; 4 Jan., 3 May 1974; Bethell, *Portrait of Chester,* 53.

9 *Ches. Observer,* 26 Feb. 1944; cf. ibid. 18 Apr. 1949.
10 Ibid. 1 Jan. 1955.
11 *Architects' Jnl.* 6 Nov. 1963, p. 936.
12 *Ches. Observer,* 8 Feb. 1968.
13 e.g. ibid. 21 May 1957.
14 Ibid. 9 Jan., 3 July 1960.
15 Ibid. 18 Feb. 1966.
16 Ibid. 27 Apr. 1957; 18 Jan. 1966; 1 Aug. 1969.
17 *Town Planning Rev.* xlvi. 384.
18 *Ches. Observer,* 5 Aug. 1966; 'Rep. of Conference for 25th Anniversary of Insall Rep.' *Chester Civic Trust Newsletter,* May 1995.

tion. The Insall Report dealt with all aspects of town planning, from traffic management to tree-planting, in relation to the city's historic fabric. It asserted that the restoration of old buildings could enhance both their own value and that of the whole city centre, and provided a realistically costed 15-year programme which identified the buildings most in need of saving.[1] The council's director of technical services, Cyril Morris, put many of Insall's recommendations into effect immediately. In 1969 a conservation area of 200 acres was declared, covering the city within the walls, the Roodee, and a section of the river frontage. The council began an exemplary policy of acquiring, restoring, and selling buildings, and encouraged private owners, developers, and architects to undertake similar renovation work, backed by council and government grants. A conservation officer was employed to liaise with local residents, for instance in King Street, where individual owners rehabilitated their houses. A new conservation rate of 1*d.* in the pound, at the time unique in English cities, was expected to raise £30,000 a year for a conservation fund.[2] In 1970 the council appointed Insall and Associates as its conservation consultants, in which role they continued until 1987; they instituted a phased programme and reported on progress in 1976 and 1986.[3]

Three of the thirteen separate areas of individual character mapped by Insall and Associates were identified as action areas. The first to be the subject of detailed plans by the consultants was the Bridgegate area in 1970, followed by Watergate Street in 1973. The Bridgegate plan was approved in 1973,[4] and work financed equally by local and central government was completed in 1980. It began with the renovation of older buildings on the west side of Lower Bridge Street such as Shipgate House and Gamul House, and of terraces in the adjoining Gamul Place, which had been neglected by their owner, the county council. Sympathetically designed residential units were built to replace low-grade property and to fill empty sites. After 1974 the Falcon Inn at the top end of Lower Bridge Street was saved as a public house by a small charitable trust set up for the purpose, and new uses were found for three redundant churches in the area, St. Michael, St. Olave, and St. Mary. An empty building in Duke Street became the county record office.[5]

Archaeology. Before the late 1960s Chester also neglected the archaeological record. The work of Professor Robert Newstead (d. 1947) was largely unrecognized.[6] Such indifference ignored the potential contribution of the excavated archaeology to the tourist trade. Excavation by Ian Richmond in the 1940s in the central clearance area revealed the Roman army's headquarters building in Goss Street and the ditch fronting the Roman west wall in Princess Street.[7] In the 1960s redevelopment of the city centre provided a unique opportunity to discover more of the Roman fortress. The excavations, which were funded by the government and the corporation, revealed the plan of a unique elliptical building and Roman floors on the Forum site, and the full extent of the bathhouse, together with part of a barrack block, under the Grosvenor Centre. The destruction of the remains of the baths, still of great size and a high degree of preservation, provoked much controversy.[8]

The walls were the city's most potent tourist attraction.[9] Despite proposals by Greenwood in 1945 and Grenfell Baines in 1964, the council failed to ensure that their surroundings were cleared and landscaped. Their very survival was always precarious, for the friable stone of which they were built made them expensive to conserve and repair. Only after the Insall Report of 1968 were the walkways even cleaned efficiently.[10]

The greatest test of the council's commitment to uncovering Chester's ancient history was its attitude to the Roman amphitheatre. In 1949 the Ministry of Works offered to excavate it if given guardianship.[11] The council agreed, and work began in 1960. Since Dee House remained in private hands, only the section already owned by the city and the Archaeological Society could be excavated. The work proceeded slowly throughout the 1960s, partly because of difficulty in shoring up the adjoining higher ground. When it was completed in 1971, there was much disappointment among the general public that there was little to see. By 1974, the improvement committee, however, was prepared to state publicly that the amphitheatre was 'one of the greatest unrealized assets in the city',[12] but its future remained a matter of debate in 2000. Little interest was taken in any aspects of Chester's archaeology other than the Roman period.[13]

1 Insall, *Chester: Study in Conservation.*
2 *Ches. Observer*, 5 Dec. 1969.
3 C. M. Morris and D. W. Insall, *Chester: Conservation Review Study, 1976* (copy in Chester City Cl. Conservation Dept., Oct. 2000); D. W. Insall and C. M. Morris, *Conservation in Chester: Chester City Cl. Conservation Review Study, 1986* (1988).
4 *Ches. Observer*, 24 July 1970; 23 July 1971; 16 Mar., 18 May 1973.
5 D. W. Insall, *Conservation in Action: Chester's Bridgegate* (H.M.S.O. 1982); *Chartered Surveyor Weekly*, 15 Mar. 1984, p. 722.
6 *Ches. Observer*, 22 Feb. 1947, obituary; 26 Oct. 1957.

7 Ibid. 29 Sept. 1945; 12 June 1948.
8 Ibid. 24 July 1964; 5 Nov. 1965; 5 Sept., 12 Oct. 1969; R. Newstead and J. P. Droop, 'Excavations at Chester, 1939: Princess Street Clearance Area', *J.C.A.S.* xxxiv. 5–47; D. F. Petch, 'Filling the Gaps: A Decade of Growth, 1962–73', ibid. lxxii. 57–72.
9 Prof. Ian Richmond quoted in *Ches. Observer*, 22 Jan. 1965.
10 Ibid. 22 Jan., 6 Aug. 1955; 7 Nov. 1959; 22 May 1969; Insall, *Chester: Study in Conservation*, 106–11.
11 *Ches. Observer*, 2 July 1949; P.R.O., WORK 14/1590.
12 *Ches. Observer*, 9 July, 27 Aug. 1971; 13 Sept. 1974.
13 e.g. *J.C.A.S.* xxxvi–lviii, *passim.*

HOUSING AND SUBURBAN DEVELOPMENT, 1945–74

The city's problems in providing sufficient houses after the Second World War were exacerbated by the fact that many workers at Ellesmere Port, Shotton, and elsewhere chose to live in the city because of its attractiveness as a residential area.[1] Immediately after the war, the council built 160 prefabricated houses from components produced at the aircraft factory at Broughton. With higher levels of government subsidy, and despite difficulties in finding sites, it went on to build almost 6,700 houses between 1947 and 1974, far more than the 1,600 completed between 1914 and 1939.[2]

Even so, the housing problem remained acute. When the government restarted its slum-clearance policies in 1954, there were still 1,000 families in accommodation which on average shared a tap between six houses and a lavatory between eight.[3] As earlier, tenants in the clearance areas were inhibited from moving to new council houses by the higher rents charged for them. Nevertheless, by 1964 there had been over 1,000 demolitions,[4] and in 1972, encouraged by the 1969 Housing Act, the housing committee announced that further slum clearances were necessary and that because of high demand it would continue to build 300 council houses a year. By then those who needed rehousing included a greater proportion of single, widowed, divorced, and elderly people wanting smaller accommodation.[5] From the outset, planners tried to ensure that mistakes made between the World Wars were not repeated, and provided new housing estates with open spaces, community centres, health clinics, libraries, churches, and old people's homes.[6] The pre-war Lache estate acquired a community centre in 1955.[7] At Blacon, developed entirely after 1945, there were eleven schools, two shopping centres, an old people's home, a library, a community centre, a public house, and five churches by 1970.[8] At Newton, however, although a full range of community services was planned in 1955, there were still no playing fields, community centre, or old people's home in 1972.[9]

Post-war council housing was concentrated in the areas added to the county borough in 1936. A very large estate was built at Blacon, and smaller ones adjoining each other in Newton and Upton. At Blacon, where temporary dwellings had been erected in 1946,[10] the building of some 684 houses was approved in 1949, 600 of them in a single section focused on Blacon Avenue, which was also to have 24 shops and a community centre.[11] Another 50 houses were approved in 1950,[12] and building continued into the 1950s on a generous layout with plenty of open space in the form of broad roadside verges and larger greens on the main thoroughfares, Blacon Avenue north of the railway line, and Western Avenue south of it. East of the latter, the streets around Fowler and Wemyss Roads were lined with widely spaced semi-detached houses, while Blacon Avenue was developed with the neo-Georgian shops and flats of the Parade, and, stretching east, terraces with the flavour of pre-war garden-suburb cottages. In the early 1960s the estate was extended north along concentric rings of streets, including Stamford Road and Hatton Road north of the Parade, where a second block of shops and flats, modern in style, was built in 1964–6.[13] By then the city-wide shortage of development land influenced the layout of the southern neighbourhood, where two 12-storeyed blocks of flats and a compact square of shops were built; other multi-storey blocks were planned but not built, largely because they were unpopular with tenants and expensive to erect.[14] Building continued into the 1970s with low-rise housing at higher densities, mainly short terraces of mixed construction, until by *c.* 1980 the estate was built up.

A spacious layout prevailed also at Newton and Upton. The Newton Hall estate was built between 1957 and 1960, Plas Newton between 1960 and 1966,[15] and Upton Park, stretching east from Stanton Drive and Dickson's Drive to Wealstone Lane, between 1954 and 1961.[16] Churches, schools, and other community facilities were sited on slices of open land between Newton Lane and Kingsway in Newton, west of Wealstone Lane in Upton, and in the grounds of Plas Newton Hall, with shops in a commercial centre on Newton Lane. The largest of the other council devel-

1 e.g. *Ches. Observer*, 31 Aug. 1957.

2 Ibid. 2 May 1969; Ministry of Health (later Ministry of Housing and Local Government), *Housing Returns for Eng. and Wales, 1946–74*; *Greater Chester District Plan: Technical Rep.* (1977), pp. 16–20; C.C.A.L.S., ZCA 11; ZDTR 5/92, tables 10 and 12, pp. 267, 269. Plate 61 for prefabs.

3 *Ches. Observer*, 10 Nov. 1956.

4 Ibid. 10 Mar. 1956; 21 Oct. 1969; *Chester City Cl. Mins. 1963/4*, by indexed refs. to Housing: Slum Clearance; C.C.A.L.S., ZDHO 26–7.

5 *Ches. Observer*, 29 Dec. 1972; 13 Dec. 1974; cf. *Greater Chester District Plan: Technical Rep.* (1977), pp. 19–22.

6 Greenwood, *Chester*, 56–8; *Ches. Observer*, 13 July 1946.

7 *Ches. Observer*, 12 Feb. 1955.

8 Ibid. 3 July 1970.

9 Ibid. 26 Feb. 1955; 9 June 1972; 1 June 1973.

10 *Chester City Cl. Mins. 1944/5* and *1945/6*, by indexed refs. to Housing: Temporary.

11 C.C.A.L.S., ZDS 3/1270, 1273.

12 Ibid. ZDS 3/1296–7.

13 *Kelly's Dir. Chester* (1966), 116.

14 *Chester City Cl. Mins. 1965/6*, pp. 307, 432, 1001; *Ches. Observer*, 4, 18 Mar., 7 Oct. 1966.

15 C.C.A.L.S., TS. list of class ZDHO.

16 Ibid. ZDLC 3/14; rest of para. and much of rest of this section based on observation.

opments was at Hoole, around a long road looping north from Hoole Lane to Hoole Road. Otherwise council housing was restricted to small pockets, for example at Melrose Avenue north of the railway and canal off Vicars Cross Road, and tucked into the Lache estate, where a small site off Willow Road was developed in the late 1960s or early 1970s with terraces similar to those built in the later phases at Blacon. Chester was subject to only one, very limited attempt at comprehensive redevelopment in the 1960s, when an area of 19th-century housing between City Road and Crewe Street near the railway station was replaced by a mixed development of two 11-storeyed blocks of flats and 4-storeyed walk-up blocks, with one or two 19th-century buildings preserved.

Most houses on all the outer estates were plain and brick-built with shallow-pitched roofs, and were arranged in straight terraces or semi-detached pairs. The walk-up blocks of flats, including those in the spine road through the Newton Hall estate, Coniston Road, were similarly conservative but flat-roofed; even the multi-storey slab blocks were brick-clad, and low compared with tower blocks in other cities.

Between 1961 and 1971 the amount of council housing increased by 6 per cent to 30 per cent of the housing stock and private accommodation for owner-occupiers by 4 per cent to 52 per cent, while privately owned rented accommodation fell from 28 per cent to 18 per cent. Only in the 1970s, after severe cuts in public funds for housing, did private house-building within the county borough exceed that by the council.[1] There was more private building in Upton and Great Boughton, outside the borough boundary, and the influx of middle-class house purchasers into Chester as a whole was so marked that in the late 1960s estate agents reported that the city was becoming a dormitory for middle and higher income groups.[2]

Immediately after the war, particularly in 1946–7, many large houses in areas such as Curzon Park and Stanley Place were divided into flats.[3] Building of individual houses in established roads, especially at the west end of Curzon Park, restarted in the late 1940s, as did medium-sized developments such as the Grosvenor estate's 40 houses in Brown's Lane, Handbridge,[4] and the 23 houses off Earlsway, Curzon Park, designed by A. R. Keane for Walker and Dawson in 1947.[5] The first very large scheme to be approved, in 1949, was the Newton and Upton estate proposed by the Newton Upton Land Co., which involved 177 houses.[6]

Individual private houses were built in the early 1950s at Blacon,[7] and throughout the 1950s and 1960s along main roads, cheek by jowl with pre-war homes, for example in Lache Lane and in Saughall Road, Blacon, where bungalows had been popular since the 1930s.[8] Existing suburbs also grew or were finally completed. In Curzon Park, empty plots were filled on the south side of Curzon Park North and in Curzon Park South, and some large gardens were subdivided. At Queen's Park, houses were built on the south side of Lower Park Road away from the river Dee, spreading east into Elizabeth Crescent c. 1964, and as a single scheme into Queen's Drive. North of the city centre, houses off Mill Lane continued the development of the isolated 19th-century speculation at Upton Park, and development continued until the 1970s along the east and north sides of Upton-by-Chester golf course. Groups of houses or estates of middle-income type were kept small, for example the Lache Hall estate, begun in 1959 south of Circular Drive, and the Queen's Drive group. Nearer the centre, building continued on very small pockets of land off Liverpool and Parkgate Roads, for example in Garth Drive in 1953–4,[9] and Dawson Drive, and more houses were squeezed into the closes already developed, such as Abbots Grange and Abbots Park, where additional culs-de-sac were formed c. 1960.

Throughout the 1950s and 1960s cheaper private housing was built next to council estates. At Blacon 44 houses in Western Avenue and Highfield Road were designed for sale by the council itself in 1960, and at Lache c. 1960–2, Oldfield and Snowdon Crescents and Clifford Drive were laid out like adjacent council-estate roads. One of the largest schemes was at Upton and Newton, where the east end of Plas Newton Lane and the area south of it was developed with over 100 semi-detached houses and bungalows along streets including Ullswater Crescent, Ambleside, and Derwent Road; planned in 1955, the scheme was not completed until the mid 1960s,[10] and was continued east into Ethelda Drive and Kennedy Close from 1963. Similar housing was scattered throughout the area north of Vicars Cross Road, for example in Green Lane and Queens Road, and was built in Hoole from 1954–5 in Kilmorey Park Avenue and Woodfield Grove. Other groups were built from 1958–60 on the western edge of Blacon, south of Highfield Road, and at Blacon Point farm by Invincible Homes.

Sites between existing housing and new or improved roads were also exploited. In Hoole, cheap semi-detached housing in Pipers Lane was built as a fringe between council housing to the west and the bypass (A41) on the east. In Lache, an estate approved in 1966–7 was built between Lache Lane and Wrexham Road, with its focus a sizeable shopping parade on Five Ashes Road.

1 *Greater Chester District Plan: Technical Rep.* (1977), pp. 17–18.
2 Insall, *Chester: Study in Conservation*, 73.
3 e.g. C.C.A.L.S., ZDS 3/965, 978, 981–2, 1014, 1016.
4 Ibid. ZDS 3/959.   5 Ibid. ZDS 3/1065.
6 Ibid. ZDS 3/1256.
7 e.g. ibid. ZDS 3/1417–18.
8 Ibid. ZDS 3/1465.
9 Ibid. ZDS 3/1406, 1458; *Kelly's Dir. Chester* (1954), 53.
10 *Kelly's Dir. Chester* (1962), 147; (1964), 151; (1966), 154.

There was almost no innovation in the design of speculative houses built in Chester after 1945 even among expensive architect-designed homes, one of the modest exceptions being the International Modern-style house designed at no. 11 Curzon Park North by T. O. Pottinger & Partners in 1967–8.[1] Indeed, most houses of the 1950s were indistinguishable from those built between the World Wars, and some of *c.* 1955 in Daleside, Upton,[2] still had the metal windows and

Art Deco styling considered particular to inter-war architecture. Cheap speculative housing was of brick and had little embellishment beyond shallow bay windows with some tile-hanging. The same house types continued to be built into the 1960s, when the Scandinavian-influenced style characterized by low-pitched roofs, weatherboarding, and large horizontal expanses of window also became popular.

SOCIETY AND CULTURE, 1945–74

Health.[3]   The establishment of the National Health Service consolidated earlier gains in some aspects of public health. In 1948, because of immunization, there were no cases of diphtheria for the first time in Chester's recorded medical history. In the 1950s treatment with new antibiotics and vaccination virtually eradicated tuberculosis. Whereas in 1932 there had been about 200 cases and 40 deaths, in 1962 only two people died of the disease. Such improvements brought other diseases to the fore: by the early 1960s lung cancer had overtaken tuberculosis as a major cause of death; coronary heart disease was also increasing, and in the 1950s there was a virulent epidemic of polio-myelitis.

In 1945 the infantile death rate was a matter for concern. It had fallen as low as 56 per thousand live births in the late 1930s, but during the war rose again into the upper 70s. The reasons, which were extensively debated in local newspapers, were thought to be bad housing, maternal undernourishment through poverty, and deficiencies in health care. There were no resident consultant paediatricians, gynaecologists, or obstetricians, no specially trained children's nurses, no special children's wards, and insufficient maternity beds.[4] In 1947 the infantile death rate in Chester rose to 81.2 per thousand live births, almost twice the national average, and the Ministry of Health instituted a local inquiry into the possible causes. Before the report was published and its recommendations effected, the corporation had appointed specialist medical and nursing staff at the City Hospital, and provided dedicated children's beds and a premature baby unit. Within two years infantile mortality fell to 20.1 per thousand live births. Thereafter there was further improvement, and by 1965 infant mortality was 14.6 per thousand live births, appreciably lower than the national average.

Despite improvements at the City Hospital there were still insufficient maternity beds, until in 1971 a new maternity unit was provided at what was later called the Countess of Chester Hospital in Liverpool Road.[5]

Under the 1948 National Assistance Act destitute old people were moved from the City Hospital, formerly the poor-law workhouse, to Sealand House, which replaced the former infectious diseases hospital in Sealand Road. Other residential homes for the elderly were established later.[6] In general Chester's health record improved dramatically between 1945 and the mid 1960s. Although better health services were the main cause, other factors included the alleviation of poverty and malnutrition, full employment, and the falling numbers of those living in overcrowded and defective houses.

Culture and Leisure.   With the spread of television there was a decline in cinema-going from the 1950s; the Music Hall cinema became a retail shop, the Gaumont a bingo hall, and by the early 1970s, when audiences began to recover, there were only two cinemas left.[7] The Royalty Theatre closed in 1966 after an unsuccessful attempt to turn it into a cabaret club.[8] In 1968 a new civic theatre, the Gateway, opened in the Forum Centre.[9] Attempts to persuade the council to fund an arts centre as a home for the city's numerous drama, music, and arts societies failed, and the cathedral remained the only suitable venue for large orchestras and audiences over 1,000.[10]

In 1961 the corporation's only contribution to arts provision was £550 pledged to cover the losses incurred by the Hallé and Liverpool Philharmonic concerts.[11] In 1967 for the first time it funded a Chester Festival, of which the central event was an adaptation of the Chester mystery plays on Cathedral Green. After

---

1   Pevsner, *Ches.* 175.

2   *Kelly's Dir. Chester* (1954), 387; (1956), 366.

3   Acct. based, except where stated otherwise, on *Annual Reps. of M.O.H.* (1932–72): copies in C.C.A.L.S., ZDH 2/10–18; ZDH 4/3–15.

4   *Ches. Observer*, 11 May 1946.

5   *V.C.H. Ches.* v (2), Medical Services: National Health Service.

6   C.C.A.L.S., ZCA 9, statement to Sir John Maude, p. 15.

7   *V.C.H. Ches.* v (2), Places of Entertainment: Cinemas; *Ches. Observer*, 7 Feb. 1959.

8   *Ches. Observer*, 19 June 1966.

9   Ibid. 22 Nov. 1968.

10   Ibid. 13 Oct. 1967; 13 Feb. 1968; 6 Oct. 1972; Greenwood, *Chester*, 59; *Chester City Cl. Mins. 1971/2*, pp. 548–9, 653; *Chester District Local Plan: First Draft for Public Consultation, Mar. 1996*, p. 218 (copy at C.H.H.).

11   *Ches. Observer*, 29 June 1961.

criticism of the council's parsimony, arts expenditure increased, primarily in the form of subsidies to the Gateway theatre.[1]

In 1948 the Chester City Record Office was established.[2] Nothing, however, was done to improve the central library, although the need for a new building had long been recognized, and the county council had in 1966 agreed to share in its cost.[3] At the Grosvenor Museum, which was more favoured, a professional archaeologist was appointed curator in 1948, and in 1953 a new Roman gallery was named after Professor Newstead. In 1966 the museum was also provided with an art gallery.[4]

The cathedral was crucial to the city's cultural life. The clergy, especially successive deans, cultivated good relations with the local community, the Army, and the corporation, through special annual services and organizations such as the Old Choristers' Association and the Friends of the Cathedral. They also hosted large orchestral concerts and performances of the mystery plays. The bishop maintained close contact with Chester College, the expansion of which after the war had a big impact on the cultural life of the city, and in the 1960s the cathedral clergy as a whole gave strong support to the bid to locate a university in Chester.[5]

Chester was reasonably well endowed with open spaces laid out for organized sports, but there was a shortage of appropriately sited land for recreation and children's play.[6] In 1945 the need for a park in the southern part of the city was recognized, and the duke of Westminster gave the corporation 46 acres at Hough Green;[7] Westminster Park, however, was not developed until 1966 when a nine-hole golf course, tennis courts, football pitches, and a running track were planned.[8] City and county co-operated on the construction of the Northgate Arena leisure centre, built on the site of Northgate station and completed in 1977.[9]

LOCAL GOVERNMENT, 1974–2000

Local Government Reorganization. The extensive discussions on the future of local government in Cheshire which followed the appointment of the Redcliffe-Maud Commission in 1966 made it clear that the county borough alone was too small to survive as a separate administrative unit. In the end Cheshire continued as a county council and Chester district council was created as a second-tier authority which united the county borough with Chester and Tarvin rural districts.[10] There was widespread relief that the city was not merged into Merseyside, as the commission had proposed, and a recognition that the county borough and the county had common interests. The county council was already a powerful presence in the city, and there were personal links between some county and city councillors, brought together by common membership of political parties, churches, and masonic lodges. The city had been losing its powers since 1945 to county or regional bodies, was not large enough to afford desirable but expensive public services on its own, and was already jointly providing secondary education with the county. Their collaboration was extended before 1974 to library and leisure facilities in Chester. Despite fears of being swallowed up in a much larger local authority and wild talk of selling the corporation buses to Crosville rather than lose them to the county (quelled when it became clear that the new district council could continue the bus service), there were also hopes expressed by the editor of the Conservative local newspaper, the *Cheshire Observer*, that 'reform should give us better government than we have had in the past'.[11]

The new district council which came into being in 1974 thus united the city with the extensive suburban housing estates at Upton and Great Boughton which had previously lain outside its boundary, but also with large swathes of countryside. In deference to Chester's historic past, the district was granted a royal charter which conferred on it the title of city and allowed the chairman of the new council to be called mayor. In 1992, on a visit to Chester, the Queen elevated the title to lord mayor. The ancient offices of alderman and sheriff were discontinued, along with the last vestiges of the borough's portmoot, Pentice, and passage courts, though the city was allowed to describe the ceremonies by which it admitted freemen as being 'in the Pentice court'. The county borough's town clerk and treasurer became chief executive and treasurer of the new district, which initially had seven main committees to discharge its responsibilities for planning and development regulations (subject to the formulation of policy at county level), environmental health, open spaces,

1 Ibid. 13 Oct. 1967; 31 Mar. 1972.

2 *Archives and Records*, ed. Kennett, 8.

3 *Ches. Observer*, 15 Sept. 1962; 25 July 1966; 2 Apr. 1971.

4 Ibid. 5 Aug. 1966; *V.C.H. Ches.* v (2), Museums.

5 *Ches. Observer*, 25 June 1955; 28 Jan. 1961; 29 Sept. 1972.

6 Ibid. 10 July 1970; *Greater Chester District Plan: Technical Rep.* (1977), pp. 90–4.

7 C.C.A.L.S., ZCA 9, statement to Sir John Maude; *Ches. Observer*, 1 June 1946.

8 *Ches. Observer*, 2 Dec. 1966.

9 Ibid. 20 July 1973; 8, 20 Mar. 1974; *Chester City Cl. Mins. 1972/3*, pp. 907–8; *1973/4*, p. 621; *V.C.H. Ches.* v (2), Sport after 1700: Public Facilities.

10 *Ches. Observer*, 21 Oct. 1966; 26 Mar. 1970; 19 Feb. 1973; *Chester City Cl. Mins. 1970/1*, p. 951; Lord Redcliffe-Maud and B. Wood, *Eng. Local Government Reformed*, 5, 46–7, map 1 [176–7].

11 *Ches. Observer*, 12 Nov. 1971; 11 May 1973; 29 Mar. 1974.

and housing. Conservation was a joint responsibility of county and district.[1]

After 1974 at least three quarters of the rates went to the county to pay for the functions such as education and social services which it now provided. Despite government cushioning of the impact of reorganization, the district's rates rose in the first year by an average of 39 per cent,[2] in part a measure of the earlier effectiveness of ratepayer pressure in keeping the county borough's rates low. After 1979 government policy was that the private sector should deliver many local services. Spending restrictions severely curtailed what local authorities were able to do, and in many areas stimulated a preference among the public for better funded unitary authorities. In Cheshire, however, when further reorganization of local government was projected between 1992 and 1994, Chester city council's bid for unitary status was undermined by clear evidence that the reforms of 1974 had taken root and had strong local support. The Local Government Commission's recommendation was therefore for no change.[3]

Politics. The parliamentary seat was held by the Conservatives with comfortable majorities in general elections between 1974 and 1987, but tactical voting by anti-Tory electors reduced the margin to 1,100 in 1992 and put a Labour M.P. in for the first time in the landslide of 1997.[4]

Chester district was divided for local electoral purposes into 27 wards, 15 of which covered the built-up area of the city. Of the 60 councillors, 41 represented those urban wards. Each year a third of the seats were contested, with county council elections taking place in the fourth year. Party politics dominated the district council's affairs far more than they had the county borough's before 1974. The first council consisted of 42 Conservatives, 15 Labour, 2 Independents, and 1 unidentified. The rural seats were held by Conservatives or Independents, a pattern which continued in 2000. Within the urban area, Labour strength was confined mainly to the council estates, particularly Blacon, whose wards returned 13 of the party's first group of councillors. The main feature of later elections was the growth in Liberal Democrat support from the later 1980s, mostly at the expense of the Conservatives in the suburban wards dominated by privately owned housing. After the 1992 elections the Conservatives had 22 seats, Labour 19, and the Liberal Democrats 16, with 3 others, necessitating co-operation between the parties. From 1998 the urban part of the district had an extra ward but only 38 councillors. In 1999 there were 22 Labour councillors, 18 Liberal Democrats, 18 Conservatives, and 2 others.[5]

THE ECONOMY, 1974–2000

In the last quarter of the 20th century Chester enhanced its role as a sub-regional centre for west Cheshire and north-east Wales, its buoyant economy generally riding above periods of national recession and mainly dependent on a wide range of employment in retailing, tourism, the professions, and the public sector. The city also became important as a provider of financial services through the arrival of several national firms. Employment in manufacturing was declining, and continued to depend on a few large industrial plants outside the city. The closure of the Shotton steelworks in 1979 was a heavy blow, depriving many Chester residents of their jobs,[6] but the other main industrial firms in the region, Vauxhall Motors and ICI

at Ellesmere Port, British Aerospace at Broughton, British Nuclear Fuels (later Urenco) at Capenhurst, and a newcomer, Toyota Motors near Wrexham, remained significant throughout the period. They were not only the main source of manufacturing jobs for Chester's workforce, but also supported the prosperity of the wider area on which Chester's service-based economy depended.[7] There were no large manufacturing concerns within the city. Characteristically it instead housed the administrative offices of firms which made things elsewhere, besides a small number of hi-tech manufacturing plants. Many of them were new to the city after 1974, and many were foreign-owned. Corporate headquarters new to the city

1 *Ches. Observer,* 29 Mar. 1974; *Chester City Cl. Mins. 1971/2* and *1972/3,* by indexed refs. to Local Government Reorganisation, esp. *1971/2,* p. 374.

2 *Ches. Observer,* 10 May 1974; C.C.A.L.S., ZDTR 5/93, 5/96; cf. ibid. 5/107.

3 *Local Government Review: Ches. Districts' Proposals* (1994): copy at C.H.H.; *Chester News: Chester City Cl.'s Newspaper for Residents of Chester District,* summer 1994: copy in Chester City Cl. Communications Unit; Chester City Cl. Econ. Development Unit, *Support for a Unitary Authority* (1994); Ches. Co. Cl., *Local Government Review: Rep. to Local Government Com. for Eng.* (1994); Local Government Com. for Eng., *Final Recommendations on Future of Local Government of Ches.: Rep. to Secretary of State for Environment* (1994).

4 *Brit. Parl. Election Results, 1974–83,* ed. F. W. S. Craig, 98; *1983–97,* ed. C. Rallings and M. Thrasher, 74; *Guardian,* 3 May 1997, p. 5.

5 *Chester District Cl. Mins. 1973/4,* pp. 1–5; *Ches. Current Facts & Figures,* sheet El 50/Jun 95, May 96, May 99 (Ches. Co. Cl. Research and Intelligence); City of Chester (Electoral Changes) Order 1998 (Statutory Instrument 1998, no. 2866); *V.C.H. Ches.* v (2), Local Government Boundaries: Ward Boundaries.

6 Ches. Co. Cl., *County Structure Plan: Rep. of Survey* (1977); Ches. Co. Cl., *Strategy Plan* (1983).

7 Inf. from Chester City Cl. Econ. and Tourism Development Unit, Aug. 1996; Ches. Co. Cl. Research and Intelligence, *Ches. Econ. Rep. 1999,* 56–69.

included Shell Chemicals U.K.; the Continental Can Co., subsidiary of a German firm, which made drinks cans at Rugby (Warws.); and Harman U.K. Ltd., which made audio equipment in Cambridge. Specialist manufacturers included Deva Manufacturing Services Ltd., high-precision engineers; Barry U.K., the British subsidiary of a French chocolate maker; and the Original Bradford Soap Works, the European branch of an American firm. All three built new factories on new industrial estates in Chester in the 1990s.[1] The manufacturing sector as a whole employed less than 19 per cent of the employed workforce in 1981, and less than 13 per cent in 1991, well below the national averages. Two thirds of the city's manufacturing workers were employed outside Chester district.[2]

County council planning policies throughout the period recognized that manufacturing jobs in Ellesmere Port and beyond Cheshire were complemented by service employment in Chester, and sought to encourage Chester district council to concentrate on attracting more service jobs.[3] It did so in part by allotting land for offices on the periphery of the city, a process closely bound up with planning issues. It was made easier by the fact that in 1984 the whole district, as part of the Wirral and Chester travel-to-work area, was designated a Development Zone eligible for government grants, largely on the strength of very high levels of unemployment in Birkenhead and parts of Ellesmere Port. Development status (downgraded to Intermediate status in 1993) helped Chester district council to set up an employment development unit in 1986, advertise the city's attractions to businesses, and provide the infrastructure for new industrial, business, and retail parks.

Sites for new industry were established west of the city centre along Sealand Road, first in an extension of the Sealand industrial estate, next by the creation of the Stadium industrial estate on the opposite side of the road, on the site vacated by Chester City Football Club in 1990, and finally at Chester West employment park, an 84-acre greenfield site further out on the south side of the road. The first businesses to set up there included an American printing firm, New England Business Stationery; a regional computerized stock-control centre for Boots; a printing works for the Thomson International newspaper group; and offices for Pearl Assurance. In the early 1990s the district council laid out Chester Gates by the M56

north of the city, 37 acres for warehousing and distribution depots.[4]

Of far greater significance for local employment was the private development of Chester business park, opened in 1988 on 150 acres beyond the southern outskirts of the city east of Wrexham Road. It incorporated (as offices) the picturesque farmhouse and outbuildings of the former Wrexham Road farm, built by John Douglas for the Grosvenor estate in 1877–84,[5] but was otherwise a greenfield site which provided high-quality and often architect-designed office accommodation in a landscaped setting. Close to the motorway network and thus within fairly easy reach of Manchester international airport as well as the private airfield at Hawarden, it attracted several large firms new to Chester. Among the first was the administrative headquarters of Shell Chemicals U.K., whose domestic-style pavilion with a hipped roof, by Leach Rhodes and Walker,[6] set the pattern for most which followed. Other notable buildings were those for Marks & Spencer Financial Services, by Aukett Associates,[7] and the palatial, Palladian-styled complex which by 1999 could accommodate up to 2,000 employees of MBNA International Bank, the British arm of a large American bank. Other firms which set up at Chester business park included the business services arm of the pharmaceutical company Bristol-Myers Squibb, and Trinity International, a holding company with interests in regional newspapers, paper, and packaging, which bought the Mirror Group of newspapers in the late 1990s and became Trinity Mirror PLC.[8]

The growth and diversity of the service sector was the main reason for Chester's economic success in the period. Despite the retrenchment of the public sector under both Conservative and Labour governments after 1979, Chester's long-established position as a regional administrative centre meant that employment levels in public administration and services remained high. The district and county councils each employed about 1,000 people in the 1990s, the Royal Mail and Chester College each about 500, and the Countess of Chester Hospital some 2,500. The city was also the headquarters of smaller employers as diverse as the county police force, the Chronicle group of local newspapers, Chester City Transport, and the diocesan administration.[9]

Even more striking was the growth of financial services, which came to provide a very large number

1 *Key Brit. Enterprises 2000* (Dun & Bradstreet), i. 824, 989; ii. 215; *Chester: Not Just a Pretty Place* (Chester City Cl. Econ. Development Unit publicity pack [1993]): copy at C.H.H.

2 *Census*, 1981, *Key Statistics for Urban Areas: North*, p. 38; 1991, *Key Statistics for Urban and Rural Areas: North*, p. 179; inf. from Chester City Cl. Econ. and Tourism Development Unit, Aug. 1996.

3 Para. based on Ches. Co. Cl., *County Structure Plan: Rep. of Survey* (1977); Ches. Co. Cl., *Strategy Plan* (1983); *Ches. 2000: Co. Structure Plan Rev.: Explanatory Memorandum* (1990), 134–5; Ches. Co. Cl. Research and Intelligence, *Ches. Econ. Rep. 1999*;

Assisted Areas Order 1984 (Statutory Instrument 1984 no. 1844); Assisted Areas Order 1993 (Statutory Instrument 1993 no. 1877).

4 *Chester Industrial and Commercial Business Dir. 1990*, 5–6; *Chester: Not Just a Pretty Place*.

5 E. Hubbard, *Work of John Douglas*, 93–5.

6 *Architects' Jnl.* 24 Feb. 1988, p. 15.

7 Inf. from Mr. de Figueiredo.

8 *Chester Business Dir. 1990*; *Chester: Not Just a Pretty Place*.

9 Inf. from Chester City Cl. Econ. and Tourism Development Unit, Aug. 1996; *Key Brit. Enterprises 2000*, i. 708–9, 860.

of managerial, administrative, clerical, and call-centre jobs. In Chester district as a whole, their number grew from 10,800 in 1991 to 15,000 in 1997, most of whom were employed in the city centre or at Chester business park.[1] The one important firm of local origin was North West Securities, renamed Capital Bank in 1997. In the 1970s and 1980s it continued to grow and diversify by operating financial services on behalf of other organizations such as the Automobile Association and the National Farmers' Union, employing 4,500 people in 1997 and almost 6,000 in 1999. It built two further office blocks in City Road in 1987–8 and a training centre at Chester business park, and in the later 1990s refurbished as its headquarters the former Western Command building overlooking the Dee from Queen's Park, adding an oversized portico.[2] The main financial services employers at the business park, Marks & Spencer and MBNA, employed almost 2,500 people between them in 1999 and were then still growing.[3]

Many older and much smaller providers of financial and professional services continued to occupy offices in the city centre. In 1990 Chester had at least 20 firms of accountants, 21 of solicitors, 11 of architects, 37 insurance brokers, and 10 advertising agencies. The three largest firms of consulting engineers and the two largest estate agents each employed over 100 people.[4] Office accommodation for several hundred very small businesses was provided by the refurbishment and adaptation in the 1990s of two city-centre industrial buildings, the Steam Mill by the canal and the Cheshire Enterprise Centre, the latter in a former goods depot at Chester General station.[5]

Chester's importance as a shopping centre remained high throughout the period, though by the late 1990s it was beginning to be challenged by out-of-town developments elsewhere in the region. The distributive trades and catering employed significantly above the national average, some 24 per cent of the Chester workforce in 1991.[6] As elsewhere, the 1980s and 1990s saw greatly increased competition among the main supermarkets who invested in large new stores away from the town centre, leading to the closure of smaller food shops both there and in local shopping centres throughout the city. Sainsbury's opened on the eastern outer ring-road, Safeway at Bache, and Kwik Save on Sealand Road.[7] Only Tesco retained a presence in the city centre, at Frodsham Street. Local shops survived in fairly large numbers in Hoole, but the big council estates at Blacon and Newton suffered a decline

in their shopping facilities.[8] The catchment area for the city-centre shops remained very wide and indeed was probably extended by the improvement of the local motorways and trunk roads: in the late 1990s it was reckoned to extend to Colwyn Bay, Wrexham, Whitchurch, Nantwich, Winsford, Northwich, Runcorn, Widnes, Ellesmere Port, and in west Wirral almost as far as Hoylake. The city centre, however, had almost reached full capacity: shop vacancies were low and it was increasingly difficult to meet the strong demand by the largest retailers for expanded premises, though Marks & Spencer, Littlewoods, and BHS all managed to increase their sales space in the mid 1990s. Chester was very attractive to chain stores of all sizes and types, and in 1997 ranked 16th nationally for their presence, far above its population ranking. Rentals in the most desirable locations, including Eastgate Street and Foregate Street, were as high as in Liverpool and Manchester city centres, and on some measures Chester was placed in the top five retail locations in Britain in the early 1990s.[9] The lack of any sizeable new retail development in that decade, however, especially a third enclosed shopping area to add to the Grosvenor Centre and the Forum, caused Chester to fall in the principal national ranking of retail centres from 9th in 1989 to 23rd in 1994. In the late 1990s the city centre nevertheless retained what by most standards was a very large array of shops. Besides the chain stores, it included the longest-established department store, Browns (owned by the Debenham Group), many antique shops, and specialist food retailers of a type in sharp decline in most towns of Chester's size, such as fishmongers, game butchers, and cheese shops.

From the mid 1990s, however, new out-of-town shopping centres threatened Chester's regional pre-eminence for comparison shopping. The huge Trafford regional shopping centre in Greater Manchester, opened in 1998, initially had less impact than was feared in Chester's core catchment area, especially south and west of the city, but two other developments nearer Chester looked set to divert much of its custom. The Cheshire Oaks outlet mall at Ellesmere Port, opened in 1995 and extended in the later 1990s, was the largest development outside North America of cut-price retail outlets selling goods direct from the factory, and by 2000 was attracting 6 million visitors a year. The Broughton Park shopping centre opened in 1999 with 300,000 square feet of shops[10] in a part of northeast Wales which had hitherto looked almost entirely to Chester for its major shopping facilities. Chester's

1 Ches. Co. Cl. Research and Intelligence, *Ches. Econ. Rep. 1999*, 75.
2 [Holland], *Memories of Chester*, [10–15]; *Chester Business Dir. 1990*, 5.
3 *Key Brit. Enterprises 2000*, i. 241, 623–4; ii. 749, 812.
4 *Chester Business Dir. 1990*.
5 Personal observation.
6 *Census, 1981, Key Statistics for Urban Areas: North*, p. 38;

1991, *Key Statistics for Urban and Rural Areas: North*, p. 179.
7 Rest of para. based on Nathaniel Lichfield & Partners, *Chester Shopping Study Review, 1997* (copies in Chester Public Libr. ref. colln. and C.H.H.), esp. i. 1–41.
8 Ibid. ii. 18–23; personal observation.
9 *Chester News*, summer 1994, p. 4.
10 Ches. Co. Cl. Research and Intelligence, *Ches. Econ. Rep. 1999*, 74.

own retail parks, Greyhound retail park and Chester retail park, both on the western edge of the city, with 19 and 6 stores respectively, were small in comparison, besides being disadvantageously sited in relation to the new competitors.

The significance of tourism to Chester's economy grew enormously between the mid 1970s and 2000.[1] Chester zoo, on the north-eastern outskirts at Upton Heath, was the second biggest tourist attraction in the North-West but enticed visitors into the city centre only to a limited extent. Within the city the most visited places were the cathedral, walls, and Rows. Apart from the cathedral, the other paid-for attractions there drew only small numbers, and even in the 1990s such free sites as the castle and the canal basin were relatively undeveloped. Despite the recessions of the

1970s and 1980s, the number of both day-trippers and staying visitors rose rapidly to an estimated 1 million in 1983 and 6½ million in 1995, who were believed to spend £38 million and £150 million annually in the city centre. Even in 1983 tourism was reckoned to support 4,000 jobs. British visitors were predominantly from the better-off social groups, and there were also many overseas tourists from North America, western Europe, and Australasia. Surveys showed that the main reasons for visiting Chester were its buildings and history, the general ambience, and the shops. The importance of the city-centre environment to tourism thus helped to keep conservation at the forefront of the political agenda locally, as well as making the council increasingly vigilant for opportunities to attract more visitors.

TOWN PLANNING AND THE BUILT ENVIRONMENT, 1974–2000

Traffic. Perhaps the greatest of Chester's difficulties in balancing economic development against environmental damage was the traffic generated by the city's success as a commercial, business, and tourist centre.[2] Much through traffic was diverted round the city by the southerly bypass opened in 1977 and a more effective easterly bypass in the early 1990s.[3] The outstanding part of the complete ring-road which had been demanded since the 1920s was a western bypass linked to a further bridge over the Dee, but only the sections from Liverpool Road to Sealand Road (Countess Way and the Chester Western Bypass) had been built by 2000, leaving the western stretch of the inner ring-road and the Grosvenor Bridge frequently congested.

It was still feared in the 1990s that more Draconian measures to restrict vehicular access to the city centre would damage the commerce on which its prosperity depended.[4] Pedestrianization of the central streets was phased in between 1982 and 1990, closing Northgate, Eastgate, St. Werburgh, Bridge, and Watergate Streets, and the Cross, except for access. The completion in 1983 of a new bus exchange between Hunter Street and Princess Street, for Chester City Transport buses, and the provision of the Delamere Street bus station, for long-distance services, had already liberated Town Hall Square from traffic and allowed the area in front of the

town hall and the new library to be paved. Park-and-ride schemes were introduced in the late 1980s, large car parks being sited on the outskirts of the city.

Conservation and Renewal in the City Centre. The district council's planning policies after 1974 continued to recognize the value of Chester's architectural inheritance and to carry out the programmes started as a result of the Insall Report of 1968.[5] By 1975, European Architectural Heritage Year, work was sufficiently advanced for Chester to be chosen as one of four official British projects.[6] The city centre became a magnet for those studying conservation methods and continued to win European prizes, notably the Europa Nostra silver medal in 1983 and 1989.[7]

The city council's conservation fund was allowed to run down in the later 1970s but was reinstated in real terms in the 1980s, when the annual budget was never less than £200,000, matched from government funds. There was also support from the European Regional Development Fund. By 1986 over 600 buildings had been renovated and restored to use, including the Dutch Houses in Bridge Street and Bishop Lloyd's House. Many environmental improvements had also been made, for example to the river bank and the cathedral precinct.[8] The renovation of Godstall Lane in 1980 and the Eastgate Street Row project of 1991–3,

1 Para. based on J. F. N. Collins and C. M. Morris, *Chester Tourism Survey, 1976*; Eng. Tourist Bd., *Chester Tourism Study,* [*1983*]; Land Use Consultants, *Visitors to Chester: Rep. to Eng. Tourist Bd. and Civic Trust* (1987); Bennett Associates, *Chester Tourism Survey, 1993* (copies of all at C.H.H.).

2 Section based, except where stated otherwise, on *Chester at the Crossroads: Chester Traffic Study* (1990); C. Cuthbert and P. Messenger, 'Managing Traffic in Historic Towns', *Practice Digest of Eng. Historic Towns Forum,* no. 3 (Mar. 1989), pp. 20–1 (copy at C.H.H.); Chester City Cl., Conservation Dept., file

CP/G/10 Europa Nostra: submission.

3 *V.C.H. Ches.* v (2), Roads and Road Transport: Roads (Bypasses).

4 e.g. *Chester Chron.* 24 Sept. 1993.

5 *Country Life,* 9 June 1983, p. 1545; *Chartered Surveyor Weekly,* 15 Mar. 1984, p. 722.

6 *Town Planning Rev.* xlvi. 383.

7 Chester City Cl., Conservation Dept., file CP/G/10 Europa Nostra: press release, 30 Jan. 1990; inf. from Mr. D. W. Insall.

8 Insall and Morris, *Conservation in Chester,* esp. 21, 97, 123.

the latter designed by the Biggins Sargent Partnership for the corner of Eastgate Street and Northgate Street, revived a run-down and underused area immediately next to the Cross.[1]

The council's view in the 1990s was that there was still scope for renewal and redevelopment within the central area of Chester,[2] but its planning regulations also acknowledged that new building could be environmentally damaging. Where possible, older buildings were adapted to new uses and new buildings were concealed by existing façades. Among the most successful examples was the new central library of 1981–4, hidden by the county architect behind the decorative brick and terracotta front of the former Westminster Coach and Motor Car Works of 1913–14.[3] Some buildings were reproduced exactly, such as the house in Lower Bridge Street fronting Heritage Court, a development of offices designed by Forbes Bramble Associates in 1989–91 to resemble early 19th-century houses.[4] Similar techniques were less successful along Foregate Street, where restored or poorly reproduced Georgian fronts bore no relation to what lay behind. On the rim of the historic city centre, industrial buildings along the canal were converted into offices, hotels, and bars.

Both Cestrians and planners were particularly sensitive about buildings near the cathedral and town hall. The appearance of the Forum Centre was viewed with dismay, and in 1993 it was called 'perhaps the worst piece of modern urban planning in the centre of any historic city in England'.[5] In 1993–5 the cantilevered upper storeys were cut back, and a new façade, more subdued in colour and post-modern classical in style, was applied by Leslie Jones.[6] The refurbishment was castigated as 'superficial, façadist and motivated more by commercial considerations than by civic pride', a wasted opportunity to revive what should have been Chester's civic and cultural heart.[7] More successful smaller-scale commercial work included James Brotherhood and Associates' Rufus Court (1991), where offices entered from the city walls were placed above shops reached from Abbey Green.[8]

Chester's black-and-white style was echoed in many buildings of the late 20th century, weakly stylized, for example, on the oversized Moat House Hotel and car park with which the architects Parry, Boardman, and Morris extended the Forum development over Trinity Street to St. Martin's Way (the inner ring-road).[9] The city's 19th-century Domestic Revival style in red brick was also resurrected, as, for instance, in the intricate brick gables of the small precinct off Frodsham Street which replaced Mercia Square, demolished in 1989–90. The most blatant piece of scene-setting, in the spirit of late Victorian Chester but inspired by schemes such as the Riverside development at Richmond (Surr.), was Grosvenor Court, a courtyard development of open-plan offices planted on an unpropitious island site at the junction of the inner ring-road and the Bars. Though of one date (1989) and with one designer and developer, the Stannanought Partnership, the group was made to look as if had evolved, by being disguised as 18th-century terraced houses and 19th-century Grosvenor estate buildings.[10]

Rebuilding along the inner ring-road gave rise during the 1970s and early 1980s to such bulky structures as the Northgate Arena and office blocks along Pepper Street, designed with the dark brick and heavy rooflines then fashionable, giving them undeserved prominence in the townscape. In the late 1980s and 1990s differently styled but equally prominent buildings appeared, such as the offices for North West Securities (later Capital Bank) close to the railway station off City Road.

Archaeology. The preservation of the city walls exemplified the way in which conservation was linked to archaeology, and it was not accidental that from the late 1960s the Department of the Environment supported both conservation and archaeological investigations. An archaeological unit was set up in 1972 at the Grosvenor Museum and became a separate service run by the city council in 1989. Under the 1979 Ancient Monuments and Archaeological Areas Act the development of sites designated as being of archaeological importance came under the control of local authorities and could be investigated and recorded ahead of any redevelopment. Significant finds from the Roman period were thus made at Abbey Green (defences, kitchens, and centurions' houses) and on the library and bus exchange site (a barracks and two other large buildings). Further investigation of the elliptical building under the Forum Centre did not reveal its purpose, but a publicly funded multidisciplinary study of the Rows confirmed their 13th-century origins.[11] Limited archaeological work was undertaken at the amphitheatre in 2000 as part of a plan to promote the site as a tourist attraction.[12]

Open Spaces. Planners thought Chester fortunate because it contained 'green wedges' separating the

1 Boughton, *Picturesque Chester*, no. 136.
2 Building Design Partnership, *Chester: Future of Historic City*.
3 Boughton, *Picturesque Chester*, no. 154.
4 Inf. from Mr. F. Bramble.
5 R. K. Morriss, *Buildings of Chester*, 41–2.
6 Ches. Co. Cl. Planning Dept., planning approval 93/1262/CAC; Boughton, *Picturesque Chester*, no. 152; *Chester Chron.* 2 Sept. 1993; 8 Sept. 1994.
7 *Chester Civic Trust Newsletter*, autumn 1993.
8 Inf. from Mr. de Figueiredo.
9 Ibid.
10 Ibid.
11 *The Past Uncovered* [newsletter of Chester Archaeology], June 1996.
12 Ibid. summer 2000.

city from its suburbs and providing a landscape setting. The open spaces included the Roodee, Curzon Park golf course, Westminster Park, and the Meadows, but their extent was less than the norm for a city of Chester's population. Provision for organized games was adequate but unevenly distributed, being especially deficient in the large council estates at Lache and Blacon.[1] The importance of the river Dee and the canal both for the attractiveness of the urban environ-

ment and for recreation was recognized, but plans for enhancing them were curtailed by financial constraints, and few of Grenfell Baines's imaginative proposals of the early 1970s were put into effect.[2] The Meadows were neglected and little used because of poor drainage and access, though by the 1990s those features were seen as assets and plans were made to develop the area as a wetland habitat grazed by cattle.[3]

HOUSING AND SUBURBAN DEVELOPMENT, 1974–2000

Although Chester's population was falling from 1971,[4] house-building continued apace, mostly in the private sector. By 1991 there were over 33,000 houses in the urban wards, of which 68 per cent were owner-occupied.[5] Demand for housing in the city was led by managers working in Merseyside, Greater Manchester, and north Wales, and house prices in Chester were consequently among the highest in the North-West, 14 per cent above the national average in 1992.[6]

One of the reasons for high house prices was the shortage of building land on the outskirts of the city. The district council remained committed to encouraging new residents into Chester, a principal reason for its proposal in the mid 1990s to breach the green belt south of the city. Local people also needed housing, in part because of the greater number of single-person households. The loss of residents within the city walls was another matter of concern. In 1975 there were *c.* 1,500 residents in the inner city, half the number in 1961.[7] To utilize existing space better and tempt residents back, dwellings suited to professional and single people and childless couples were created on the upper floors of the Rows and other city-centre premises. Small housing units were also built within the conservation area and on reclaimed land such as the site of Northgate station west of Victoria Road, where between 1985 and 1991 Northgate Village was built,[8] with very small terraced houses and blocks of flats grouped at high density round courts shared by pedestrians and vehicles.

The council's ability to provide social housing was severely limited by government financial restrictions. In 1977 plans were made for a steady programme of

new building for families on the housing list and to replace unfit dwellings. Government policies prevented its completion, and land assigned for council houses was later turned over to the private sector and housing associations. Despite council co-operation with the private sector, the waiting list continued to expand beyond the 3,250 families needing accommodation in 1976.[9] The difficulty in remedying the situation was exacerbated by the government's 'Right to Buy' policy of 1980, which seriously depleted the existing housing stock. Chester had been selling council houses since the early 20th century, but until 1980 always built more than it released. Between 1980 and 1993, however, the stock fell by almost 2,000. By 1994 only 15.6 per cent of the housing in Chester was council-owned, there was a waiting list of 3,750 families, and 109 families were homeless. Financial constraints also hindered the refurbishment of older council houses. In 1993, for example, over 3,000 of them lacked central heating, and by 1994 some 3 per cent in the district as a whole were reported unfit for human habitation and 74 per cent in need of much improvement; the government, however, would not approve the 10-year investment programme of £8.3 million a year said to be required.[10]

Private house-building for families with the highest incomes followed the pattern established in the 1950s. Most took place within or as extensions to existing suburbs, and only a little in small groups on greenfield sites. Typical in its North American-influenced style was a development off Eaton Road in the 1970s and 1980s of detached houses with open front lawns. More original was Claverton Court, built in Queen's Park *c.* 1980 for the Architects' Benevolent Fund to designs by Brock

1 *Greater Chester District Plan: Technical Rep.* (1977), pp. 90–1.
2 Inf. from Mr. Insall.
3 Chester City Cl., Leisure Services Committee papers, 28 Nov. 1991, enclosure J: draft management plan for the Meadows; 23 Jan. 1992, enclosure F: interim progress rep. on consultation; *Chester Riverside Study*, section FR5A.
4 *V.C.H. Ches.* v (2), Population.
5 *Chester District Ward Atlas: Summary of Key Inf. from 1991 Census* (Chester City Cl. Econ. and Tourism Development Unit, 1993: copy at C.H.H.), pp. 8, 38, 40.

6 *The Times*, 19 Oct. 1989; *Ches. 2001: Chester: City and County Response* (1991); Chester City Cl., *Housing Strategy Statement, 1989* (copy at C.H.H.), 3.
7 *Greater Chester District Plan: Technical Rep.* (1977), p. 27.
8 Plaque within Northgate Village.
9 *Greater Chester District Plan: Technical Rep.* (1977), pp. 17, 19; Ches. Co. Cl., *Strategy Plan* (1983).
10 C.C.A.L.S., ZDTR 5/92, p. 267; Chester City Cl., *Housing Strategy Statement, 1993*; ibid. *1995–8* [1994], esp. 40, 58; *Ches. Current Facts & Figures*, sheet Hou 11/Oct 93 (Ches. Co. Cl. Research and Intelligence).

Carmichael, and extended in 2000.[1] The only distinguished individual house built in Chester after 1974 was the Schreiber House off Eaton Road, designed *c.* 1983 by James Gowan as a post-modern fusion between the ideas of Le Corbusier and Palladio.[2]

Houses for a slightly lower income group were built in far greater numbers, particularly in the 1980s and 1990s. The main concentrations were around the southern perimeter of the Lache estates, and south of Great Boughton in the angle between Chester Road and the Chester southerly bypass (A55). The planning principles followed national trends: at Great Boughton a spine road (Caldy Valley Road) was laid out to serve separate closes of mainly small detached houses on cramped plots. Each group was developed individually by a large house-builder. The architectural styles adopted were conservative, embracing neo-vernacular, neo-Georgian, and by the later 1990s neo-Victorian. At Great Boughton a Sainsbury's supermarket and a retail park

formed part of the development. During the 1990s there were a few schemes on brownfield sites, for example a block of flats and some houses on a former factory site south of Overleigh Road, Handbridge, and an extensive area of flats and houses, eclectic in style, designed by Jane Derbyshire and David Kendall for Bryant Homes on the site of the Royal Infirmary west of the inner ring-road. Some new housing was tucked into spaces within the city centre, for example a modest terrace behind King Street and two schemes by Robin Clayton between Duke Street and the city walls, but few of those developments were architecturally noteworthy.[3] The most distinctive new housing was probably Salmon's Leap, designed in 1976 by Gilling Dod and Partners for a restricted site close to the river in Handbridge,[4] and the discreet infill designed to Donald Insall and Associates' concept as part of the rehabilitation of Lower Bridge Street, such as Insall's houses of the early 1980s in Castle Street, Castle Place, and St. Mary's Hill.[5]

SOCIETY AND CULTURE, 1974–2000

Health and Poverty.   After 1974 the health of Cestrians was not an issue for particular concern, as average death rates were close to those for the county and nationally, mostly between 11 and 12 per thousand. The most common causes were heart disease, lung cancer, and strokes. Averages, however, concealed great differences between areas of the city, and a report of 1994 demonstrated the connexion between sickness and poverty: the incidence of all the main life-threatening diseases was higher in those parts of the city where deprivation could be identified.[6] In the 1990s both statutory and voluntary agencies in Chester understood that poverty was increasing and that the widening gap between rich and poor nationally was mirrored locally. The causes identified included unemployment, old age, sickness, and large families, all familiar since the 1930s or earlier, besides the new factor of far more extensive single parenthood. Government constraints on local authority spending prevented due attention being paid to poverty, but Chester's image as a wealthy area was also an inhibiting factor. An investigation by Cheshire county council into family stress identified three of the city's wards as being among the 33 areas in the county where the problem was worst: Lache ranked second worst, Blacon Hall seventh, and Dee Point (also in

Blacon) thirtieth. In 1993 unemployment reached 40 per cent in parts of Lache, when the Chester district average was 7.8 per cent.[7]

Culture and Leisure.[8]   Cultural provision changed little after 1974 and was left largely to the private sector. Cinema-going revived considerably, and a multi-screen cinema was built away from the city centre on the Sealand retail estate, where car parking was plentiful. The Odeon survived in Northgate Street. The civic theatre, the Gateway, was moderately successful, but suffered from a poor location and cramped premises in the Forum Centre. Lobbying continued for a concert hall and arts complex. In the mean time orchestral concerts were still held in the cathedral, where a summer music festival was staged every year.[9] 'Cultural tourism', one of few growth areas in the 1990s, was seen as essential in helping the city to compete successfully with its rivals for the tourist trade.[10] Libraries were a county service, but the district council obtained powers in 1974 to continue operating an archives service at the Chester City Record Office in the town hall. It closed the office in 2000, however, and transferred the city's records to a joint service run by the county at Duke Street.[11]

---

1 Inf. from Mr. de Figueiredo.
2 *Archit. Rev.* 4 Feb. 1983, pp. 39–43.
3 Inf. from Mr. de Figueiredo.
4 C.C.A.L.S., ZDLC 3/14.
5 *Baumeister*, Dec. 1982, pp. 1212–14.
6 *Ches. Current Facts & Figures*, sheet Pop 52/Aug 93, Jul 99; sheet Pop 53/Jan 94, Aug 95, Jul 99 (Ches. Co. Cl. Research and Intelligence); Chester City Cl., *Annual Rep. of Director of Public Health, 1994.*
7 Chester College, *Research for Chester's Anti-Poverty Strategy, Rep. 2: Anti-Poverty Action and Policy in Chester* (1995); Chester

City Cl., *Inf. on Poverty Issues in Chester* (1995); Chester City Cl., *Preliminary Poverty Profile of Chester* (1993); *Chester District Ward Atlas*, pp. 30, 54, 56.
8 See also *V.C.H. Ches.* v (2), Leisure and Culture.
9 *Chester District Local Plan: 1st Draft, 1996*, p. 218; *Chester Chron.* 24 Sept. 1993; *V.C.H. Ches.* v (2), Places of Entertainment.
10 *Chester District Local Plan: 1st Draft, 1996*, p. 217; *Chester Chron.* 8 Jan. 1993.
11 *Archives and Records*, ed. Kennett, 8–9; personal knowledge.

1 *The shrine of Minerva found in the Roman quarry in Handbridge, 1725.*
Drawn by William Stukeley. Engraving

2 *Masonry of the Roman east gate, 1768. Etching by Musgrove for Joseph Hemingway's* History of Chester *(1831)*

ROMAN CHESTER

3 'Chester ware' pot and part of the silver treasure buried in the late 10th century and excavated at Castle Esplanade in the 1950s

4 13th-century pottery imported to Chester from the Saintonge

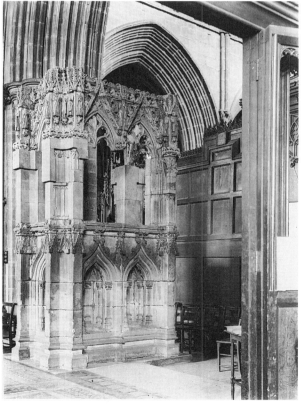

5 A lead seal matrix of Bishop Peter of Chester (1075–85)

6 St. Werburg's shrine as re-erected in the 1880s behind the high altar of Chester cathedral

REMAINS OF EARLY MEDIEVAL CHESTER

7 *Interior in 1812, looking from the north transept into the crossing and nave. Drawn by Charles Wild (1781–1835), engraved by H. Le Keux*

8 *Exterior from the north-east in 1838, before restoration and the tidying of the ruins in the 1860s and the collapse of the north-west tower in 1881. Drawn by W. Tasker (1808–52). Lithograph*

ST. JOHN'S CHURCH

9 *St. Michael's from the south-west, showing the chancel as rebuilt c. 1678 and the tower added 1708–10. All rebuilt 1849–51*

10 *St. Bridget's from the north-east in 1816, with Lamb Row (left), showing the church as rebuilt 1690 and refaced 1785. Demolished 1829*

11 *Holy Trinity from the south-east, after the spire was removed in 1811. South side as rebuilt 1678, and tower as rebuilt 1728. Replaced on the same site 1864*

MEDIEVAL PARISH CHURCHES DRAWN AND ETCHED BY

12 *St. Martin's from the north-west,
showing it as rebuilt in brick
with stone dressings in 1721.
Demolished 1964*

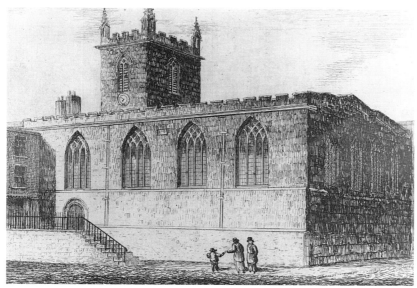

13 *St. Peter's from the south-east,
after the Pentice was removed
from the south side in 1803*

14 *St. Mary's from the north-west*

GEORGE BATENHAM IN THE EARLY 19TH CENTURY

15 *Before the Victorian restorations, showing the work done by Thomas Harrison from 1819.*
Drawn by J. Shaw, lithograph by R. Groom

16 *After thorough restoration by Giles Gilbert Scott, 1868–76.*
Drawn by S. Read. Engraving

THE CATHEDRAL FROM THE SOUTH-EAST

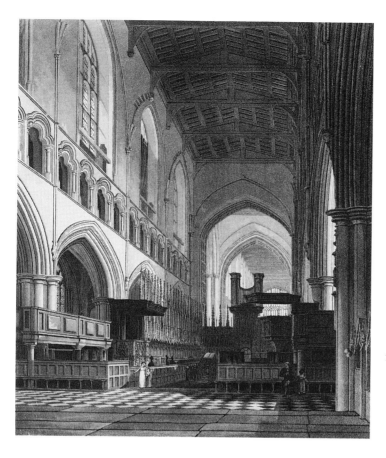

17 *The choir, looking west in 1813, showing Bishop Peploe's seating and marble floor of the 1740s. Drawn and etched by Charles Wild (1781–1835) for his* An Illustration of the Architecture of the Cathedral. *Aquatint by M. Dubourg*

18 *The chapter house, probably c. 1780. Drawn by Moses Griffith (1747–1819), lithograph by W. Crane*

THE CATHEDRAL: INTERIOR

19 *Old Eastgate, from outside the walls, probably soon before its demolition in 1768. Etching*

20 *New Eastgate, as rebuilt in 1768. Drawn by G. Wilkinson. Etching*

21 *Old Northgate, with debtors' gaol over the gateway, shortly before demolition in 1808. Drawn by T. Hunter. Aquatint*

THE CITY GATES

22 *Old Bridgegate, 1780, from outside the walls, showing the octagonal water tower. Wash drawing by G. Wilkinson*

23 *New Bridgegate, by Joseph Turner, completed 1781, from inside the walls in 1857. Drawn by John Romney (1786–1863). Engraving*

24 *New Northgate, by Thomas Harrison, completed 1810. Drawn by George Batenham, 1815*

THE CITY GATES

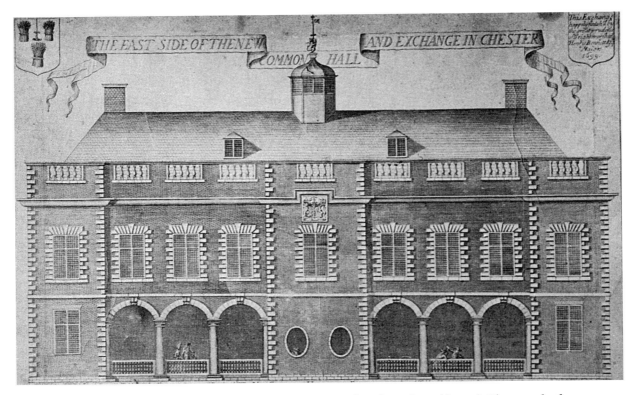

25 *The Exchange, 1699, from the east, facing Abbey Gate. Drawn by John Jackson (d. 1718). Photograph of an engraving*

26 *Chester town hall, 1865–9* (centre) *and market hall, 1863, demolished 1967* (left), *linked by the market hall extension of 1882. Photograph c. 1890*

CIVIC BUILDINGS

27 *From the south with new St. Bridget's church* (foreground). *Etching*

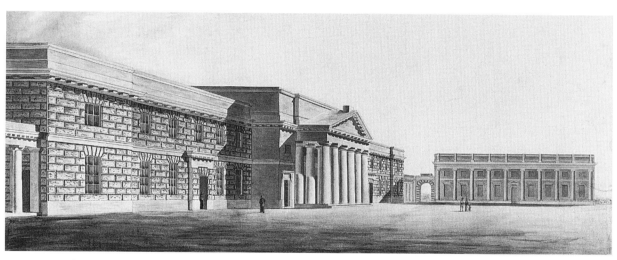

28 *In 1804, showing the main block with the portico leading to the new shire hall* (centre), *the archway to the upper ward, and the armoury* (right). *Drawn by the architect, Thomas Harrison. Lithograph*

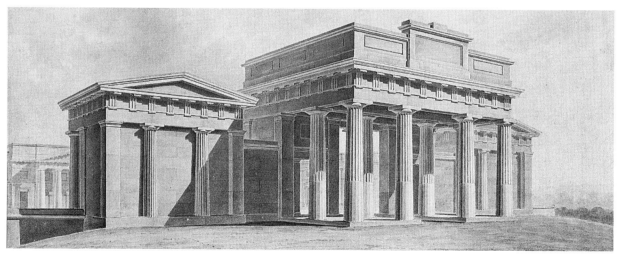

29 *The propylaeum as completed in 1813. Drawn by Thomas Harrison. Lithograph*

CHESTER CASTLE

30 *Smith's almshouses, formerly the common hall. Undated print*

31 *Lamb Row* (centre) *and the Two Churches, St. Bridget's* (left) *and St. Michael's* (right), *before the demolition of Lamb Row and St. Bridget's in the 1820s. Drawn by C. F. Wicksteed (d. 1846). Undated engraving*

32 *Eastgate Row in 1817, showing two 13th-century stone arches and new bow-fronted shop windows at no. 32, in a more realistic depiction than most made in the 19th century. Drawn by George Pickering (1794–1857), engraved by Charles Heath (1785–1848)*

33 *Stone-vaulted medieval undercroft below Prichard and Dodd's carpet warehouse, no. 12 Eastgate Street, before demolition in 1861. Drawn by George Measom for Thomas Hughes's* Stranger's Handbook to Chester *(1856). Etching by Gilks*

THE ROWS

34 *Chester in the mid 19th century from the city walls near Bonewaldesthorn Tower, showing Yoxall's Chester Infirmary (1761), Harrison's city gaol (1809), with gibbet over the western gate, and the rear of Georgian houses in Stanley Place. Artist and date unknown. Etching*

35 *Chester Lunatic Asylum, Bache, by William Cole junior, opened 1829. Drawn by Musgrove for Hemingway's* History of Chester (1831). *Engraving by Dean*

PUBLIC BUILDINGS

36 *Matthew Henry's chapel (Unitarian, formerly Presbyterian), Trinity Street, in 1847. Built 1700, demolished in 1962. Drawn by John Romney (1786–1863). Engraving*

37 *St. Werburgh's Roman Catholic church, Queen Street, probably c. 1838. Opened 1799, demolished 1966. Drawn by T. Bailey. Lithograph by Bailey and Owen*

38 *Methodist New Connexion chapel, Pepper Street, in 1850. Opened 1835, closed as a chapel 1920. Drawn by J. C. Rowland. Lithograph*

39 *Queen Street Independent (Congregational) chapel, built in 1777, showing the neo-Grecian façade added in 1838 and retained when the chapel was demolished in 1978. Drawn by T. Bailey. Lithograph by Evans and Howarth*

NON-ANGLICAN CHURCHES

40 *The Dee with the Dee Bridge, the Dee Mills* (centre)*, the Floating Baths* (right of bridge)*, and the Groves* (right)*,
photographed soon after the Groves were extended in 1881*

41 *Overleigh cemetery as laid out to T. M. Penson's designs, 1848–50, showing entrance lodges on Grosvenor Road*
(rear) *and River Lane* (front left)*, the neo-Romanesque Anglican chapel* (rear centre)*, and the nonconformist
chapel* (front right)*. Drawn by R. G. Clark. Lithograph by J. M'Gahey*

42 *Chester regatta, 1854, showing a contest of coxed fours between Chester Royal and Manchester Nemesis rowing clubs, elegant crowds on the bank below Sandy Lane* (foreground), *lower-class spectators thronging marquees, and a fairground on the Meadows. Drawn by Evans and Gresty. Engraving*

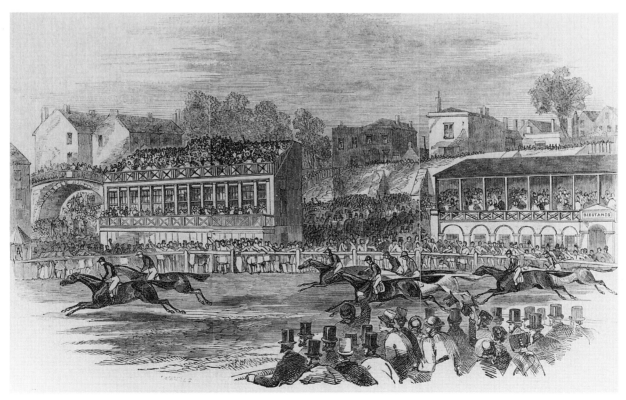

43 *Chester Cup Day at Chester Races, 9 May 1846, showing Harrison's grandstand* (left), *the Dee stand of 1840 used by middle-class spectators* (right), *and people watching for free from the Watergate and city walls. Engraved by Ebenezer Landell's assistants for the* Illustrated London News

44 *Chemical works in Skinner Street, near the Dee Bridge, 1820, showing a furnace which may be a limekiln (centre right), fed from a barrow-way. Drawn by F[rancis] N[icholson] (1753–1844). Aquatint*

45 *Covered canal boat-building and repair dock in use at Tower Wharf in the early 20th century*

46 *Hallmarking silver in the Chester assay office in Goss Street, probably shortly before its closure in 1962*

47 *The canal wharf in the earlier 19th century, showing a warehouse* (right), *the Canal Tavern* (left), *the unloading of a packet boat on the service from Liverpool, and in the distance* (top left) *the northern city walls. Undated lithograph*

48 *Clare's Court, off Charles Street, 1930, where six houses shared a single tap and two W.C.s; closed off* (rear) *by the Hydraulic Engineering Co. works*

49 *Posnett's Court, looking north to the back of houses and shops fronting the south side of Watergate Street, 1930*

50 *No. 1 Bridge Street, by T. M. Lockwood (1888), probably the most photographed group of buildings in Chester. Photograph 1896*

51 *Parke's Court, off Love Street, 1930, showing* (centre) *a low building housing shared W.C.s*

52 *Atholl Place, off Crook Street, where ten houses shared two W.C.s and one tap, 1930*

53 *The spectacular range of commercial buildings by John Douglas (1895–9) on the east side of St. Werburgh Street. Photograph c. 1900*

54 *The markets in the earlier 19th century. Etching*

55 *Shops at the south end of Northgate Street, photographed c. 1860s*

56 *Factories at the Handbridge end of the Dee causeway,
on the site of the medieval fulling mills, showing
Hooley's candle works (left) and Jones's tobacco
factory. Photograph c. 1925 by R. W. Morris*

57 *King Charles's Tower on the city walls, as occupied in
the early 20th century by a private museum*

58 *Brickmaking on Hough Green in 1796. Drawn by W. Turner. Engraving by J. Walker*

59 *Watling Crescent, Lache*

60 *Houses on the Eaton Road estate*

61 *Prefabricated bungalows in Blacon*

EARLIER 20TH-CENTURY COUNCIL HOUSING

INDEX

THIS index is confined to persons (including businesses) and places; an index to subjects, together with a complete index to persons and places in both parts of vol. v, will be published in part 2. Buildings, streets, and other minor place names have been indexed under their own name and not as subheadings under Chester or other parish names. All places may be assumed to be in Cheshire unless otherwise indicated. Peers have been indexed under family names, and women, as far as possible, under their maiden names.

THE V.C.H. CHESHIRE APPEAL

The following individuals and organizations contributed generously to an appeal for funds which enabled this volume to be completed.

SUBSCRIBERS

Sir Richard Baker Wilbraham, Bt., Rode
A. G. Barbour, Esq., Bolesworth
H. M. Bibby, Esq., Llansannan, Denb.
Mr. and Mrs. F. R. Brace, Mollington
Gyles Brandreth, Esq., London
Mr. and Mrs. Stephen Brown, Huntington
† G. Burkinshaw, Exeter
Dr. and Mrs. A. J. P. Campbell, Tattenhall
Mr. and Mrs. T. D. Carnwath, Sandiway
D. H. B. Chesshyre, Esq., College of Arms, London
Mr. and Mrs. K. G. H. Cooke, Kelsall
Professor J. Davies, Liverpool
S. de Ferranti, Esq., Henbury
Mrs. D. Dunn, Manley
E. P. Foden, Esq., Sandbach
C. F. Foster, Esq., Arley
Mr. and Mrs. C. M. Frazer, Kew, Surr.
Sir William Gladstone, Bt., Hawarden, Flints.
Lyndon Harrison, Esq., M.E.P., Chester
M. Hassall, Esq., London
E. M. Hawes, Esq., Kingsley
Mr. and Mrs. E. J. W. Hess, Wheatley, Oxon.
Mr. and Mrs. J. P. Hess, Chorlton by Backford
Mrs. R. H. Hobhouse, Nercwys, Flints.
Dr. T. D. S. Holliday, Chester
P. T. Hughes, Esq., Churton
Mr. and Mrs. D. M. Kermode, Little Neston
Mr. and Mrs. V. A. Knight, Chester
Mr. and Mrs. F. A. Latham, Alpraham
Mrs. R. F. McConnell, C.B.E., D.L., Chester
Mrs. S. M. McRoberts, Romiley
Mr. and Mrs. J. B. Makinson, Chester

The Hon. Mary Morrison, D.C.V.O., Fonthill Bishop, Wilts.
Dr. D. Nuttall, Dodleston
Mr. and Mrs. D. Okell, Great Barrow
J. H. Peacock, Esq., Little Sutton
Mr. and Mrs. D. O. Pickering, Higher Kinnerton, Flints.
Dr. and Mrs. C. Pownall, Chester
H. S. Proudlove, Esq., Chester
Ms. E. A. Renshall, Leeds
† Canon M. H. Ridgway, Rhyd y Croesau, Oswestry, Salop.
J. K. Shanklin, Esq., Dodleston
Mr. and Mrs. D. H. L. Shone, Wimborne, Dors.
J. Treloar, Esq., Huntington
M. A. T. Trevor-Barnston, Esq., D.L., Crewe by Farndon
Mr. and Mrs. A. W. Waterworth, Kingsley
Mrs. P. A. Wendt, Upton by Chester
Anne, Duchess of Westminster, Eccleston
Mr. and Mrs. G. Wolf, Disley

Barclays Bank plc, Chester
Cheshire County Council Archaeology Service
Cheshire County Council Conservation Action
Chester Society of Natural Science, Literature, and Art
Delamere Local History Group
Department of History, University College Chester
Duchy of Lancaster Estate Office, Crewe
Frodsham and District Local History Group
The Louis Nicholas Residuary Charitable Trust
Shell Chemicals UK Ltd., Chester
Simon Engineering Charitable Trust
Vauxhall Motors Ltd., Ellesmere Port
Wilmslow Historical Society
C. P. Witter Ltd., Chester

CONTRIBUTORS

Canon E. M. Abbott, Claughton, Birkenhead
Professor and Mrs. C. T. Allmand, Liverpool
Mr. and Mrs. M. A. Anderson, Burton
J. H. Beckett, Malpas
Sir Derek and Lady Bibby, Willaston
† Col. H. L. Birch, Tattenhall
R. E. Birkett, Esq., Macclesfield
W. K. Blinkhorn, Esq., Whiston, Lancs.

J. Blundell, Esq., Congleton
P. H. W. Booth, Esq., Birkenhead
Col. William Bromley-Davenport, Capesthorne
Dr. J. D. Bu'lock, Marple
Mrs. J. W. Burn, Rhyl, Flints.
P. Carden, Esq., Westbury, Salop.
Lord Carlisle of Bucklow, Mobberley
Mrs. J. Cooper, Haslington